EXAM✓CRAM

CompTIA® A+®
Core 1 (220-1101)
and Core 2
(220-1102)

David L. Prowse

Pearson

CompTIA® A+® Core 1 (220-1101) and Core 2 (220-1102) Exam Cram

ISBN-13: 978-0-13-763754-6
ISBN-10: 0-13-763754-3

Library of Congress Control Number: 2022933630

4 2022

Trademarks

Warning and Disclaimer

Special Sales

For information about buying this title in bulk quantities, or for special sales opportunities (which may include electronic versions; custom cover designs; and content particular to your business, training goals, marketing focus, or branding interests), please contact our corporate sales department at corpsales@pearsoned.com or (800) 382-3419.

For government sales inquiries, please contact governmentsales@pearsoned.com.

For questions about sales outside the U.S., please contact intlcs@pearson.com.

Editor-in-Chief
Mark Taub

Director, ITP Product Management
Brett Bartow

Executive Editor
Nancy Davis

Development Editor
Christopher A. Cleveland

Managing Editor
Sandra Schroeder

Senior Project Editor
Tonya Simpson

Copy Editor
Kitty Wilson

Indexer
Ken Johnson

Proofreader
Charlotte Kughen

Technical Editor
Chris Crayton

Publishing Coordinator
Cindy Teeters

Cover Designer
Chuti Prasertsith

Compositor
codeMantra

Pearson's Commitment to Diversity, Equity, and Inclusion

Pearson is dedicated to creating bias-free content that reflects the diversity of all learners. We embrace the many dimensions of diversity, including but not limited to race, ethnicity, gender, socioeconomic status, ability, age, sexual orientation, and religious or political beliefs.

Education is a powerful force for equity and change in our world. It has the potential to deliver opportunities that improve lives and enable economic mobility. As we work with authors to create content for every product and service, we acknowledge our responsibility to demonstrate inclusivity and incorporate diverse scholarship so that everyone can achieve their potential through learning. As the world's leading learning company, we have a duty to help drive change and live up to our purpose to help more people create a better life for themselves and to create a better world.

Our ambition is to purposefully contribute to a world where

- ▶ Everyone has an equitable and lifelong opportunity to succeed through learning.

- ▶ Our educational products and services are inclusive and represent the rich diversity of learners.

- ▶ Our educational content accurately reflects the histories and experiences of the learners we serve.

- ▶ Our educational content prompts deeper discussions with learners and motivates them to expand their own learning (and worldview).

While we work hard to present unbiased content, we want to hear from you about any concerns or needs with this Pearson product so that we can investigate and address them.

Please contact us with concerns about any potential bias at https://www.pearson.com/report-bias.html.

Contents at a Glance

Part II: Introduction to Core 2 (220-1102)

Table of Contents

CORE 2 (220-1102): DOMAIN 3.0: SOFTWARE TROUBLESHOOTING

About the Author

David L. Prowse has more than 20 years of experience in the IT field and loves to share his knowledge with readers, viewers, and students. Dave is an advocate of lifelong learning, self-improvement, building confidence, and the sharing of knowledge, and he promotes these ideas in his books, videos, and classes. He answers questions at his websites: https://dprocomputer.com (for A+) and https://prowse.tech (for Linux).

Acknowledgments

I'd like to give special recognition to:

Nancy Davis, *Executive Editor Perfectamundo*. Thank you so much for giving me the opportunity to write this book and for overseeing the project. Your support and humor have been crucial. The "supertome" is complete!

Chris Cleveland, *Development Editor Legend*. Can't ask for a better DE. It's hard to understand the madness involved when writing a book. Chris gets it…and fixes my big mess without any fuss.

Chris Crayton, *Technical Editor Extraordinare*. I wouldn't work with anyone else. Chris has the innate ability to ascertain what's *wrong*. My extreme thanks to the unrivaled TE.

Also, I'd like to thank the Pearson production team. Without you, this book wouldn't have made it to the presses. I'm serious here: Writing a book is tough work, and this edition of the *A+ Exam Cram* was the toughest to date. Publishing a book takes a team of professional and talented people. My thanks to everyone else at Pearson for your expertise and help throughout this project.

Going beyond the people directly involved in this book, I'd also like to thank:

Denise Lincoln. Thank you for being patient and for providing content to this project. Videos are coming soon…I promise!

Dave Dusthimer. Dave was the one who gave me my start writing books many years ago. He and Betsy Brown stood by me when I didn't know a participle phrase from a gerund. A thousand thank yous!

And let's not forget the many readers over the years who have emailed me with questions, comments, and suggestions about how to make the book better—most especially those happy readers who passed the exams and have found employment in the IT field. Those emails make it all worth it.

Finally, the biggest thanks goes to my family. You stuck by me through all the due dates, early hours, late hours, aggravation, and my random technical blather that I expect everyone to understand (or care about). Without your support, this book would not be possible. You have my eternal gratitude.

About the Technical Reviewer

Chris Crayton is a technical consultant, trainer, author, and industry-leading technical editor. He has worked as a computer technology and networking instructor, information security director, network administrator, network engineer, and PC specialist. Chris has authored several print and online books on PC repair, CompTIA A+, CompTIA Security+, and Microsoft Windows. He has also served as technical editor and content contributor on numerous technical titles for several of the leading publishing companies. He holds numerous industry certifications, has been recognized with many professional and teaching awards, and has served as a state-level SkillsUSA final competition judge. Chris tech edited and contributed to this book to make it better for students and those wishing to better their lives.

We Want to Hear from You!

As the reader of this book, *you* are our most important critic and commentator. We value your opinion and want to know what we're doing right, what we could do better, what areas you'd like to see us publish in, and any other words of wisdom you're willing to pass our way.

We welcome your comments. You can email to let us know what you did or didn't like about this book—as well as what we can do to make our books better.

Please note that we cannot help you with technical problems related to the topic of this book.

When you write, please be sure to include this book's title and author as well as your name and email address. We will carefully review your comments and share them with the author and editors who worked on the book.

Email: community@informit.com

Reader Services

Register your copy of *CompTIA A+ Core 1 (220-1101) and Core 2 (220-1102) Exam Cram* at www.pearsonitcertification.com for convenient access to downloads, updates, and corrections as they become available. To start the registration process, go to www.pearsonitcertification.com/register and log in or create an account*. Enter the product ISBN 9780137637546 and click Submit. When the process is complete, you will find any available bonus content under Registered Products.

*Be sure to check the box that you would like to hear from us to receive exclusive discounts on future editions of this product.

Introduction

Welcome to the *CompTIA A+ Core 1 (220-1101) and Core 2 (220-1102) Exam Cram*. This book prepares you for the CompTIA A+ Core 1 (220-1101) and Core 2 (220-1102) certification exams. Imagine that you are at a testing center and have just been handed the passing scores for these exams. The goal of this book is to make that scenario a reality. My name is David L. Prowse, and I am happy to have the opportunity to serve you in this endeavor. Together, we can accomplish your goal to attain the CompTIA A+ certification.

Target Audience

The CompTIA A+ exams measure the necessary competencies for an entry-level IT professional with the equivalent knowledge of at least 12 months of hands-on experience in the lab or field.

This book is for persons who have experience working with desktop computers and mobile devices and want to cram for CompTIA A+ certification exams—*cram* being the key word. This book does not cover everything in the computing world; how could anyone do so in such a concise package? However, this guide is fairly thorough and should offer you a lot of insight—and a whole lot of test preparation.

If you do not feel that you have the required experience, have never attempted to troubleshoot a computer, or are new to the field, then I recommend the following:

▶ Attend a hands-on A+ class with a knowledgeable instructor.

▶ Consider purchasing the CompTIA A+ Core 1 (220-1101) and Core 2 (220-1102) Video Course, which goes into a bit more depth than this text and shows technology concepts from a hands-on perspective.

Essentially, I have written this book for three types of people: those who want a job in the IT field, those who want to keep their job in the IT field, and those who simply want a basic knowledge of computers and want to validate that knowledge. For those of you in the first group, the latest version of the CompTIA A+ certification can have a positive career impact, increasing the chances of securing a position in the IT world. It also acts as a stepping stone to more advanced certifications. For those in the second group, preparing for the exams serves to keep your skills sharp and your knowledge up to date, helping you to remain a well-sought-after technician. For those of you in the third group, the knowledge within this book can be helpful in any career path you decide to take, and it can be beneficial to just about any organization you might work for—as long as that organization uses computers!

Regardless of your situation, one thing to keep in mind is that I write my books to teach you how to be a well-rounded computer technician. While the main goal for this book is to help you become A+ certified, I also want to share my experience with you so that you can grow as an individual.

About the CompTIA A+ Certification

This book covers the CompTIA A+ 220-1101 and 220-1102 exams, also known as Core 1 and Core 2, respectively. To obtain the CompTIA A+ certification, you must pass *both* exams. These exams are administered by Pearson Vue and can be taken at a local test center or online.

Passing the certification exams proves that you are an experienced problem solver and can support today's IT technologies.

Before doing anything else, I recommend that you download the official CompTIA A+ objectives from CompTIA's website. The objectives are a comprehensive bulleted list of the concepts you should know for the exams. This book directly aligns with those objectives, and each chapter specifies the objective covered in the pages that follow.

For more information about how the A+ certification can help your career or to download the latest objectives, access CompTIA's A+ web page at https://www.comptia.org/certifications/a.

About This Book

This book covers what you need to know to pass both CompTIA A+ exams. It does so in a concise way that allows you to memorize the facts quickly and efficiently.

We have organized this book into two parts, together comprising 65 chapters, all pertaining to the objectives covered on the exams. The first part of the book—Chapters 1 through 29—applies to the Core 1 (220-1101) exam. The second part of the book—Chapters 31 through 64—applies to the Core 2 (220-1102) exam. At the beginning of each of those parts, you will find a handy checklist you can use as you prepare for the exams. Chapter 65 discusses how to get ready for the real exams and gives some tips and techniques for passing the exams.

For this edition of the book, I decided to organize the content based on the order of the official CompTIA objectives. Typically, you will find one objective per chapter. Less commonly, a chapter will cover two objectives, and in a couple of instances, an objective will stretch across two chapters. The corresponding CompTIA objective or objectives are listed verbatim at the beginning of each chapter and in the subsequent major heading(s). Organizing the book this way enables you to easily locate whatever objective you want to learn more about. In addition, you can use the index to quickly find the concepts you are after.

Regardless of your experience level, I don't recommend skipping content. This book is designed to be read completely. The best way to study is to read the entire book. Then, go back and review the 220-1101 portion and take the real CompTIA 220-1101 exam. Afterward, review the 220-1102 portion and take that exam. The two exams are inextricably linked. It's a good idea to get the whole picture first and then break it down by the exam. While this might not be possible based on time constraints, I still strongly recommend it as the best study method.

> **Note**
>
> I do *not* recommend taking both exams on the same day. Instead, space them apart by at least a week to allow yourself time to prepare.

Chapter Format and Conventions

Every Exam Cram chapter follows a standard structure and contains graphical clues about important information. The structure of each chapter includes the following:

▶ **Opening topics list:** This defines the CompTIA A+ objective(s) to be covered in the chapter.

▶ **Topical coverage:** The heart of the chapter, this text explains the topics from a hands-on and a theory-based standpoint. The text includes in-depth descriptions, tables, and figures geared to build your knowledge so that you can pass the exams.

▶ **Cram Quiz questions:** At the end of each chapter is a quiz. The quizzes, and ensuing explanations, are meant to help you gauge your knowledge of the subjects you have just studied. If the answers to the questions don't come readily to you, consider reviewing individual topics or the entire chapter. In addition to being in the chapters, you can find the Cram Quiz questions at the book's companion web page, at www.pearsonitcertification.com. The questions are separated into their respective 220-1101 and 220-1102 categories for easier studying when you approach each exam.

▶ **Exam Alerts, Sidebars, and Notes:** These are interspersed throughout the book. Watch out for them!

> **ExamAlert**
>
> This is what an Exam Alert looks like. An alert stresses concepts, terms, hardware, software, or activities that are likely to relate to one or more questions on the exams.

▶ **Challenges:** New to this edition, I've added skill challenges that are designed to build your hands-on skills for the IT field. There are corresponding videos on the companion website. Note that these challenges are optional, but I strongly suggest that you attempt them if you have the time.

Additional Elements

Beyond the chapters, there are a few more elements that I've thrown in for you:

▶ **Practice exams:** These are located at the end of Part I and Part II. There is one practice exam for each CompTIA A+ exam. These practice exams (and additional exams) are available as part of the custom practice test engine at the companion web page also. They are designed to prepare you for the multiple-choice questions that you will find on the real CompTIA A+ exams.

▶ **Real-world scenarios:** These are located on the companion web page as PDFs. They describe actual situations with questions that you must answer and potential solutions with supporting videos and simulations. These scenarios are designed to help prepare you for the performance-based questions within the real CompTIA A+ exams.

▶ **Cram Sheet:** The tear-out Cram Sheet located at the beginning of the book is designed to jam some of the most important facts you need to know for each exam into one small sheet, allowing for easy memorization. It is also available in PDF format on the companion web page. If you have an e-book version, this might be located elsewhere in the e-book; run a search for the term "cram sheet," and you should be able to find it.

The Hands-On Approach

It is incredibly important that you apply what you learn in this book to real hardware and software. This is the kinesthetic approach that I have recommended for years. It works! Practice as much as you can on Windows, mobile devices, computer hardware, network devices …whatever you can get your hands on.

In this book, I give as many use cases and actual technology examples as possible, including command usage, operating system navigation, troubleshooting techniques, and so on. Also, every so often, this book refers to a computer called *AV-Editor*. This is a computer that I built to act as a powerful audio/video editing workstation. By referencing computer technology in actual scenarios, I hope to infuse some real-world knowledge and to solidify the concepts you need to learn for the exams. This hands-on approach can help you to visualize concepts better. I recommend that every computer technician build their own computer at some point (if you haven't already). This can help to reinforce the ideas and concepts expressed in the book.

You should also work with multiple operating systems while going through this book: primarily Windows but also Linux, macOS, Android, iOS, and Chrome OS. Consider dual-boots, virtual machines, and emulators to learn more about these systems. However, if at all possible, the best way to learn is to run individual computers. This will ensure that you discover as much as possible about the hardware and software of each computer system and how they interact with each other.

This book frequently refers to various support websites. Have a browser open all the time and be ready to perform more research as you read through the book.

Goals for This Book

I have three main goals in mind while preparing you for the CompTIA A+ exams.

My first goal is to help you understand A+ topics and concepts quickly and efficiently. To do this, I try to get right to the facts necessary for the exam. To drive these facts home, the book incorporates figures, tables, real-world scenarios, and simple, to-the-point explanations. Also, in the introductions for the Core 1 and Core 2 sections, you will find preparation checklists that give you an orderly, step-by-step approach to taking the exams. Be sure to complete all items on the checklists! For students of mine who truly complete every item, there is an extremely high passing rate. Finally, in Chapter 65, you will find some important test-taking tips that I've developed over the years.

My second goal for this book is to provide you with an abundance of *unique* questions to prepare you for the exams. Between the Cram Quizzes and the practice exams, that goal has been met, and I think it will benefit you greatly. Because CompTIA reserves the right to change test questions at any time, it is difficult to foresee exactly what you will be asked on the exams. However, to become a good technician, you must know the *concepts*; you can't just memorize questions. Therefore, each question has an explanation and maps back to the chapter covered in the text. I've been using this method for more than a decade with my students with great results.

My final goal is to provide support for this and all my titles, completing the life cycle of learning. I do this through my personal website (https://dprocomputer.com), which provides additional resources for you, including an errata page (which you should check as soon as possible) and is set up to take questions from you about this book. I'll try my best to get to your questions ASAP. All personal information is kept strictly confidential.

Good luck in your certification endeavors. I hope you benefit from this book. Enjoy!

Sincerely,

David L. Prowse

https://dprocomputer.com

Figure Credits

Introduction to Core 1 (220-1101)

Welcome to the Core 1 (220-1101) section of this book. This portion of the CompTIA A+ certification focuses on computers such as laptops, smartphones, tablets, and PCs; computer networking; virtualization and cloud computing; and troubleshooting of hardware and networks. That's a great deal of things to know—but you can do this. Take it slow, study hard, and stay positive. Do these things, and you will succeed.

The Core 1 content of this book comprises Chapters 1 through 29. For the most part, I've written the content to match the order of the objectives. This way, you can follow along with the official CompTIA A+ objectives and mark them up as you wish while you progress through the book. After Chapter 29, you will find a practice exam that is designed to test your knowledge of the 220-1101 objectives.

Core 1 (220-1101) Domains

The CompTIA A+ Core 1 exam objectives are broken down into five domains:

- ▶ 1.0—Mobile Devices
- ▶ 2.0—Networking
- ▶ 3.0—Hardware
- ▶ 4.0—Virtualization and Cloud Computing
- ▶ 5.0—Hardware and Network Troubleshooting

After this introduction, we'll address these objectives in order, starting with Chapter 1, "Laptop Hardware and Components." Be sure to study each of the domains! To do this properly, I suggest that you get your hands on as much technology gear as you can: PCs, laptops, mobile devices, printers, SOHO routers, and so on. Work with as much of this technology as possible so that you can learn how the hardware and devices really work. Then apply that knowledge to the objectives and the content in this book.

Core 1 (220-1101) Checklist

You must be fully prepared for the exam, so I created a checklist that you can use to make sure you are covering all the bases as you study. Take a look at the following table and make sure you check off each item before attempting the 220-1101 exam. Historically, my readers and students have benefited greatly from this type of checklist. Use the table as a guide for ordering your studies. I suggest you bookmark this page and refer back to it as you complete each item.

Exam Preparation Checklist

Step	Item	Details	220-1101 Status
1.	Read the Core 1 (220-1101) content.	Thoroughly read Chapters 1 through 29.	
2.	Review the Exam Alerts.	The little boxes with Exam Alerts are interspersed throughout the book. Review them and make sure you understand every one.	
3.	Review the Cram Quizzes.	Cram Quizzes are categorized by exam. You can review them in the text or on the companion website.[1]	
4.	Complete the practice exam in the book.	Directly after Chapter 29 is a 220-1101 practice exam. Your goal should be to get at least 90% correct on the exam on the first try. (100% would be preferable!) If you score less than 90%, go back and study more!	
5.	Study the Core 1 Real-World Scenarios.	These can be found on the companion website. Complete them by reading and answering the scenarios and questions within the PDFs and accessing the corresponding videos and simulations.	
6.	Create your own cheat sheet.	Although there is a Cram Sheet in the beginning of this book, you should also create your own. The act of writing down important details helps commit them to memory. Keep in mind that you will not be allowed to take your own cheat sheet or the Cram Sheet into the actual testing room.	

Step	Item	Details	220-1101 Status
7.	Register for the exam.	Do not register until you have completed the previous steps; you shouldn't register until you are fully prepared. When you are ready, schedule the exam to commence within a couple days so that you won't forget what you have learned! Registration can be done online. Register at Pearson VUE (https://home.pearsonvue.com). It accepts payment by major credit cards for the exam fee. You need to create an account to sign up for exams.	
8.	Read the test-taking tips.	These can be found in the last chapter of the book and on the companion website.	
9.	Study the Cram Sheet and cheat sheet.	The Cram Sheet is a fold-out in the beginning of this book. It is also on the companion website. Study from the Core 1 portion of the Cram Sheet and your cheat sheet during the last 24 hours before the exam. (If your exam is delayed for any reason, go back to step 3 and retake the Cram Quizzes and practice exam 24 hours prior to your test date.)	
10.	Take the exam!	When you pass, place that final check mark in the box! Good luck!	

[1]Some electronic editions of this book do not have access to the practice test software.

ExamAlert

Do not register for the exam until you are thoroughly prepared. Meticulously complete items 1 through 6 in the checklist before you register.

Note

Remember: It's not mandatory, but I recommend going through the entire book (Core 1 and Core 2). Then, return to the Core 1 portion and review it carefully, going through the steps in the checklist. It takes more time, yes—but this is a proven method that I have used with CompTIA A+ exams since the turn of the millennium!

CORE 1 (220-1101)

Domain 1.0: Mobile Devices

CHAPTER 1

Laptop Hardware and Components

This chapter covers the following A+ 220-1101 exam objective:

▶ 1.1 – Given a scenario, install and configure laptop hardware and components.

Welcome to the first chapter of this book! In this chapter, we focus on laptop hardware only. Software will be covered later in the book. The core of this chapter deals with laptop hardware and device replacement. By that I mean laptop power and batteries, keyboards, memory, storage drives, and so on. You might come into contact with laptops old and new that need to be repaired and/or upgraded. This chapter addresses many of those scenarios. Let's get to it.

> **ExamAlert**
>
> **Objective 1.1** focuses on the following concepts: battery, keyboard, random-access memory (RAM), storage drives, wireless cards, and physical privacy and security components.

> **Note**
>
> Don't forget, a complete list of the Core 1 (220-1101) objectives can be found on the companion website for this book (see the Introduction for details) and on CompTIA's website: https://certification.comptia.org/certifications/a.

Introduction to Laptops

Ah, the laptop. The beauty of laptops is that they are portable, and all the connections are right at your fingertips. However, quite often there is a trade-off in performance and in price—that is, in comparison to PCs. This chapter assumes a basic knowledge of laptops and jumps straight into how to install and configure laptop devices.

Laptops were originally designed for niche markets but today are often used in businesses, schools, and at home. Laptops (also known as notebooks or portable computers) have integrated displays, keyboards, and pointing devices, making them easy to transport and easy to use in confined spaces. What makes them work when they are not plugged in? The battery, of course! Let's dive right in to laptop power and batteries.

Power

Laptops are designed to run on battery power, but laptops can run only several hours on these batteries. So, a laptop comes with an AC power adapter to plug into an AC outlet; this adapter should always be carried with the laptop. How many times have I heard users say they've forgotten their AC adapter! Recommend to users that they always put the AC adapter back in the laptop case—or use two: one for the workplace and one for "going mobile."

The worst-case scenario is when a laptop won't turn on! Without power, a user can't do anything. When troubleshooting power problems, envision the entire chain of power in your mind (or write it on paper)—from the AC outlet to the

AC adapter to the DC jack and all the way to the Power button. There are a few things you can check if it appears that a laptop is not getting any power.

▶ **Check the power LED:** Check the power light on the AC adapter. If this is off, not only will the laptop not get power but the battery won't charge. Most laptops also have a power LED on the front of the case or just above the keyboard. If this lights up, then maybe it isn't a power problem at all. For example, the user might start the laptop, see nothing on the display, and determine that the laptop has no power—when, in reality, it is a display issue.

> **Note**
>
> Many laptops also have storage drive and wireless LEDs, which can tell you more about the status of the laptop when you can't see anything on the screen. Use them!

▶ **Check connections:** Verify that the laptop is firmly connected to the AC adapter and that the AC adapter is firmly connected to the AC outlet. Sometimes a user presses the power button, expecting the laptop to start, without realizing that the battery is discharged and that the AC adapter is not connected. Also, check for damage. Inspect the DC jack that is on the side of the laptop; it is soldered onto the motherboard of the laptop. Make sure it isn't loose or damaged. Sometimes the battery charges only if the output cord of the AC adapter is held at an angle—probably because the laptop was transported while the output cord was plugged into the laptop, causing damage to the DC jack. Also make sure that the user is attempting to connect to the actual DC jack, and not an audio port, security port, or something else. The DC jack is sometimes labeled. For example, it might show that it requires 19-V DC. This must be exact, which is covered by using the correct adapter—as explained in the following bullet.

▶ **Make sure the user uses the right power adapter:** Swapping power adapters between two different laptops is not recommended, but users try to do it all the time. Two different laptop models made by the same manufacturer might use what appear to be similar power adapters, with only 1 or 2 volts separating them; however, the laptop usually won't power on with that "slightly" different power adapter. Laptop AC adapters are known as fixed-input power supplies, meaning they work at a specific voltage. An adapter is not meant to be used on another model laptop. Unfortunately, a user might have plugged in the incorrect power adapter;

the laptop then worked fine for 4 or 5 hours because it was actually running on battery power, but the user might not have noticed the laptop wasn't charging, even though the system should have notified the user when the battery was low (and critical). Another power adapter–related issue could be that the user is trying to work in another country. To do this, the user needs an auto-switching AC adapter, meaning that it can switch from 120 to 240 VAC automatically. Some laptops do not come with auto-switching AC adapters, but after-market versions can be purchased for many models of laptops. Remember that an additional adapter might be necessary to connect to AC outlets in foreign countries.

▶ **Check the battery and voltage:** It might sound silly, but check if the battery has been removed for some odd reason. Also, check if the battery is fully inserted into the battery compartment. There is usually a locking mechanism that should hold the battery in place. Finally, test the battery's voltage. Batteries last a finite amount of time. They can be recharged by the laptop only so many times (known as cycles) before failure. After several years, the battery won't hold a charge any longer or will lose charge quickly. In some cases, you can try discharging and recharging the battery a few times to "stimulate" it, but in most scenarios, an extremely short battery life means that the battery must be replaced. An old or failing battery can cause the system to overheat or could cause operating system freeze-ups or slow performance. In general, lithium-ion batteries last longer when the laptop is operated and stored at the right temperature ranges. Acceptable operating range for laptops is 50 to 95°F (10 to 35°C), and acceptable storage range is –4 to 140°F (–20 to 60°C). Watch out for swollen batteries, which could be caused by age, overcharging, or manufacturer defect. If a battery is user-removable, it will often require the removal of a couple of screws. Use caution in attempting to remove it and be sure not to puncture it. Store it in a dark, cool container until you can recycle it. If it is a non-user-serviceable battery, bring/send the device to the nearest authorized repair center and, as before, keep the entire device within a cool container that light cannot get to.

▶ **Check whether standby, sleep/suspend, or hibernate mode has failed:** If users regularly put their laptops into standby or hibernate modes, they could encounter issues once in a while. In some cases, the Power button needs to be held down for several seconds to reboot the machine out of a failed power-down state. This might have to be done with the battery removed. If either of these modes failed, check within the OS for any relevant information and possibly turn off hibernation and/or standby mode until the situation has been rectified. (On a slightly different note, sometimes laptops take a long time to come out of standby mode, and it's not necessarily an issue with standby but a case of the lid switch being stuck. It looks like a power issue, but it's a simple hardware fix.)

▶ **Reconnect the power button:** In rare cases, the power button might have been disconnected from the system board, or a new one may be required because the button mechanism failed. To fix this, the laptop must be opened, but often the power button is easily accessible once you do so.

▶ **Discharge the motherboard:** Another uncommon scenario is when there is a charge stored in some capacitance somewhere in the laptop—most likely the motherboard. This can cause the laptop to fail to turn on. LEDs do not light, even when the laptop is plugged in. It could be due to a power surge or other irregularity, or it may be an issue with the laptop's power system. You can discharge the motherboard by disconnecting the power, removing the battery, and then pressing and holding the power button for 30 seconds or so. This will remove any residual voltage from the motherboard and, depending on the laptop, might reset some BIOS/UEFI settings, which would have to be reconfigured later. Some people call this the *30-second trick* (although it could take less time or more), or a laptop *hard reset*, though that is not really an accurate term. What you are really doing here is discharging the motherboard, but be ready for other terms used by various technicians in the field.

▶ **Check the AC outlet:** Make sure the AC outlet that the user has plugged the laptop into is supplying power. A simple test would be to plug a lamp, clock, or other device into the outlet, but a more discerning and safer test would be to use a receptacle tester or circuit analyzer. For more information on testing AC outlets, see Chapter 18, "Power."

ExamAlert

Power is crucial! When troubleshooting, go through the entire power system step by step, including the power button, battery, DC jack, AC adapter, and AC outlet.

Keyboards/Keys

The keyboard is the most important input device on a laptop (or a PC). One of the great things about the keyboard is that you can use it exclusively, even if you don't have a pointing device or a touchpad available (or functional). You can do just about anything within the system with the keyboard.

Figure 1.1 shows an example of a typical laptop keyboard. Take a look at the keyboard on your laptop and identify the various keys. Also, look for similarities and differences between the keyboard in the figure and yours. If you don't have a keyboard, go to the Internet and search for images of current laptop keyboards.

FIGURE 1.1   **A typical laptop keyboard**

Special Function Keys

Some laptops have keyboards similar to the 101-key keyboard found on a PC and include a numeric keypad; these laptops are larger than most and are known as *desktop replacements*. However, most laptops are designed with a small form factor in mind, and this means a smaller keyboard. For example, the keyboard shown in Figure 1.1 has 86 keys. But, as shown in Figure 1.2, a user has the option of using the Fn key (Function key). The Fn key is a modifier key used on most laptops. It is designed to activate secondary, or *special*, functions of other keys. For example, in Figure 1.2, the F12 key has the secondary function of turning the wireless connection on or off—but only if you press the Fn key at the same time that you press the F12 key. To make it easier to read, Figure 1.2 breaks up the Fn key and the F1–F12 function keys, so you can see each of them better. But remember that the Fn key is usually toward the lower-left corner of the keyboard, and the function keys (F1–F12) are situated at the top of the keyboard.

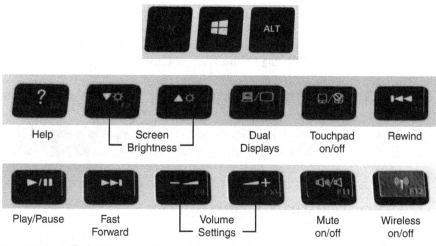

FIGURE 1.2   **Typical function keys and their tasks**

Thanks to the Fn key and the F1–F12 function keys, much more functionality can be incorporated into the keyboard without the need for additional keys. This idea has since grown to include all kinds of controls; for example, controls for using the media player (play/pause/fast forward/rewind), putting the computer to sleep; enabling wireless, the keyboard backlight, and the touchpad; adjusting screen orientation; and a variety of other functions, including enabling an external monitor. On the laptop shown in this example, the F4 key seconds as a display toggle between the built-in display and an external monitor. Take a look at Figure 1.2 and attempt to identify what each of the function key images represents.

> ## ExamAlert
>
> Use the Fn key in combination with the F1–F12 function keys to configure many things, including media options, Wi-Fi access, brightness, the touchpad, and an external monitor.

But all this key configuration is up to the manufacturer, and any key can be given a secondary function. This enables things like the numeric keypad and the number lock key, which might be abbreviated as Num Lock, or num lk. (This could also be an individual key.) Sometimes, users forget about the Num Lock key, and when they try to type, strange garbled code comes out! This is because the numbers are sharing keys used by letters and symbols. Simply press the Num Lock key once to fix the problem. This is also common if the user works with an external keyboard at the office and disconnects it when leaving the office. However, today's operating systems and programs are pretty good at sensing things such as an enabled Num Lock or Caps Lock key.

> **ExamAlert**
>
> If available, press the Num Lock key to enable/disable the numeric keypad on a laptop. If the Num Lock indicator light is on, then the numeric key is enabled.

Troubleshooting Keyboards

I have had many people tell me that their laptop's keyboard isn't working properly. Over time I've noticed several culprits: overuse, loose ribbon cables, spilled coffee, or users simply pounding the tar out of the keyboard! It happens. The telltale signs include bent or warped keyboards and missing keycaps. Whatever the cause, here are a couple of actual problems you might encounter:

▶ **Stuck keys:** Sticking keys could be a result of overuse, damage to an individual key's switch, or liquid spilled on the keyboard. (If a stuck key is the worst that happens due to a liquid spill, consider yourself lucky!) A stuck key can be identified by the key failing to work in the operating system or the BIOS/UEFI reporting an error. Use an external keyboard to troubleshoot further. By removing the keycap and cleaning the keyswitch underneath, you can usually fix the problem. If not, the entire keyboard will probably have to be replaced.

> **Note**
>
> The Basic Input/Output System (BIOS) is the underlying setup system for a laptop or PC. We'll discuss that and the Unified Extensible Firmware Interface (UEFI) more in Chapter 16, "Motherboards and Add-on Cards."

▶ **Loose connection:** If a laptop is moved around and jostled a lot, as many laptops are, it could possibly cause loose connections. One of these is the ribbon cable that connects the keyboard to the motherboard. To fix this, the keyboard must be lifted away from the laptop and the ribbon cable attached securely.

▶ **Damaged keyboard:** Users who inadvertently drop heavy items onto the keyboard or operate the keyboard with a heavy hand might cause a warped or bent keyboard. Some brands of laptops suffer from this more than others. This is usually impossible to repair; the keyboard often needs to be replaced.

When replacing a keyboard, be sure to shut down the laptop, unplug it, and disconnect the battery. Then employ electrostatic discharge (ESD) prevention measures. Among other things, that means using an antistatic strap and antistatic mat. I speak more to this in Chapter 59, "Safety Procedures." You'll need a very small Phillips-head screwdriver and/or small Torx screwdriver—as low as T8 or even T6—some things to add to your computer repair toolkit!

> **Note**
>
> ESD can occur when two objects with different voltages come into contact with each other.

Try to document the process as you go. Write down what you see and how and where cables and screws were attached. Also make note of how devices were oriented before they were removed. Label any parts that you remove for easier identification later on. Take pictures with your smartphone or another camera as you go through the disassembly process. If available, refer to the manufacturer's documentation that came with the laptop.

When you are done with the repair, verify that the new keyboard works by testing every key using Notepad or another text editor or word processor and by testing Fn-enabled keys as well.

If a user needs access to a laptop right away (before it can be repaired), a temporary solution would be to connect a USB or wireless keyboard. This *should* be recognized automatically by the operating system, though a BIOS/UEFI configuration might be necessary.

Touchpad

Whereas a PC uses a mouse, a laptop uses a built-in pointing device. The bulk of laptops come with a pointing device known as a touchpad. By gliding a finger across the touchpad surface, a user can move the cursor on the screen. Touchpads might also come with two buttons that take the place of a mouse's buttons. In portable computing lingo, the word "click" is replaced with the word "tap." In addition to using the buttons, many touchpad surfaces can also be tapped or double-tapped upon, just by tapping with the finger. Touchpads can be replaced, though it is uncommon to do so; they are often connected by two cables similar to the flex cable that connects the keyboard. However, you might have to remove other devices first to get at the touchpad. You might also have to work from the bottom and from the top of the laptop; it depends on the brand of laptop.

Now and again you will encounter users reporting that when they type on the keyboard, the mouse pointer scrolls across the screen. This is sometimes referred to as a "ghost cursor," "cursor drift," or "pointer drift." It could occur because a part of the user's hand, or even the user's sleeve, is brushing against the touchpad or touchscreen. It could also be caused by paired Bluetooth devices such as an external mouse or mouse/keyboard combination, especially if the person is moving about and the external device is in a backpack. To remedy this, pointing devices can be turned off within the operating system, usually through the laptop manufacturer's software. Watch out for situations in which the entire device might have been disabled or perhaps just the pad portion of the touchpad was disabled. It can be disabled in the OS and with a function key on some laptops. It's also possible to disable tapping capability of the touchpad while still allowing movement of the cursor. In rarer cases, a ghost cursor occurring while working in the operating system or in an application can be caused by an incorrect or bad device driver. (A device driver is a small program that controls the device and acts as a software interface between the device and the OS.) If you suspect a driver issue, then reinstall or update the mouse/touchpad driver and the video driver and update the OS as well.

> **Note**
>
> Another type of pointing device is a pointing stick, known within Lenovo laptops as the TrackPoint. This device is implemented as a small rubber cap (that looks like an eraser head) just above the B key or as two buttons that work essentially the same as a touchpad's buttons.

Of course, external mice can be connected to a laptop or its docking station as well. These would be connected to USB ports or could be wireless devices.

Random-Access Memory (RAM)

Laptops use double data rate (DDR) memory. But in laptops it's miniaturized and is known as a small outline dual inline memory module (SODIMM). Two common types of SODIMMs in laptops are DDR3 (which has 204 pins) and DDR4 (which has 260 pins). Different versions of SODIMM memory are not compatible. For example, normally you can't put a DDR4 SODIMM into a DDR3 SODIMM slot. SODIMM DDR speeds are similar to their PC equivalents. We'll discuss the different types of DDR and their speeds and data transfer rates in Chapter 14, "RAM."

> **ExamAlert**
>
> Know that SODIMM DDR3 has 204 pins and SODIMM DDR4 has 260 pins. Understand the pin format differences between them and standard DIMMs (used in PCs).

Random-access memory (RAM) has a center notch that helps to orient the RAM during installation. This notch will usually be in a different location depending on the SODIMM version.

Before installing any new RAM, check compatibility. Remember to consult the laptop's documentation to find out exactly how much RAM and which type of RAM the laptop will accept. When you have purchased compatible RAM, installing it to a laptop is usually quite simple. RAM is often located on the bottom of the laptop, underneath an access cover. In other laptops, it might be underneath the keyboard, or there could be one stick of RAM under the keyboard and a second (usually for add-ons) under an access cover underneath the laptop. Consult your laptop's documentation for the exact location of the RAM compartment. Table 1.1 shows the steps involved in adding RAM to a laptop. Keep in mind that SODIMMs and their corresponding memory boards are more delicate than their counterparts in a desktop computer.

TABLE 1.1   **Installing a SODIMM in a Laptop**

Step	Procedure
1. Prepare the laptop for surgery!	Shut down the laptop, unplug it, and disconnect the battery. Then employ ESD prevention measures.
2. Review your documentation.	Review your documentation to find out where RAM is located. For this step, assume that the RAM can be added to an area underneath the laptop.
3. Locate the memory.	Quite often, you will need to remove the bottom cover of the laptop. Be ready to document and store the many screws somewhere safe. On older laptops, there might be two screws that you need to remove to open a memory compartment door. Often, these are captive screws and will stay in the door. But if they are not, label them and store them in a safe place.
4. Remove the old RAM.	If you are upgrading, remove the current RAM by pushing both of the clips out. The RAM should pop up. If it does not, lift the RAM at a 45-degree angle. Gently remove the RAM, holding it by the edges.
5. Insert the RAM.	There could be one or two slots for RAM. One of them might already be in use. Many laptops support multichannel memory. If this is the case and you install a second memory module, the best option is to select one that is identical to the first, though that is not always necessary.
Insert the memory module at a 45-degree angle into the memory slot, aligning the notch with the keyed area of the memory slot. Press the module into the slot; then press the module down toward the circuit board until it snaps into place (GENTLY!). Two clips (one on either side) lock into the notches in the side of the memory module. Press down again to make sure it is in place. See Figure 1.3 for an example of an installed SODIMM. Note the locking clips holding the memory module into place.
6. Close the laptop and then test.	Attach the cover (or compartment). You might want to wait on screwing it in until you test the laptop. Then boot the computer into the BIOS/UEFI and make sure it sees the new memory module(s). Finally, boot into the operating system, make sure that it sees the new total amount of RAM, and then verify whether applications work properly.

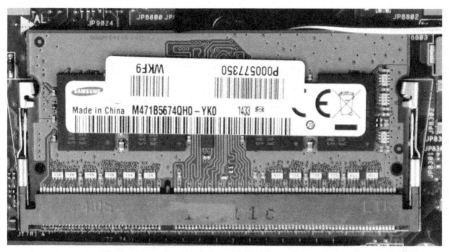

FIGURE 1.3 **Installed SODIMM**

Sometimes upgraded memory fails to be identified by the BIOS/UEFI. This usually means that the memory was not installed properly. Turn off the computer, reseat the RAM modules, and then reboot. This usually fixes the problem.

Occasionally a laptop fails to boot and emits a series of continuous beeps. This could be due to faulty memory. However, it could simply be that the memory contacts are dirty. As mentioned before, laptops are often mistreated and are used in a variety of environments. Pop the memory hatch and inspect the RAM modules. If they require cleaning, use compressed air or try using a RAM cleaner. Plug the modules back in and verify functionality by rebooting the system several times. If they still don't work, try swapping out the RAM with known good modules.

Storage Drives

While RAM excels at storing data temporarily, a laptop needs something to store data permanently (that is, until it is erased). Storage drives allow for this "permanent" storage of data.

> **Note**
>
> Storage drives are often referred to as "hard drives." While this term is probably not accurate for a drive being used in a laptop today, it is still a commonly used term that you should be ready for.

Storage drives *will* fail; it's just a matter of when. Laptop storage drives are even more susceptible to failure than those in desktop computers due to their mobility and the bumps and bruises that laptops regularly sustain.

Many laptops come with Serial ATA (SATA) drives, which incorporate two connectors: a 7-pin data connector and a 15-pin power connector. The bulk of the storage drives in laptops are 2.5 inches wide, though ultra-small laptops and other small portable devices might use a drive as small as 1.8 inches. See Figure 1.4 for an example of a 2.5-inch SATA solid-state drive (SSD). Note the smaller data connector and larger power connector.

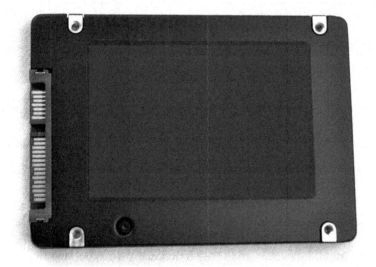

FIGURE 1.4   **A typical 2.5-inch SSD**

SATA drives are broken down into three categories:

▶ **SSD:** Has no moving parts and generally uses NAND-based flash memory to store data

▶ **Magnetic disk:** Also known as a hard disk drive, a magnetic-based drive that uses an actual mechanical disk and an arm with a read/write head to store data to the disk

▶ **Hybrid:** A hybrid drive that uses a magnetic disk as well as SSD cache memory—so it combines the capacity of a magnetic disk with the performance of an SSD

We discuss the various types of storage drives in Chapter 15, "Storage Drives."

ExamAlert

Know that laptop storage drive types include SSD, magnetic disk, and hybrid. Also, be aware that they have either 2.5- or 1.8-inch form factors.

One of the ways to make an older laptop run faster is to replace the storage drive. For example, if a laptop contains a SATA magnetic disk, you might opt to replace it with an SSD or perhaps a hybrid drive, or perhaps even an M.2 drive, if the laptop has an M.2-compatible slot on its motherboard. These options can offer greater data transfer rates as well as improvements in overall system efficiency. Upgrades such as these might also need to be performed if the original drive fails. At that point, you'll probably need to rescue some data from the original drive.

Note

Be careful with M.2 drives. They create a lot of heat, and in a laptop's tight environment, overheating is a possibility.

Of course, to rescue data from a drive, you must first remove it. Laptop drives can be accessed from one of three places. The first, and maybe the most common, is from the bottom; this requires removing either the entire bottom cover or an access panel. The second is from underneath the keyboard. And the third is from the side of the laptop where the drive is located, in some kind of caddy. These last two options are much less common than the first. In any of the three scenarios, there is usually some kind of rubber molding or bracket that has to be removed or unscrewed from the drive when replacing it. Hold on to this item for the new drive. In any case, I employ antistatic measures and *use care* when working around any connections inside the laptop; they are more fragile than their PC counterparts.

Communications

Communicating quickly and efficiently with other computers and wireless devices is key in business and home environments. To do so, laptops use a variety of different devices, including the following:

▶ **Wired and wireless networking:** Most laptops today come equipped with wired Ethernet and Wi-Fi to connect to a local area network (LAN) or a wireless local area network (WLAN). The wired connection has an

RJ45 port and can typically transfer data at 1000 Mbps, auto-negotiating its speed to the network it is connected to. Wireless networking connections are made with an internal Mini PCIe card that can potentially connect to 802.11a, b, g, n, ac, and ax networks. For more information on wireless protocols, see Chapter 7, "Wireless Protocols." It is also possible to connect wired or wireless network adapters to USB ports. There is often a WLAN button (or Wi-Fi button) that can enable/disable a laptop's built-in wireless adapter. It usually shares a function key. Keep this in mind when troubleshooting. If this is disabled, the laptop cannot connect wirelessly, even if the device is enabled in the operating system. Many laptops use proprietary software for the configuration of wireless network connections instead of using the built-in Windows WLAN AutoConfig service. In some cases, it might be easier to disable the proprietary application and use Windows instead.

ExamAlert

If a laptop can't connect to a wireless network, try pressing the Wi-Fi button—either a button associated with a function key or a standalone button near the keyboard.

▶ **Bluetooth:** Bluetooth modules enable a laptop to connect to other Bluetooth devices, such as headsets and phones, over short distances, thus joining or creating a personal area network (PAN). A Bluetooth module might be included inside the laptop as an individual card or as a combo Bluetooth/WLAN card. External USB and remote controls are also available. For more information on Bluetooth, see Chapter 3, "Mobile Device Accessories and Ports." Many laptops come with WLAN and Bluetooth capabilities; however, the two technologies can possibly compete over frequencies. If the WLAN connection runs at 2.4 GHz, you might need to recommend that a user make use of only one technology at a time, if possible. Function keys or individual buttons are often available on a laptop for enabling/disabling Wi-Fi and Bluetooth. If not, it can be done within the operating system (for example, in the Notification Area in Windows).

▶ **Cellular:** Wireless wide area network (WWAN) cellular connections can be made in a variety of ways. Some laptops are designed with built-in Mini PCIe or M.2 cellular modules. Some telecommunications providers offer cellular connections via USB-based devices as well.

Laptop wireless cards can be added to laptops or upgraded if needed. You will find combination cards that offer Wi-Fi and Bluetooth. These often use the M.2 form factor. Such a card has one antenna for each technology. After employing antistatic methods and opening the laptop, you'll find that the M.2 card is connected with a single screw. The connector edge of the card will often have two divots—showing you how it should be oriented. After installation, be sure to use insulating tape to cover the antenna leads and to wrap around the antenna wires if they come into close contact with any power wires/connections. Finally, route the wires carefully. Often, they will terminate in the laptop's hinge or similar endpoint.

If there is no option for upgrade, meaning there is no M.2 slot for wireless, then a laptop can still access Wi-Fi and Bluetooth by way of an external, low-profile mini-USB device.

> **ExamAlert**
>
> Know the various ways that a laptop could communicate with other computers, including wired and wireless Ethernet, Bluetooth, and cellular WAN connections.

Physical Privacy

A laptop can be secured through the use of cable locks, biometrics, and by disabling NFC. Let's briefly discuss each of those.

One way to physically secure a laptop is to use a cable lock. This works in a similar fashion to a bicycle lock. It consists of a very strong cable that is difficult to cut through—often galvanized, multi-stranded steel—with a lock on one end and a loop on the other. This allows the user to secure the laptop in a variety of ways, such as to a table, desk, and so on. Some companies incorporate metal loops or eye bolts near workstations to use with the cable lock for increased security. The lock itself will often adhere to lock-picking protection standards and is usually a tubular cam lock. Many laptops come with a security slot to be used with cable locks; the tubular lock is inserted into the slot and turned 90 degrees to lock it or unlock it. This, of course, is only one anti-theft solution for laptops, but it is one that is commonly used by organizations, corporations, and individuals.

Biometrics is the science of identifying human beings based on their physical characteristics, such as a thumbprint, retina scan, voice pattern, facial recognition, and so on. A USB-based biometric reader can be connected to a laptop, which then requires an additional form of identification from the user before the user can log in—for instance, a thumbprint. This secures the laptop further through what is known as multi-factor authentication (MFA); the user must provide his or her thumbprint, as well as a username and password to gain access to the computer. For more information on biometrics, see Chapters 43, "Physical Security," and 44, "Logical Security."

Near-field communication (NFC) is a technology that allows two mobile devices to "beam" information to each other wirelessly if they are in close proximity. A device such as a laptop that is equipped with NFC will employ near-field scanning techniques in order to communicate with other NFC-enabled devices. Because NFC is a two-way, short-range communications technology, it opens the door for an attacker to attempt to gain access to the laptop's data with a third-party app/scanner. If NFC is deemed too great a security risk (and for many organizations it is), then it can be individually disabled in the operating system's settings, or you could set the laptop to operate in airplane mode to turn off all wireless transmissions. See Chapter 3 for more information about NFC.

> **ExamAlert**
>
> Turning on airplane mode will disable wireless transmissions such as NFC; however, it can also disable your ability to connect to Wi-Fi or send/receive calls. Remember this for troubleshooting purposes!

> **Note**
>
> Know that you can increase the security for your laptop, but there is never a 100% secure solution because any security technique can be bypassed given time, persistence, and ingenuity. So, for example, a cable lock can help, but don't rely solely on that—or on any other single security precaution.

Wrap-up of Chapter 1

That wraps up this first chapter. I recommend you review the ExamAlerts and any notes that you have taken before you continue to the Cram Quiz. Do this for the rest of the book as well.

What follows is your first cram quiz. This will help to reinforce the concepts you have learned. Good luck!

Cram Quiz

Answer these questions. The answers follow the last question. If you cannot answer these questions correctly, consider reading this chapter again until you can.

1. What is the module format for a stick of SODIMM DDR4 RAM?

   ○ **A.** 1.8-inch

   ○ **B.** 204-pin

   ○ **C.** 260-pin

   ○ **D.** 2.5-inch

2. You just added a second memory module to a laptop. However, after rebooting the system, the OS reports the same amount of memory as before. What should you do next?

   ○ **A.** Replace both memory modules.

   ○ **B.** Run Windows Update.

   ○ **C.** Replace the motherboard.

   ○ **D.** Reseat the laptop memory.

3. Which of the following are ways that a laptop can communicate with other computers? (Select all that apply.)

   ○ **A.** Bluetooth

   ○ **B.** WLAN

   ○ **C.** DC jack

   ○ **D.** Cellular WAN

4. Which of the following are possible reasons that a laptop's keyboard might fail completely? (Select the two best answers.)

   ○ **A.** A key is stuck.

   ○ **B.** A ribbon cable is disconnected.

   ○ **C.** The user spilled coffee on the laptop.

   ○ **D.** The keyboard was disabled in the Device Manager.

5. A user doesn't see anything on his laptop's screen. He tries to use AC power and thinks that the laptop is not receiving any. Which of the following are two possible reasons for this? (Select the two best answers.)

   ○ **A.** He is using an incorrect AC adapter.

   ○ **B.** The AC adapter is not connected to the laptop.

   ○ **C.** Windows won't boot.

   ○ **D.** The battery is dead.

6. One of your customers reports that she walked away from her laptop for 30 minutes, and when she returned, the display was very dim. She increased the brightness setting and moved the mouse but to no effect. What should you do first?

   ○ **A.** Replace the LCD screen.

   ○ **B.** Check the operating system for corruption.

   ○ **C.** Connect an external monitor to verify that the video card works.

   ○ **D.** Check whether the laptop is now on battery power.

7. You are helping a customer with a laptop issue. The customer says that two days ago the laptop was accidentally dropped while it was charging. You observe that the laptop will not turn on and that it is connected to the correct power adapter. Which of the following is the most likely cause?

   ○ **A.** The battery

   ○ **B.** The power adapter

   ○ **C.** The storage drive

   ○ **D.** The DC jack

   ○ **E.** The BIOS/UEFI

8. You want to reduce the risk of your laptop being stolen. Which of the following is the best option?

   ○ **A.** Incorporate biometrics

   ○ **B.** Disable NFC

   ○ **C.** Use a cable lock

   ○ **D.** Enable MFA

9. A user cannot make contactless payments using NFC, connect to the Internet, or send/receive calls from their mobile device. The user is able to boot the device and sign on. Which of the following is most likely the cause of the problem?

   ○ **A.** Failed power-down state

   ○ **B.** Airplane mode

   ○ **C.** Biometric authentication

   ○ **D.** ESD has occurred

Cram Quiz Answers

1. **C.** DDR4 SODIMM modules have 260 pins. DDR3 is 204-pin. 1.8-inch is the size associated with smaller storage drives used in some laptops. 2.5-inch is the standard size for SSD storage drives.

2. **D.** The next step you should take is to reseat the memory. SODIMMs can be a bit tricky to install. They must be firmly installed, but you don't want to press too hard and damage any components. If the laptop worked fine before the upgrade, you shouldn't have to replace the modules or the motherboard. Windows Update will not find additional RAM.

3. **A, B, and D.** Some of the methods that laptops use to communicate with other computers include Bluetooth, WLAN, and cellular WAN wireless connections, plus wired connections like Ethernet (RJ45) and, for older laptops, dial-up (RJ11). The DC jack is the input on the laptop that accepts power from the AC adapter.

4. **B and C.** A laptop's keyboard could fail due to a disconnected or loose keyboard ribbon cable. It could also fail if a user spilled coffee on the laptop, dropped it on the ground, and so on. One stuck key will not cause the entire keyboard to fail, and on most laptops, the keyboard cannot be disabled in the Device Manager. It can be uninstalled but not disabled.

5. **A and B.** An incorrect adapter will usually not power a laptop. The adapter used must be exact. And, of course, if the laptop is not properly plugged in to the adapter, it won't get power. Windows doesn't play into this scenario. And if the battery were dead, it could cause the laptop to fail to power up, but only if the AC adapter were also disconnected; the scenario states that the user is trying to use AC power.

6. **D.** It could be that the laptop is now on battery power and is set to a dimmer display and shorter sleep configuration while on battery. The laptop may not be getting AC power from the AC outlet for some reason. The battery power setting is the first thing you should check; afterward, start troubleshooting the AC adapter, cable, AC outlet, and so on. It's too early to try replacing the display; try not to replace something until you have ruled out all other possibilities. A dim screen is not caused by OS corruption. There's no need to plug in an external monitor; you know the video adapter is working, it's just dim.

7. **D.** The DC jack was probably damaged when the laptop was dropped. It may have been plugged in (charging) and fallen on the plug that connects to the DC jack (which is easily damaged on many laptops). The customer probably used the laptop until the battery became discharged before noticing that the laptop wouldn't take a charge anymore—and now it won't turn on at all. So the battery is probably not the issue. A power adapter can be damaged, but the DC-in jack is more easily damaged. The storage drive and the BIOS/UEFI normally will not affect whether the laptop will turn on.

8. **C.** To best reduce the chance of theft, use a cable lock. This is a physical cable that can be wrapped around a sturdy object and locked to the laptop, keeping it *relatively* secure from theft. Incorporating biometrics means implementing a thumbprint scan or other physical characteristic scan into the authentication process. Disabling NFC means that near-field communications will be turned off, and data can't be "beamed" to other devices. Enabling MFA means that you are implementing multi-factor authentication—for example, combining a password and biometrics. While none of the incorrect answers can reduce the risk of a laptop being stolen, they do decrease the chance of *data* being stolen. As you can guess, computer security can be incredibly deep. That's why I dedicate Chapters 43 through 52 of this book to it!

9. B. Turning on airplane mode (the most likely cause of the problem) will disable wireless transmissions, including NFC. This is great for security purposes, but it can also disable the ability to connect to Wi-Fi networks or send/receive calls. A failed power state would render the entire device unusable; however, the question says the user was able to boot and sign on to the device. Biometric authentication is most likely not the cause of the problem in this scenario because the user is not having problems signing on to the device. Electrostatic discharge (ESD) can occur when two objects with different voltages come into contact with each other. ESD can wreak havoc with electronic components, but it is not the most likely problem here because the device appears to be working normally in all other regards—plus it's somewhat uncommon for mobile devices.

The real issue here is *user error*: The user did not remember that the device was in airplane mode. When you troubleshoot problems, remember that they are often user related!

Good going, you completed the first chapter! I'll meet you at the next one.

CHAPTER 2

Mobile Device Display Components

This chapter covers the following A+ 220-1101 exam objective:

▶ 1.2 – Compare and contrast the display components of mobile devices

As a technician, you should understand the differences between the various laptop display types, including LCD, LED, and OLED. Going further, you need to know the basics about the display's inverter and digitizer technology. Finally, be sure to know how other components are installed that might be located in the display area of a laptop—for instance, webcams, microphones, and Wi-Fi antennas.

Note

The CompTIA A+ objectives list important concepts that you need to know for the exam, but the list is not *finite*. By this, I mean that there might be other associated technologies that are not listed but that you might be tested on. So, at times, I add content to this book that goes further than the listed objectives. Be ready to study beyond the objectives to fully prepare for the exam—*and* for the real world.

Display Types

A laptop might use one of a few types of displays, depending on the age and the price of the laptop. These include LCD, LED, and OLED:

▶ **LCD:** The liquid-crystal display (LCD) is a flat-panel display that consists of two sheets of polarizing material surrounding a layer of liquid-crystal solution. It connects to the motherboard by way of a flex ribbon cable or an all-in-one power/signal cable and gets its power from an inverter board. Most LCD screens are thin-film transistor (TFT) active-matrix displays, meaning they have multiple transistors for each pixel. These transistors are contained within a flexible material and are located directly behind the liquid-crystal material. In general, LCDs generate a small amount of heat and cause little in the way of interference and emissions. However, they use more electricity than newer types of displays because they utilize a high-powered bulb, quite often a cold cathode fluorescent lamp (CCFL). LCD screens can be broken down into several types of active-matrix technologies, including

   ▶ **TN:** Twisted nematic (TN) displays use liquid crystals that can twist to allow light to pass through. This is an older technology that was used on small mobile devices but is not seen as often today.

   ▶ **IPS:** In-plane switching (IPS) and Super-IPS are LCD technologies that align liquid crystals on a plane parallel to a glass substrate. IPS provides for a wider viewing angle than TN and was very popular on laptops for a long time.

▶ **VA:** Vertical alignment (VA) displays align liquid crystals vertically to a glass substrate. VA can offer a higher contrast ratio and deeper black levels compared to IPS, but they sacrifice viewing angle in the process.

▶ **LED:** Light-emitting-diode (LED) monitors utilize two-terminal electronic components known as diodes to display images. These diodes are red, green, and blue (RGB)—the "primary" colors when it comes to computer monitors. LEDs use less power than traditional LCDs and are therefore more efficient. LED monitors use a different backlight than traditional LCD monitors. Whereas older LCD monitors use a CCFL as the illumination source, LED monitors use light-emitting diodes, which release photons; this process is known as *electroluminescence*. It is so much more energy efficient that you will find hybrid designs known as LED-backlit LCDs. Such a device does not use a CCFL but instead uses diodes with an LCD screen.

▶ **OLED:** OLED stands for *organic* light-emitting diode. The main advantage of OLED over LED is manufacturing cost; OLEDs can be printed onto just about any substrate using simple printing processes—and they can be incredibly small (even one per pixel), all lighting individually. The technology uses an organic compound to emit light in response to an electric current. OLED displays have the best black levels, but you might opt for a different type of LED if you are more concerned with brightness and some other specifications. One example is QLED (quantum dot light-emitting diode), which has a quantum dot layer built in to it which enhances colors and the brightness of images.

Inverter and Backlight

A typical laptop's LCD display incorporates a backlight and an inverter. The backlight is a bulb (for example, a CCFL). It emits light through the screen so that you can see the images that the computer is attempting to display. The inverter—or, more accurately, the *screen* inverter—is a device that converts direct current (DC) that comes from the motherboard into alternating current (AC) to be used by the display's backlight. This section focuses on LCDs because LEDs (and OLEDs) don't need an inverter; they are DC only by design and don't use a CCFL or similar lamp.

ExamAlert

Know that a screen inverter's job is to convert DC voltage from the motherboard into AC voltage to be sent to the backlight.

The video display in a laptop is integrated; however, while this is a main feature of the portability of laptops, it can be a point of failure as well. Minor issues such as intermittent lines on the screen suggest that the display cable needs to be reconnected or replaced. However, complete display failures suggest a worse problem that will take longer to repair. Aside from a damaged screen, LCD display failures can be broken down into a couple categories: a damaged inverter or a worn-out backlight.

Damaged Inverter

To review, on a laptop with an LCD-based screen, the LCD is usually lit by a CCFL (basically a bulb); it is that LCD backlight which requires AC power. The backlight is driven by a high-voltage inverter circuit. Because the inverter runs at high voltage, and possibly at high temperatures, it is prone to failure. If the inverter fails, the display will go dark; however, an external monitor should work properly. Another possibility is that the backlight has failed. You can verify if it is an inverter/backlight issue by shining a flashlight directly at the screen; this works best in a dark room. When you do this, you should be able to make out the operating system! This means that the display is getting the video signal from the motherboard and the problem, most likely, is indeed the inverter or the backlight. If the display's cable that connects the LCD to the motherboard were loose or disconnected, or if the video adapter failed, nothing would show up on the screen at all. The inverter circuit is usually situated on its own circuit board. The inverter often has two connectors: one for the high-voltage connection that leads to the power source and one for a cable that connects to the display. Disconnect these and carefully remove the inverter. Always hold circuit boards by the edges and try not to touch any actual circuits or chips.

> **ExamAlert**
>
> Warning! The inverter should not be handled if the laptop is on! Incorrect handling could result in personal injury. Be sure to turn off and unplug the laptop and remove the battery before removing an inverter.

Worn-Out Backlight

A laptop's backlight usually lasts a long time. However, at some point, the lamp starts to wear out. You might notice a dimmer screen than before, or a reddish/pinkish hue to the screen, or maybe a loss of color. All of these things indicate the possibility of a worn-out lamp.

To replace either the inverter or the lamp, you need to disassemble the display. This usually means removing a screen bezel and taking out the screen, which gives way to those items. Be ready to have mobile device tools on hand, especially a thin but strong plastic shim. Consider purchasing a pry tool repair kit that includes a variety of shims, prying tools, and so on. Don't forget to keep a variety of small screwdrivers on hand.

> **Note**
>
> As you can guess, LED and OLED screens do not suffer as many failures as CCFL-based LCDs do, mainly because LEDs and OLEDs do not incorporate (or need) an inverter or a lamp. Consider that when making technology purchases.

Digitizers and Touchscreens

A touchscreen—also known as a *digitizer* screen—is a screen that allows for tapping or writing on the screen. Many allow users to simply use their finger, while others also allow for the use of a stylus. A *stylus* is a writing tool, usually a thin plastic "pen" type of device used to take the place of a mouse; it enables you to tap and "write" on the digitizer with great accuracy.

These methods are widely used in smartphones, tablets, handheld computers, Chromebooks, and some laptops. For example, usually, when you sign for a package from a shipping company, you sign with a stylus on a touchscreen/digitizer instead of using pencil and paper.

More accurately, a digitizer is a device that converts tapped or written impulses (analog) on the screen into instructions (digital) for the operating system to follow.

Removal of a touchscreen requires some disassembly. Screen bezels, plastics, and so on have to be removed before the screen can be unscrewed and disconnected.

> **Note**
>
> Be prepared to have very small screwdrivers available. Laptop and mobile device repair kits often come with these types of screwdrivers. Also be prepared for more "proprietary" types of screws that require fewer common screwdrivers.

There are also digitizer overlays that can be added to a laptop screen. Generally, these touchscreen kits are strapped on to the display with Velcro and connect via USB. Be ready to install custom drivers and perform touchscreen orientation and/or calibration.

Webcam and Microphone

Webcams are great for communication, but sometimes they fail, and in some cases they are considered security vulnerabilities. In the event that a webcam has to be replaced, or just removed altogether, you can follow a few simple steps. First, employ antistatic measures. Then, remove the bezel from the display. The webcam module should then be visible above the display screen. Often, it is just connected with a small plug and no screws or attachment of any kind. Next, *carefully* disconnect it with your shim or other thin prying tool (non-metal), place it in an antistatic bag, and label the bag for later use. Hold on to any tape or sticky material that keeps the webcam in place. Next, replace it with an identical part. Be very careful when connecting the power for the new webcam; the plug is often delicate. Use (or reuse) tape to fasten the webcam in the right spot (if necessary). Then, attach the bezel to the display once again. Finally, test the webcam's video and audio with an application such as the built-in Windows Camera program.

Some people use tape to cover their webcams for security or privacy purposes, but depending on the policies of your organization, this might not be enough, and you will have to remove webcams altogether. Some companies offer filler items to fill the gap where the camera lens normally goes.

A laptop might have a function key that can disable the webcam. It can also be disabled in the operating system, so be sure to check those options before replacing a webcam.

The microphone on a laptop is often part of the webcam module (for example, to the left of the lens). In such a case, removing the webcam module removes the microphone. The microphone could also be disabled in the operating system. For example, in Windows, you would do this in the Recording tab of the Sound dialog box. As mentioned, some people use tape to cover their webcams, and they also use tape to cover the microphone openings; however, depending on the type of tape, it might muffle the recorded sound but not eliminate it. Once again, for security purposes, it may be necessary to disable the webcam altogether or remove it.

> **ExamAlert**
>
> Know where to find the webcam and microphone within a laptop display and know how to disable them.

Some companies opt to disable webcams (and associated microphones) and instead use external USB-based webcams to achieve better security as well as better performance so that the users can physically disconnect webcams when they are not in use.

Wi-Fi Antenna Connector and Placement

A Wi-Fi antenna is used to connect to a wireless network, also known as a wireless local area network (WLAN). Wi-Fi antennas can be found inside a laptop as well as externally. If an antenna is inside the laptop, it is usually some type of module—either an M.2 card (as shown in Figure 2.1) or a PCI Express Mini Card (also known as a Mini PCIe card).

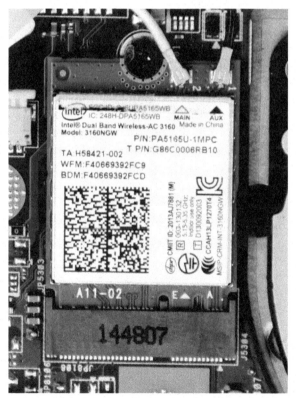

FIGURE 2.1   A typical internal Wi-Fi module using the M.2 form factor

ExamAlert

Be able to identify M.2 and Mini PCIe cards by name and by sight.

Usually, this module can be identified quickly by removing the bottom cover of the laptop. It is connected to a slot and is attached with either one screw (for M.2) or two screws (for Mini PCIe). M.2-based cards have up to 67 pins and might use the 2230 standard (22×30 mm) or the 1216 standard (12×16 mm), among others. The one in Figure 2.1 uses the 2230 standard. Full-size Mini PCIe cards are 30×50.95 mm and use a 52-pin edge connector.

Be careful when installing an M.2 or Mini PCIe card; the contacts can be easily damaged. Place even pressure on both sides and press the card into the slot evenly so it goes in straight, without any side-to-side movement. If a Wi-Fi antenna cable already exists in the laptop, reuse it by connecting the wire ends to the contacts on the card. Usually there are two: one for Wi-Fi and one for Bluetooth (BT). If there is no antenna, install a new one and route it through the laptop hinge and around the display as far as it can go. The longer the antenna, the better the reception.

Of course, external Wi-Fi adapters can be used, connecting to USB or an RJ45 port. With external adapters, antennas (if there are any) can be pointed in the direction that you desire. Or, the adapter can be moved from a USB port on one side of the laptop to a USB port on the other side. Just remember to consider using USB 3.0 or higher; blue ports or better. Also, keep the module away from any sources of interference. If it has actual antennas that you can move, first attempt a 90-degree angle, and if that doesn't work, experiment! However, many external Wi-Fi modules that connect via USB are small, self-contained devices with the antenna embedded inside. So, the choice of USB port is really your only option in that scenario when it comes to antenna placement.

Wi-Fi transmissions rely on the IEEE 802.11 standards, including 802.11ax, ac, n, g, and b (listed here from fastest to slowest). We'll discuss those protocols more in Chapter 7, "Wireless Protocols."

Every Wi-Fi adapter has its own unique media access control (MAC) address, also known as a MAC ID. This identification number is usually printed on a sticker on the Wi-Fi adapter, and it is programmed into the ROM of the adapter. It differentiates the Wi-Fi adapter from all other network adapters on your network and around the world. Regardless of the type of network adapter, the MAC address is a 48-bit number, described using hexadecimal numbering (for example, 68-05-CA-2D-A4-B3). The number is also referred to as a physical address in the Windows command-line interface. If you have an internal Wi-Fi adapter, you can find out the MAC address in Windows by typing **ipconfig /all** in the Command Prompt or the PowerShell. (In macOS or Linux, you can use **ip a** or **ifconfig**.) We'll discuss the MAC address more in Chapter 6, "Network Devices."

Cram Quiz

Answer these questions. The answers follow the last question. If you cannot answer these questions correctly, consider reading this chapter again until you can.

1. Which kind of video technology do most laptop LCDs use?

   ○ **A.** TFT active matrix

   ○ **B.** Passive matrix

   ○ **C.** OLED

   ○ **D.** MAC ID

2. Which of the following uses an organic compound that emits light?

   ○ **A.** TFT active matrix

   ○ **B.** IPS

   ○ **C.** OLED

   ○ **D.** LCD

   ○ **E.** LED

3. Which of the following are possible reasons a laptop's LCD suddenly went blank with no user intervention? (Select the two best answers.)

   ○ **A.** Damaged inverter

   ○ **B.** Damaged LCD

   ○ **C.** Burned-out backlight

   ○ **D.** Incorrect resolution setting

4. Which of the following allows you to access a WLAN?

   ○ **A.** LED

   ○ **B.** Webcam

   ○ **C.** Digitizer

   ○ **D.** Stylus

   ○ **E.** Wi-Fi card

5. You have been tasked with replacing a Wi-Fi/Bluetooth card in a laptop. You open the laptop and find a card that uses the 2230 standard. What type of card is this?

   ○ **A.** Mini PCIe

   ○ **B.** M.2

   ○ **C.** Digitizer

   ○ **D.** RJ45

Cram Quiz Answers

1. **A.** TFT active-matrix displays are the most common in laptops that use LCDs. Passive-matrix screens have been discontinued, but you *might* see an older laptop that utilizes this technology. OLED technology is a newer and different technology that is not based on TFT displays but instead uses emissive display technology, meaning that each dot on the screen is illuminated by a separate diode. OLED displays can, however, be passive-matrix or active-matrix controlled. The MAC ID is the hexadecimal address associated with a network adapter, such as a Wi-Fi adapter or network card.

2. **C.** OLED (organic light-emitting diode) displays use an organic compound or film that emits light. TFT active matrix implies LCD, and neither TFT nor LCD uses organic compounds the way OLED does. In-plane switching (IPS) is a type of LCD technology that increases the available viewing angle compared to older technologies, such as twisted nematic (TN) matrix LCDs. However, IPS is generally considered inferior to OLED screens when it comes to brightness and contrast ratio when viewed from an angle. LED screens use a film and diode, but not organically in the way that OLED does, and not at such a small size.

3. **A and C.** A damaged inverter or burned-out bulb could cause a laptop's display to go blank. You can verify whether the LCD is still getting a signal by shining a flashlight at the screen. A damaged LCD usually works to a certain extent and will either be cracked, have areas of the Windows interface missing, or show other signs of damage. An incorrect resolution setting can indeed make the screen suddenly go blank (or look garbled), but that scenario will most likely occur only if the user has changed the resolution setting—and this question specifies "with no user intervention."

4. **E.** A Wi-Fi card, also known as a Wi-Fi network adapter, allows you to connect to a WLAN (wireless local area network), which is essentially another name for a Wi-Fi network. LED is a type of display. A webcam is used to communicate visually and audibly with others or to record oneself. A digitizer is a device that converts tapped or written impulses on a screen into digital information that the operating system can use. A stylus is a writing device used with a digitizer or touchscreen.

5. **B.** The 2230 standard is a kind of M.2 size measuring 22×30 mm. It is common in laptops for use with Wi-Fi and Bluetooth. In comparison, a PC often uses a 2280 M.2 card. Mini PCIe is an older type of card slot that might be used for Wi-Fi cards, but it does not use measurements such as 2230 or 2280 the way that M.2 does. A digitizer is not a port at all but a device that converts tapped impulses into digital information. An RJ45 port is a networking port that allows a laptop to communicate with the rest of the network in a wired fashion—that is, if the laptop has such a port!

Great job so far! Two chapters down!

CHAPTER 3

Mobile Device Accessories and Ports

This chapter covers the following A+ 220-1101 exam objective:

▶ **1.3** – Given a scenario, set up and configure accessories and ports of mobile devices.

Mobile device connectivity is imperative. For the exam, you need to know the physical ports used for charging and synchronizing and for communicating with external devices. Then, of course, there are various wireless connectivity options available on today's mini-powerhouse computers. Let's not forget that people love to accessorize: headsets, speakers, add-on memory, the list is long. Be ready to provide support for a plethora of ports and gadgets!

Connection Types

Depending on what you need to accomplish with your mobile device, you might require a wired or a wireless connection. Let's discuss these now.

Wired Connections

Wired connections use physical ports. If you have ever plugged in a mobile device to charge it, then you have used a wired connection.

The most common wired connection is USB. USB has been around for a long time and has gone through several versions and port changes. USB is used by devices that run Android and Windows (among others). However, aside from USB-C, iOS-based devices from Apple use the proprietary Lightning connector. Figure 3.1 shows examples of the ports and connectors that you should know for the exam, including Mini-USB, Micro-USB, USB-C, and Lightning.

Almost all device charging cables use a standard Type A USB port on the other end, regardless of the connector type that is used to attach to the device. This allows connectivity to the majority of charging plugs and PCs and laptops in the world. However, there are tons of adapters out there, so be ready.

As of the writing of this book (2022), USB-C is common for many Android-based smartphones and tablets. Previously, and for many years, Android devices used Micro-USB, but USB-C has been the dominant port on new devices since at least 2019. Even some Apple devices started using it in 2019. On the other hand, Mini-USB is quite uncommon, but you might see it on older devices, such as accessories for smartphones.

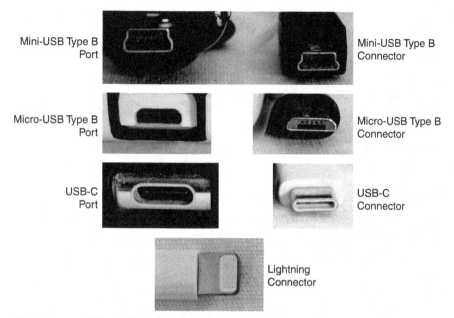

Mini-USB Type B Port

Mini-USB Type B Connector

Micro-USB Type B Port

Micro-USB Type B Connector

USB-C Port

USB-C Connector

Lightning Connector

FIGURE 3.1   **USB and Lightning ports and connectors**

ExamAlert

Know your mobile device ports and connectors. Remember that Android devices generally use USB-C (with older ones using Micro-USB), and iOS-based devices use USB-C or Lightning.

Note

We cover more about ports and connectors in Chapter 13, "Cables and Connectors."

Another purpose of a wired port is to make it possible to tether the mobile device to a desktop or laptop computer (usually via the computer's USB port). This tethering can allow a desktop computer or laptop to share the mobile device's Internet connection. Tethering functionality can be very useful in areas where a smartphone has cellular access but the PC/laptop cannot connect to the Internet. Once the physical USB connection is made, USB tethering can be turned on in the OS settings (where you will usually find the Mobile Hotspot option as well). Keep in mind that Wi-Fi capability on a smartphone is usually disabled when USB tethering is enabled and that the user must have hotspot service with their cellular provider for USB tethering to work.

Some mobile devices can also be equipped with serial interfaces (RS-232) or adapters from USB to serial. This allows for testing of devices and connectivity to various networking equipment and industrial devices. We will discuss serial interfaces and RS-232 in Chapter 13.

Wireless Connections

Wireless technologies are what really make a smartphone attractive to users. Most people would rather do without cables, and technologies such as Bluetooth, near-field communication (NFC), and hotspots make a smartphone functional and easier to use.

Given the inherent mobility of smartphones and tablets, most technologies regarding communications and control are wireless. If designed and configured properly, wireless connections offer ease of use, efficiency, and even great speed. We'll discuss Wi-Fi, cellular, GPS, and similar data-related wireless technologies later in the book. For now, let's focus on wireless connections used by mobile devices to communicate with accessories and other mobile devices.

One of the wireless technologies most commonly used is Bluetooth. Bluetooth enables users to incorporate wearable technology (such as headsets, earpieces, earbuds, and smartwatches) with their existing mobile devices. But the technology goes much further; for example, it allows for the streaming of music to external speakers and an automobile's music system. Bluetooth is usually limited to about 33 feet (10 meters), which is the maximum transmission distance for Class 2 Bluetooth devices.

Another commonly used wireless technology is the mobile hotspot. When enabled on a properly equipped smartphone or tablet (with 4G or faster connection), a hotspot allows a user to connect desktops, laptops, and other mobile devices (wirelessly, of course) through the device running the hotspot, ultimately allowing access to the Internet. This can be a great way to connect your laptop or other computer if Wi-Fi goes down, often with speeds rivaling wired Internet speeds. But remember, there's usually a catch! Many providers charge for data usage (unless you have a corporate plan). Because of this, a hotspot is often used as a secondary connection or as a backup plan. In addition, the further the hotspot-enabled mobile device is from a cell tower, the lower the data transfer rate. So know the pros and cons of running a hotspot on a mobile device.

> **ExamAlert**
>
> Understand the difference between configuring USB tethering (which is wired) and creating a mobile hotspot (which is wireless).

Next, let's discuss near-field communication (NFC). This allows smartphones to communicate with each other via radio frequency by touching the devices together or, in some cases, by simply having them in close proximity to each other. NFC uses the radio frequency 13.56 MHz and can transmit 100 to 400 kb/s. It doesn't sound like much—it transfers more slowly than Bluetooth, for example—but it's usually plenty for sending and receiving contact information, MP3s, and even photos. Besides working in peer-to-peer mode (also known as ad hoc mode), a full NFC device can also act like a smart card performing payment transactions and reading NFC tags. If you are not sure whether your device supports NFC, check the settings in the mobile OS. Most smartphones incorporate NFC technology.

> **ExamAlert**
>
> NFC is used for close-proximity transactions, such as contactless payments.

Accessories

Well, a person has to accessorize, right? It almost seems a requirement with today's mobile devices. Probably the number-one thing that people do to augment their device is to protect it—using protective covers or cases, plastic or glass-based screen protectors, waterproofing, car mounts, and so on.

Then there's add-on storage. You can never have enough memory, right? Adding long-term storage is usually accomplished with the addition of a microSD card (for example 32, 64, or 128 GB). It is common for people who shoot a lot of videos (or a whole lot of photos) to need more memory than the mobile device comes with when purchased. Some devices allow for add-on storage via a slide-out tray on the side of the device. Others don't allow upgrades.

Next on the list are audio accessories. The 3.5 mm audio jack (*if you have one*) allows a user to connect headsets, earbuds, or small speakers. Or you can connect a 3.5 mm-to-3.5 mm cable from your phone to the auxiliary port of your car radio or your all-in-one music device—though Bluetooth is usually the easier option. When it comes to music, you can connect a mobile device to anything, such as TVs and music players, given the right cable or adapter. A person can even use a device when performing a live event. The possibilities are endless. And today's mobile device audio ports can be programmed in such a way as to accept special credit-card readers and a host of other devices. Appliance repair persons and other workers who need to be paid onsite might make use of this technology, though that can also be accomplished in a wireless fashion.

Most of today's devices cannot be opened by the consumer without voiding the warranty. So, replacing a battery is not as easy as it once was. To do this, a heat gun and proper shims are required. However, if not done correctly, it can defeat the IP rating (more on IP code in a bit). That's why manufacturers require that battery replacements be done at authorized repair centers. More important when it comes to accessories are battery chargers. Smartphones and tablets can be charged with their included AC chargers or possibly with wireless chargers, where the unit is laid down directly on the charger. A user might also opt to use a "power brick," which stores a charge for a long time. Keep in mind that these battery packs take a long time to charge up themselves.

IP Code

Many smartphones and other handheld computers are certified as being ingress protection (IP) compliant. Ingress protection means protection against dust and water, which are tested separately. There are a lot of different IP ratings, but let's use IP68 as an example. The first digit, 6, deals with dust and means that the device is dust tight and that no ingress of dust can occur. The second digit, 8, means that the device can be immersed in water up to and beyond 1 meter, generally for 30 minutes, though this can vary. The exact depth and length of time is up to the manufacturer, so IP68 could be slightly different from one device to the next. Regardless, the manufacturer must test the device and prove that it is IP compliant before the rating can be applied to that particular model.

Docking Stations and Port Replicators

A docking station expands a laptop so that it can behave more like a desktop computer. By connecting a laptop to a docking station and adding a full-size keyboard, mouse, and monitor, the user doesn't actually touch the laptop except perhaps to turn it on. Some laptops can *hot dock*, meaning they can connect to a docking station while powered on. The docking station recharges the laptop's battery, and possibly a second battery, and has connections for video, audio, networking, and expansion cards. Docking stations might even have an optical disc drive, an additional hard drive, and additional display and USB ports; it all depends on the brand and model. If all these extras aren't necessary, a user might require only a *port replicator*, which is a similar device but has only ports (for example, video, sound, network, and so on). Sometimes these are just referred to as docking stations as well.

> **ExamAlert**
>
> Note the difference: A laptop is placed, or "docked," into a docking station. In contrast, a port replicator is connected to a laptop simply to provide additional ports.

Drawing Pads, Touchpads, and Touch Pens

A mobile device's screen is often small, and it can be difficult to manipulate with your fingers. Sometimes a mobile device is not entirely accessible to your hands, perhaps because it is being used as a desktop replacement. And so, necessity breeds invention—in this case easier manipulation in the form of drawing pads, touchpads, and touch pens.

A drawing pad is a flat tablet that allows you to use a stylus to "draw" on the screen of a mobile device. It can be used in illustration programs, slideshows, teaching utilities, and complex programs that have very tight interfaces where the tip of a stylus will work much better than your finger.

A stylus is often referred to as a touch pen or stylus pen. A touch pen can be used by itself with a mobile device to increase the accuracy of input to the screen.

A touchpad (or trackpad) is used to take the place of a laptop's touchpad; it is much larger and easier to manipulate. It is usually connected via USB or Bluetooth.

Always check whether a mobile device's operating system will support any of these devices before purchasing and installing them. Installing such accessories is usually very easy as they are typically either plug and play or configured within the Bluetooth properties.

We could go on for days about the accessories available for mobile devices, and we'll discuss the concepts more later in the book, but that should be enough for the exam for now. Remember, protecting a mobile device and protecting its memory capacity are crucial. The rest of the things we have discussed enable a user to increase functionality or just plain make it more fun, but these things are usually not essential to the device performing its job. Plus, in a bring your own device (BYOD) or choose your own device (CYOD) environment, the users are often quite limited when it comes to accessorizing to prevent compatibility issues and to avoid security vulnerabilities.

Cram Quiz

Answer these questions. The answers follow the last question. If you cannot answer these questions correctly, consider reading this chapter again until you can.

1. Which type of charging connector would you find on an iPad?
   - ○ **A.** Micro-USB
   - ○ **B.** Lightning
   - ○ **C.** Thunderbolt
   - ○ **D.** IP68

2. You are required to add long-term storage to a smartphone. Which type would you most likely add?
   - ○ **A.** DDR4
   - ○ **B.** microSD
   - ○ **C.** LPDDR4
   - ○ **D.** SSD
   - ○ **E.** SIM

3. The organization you work for allows employees to work using their own mobile devices in a BYOD manner. You have been tasked with setting up the devices so that they can "beam" information back and forth between each other. What is this known as?
   - ○ **A.** Mobile hotspot
   - ○ **B.** IoT
   - ○ **C.** CYOD
   - ○ **D.** IR
   - ○ **E.** NFC

4. Which of the following can be useful in areas where a smartphone has cellular access but a PC (or laptop) cannot connect to the Internet?

   ◯ **A.** Proprietary vendor-specific connector

   ◯ **B.** Accessories

   ◯ **C.** IP codes

   ◯ **D.** Tethering

5. A user has asked you to provide her with a more accurate way of manipulating her smartphone screen. She is part of a mobile sales force and needs to be able to work quickly and efficiently. Which of the following is the easiest and best solution?

   ◯ **A.** Connect an external monitor so that the images on the screen will be bigger.

   ◯ **B.** Configure a drawing pad to work with the smartphone.

   ◯ **C.** Set up a touch pen to access the screen directly.

   ◯ **D.** Add an external touchpad to the device.

Cram Quiz Answers

1. **B.** The Lightning connector is one of Apple's proprietary charging and synchronization connectors used by iPads and iPhones, although Apple also uses USB-C. Micro-USB is used by older Android-based mobile devices, and USB-C is more common on newer Android-based devices. Thunderbolt is a high-speed hardware interface used in desktop computers, which we will discuss more in Chapter 13. IP68 deals with ingress protection against dust and water.

2. **B.** You would most likely add a microSD card (if the smartphone has a slot available for add-ons or upgrading). This is the most common method for adding long-term storage. DDR4 is a type of RAM; it is not used for adding long-term memory storage. Some smartphones use LPDDR4 as their main memory, but this is part of the system on a chip (SoC) and not accessible to the typical user. An SSD is a solid-state drive, which generally means a hard drive that is installed to a PC or laptop, connected either as SATA or M.2. SSDs are too large for smartphones and tablets. A SIM is a subscriber identity module, usually represented as a small card (mini-SIM) used in smartphones that securely stores authentication information about the user and device, such as the International Mobile Subscriber Identity (IMSI), which we will discuss more in the following chapter.

3. **E.** "Beaming" the information back and forth can be accomplished in a couple of ways, primarily by using near-field communication (NFC). This can only be done if the devices are in close proximity to each other. NFC is commonly used for contactless payment systems. Another potential option would be Apple's AirDrop, but this relies on Bluetooth (for finding devices) and Wi-Fi (for transmitting data), and of course relies on using Apple-based devices. A mobile hotspot enables a smartphone or tablet to act as an Internet gateway for other mobile devices and computers. IoT stands for the Internet of Things. The question says that

employees can use their mobile devices in a BYOD manner, but CYOD is a bit different. This means that employees can *choose* a device to use for work purposes (most likely whichever type they are more familiar with). Whether the employees can use those devices for personal purposes usually depends on company policy. IR stands for infrared, which is not commonly found on smartphones.

4. **D.** Tethering can allow a desktop computer or laptop to share the mobile device's Internet connection. Tethering functionality can be very useful in areas where a smartphone has cellular access but a PC/laptop cannot connect to the Internet. Mobile device accessories such as headsets, speakers, game pads, extra battery packs, and protective covers are useful, but they are not used to connect to the Internet. IP codes (for example, IP68) are used to classify and rate the degree of protection against dust and water.

5. **C.** The best option is to set up a touch pen to access the smartphone's screen directly. A smartphone may come with a touch pen (also known as a stylus pen or simply a stylus); or it may be able to have a touch pen added later. A touch pen enables a person to input information to the screen more accurately. The other devices listed will make mobility more difficult (if not impossible). The next best answer would be an external touchpad, but it isn't the easiest solution. If the user finds that she needs the touchpad more often, then a better, more permanent solution might be to use a tablet computer instead of a smartphone.

Chapter 3 is in the books, so to speak. Excellent work! Keep going!

CHAPTER 4

Mobile Device Network Connectivity and Application Support

This chapter covers the following A+ 220-1101 exam objective:

▶ **1.4** – Given a scenario, configure basic mobile-device network connectivity and application support.

Nice to see you again! This is the last chapter dealing with mobile devices. Here we'll be discussing networking and synchronization. As those are big topics, this is a relatively big chapter (for this book at least). Take it one step at a time, and you should be fine.

Users need Wi-Fi, Bluetooth, and email. They need cellular connections for voice calls as well as for data. And let's not forget the need to synchronize data to computers, automobiles, and the cloud. That's what this chapter is all about. Now that you know, it's time to begin.

> **ExamAlert**
>
> **Objective 1.4** concentrates on the following concepts: wireless/cellular technologies, Bluetooth setup, location services, mobile device management (MDM) and mobile application management (MAM), email configuration, and mobile device synchronization.

> **Note**
>
> For simplicity, most of the time I use the term *cellular* to refer to smartphone connectivity to a telecommunications provider, meaning 3G, 4G, 5G, and so on.

Enabling Wireless Functions

You will most definitely be called upon to enable and disable various wireless and cellular functionality. In this section we'll discuss how to connect to Wi-Fi, set up a mobile hotspot, and turn on airplane mode.

Cellular connections such as 3G, 4G, LTE, 5G, and beyond are commonplace on smartphones. If you purchase a smartphone from a telecommunications provider, then you get cellular access. It is enabled by default, and it functions unless you turn on airplane mode. We'll talk more about cellular technologies later, but for now keep in mind a couple things:

 ▶ Cellular connections can be slow when transmitting data. That could be due to the distance from the nearest cell tower, the connection speed, or a general lack of service availability.

 ▶ Cellular connections can cost the customer money. That's why all mobile devices are equipped with an embedded wireless antenna to connect to wireless LANs (WLANs). This Wi-Fi antenna can potentially allow access to 802.11a, b, g, n, ac, and ax networks. The wireless connection works similarly to a wireless connection on a PC, laptop, or tablet. See Chapter 9, "SOHO Network Configuration," for a detailed description of connecting to wireless networks.

In general, a mobile device must search for wireless networks before it can connect. This is done in the wireless settings of the device. Figure 4.1 shows a typical Wi-Fi settings screen.

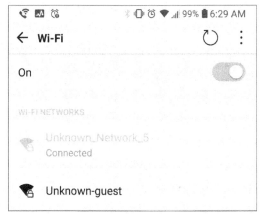

FIGURE 4.1 Wi-Fi settings screen in Android

In the Wi-Fi settings screen, perform the following general steps:

1. Most devices usually scan for wireless networks automatically and list them for you, or you can tap **Add Wi-Fi Network** (or something similar) to add one manually.

2. When adding a network manually, enter the service set identifier (SSID) of the wireless access point (WAP).

3. Enter the passcode for the network. If the code is correct, then the wireless adapter in the mobile device gets an IP address, allowing it to communicate with the network. Remember to use the latest wireless protocol available to you (such as WPA2 or WPA3). Update the mobile device if it isn't compatible.

4. Check for the universal wireless icon at the top of the screen (in the notification bar) to verify connectivity.

ExamAlert

Understand how to connect to a Wi-Fi network in Android, iOS, and iPadOS.

If you bring your mobile device into a secure area or onto an airplane, you will most likely be asked to place the device in *airplane mode*. This mode disables all wireless connectivity, including (but not limited to) cellular, Wi-Fi, and Bluetooth. You can put a device in this mode by pressing and holding the power button and selecting airplane mode or by accessing the quick settings dropdown menu (Android) or Control Center (iOS).

Once in airplane mode, you should see the airplane icon in the notification bar. However, keep in mind that this is primarily designed to disable cellular access. On many devices, a user can still re-enable Wi-Fi, Bluetooth, or NFC even when airplane mode is on. Sometimes a user might complain that there is no wireless connectivity. If so, check if the device has been inadvertently placed into airplane mode and disable it from the same locations mentioned previously.

So, you know how to set up Wi-Fi. But what if you want to share that connection with other computers, such as laptops or tablets? That's where the mobile hotspot comes in. When you configure a *mobile hotspot*, the mobile device shares its Internet connection with other Wi-Fi-capable devices. For example, if a user has a smartphone that can access the Internet through a cellular network, it can be configured to become a portable Wi-Fi hotspot for other mobile devices (or desktops/laptops) that are Wi-Fi capable but have no cellular option. Beware of the hotspot option; most providers have a fairly low consumer bandwidth threshold for data transferred through the hotspot by default, even if the plan is called "unlimited." This data transmission limit (often referred to as a "data cap") is a service provider–imposed limit on the amount of data that can be sent and received by a customer over the course of a month or other time period. When the customer surpasses the cap, additional fees can be applied to the customer's account. To guard against this, there are Internet usage monitoring apps available that will give a warning when approaching the cap.

Enabling hotspots is easy and is usually done in the network settings section of the device. Figure 4.2 shows an example of this. The first time you enable the hotspot, you will be asked to supply a password and the wireless protocol to be used, which can be modified later. As of this writing, it is recommended to use WPA2/WPA3 and, of course, set a strong password. An example of the configuration screen is also shown in Figure 4.2.

When a hotspot is enabled on a smartphone, Wi-Fi is automatically disabled. So, the smartphone will only be able to connect via the cellular network—but it is designed this way on purpose, expecting to be used only when there is no Wi-Fi connection available. Other Wi-Fi-ready systems (laptops, PCs, tablets, etc.) need only look for and connect to the Wi-Fi network that was created (for example, *Hotspot-dpro* in Figure 4.2). Running a mobile hotspot can also be a great backup option in the event that the main Internet connection in a small office or home office fails temporarily.

Enabling a HotSpot

Configuring a HotSpot

FIGURE 4.2   Hotspot configuration in Android

Bluetooth

Bluetooth is a wireless standard for transmitting data over short distances. It is commonly implemented for multimedia purposes and for connecting to mobile device accessories.

To connect a Bluetooth device to a mobile device, Bluetooth first needs to be enabled. Then the Bluetooth device needs to be synchronized to the mobile device. This is known as *pairing*, or *linking*. It sometimes requires a PIN code, depending on how the remote device is configured. Once synchronized, the device should automatically connect and should function at that point. Finally, the Bluetooth connection should be tested. Following are the steps involved in connecting a Bluetooth device to a typical mobile device. Before you begin, make sure the Bluetooth device is charged (if applicable). The typical procedure for making a Bluetooth connection is as follows:

1. Turn on Bluetooth in the Settings of the mobile device.

2. Prepare the device by turning it on and pressing (and sometimes holding) the Bluetooth button.

3. Scan for devices on the mobile device.

4. Pair to the desired device.

5. Enter a PIN code if necessary. Some devices come with the default PIN 0000.

When finished, the screen will look similar to Figure 4.3. Note the Bluetooth icon at the top-middle of the screen. It almost looks like an uppercase *B* made of triangles. (Really, it's two Roman runes merged together, but I digress.) This icon indicates whether Bluetooth is running on the device. It will remain there even after you disconnect the Bluetooth device but in a grayed-out state. To disconnect or reconnect a Bluetooth device, simply tap the device on the screen. It will remain paired but nonfunctional until a connection is made again. (Typically, devices are listed in bold if they are connected.) You can also unpair and/or forget a Bluetooth device in the settings for that device. Unpairing removes the link between the smartphone and the Bluetooth device, but the mobile device will remember the Bluetooth device. "Forgetting" removes the connection altogether.

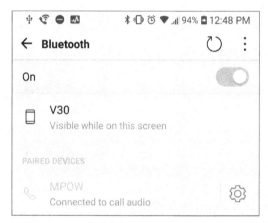

FIGURE 4.3 Bluetooth paired devices screen in Android

A Bluetooth device can be connected to only one mobile device at a time. If you need to switch a Bluetooth device from one mobile device to another, be sure to unpair or disconnect it or, going further, "forget" it from the current connection before making a new one.

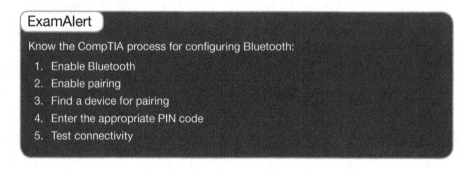

ExamAlert

Know the CompTIA process for configuring Bluetooth:

1. Enable Bluetooth
2. Enable pairing
3. Find a device for pairing
4. Enter the appropriate PIN code
5. Test connectivity

Email Configuration

Although there are many other types of communication available to mobile users, email still accounts for an important percentage. You should know how to configure a mobile device for web-based email services such as Gmail, Yahoo!, and so on. You should also know how to configure Post Office Protocol Version 3 (POP3), Internet Mail Access Protocol (IMAP), and connections to Microsoft Exchange Server.

Integrated Commercial Provider Email Configuration

Mobile devices can access web-based email through a browser, but this is not necessary today because most commercial providers offer integrated email configuration for mobile operating systems. For example, most Android-based devices come with a Gmail application ("app") built in, allowing a user to access Gmail directly, without having to use the browser. A device also might have a proprietary email application. Apple iOS devices allow connectivity to Gmail, Yahoo!, and a host of other email providers as well. Apple users might also connect to iCloud for mail features. Users of other devices might use Microsoft's Outlook on the Web (part of a Microsoft 365 subscription), or for more users and for collaboration, a company might opt for Exchange Online. As you can see, there are a lot of options when it comes to mail services for mobile devices.

Connecting to these services is simple and works in a fashion that is similar to working on a desktop or laptop computer. Choose the type of provider you use, enter a username (the email address) and password (and, on Apple devices, an Apple ID), and the user will have access. In more advanced cases, a user may have to select the protocol and ports to be used. That's where you as the administrator come in—and we'll discuss those protocols and ports in a little bit.

When troubleshooting user issues with email, make sure that the username and password are typed correctly. Using onscreen keyboards often leads to mistyped passwords. Also make sure that the mobile device is currently connected to the Internet.

Corporate and ISP Email Configuration

When you need to connect a mobile device to a specific organization's email system, it gets a little more complicated. You need to know the server that you want to connect to, the port you need to use, and whether security is employed.

Look at the following email configuration information and Figure 4.4 for an example:

▶ **Incoming server name:** secure.dpro42.com

▶ **POP3 port (SSL/TLS):** 995

▶ **Outgoing server name:** secure.dpro42.com

▶ **SMTP port (SSL/TLS):** 465

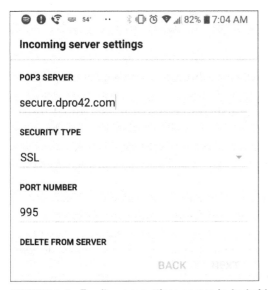

FIGURE 4.4   Email server settings screen in Android

The figure shows manual configuration of an email client in Android. At this stage, the email client is asking for the incoming server, meaning the one used for receiving mail. It just so happens that the same server takes care of incoming mail and outgoing mail: secure.dpro42.com; but sometimes it could be two different servers. So, you add the name of the server into the POP3 Server field. Then you specify the security type. In this case, you select Secure Sockets Layer (SSL) instead of "no security," which is important. Most of the time you want to have encrypted email sessions to your email server to prevent eavesdropping and tampering. This could be SSL or Transport Layer Security (TLS), depending on the server configuration. Then you select the port, which, according to the previous documentation, is 995. That is the default secure port for POP3 email connections that make use of SSL/TLS; however, this port number can vary depending on what protocol you are using for email and what type of security you implement. As a technician configuring the client email, you must go by the documentation provided by the network administrator (or just "admin" for short). As an admin, it's generally a good idea to go with the default secure port numbers, but in reality, you can choose which port to use (within reason), and as long as the client configures that port to connect, it should be successful. See Table 4.1 for a list of original and secure ports used by the various email protocols.

TABLE 4.1   Email Configuration Example

Email Protocol	Original Port Number	Secure Port Number
SMTP	25	465 or 587
POP3	110	995
IMAP	143	993

ExamAlert

Know the email protocols/ports: SMTP = 25/465/587; POP3 = 110/995, IMAP = 143/993.

I say Table 4.1 shows the "original" port numbers because these are what we used for many years until encrypted email sessions became necessary. The secure port numbers are defaults, but they can vary, depending on whether you have to select TLS or whether another secure technology is used; in addition, the admin simply might decide to go with a different port number. Here's the thing: Most ports can work in a secure fashion—if configured properly—but you should know the most common defaults in Table 4.1 for the exam. These are what email server programs and client applications will typically default to.

Note

Another protocol you might implement when setting up secure email is S/MIME (Secure/Multipurpose Internet Mail Extensions). This is used for authentication and message integrity and is built into some email clients.

Cellular Radio Technologies

Hey, listen! Without a properly working radio in your smartphone, you won't hear anything. This section is designed to teach you the basics about cellular voice calls and data transmissions. You see, most people can't live without their phones—and ultimately, phones are radios.

Originally, cellular phones used the Global System for Mobile Communications (GSM) to make voice calls and GSM or the General Packet Radio Service (GPRS) to send data at 2G speeds through the cellular network. Extensions of these standards—the Universal Mobile Telecommunications System (UMTS) and Enhanced Data rates for GSM Evolution (EDGE)—are used to attain 3G speeds. 4G and 4G LTE speeds can be attained only when a mobile device complies with the International Mobile Telecommunications Advanced (IMT-Advanced) requirements, has a 4G antenna, and is in range of a 4G transmitter. LTE builds on 4G by using an updated radio interface/antenna in the mobile device and by utilizing core network infrastructure improvements. The fifth generation of cellular, 5G, is known as the ITU IMT-2020 standard and has data transfer rates of up to 20 gigabits per second (Gbps).

ExamAlert

Know the different cellular standards and that 5G can transmit at 20 Gbps.

Most devices cannot shut off the cellular antenna by themselves (unless you shut down the device itself). However, every device manufactured now is required to have an airplane mode, which turns off any wireless antenna in the device, including disabling the connection to the cellular network and disabling Wi-Fi, and Bluetooth. You will find that some airlines don't consider this to be acceptable and for security purposes will still ask you to turn off your device altogether, either for the duration of the flight or at least during takeoff and landing. Some devices can also limit or disable cellular *data* usage—often known as "mobile data."

Let's get a little more into it and briefly discuss some additional mobile technology and acronyms, such as PRL updates, baseband updates, and radio firmware.

PRL stands for preferred roaming list. It is used by cellular providers (such as Verizon and U.S. Cellular) that utilize code division multiple access (CDMA) technology instead of GSM. PRL is a database that contains information about the provider's radio bands, sub-bands, and service provider IDs. Ultimately, it allows a phone to connect to the correct tower. Without the database, the phone might not be able to roam outside the provider's network. When necessary, PRL information is sent as an update over the air. However, you can also update it manually by dialing a number that is unique to each provider. You can find the PRL version number you are using within the About section on some phones.

ExamAlert

PRL updates help you get better coverage by keeping your device on preferred networks.

When a phone uses GSM, that technology and its radio functions are controlled by a chip and software package that is collectively referred to as "baseband." Baseband updates are necessary to communicate properly with GSM cell towers. If an older phone won't update properly, it must be taken to the provider for a wired, manual update. Baseband is also referred to as radio firmware as it controls network connectivity for GSM. Other wireless antennas, such as Wi-Fi and GPS antennas, are controlled by the operating system's drivers.

Note

Do not attempt a radio firmware (baseband) update if your phone does not require it. A faulty update can easily make the phone inoperable.

You can find the versions of most of these technologies (and the types of radio technology used) in the About (or About device) section on a device. Take a look at your own mobile device's settings, such as the radio technologies you are connecting to, the baseband version, and the IMEI. You might also consider using a cellular analyzer app to see this data—as well as data concerning cellular towers—in a more visual and centralized manner.

All of these radio network technologies can be affected by a mobile phone update, such as a version update. To prevent network connectivity issues, consider waiting until a new mobile OS version has been thoroughly tested before you update a phone.

Location Services

Location services (or location-based services) is a somewhat ambiguous term and can take form as one of two things: GPS and cellular location. It's a generalized term that refers to software services that work with geographic data in order to provide services and information to users—or, to track user location. On a mobile device, location services (or simply "location") can be enabled or disabled in the settings of the mobile device. If enabled, GPS apps and other location-based programs will function. If disabled, the mobile device is "taken off the grid" to a certain extent. This can be beneficial if a user wants to prevent particular types of tracking, such as geotagging—which allows location data to be attached to images, videos, SMS messages, and website postings, providing permanent and searchable data about the user (a privacy concern for sure). Most devices allow a user to disable location services but then selectively use individual location features as desired.

> **Note**
>
> Corporate access policies can also be controlled by location data. For example, geofencing, which uses location-based services, can trigger an action when a mobile device enters or exits a specific geographic area called a geofence.

Let's define GPS and cellular location now.

GPS

The Global Positioning System (GPS) is a satellite-based navigation system that provides geolocation to properly equipped GPS devices, including smartphones and dedicated GPS devices. If you have a smartphone, you probably use some kind of GPS app, but there are also dedicated smart GPS systems for vehicles that can work independently and possibly integrate with your smartphone and social media via Wi-Fi and Bluetooth. The beauty of these is that the bulk of the CPU in the device is dedicated to GPS. If you have ever run GPS on a smartphone while other apps are running and experienced slow performance, then you can understand why a dedicated GPS system might be a valid option for delivery drivers, those in the transportation industry, or those who simply want more accurate and efficiently presented GPS data.

Many vehicles offer systems with touchscreens that can integrate with a person's smartphone and GPS apps. The most common of these systems are Apple CarPlay and Android Auto. To use such a system, the vehicle must be compatible, and the smartphone must have the correct app installed; often the device must be connected in a wired fashion via USB. In this scenario, a technician should make sure that the vehicle's firmware and software are updated, that the smartphone's vehicle connectivity software and GPS software are updated, and that a *quality* cable is used. This way, the user can be properly "geolocated," and GPS directions will be up to date.

> **ExamAlert**
>
> Know that GPS technology is integrated into mobile devices to help a user navigate while driving (among other things) but that it will be useless if location services is disabled.

Cellular Location

Cellular location is a method of locating a mobile device with the use of cellular technologies. For example, by using GSM and a smartphone's signal strength, it is possible to estimate the distance of the smartphone to a cell tower. Going further, it is possible to use multiple towers' radio signals (known as multilateration) to "triangulate" a more exact location of the smartphone. This is an example of *mobile phone tracking*.

IMEI and IMSI

Another related concept is mobile device identification technology—namely International Mobile Equipment Identity (IMEI) and International Mobile Subscriber Identity (IMSI). IMEI identifies phones used on 3GPP-based networks (GSM, UMTS, and LTE). You can find this ID number in Settings, and on older phones it is printed inside the phone, either on or near the battery. It is used only to identify the device. However, IMSI is used to identify the user. For GSM, UMTS, and LTE networks, this ID is loaded into the subscriber identity module (SIM) card. For CDMA networks, the ID is loaded directly into the phone or to a removable user identity module (R-UIM), which is similar to a SIM card.

Synchronization Methods

A person might want to synchronize a mobile device's data somewhere else so that he or she can have access to that data from anywhere. This synchronization also offers peace of mind: If the mobile device is lost or stolen, the data will be available on the other system when a new mobile device is procured. And, of course, even though mobile devices today can store a lot of data, there's always the need for more storage. External systems allow for a much greater amount of storage, as well as redundancy of data.

A person can choose to synchronize data to an individual computer that is physically nearby, or to an automobile, or to the cloud, which is the most common option.

Synchronizing to the Cloud

For simplicity, we can refer to the cloud as any computer that you synchronize to on the Internet. Generally, this means using some type of service. You might synchronize your mobile device's data to Google Drive, Microsoft OneDrive, Apple iCloud, Dropbox, or one of several other services. Making this happen entails creating an account, installing the appropriate app on the mobile device (if it is not already there), and specifying what folders, files, and other data you would like to synchronize. The first time you synchronize your device's data, the application will copy the data over to the cloud recipient. Subsequent synchronizations will copy new files and append changed files.

> **Note**
>
> You might also opt for a service such as Nextcloud, which you can run locally on your own server, as well as connect to in the cloud. Check it out!

When it comes to popular services such as Gmail, you might question whether you really are "synchronizing" anymore. You are. It's just that the data is all stored on the service's servers, and you are simply accessing it from a mobile device or PC. A person who signs up for a Gmail account allows Google to automatically synchronize mail, contacts, and the calendar so that the information can be viewed on the mobile device or on the PC (when connected to the Google website).

However, because the data is stored on a Google server, security should be a concern. If you choose to use Gmail (or another similar service), you should use an extremely strong password and consider changing it periodically (for example, every 6 to 12 months). Also, if possible, incorporate two-factor authentication (such as using a password and some kind of biometrics or encrypted key technology in conjunction with the password). Beyond this, use a secure browser when connecting to Gmail from a desktop computer. On the mobile device side, make sure the Gmail app is updated often to ensure that any security vulnerabilities are patched. The same concepts hold true for other similar services. Utilizing the cloud presents many configuration and security concerns, which we will discuss further in the networking chapters of this book.

> **Note**
>
> Keep in mind that you might also *back up* your data, but this is different from synchronization. For example, you might back up an Android-based device's apps, call history, contacts, device settings, SMS text messages, and other items that are normally stored locally. You could back up this data to a server on the cloud owned by the manufacturer of the mobile device, or you could use a separate service, such as Google Drive. Either way, this is done separately from synchronization.

Synchronizing to the Desktop

Today, synchronizing to the desktop is not nearly as common as syncing to the cloud. But it might be necessary, or desired, by some users. When you connect mobile devices to a Windows PC via a USB connection, they are typically seen automatically and are represented as devices in File Explorer under This PC. On the mobile device, you might have to change the USB options from Charging to File Transfer or another similar option in order to see the device in Windows. At this point, you can copy files back and forth between the mobile device and the PC manually or rely on automatic synchronization software from the manufacturer of the mobile device or from a third party.

Windows devices can be synchronized together with the Sync Center. This allows you to choose individual synchronize settings such as Theme, Passwords, Language preferences, Ease of Access, and other Windows settings, but a user would have to sign in with a Microsoft account in order to synchronize.

> **Note**
>
> Exchange ActiveSync can be used to synchronize email, contacts, and calendars between a variety of devices (iOS-based devices, Windows devices, etc.) with Microsoft Exchange Server.

To synchronize data—contacts, calendars, and so on—from Apple devices to a PC requires the use of iTunes for Windows. From iTunes, a user selects Sync Contacts or Sync Calendars, for example. Calendar items can also be synced from the Apple-based device (such as an iPad) by going to **Settings > Mail, Contacts, Calendars**. Then scroll down and select **Sync**. iCloud can also be downloaded for Windows.

Synchronizing to the Automobile

It had to happen—computers in cars. People want to harness the power of their smartphone in conjunction with their automobile's computer and display. It's easy with tools such as Android Auto and Apple CarPlay. These apps can be used independently on a mobile device or can be synchronized to an automobile's computer if it has the proper firmware/software installed. Then, the user can make use of the automobile's larger screen for easier accessibility, better viewing, and increased safety. Generally, these platforms are supported on higher-level trims of a vehicle. For integration of these platforms, the mobile device usually has to be plugged in via USB, and a high-quality cable should be used to avoid interruptions.

In reality, this isn't as much "synchronizing" as it is screen sharing. The larger screen in the automobile is used to display, and control, the common apps you might need: phone, maps, music player, and so on. Apple CarPlay and Android Auto both limit the number and types of apps you can use in the automobile for safety reasons.

Figure 4.5 shows an example of Android Auto running on a smartphone connected to an automobile via USB. Of course, most smartphones can multitask, so you can potentially use both screens at the same time with different apps running on each—when parked, of course!

FIGURE 4.5   Example of Android Auto

If a vehicle does not support Android Auto or Apple CarPlay, it might support Bluetooth (BT). If that is the case, then a smartphone or tablet can be synchronized to the vehicle via BT by pairing the automobile to the device in the same manner described earlier in the chapter. Then the user can operate voice calling and texting hands-free. If the vehicle is not equipped with any computer or BT integration, then a replacement head unit (stereo) can be purchased to allow BT and USB integration as well as Apple CarPlay or Android Auto.

> **Note**
>
> As of the writing of this book, if you use Android and are using the smartphone only (with no vehicle screen), the GPS-based navigation software is simply known as Maps or, if enabled, Google Assistant Driving Mode. If used in conjunction with the vehicle's screen, it is known as Android Auto.

Mobile Device Management (MDM)

For networks with a lot of users, consider third-party offerings from companies that make use of mobile device management (MDM) platforms. These are centralized software solutions that allow admins to control, configure, update, and secure remote mobile devices such as Android, iOS, and so on, all from one administrative console. The MDM software can be run from a server within an organization or administered within the cloud. MDM makes the job of a mobile IT administrator at least manageable. From the central location, the administrator can carry out the tasks of application management, content management, and patch management. The admin can also set up more secure levels of mobile device access control. *Access control* is the methodology used to allow access to computer systems.

For larger organizations, MDM software makes it easy for an admin to view inventory control, such as how many devices are active for each of the mobile operating systems used. It also makes it simpler to track assets, such as the devices themselves, and the types of data each contains. In addition, MDM software makes it less complicated to disable unused features on multiple devices at once, thereby increasing the efficiency of the devices, reducing their footprint, and ultimately making them more secure. For instance, an employee who happens to have both a smartphone and a tablet capable of making cellular calls doesn't necessarily need the latter. The admin could disable the tablet's cellular capability, which would increase battery efficiency as well as security for that device. Insecure user configurations such as rooting and jailbreaking can be blocked from MDM, as can sideloading—the art of loading third-party apps from a location outside the official application store for that device.

Finally, application control becomes easier thanks to *mobile application management (MAM)*. With MAM, applications can be installed, uninstalled, updated, and secured from a central location. Even devices' removable storage (often USB based) can be manipulated—as long as the removable storage is currently connected to the device. We'll discuss MDM more in Chapter 49, "Mobile Device Security."

> **ExamAlert**
>
> Understand that MDM is software that is used to update and secure mobile devices from a central location. MAM focuses on managing specific corporate mobile applications.

Cram Quiz

Answer these questions. The answers follow the last question. If you cannot answer these questions correctly, consider reading this chapter again until you can.

1. Which of the following connections require a username, password, and SMTP server? (Select the two best answers.)
   - A. Bluetooth connection
   - B. Wi-Fi connection
   - C. POP3 connection
   - D. Exchange connection
   - E. IMAP connection

2. When manually configuring a Wi-Fi connection, which step occurs after successfully entering the SSID?
   - A. Select POP3.
   - B. Check whether the device is within range of the WAP.
   - C. Enter a passcode for the network.
   - D. Scan for networks.

3. Which of the following allows other mobile devices to wirelessly share a mobile device's Internet connection?

- ○ **A.** NFC
- ○ **B.** Airplane mode
- ○ **C.** IMAP
- ○ **D.** Mobile hotspot

4. Which of the following identifies the user of a device?

- ○ **A.** IMSI ID
- ○ **B.** IMEI ID
- ○ **C.** S/MIME
- ○ **D.** VPN

5. Which of the following is used to synchronize contacts from an iPad to a PC? (Select the best answer.)

- ○ **A.** Gmail
- ○ **B.** Google Play
- ○ **C.** iTunes
- ○ **D.** Sync Center

6. You oversee a midsized enterprise and are supporting 300 smartphones. Which of the following would best allow you to configure them from a centralized location?

- ○ **A.** GPS
- ○ **B.** MDM
- ○ **C.** Location services
- ○ **D.** PRL

7. What should you do after you have found a Bluetooth device for pairing? (Select two.)

- ○ **A.** Enter the appropriate PIN code
- ○ **B.** Enable Bluetooth
- ○ **C.** Disable pairing
- ○ **D.** Test connectivity

8. What is the secure port for POP3 email connections that make use of SSL/TLS?

- ○ **A.** 110
- ○ **B.** 465 or 587
- ○ **C.** 993
- ○ **D.** 995

Cram Quiz Answers

1. C and E. POP3 and IMAP email connections require an incoming mail server (either POP3 or IMAP) and an outgoing mail server (SMTP). Bluetooth and Wi-Fi connections do not require a username or SMTP server. Bluetooth might require a PIN, and Wi-Fi will almost always require a passcode. Exchange connections require a username and password but no SMTP server. Exchange Server acts as the incoming and outgoing mail server.

2. C. After you enter the correct SSID, you enter the passcode (or passphrase) for the network. POP3 has to do with configuring an email account. If you have already entered the SSID, then you should be within range of the wireless access point (WAP). Scanning for networks is the first thing you do when setting up a Wi-Fi connection.

3. D. Mobile hotspot technology (sometimes referred to as Wi-Fi tethering) allows a mobile device to share its Internet connection with other Wi-Fi-capable devices. Another possibility would be USB tethering, but that is done in a wired fashion. NFC, which stands for near-field communication, is a technology that allows two mobile devices to send information to each other when they are in close proximity. Airplane mode disables all wireless connectivity, including (but not limited to) cellular, Wi-Fi, and Bluetooth. IMAP is another email protocol similar to POP3.

4. A. International Mobile Subscriber Identity (IMSI) or an IMSI ID is used to identify the user of a device. IMEI, which stands for International Mobile Equipment Identity, identifies the phone used. In other words, the IMEI ID identifies the device itself. S/MIME (Secure/Multipurpose Internet Mail Extensions) is used for authentication and message integrity and is built into some email clients. In other words, it is used to encrypt email. Virtual private network (VPN) technology is used to make secure connections by tunneling through the provider's radio network.

5. C. PC users need iTunes to synchronize contacts and other data from an iPad to a PC. While Gmail can work to synchronize contacts, it is completely based on web storage; nothing is actually stored on the iPad. Google Play is a place to get applications and other items for Android. Sync Center is a Control Panel utility that enables synchronization across Windows devices.

6. B. Mobile device management (MDM) allows a person to centrally administer many mobile devices from a single workstation. Global Positioning System (GPS) is a satellite-based navigation system that allows a mobile device to help you find your way to wherever it is you want to go. Location services is a more generic term that means any and all services that help to locate a mobile device and provide mapping information to apps. Preferred roaming list (PRL) is a database (used by CDMA-based phones) that contains telecommunication provider data.

7. **A and D.** CompTIA lists the Bluetooth connection process in the following order: Enable Bluetooth, enable pairing, find a device for pairing, enter the appropriate PIN code, and finally, test connectivity.

8. **D.** The secure port for POP3 email connections that make use of SSL/TLS is 995. Port 110 is the POP3 default non-encrypted port. Ports 465 and 587 are the secure port numbers for SMTP. Port 993 is the secure port number for IMAP.

You're doing great! Take some time to review this chapter—which is longer than most—and then review the entire first domain (Chapters 1 through 4) before you move on to Domain 2.0: Networking.

And listen, you never know when a chapter is going to end—until it ends.

CORE 1 (220-1101)

Domain 2.0: Networking

CHAPTER 5

TCP and UDP Ports and Protocols

This chapter covers the following A+ 220-1101 exam objective:

▶ **2.1** – Compare and contrast Transmission Control Protocol (TCP) and User Datagram Protocol (UDP) ports, protocols, and their purposes.

We're back. Welcome to Domain 2.0: Networking. Knowing how to build computers and configure mobile devices is all well and good, but if they can't communicate with each other, very little gets done. That means you as the technician should have a good understanding of networking connections between computers on the local area network (LAN) and over the Internet. This chapter and the seven that follow will set the foundation for your networking knowledge.

This first networking chapter discusses the TCP/IP ports and protocols that you should know for the exam (for example, Domain Name System [DNS] on port 53). To prepare for this objective, we'll discuss the differences between TCP and UDP, why you would use each, and which protocols use them. Then we'll get into individual protocols such as FTP, HTTP, RDP, and many more. These protocols are at the core of network communications between computers. And now, it's time to dive into the first of the networking objectives.

ExamAlert

Objective 2.1 concentrates on the following concepts: ports and protocols such as FTP, SSH, Telnet, SMTP, DNS, DHCP, HTTP, POP3, NetBIOS/NetBT, IMAP, SNMP, LDAP, HTTPS, SMB/CIFS, and RDP. It also covers the differences between TCP and UDP.

Note

It's imperative that you know this section—for the exam and for the real world. You need to know more than the acronyms and port numbers; you also need to understand how the protocols work in real-world scenarios with real hardware and software. We'll try to incorporate these "use cases" as often as possible.

TCP vs. UDP

Network sessions on an IP network are normally either TCP or UDP sessions. Let's briefly discuss these two.

Transmission Control Protocol (TCP) sessions are known as *connection-oriented sessions*. This means that every packet that is sent is checked for delivery. If the receiving computer doesn't receive a packet, it cannot assemble the message and will ask the sending computer to transmit the packet again.

TCP establishes network connections with a *three-way handshake*, a process that includes three steps:

1. **SYN:** The client computer attempts to initiate a session to a server with a synchronize packet of information. (This is known as a SYN packet.)

2. **SYN + ACK:** The server responds to the client request by sending a synchronization/acknowledgment packet. (This is known as a SYN-ACK packet.)

3. **ACK:** The client sends an acknowledgment packet to the server. (This is known as an ACK packet.)

Once the server receives that ACK packet, it acknowledges the session, and the network connection is established. This is also known as a *TCP socket connection*. With TCP, the synchronization, acknowledgment, and sequencing of packets guarantees delivery. Not a single packet is left behind! In addition, TCP uses a method known as *flow control*, which prevents a sender from overwhelming a server by sending too many packets too quickly.

User Datagram Protocol (UDP) sessions are known as *connectionless sessions*. One example of UDP usage is with streaming media sessions. With UDP, if a packet is dropped, it is not asked for again. Let's say you are listening to some streaming music, and you hear a break in the song or a blip of some kind. That indicates some missing packets, but you wouldn't want those packets back because by the time you get them, you would be listening to a totally different part of the music stream! Unlike TCP, UDP does not use a handshake process or flow control. It's expected that you might lose packets in UDP streams but not when making TCP connections.

Both TCP and UDP utilize protocols and ports to make connections. Let's further discuss these protocols and ports now.

Ports and Protocols

Computers use many ports and protocols to transmit information. The protocol used is based on the type of data being transmitted and the application being used. We'll begin with HTTP and HTTPS.

HTTP vs. HTTPS

For two computers to communicate, they must both use the same protocol. For an application to send or receive data, it must use a particular protocol designed for that application, and it must open a port on the network adapter to make a connection to another computer.

For example, let's say you want to visit a website. You type the name of that website into the address bar of a web browser, and one of two protocols will be initiated: HTTP or HTTPS. Take a look at Table 5.1.

TABLE 5.1 **Comparing HTTP and HTTPS**

Protocol	Full Name	Default Port Number
HTTP	Hypertext Transfer Protocol	80
HTTPS	Hypertext Transfer Protocol Secure	443

HTTP and HTTPS both use TCP as their connection mechanism. HTTP was used for decades, but its use has been reduced drastically in favor of the more secure HTTPS. For security reasons, most websites that you connect to today use HTTPS. Primarily, HTTPS is designed to keep a user's information private and to prevent tampering and eavesdropping. Try connecting to some of your favorite websites and identify which protocol is being used. Most of them should use HTTPS, and those that are not should be avoided.

Let's say you open a web browser and connect to one of my websites by typing
dprocomputer.com. When you do so, the address is automatically changed
to https://dprocomputer.com. (If you can't see the full web address and the
HTTPS protocol, simply click on the domain name you typed.) That domain is
configured to use HTTPS for security. HTTPS is the protocol that makes the
connection to the dprocomputer.com web server. The HTTPS protocol selects
an unused port on your computer (known as an *outbound port*) to send and receive data to and from dprocomputer.com. On the other end, dprocomputer.com's
web server has a specific port open at all times, ready to accept sessions. In most
cases, the web server's port is 443, which corresponds to the HTTPS protocol.
This is known as an *inbound port*. Figure 5.1 illustrates this.

FIGURE 5.1 **HTTPS in action**

The local computer on the left in Figure 5.1 has been given the IP address
10.252.0.141. This is a private internal address. It uses port 3515 to go out to
the Internet and start a session with dprocomputer.com. For security purposes,
this is a dynamically assigned port and will be different every time you connect
to another web server, but it will normally be somewhere in the thousands.
The session is accepted by dprocomputer.com's web server, using the public
IP address 216.97.236.245 and inbound port 443. Conversely, if you want to
run your own web server at home and sell widgets and such, that web server
needs to have port 443, or the less secure port 80, open to the public at all
times. If it were ever closed, you would lose sales! Computers that connect to
your web server would use dynamically assigned ports.

HTTPS is used by the majority of websites today. It is recommended because
of the secure connection it makes—which it does via a secure protocol such as
Transport Layer Security (TLS) and using an encrypted certificate. We'll discuss this process more in Chapters 43 through 52, which focus on security.

> **ExamAlert**
>
> Use HTTPS for web servers whenever possible—usually on port 443. Also remember
> that HTTPS is connection oriented (as it uses TCP).

Email Protocols

For people who share written communications with each other, email protocols are a must. Email is sometimes accomplished using a web browser (HTTPS) or within an app that works in the same manner. This is great for home users and for small businesses. However, for larger organizations using desktop computers, or if you simply need to connect directly to specific email servers, you'll have to configure email protocols. When setting up an email client, you might need to know the protocols and ports involved. Email can be sent and received, so you will have to configure an outbound server and an inbound server—which could be one and the same. Generally, the outbound server will use SMTP, and the inbound server will use either POP3 or IMAP:

▶ **SMTP:** Simple Mail Transfer Protocol sends email. When you send email from the email client, it goes to an SMTP server and is then sent off to its destination. The email server could be at an Internet service provider (ISP) or could be supplied by the organization you work for, and it could be either in-house or in the cloud. A good way to remember this acronym is by using the mnemonic device *Send Mail To People*. The original default port for SMTP was 25, but to make use of an SSL- or TLS-encrypted session, you would use either port 587 or port 465, depending on the type of encryption used and which protocol your ISP or administrator (or *you*) has selected.

▶ **POP3:** Post Office Protocol Version 3 is very common and is used by email clients to retrieve incoming email from a mail server. The original POP3 server port was 110, but for secure transmissions, the default port is 995.

▶ **IMAP:** Internet Message Access Protocol is an email protocol that enables messages to remain on the email server so they can be retrieved from any location. IMAP also supports folders, so users can organize their messages as desired. IMAP email servers used port 143 for many years, but for secure transmissions, they use 993 by default.

ExamAlert

Know your secure ports! SMTP uses 587 or 465, POP3 uses 995, and IMAP uses 993.

On the client side, you must specify the server name and the correct ports for both the sending and receiving of email. The protocols and ports must exactly match the configuration of the email server(s). Email clients include Outlook,

Thunderbird, and a host of others. You can also use the Gmail application to connect to separate accounts using these protocols.

On the server side, there are several options available; for example, Microsoft Exchange can handle SMTP, POP3, and/or IMAP, as well as HTTPS connections from web browsers and from mobile devices by using Exchange ActiveSync, which is part of Exchange Online. Configuration of email servers is beyond the scope of the A+ exams.

FTP, SSH, and Telnet

If you need to communicate with an external host to send and receive files and/ or run commands on the external host, you might be interested in FTP or SSH. Telnet, on the other hand, is deprecated, as it is insecure, and should be avoided. This is what you need to know about these protocols:

▶ **FTP:** File Transfer Protocol allows computers to transfer files back and forth. When you connect to an FTP server, that FTP server has port 21 open. Some type of FTP client software is necessary to connect to the FTP server; this could be done in the command line within the FTP shell or by using a GUI-based application (such as FileZilla). However, default FTP is not considered secure today. Instead, organizations usually prefer SFTP (discussed in the next bullet), or FTP Secure (FTPS), which uses SSL/TLS and utilizes port 989 and 990. So far, all the FTP options I've listed have been connection oriented. But Trivial File Transfer Protocol (TFTP), which is commonly used for booting a system from a network, is connectionless.

> **Note**
>
> The exam objectives list FTP port 20. Historically, after connecting to an FTP server on port 21, a client would use port 20 for the actual data transfer. That is still possible, but today, most FTP client programs randomly and dynamically assign ports for data transfer.

▶ **SSH:** Secure Shell enables the remote control of computers and enables data to be exchanged between computers on a secured channel. This protocol offers a more secure replacement to FTP and Telnet. To access a Secure Shell server, the server must have port 22 open. There are additional protocols that use SSH as a way of making a secure connection. One of them is the commonly used Secure FTP (SFTP). As mentioned, regular FTP can be insecure. SFTP provides file access over a reliable data stream that is generated and protected by SSH. Other protocols that "ride" on SSH include SCP and rsync. SSH is an example of a connection-oriented protocol that uses TCP.

▶ **Telnet:** Short for Telecommunication network, Telnet provides remote access to other hosts using the command-line interface (CLI). It uses port 23 but is an insecure and somewhat deprecated protocol. However, because some companies *might* still use it to access routers and other hosts, and to test and manage network connectivity, you might see a question about it on the exam. Generally, Telnet is disabled, if it even exists, in the OS. If you are wondering if it is enabled in Windows, you can do a quick check for it in the Services console window (**Run > services.msc**). If it is not listed, then it is not enabled. It can be enabled or disabled in the **Turn Windows features on or off** window. (By default, only the Telnet client is listed in Windows.)

DHCP

Dynamic Host Configuration Protocol (DHCP) is used to automatically assign IP addresses to hosts. These hosts could be computers, printers, servers, routers, and so on. In most small office/home office (SOHO) networks, a router uses DHCP to assign IP addresses to the client computers. However, your ISP will also use DHCP to assign an IP address to you; usually your router gets this. Finally, small-to-midsized businesses (SMBs) and enterprise organizations alike use DHCP—often implemented as a separate server.

The DHCP service makes life easier for a network administrator by automatically assigning IP addresses, subnet masks, gateway addresses, DNS servers, and so on from a central location. If you get your address from a DHCP server, you are getting your address assigned dynamically, and it could change periodically. That's because a lease is attached to the IP address, which only lasts for a certain amount of time (a month, a week, or even less). Computers that obtain IP addresses from a DHCP server have the advantage of automatically getting new addressing when they are moved to a different network segment. However, some computers require a static address—one that is assigned by a network administrator manually. It is better in many situations for servers and printers to use static addresses so you know exactly what the address is and so it won't change.

By default, in a typical IPv4 network, the DHCP server needs to have inbound port 67 open, and a DHCP client uses port 68 to connect out to that DHCP server. We would refer to such a DHCP server as a "DHCPv4" server.

(DHCPv6 servers use port 547, and clients use port 546. We'll discuss the differences between IPv4 and IPv6 later in the book.) DHCPv4 servers are connectionless, which means they use UDP as the main transport protocol. By the way, DHCP is also sometimes referred to as *BOOTP*—short for Bootstrap Protocol.

> **ExamAlert**
>
> Typical DHCPv4 servers use port 67 and clients use port 68. Remember that DHCP is considered connectionless (as it uses UDP).

We'll discuss DHCP further in Chapter 10, "Network Configuration Concepts."

DNS

Domain Name System (DNS) is the group of servers on the Internet that translates domain names to IP addresses. For instance, a domain name such as *example.com* might translate to the IP address 93.184.216.34. When you connect to a website by name, the DNS server takes care of resolving the name to the IP address so that your computer and the web server can communicate via IP. To find out the DNS server that your Windows computer talks to, type the command **ipconfig/all** in the Command Prompt, and you will see the IP address of that DNS server.

A DNS server has inbound port 53 open by default. We'll discuss DNS servers further in Chapter 8, "Networked Hosts," and in Chapter 10.

LDAP

Lightweight Directory Access Protocol (LDAP) is used to access and maintain distributed directories of information (such as the kind involved with Microsoft domains). Microsoft refers to this as Active Directory (AD), and also directory services or domain services. It includes the user accounts, computer accounts, groups, and the authentication and permissions involved with those accounts—collectively known as a Windows domain. To implement a Windows domain, at least one Windows server must be promoted to a domain controller. When you do this, LDAP is installed and runs on inbound port 389 by default. A more secure version of LDAP (Secure LDAP) runs on port 636.

RDP

To facilitate connections to remote computers and allow full remote control, Microsoft uses the Remote Desktop Connection program, which is based on Remote Desktop Protocol (RDP).

RDP works in three ways. First, users can be given limited access to a remote computer's applications (such as Word or Excel). Second, administrators can be given full access to a computer so that they can troubleshoot problems from another location. Third, another part of the program, known as Remote Assistance, allows users to invite a technician to view their desktops in the hopes that the technician can fix any encountered problems. These invitations can be made via email. The RDP port, 3389, is also used by Remote Desktop Services, which is the server-based companion of Remote Desktop Connection.

Figure 5.2 shows the results of running a **netstat** command on a Windows server. You can see that port 3389 is open, which allows for remote control of the server (which is exactly what the figure shows happening). Inbound port 389 is also open, indicating that LDAP is running and that the server is indeed a domain controller.

```
Active Connections

  Proto  Local Address          Foreign Address        State
  TCP    0.0.0.0:88             0.0.0.0:0              LISTENING
  TCP    0.0.0.0:135            0.0.0.0:0              LISTENING
  TCP    0.0.0.0:389            0.0.0.0:0              LISTENING
  TCP    10.252.0.103:139       10.252.0.141:50522     ESTABLISHED
  TCP    10.252.0.103:139       10.252.0.141:50523     ESTABLISHED
  TCP    10.252.0.103:139       10.252.0.141:50524     ESTABLISHED
  TCP    10.252.0.103:3389      10.252.0.254:3633      ESTABLISHED
  TCP    10.252.0.105:53        0.0.0.0:0              LISTENING
  TCP    10.252.0.105:139       0.0.0.0:0              LISTENING
```

FIGURE 5.2   LDAP and RDP ports on a Windows server

More Protocols and Ports

There are a few more protocols that you should know for the exam, including SMB/CIFS and SNMP:

▶ **SMB:** The Server Message Block protocol provides access to shared items such as files and printers. These are actual packets that authenticate remote computers through what are known as interprocess communication (IPC) mechanisms. They can communicate directly over TCP using port 445 or by working with the legacy NetBIOS/NetBT protocol using a port between 137 and 139. In the past, SMB was also referred to as the Common Internet File System (CIFS) protocol.

▶ **SNMP:** Simple Network Management Protocol is used as the standard for managing and monitoring devices on a network. It is used to manage routers, switches, UPS devices, and computers and is often incorporated in software known as a network management system (NMS). The NMS is the main software that controls everything SNMP based; it is installed on a computer known as a manager. The devices to be monitored are known as managed devices. The NMS installs a small piece of software known as an agent that allows the NMS to monitor those managed devices and alert the SNMP manager software—and ultimately the administrator. If there is an alert to be sent to an administrator, it is known as a trap. SNMP by default uses port 161, and SNMP traps use port 162.

▶ Wow, that was a mouthful of acronyms. Study them and their port numbers! Use Table 5.2 to help. You will note that there are secure versions of some of the protocols and that each uses a different port number than the insecure version. You will also see in this table whether a protocol rides on TCP, or UDP, or both. I listed the protocol name in the first column, but the table is sorted by port number for easier reference.

TABLE 5.2 **Protocol and Port Listing**

Protocol	Original Port	Secure Port	TCP/UDP Usage
FTP	21	989/990	TCP
SSH	22	22	TCP or UDP
Telnet	23	Not considered a secure protocol	TCP or UDP
SMTP	25	587 or 465	TCP
DNS	53		TCP or UDP
DHCP	67 (server) 68 (client)		UDP
HTTP	80	443 (HTTPS)	TCP
POP3	110	995	TCP
NetBIOS/NetBT	137–139		TCP or UDP
IMAP	143	993	TCP
SNMP	161		UDP
SNMPTRAP	162		TCP or UDP
LDAP	389	636	TCP or UDP
SMB	445		TCP
RDP	3389		TCP or UDP

Cram Quiz

Answer these questions. The answers follow the last question. If you cannot answer these questions correctly, consider reading this chapter again until you can.

1. Which protocol uses port 22?

   ○ **A.** FTP

   ○ **B.** Telnet

   ○ **C.** SSH

   ○ **D.** HTTPS

2. Which of these would be used for streaming media?

   ○ **A.** TCP

   ○ **B.** RDP

   ○ **C.** UDP

   ○ **D.** DHCP

3. Which ports are used by the IMAP protocol?

   ○ **A.** 53 and 68

   ○ **B.** 80 and 443

   ○ **C.** 110 and 995

   ○ **D.** 143 and 993

4. A user can receive email but cannot send any. Which protocol is not configured properly?
   - ○ **A.** POP3
   - ○ **B.** FTP
   - ○ **C.** SMTP
   - ○ **D.** SNMP

5. Which of the following is the default inbound port of a DHCPv4 server?
   - ○ **A.** 67
   - ○ **B.** 22
   - ○ **C.** 995
   - ○ **D.** 3389

Cram Quiz Answers

1. **C.** SSH (Secure Shell) uses port 22. FTP uses port 21, Telnet uses port 23, and HTTPS uses port 443.

2. **C.** User Datagram Protocol (UDP) is used for streaming media. It is connectionless, whereas TCP is connection oriented and not a good choice for streaming media. RDP, which stands for Remote Desktop Protocol, is used to make connections to other computers. DHCP, which stands for Dynamic Host Configuration Protocol, is used to assign IP addresses to clients automatically. Don't forget: DHCP is connectionless and uses UDP, too!

3. **D.** Internet Message Access Protocol (IMAP) uses port 143 by default and port 993 as a secure default. DNS uses port 53. DHCP uses port 68. HTTP uses port 80. HTTPS uses port 443. POP3 uses port 110 and 995 as a secure default. Know those ports!

4. **C.** Simple Mail Transfer Protocol (SMTP) is probably not configured properly. It deals with sending mail. POP3 receives mail. FTP sends files to remote computers. SNMP is used to manage networks.

5. **A.** The default inbound port of a DHCPv4 server is 67 (and clients use port 68 outbound). Port 22 is the inbound port of an SSH server. Port 995 is the secure inbound port of a POP3 server. Port 3389 is the default inbound port of a server that is running RDP.

Another chapter done! Memorize those protocols and port numbers, take a quick breather, and move on!

CHAPTER 6

Network Devices

This chapter covers the following A+ 220-1101 exam objective:

▶ **2.2** – Compare and contrast common networking hardware.

In this second chapter about networking, we will discuss networking devices—the devices that make communications happen between computers. Need your computers to talk to each other in a wired fashion? You want a switch. Need them to communicate wirelessly? Use a wireless access point. Want to connect two or more networks or connect to the Internet? Routers do just this. These are just a few examples of networking devices that make our computers more "talkative." And know this: Some are multifunction devices, meaning that they can do the work of more than one network device.

While you read this chapter, apply what you learn to the devices in your own network. Whenever you encounter a device, think about its function in a network environment. The A+ Core 1 (220-1101) exam covers only the basics about networking, but it is still a lot of material to cover, so let's get to it!

> **ExamAlert**
>
> **Objective 2.2** focuses on the following concepts: routers, switches, access points, patch panels, firewalls, Power over Ethernet (PoE), hubs, cable modems, digital subscriber line (DSL), optical network terminals (ONTs), network interface cards, and software-defined networking (SDN).

Switches

A *switch* is a central connecting device that computers connect to in a wired fashion. Each computer is connected to its own physical port on a switch. The switch is in charge of sending data directly to the correct computer instead of broadcasting it out to every port (the way an older hub would). It does this by identifying the media access control (MAC) address of each computer. The MAC address is the physical address (for example, 00-0C-29-C6-XX-XX) that is programmed into the network adapter. (In Windows, run a quick **ipconfig /all** to find out your MAC address, also called a "physical address.") By identifying each computer's MAC address, the switch can effectively make every port on the switch an individual entity. To further accomplish this, switches employ a matrix of copper wiring—and everything is interconnected between the ports.

Switches are intelligent, and they use their intelligence to pass information to the correct port. This means that each computer has its own bandwidth (for example, 1000 Mbps). In today's networks, switches are commonly found in 1000 Mbps (1 Gbps), 10 Gbps, and 40 Gbps networks.

> **ExamAlert**
>
> A switch is responsible for transmitting data from two or more wired computers. It often works at data transfer rates of 1000 Mbps or 10 Gbps.

Switches work within the Ethernet standard, which is the most common networking standard used today. It was ratified by the IEEE and is documented in the 802.3 set of standards. For example, a typical Ethernet network running at 1000 Mbps and using twisted pair cable is classified as 802.3ab. 10 Gbps Ethernet over twisted pair cable is 802.3an.

Understand the difference between a managed switch and an unmanaged switch. Managed switches can be configured when accessed from a browser or from the command line, using SSH or a similar configuration tool. For example, you can change a device's IP address, turn on Spanning Tree Protocol (STP) to avoid network looping, enable system logging (syslog), and monitor the switch and other devices with SNMP. On the other hand, unmanaged switches don't have these capabilities; they simply connect devices and computers together for transmission of data over the Ethernet network. Unmanaged switches provide an inexpensive method of adding computers to your network.

> **ExamAlert**
>
> A managed switch can allow an admin to control settings and network traffic. An unmanaged switch simply allows LAN devices to communicate without user intervention.

As mentioned, a switch connects computers together in a wired fashion. From a design standpoint, this is known as a *star topology* (or hub-and-spoke topology), with the switch in the center of it all. A switch is also the basis for a local area network (LAN). But what if you want to connect two LANs together? Enter the router.

Routers

A *router* is used to connect two or more networks to form an internetwork. Routers are used in LANs and WANs and on the Internet. A router is a device that routes data from one location to another, usually by way of IP addresses and IP network numbers. Routers are intelligent and even have their own operating systems. A router enables connections with individual high-speed interconnection points. A common example would be an all-in-one device or multifunction network device that might be used in a home or small office. These devices route signals for all the computers on the LAN out to the Internet. Larger organizations use more advanced routers that can make connections to multiple various networks as well as the Internet.

> **ExamAlert**
>
> Know that a router connects networks and uses software-configured network addresses to make forwarding decisions.

Wireless Access Points

A *wireless access point (WAP)*—or simply an access point—enables data communications over the air when a computer is equipped with a wireless networking adapter. The WAP and the wireless networking adapter transmit data over radio waves either on the 2.4 GHz, 5 GHz, or 6 GHz frequencies. Wireless access points are everywhere you look: hotels, restaurants, shopping centers, you name it. They allow people to easily connect to the Internet with smartphones, tablets, and laptops.

WAPs are also included in most multifunction network devices, known as SOHO (small office/home office) routers or simply routers. They enable wireless computers to not only communicate with each other but also access the Internet. Whereas switches deal with wired networks, WAPs deal with wireless connections. WAPs are also based on Ethernet, but now we are talking about the IEEE 802.11 group of standards, which defines wireless LANs (WLANs), simply referred to as Wi-Fi. A WAP acts as a central connecting point for Wi-Fi-equipped computers. Like a switch, a WAP identifies each computer by its MAC address.

> **ExamAlert**
>
> A wireless access point (WAP) is responsible for transmitting data between two or more wireless computers, usually at 6 GHz, 5 GHz, or 2.4 GHz frequencies.

Firewalls

A *firewall* is a hardware appliance or software application that protects a computer from unwanted intrusion. In the networking world, we are more concerned with hardware-based devices that protect an entire group of computers (such as a LAN). When it comes to small offices and home offices, firewall functionality is usually built into the router. In larger organizations, a firewall is a separate device—or it could be part of a more complex all-in-one solution. A firewall stops unwanted connections from the outside and can block basic network attacks. We'll discuss firewalls more in Chapters 43, "Physical Security," 44, "Logical Security," and 51, "SOHO Security."

> **ExamAlert**
>
> A firewall provides controlled access between networks. Firewalls can be hardware or software based and are essential to network security.

Network Interface Cards

A network interface card (NIC, pronounced "nick"), also known as a network adapter, is a physical device that can be added to a computer or networking device that has an open and compatible slot. For example, a computer with an open PCI Express slot (x1 or x4) can be used with a NIC for connectivity to a computer network. Most PCs and laptops have NICs built into the motherboard; these are known as *integrated NICs*. However, workstations and servers often require more powerful, separate, network interface cards, or require multiple NICs. A server may use special network cards that have two, four, or more RJ45 ports to allow for increased data throughput as well as higher availability. We'll discuss NICs further in Chapter 16, "Motherboards and Add-on Cards."

Hubs

The *hub* is the original connecting device for computers on a LAN. It creates a simple shared physical connection that all computers use to send data. It's a basic device that has multiple ports, usually in intervals of four. Internally, a hub actually has only one main circuit that all the ports connect to. (In contrast, a switch has a matrix of circuits.) A hub regenerates and passes on the electrical signals initiated by computers, broadcasting data out to all computers on the network. The computer that it is meant for accepts the data; the rest of the computers drop the information. Because of this broadcasting and sharing, this device allows only two computers to communicate with each other at any given time.

In the days of 10 Mbps and 100 Mbps networks, hubs were common. Although hubs are still included in the A+ objectives, in most instances today, hubs have given way to switches.

Patch Panels

A *patch panel* is a physical hardware device that acts as a termination point for all of the network cables in a building. It is often located in a wiring closet, server room, or data center, depending on the size of the organization. It consists of multiple RJ45 ports on the front that connect to switches by way of twisted pair patch cables and 110 IDC termination points on the back for connecting all of the individual wires in twisted pair cables. Those cables lead out to the various computer ports in the building. While it isn't necessary to have a patch panel, it makes for easier and more reliable patching of ports. A typical physical data path from a user to a server is Computer > RJ45 jack > twisted pair cable > patch panel > switch(s) > server.

Power over Ethernet

Power over Ethernet (PoE) is an Ethernet standard that allows for the passing of electrical power in addition to data over Ethernet cabling. It is described in several IEEE 802.3 standards (for example, IEEE 802.3bt-2018). PoE can deliver between 15.4 and 100 watts maximum to a variety of devices, as long as the sending and receiving devices are both PoE compliant.

PoE is an excellent solution for devices that require specific placement but where no electrical connection can be made (for example, with outdoor video cameras or WAPs that need to be mounted to the ceiling). In these cases, all that needs to be run is a twisted pair network cable, which takes care of power *and* data. No AC electrical connection is necessary.

PoE technology is broken down into the two devices:

▶ **Power sourcing equipment (PSE):** This could be a switch or other similar device.

▶ **Powered device (PD):** This could be an IP-based camera, an IP phone, a wireless access point, a router, a mini network switch, an industrial device, a lighting controller, and more. If the device to be powered is not PoE compliant, then a PoE splitter can be used in between the device to be powered and the network connection.

> **ExamAlert**
>
> Power over Ethernet (PoE) devices include power sourcing equipment (PSE) and a powered device (PD).

For organizations with a group of remote devices, a 24- or 48-port PoE-enabled switch is the way to go. For a smaller organization that only has one or two remote devices that need to be powered, a *PoE injector* is a decent, cheaper PSE solution. This device is installed where the main network switch is and plugs into one of the switch's ports. It is also powered normally from an AC outlet. But the injector has a second RJ45 port that is used to connect out to the remote device. This port sends Ethernet data as well as power over the Ethernet connection. This way, the organization can get power and data to a PoE-compliant access point, IP camera, or other device that needs to be located in an area where it would be difficult (not to mention expensive) to add an electrical outlet. However, the correct type of cabling must be used to handle the amperage required. Generally, this is Category 5 twisted pair cabling and higher.

Table 6.1 shows some of the IEEE standards for PoE, their associated maximum power levels, and the modes of power usage. Mode A delivers power on the two data pairs of wires in a twisted pair connection. For example, using the T568B wiring standard, this would be the orange and green pairs, or wires 1, 2, 3, and 6. Mode B delivers power on the spare pairs, which in T568B would be the blue and brown pairs, or wires 4, 5, 7, and 8. However, it's more common in newer standards to use all four pairs of wires in a twisted pair cable. This is done using phantom power, which allows for data *and* power to be sent on each pair of wires. For more information about the T568B wiring standard, see Chapter 13, "Cables and Connectors."

ExamAlert

Newer versions of PoE use all four pairs of wires on a twisted pair cable and also implement phantom power—allowing data and power to be sent simultaneously over all pairs.

TABLE 6.1 **IEEE PoE Standards**

Standard	Maximum Provided Power (watts)	Power Modes
802.3af (Type 1) (PoE)	PSE: 15.4 W PD: 12.95 W	Mode A and Mode B
802.3at (Type 2) (PoE+)	PSE: 30 W PD: 25.5 W	Mode A and Mode B
802.3bt (Type 3) (PoE++)	PSE: 60 W PD: 51 W	Mode A, Mode B, and 4-pair
802-3bt (Type 4) (PoE++)	PSE: 100 W PD: 71 W	4-pair only

Note

The second column of Table 6.1 shows the power sourcing equipment (PSE) first and the powered device (PD) second. Power dissipation over the twisted pair cable is between 10% to 30%, depending on the standard.

You should also consider *load testing* a PoE system. Do this before anyone uses it to make sure that the system can handle the amount of electricity you plan to send over it. Load testing has the added benefit of making a PoE-enabled switch work more efficiently. For example, a typical Type 2 PD will be rated as a 30 W device. However, many of those PDs will be able to function with less power, and you can configure each one's power usage on a port-by-port basis at the PoE-enabled switch.

Cable/DSL Modems

Essentially, a cable or DSL modem is a device that allows a computer (or SOHO network) to access the Internet. Cable Internet and digital subscriber line (DSL) Internet connections use separate devices to connect. For example, a person with a cable Internet connection will use a device that has an RG-6 port for the provider's incoming coaxial cable. A DSL modem, on the other hand, will have an RJ11 port that makes use of a person's telephone line. Both, however, use an RJ45 port that connects to the consumer's computer or SOHO router by way of a twisted pair patch cable.

> **Note**
>
> The term *modem* is a combination of the words *mo*dulate and *dem*odulate. It origi- nated with the dial-up modem that uses a standard telephone phone line. While it is arguable whether cable and DSL Internet devices are actually "modems," the plain truth is that the term is commonly used—even by some manufacturers.

Network Interface Devices

A network interface device (NID) is a device installed at the perimeter of a customer's premises. It is the connection point between a provider's cabling and the customer's cabling—also known as a demarcation point, or demarc. It is often a gray box on the outside of a building that is maintained by providers of cable Internet, cable TV, DSL, or fiber optic–based services, though it could be inside the building as well. It could act as a basic wiring termination point or provide more functionality, intelligence, and possibly power, depending on the technology involved. (A NID goes by several other names, including network interface unit, telephone network interface, or network termination device.)

One example of a NID is an *optical network terminal (ONT)*. When you see the word *optical*, think fiber optic cables, which have the ability to transmit massive amounts of data. In some urban areas, businesses and homes can get fiber to the premises, which means that a fiber optic cable is run directly to the premises by the provider. It terminates at an ONT, where it can be split off for services such as voice, data, and television, which will usually run on copper-based cables from the ONT to the inside of the customer's premises. The ONT (and any type of NID) is normally accessible only by employees of the fiber optic provider.

> **Note**
>
> Don't confuse an optical network terminal (ONT) with an optical line terminal (OLT). An OLT is an endpoint for fiber optic cables that are run *inside* an organization's premises for use with high-speed data transfer between hosts and/or networks.

Software-Defined Networking

Software-defined networking (SDN) is a type of centralized network management that is dynamic and programmable. It separates the data that is transmitted by network devices from the administration of those devices. This can be helpful in a network that has many switches and routers. SDN is used to aid with traffic engineering, routing, switching, monitoring, load balancing, and security.

In a network that uses SDN, there is a separate system known as a controller that talks to all the routers and switches and other network devices. Ultimately, the SDN approach deals less with individual protocols on individual devices and more with the SDN controller's instructions to the devices. The controller tells routers and switches what to do with particular types of packets, applying rules as set by the administrator of the controller. For example, an admin might set a rule for a switch with the IP address 10.0.0.1 (known as a match) which specifies that certain packets are dropped (which is the action taken). This eliminates that type of packet from being forwarded by that switch. You can also use SDN software to more efficiently control large numbers of virtual machines and categorize them by virtual LANs, allowing them to be grouped and administered easily, even if they are physically moved. This makes the network more agile.

The most commonly known SDN protocol is the OpenFlow protocol (which is open source, meaning anyone can use it), although companies (such as Cisco) have entered the market with their own proprietary SDN solutions.

Cram Quiz

Answer these questions. The answers follow the last question. If you cannot answer these questions correctly, consider reading this chapter again until you can.

1. Which of the following is most often used to connect a group of computers in a LAN? (Select all that apply.)

   ○ **A.** Router
   ○ **B.** Switch
   ○ **C.** Bridge
   ○ **D.** WAP

2. What device protects a network from unwanted intrusion?

   ○ **A.** Switch
   ○ **B.** Router
   ○ **C.** Access point
   ○ **D.** Firewall

3. Which of the following network devices moves frames of data between a source and destination, based on their MAC addresses?

   ○ **A.** Hub
   ○ **B.** Switch
   ○ **C.** Router
   ○ **D.** Modem

4. Which of the following network devices allows a remote device to obtain Ethernet data as well as electrical power?

   ○ **A.** PD
   ○ **B.** PoE injector
   ○ **C.** Firewall
   ○ **D.** Router

5. Which of the following devices can be configured when accessed from a browser or SSH or similar configuration tool?

   ○ **A.** Managed switch
   ○ **B.** Unmanaged switch
   ○ **C.** Patch panel
   ○ **D.** Network interface card

6. Which of the following acts as a demarcation point for fiber optic services?

- ○ **A.** SDN
- ○ **B.** ONT
- ○ **C.** Patch panel
- ○ **D.** NIC

Cram Quiz Answers

1. **B and D.** Computers in a LAN are connected by a central connecting device, the most common of which are switches and wireless access points (WAPs). Hubs can also be used, but those are deprecated devices; they are predecessors of switches. A router is designed to connect two networks. Now, you might say, "Wait! My router at home has four ports on the back for computers to talk to each other." Well, that is actually the switch portion of a SOHO "router." The actual *router* functionality is in the connection between the two networks—your switched LAN and the Internet. A bridge is used to connect two LANs or separate a single LAN into two sections.

2. **D.** A firewall is a hardware appliance or software application that protects one or more computers from unwanted intrusion. A switch is a device that connects multiple computers together on a LAN. A router is used to connect two or more networks. An access point (or wireless access point) allows Wi-Fi-enabled computers and devices to communicate on the LAN wirelessly.

3. **B.** A switch sends frames of data between computers by identifying the systems by their MAC addresses. A hub broadcasts data out to all computers. The computer that it is meant for accepts the data; the rest of the computers drop the information. Routers enable connections with individual high-speed interconnection points and route signals for all the computers on the LAN out to the Internet. A modem is a device that allows a computer to access the Internet by changing the digital signals of the computer to analog signals used by a typical land-based phone line.

4. **B.** A Power over Ethernet (PoE) injector sends Ethernet data and power over a single twisted pair cable to a remote device. A PD, which stands for "powered device," is a PoE-compliant remote device that is receiving the power. A repeater extends the distance of a network connection. A firewall is a device (or software) that secures ports on a network or on an individual system. A router makes connections from one network to another or from the LAN to the Internet.

5. **A.** Managed switches can be configured when accessed from a browser or SSH or similar configuration tool. For example, you can change the device's IP address, configure ports, and monitor the switch and other devices using SNMP. On the other hand, unmanaged switches don't have these capabilities; they simply connect devices and computers for transmission of data over the Ethernet network. A patch panel is a physical hardware device that acts as a termination point for all of the network cables in a building. A network interface card (NIC)

allows for connectivity to a computer network. It is a physical device that can be added to a computer or networking device that has an open and compatible slot.

6. **B.** An optical network terminal (ONT) is a type of network interface device (gray box) used to take an incoming fiber optic line from a provider and split it off to a customer's premises for the purposes of Internet access, voice calls, and television. Often, the cables that go from the ONT to the inside of the customer's premises are copper based (coaxial or possibly twisted pair). Software-defined networking (SDN) is a method of administering multiple network devices with a controller program. A patch panel is a device that terminates twisted pair cables on one side and has ports for patch cables on the other (to be connected to a switch). A network interface card (NIC) is an adapter card that can be installed to a PC that allows the system to access a wired network. Don't confuse a NIC with a NID!

You are unstoppable. Be sure to review the Exam Alerts and continue!

CHAPTER 7
Wireless Protocols

This chapter covers the following A+ 220-1101 exam objective:

▶ **2.3** –Compare and contrast protocols for wireless networking.

Welcome back! Sometimes you will wire computers to the network, and other times—perhaps more often—you will use wireless. Wireless takes the cable out of the mix and allows for mobility and ease of use. But I caution you: The air is shared! So, when planning your wireless technologies, especially Wi-Fi, you have to take into account such things as frequencies, desired data transfer rates, distance between devices, and much more. This is a shorter chapter, but it is chock full of technical information.

In this chapter, we'll discuss the IEEE 802.11 wireless protocols and some other wireless standards available for mobile devices. Bluetooth and NFC are also listed in the CompTIA objective, but we covered them previously in Chapters 3, "Mobile Device Accessories and Ports," and 4, "Mobile Device Network Connectivity and Application Support"; make sure you know them. Here we go!

802.11 Wireless

To standardize *wireless LAN (WLAN)* communications—also known as Wi-Fi—the Institute of Electrical and Electronics Engineers (IEEE) developed the 802.11 series of protocols. The 802.11 standard defines the various speeds, frequencies, and protocols used to transmit data over radio waves in small geographic areas using unlicensed spectrums.

There are several different 802.11 derivatives you need to know for the exam: 802.11a, 802.11b, 802.11g, 802.11n, 802.11ac, and 802.11ax. Table 7.1 shows these technologies and the characteristics that differentiate them.

TABLE 7.1 **802.11 Standards**

802.11 Version	Maximum Data Rate	Frequency
802.11a	54 Mbps	5 GHz
802.11b	11 Mbps	2.4 GHz
802.11g	54 Mbps	2.4 GHz
802.11n (Wi-Fi 4)	600 Mbps	5 and/or 2.4 GHz
802.11ac (Wi-Fi 5)	3.5 Gbps	5 GHz
802.11ax (Wi-Fi 6)	9.6 Gbps	5 and 2.4 GHz

Note

The data rates in Table 7.1 are potential maximums. Typical numbers will be less and are limited by factors such as bandwidth, interference, and the distance of a wireless device from the transmitter.

One thing I left out of the table is coverage, or distance. It is difficult to put an exact number on the maximum wireless transmission distances for each standard because it depends on the signal strength of the WAP's antenna, the use of additional features, and environmental factors such as obstructions and interference. But generally, the wireless range from WAP to client increases with each standard listed in the table.

> **Note**
>
> New technologies being developed as of the writing of this book use higher frequency ranges and can transmit much more data per second. Always be on the alert for emerging networking technologies!

The data transfer rates of newer wireless network technologies are increased using a concept known as *multipath propagation*. This occurs when an antenna (or antennas) receives radio signals on two or more paths. A common example of this is multiple-input, multiple-output (MIMO) technology, which is incorporated into 802.11n, ac, and ax wireless networks. For example, a typical 802.11ac wireless device uses three or four antennas; the 802.11ac standard complies with multiuser MIMO (or MU-MIMO), which can have four simultaneous downlinks.

Depending on the frequency used, there are different channels that can be utilized by the average home or company. We touched on these previously, but let's summarize them in Table 7.2 and then look more closely.

TABLE 7.2 **2.4 GHz and 5 GHz Channels**

Frequency	Typical Channels	Example
2.4 GHz	1 through 11	802.11g
5 GHz	36, 40, 44, 48, 149, 153, 157, 161, 165	802.11ac and 802.11ax

> **Note**
>
> Though it's not listed in Objective 2.3, I suggest you also look into 6 GHz. It has a larger frequency width and the potential to offer more channels than 5 GHz. As of the writing of this book, the 802.11ax standard can also use the 6 GHz range, but it must be with compatible Wi-Fi *6E* devices.

Let's take it to the next level. More accurately, 2.4 GHz, 5 GHz, and 6 GHz are frequency *ranges*. The exact range for these will vary from one country to the next. For example, the range for 2.4 GHz Wi-Fi in the United States is between 2.412 GHz and 2.462 GHz, broken up as channels 1 through 11—each spaced 5 MHz apart from the next. When you set up a 2.4 GHz Wi-Fi network, it has a *channel width* associated with it. By default, this is often 20 MHz—an amount that spans multiple channels. I therefore usually recommend placing wireless networks (and access points) on separate channels that are distant from each other. In the United States, the 2.4 GHz non-overlapping channels are 1, 6, and 11. For example, one Wi-Fi network could be on channel 1 (2.412 GHz) and the next could be on channel 6 (2.437 GHz), which allows for 25 MHz of space—which in most cases is more than enough to avoid interference.

However, to increase data rates, you can increase the channel width on many routers to 40 MHz for 2.4 GHz networks and up to 80 MHz for 5 GHz networks. This is known as *channel bonding*. As you can guess, the chance for interference increases as well, so this notion can be risky. If we used 40 MHz channel bonding with our previous example, we would have interference from one Wi-Fi network to the next. Channel 6 is too close to channel 1 in this case. We would need to go to at least channel 9 (2.452 GHz) to avoid overlapping of the two Wi-Fi networks. The same goes for 5 GHz Wi-Fi networks. For example, channel 36's center frequency is actually 5.180 GHz. Channel 40 is 5.200 GHz. That is 20 MHz of channel width. If we wanted a separate Wi-Fi network on each of those channels, it would work fine by default, but if we wanted to perform channel bonding, then we would have to select another channel, such as channel 149 (5.755 GHz), which would allow for 40 or 80 MHz channel bonding and, possibly, higher data rates.

> **Note**
>
> All the wireless frequencies and channels that we have discussed so far are *unlicensed*. This means that anyone can use them, and they are not reserved for any government or organizational entity.

But air is free, right? So, we should perform a wireless site survey and identify other companies' and homes' Wi-Fi networks that are nearby. They could be using channels that are too close and cause interference. A *Wi-Fi analyzer* program is the best way to go when it comes to seeing who is using which frequencies and then selecting frequencies that you can use (even with channel bonding) without causing overlap and interference. Vendors develop these programs for Windows, Android, and iOS. A Wi-Fi analyzer makes it easier for a person to discern where Wi-Fi networks exist in a given frequency range by showing the information in a graphical format, such as a chart or something similar. It also shows the strength of the signal of each network. All this information can help you decide on the right channel to use when you are performing your wireless site survey.

> **ExamAlert**
>
> Don't stand so close to me! Seriously, make sure your selected Wi-Fi channel is in its own "space" by investigating the airwaves with a Wi-Fi analyzer.

Long-Range Fixed Wireless

The term "long-range fixed wireless" has no formal definition. However, we could apply it to any wireless technology that can send data more than 100 meters (or so) and uses equipment that is stationary, or "fixed."

One example of fixed wireless would be a small office or home office that purchases a fixed wireless Internet plan from a communications provider, or *wireless Internet service provider (WISP)*. Such a plan requires the use of a capable device that is mounted in a fixed position to the building or the home. This type of plan is common in rural areas that do not have broadband Internet access and is also used in mobile home parks, assisted living facilities, and other areas where service providers may have a difficult time laying fiber-optic and/or coaxial cable due to environmental factors. Due to recent rule changes, such plans are also seen more in metropolitan areas as well.

Some long-range fixed wireless services use unlicensed frequency ranges (or bands), such as 900 MHz, 1.8 GHz, 2.4 GHz, and 5 GHz. Other services make use of licensed frequencies, some of which may use the UHF band (300 MHz to 3 GHz) and the Local Multipoint Distribution Service (LMDS) on the 26 and 29 GHz bands. Licensed frequencies have the potential for better quality of service (QoS) and higher Internet speeds.

In general, a long-range fixed wireless device requires power from the electrical grid (public utilities) as opposed to other mobile access points that are powered by batteries. In the United States, the Federal Communications Commission (FCC) oversees regulations for the use of fixed wireless technology, including frequency bands that can be used, types of antennas that are allowed, and how those antennas distribute signals.

RFID

Radio-frequency identification (RFID) is a wireless technology used to read information that is stored on tags that can be attached to, or embedded in, just about anything. They are used in many industries and have many uses, such as access control, commerce, advertising, manufacturing, agriculture, and so on.

For example, RFID tags can be used in a retail store to help with the tracking of inventory and protection from theft. Tags are attached to clothing or other items and are read by an RFID reader as part of the checkout process. After a customer pays for an item, the RFID reader deactivates the item's tag. To detect cases of customers failing to pay for items, an RFID detector placed at the entrance/exit reads tags and sends alerts. These readers and detectors must be nearby, but not necessarily within line of sight, which is an improvement over a basic barcode system. In addition, an RFID tag can hold a lot more information and can be programmed, if necessary. For readers that can track items over larger distances—beyond close proximity—an active RFID system would be necessary, where the reader is AC powered.

When it comes to computers, networks, and authentication, RFID plays a vital role. For instance, as part of an access control solution, RFID tags are used as ID badges—proximity cards, dongles, and so forth—and can take the place of older and less secure magnetic stripe cards. Entrances to a building, specific offices, server rooms, data centers, and so on can be equipped with RFID readers. Simply placing an RFID badge on or near the reader activates the reader so it can verify the ID of the employee. Of course, badges can be stolen; that's why a second factor of authentication is common, such as a passcode, which we will discuss in the security chapters. RFID is also present in smartphones and some other computing devices. Many smartphones are furnished with NFC, which is actually a subset of RFID. These readers are often locked down so that they can only read tags from a certain manufacturer or for a specific purpose.

And that closes out this section on the electromagnetic spectrum. Transmission of data over radio waves can be done in many ways. Be sure to know the basics of each technology discussed in this chapter.

Cram Quiz

Answer these questions. The answers follow the last question. If you cannot answer these questions correctly, consider reading this chapter again until you can.

1. Which of the following would a company most likely use for authentication to a server room?

   ○ **A.** 802.11ac

   ○ **B.** Fixed wireless

   ○ **C.** RFID

   ○ **D.** MIMO

2. Which standard can attain a data transfer rate of 1 Gbps over a wireless connection?

   ○ **A.** 802.11a

   ○ **B.** 802.11b

   ○ **C.** 802.11g

   ○ **D.** 802.11ac

   ○ **E.** 802.3ab

3. Which of the following is often broken down into groups of channels including 1–5, 6–10, and 11?

   ○ **A.** 802.11ac

   ○ **B.** 2.4 GHz

   ○ **C.** 5 GHz

   ○ **D.** 802.11a

4. You are servicing a customer with a cable broadband Internet connection and an 802.11ac wireless network that is experiencing interference from a nearby office. The customer's WAP is mounted to the ceiling. Which of the following is the easiest and best solution?

   ○ **A.** Move the wireless access point to another location.

   ○ **B.** Reconfigure the WAP to use 2.4 GHz instead of 5 GHz.

   ○ **C.** Change the broadcasting channel on the WAP to one that is not used by any neighbors.

   ○ **D.** Recommend a long-range fixed wireless service.

5. Which wireless system is composed of readers and tags and can be used for access control, commerce, advertising, manufacturing, and agriculture?

    ○ **A.** 802.11ax

    ○ **B.** Wi-Fi 6

    ○ **C.** RFID

    ○ **D.** FCC

Cram Quiz Answers

1. C. RFID (radio-frequency identification) is commonly used for access to areas of a building such as a server room. It is often implemented as a proximity-based ID card or badge. The other options are not usually associated with authentication. 802.11ac is a WLAN (Wi-Fi) standard that runs on 5 GHz and can provide 1 Gbps of data transfer. Fixed wireless is a wireless service that uses a fixed wireless device to provide Internet access to users in a building or a home. MIMO (multiple-input, multiple-output) is a multiple propagation technology used to increase data transfer in 802.11n and 802.11ac wireless networks, which is further enhanced with MU-MIMO in 802.11ax.

2. D. 802.11ac (and 802.11ax) can attain speeds in excess of 1 Gbps over wireless. 802.11a and g have a typical maximum of 54 Mbps. 802.11b (rarely used today) has a maximum of 11 Mbps. 802.3ab is the IEEE specification for 1 Gbps transfer over twisted pair cables; it is wired, not wireless (and is also known as 1000BASE-T).

3. B. In the United States, the 2.4 GHz frequency range is broken into three categories: Channels 1–5, 6–10, and 11. By placing separate wireless networks on separate distant channels (such as 1 and 11), you can avoid overlapping and interference. 802.11ac and 802.11a are standards, not frequencies. 5 GHz uses channels such as 36, 40, 149, 153, and so on.

4. C. The easiest (and best) solution to this scenario would be to change the WAP's broadcasting channel to one that is not used by any neighbors. That would first require a wireless site survey to find out what frequencies are being used. Moving the wireless access point is a potential solution but would require a bit of hands-on work because the WAP is mounted to the ceiling. Reconfiguring the WAP to use 2.4 GHz doesn't ensure a reduction in interference; you would still need to do a wireless site survey to make sure there is no channel overlap, which is actually more likely with 2.4 GHz than with 5 GHz. And if you are doing a survey anyway, you might as well find an open channel on the 5 GHz band. A long-range fixed wireless service is the most expensive, time-consuming, and difficult solution on the list, and it isn't necessary because the customer already has broadband Internet access!

5. **C.** Radio-frequency identification (RFID) is a wireless technology used to read information that is stored on tags. The IEEE 802.11ax standard, also referred to as Wi-Fi 6, operates using the 2.4 GHz and 5 GHz frequency bands (and 6 GHz for Wi-Fi 6E). In the United States, the Federal Communications Commission (FCC) oversees regulations for the use of fixed wireless technology, including frequency bands that can be used.

You are doing fantastic! Great job with the chapter. Keep going. There's lots more!

CHAPTER 8

Networked Hosts

This chapter covers the following A+ 220-1101 exam objective:

▶ **2.4** – Summarize services provided by networked hosts.

Let's get a little bit deeper into networking. In this chapter, we'll focus mostly on servers. I'm referring not only to commonly known servers such as web servers, file servers, and email servers but also servers that provide less-well-known underlying services, such as DHCP servers, authentication servers, and load balancers. This chapter also briefly describes Internet appliances, legacy/embedded systems, and IoT devices. Rock on.

ExamAlert

Objective 2.4 concentrates on the following concepts: server roles (DNS, DHCP, file servers, print servers, mail servers, syslog, web servers, AAA), Internet appliances, legacy/embedded systems, and IoT devices.

Server Roles

Servers take care of centralizing data, allowing access to a network, making connections to printers, controlling the flow of email, and much more. Whatever the role, the concept of the server is to do it in a centralized fashion, reducing the burden on client computers. Regardless of whether a server is in the organization's LAN or in the cloud, it will have the same purpose.

If the data you need is not stored at the local computer, then you look to servers to provide it. In the following sections, we'll discuss the various server roles that you should know for the exam: file servers that provide access to data files of all kinds; web servers that provide websites and e-commerce; email servers that provide a central administration and storage point for email messages; and print servers that provide the ability to print to remote printers. We'll also get a bit more technical and cover some of the essential servers on a midsized to large computer network, including DHCP, DNS, proxy, syslog, and authentication servers.

File Servers

File servers store, transfer, migrate, synchronize, and archive files. Any computer can act as a file server of sorts. All you need to do is create a share on your local system and point remote computers to that share, either by browsing or through a mapped network drive. On a typical Windows client computer, however, those shares are limited in the number of simultaneous connections allowed (usually 20 maximum). So, for larger network environments, you need a real server of some sort. Examples of actual server software include Microsoft Windows Server and the various types of Linux server versions, such as Red Hat Enterprise Linux (RHEL) and Ubuntu Server. Like most other servers, a file server can be a physical box or a virtual machine, and it can be located within the LAN or in the cloud.

> **Note**
>
> You could also purchase or build a network-attached storage (NAS) server, which is a basic box that often contains two or more storage drives and connects directly to the network. A NAS server usually runs some variant of Linux. We'll discuss NAS further in Chapter 15, "Storage Drives."

Web Servers

A *web server* houses the website of an organization. Examples of web servers include Microsoft's Internet Information Services (IIS), which is part of Windows Server, and Apache HTTP Server (for Linux and FreeBSD). Small and midsized companies often host their websites with an external provider. Larger companies might choose to host their websites on web servers physically located in their data centers, though many also choose to use the cloud. An organization's choice usually depends on the resources and human power available.

Print Servers

Print servers are basic servers that take control of multiple printers on the network. All caching of information, spooling, printer pooling, sharing, and permissions are controlled centrally by the print server. While a Windows client computer (or another client) could act as a print server, and you can also purchase a basic print server device that plugs into your network, enterprise-level print servers run software such as Windows Server so that they can handle lots of simultaneous print requests from client computers.

Mail Servers

Mail servers (or *email servers*) are part of the message server family. When we refer to a *message server*, we mean any server that deals with email, faxing, texting, chatting, and so on. But for the purposes of the A+ exams, we concentrate strictly on the email server. The most common of these is Microsoft Exchange. An Exchange server might run POP3, SMTP, and IMAP, and allow for Outlook connections via a web browser. That's a lot of protocols running. So, it's not surprising to hear some Exchange admins confess that running an email server can be difficult at times.

For the A+ exams, you should know how to connect a client to an email server such as Microsoft Exchange. This is done by using appropriate email client software (such as Outlook) and knowing the server name, the protocols and ports used, the username and password, and whether there is additional security involved. For more about email client configuration, see Chapter 4, "Mobile Device Network Connectivity and Application Support."

Proxy Servers

A *proxy server* is used primarily as a go-between for a client and the website accessed. It is commonly used to cache information so that the information exists on the proxy server, and another user accessing the same web page won't have to get it from the Internet; this increases general performance and efficiency. For a client computer to use a proxy server, the web browser needs to be configured properly (as described in Chapter 37, "Windows Networking"). In addition, the proxy server can analyze data as it passes through and filter it accordingly; this is referred to as content filtering. Plus, you can have proxies for FTP, SMTP, and other protocols. There are also proxies that reside on the Internet and are designed to hide users' IP addresses, allowing users to browse the web anonymously. Quite often, organizations block these types of connections.

To protect a web server, an organization might implement a *reverse proxy*. This device is placed in the area of the network where the web server resides. Requests from clients on the Internet are forwarded by the reverse proxy to the web server so that the clients will be unaware of the identity of the web server. Reverse proxies can also be used for encryption of web sessions and for load balancing, where client requests can be distributed to multiple web servers.

DHCP Servers

Some servers have less tangible—though no less important—duties. For example, the *DHCP server* is in charge of handing out IP addresses to clients. But don't underestimate this function; if an organization has a couple thousand computers that rely on obtaining IP addresses from a DHCP server, it becomes one of the most important servers on the network. If it fails, computers will have great difficulty doing anything on the network. DHCP server functionality is built into Windows and Linux servers, SOHO routers, and many other devices. Whenever a device or computer obtains an IP address automatically, chances are that a DHCP server was involved. We'll discuss DHCP further in Chapter 10, "Network Configuration Concepts."

DNS Servers

A *Domain Name System (DNS) server* takes care of resolving domain names to IP addresses. For instance:

```
example.com  =  93.184.216.34
```

Try running the **ping** command in the Command Prompt and ping a domain name of your choice, perhaps:

```
ping example.com
```

The results should display the IP address of that domain. This is a basic example of DNS being performed. DNS servers also take care of reverse DNS—or resolving IP addresses to domain names.

In smaller networks, the DNS server is at the ISP. However, larger networks might decide to run DNS servers internally. In fact, it becomes a necessity for a company that has a domain controller because the domain relies on DNS name resolution for just about everything that needs to be accessed. DNS functionality can be implemented in most server operating systems, such as Windows Server or Linux. We'll discuss DNS further in Chapter 10.

> **ExamAlert**
>
> A DNS server resolves hostnames to IP addresses and vice versa.

Syslog Servers

Syslog is a protocol that can take logged event information from a router or other network device and send it to a logging server—also known as a *syslog server*. The syslog server uses special software to store these logs in real time and is designed so that is easy for administrators to read, analyze, and save the information. This information might consist of status, events, diagnostics, entry attempts, and so on. Best of all, the administrator can do all this from his or her workstation, without having to log in to each network device separately. Linux has syslog integrated with the operating system, but there are third-party examples of syslog, too, including Kiwi Syslog Server, PRTG, and Syslog Watcher.

AAA Servers

In the computer security world, AAA stands for authentication, authorization, and accounting. The terms can be broken down as follows:

▶ **Authentication:** Establishing a person's identity with proof and confirming it via a system. Typically, this requires a digital identity of some sort, a username/password, security card, biometric data, or other authentication scheme—and hopefully more than one!

▶ **Authorization:** Giving a user access to certain data or areas of a building. Authorization happens after authentication and can be determined in several ways, including via permissions, access control lists, time-of-day restrictions, and other login and physical restrictions.

▶ **Accounting:** Tracking data, computer usage, and network resources. Often it means logging, auditing, and monitoring data and resources. Part of this concept is the burden of proof. If it is believed that someone committed an unauthorized action, a security administrator must provide proof that it happened. When you have indisputable proof of something users have done and they cannot deny it, this is known as non-repudiation.

A server can oversee one or more of these security functions.

For example, an *authentication server* acts as a central repository of user accounts and computer accounts on the network. All users in a given network log on to this server. The most common example of this would be a Windows Server system that has been promoted to a domain controller (meaning it runs Active Directory). This type of server validates the users who attempt to log on. Authentication servers utilize some kind of authentication protocol, such as the Lightweight Directory Access Protocol (LDAP), or Kerberos, or both, as is the case for a Windows domain controller.

One example of a server that oversees the entire AAA family of protocols is a Remote Authentication Dial-In User Service (RADIUS) server. RADIUS servers can act as the backend for WLAN authentication and with port-based network access control protocols such as 802.1X. We'll cover these concepts later in the book.

> **ExamAlert**
>
> Know the differences between file servers, web servers, print servers, email servers, proxy servers, DHCP servers, DNS servers, syslog servers, and AAA servers. You might also want to tie in these concepts to the ports that the servers use (see Chapter 5, "TCP and UDP Ports and Protocols").

So, there's a little primer on servers. The server is the home of the systems administrator/network administrator. A lot of you reading this are probably very interested in servers. The Core 1 (220-1101) A+ exam focuses more on the client side of things, but you should attempt to learn as much as you can about the various servers we just discussed. Ultimately, you will be working on them!

Internet Security Appliances

A variety of security and networking devices can be used to block unauthorized access, decrease garbage messages, and increase availability. Firewalls, UTMs, and IDS and IPS solutions can help block access to a system or network. These are examples of Internet appliances—or, more accurately, Internet *security* appliances. Spam filters can be used to reduce the amount of junk email that an organization receives. And load balancers can be used to distribute data in an efficient manner so that servers are not "overloaded." Let's discuss these networked hosts now.

Network Firewall

Almost every organization has a *network firewall* protecting its network. Such a firewall is usually a rack-mountable device that connects to the LAN on one side and to the Internet on the other (and possibly to a secondary network using a third connection). The primary function of a network firewall is to close ports (such as HTTP port 80) to prevent unwanted intrusion. A typical firewall implementation closes all inbound ports so that external users are blocked from access to the LAN of an organization. However, in some cases, you will find that a port on a firewall was opened previously to allow communication by a service or an application that is no longer in use. If that happens, you need to disable (or close) that port or delete the rule that was created for that type of communication. These rules are also known as access control lists (ACLs).

UTM

A firewall can be part of a *unified threat management (UTM)* gateway solution as well. UTM incorporates the features of a firewall along with antivirus, antispam, content filtering, and intrusion prevention for the entire network. It might also incorporate data loss prevention (DLP) by way of content inspection. The idea behind UTM is that it can take the place of several units doing separate tasks and consolidate them into one easily administered system. The drawback to this is that it can act as a single point of failure. So, many organizations will consider secondary UTM units or fallback firewalls.

> **Note**
>
> You might not hear the term UTM used much today, but it's still on the A+ objectives, so know it!

IDS/IPS

It's important that you understand two other terms, IDS and IPS, and that you know the difference between them. An *intrusion detection system (IDS)* can determine whether an unauthorized person has attempted to access the network and then alert the systems administrator of its findings. In this case, an admin is alerted to the problem, but the unauthorized user might actually gain access to the network; the damage might be done before the admin has a chance to rectify the situation. Building on this concept, an *intrusion prevention system (IPS)* not only detects unauthorized access to the network but attempts to thwart it, making the admin's job somewhat easier. IDS and IPS solutions are available as security appliances for an entire network, and when they are, they are also referred to as network-based IDS (NIDS) and network-based IPS (NIPS), respectively. They are often incorporated into UTM devices, most commonly NIPS. However, IDS and IPS solutions are also available for individual hosts. In this case, they are referred to as host-based IDS (HIDS) and host-based IPS (HIPS).

Spam Gateway

Have you ever received an email asking you to send money to some strange person in a faraway country? Or an email offering extremely cheap Rolex watches? Or the next best penny stock? All of these are examples of spam. Spammers abuse electronic messaging systems such as email, texting, social media, broadcast media, instant messaging, and so on.

For the A+ exams, you need to be most concerned with spam email. There are many ways to try to reduce the amount of spam that is received. Of these anti-spam techniques, email filtering is at the top. One example of email filtering is the use of a *spam gateway*, also known as a gateway spam filter or email security gateway. This is a software solution that is either incorporated into an email server or installed as a virtual appliance—generally, just behind an organization's firewall (that is, on the LAN). Anti-spam policies and filtering can be configured in Microsoft Exchange Server (with Exchange Online Protection, or EOP) or with third-party offerings. Organizations using Microsoft 365 and Exchange are automatically protected to a certain extent from spam (or junk) email.

Load Balancer

Load balancing is the process of distributing tasks over all available resources. The "load" is essentially the packets of data that are sent across the network.

Say that you have three file servers taking care of requests for files from clients. Ideally, you would want each of those servers to work at the highest level of efficiency, and one way to ensure that would be to have the client requests for files distributed equally to those servers. A load balancer is a hardware or software solution that monitors the servers in question and routes client requests to servers in a uniform fashion, making sure that no servers are overloaded and that no servers are idle. Essentially, a load balancer provides for the balancing of IP traffic across a set of servers. The concept of load balancing is popular with web servers and can be used with other technologies as well.

A properly configured load balancer can distribute the network load and any client requests efficiently among servers, ensure high availability/redundancy of those servers, and offer flexibility when servers need to be added or removed. There are a variety of load-balancing algorithms that you can employ, including

▶ **Round robin:** Client requests are distributed across all servers sequentially.

▶ **Least connections:** New client requests are sent to the server with the fewest concurrent connections.

The concept of load balancing is closely linked to high availability (HA) and clustering.

ExamAlert

A load balancer provides for equal distribution of IP traffic among a set of servers, increasing redundancy and performance.

Embedded Systems and IoT

Some groups of networked hosts are designed to run on-premises only—and you are sure to see them at some point. These include embedded devices in industrial systems, such as Supervisory Control and Data Acquisition (SCADA), and devices that are part of the Internet of Things (IoT), such as smart security systems and fire alarms, medical sensors, and appliances. They all connect to the network, so networking knowledge is crucial!

Embedded Systems

Embedded systems are devices that have integrated CPU and RAM and can process information internally without the need for a controlling system. They are commonly found in home appliances, office automation, thin clients, security systems, telecommunications, automotive, medical, assembly systems, and more.

One place where you will find embedded systems is in heating, ventilation, and air conditioning (HVAC). Larger infrastructures—electrical power grids, water treatment plants, gas/oil pipelines, hydroelectric systems, sewage systems, traffic systems, building controls, and so on—often use SCADA systems. Compared to typical home offices and small offices, SCADA solutions must be heavily secured because they are often used in protected environments and infrastructures. Teams of engineers are employed to design and secure SCADA solutions.

Some buildings might require *legacy systems* to control their older HVAC, plumbing, and other technologies. Some of these legacy systems might be single-board computers such as a PC/104 embedded system, which typically runs at 33 MHz and has 16 to 32 MB of RAM. (Note that the last sentence says MHz and MB—instead of GHz and GB—which helps you see what I mean by *legacy*!) These boards can go bad over time and need to be replaced. Or, a particular technology might be controlled by a legacy thin client computer with an embedded operating system—and no hard drive. These are also generally single-board designs where a failure means a total board or unit replacement.

If you are in charge of this type of technology, be ready to scour the Internet and locate reliable distributors so that you can get quality replacements at a decent price.

IoT

The *Internet of Things (IoT)* is a global network of physical objects that have embedded processors (of some sort) that can communicate with computers across the Internet.

Collectively, tablets, smartphones, e-readers, and other mobile devices—not to mention their wearable counterparts—make up a portion of the IoT. But IoT devices also include household appliances such as smart refrigerators, digital thermostats, home automation devices, and so on. However, IoT isn't limited to just personal devices; it also includes devices used in the medical, manufacturing, and transportation industries, among others. Depending on the organization you work for, you will need to install, configure, secure, and troubleshoot a specific subset of IoT devices. If you apply the methods and techniques in this book, you will be able to work with any device in any market.

Strictly speaking, technicians (and many consumers) look at IoT as a group of technology goodies found in home automation, within appliances, and as voice-activated digital assistants—devices that go beyond desktops, laptops, smartphones, and tablets. The key is that they connect to the network and ultimately to the Internet to receive updates and so that they can be controlled from a mobile device or other computing system.

IoT devices include thermostats, light switches, security cameras, door locks, refrigerators (and other appliances), and smart speakers. In some cases, these "smart" devices incorporate Bluetooth Low Energy (BLE) technology, which uses less power than a standard Bluetooth device. Ultimately, IoT devices connect to the Internet and collect and exchange data. Configuring these devices is usually an intuitive process. It is important to pay attention to how they are connected to the network and how they are secured because IoT devices all connect to the Internet, and the apps that control them may or may not have the most brilliant programming—and security vulnerabilities abound.

Some of the ways to increase security include updating IoT devices' firmware and associated apps, updating SOHO routers (or other routing devices), keeping IoT devices on a separate network, using Bluetooth PIN codes, using strong passwords (and possibly multi-factor authentication), and carefully selecting and monitoring cloud-based services that are used by the IoT devices.

Cram Quiz

Answer these questions. The answers follow the last question. If you cannot answer these questions correctly, consider reading this chapter again until you can.

1. While looking at the details of a server in your provider's control panel, you notice that it says "Apache" in the HTTP summary. What kind of server is this?
   - ○ **A.** File server
   - ○ **B.** Web server
   - ○ **C.** Email server
   - ○ **D.** Authentication server

2. Which type of server acts as a go-between for clients and websites?
   - ○ **A.** Proxy server
   - ○ **B.** Print server
   - ○ **C.** Syslog server
   - ○ **D.** DHCP server

3. Which type of server runs Microsoft Exchange?
   - ○ **A.** File server
   - ○ **B.** Authentication server
   - ○ **C.** Email server
   - ○ **D.** Web server
   - ○ **E.** SCADA

4. Which type of device category would a smart thermostat fall under?
   - ○ **A.** SCADA
   - ○ **B.** IoT
   - ○ **C.** Load balancer
   - ○ **D.** Spam gateway

5. You have been tasked with installing a solution that will proactively prevent Internet attacks from reaching the LAN. Which of the following devices is the best solution?
   - ○ **A.** Proxy server
   - ○ **B.** IDS
   - ○ **C.** Authentication server
   - ○ **D.** IPS

CramQuiz

Cram Quiz Answers

1. **B.** Apache is a type of web server that runs on Linux. It is also known as Apache HTTP Server. File servers are used to store and transfer files but not websites. Email servers deal with the sending and receiving of email via POP3, IMAP, and SMTP. Authentication servers verify the identity of users logging in and computers on the network.

2. **A.** A proxy server is a caching server used to store commonly accessed websites. Such a server can be incorporated into a web server but often runs as a stand-alone server. A print server manages network printers and their spooling of print jobs, priorities, and so on. A syslog server gathers logging data from network devices and allows for the easy analysis of those logs from a client workstation. A DHCP server hands out IP addresses (and other TCP/IP information) to client computers.

3. **C.** Microsoft Exchange is a type of email server software. While you could run multiple services on a single server—for example, you could run a web server and an email server on the same machine—doing so isn't recommended. Unless you have a small office, all servers (such as file servers, authentication servers, email servers, DHCP servers, and so on) should be separate entities. SCADA is not a server; it stands for Supervisory Control and Data Acquisition and is a type of system used to control larger organizations' infrastructures, such as heating/cooling, electricity, and so on.

4. **B.** A smart thermostat is a type of Internet of Things (IoT) device. SCADA is an industrial system that controls an organization's infrastructure facilities. A load balancer is in charge of distributing IP traffic among multiple servers. A spam gateway is an email filtering device that removes unwanted spam (or junk) email from all email accounts on the network.

5. **D.** An intrusion prevention system (IPS) is a solution that can detect *and* prevent attacks from entering a LAN or an individually protected server. An IDS, on the other hand, only *detects* attacks and doesn't prevent them. A proxy server is used to cache and monitor Internet traffic and other types of traffic. An authentication server is used to identify users and allow/disallow access to a system or network based on the users' credentials.

A wise person once said, "Learning is a life-long endeavor." Continue!

CHAPTER 9

SOHO Network Configuration

This chapter covers the following A+ 220-1101 exam objective:

▶ **2.5** – Given a scenario, install and configure basic wired/wireless small office/home office (SOHO) networks.

In the last chapter, we discussed a lot of theory about servers, services, and networked hosts. Now, let's get more hands-on, especially with TCP/IP configurations. In this chapter, we'll discuss IP addressing, dynamic IP assignment, name-to-IP address resolution, and gateway IP addressing.

Without IP addresses, computers can't communicate, so it's vital that you know IP addressing frontward and backward. This could be considered one of the most important chapters in the book, and it's packed with information. It's time to network!

> **ExamAlert**
>
> **Objective 2.5** focuses on the following concepts: Internet Protocol (IP) addressing; IPv4 and IPv6; Automatic Private IP Addressing (APIPA); and static, dynamic, and gateway addressing.

Configuring IPv4

Let's look at how to configure IPv4 addresses in Windows 10. First, you navigate to the Internet Protocol (TCP/IP) Properties window, which I often refer to as the IP Properties dialog box. To do this, open the **Network Connections** window (search for it, or go to **Run** and type **ncpa.cpl**). Then right-click the **Ethernet** icon and select **Properties**. Finally, highlight **Internet Protocol Version 4** and then click the **Properties** button.

> **Note**
>
> Navigation may differ slightly depending on the version of Windows and the way it is configured. Be ready for alterations over time and be ready to use the search tool to simplify the process (or the Run prompt, whenever possible).

The first item to be configured is the IP address, which is the unique assigned number of a computer on the network. An IPv4 address consists of four octets, with each octet's value ranging between 0 and 255. The octets are separated by dots (for example, 192.168.0.100). The binary equivalent of 0–255 would be 00000000 through 11111111. For example, 192 is equal to 11000000 in binary. Because each octet contains 8 bits and there are four octets, the IP address collectively is a 32-bit number but is normally expressed in dotted-decimal notation.

There are two main types of addresses: dynamic and static. Dynamically assigned addresses are more common for a client computer; with this type of address, a computer seeks out a DHCP server so that it can get its IP information automatically. Figure 9.1 shows a radio button labeled **Obtain an IP address automatically**. When you select this, the rest of the information becomes grayed out, and the computer attempts to get that IP information from a DHCP server (such as a SOHO router or Windows Server). That DHCP server has a range of IP addresses configured by an administrator—also known as a DHCP scope. One of those addresses in the range will be selected for the client computer.

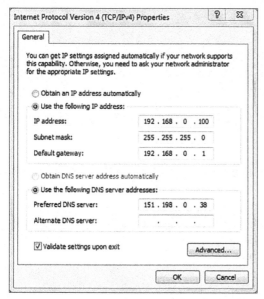

FIGURE 9.1   Internet Protocol Version 4 Properties dialog box in Windows

For client computers, DHCP is common; in fact, it's the default configuration for Windows. On the other hand, static addresses are generated when you configure the IP information manually. Figure 9.1 shows an example of statically configured IP settings. The computer is configured to use the address 192.168.0.100, but the IP address differs from machine to machine, depending on several factors. Remember that the address should be unique for each computer on the network.

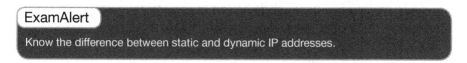

ExamAlert

Know the difference between static and dynamic IP addresses.

IP addresses can also be self-assigned by the computer. In Windows, this process is known as *Automatic Private IP Addressing (APIPA)*, and it occurs when a computer cannot contact a DHCP server to obtain an IP address. When APIPA self-assigns an address, the address is on the 169.254.0.0 network. Addresses on this network are also known as *link-local* addresses.

ExamAlert

APIPA (Automatic Private IP Addressing) is a system used on Windows to automatically self-assign an IP address in the 169.254.x.x range in the absence of a DHCP server.

IP addresses are divided into two sections: the network portion, which is the number of the network the computer is on, and the host portion, which is the number of the individual computer. The subnet mask defines which portion of the IP address is the network number and which portion is the individual host number. In this case, the subnet mask is 255.255.255.0. The 255s indicate the network portion of the IP address. So, 192.168.0 is the network this computer is a member of. The 0s (or, in this case, only one zero) indicate the host number, so 100 is the individual number of this computer. Quite often the subnet mask is configured automatically by Windows after you type the IP address.

The gateway address is the IP address of the host that enables access to the Internet or to other networks. The IP address of the gateway should always be on the same network as the computer(s) connecting to it. In Figure 9.1, you can see that it is because the first three octets are 192.168.0. If a computer is not configured with a default gateway address, it cannot connect to the Internet.

ExamAlert

To use the gateway, computers must be on the same network number as the gateway device.

The DNS server address is the IP address of the host that takes care of domain name translation to IP. When you use your browser to connect to a website, you might type something like **www.dprocomputer.com**. What you need to remember, however, is that computers actually communicate using IP addresses, not names. So, the DNS server takes care of translating the name dprocomputer.com to its corresponding IP address and forwarding that information back to your computer. When your computer knows the IP address of the website, it can start a session with the website and transmit and receive files. Notice in Figure 9.1 that the DNS server address is on a completely different network from my computer. This is typical; in this case, the DNS server is run by the Internet service provider (ISP) that provides me with my Internet connection. However, DNS servers can also be run internally by a company; this happens most often with larger companies.

Notice the checkbox labeled **Validate settings upon exit**. If you set up a static IP address on a computer, you should select this checkbox. This way, when you click the **OK** button for the IP Properties dialog box, Windows checks whether the configuration works properly and lets you know when any basic errors arise. The IP configuration might have an incorrect DNS server, gateway address, or IP network number.

Challenge 1: Configuring IP with PowerShell

Tired of clicking around the GUI? Use PowerShell! For example, to set a static IP address for a Windows computer, the syntax would be

```
netsh interface ip set address "connection name" static
<IPv4 address> <IPv4 mask> <gateway>
```

Here's a real example:

```
netsh interface ip set address "Ethernet" static 192.168.0.100
255.255.255.0 192.168.0.1
```

Try configuring a new IP address on a (test) Windows system now. Because this is an important task, you need to run PowerShell as an administrator. To do this, go to **Start > Windows PowerShell**, click the down arrow, right-click **Windows PowerShell**, and select **Run as administrator**. Alternatively, you can open the Run prompt (Windows+R), type **powershell**, and then press Ctrl+Shift+Enter. Remember to return your computer back to normal when you are done. If your system was obtaining an IP address automatically from a DHCP server, then you could reset that in the IP Properties dialog box or use the following syntax:

```
netsh interface ip set address "connection name" dhcp
```

Chances are, you'll need PowerShell in the field. Find it and use it.

You're not done yet! If your IP Properties dialog box is set to **Obtain an IP address automatically**, then you will also see the Alternate Configuration tab. This allows you to have a secondary IP configuration. Let's say that you use a laptop at work and get your IP address from a DHCP server, but you also go on the road as part of your job. The alternate configuration would kick in automatically when you are away from the office and allow you access to the Internet or to virtual private networks, depending on your configuration.

The alternate configuration can be on a completely different IP network from the main configuration.

Speaking of secondary IP addresses, every computer running TCP/IP has an additional address known as a *loopback* address. By default, this is 127.0.0.1, and it can be used to test TCP/IP on the local machine, regardless of whether the system is plugged into the network. Try running **ping 127.0.0.1** or **ping loopback -4** in PowerShell or the Command Prompt to test your system internally. Remember that replies are good!

Private vs. Public Addresses

Let's consider the difference between private and public IP addresses.

▶ **Private:** Private IP addresses are internal to your network and do not communicate directly with the Internet. The IP address assigned to the client in Figure 9.1 (192.168.0.100) is an example of a private IP address. Contrast this with

▶ **Public:** A public IP address is an address that communicates directly with the Internet. The DNS server IP address in Figure 9.1 (151.198.0.38) is an example of a public IP address.

You use private IP addresses on LANs and internal networks to provide a certain level of protection and anonymity to client computers, as well as to conserve IPv4 addresses in general. However, the client computers need to access the Internet, and so your network needs some sort of gateway device that connects all of the private systems to the Internet by way of a public IP address. Similarly, if you have a server that needs to be accessed by users on the Internet, it needs to have access to a public IP address—either directly or indirectly.

Private IP network numbers can be used by anyone in the internal network. The reserved private IP address ranges include

▶ **Class A addresses:** 10.0.0.0–10.255.255.255

▶ **Class B addresses:** 172.16.0.0–172.31.255.255

▶ **Class C addresses:** 192.168.0.0–192.168.255.255

Public IP addresses are assigned to customer equipment by ISPs. The Internet Assigned Numbers Authority (IANA) is responsible for global coordination of public IP addresses.

Let's look at an example of a device that uses both types of addresses—a typical small office/home office (SOHO) router.

A SOHO router normally obtains a public IP address from the ISP; it is dynamically assigned and is also known as the WAN address. The public address is visible on the Internet. The router also has a private address (or LAN address), which is visible only to the computers on the network. That is the address you use to log in to the router (for example, 192.168.0.1 or 192.168.1.1) and also acts as the gateway address for the clients on the network. Figure 9.2 shows the LAN and WAN settings on a typical SOHO router.

LAN	
MAC Address:	30-B5-C2-B2-59-E6
IP Address:	192.168.0.1
Subnet Mask:	255.255.255.0

WAN	
MAC Address:	30-B5-C2-B2-59-E7
IP Address:	64.121.138.225
Subnet Mask:	255.255.240.0
Default Gateway:	64.121.128.1
DNS Server:	208.59.247.45 , 208.59.247.46

FIGURE 9.2   LAN and WAN settings on a typical SOHO router

As you can see in this figure, the router's LAN address is 192.168.0.1. This device makes use of DHCP, which can be turned on or off. When on, it automatically assigns IP addresses to most of the clients on this network, starting with 192.168.0.100 and ascending from there—192.168.0.101, 192.168.0.102, and so on. The router and all of the clients are on the same local area network number (192.168.0.0), using the same subnet mask (255.255.255.0), which means they can all communicate with each other.

The public address allows the entire network access to the Internet. The router acts as the connection between the private and public networks. It allows for the transmission of data between the clients and the Internet, using a technology called network address translation (NAT).

NAT modifies IP addresses as information crosses a router. It hides an entire IP address space on the LAN (for example, 192.168.0.1 through 192.168.0.255). Whenever an IP address on the LAN wants to communicate with the Internet,

NAT converts the IP address to the public IP address of the router (for example, 64.121.138.225), which is whatever IP address the ISP assigned to the router. This way, it looks like the router is the only device making the connection to remote computers on the Internet, providing a modicum of safety for the computers on the LAN. To summarize, with NAT, a single public IP address does the work for many private IP addresses in the LAN.

> **ExamAlert**
>
> Private IP addresses are internal and do not connect directly to the Internet. Public IP addresses allow direct connectivity to the Internet and are visible by anyone with an Internet connection.

Classful vs. Classless IP Addresses

The IPv4 system of IP addresses is divided into classes A, B, and C, where specific subnet masks correspond to each class; this is known as classful IP addressing. For example, class C addresses use subnet mask 255.255.255.0. While IP address classes can still be used, most companies today opt for a network that is classless, using CIDR (Classless Inter-Domain Routing)—pronounced "cider." With CIDR, any subnet mask can be used for any IP network.

The important part to understand is that the 255s of a subnet mask relate to the network portion, and the 0s correspond to the host portion of the IP address. For example, if the IP address 10.252.0.101 uses the subnet mask 255.255.0.0, then the network portion is 10.252. The IP address and subnet mask can be written together in the following manner: 10.252.0.101/16. You probably won't see this concept on the A+ exams, but for more information about classful and classless IP addresses, see the post "IPv4 Classes and CIDR" on my website: https://dprocomputer.com/?p=2907.

Configuring IPv6

Although acceptance has been slow over the years, IPv6 is the next generation of IP addressing. IPv6, which is used on the Internet and on some LANs and WANs, is designed to address the inadequacies of IPv4. One of the main reasons for the development of IPv6 was the rapidly approaching global shortage of IPv4 addresses. Whereas IPv4 (a 32-bit system) can have approximately 4 billion total theoretical addresses, IPv6 (128-bit) can have a total of 340 *undecillion* theoretical addresses—a far greater total. Various limitations of the system will drastically reduce that number, but the remaining result is still orders of magnitude above and beyond the IPv4 system. However, IPv6 is also known for security. One feature of IPv6 security is IPsec (IP Security), which authenticates and encrypts data packets that are sent over IP networks. IPsec is a fundamental piece of the IPv6 puzzle and, if used properly, it can offer much more secure communications than IPv4. IPv6 also supports larger packet sizes, known as jumbograms. Table 9.1 summarizes some of the differences between IPv4 and IPv6.

TABLE 9.1 **IPv4 vs. IPv6**

IPv4	IPv6
32-bit	128-bit
4 billion addresses	340 undecillion addresses
Less secure	More secure; uses IPsec
65,536-byte maximum packet size	4 billion-byte maximum packet size

IPv6 addresses are 128-bit hexadecimal numbers that are divided into eight groups of four numbers each. The most commonly used type is the unicast address, which defines a single IP address on a single interface (such as a network adapter). Windows auto-configures a unicast address when IPv6 is installed. The address starts with FE80, FE90, FEA0, or FEB0. Collectively, this range is shown as FE80::/10, and it comprises all of the link-local addresses for IPv6. These link-local addresses are often based on the MAC address of the network adapter. Every Windows computer with IPv6 installed also receives the loopback address ::1. The IPv6 address ::1 is the equivalent to IPv4's loopback address 127.0.0.1. To test it, type **ping ::1** or **ping loopback -6** in PowerShell or the Command Prompt.

> **ExamAlert**
>
> Know the loopback addresses for IPv6 and IPv4.

Here's an example of an IPv6 address:

2001:7120:0000:8001:0000:0000:0000:1F10

An IPv6 address is broken down into three sections: the global routing prefix (in this case, 2001:7120:0000), a subnet (in this case, 8001), and the individual interface ID (in this case, 0000:0000:0000:1F10).

This is the full address, but you will more commonly see truncated addresses. There are two ways to truncate, or shorten, an IPv6 address. The first is to remove leading zeros. Any group of four zeros can be truncated to a single zero; basically zero is always zero, so the additional zeros are not necessary. Also, a single consecutive group of zeros can be truncated as a double colon (::). The example shows 12 consecutive zeros that can be truncated to a double colon. (A double colon can be used only once in an address.) The following is the end result of both of these abbreviations:

2001:7120:0:8001::1F10

ExamAlert

Understand how IPv6 addresses can be truncated.

Although it is not common, IPv6 addresses can be assigned statically as well; this can be done within the Internet Protocol Version 6 Properties dialog box, which can be accessed from Local Area Connection Properties.

Cram Quiz

Answer these questions. The answers follow the last question. If you cannot answer these questions correctly, consider reading this chapter again until you can.

1. Which of these addresses needs to be configured to enable a computer access to the Internet or to other networks?

   ○ **A.** Subnet mask

   ○ **B.** Gateway address

   ○ **C.** DNS address

   ○ **D.** MAC address

2. Which technology assigns addresses on the 169.254.0.0 network?

   ○ **A.** DHCP

   ○ **B.** Static IP

   ○ **C.** APIPA

   ○ **D.** Class B

3. You want to test the local loopback IPv6 address. Which address would you use?

   ○ **A.** 127.0.0.1

   ○ **B.** ::1

   ○ **C.** FE80::/10

   ○ **D.** ::0

4. Which of the following IP addresses would you configure so that the computer can take advantage of hostname-to-IP address resolution?

   ○ **A.** 127.0.0.1 (local loopback)

   ○ **B.** 192.168.0.1 (gateway)

   ○ **C.** 8.8.8.8 (DNS)

   ○ **D.** 255.255.255.0 (subnet mask)

5. Of the following, which is a common use for NAT?

   ○ **A.** Defining the network portion of an IPv4 address

   ○ **B.** Connecting multiple computers using a single public IP address

   ○ **C.** Resolving hostnames to IP addresses

   ○ **D.** Automatically assigning TCP/IP addresses

Cram Quiz Answers

1. **B.** The gateway address must be configured to enable a computer access to the Internet through the gateway device. By default, the subnet mask defines the IP address's network and host portions. The DNS server takes care of name resolution. The MAC address is the address that is burned into the network adapter; it is configured by the manufacturer.

2. **C.** If you see an address with 169.254 as the first two octets, then Automatic Private IP Addressing (APIPA) is in use. This is the link-local range for IPv4. Dynamic Host Configuration Protocol (DHCP) assigns IP addresses automatically to clients but by default does not use the 169.254 network number. Static IP addresses are configured manually by the user in the IP Properties window. Class B is a range of IP networks from 128 through 191.

3. **B.** You would use the ::1 address, which is the local loopback address for IPv6. 127.0.0.1 is the local loopback address for IPv4. FE80::/10 is the range of unicast auto-configured addresses. ::0 is not valid but looks similar to how multiple zeros can be truncated with a double colon.

4. **C.** You would use a DNS server IP address. 8.8.8.8 is an example of a DNS server IP address run by Google. Anyone in the United States and many other countries is allowed to use it for DNS resolution. Remember that the DNS server is in charge of resolving (or translating) hostnames and domain names to their respective IP addresses. Note that in this example (and in Figure 9.1), the DNS server uses a public IP address. However, depending on your network configuration, clients might be set up with a DNS server that uses a private IP address (such as 192.168.1.1), which simply means that DNS is being forwarded by that system out to a DNS server on the Internet. 127.0.0.1 (the local loopback address) is the internal loopback address on any system running TCP/IP. The gateway address (for example, 192.168.0.1) allows a system access to the Internet or to other networks. The subnet mask (for example, 255.255.255.0) defines the network and host portions of an IP address.

5. **B.** Network Address Translation (NAT) is used to convert private IP addresses to public IP addresses. It allows for the connection of multiple private computers through a single public IP address (usually using some sort of router). The subnet mask defines the network portion of an IP address. DNS is in charge of resolving hostnames to IP addresses. DHCP is responsible for automatically assigning TCP/IP addresses.

Whoa! That was a power packed chapter. I strongly suggest you *carefully* review this one. Keep up the great work!

CHAPTER 10

Network Configuration Concepts

This chapter covers the following A+ 220-1101 exam objective:

▶ 2.6 — Compare and contrast common network configuration concepts.

Let's get deeper into network configurations. There are two technologies that are integral to just about every network out there: DNS and DHCP. DNS provides name resolution, and DHCP provides automatic IP addressing. Without these two services, not much would get done in a typical organization, and not much fun would be had at home! DNS and DHCP are fundamental networking services that allow systems to interoperate properly.

Of course, it's great to develop systems and networks in a physical, tangible way, but it isn't always the most sensible way. Sometimes, going *virtual* is the best solution. Anything can be virtualized, from individual computers to entire networks. In this chapter, we'll briefly cover two virtual technologies: VLANs and VPNs. A VLAN helps to organize a LAN in a virtual manner. A VPN allows for external connections to a network while making it appear that the user is physically working at that network.

DNS

The Domain Name System (DNS) is a worldwide system of domains, hosts, and DNS servers. The primary function of DNS is to resolve hostnames to IP addresses. This "translation" takes place all the time between computers. For an example, see the section "DNS Servers" in Chapter 8, "Networked Hosts." In that example—and any time a client connects to a domain—a DNS server somewhere on the Internet (or possibly in an organization's LAN) oversees hostname-to-IP resolution. Once that is done, the computer can communicate directly with the host via the IP address, which is how all data packets are sent.

Sometimes, you'll connect to a domain such as dprocomputer.com. And sometimes you'll connect to a specific host within a domain—for example, server1.dprocomputer.com. In this example, server1 is the hostname, and dprocomputer.com is the domain name. Together, they form a *fully qualified domain name (FQDN)*, also sometimes referred to as an *absolute domain name* or simply as a *DNS name*.

As mentioned, a DNS server does the actual resolution work. DNS servers house the records of various systems. A common DNS record type is the *address record*. An address record (A record for short) stores the IPv4 address of a host or of a domain, as well as the corresponding name. It is used to do forward lookups of a system, which means it resolves from name to IP address. This is a very common type of DNS record, but there are plenty of others. Table 10.1 shows some of the most common resource records (RR) that you will encounter.

TABLE 10.1 **DNS Record Types**

Record Type	Description
A record	Stores the IPv4 address of a domain or host for forward lookup (name to IP address). Example on a DNS server: `server1.example.com   A   10.0.2.4`
AAAA record	Stores the IPv6 address of a domain or host.
NS record	Name Server record. Stores the DNS server record.
SOA record	Start of Authority record. Stores the administrative information for a domain.
MX record	Mail Exchange record. Directs mail to an email server. Example on a DNS server: `example.com.   1936   IN   MX   10   mail.example.com.`
PTR record	Pointer record. Does reverse lookup (IP to name). Example on a DNS server: `4.2.0.10.in-addr.arpa.   PTR   server1.example.com.`
TXT record	Used for administrative text-based notes and with email authentication methods.

DNS resource records are written into zone files, either statically by the administrator or dynamically by a system. Table 10.1 shows an example of an A record. This example shows that the hostname is server1.example.com, the type is an address record, and the IP address of that host is 10.0.2.4. This type of record is used for forward lookups (from name to IP address), and the record is stored in a forward lookup zone. However, sometimes systems need to go in reverse, using the IP address to find out the hostname. In such a case, you need a pointer record (PTR). Table 10.1 shows an example of this, where the IP address is shown in reverse (4.2.0.10) and the hostname is also listed. This type of record is written into a reverse lookup zone.

ExamAlert

Be able to identify DNS Address (A and AAAA) records, Mail Exchange (MX) records, and Text (TXT) records for the exam.

Table 10.1 also shows an example of a Mail Exchange (MX) record. In this case, if a person were to send mail within the example.com domain, that mail would be forwarded to the mail.example.com host. As you can imagine, email and DNS are heavily intertwined.

Email Authentication Methods

Do you want to know what the biggest challenge is for email administrators? Spam. You could say it's the bane of humankind! So, it follows that an email administrator needs to pay strict attention to spam management. We've already mentioned that this can be done with the use of filters at both the server and the clients. However, there are some other methods and protocols that an admin can employ to reduce spam and email spoofing in general. (With email spoofing, a sender uses a forged sending address, such as with spam and phishing.) Here are a few methods for detecting email spoofers and reducing spam email:

▶ **DomainKeys Identified Mail (DKIM):** DKIM is an authentication method for email that attempts to detect email spoofers. DKIM enables the email recipient to check the domain that an email supposedly came from using a digital signature. A receiving email server can check the DKIM signature—which is part of the email header—and verify it by doing a DNS lookup and then checking the public key that is associated with that domain. DKIM records are listed in a DNS server with a domainkey subdomain label such as selector._domainkey.example.com. Here is an example of a DKIM TXT record in DNS:

```
selector._domainkey.example.com.  TXT v=DKIM1;p=<public key>
```

Here we see the FQDN (selector._domainkey.example.com), the resource record type (TXT), and the version of DKIM (1). We can also see that we are using a public key, perhaps an RSA key. (Public keys are long hexadecimal strings of information, and for simplicity I just used **<public key>** here.)

▶ **Sender Policy Framework (SPF):** SPF also detects email spoofers. A receiving email server can attempt to check mail by verifying the IP address of the domain that the mail claims to have come from. It does this by checking the DNS records for that domain and systems. Unlike DKIM records, SPF records only use the domain name in their records. Here's a basic example of an SPF TXT record in DNS:

```
v=spf1 ip4:93.184.216.34 include:example.com -all
```

This indicates that you are using SPF version 1, and it defines the IP address of the mail server (93.184.216.34) and the domain name (example.com).

▶ **Domain-based Message Authentication, Reporting & Conformance (DMARC):** This email authentication protocol helps protect email domains from spoofing and other unauthorized use. It is used in conjunction with the older DKIM and/or SPF methods, which by themselves are less potent solutions. For example, SPF cannot check the From field of an email header, but DMARC can. DMARC enables an admin to publish a policy in the DNS server's records that states which mechanism to use and what to do in the event of failures. DMARC records might be listed in a DNS server with a DMARC subdomain label such as:

`_dmarc.example.com.`

Here's a more advanced example of a DMARC TXT record on a DNS server:

`"v=DMARC1;p=reject;pct=100;rua=mailto:postmaster@example.com"`

This example specifies several things: First, you are using DMARC version 1; second, there is a policy for "rejecting" emails; third, it will do this for 100% of the email messages; and fourth, reporting (rua) will go to the email address postmaster@example.com. For more information on DMARC, visit https://dmarc.org.

> **Note**
>
> Don't confuse the email authentication protocol DMARC with the term demarc (short for demarcation point), which is mentioned in Chapter 6, "Network Devices."

> **Note**
>
> For more information about DNS, see IETF RFC 1591: https://datatracker.ietf.org/doc/html/rfc1591. Also consider looking into commonly used DNS server software, such as BIND: https://www.isc.org/bind/.

DNSSEC

For a computer to do anything today, proper credentials have to be supplied and verified. However, DNS by itself does not check for credentials. Case in point: An attacker can cause DNS poisoning by delegating a false name to the DNS server and providing a false address for the server. That can then spread to other DNS servers. Enter DNSSEC. The Domain Name System Security Extensions (DNSSEC) protocol was developed to strengthen DNS through the use of digital signatures and public key cryptography. It protects against attacks by providing a validation path for records. Although you might not see it on the A+ exams, DNSSEC is an integral part of today's DNS technology. To learn more, see the IETF RFCs 4033, 4034, and 4035.

What can I say? DNS is massive; there are a lot of moving parts. We're just scratching its surface in this book. People just expect it to work, but to make it work well, an admin must configure and secure it properly and monitor it carefully.

DHCP

In Chapter 8, we discussed DHCP as a service and what a DHCP server does. To review, a DHCP server is used to automatically assign IP addresses (and other pertinent IP information) to clients. Now let's get into some more fine-grained DHCP concepts.

DHCP Process

DHCP clients get their IP addresses from a DHCP server through the use of a four-step process referred to by the acronym DORA, which stands for discovery, offering, request, and acknowledgement. Let's briefly discuss this process now, using TCP/IP version 4 (or simply IPv4) as our example. In this scenario, the DHCP server uses the IP address 192.168.1.1:

1. **Discovery:** Normally, a client computer is configured to automatically obtain an IP address from a DHCP server. When a typical client on a network is first booted, it attempts to discover DHCP servers by broadcasting over the network. Broadcasting essentially means sending a message to all recipients on the network at the same time. The client computer does this because it doesn't have an IP address yet and doesn't know the IP address of the DHCP server. If a DHCP server exists on the network, and that server is listening for requests, the client will discover it. With IPv4, the DHCP server uses inbound port 67 to listen for DHCP requests. The client uses outbound port 68 to discover a DHCP server. Once a DHCP server is discovered, the next step occurs.

2. **Offering:** For simplicity, let's say there is a single DHCP server on the network. (This is common.) If that DHCP server is listening and has been discovered, it then makes an offer to the client. The offer usually consists of an IP address, a subnet mask, a gateway address, and a DNS server IP address, though it could include more information. The IP address that is offered to the client is selected from a range of IP addresses that the server has been preconfigured to provide. This preconfiguration is done by the admin and is also known as an IP pool, or a *DHCP scope*. In this example, let's say the admin has configured

the scope as a range of IP addresses spanning 192.168.1.101 through 192.168.1.200. That's a range of 100 addresses, so the server could hand out addresses to 100 clients in total before running out. If the client in this example were the first one to be used on the network, it would normally be offered the first IP address in the scope (in this case, 192.168.1.101), although it is possible to configure the DHCP server to hand out addresses dynamically instead. In a SOHO network, the scope is part of the same IP network that the DHCP server is on—in this case, 192.168.1 (also referred to as 192.168.1.0).

> **ExamAlert**
>
> A DHCP scope is a range of IP addresses that a DHCP server can hand out to clients.

3. **Request:** In most cases, especially if there is a single DHCP server, the client requests the IP address and additional TCP/IP information that has been offered by the DHCP server. That means that the client is agreeing to use the IP address, and it lets the server know this.

4. **Acknowledgment:** In the last step, the server acknowledges that the client has requested the offered IP configuration. It then creates an *IP lease* for the client. The lease is available for a limited time, and that time is specified in the DHCP server's configuration file. It could be as little as 1 hour (3600 seconds), or it could be 24 hours, or possibly 8 days, depending on the environment, organizational policies, type of system used, and administrator preferences. The lease information is written to a file on the server. That information typically includes the IP address the client will be using (in this example, 192.168.1.101), the client's MAC address, the length of the lease, and possibly the hostname of the client. The server confirms with the client, and the client can now communicate over the network via TCP/IP. At this point, the server knows not to hand out the 192.168.1.101 IP address to any other clients. Instead, the next client that boots on the network will most likely receive the 192.168.1.102 IP address.

> **ExamAlert**
>
> An IP lease is the amount of time that a client can use an assigned IP address in a DHCP system.

Table 10.2 summarizes the four-step DORA process.

TABLE 10.2 **DHCP Four-Step Process—DORA**

Step	Description
Discovery	The client looks for and discovers a DHCP server.
Offering	The server offers an IP address to the client.
Request	The client picks an address and requests that it be assigned.
Acknowledgment	The server acknowledges the request, and the client can then use the IP address for a set amount of time, which is known as a *lease*.

> **Note**
>
> The DORA process happens in a flash, and oftentimes, only half of the process is necessary. Remember that an IP lease is finite. When it expires, the client typically requests the same IP address again (if the client is still a part of the network). The original dynamic address is stored at the client computer, so the client simply requests the same IP address, which means only the request and acknowledgment steps are required—so the process in this case is simply RA. In many situations, the client receives the same IP address, but this is not always the case. Be prepared for clients to obtain new IP addresses at random.

DHCP Reservations

Sometimes, you may want to reserve certain IP addresses within a DHCP scope—such as for servers or other special systems. *DHCP reservations* are IP addresses within the DHCP scope that are permanently reserved for special computers/devices that need to use DHCP but don't want the IP address to change over time (which can happen periodically in DHCP environments). These special computers/devices might include printers or web servers, for example.

An IP reservation is configured at the DHCP server and specifies the IP address to be reserved and some type of identifying information about the client that it is reserved for—typically the client's MAC address. That client will be allowed to use the IP address exclusively, without any concern that it will change over time. In this example, an IP reservation isn't really necessary because there are open IP addresses on the network (from 192.168.1.2 to 192.168.1.100 and from 192.168.1.201 to 192.168.1.254). However, you might encounter a DHCP scope that was originally configured to use the entire range of usable IP addresses in a given network (for example, 192.168.1.2–192.168.1.254, excluding the DHCP server on 192.168.1.1). If you want to have servers with exclusive IP addresses that will not change, you need to set up reservations for those servers within that DHCP scope.

ExamAlert

DHCP reservations are IP addresses within the DHCP scope that are permanently reserved.

Note

For more information about DHCP, see RFC 2131: https://datatracker.ietf.org/doc/html/rfc2131. Also, for a real (and commonly used) DHCP server example, learn more about ISC Kea by visiting https://www.isc.org/kea/.

VLANs

A virtual LAN (VLAN) is implemented primarily to segment a network. But it can also be used to reduce data collisions, organize the network, potentially boost performance, and, possibly, increase security. A device such as a switch often controls a VLAN. A VLAN compartmentalizes a network and can isolate traffic. VLANs can be set up in a physical manner; for example, with a port-based VLAN, a switch's physical ports are grouped and configured to act as individual VLANs. To set up a VLAN this way, you would need a managed switch—one that you can log in to and configure for VLAN use. But there are lots of switches from different manufacturers out there, right? So, the Institute of Electrical and Electronics Engineers (IEEE) developed the 802.1Q networking standard, which supports and ensures interoperability of VLAN technologies from different vendors.

There are also logical types of VLANs, such as protocol-based VLANs. A VLAN can be set up in such a way that each VLAN is on a different IP network number (for example, 192.168.0.0, 192.168.1.0, 192.168.2.0, and so on). Or, you could take it to the next level and incorporate a technology called IP subnetting, which involves dividing a network into two or more subnetworks by changing the subnet mask that is used (for example, from 255.255.0.0 to 255.255.240.0). Some administrators prefer the use of IP subnetting over VLANs, and some use them together; for example, they might use a group of physical port-based VLANs, each of which is on a different IP subnetwork.

> **ExamAlert**
>
> Remember that VLANs are commonly used for network segmentation.

> **Note**
>
> VLANs and subnetting go a bit beyond what a typical A+ technician will be asked to perform, but you should know the basic definitions for these terms. To learn more about subnetting, see my blog post "Subnetting Introduction, Tables and Tools": https://dprocomputer.com/?p=1185.

VPNs

Let's say you want to connect to your network, but you are at a remote location. Enter the VPN. Virtual private networks (VPNs) were developed so that data commuters, salespeople, and others could connect to the office from a remote location. If a VPN is set up properly, the remote logon connection is seamless, and it appears as if you are actually on the LAN in the office. You log on just as you would if you were at your desk at headquarters. A VPN gives a user access to all the resources available when logging on locally. VPNs take advantage of the infrastructure of the Internet and fast connections (such as cable, fiber, DSL, and so on).

In Windows, a VPN connection can be identified by an additional network connection in the notification area, as an additional network connection when using the **ipconfig** command, or as a pop-up window that appears during the logon process. Connections to VPNs can be initiated in a couple of ways in Windows:

▶ Go to **Start > Settings > Network & Internet > VPN**. Then click the **+** sign (Add a VPN connection).

▶ Navigate to the Network and Sharing Center. Select the **Set up a new connection or network** link. From there, select **Connect to a workplace** and **VPN**.

There are also third-party offerings from companies such as Cisco and Check Point. Regardless of the software used, you need to know VPN-specific details such as the VPN provider, the IP address or name of the VPN server you are connecting to, or the username and password to get into the VPN. Alternate IP configurations are sometimes used with VPN connections so that the main IP configuration is not disturbed, especially if it is configured statically.

ExamAlert

Know that a VPN extends a LAN by establishing a secure connection tunnel through a public network such as the Internet.

Cram Quiz

Answer these questions. The answers follow the last question. If you cannot answer these questions correctly, consider reading this chapter again until you can.

1. Your system needs to renew its IP address from a DHCP server. What has expired?
   - ○ **A.** IP lease
   - ○ **B.** IP reservation
   - ○ **C.** DHCP scope
   - ○ **D.** MAC address

2. Which type of DNS record associates an IPv6 address with a hostname?
   - ○ **A.** A
   - ○ **B.** AAAA
   - ○ **C.** SOA
   - ○ **D.** MX

3. Which of the following is the best solution for protecting email domains against spoofing and other unauthorized uses?
   - ○ **A.** SPF
   - ○ **B.** DORA
   - ○ **C.** DMARC
   - ○ **D.** VLAN

4. You have been tasked with compartmentalizing a network. Which of the following technologies should you use?
   - ○ **A.** APIPA
   - ○ **B.** VPN
   - ○ **C.** VLAN
   - ○ **D.** IPv6

5. Which of the following DNS record types directs email to an email server?

   ○ **A.** A

   ○ **B.** AAAA

   ○ **C.** TXT

   ○ **D.** MX

Cram Quiz Answers

1. **A.** The IP lease has expired. When this happens, the client needs to renew the address (or seek a new one from another DHCP server). An IP reservation is a reserved address to be used exclusively by a server or another special system. A DHCP scope is the range of IP addresses that a DHCP server assigns to clients. A MAC address is a unique address written to a network interface card.

2. **B.** An AAAA record associates an IPv6 address with a hostname for use with forward lookup (name to IP address). An A record associates an IPv4 address with a hostname. SOA is the Start of Authority record. MX is a Mail Exchange record, which directs email to the proper email server.

3. **C.** The best listed solution is DMARC, which enables an admin to make use of the SPF or DKIM protocols (or both) in a more secure way. SPF by itself is not as functional as DMARC. DORA is the four-step DHCP process. A VLAN is a virtual LAN, designed to organize and compartmentalize a LAN.

4. **C.** You would create a virtual LAN (VLAN). Another valid option would be to implement IP subnetting. APIPA (also known as link-local) is an IP technology that auto-assigns addresses on the 169.254 network. A virtual private network (VPN) allows remote clients to connect to a network over the Internet using a secure tunnel. IPv6 in and of itself does not compartmentalize the network. However, an IPv6 network that has been *subnetted* would be acceptable.

5. **D.** The DNS Mail Exchange (MX) record directs mail to an email server. An A record type stores the IPv4 address of a domain or host for forward lookup (name to IP address). An AAAA record stores the IPv6 address of a domain or host. A TXT record is used for administrative text-based notes and with email authentication methods. Know those DNS record types!

Do you like bad dad jokes? Your New Year's *resolution* should be to know DNS, DHCP, and virtual networking concepts. Anyway...nice work so far!

CHAPTER 11
Network Types

This chapter covers the following A+ 220-1101 exam objective:

▶ **2.7** – Compare and contrast Internet connection types, network types, and their features.

In this chapter, we discuss the types of Internet connections available to the typical small office/home office (SOHO) user, as well as the basics of enterprise Internet connectivity. But first we'll cover computer network *types*—such as local area networks and wide area networks. Be prepared; there are a lot of acronyms when it comes to network types. Be ready to take notes and write down each acronym and what it stands for as we progress through the chapter.

> **ExamAlert**
>
> **Objective 2.7** concentrates on the following concepts: Internet connection types (cable, DSL, fiber, satellite, cellular, and WISP), and network types (LAN, WAN, PAN, MAN, SAN, and WLAN).

Network Types

It's important to know how networks are classified. Two common terms are LAN and WAN. But you should also know the terms MAN, SAN, PAN, and WLAN. Let's begin with LAN and WAN.

LAN and WAN

A local area network, or *LAN*, is a group of computers and other devices usually located in a small area: a house, a small office, or a single building. The computers all connect to one or more switches, and a router allows the computers access to the Internet. Generally, there are no other routers internally. Technicians might use phrases such as "Connect the computer to the LAN" or "How many computers are on your LAN?" A LAN is usually based on a network design called the star, or hub-and-spoke, topology, where all hosts connect to a central connecting device such as a switch, an access point, or a SOHO router. Figure 11.1 shows an example of a typical LAN configured using the hub-and-spoke/star topology.

A wide area network, or *WAN*, is a group of one or more LANs over a large geographic area. Let's say a company has two LANs: one in New York and one in Los Angeles. Connecting the two would result in a WAN. However, to do this, the company would require the help of an Internet service provider (ISP) or a telecommunications company. This provider would supply the high-speed connection required for the two LANs to communicate quickly. Each LAN would need a router for the two to connect to each other. A network administrator or network engineer or facilities department would be in charge of selecting an Internet service for the link between the offices. We'll discuss some of those Internet service options later in the chapter.

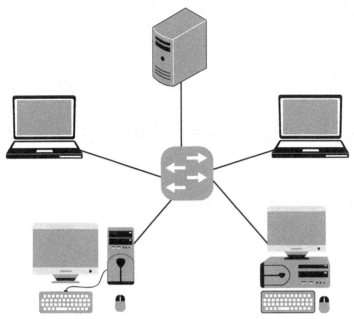

FIGURE 11.1 **A typical LAN using the hub-and-spoke/star topology**

MAN

There is a smaller version of a WAN known as a metropolitan area network (*MAN*) and sometimes called a municipal area network. Say that a company has two offices in the same city and wants to make a high-speed connection between them; the connected offices' networks form a MAN. It's different from a WAN in that it is not a large geographic area, but it is similar to a WAN in that an ISP is needed for the high-speed link.

SAN

A storage area network (SAN) is a dedicated network designed specifically for the storage of data. Moreover, it is a network of data storage devices that are connected together on a typical LAN or by way of a special high-speed fiber optic connection such as Fibre Channel. The network consists of components such as network-attached storage (NAS) devices, RAID arrays, tape backup devices, and a switch to connect it all together. The idea is to allow for high-speed access to data without bogging down the servers that control and request that data. This separates the servers' functionality from the data storage and also allows for an admin to potentially make data more secure, redundant, and highly available. SANs are subsets of LANs and offer block-level data storage that appears within the operating systems of the connected devices as locally attached devices.

> **ExamAlert**
>
> Fibre Channel is widely used for high-speed fiber networking and has become common in enterprise SANs.

WLAN

A wireless local area network (*WLAN*) is really a subdivision of a LAN. A WLAN is formed when multiple computers are connected by way of one or more wireless access points. (I use the term "computers" loosely here to refer to PCs, laptops, tablets, smartphones, IoT devices, and so on.) WLAN protocols are defined in the IEEE 802.11 set of technical standards. Common standards that you should know include 802.11a, b, g, n, ac, and ax. For more information on WLANs and Wi-Fi, refer to Chapter 7, "Wireless Protocols."

WMN

Another network type is a wireless mesh network (*WMN*). Generally, with a mesh, wireless access points (or nodes) have multiple connections to each other in a matrix (or *mesh*) pattern. Implementing a mesh can help greatly with redundancy and availability.

In a WMN, multiple wireless access points are used on the same channel. This allows for greater coverage in larger environments. As mobile devices move around the building or buildings, they quickly transition from one access point to another. In a WMN, the APs do not have to be physically cabled to a wired port, as is the case with a traditional AP or wireless extender. However, the APs must have built-in mesh capability, which often means increased cost. This technology can provide a more efficient solution than traditional wireless extenders, and it also enables centralized management. A WMN can be used in larger infrastructures and also in simpler SOHO environments (where it might be referred to as mesh Wi-Fi, Wi-Fi ad hoc, or a similar name).

PAN

A personal area network (*PAN*) is a smaller computer network used for communication by small computing devices. Take this to the next level by adding wireless standards such as Bluetooth, wireless USB, NFC, Zigbee, or Z-Wave, and you get a wireless PAN (*WPAN*). PANs are sometimes ad hoc, meaning there is no single controlling device, server, or access point. However, they might be controlled by a hub and gain access to the Internet from that device.

> **ExamAlert**
>
> Be able to define, compare, and contrast LAN, WAN, MAN, SAN, WLAN, and PAN.

Internet Connection Types

There are a lot of different options for connecting to the Internet, including fiber-based systems, DSL, cable Internet, the venerable dial-up, and more. The type of Internet connection dictates download speeds to the clients on a network. Let's discuss some of the options available, starting with cable Internet.

Cable Internet

Broadband cable, used for cable Internet and cable TV, is very common in the United States and many other countries. It offers download transfer rates from 50 Mbps to 1000 Mbps (depending on the ISP). Upload speed is almost always slower—a fraction of the download speed. Like most other Internet connectivity options, cable Internet is shared by the customer base. The more users who are on the Internet, the slower it becomes for everyone. Cable Internet is a common option for home use and for SOHO networks that use a router to allow multiple computers access to the Internet via a cable. An RG-6 coaxial cable is run into the home or office and connected to a cable modem by way of a screw-on F-connector. The cable modem also has an RJ45 connection for patching to the router or to an individual computer's network adapter.

> **Note**
>
> We'll discuss cables and ports in Chapter 13, "Cables and Connectors."

> **ExamAlert**
>
> Know that cable Internet connections use RG-6 coaxial cable and F-connectors to the cable modem.

> **Note**
>
> Dial-up Internet is still used by some people around the world. It is based on POTS (plain old telephone service) and landlines that connect to phones and dial-up modems by way of an RJ11 connection, resulting in a typical data transfer rate of 56 Kbps—much slower than today's broadband Internet solutions. This is the only solution for people in some rural areas and also areas where it is impossible to get access to any broadband technologies.

DSL

Digital subscriber line (DSL) builds on dial-up by providing full digital data transmission over phone lines but at higher speeds. DSL modems connect to the phone line and to the PC's network adapter or to a SOHO router to enable sharing among multiple computers. One of the benefits of DSL is that you can talk on the phone line and transmit data at the same time. There are several derivatives of DSL, including

▶ **ADSL (Asymmetrical Digital Subscriber Line):** ADSL enables transmission over copper wires that is faster than dial-up. It is generally geared toward consumers who need more downstream bandwidth than upstream. Because the downloading and uploading speeds are different, it is known as an *asymmetric* technology. A group of ADSL technologies offer data transfer rates of anywhere from 8 Mbps download/1 Mbps upload to 52 Mbps download/16 Mbps upload, and newer, faster technologies are being developed as of the writing of this book. ADSL is often offered to consumers who cannot get cable Internet.

▶ **SDSL (Symmetrical Digital Subscriber Line):** SDSL is installed (usually to companies) as a separate line and is usually more expensive than ADSL. With SDSL, upload and download speeds are the same, or *symmetrical*. Maximum data transfer rates for typical versions of SDSL are 1.5 Mbps and 5 Mbps (depending on the version).

Fiber

Instead of using a copper connection to the home or business the way cable Internet, DSL, and dial-up do, some companies offer fiber optic connections directly to the customer. With fiber to the premises (FTTP), optical fiber is installed and used from a central point directly to individual buildings, such as residences, apartment buildings, and businesses.

FTTP service typically runs over a fiber optic line to a network interface device (NID) at the home or office (specifically an optical network terminal); from there, it changes over to copper, which then makes the connection to the customer's router or individual computer. This copper connection could be a twisted pair patch cable (for example, a Cat 6 cable) or a coaxial cable using the Multimedia over Coax Alliance (MoCA) protocol. Examples of companies that offer FTTP include Verizon (Fios) and Google (Google Fiber).

> **Note**
>
> There are other varieties of fiber available to the customer, and they are defined by the point where the fiber ends and the copper begins. Collectively, they are referred to as "fiber to the *x*," where *x* equals the endpoint for the fiber run.

Fiber optic cables can run at much higher data transfer rates than copper-based cables. Home-based fiber optic Internet connections can typically download data between 100 Mbps and 1000 Mbps. Upload speeds are typically less, as they are in most other Internet services, but they are substantially higher than other broadband options.

Satellite

With satellite connectivity, a parabolic antenna (satellite dish) connects via line-of-sight to a satellite; it is used in places where standard landline-based Internet access is not available. The satellite is in geosynchronous orbit, at 22,000 miles (35,406 km) above the Earth. This is the farthest distance of any Internet technology. A satellite dish connects to coax cable that runs to a switching/channeling device for the site's computers. Today's satellite connections offer speeds close to those of traditional broadband access such as cable Internet.

One of the issues with satellite connectivity is electrical and natural interference. Another problem is latency. Due to the distance (44,000 miles total) of the data transfer, there can be a delay of .5 to 5 seconds. That's the highest latency of any Internet technology. Latency goes hand-in-hand with distance. In the past, satellite-based Internet connections offered high-speed downloads, but uploads were slow due to the fact that the service would use a dial-up line to upload information. Newer satellite Internet technologies allow for the upload of data to the satellite as well, and while uploads are often still slower than download speeds, it is much faster than uploading via dial-up.

Satellite-based Internet is growing quickly. For example, SpaceX has a growing constellation of orbital satellites and aims to bring Internet access to people around the world currently living without access to high-speed Internet.

Wireless Internet Service Provider

A wireless Internet service provider (WISP) is an ISP that specializes in wireless networking and builds a wireless mesh network using one of several licensed or unlicensed frequency bands. A WISP's main function is to provide Internet service to customers who cannot obtain service from cable, DSL, or fiber providers or who do not want those services. Originally, WISPs serviced rural areas and other areas where it is difficult to run cable. Today there are millions of wireless Internet customers in rural, suburban, and urban areas.

The technology starts with a fiber line that is run to the center of the geographic area that will be providing access to customers. That line is extended to a high point such as a radio tower, a tall building, or another tall structure. From there, a mounted access point of some sort is used to communicate with customers or other towers in the wireless mesh network. A customer receives a small antenna (parabolic or another type) that is installed on the customer's roof and aligned to the WISP's nearest antenna. The customer's antenna is then wired down to the customer's network. Some WISP services require that the customer's antenna be line-of-sight. Line-of-sight, or *fixed*, wireless Internet service requires the customer's reception device to face the access point at the tower or ground station of the provider—without obstruction.

> **Note**
>
> Cellular is also listed in the CompTIA objectives. For more information on cellular technologies, see Chapter 4, "Mobile Device Network Connectivity and Application Support."

Cram Quiz

Answer these questions. The answers follow the last question. If you cannot answer these questions correctly, consider reading this chapter again until you can.

1. Which of the following is a group of Windows desktop computers located in a small area?

   ○ **A.** LAN

   ○ **B.** WAN

   ○ **C.** PAN

   ○ **D.** MAN

2. What kind of cable and connector are used with cable Internet service to connect to the customer's "modem"?

  ○ **A.** Twisted pair and RJ11

  ○ **B.** 802.11ax and antenna

  ○ **C.** Fiber and ST

  ○ **D.** RG-6 and F-connector

3. Which of the following might make use of Fibre Channel connections?

  ○ **A.** WAN

  ○ **B.** SAN

  ○ **C.** DSL

  ○ **D.** Cable Internet

  ○ **E.** WISP

Cram Quiz Answers

1. **A.** A local area network (LAN) is a group of computers, such as a SOHO network, located in a small area. A wide area network (WAN) is a group of one or more LANs spread over a larger geographic area. A personal area network (PAN) is a smaller computer network used by smartphones and other small computing devices. A metropolitan area network (MAN) is a group of LANs in a smaller geographic area, such as a city.

2. **D.** Cable Internet connections use an RG-6 coaxial cable that is run from a NID to the customer's cable modem. It is connected by way of an F-connector. Twisted pair cables and RJ11 might be used by DSL or dial-up. 802.11ax is a WLAN protocol. Fiber-based services might indeed use an ST connector, but this question asks about cable Internet service.

3. **B.** A SAN (storage area network) often makes use of Fibre Channel connections and switches to connect NAS points and other data storage devices together into a super-fast network. A wide area network (WAN) is a network that connects two or more LANs together. Digital subscriber line (DSL) is a type of Internet service, as are cable Internet and wireless Internet service providers (WISPs).

Well, at this point you might be suffering from networking on the brain. But there's only one more networking chapter left. Take a small break and continue on. You're doing awesome!

CHAPTER 12
Networking Tools

This chapter covers the following A+ 220-1101 exam objective:

▶ **2.8** – Given a scenario, use networking tools.

Let's wrap up the computer networking section of this book with a shorter chapter on the types of tools used for network connectivity and network testing.

For this objective, you should know some of the cabling and networking tools that can help you create, modify, and troubleshoot network patch cables and longer network cables that terminate at patch panels and RJ45 jacks. We'll also briefly talk about network taps that can be used to analyze data, as well as Wi-Fi analyzers that can be used to identify wireless networks.

Of course, you will continue to use your networking knowledge as you progress through the book—especially as you get to the operating systems chapters—and as you advance in the IT field. One of the goals of this book is to help you retain knowledge over the long term. Remember to take notes and quiz yourself often. At the end of each domain (such as this one, Domain 2.0: Networking), review what you have learned throughout the section. This will help you transition to other areas of the book.

Network Cabling Tools

If you plan to build or troubleshoot a physical network, you need to stock up on some key networking tools that will aid you when running, terminating, and testing cable. For this short section, imagine a scenario where you are the network installer and are required to install a wired network for 12 computers.

To start, you should check with your local municipality to see if there are any rules and regulations related to running networking cable. Some municipalities require an installer to have an electrician's license. Some require only an exemption of some sort that anyone can apply for at the town or county seat. Due to the low-voltage nature of network wiring (for most applications), some municipalities have no rules regarding this wiring. But in urban areas, you will need to apply for a permit and have at least one inspection done when you are finished with the installation.

Permits and regulations aside, let's say that in this scenario, you have been cleared to install 12 wired connections to computers (known as cable "runs" or "drops"). You have diagrammed where the cables will be run and where they will terminate. All cables will come out of a wiring closet, where you will terminate them to a small patch panel. On the other end, they will terminate at in-wall RJ45 jacks near each of the computers. Wire termination is the work performed at each end of a cable that allows it to connect to a physical endpoint such as a jack or a patch panel. These are the networking tools that you will use to complete this job.

- ▶ **Cable cutter:** The first tool you should have is a good, sharp cutting tool. You need to make a clean cut on the end of the network cable; scissors will not do. Either cut pliers or other cable cutting tools are necessary.

- ▶ **Cable stripper:** A cable stripper (or wire stripper) is used to strip a portion of the plastic jacket off the cable to expose the individual wires. At this point, you can separate the wires and get ready to terminate them with a punchdown tool.

▶ **Punchdown tool:** A punchdown tool is a device that punches the individual wires down into the 110 IDC clips of an RJ45 jack and the patch panel. This punching down of the wires is the actual termination. This tool can also be used to terminate twisted pair wires to a punchdown block—either a 110 block for data or a 66 block for telecommunications.

▶ **Cable testers:** The last tool necessary for the job is a cable testing tool. There are a few options here:

  ▶ The best option is a proper network cable tester, also known as a continuity tester or cable certifier. This device has a LAN testing unit that you can plug into a port on the patch panel and a terminator that you plug into the other end of the cable in the corresponding RJ45 jack (or vice versa). This tool tests for continuity and tests each wire in the cable, making sure each one is wired properly.

  ▶ Another option is a tone generator and probe kit (also known as a toner/probe or fox and hound). This kit consists of two parts: a tone-generating device, which connects to one end of the network cable and, when turned on, sends a tone along the length of the cable; and a probing device, also known as an inductive amplifier, which can detect the tone anywhere along the cable length and at the termination point. This tool is not as good as a proper network cable tester because it tests only one of the pairs of the wires. However, it is an excellent tool for finding individual phone lines and is most commonly used for that. You can also use a multimeter to do various tests of individual lines, but it is usually not necessary if you own the other tools mentioned. The cable tester mentioned previously can usually create tone as well.

At this point, the cables have been run, terminated on both ends, and tested. The only other thing you need is patch cables. The patch cables connect the various ports of the patch panel to a switch and the RJ45 jacks to the computers.

▶ **RJ45 crimper:** You usually buy patch cables for a couple dollars each and are done with it. However, you can make them, too. To do so, you have to purchase cable as well as RJ45 plugs. Make sure that the cable and plugs meet the cabling standard you decide to use, such as Category 5e or Category 6. You attach the plugs to the cable ends with an RJ45 crimping tool. This tool can be especially handy when you need to make a crossover patch cable, which can be used to connect a computer to another computer directly. There are other types of crimpers for coaxial cable as well.

▶ **Patch tester:** Before connecting the patch cables, you should test them with a patch tester. This device has two RJ45 jacks; you plug each end of the patch cable into the tester and then press the button to make sure each wire makes a proper connection and has continuity. Remember to always test twice!

▶ **Loopback plug:** Another tool every PC tech should have is a loopback plug. It simulates a network connection and has two main functions. First, it can help find what port on a switch an RJ45 jack is wired to. You plug it into an RJ45 jack on the wall, and it bounces the signal back down the cable to the switch, lighting up the port that the cable is ultimately connected to. This tells you which port on the switch a particular cable is connected to in case it wasn't labeled previously. You can also accomplish this by connecting it to the end of a patch cable because the device usually has male and a female RJ45 connections. Second, you can test the network adapter on a PC and find out if TCP/IP is functioning properly. An easy way to do this is to plug the loopback adapter into the RJ45 port of the PC, open the command line, and then ping the IP address of the local system. The loopback plug is essentially a really short crossover connection; the appropriate pins are crossed within the device, looping the signal and data back to where it came from.

Figure 12.1 identifies some of the tools described in this section.

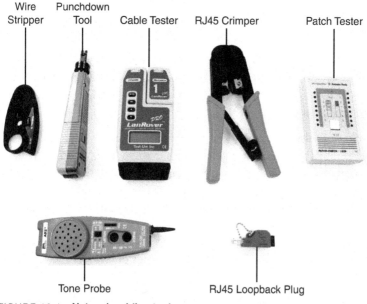

FIGURE 12.1   **Network cabling tools**

Network Tap

A network tap is a physical device used to make one or more copies of traffic from a network port. It can then send the data to a variety of different monitoring devices. This "traffic mirroring" helps a network analyst gather data, monitor the network, and check for intrusion detection among other things.

At its simplest, a network tap could be passive (USB-powered) and simply incorporate one additional port for monitoring, passing original traffic through. A more complicated device might run on AC power or could have multiple ports for data analysis. Either way, the key is to know what you want to monitor. Traffic can be taken from an individual system connected to a switch port to mimic that particular system's data flow. However, it can also be taken from an entire switch or a network port that is farther up the network chain to allow for analysis of segments of the network—or even the entire network's data. For example, have you ever wondered why the data LED of your cable modem (or other ISP-provided device) blinks incessantly, even if nothing is happening on your network? Placing a network tap in between the cable modem and the router will allow you to analyze *all* the traffic before it even hits your firewall, giving you a clearer picture of what your cable modem is actually doing.

Ultimately, packets of data can be analyzed with programs such as Wireshark, Snort, or tcpdump. If you are interested in network security, I highly recommend checking out the Wireshark packet sniffer program: https://www.wireshark.org.

Of course, a network tap could be used by malicious individuals as well; to protect against this, an organization should make sure that it has physical security measures and multi-factor authentication implemented; it should also ensure that the network is being scanned for unauthorized network taps.

ExamAlert

A network tap is a physical device used to capture and copy data packets for analysis.

Wi-Fi Analyzers

A *Wi-Fi analyzer* is a tool that can identify wireless networks—typically on 2.4 GHz and 5 GHz frequencies. This tool shows things such as the channels used by neighboring wireless networks, any overlap that might be occurring between those networks and yours, and the signal strength of access points. Wi-Fi analyzers come in two types. A Wi-Fi analyzer may be a (relatively expensive) handheld, all-in-one device with a built-in Wi-Fi antenna and incorporated analysis programs; or it may be an app for Windows, Android, or iOS. Whatever device you run the app on must have a wireless network adapter that is set up properly. Figure 12.2 shows an example of a basic Wi-Fi analyzer app that is displaying the 2.4 GHz Wi-Fi networks in the vicinity. In this example, you can see that the lower channels (1–5) are being used much more than the upper channels. This type of data should play into your decision-making process when setting up a new Wi-Fi network or when selecting an access point to connect a client to—if there is more than one.

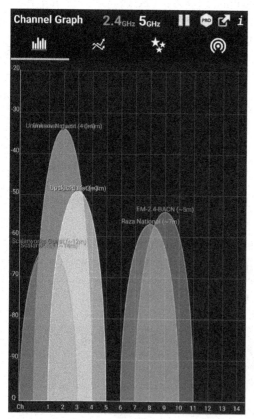

FIGURE 12.2   Wi-Fi analyzer viewing the 2.4 GHz range

ExamAlert

A Wi-Fi analyzer is a tool that can identify wireless networks and the channels/frequencies they use.

Cram Quiz

Answer these questions. The answers follow the last question. If you cannot answer these questions correctly, consider reading this chapter again until you can.

1. Which tool is used to test a network adapter without a network connection?

   ○ **A.** Punchdown tool

   ○ **B.** Cable tester

   ○ **C.** Loopback plug

   ○ **D.** Tone generator and probe

2. Your boss is concerned about overlapping wireless networks from neighboring companies using 802.11ac. Which tool should you use to analyze the problem, and which frequency should you display for analysis?

   ○ **A.** Wi-Fi analyzer; 5 GHz

   ○ **B.** Cable certifier; 5 GHz

   ○ **C.** Loopback plug; 2.4 GHz

   ○ **D.** Wi-Fi analyzer; 2.4 GHz

3. What would be required to attach RJ45 plugs to the ends of a single patch cable?

   ○ **A.** Tone and probe kit

   ○ **B.** Multimeter

   ○ **C.** Cable stripper

   ○ **D.** Crimper

4. Your organization is terminating Category 6 cable to a 110 block. Which of the following tools should you use to perform the task?

   ○ **A.** Punchdown tool

   ○ **B.** Crimper

   ○ **C.** Cable stripper

   ○ **D.** Tone generator

5. Say that you are responsible for the network security of your organization. You decide to perform packet sniffing on your switch by using Wireshark. Which of the following tools will help you to do this?

○ **A.** Tone and probe kit

○ **B.** Network tap

○ **C.** Wireless analyzer

○ **D.** Loopback plug

Cram Quiz Answers

1. **C.** To test a network adapter without a network connection, you use a loopback plug. This tool simulates a network connection. It can also be used to test a switch port. Punchdown tools are used to punch individual wires to a patch panel. Cable testers such as continuity testers test the entire length of a terminated cable. A tone generator and probe kit can also test a cable's length, but it tests only one pair of wires at a time.

2. **A.** To analyze the problem, use a Wi-Fi analyzer. Because your boss is concerned about wireless networks using 802.11ac, you should display the results for 5 GHz networks, not 2.4 GHz networks. Cable certifiers are used to check long-distance *wired* connections, such as from a patch panel to an RJ45 jack. A loopback plug is used to simulate a network connection, which can help with identifying switch ports and testing a PC's network connection.

3. **D.** RJ45 plugs are attached to cable ends with a tool called a crimper. A tone generator and probe kit is used to trace hard-to-find telecommunication and data communication cables/wires. A multimeter can be used to test the continuity of a patch cable. A cable stripper is used to strip a portion of the plastic jacket off the cable and expose the individual wires.

4. **A.** Use a punchdown tool to terminate the individual wires of a Category 6 cable to a 110 punchblock. Use a crimper to connect plugs to the ends of a cable. Use a cable stripper to remove a section of the plastic jacket of a cable. Use a tone generator to create tone at one end of a cable and then use a tone probe to find the same cable at the other end.

5. **B.** A network tap is used to intercept network traffic and make a copy of it for analysis with programs such as Wireshark. (Side note: Be sure to use a quality network tap; lesser ones will reduce your network bandwidth, which could affect everyone!) A tone and probe kit is used to trace signals on cables. A wireless analyzer (or Wi-Fi analyzer) is used to view the frequencies used in nearby wireless networks. A loopback plug is used to simulate a network connection (and test it) but can't be used as a network tap.

You did it! You've completed the networking section of this book. Great work! Be sure to review the networking chapters, ExamAlerts, and your notes before moving on to the next domain.

CORE 1 (220-1101)

Domain 3.0: Hardware

CHAPTER 13

Cables and Connectors

This chapter covers the following A+ 220-1101 exam objective:

▶ **3.1** – Explain basic cable types and their connectors, features, and purposes.

Welcome to Domain 3.0: Hardware. This domain accounts for 25% of the overall exam objectives. Every chapter covering this domain is chock full of hardware information you need to know. Treat these chapters accordingly!

Even though wireless technology usage is widespread, cables are still necessary and used in many applications. This chapter gets you familiar with all the cables and connectors you need to network systems together, add peripherals, and adapt or convert from one technology to another. Everything can be linked together!

ExamAlert

Objective 3.1 concentrates on the following concepts: network cables, peripheral cables, video cables, hard drive cables, adapters, and connector types.

Network Cables

Cable types are broken down into two categories: cables that use electricity and cables that use light. Twisted pair and coaxial cables use copper wires as their transmission media and send electricity over those wires. Fiber optic, on the other hand, uses glass or plastic as the transmission medium and sends light (photons) over those cables.

Twisted Pair

The most common type of cable used in today's networks is *twisted pair*. It is referred to as twisted pair because the copper wires inside the cable are twisted together into pairs throughout the entire length of the cable. Administrators regularly use unshielded twisted pair (UTP) cable. Typical versions of twisted pair include *Category 6* and *Category 5e* (often abbreviated Cat 6 and Cat 5e). Table 13.1 shows the various categories of twisted pair you should know for the exam and the networks they are rated for.

TABLE 13.1 **UTP Categories and Speeds**

UTP Category	Rated For
Category 5	100 Mbps networks
	(100 MHz)
Category 5e	100 Mbps and 1 Gbps networks
	(100 MHz/350 MHz)
Category 6/6a	1000 Mbps (1 Gbps) and 10 Gbps networks
	(250 MHz/500 MHz)

Note

Table 13.1 shows the UTP cables listed in the objectives. But as of the writing of this book, Cat 7 cable (1 Gbps and 10 Gbps) and Cat 8 cable (up to 40 Gbps) are available. Watch out for them!

Data transfer rate (also known as *speed* or *bandwidth*) is normally measured in bits because networks usually transfer data serially, or 1 bit at a time. 100 Mbps is 100 megabits per second. 1 Gbps is equal to 1 gigabit per second (and a network capable of this speed is known as a gigabit network), or 1000 Mbps. 10 Gbps is equal to 10 gigabits per second. Now, a cable might be rated for 10 Gbps networks (for example, Cat 6), but you probably won't attain that speed over the cable. Typically, the actual speed (known as *throughput*) might be 250 Mbps, 500 Mbps, 1 Gbps, or possibly more. The speed depends on many factors, including the frequency of the cable (for example, Cat 6 is 250 MHz and Cat 6a is 500 MHz), the technology used to send data, the encoding rate, whether duplexing is involved, the length of the cable, the quality of the installation, and so on. So, it's difficult to put a specific number to each category of cable. Just remember what network speeds each category of cable is rated for.

> **ExamAlert**
>
> Know what network speeds Cat 5, 5e, and 6/6a are rated for.

The Telecommunications Industry Association (TIA) defines standards for cabling and wiring, such as the 568A and 568B standards. Generally speaking, the most common standard you see is the 568B standard. Table 13.2 shows the color sequence for each of the eight wires (or pins) for the 568B and 568A standards. Figure 13.1 shows a close-up of the wires organized for a 568B connection.

TABLE 13.2 **568B and 568A Wiring Standards**

Pinouts	568B	Pinouts	568A
Pin 1	White/orange	Pin 1	White/green
Pin 2	Orange	Pin 2	Green
Pin 3	White/green	Pin 3	White/orange
Pin 4	Blue	Pin 4	Blue
Pin 5	White/blue	Pin 5	White/blue
Pin 6	Green	Pin 6	Orange
Pin 7	White/brown	Pin 7	White/brown
Pin 8	Brown	Pin 8	Brown

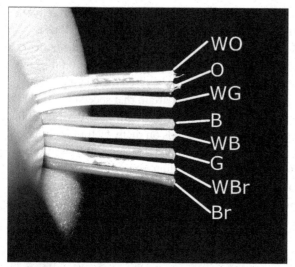

FIGURE 13.1 **Wires organized for the 568B standard**

Any physical cabling equipment used in a network must comply with the standard chosen for that network, including cables, patch panels, jacks, and connectors. The connector used with twisted pair networks is known colloquially as the RJ45 (or, more specifically, the 8P8C connector). RJ45 plugs connect to each end of the cable, and these cables connect to RJ45 sockets within network adapters and on network switches.

ExamAlert

If a computer cannot connect to the network, check the network cable first. Make sure the RJ45 plug has a solid connection.

As you can see in Figure 13.2, RJ45 plugs look a lot like the landline telephone plugs (known as RJ11 plugs). However, the RJ45 plug is larger and contains eight wires, whereas the RJ11 plug holds only a maximum of six wires (and normally only uses four).

RJ45   RJ11

FIGURE 13.2 **RJ45 and RJ11 plugs**

A standard twisted pair patch cable that you would use to connect a computer to a switch or an RJ45 jack is wired for 568B on each end. That makes it a *straight-through cable*. However, if you wanted to connect a computer directly to another computer, you would need to use a *crossover cable*. This type of cable is wired for 568B on one end and 568A on the other. You can see in Table 13.2 that certain pins are "crossed" to each other from 568B to 568A. Pin 1 on 568B crosses to pin 3 on 568A, and pin 2 crosses to pin 6. You can also use a crossover cable to connect one switch to another—although this is usually not necessary because most switches auto-sense the type of cable you plug into them.

> **Note**
>
> The way that a crossover cable's pins are wired is the basis for a loopback—a connection made to test the local computer or system (for example, an RJ45 loopback plug).

UTP has a few disadvantages:

▶ It can be run only 100 meters (328 feet) before *signal attenuation*—that is, weakening or degradation of signal—occurs.

▶ Its outer jacket is made of plastic, and it has no shielding, making it susceptible to electromagnetic interference (EMI) and vulnerable to unauthorized network access in the form of wiretapping.

Because the UTP cable jacket is made of PVCs (plastics) that can be harmful to humans when they catch on fire, most municipalities require that plenum-rated cable be installed in any area that cannot be reached by a sprinkler system. A *plenum* is an enclosed space used for airflow. For example, if cables are run above a drop ceiling, building code requires that they be plenum rated. This means that the cable has a special Teflon coating or is a special low-smoke variant of twisted pair, reducing the amount of PVC chemicals that are released into the air in the event of a fire.

> **ExamAlert**
>
> To meet fire code, use plenum-rated cable above drop ceilings and anywhere else necessary.

Because UTP is susceptible to EMI, a variant was developed known as shielded twisted pair (STP). STP includes metal shielding over each pair of wires, reducing external EMI and the possibility of unauthorized network access. A couple of disadvantages of STP include higher cost of the product and installation and the fact that the shielding needs to be grounded to work effectively. Keep in mind that all server room and wiring closet equipment—such as patch panels, punch blocks, and wiring racks—should be permanently grounded before use.

> **ExamAlert**
>
> STP cable is resistant to EMI.

Speaking of "ground," there is also specially rated cable for use underground. When twisted pair cable (for example, Cat 5e or Cat 6) needs to be run outdoors, *direct burial* cable should be used, and it should be placed approximately 8 inches underground and at least 8 inches away from any buried power lines. This cable does not degrade when exposed to the elements because it is protected by an additional plastic or metal conduit.

> **Note**
>
> Objective 3.1 lists "punchdown block," which is a place to terminate many twisted pair cables. We discuss this concept briefly in Chapter 12, "Networking Tools."

Coaxial

Coaxial cable provides another way to transfer data over a network. This cable has a single conductor surrounded by insulating material, which is then surrounded by a copper screen and, finally, an outer plastic sheath. Some networking technologies still use coaxial cable; for example, cable Internet connections use RG-6 coaxial cable (and possibly the older RG-59 cable). This cable screws on to the terminal of a cable modem using an F-connector (also called F-type connector). It is the same cable and connector used with cable TV set-top boxes (STBs) and DVRs.

Generally, RG-6 cable can be run as far as 500 to 1000 feet. The maximum distance varies because several factors play into how far the data can travel before attenuation occurs—including the frequency used and the protocol used. Its speed also varies depending on what type of transmission is sent over it. A typical RG-6 cable has a minimum bandwidth of 1 GHz, which can loosely translate to 1 Gbps, but the data throughput will most likely be capped at some number below that. For example, cable Internet providers offer different tiered download speeds (50 or 100 Mbps and so on), and some fiber optic providers (who change the cable type from fiber optic to coaxial at the house or business) might cap it at anywhere between 100 Mbps and 500 Mbps. This all varies according to the provider and how many services are being transmitted over the same line.

There are two derivatives of RG-6 that you should know: RG-6/U, which is double-shielded, and the more common RG-6/UQ, which is quadruple-shielded and is often referred to as "quad shield." It is a better option if you are running RG-6 in ceilings or near any electrical appliances.

> **ExamAlert**
>
> Make sure you know cable terminology such as RJ11, RJ45, F-connector, and RG-6 for the exam.

Optical

Optical, or fiber optic, cable is fast, and unlike copper-based cables, it is not subject to EMI. Because fiber optic cables transmit data by way of light instead of electricity, they can send signals much faster and farther than do copper wires. Optical cable can be more secure than copper-based cable as well. EMI doesn't even play into the equation because optical cables don't use electricity. Plus, fiber optic cables are more difficult to tap (splice) into than copper-based cables.

You might encounter single-mode and multimode fiber; for the most part, single-mode fiber is used over longer distances, but both types are easily capable of supporting 1000 Mbps and 10 Gbps networks and can be run farther than twisted pair cable. Straight tip (ST) and subscriber connector (SC), shown in Figure 13.3, are a couple types of connectors used with fiber. Another connector is the Lucent Connector (LC), which looks quite similar to SC.

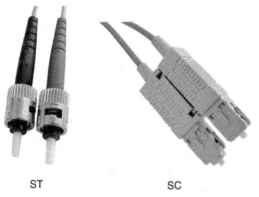

ST   SC

FIGURE 13.3 **ST and SC connectors**

ExamAlert

Be able to identify straight tip (ST), subscriber connector (SC), and Lucent Connector (LC) fiber optic connectors.

Multimode cables have a larger core diameter than do single-mode cables. It is the more commonly used fiber optic cable in server rooms and when making network backbone connections between buildings in a campus. It transmits data approximately 600 meters. Single-mode, on the other hand, is used for longer-distance runs, perhaps from one city to the next (as far as thousands of kilometers). At shorter distances, single-mode cable can go beyond 10 Gbps.

Peripheral Cables and Connectors

This is sort of the catch-all section for several types of cables: USB, Apple device cables, and serial cables.

USB

USB ports are used by many devices, including keyboards, mice, printers, flash drives, and more. A USB port enables data transfer between a device and a computer and usually powers the device as well. The speed of a USB device's data transfer depends on the version of the USB port, as shown in Table 13.3.

TABLE 13.3 **Comparison of USB Versions**

USB Version	Name	Data Transfer Rate
USB 2.0	High-Speed	480 Mbps
USB 3.0	SuperSpeed	5 Gbps
USB 3.1	SuperSpeed+	10 Gbps
USB 3.2 (USB-C)	SuperSpeed+	10/20 Gbps

Note that Table 13.3 doesn't mention the USB4 specification, which was released in 2019, provides for 40 Gbps throughput, and is compatible with Thunderbolt 3. Be ready for it! Also, you might see USB data transfer rates written as Mbit/s and Gbit/s, which mean the same thing as Mbps and Gbps. Finally, note that USB 1.0 (1.5 Mbps) and 1.1 (12 Mbps) have been deprecated. If you encounter an older computer that has only these ports, consider installing a USB adapter that adheres to a higher version of USB.

> **ExamAlert**
>
> Memorize the specifications for USB 2.0 (480 Mbps) through 3.2 (10/20 Gbps).

There are various plugs used for the different types of USB connections. Figure 13.4 illustrates these connectors.

Type A and Type B connectors are commonly used for printers and other larger devices. Mini- and Micro- connectors are often used for handheld computers, smartphones, mice, digital cameras, portable music players, and cell phones. USB-C is used for newer smartphones and other devices developed after 2017. However, some companies create proprietary cables and connectors for their devices, based on the USB specifications. Such devices cannot connect properly to Type A, Type B, and Mini- or Micro- connectors.

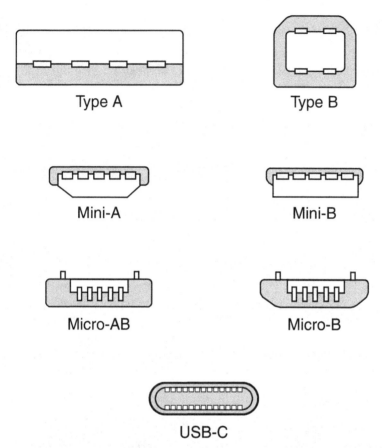

FIGURE 13.4 **USB connectors**

The USB-C connector is quite common. Aside from its increased speed, it is found on a plethora of devices, and the cable end can be connected to the port in either direction (that is, there is no "upside down"). So, unlike with older versions of USB, you can plug it in either way without having to worry (and without having to look carefully at the port). Also, it has higher power flow. It can provide up to 5 amps of current, allowing for faster charging of devices, but it is important to use quality USB-C cables that can handle the higher amperage. Finally, back to the increased speed: With USB-C, today's USB technology has progressed to the point where it can be used as a video connection (for example, to provide HD video and audio to an external monitor connected to a laptop). It is one mighty connector.

Lightning and Thunderbolt

Lightning is a proprietary port built into Apple devices such as the iPad and iPhone. It's an 8-pin connector that replaced the (now legacy) 30-pin dock predecessor. As with USB-C, the Lightning connector can be inserted face up or face down. It supports USB 3.0 speeds. As mentioned in Chapter 3, "Mobile Device Accessories and Ports," keep in mind that some Apple devices use USB-C instead of the Lightning connector.

Thunderbolt is a high-speed hardware interface developed by Intel. As of the writing of this book, this is used primarily by Apple computers. It combines elements of PCI Express and DisplayPort technologies. Versions 1 and 2 use the Mini DisplayPort connector, and version 3 uses the USB-C connector. Thunderbolt 2 provides access to 4K monitors. Because Thunderbolt is based on DisplayPort technology, it provides native support for the Apple Thunderbolt Display and Mini DisplayPort displays.

Thunderbolt can be used to transfer data at high rates to external storage devices or to displays (or both; up to six devices can be daisy-chained, or wired together in sequence). If you look at the ports of a computer and see the Thunderbolt icon next to the Mini DisplayPort port, then it is meant to be used for data transfer to peripherals. If you see a Display icon, then it can be used with a monitor. While you can physically connect a Thunderbolt device to a Mac with DisplayPort, the device will not work; however, if you connect a DisplayPort device to a Mac with Thunderbolt, the device will work. Table 13.4 describes the different versions of Thunderbolt.

TABLE 13.4 **Comparison of Thunderbolt Versions**

Thunderbolt Version	Data Transfer Rate	Connector Type	PCI Express Version Required
Version 1	10 Gbps	DisplayPort	Version 2.0
Version 2	20 Gbps	DisplayPort	Version 2.0
Version 3	40 Gbps	USB Type-C	Version 3.0

> **Note**
>
> Table 13.4 does not mention Thunderbolt 4, which was released in 2020. While the transfer rate is the same as for version 3, Thunderbolt 4 supports USB4.

> **ExamAlert**
>
> Know the Thunderbolt versions, speeds, and connection types.

Serial

The term *serial* is used with many technologies: USB, Serial Attached SCSI, bit streams over network cables, and so on; but generally, a person who refers to serial connections for peripheral devices is talking about the Recommended Standard 232 (RS-232) data transmission standard. Although it is an old technology, it is still used in many environments. For example, the RS-232 standard describes how DTEs (computers) and DCEs (dial-up modems) communicate using serial ports.

RS-232 communicates via serial cables that have either 9 wires (DE-9, also known as DB9) or 25 wires (DB-25). RS-232 has been used for many years, and it will most likely continue to be used due to its simple design and the vast array of devices out there that use RS-232 interfaces, such as handheld and mountable terminals, networking equipment, industrial machines, and analytical instruments. Because of this, you can still find motherboards with built-in RS-232 ports (usually DE-9). If a computer does not have one, and you need to access RS-232-based equipment, you can use a PCIe add-on card. For laptops and other mobile devices, you can use USB-to-RS-232 converters.

RS-232 and other Recommended Standards (such as RS-422 and RS-485) are published by the TIA, the same organization that publishes the 568B cabling standard.

> **ExamAlert**
>
> Remember that DE-9 (DB-9) is a 9-pin connector used for serial cable and RS-232 data transmissions.

Video Cables and Connectors

Your choice of video card will probably dictate the cable and connector that you use. Most of today's PCIe video cards come with either DVI, HDMI, or DisplayPort outputs. Some monitors also have VGA connections for legacy compatibility. Table 13.5 details some of the common connectors you will see in the field. Figure 13.5 shows some of the typical video ports you will use.

TABLE 13.5 **Video Card Connectors**

Connector Type	Full Name	Description
DVI	Digital Visual Interface	High-quality connections used with LCD displays. Carries uncompressed digital video; is partially compatible with HDMI. Types include ▶ **DVI-D:** Digital-only connections ▶ **DVI-I:** Digital and analog connections ▶ **DVI-A:** Analog-only connections Dual-link connections are available for DVI-D and DVI-I. Non-dual-link versions have a gap in the center of the pins, using one-third fewer pins total.
HDMI	High-Definition Multimedia Interface	Used mainly for high-definition television. Can carry video and audio signals ▶ **Type A:** Supports all HD modes; compatible with DVI-D connectors ▶ **Type B:** Double-video bandwidth; supports higher resolutions; also known as dual-link; uncommon ▶ **Type C:** Mini-HDMI; used in portable devices ▶ **Type D:** Micro-HDMI; smallest connector; also used in portable devices ▶ **Type E:** Used in automobiles; has a locking tab
DisplayPort	DisplayPort	▶ Royalty-free interface similar to HDMI; designed to be the replacement for HDMI and DVI ▶ Often has a locking tab ▶ Uses packet transmission similar to Ethernet ▶ Mini version developed by Apple
VGA (also known as SVGA)	Video Graphics Array	15-pin, usually blue, known as DE15 (also sold as DB15 or HD15). Used for older monitors that display VGA, SVGA, and XGA resolutions. Signal quality degrades over shorter distances than with HDMI, DVI, and DisplayPort.

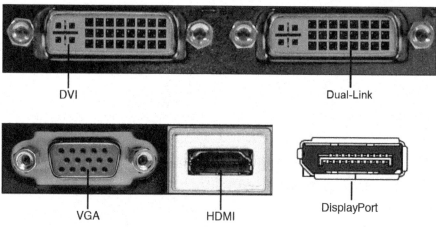

DVI   Dual-Link

VGA   HDMI   DisplayPort

FIGURE 13.5 **Typical video ports**

ExamAlert

Be able to identify VGA, HDMI, Mini-HDMI, DisplayPort, and DVI video connectors
and ports.

There are adapters, splitters, and signal boosters available for just about every
type of video connection: HDMI to DVI, DVI to VGA, and so on. In some
cases, a passive adapter or splitter works fine. In other cases, an active (AC-
powered) connection is required. This is common with DVI and HDMI,
especially if you want a clean, quality signal over any length beyond 1 meter.

Storage Drive Cables and Connectors

The three types of storage drive/hard drive cables listed in the objective are as
follows:

▶ **Serial ATA (SATA):** A very common connection for internal drives
(SATA) and external drives (eSATA). It uses a 7-pin data connector and a
15-pin power connector.

▶ **Integrated Drive Electronics (IDE):** A much older type of connection
that runs in parallel (8 bits at a time) instead of serially (1 bit at a time).
It uses a 40-pin ribbon cable for data and a 4-pin Molex connector for
power. (The chances of seeing this type of connector are slim.)

▶ **Small Computer System Interface (SCSI):** Around since the 1980s, SCSI at first was designed as a parallel technology that could run faster than IDE and other connections. Today, a common type of SCSI is Serial Attached SCSI (SAS), which can transfer data as fast as 22.5 Gbps (SAS version 4); faster speeds are being developed.

We'll be discussing some of these drive cables and connections more in Chapter 15, "Storage Drives."

ExamAlert

Know your storage drive cables, including SATA, SCSI, eSATA, and IDE.

Adapters

You can't put a square peg in a round hole (normally). Sometimes you need to make a connection, but the devices and/or cables don't match up; in such cases, you need an adapter, and there are adapters for virtually everything you might want to do. Let's say you need to make a connection to a USB Type B connector from a USB Type A connector, or you need to connect from USB to RJ45, or you need to connect from a USB to the older PS/2 connector. Well, there are adapters for all those situations and more.

Video can be especially troublesome. For example, what if your laptop has an HDMI output, but the monitor you want to connect to only has DVI and VGA? An HDMI-to-DVI output would be necessary. But remember, DVI does not normally carry audio signal the way that HDMI does, so you might also need to run an audio cable from the 3.5 mm audio output of the laptop to a set of speakers. You might need to switch from DVI to VGA or from DVI to HDMI. Be ready to use adapters and research whether the length of your connection and/or the quality of signal requires an active AC-powered adapter.

A common adapter today is the USB-to-Ethernet adapter. This type of adapter allows you to use just about any USB port and send data from the computer (or device) over an Ethernet network. There are adapters that go from USB (Type A) to RJ45, USB-C to RJ45, and so on. USB-C is preferred for many devices because it can handle higher data throughputs with less latency.

Most PC technicians carry a variety of adapters with them just in case they need them. That's something to think about for your toolkit.

Cram Quiz

Answer these questions. The answers follow the last question. If you cannot answer these questions correctly, consider reading this chapter again until you can.

1. Which of the following uses a 7-pin data connector and a 15-pin power connector?

   ○ **A.** VGA

   ○ **B.** IDE

   ○ **C.** SATA

   ○ **D.** Molex

   ○ **E.** Cat 6

2. Which type of cable would you use if you were concerned about EMI?

   ○ **A.** Plenum rated

   ○ **B.** UTP

   ○ **C.** STP

   ○ **D.** Coaxial

3. You have been tasked with connecting a newer Android smartphone to an external TV so that you can display the CEO's smartphone screen during a meeting. Which of the following adapters would typically be the best solution?

   ○ **A.** Micro-USB to HDMI

   ○ **B.** Micro-USB to DVI

   ○ **C.** USB-C to DVI

   ○ **D.** USB-C to Ethernet

   ○ **E.** USB-C to HDMI

4. Which type of cable can connect a computer to another computer directly?

   ○ **A.** Straight-through

   ○ **B.** Crossover

   ○ **C.** 568A

   ○ **D.** SATA

   ○ **E.** 568B

5. Which connector is used for cable Internet?

- ○ **A.** LC
- ○ **B.** F-connector
- ○ **C.** Direct burial
- ○ **D.** RJ45
- ○ **E.** DE-9

6. Which cable type would be suitable for longer distances, such as connecting two cities?

- ○ **A.** Coaxial
- ○ **B.** Twisted pair
- ○ **C.** Multimode fiber
- ○ **D.** Single-mode fiber

7. You need to make a high-speed connection to an external storage device that can handle 40 Gbps. Which of the following is the best solution?

- ○ **A.** USB 3.2
- ○ **B.** Thunderbolt
- ○ **C.** HDMI
- ○ **D.** Cat 6a

Cram Quiz Answers

1. C. SATA connections include a 7-pin data connector and a 15-pin power connector. VGA ports have 15 pins that are used to transmit video signal. An older IDE hard drive cable has 40 pins. Molex is a power connection that has 4 wires. Category 6 (Cat 6) cable is twisted pair cable that has 8 pins (wires).

2. C. STP (shielded twisted pair) is the only cable listed here that can reduce electromagnetic interference. However, fiber optic cable is another good solution, though it is more expensive and more difficult to install. Plenum-rated cable is used where fire code requires it; it doesn't burn as fast as regular cable, and it releases fewer PVC chemicals into the air.

3. E. Typically, you would use USB-C to HDMI. If it is a newer Android smartphone, then chances are it will have a USB-C port. If you are attempting to connect it to a TV, HDMI is the most likely port to use. Micro-USB is used with some mobile devices, but newer devices (especially Android devices) have switched to USB-C. You wouldn't want USB-C to DVI because TVs normally don't have DVI inputs. USB to Ethernet helps convert from a computer or mobile device to the Ethernet network. These devices can ultimately allow a device or computer with a USB port to access the Internet. This wired connection might be favored over wireless for its speed, quality connection, and low latency.

4. **B.** A crossover cable is used to connect like devices: computer to computer or switch to switch. Straight-through cables (the more common patch cable) connect different devices (for example, connect a computer to a switch). 568B is the typical wiring standard you see in twisted pair cables; 568A is the less common standard. A crossover cable uses the 568B wiring standard on one end and 568A on the other end. (By the way, sometimes you see these standards written as T568A and T568B.) SATA is used to connect storage drives internally to desktop or laptop computers.

5. **B.** Cable Internet connections use RG-6 coaxial cable (usually) with an F-connector on the end. LC is a type of fiber optic connector. Direct burial is a type of cable that you can purchase for underground installations. RJ45 is the connector used on twisted pair patch cables. DE-9 (or DB-9) is a serial connector used with RS-232 connections.

6. **D.** Single-mode fiber is used for longer-distance runs, perhaps from one city to the next (as far as thousands of kilometers). Coaxial is common for connections between utility poles and houses/buildings. Twisted pair is common in LANs. Multimode cables have a larger core diameter than single-mode cables. Multimode is the more commonly used fiber optic cable in server rooms and for making network backbone connections between buildings in a campus.

7. **B.** A Thunderbolt connection is the best solution to the scenario—specifically, Thunderbolt version 3, which can handle 40 Gbps over USB Type-C. USB 3.2 is limited to 10 or 20 Gbps, though it also uses the USB Type-C connection. HDMI is used for video (and audio) connections. Cat 6a is a type of twisted pair cable used in Ethernet networks; it is rated for 1000 Mbps and 10 Gbps.

Today, it seems that just about everything is *interconnected*. And sometimes, a person just needs to disconnect! As this was one of the longer chapters of the book, now is such a time. Take a break, review, and then continue!

CHAPTER 14

RAM

This chapter covers the following A+ 220-1101 exam objective:

▶ **3.2** – Given a scenario, install the appropriate RAM.

This chapter and the next one are all about how data is accessed and stored—over the short term and the long term. We use random-access memory (RAM) for the short term and storage drives over the long term. In this chapter, we'll focus on the short term and RAM.

When people talk about the RAM in their computer, they are almost always referring to the "sticks" of memory that are installed into the motherboard. This is known as *dynamic random-access memory (DRAM)*, or main memory, and often comes in capacities of 4, 8, 16, or 32 GB—or more. This type of RAM has its own speed and must be compatible with the motherboard's RAM slots. It's not the only type of RAM, but it's the type you should be most concerned with for the exam. For all practical purposes, the terms *stick*, *DIMM*, and *memory module* mean the same thing: They refer to the RAM installed in a motherboard's RAM slots.

The most important concept in this chapter is *compatibility*. There are a lot of RAM technologies to know, and you always need to determine whether a particular technology will be compatible with your motherboard. The best way to find out is to go to the RAM manufacturer's website and search for your motherboard, which should list the matching RAM.

Let's discuss the types of RAM you should know.

RAM Types

There are many types of RAM, but for the exam you need to know about two types: *desktop RAM* and *laptop RAM*. Generally, desktops use dual-inline memory modules (DIMMs), and laptops use small-outline DIMMs (SODIMMs). We discuss SODIMM types and installation in Chapter 1, "Laptop Hardware Components."

Both DIMMs and SODIMMs use RAM that is based on Double Data Rate (DDR) technology. DDR originally got its name because it doubles the data per cycle compared to older types of RAM. A typical data transfer rate for DDR version 1 was 1600 MB/s. This is not nearly enough for today's computers, so let's skip over DDR and DDR2 and move on to more common versions of RAM, including DDR3, DDR4, and DDR5.

DDR3

DDR3 was designed for lower power consumption and higher reliability while enabling higher levels of performance compared to older versions of DDR. DDR3 has 240 pins and common voltages of 1.2 or 1.5 V.

Figure 14.1 shows a typical DDR3-1333 memory module, which is also known as PC3-10600. That means that it can perform 1333 megatransfers per second (MT/s) and has a total data transfer rate of 10,600 MB/s. All the numbers you need to know are in the names!

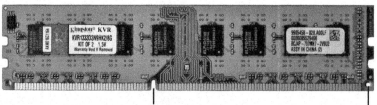

Orientation Notch   Locking Tab Notch

FIGURE 14.1   **A 240-pin PC3-10600 4-GB DIMM (DDR3-1333)**

The DDR3 module in Figure 14.1 has a sticker on the left that shows an identification code. You might not be able to read it, but it says KVR1333D3N9HK2/8G and Kit of 2, 1.5 V. The 1333 and D3 in the code tell you that this is DDR3-1333 RAM. The 8G tells you the capacity (8 GB) but only when installed as a kit of two memory modules—as the label goes on to say. Finally, it tells you that the memory runs at 1.5 volts.

Leave the sticker on the memory module. This way, the warranty will not be voided, and you can find out important characteristics of the RAM later. Often you will come across sticks of RAM just lying about, and you might not remember what they are without the code on the sticker, which tells you everything you need to know.

DDR4

At 1.2 to 1.35 V, DDR4 has a lower voltage range than most DDR3. It also has a higher module density and a higher data transfer rate. As is the case with all versions of DDR, it is not backward compatible. This type of RAM has 288 pins and has a different physical configuration than DDR3. Table 14.1 compares some typical DDR4 types, and Figure 14.2 shows an example of DDR4.

TABLE 14.1 **Comparison of DDR4 Types**

DDR4 Standard	Transfers per Second	Maximum Transfer Rate	Module Name
DDR4-2133	2133 MT/s	17,066 MB/s	PC4-17000
DDR4-2400	2400 MT/s	19,200 MB/s	PC4-19200
DDR4-2666	2666 MT/s	21,333 MB/s	PC4-21333
DDR4-3200	3200 MT/s	25,600 MB/s	PC4-25600

Note

The standards listed in Table 14.1 are based on the JEDEC standards (www.jedec.org). JEDEC develops various open standards for the microelectronics industry.

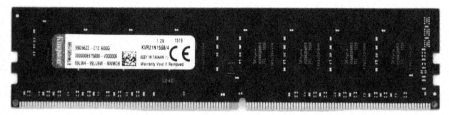

FIGURE 14.2   A 288-pin PC4-17000 4-GB DIMM (DDR4-2133)

As you have probably guessed, the RAM in Figure 14.2 can perform 2133
MT/s and has a maximum data transfer rate of 17,066 MB/s. I actually used
the memory module in Figure 14.2 within my *AV-Editor* computer. (That's the
name of the audio/video workstation I built to help describe and show A+
concepts in this book.) Or, more accurately, I used four of them in a quad-
channel configuration that we will speak of more later. Note how both connectors are slightly angled. This and the number of pins (among other things)
make it incompatible with DDR3 slots.

> **ExamAlert**
>
> Be able to identify a 288-pin DDR4 module.

DDR5

As of the writing of this book, DDR5 is the latest of the DDR standards. It was
released in 2020, and modules began arriving to the consumer market in 2021.
The voltage for standard DDR5 memory modules is 1.1 V, so it uses less power
than DDR4. Like DDR4, it has 288 pins, but there are physical differences, so
it is *not* backward compatible with DDR4. One of those physical differences is
that the module stack measures 1.0 mm—slightly smaller than DDR4's 1.2 mm.
The maximum density of a DDR5 module is 64 GB, compared to DDR4's
16 GB.

A typical speed for DDR5 is 4800 MT/s (also simply referred to as 4800 MHz).
At that speed, that RAM can transfer a maximum of 38,400 MB/s. Another
typical speed is 6400 MT/s, which can transfer a maximum of 51,200 MB/s
(or 51.2 GB/s). As with previous versions of DDR, the goals for DDR5 are to
reduce power consumption and increase bandwidth so that it can ultimately
work faster and more efficiently.

ExamAlert

Remember: DDR3 is 240-pin; DDR4 and DDR5 are 288-pin—and *none* of them are compatible with each other!

Note

Some mobile devices use *low-power* versions of DDR (known as LPDDR3, LPDDR4, and LPDDR5).

Installing RAM

Installing DRAM is fun and easy. It can be broken down into these basic steps:

1. Orient the RAM properly.

2. Insert the RAM into the slot.

3. Press down with both thumbs until the ears lock.

4. Test.

Easy! But let's take it a little further. Remember that some people refer to memory modules as DIMMs, DRAM, RAM sticks, or just plain RAM, and you could encounter any of these terms on the exam as well. Once you have selected the correct memory module for your motherboard and employed ESD prevention (by using an antistatic strap), you can install the RAM.

Be careful with the RAM and the RAM slot! They are both delicate! Hold the RAM by the edges and do not touch any pins or other circuitry on the memory module. If you need to put it down, put it down on an antistatic mat or in the container it shipped in.

Take a look at the slot; there should be a break in the slot somewhere near the middle (but not in the exact middle). This is where the notch in the memory module will go. Gently place the memory module in the slot, pins down. If the notch does not line up with the break in the slot, you might need to turn the module around. When it appears that the RAM is oriented correctly, press down with both thumbs on the top of the memory module. Keep your thumbs as close to the edge as you can so that you can distribute even pressure to the memory module. Press down with both thumbs at the same time until the tab (or tabs) on the edge of the RAM slot closes and locks on to the memory module. You should hear a click or two when it is done. You might need a bit of force to fully insert the RAM—but don't go overboard! If the motherboard is bending excessively, you are using too much force. If this is the case, make sure that the RAM is oriented correctly; the notches should match up, and the RAM should be straight within the slot. Figure 14.3 shows a bank of DDR4 memory modules installed into the gray DIMM slots in a quad-channel configuration. Each of these is 4 GB, giving a total of 16 GB of RAM.

Channel A, DIMM A1   Channel B, DIMM B1

Channel D, DIMM D1   Channel C, DIMM C1

FIGURE 14.3   Installed bank of DDR4 memory modules

Now, the most important thing to do with any installation is to *test*. With the case still open, boot the computer, access the BIOS/UEFI, and make sure that the system recognizes the new RAM as the right type and speed. The amount is often on the main page, but you might need to look deeper for the exact configuration, depending on the motherboard. Next, access the operating system (after the OS is installed) and make sure it boots correctly. Complete several full cycles and warm boots. Also, at some point, you should view the RAM within the operating system. For example, in Windows, use the System Window or the Task Manager to verify that the operating system sees the correct capacity of RAM:

▶ **System Window:** Go to **Settings > System > About**, or **Control Panel > All Control Panel Items > System**. The total RAM should be listed within this window.

▶ **Task Manager:** You can view the Task Manager by right-clicking on **Start** or on the taskbar and selecting **Task Manager**. There are several other ways to open this. I like this one: Press Windows+R to bring up the Run prompt and type **taskmgr**. When it is open, go to the Performance tab and view the Memory section. It should show the total physical memory as well as the memory that is in use. Figure 14.4 shows a computer running Windows 10 Pro, displaying 32 GB of RAM in the Task Manager or, more accurately, 31.9 GB, as circled toward the upper left of the figure. The in-use amount is 6.1 GB.

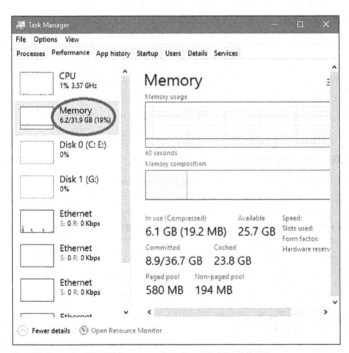

FIGURE 14.4 **Task Manager showing 32 GB of RAM**

> **Note**
>
> There are plenty of good third-party tools for analyzing RAM as well, such as CPU-Z.

Another good test of RAM is to make sure you can open several applications at once without any issues or delays. Finally, if everything looks okay, close up the case, and if all went well, congratulate yourself on another job well done!

> **ExamAlert**
>
> Know how to select, install, and verify RAM.

There are a couple of other important things to mention here.

First, if you were for some reason to install two different speeds of RAM, the system would most likely run at the lower of the two speeds. This is an example of *underclocking*, and it means you won't get the most out of the computer. However, a mismatch like this could also cause the system to fail because some motherboards insist that the modules be identical.

Second, if you install the very latest type of RAM that is supposed to be compatible with a motherboard, be prepared to update the BIOS/UEFI so that the system can recognize the new RAM. The firmware update (also known as a "flash") is one of the most important jobs a PC technician will perform.

A Final Word About Installing RAM

The main thing to remember when working with RAM is that it needs to be compatible with the motherboard. Check your motherboard's documentation regarding capacity per slot (or channel), channel/slot configuration, maximum capacity, and speed. The best thing to do is to run a search on your particular motherboard at the RAM manufacturer's website to obtain a complete list of compatible RAM and then cross-reference that with your motherboard's manual.

RAM Technologies

Once you have chosen the type of RAM to use, you must then decide on more technical details, such as the configuration of channels, which will be dictated in part by the motherboard. Your particular solution might also require the use of error correction memory, which is less common for desktop PCs and laptops but might be necessary for more customized computers. Let's begin with memory channels.

Single-Channel vs. Multichannel Architectures

Single-channel is the original RAM architecture for PCs. It means that there is a 64-bit address bus (or data channel) between the memory and the memory controller (usually within the CPU). One or more sticks of RAM can be installed into the motherboard, but they share the same channel.

Dual-channel is a technology that essentially doubles the data throughput. Two separate 64-bit channels are employed together, resulting in a 128-bit bus. To incorporate this, the proper motherboard has color-coded matching banks divided into Channel A and Channel B. Triple-channel architecture accesses three memory modules at the same time and is, in effect, a 192-bit bus.

Quadruple-channel (or simply quad-channel) architecture takes this idea to the next level. It works only when four identical memory modules are placed in the correct slots. Quad-channel is common in computers that use DDR4 or higher. Four 64-bit-wide buses work together, and a module of RAM must be installed in each of the four banks for best results. If only three modules are installed (thus only three banks are used), the architecture downgrades to triple-channel automatically. Likewise, if only two are used, the motherboard scales back to dual-channel architecture. However, in some cases, the reduction in performance is negligible.

Figure 14.5 shows an example of a motherboard's RAM slots making use of quad-channel technology. As you can see in the figure, there are four banks, each with two slots (one of which is black and one of which is gray). By installing a memory module into each of the gray slots (known as A1, B1, C1, and D1), you can harness the collective power of the quad-channel technology.

This is the configuration used in the AV-Editor computer. Of course, you can add another four memory modules if you wish (in the black slots). The ASUS motherboard used in this computer can handle 64 GB of RAM total.

Channel B, DIMM B1 and B2

Channel A, DIMM A1 and A2

Channel C, DIMM C2 and C1

Channel D, DIMM D2 and D1

FIGURE 14.5   **A motherboard with quad-channel-capable RAM slots**

ExamAlert

Know the difference between single-, dual-, triple-, and quad-channel for the exam.

ECC vs. Non-ECC

Error correction code (ECC) in RAM can detect and correct errors. Real-time applications might use ECC RAM. When using ECC, additional information needs to be stored, and more resources are used in general. This RAM is the

slowest and most expensive of RAM types. DDR ECC modules are identified with either the letter E or ECC (for example, PC3-10600E). DDR5 has
another advantage: on-die ECC. This provides further protection against
single-bit errors in DDR5 memory modules. For every 128 bits of data, DDR5
stores an additional 8 bits for ECC. If ECC is enabled, whenever data is read,
the actual data and the ECC data are read together, and so DDR5 can repair
single-bit errors on any data bits right away.

> **ExamAlert**
>
> Know that ECC RAM can prevent data loss and potential system crashes by auto-
> matically correcting memory errors.

Virtual RAM

Virtual RAM is a term that can be applied to several technologies. Two examples
include Windows virtual memory and virtual RAM, as it is configured on a smartphone. Both of these address the problem of limited RAM by using other, long-term
storage in the place of RAM—this becomes *virtual RAM*.

In Windows, virtual memory is space used to emulate RAM on a storage drive of
some sort: hard disk drive, solid-state drive, flash drive, and so on. It's also known
as a paging file. Let's say you are working on a laptop that has only 2 GB of RAM.
That amount might not be enough for today's applications and processes. When the
memory in use by all the existing processes in Windows goes beyond the amount of
physical RAM that is installed, Windows moves pages of information to the storage
drive. The beauty of this is that a typical PC or laptop now has virtually unlimited
storage. The drawback is that the virtual storage space will be much slower than
physical RAM.

The Windows utility for virtual memory can be accessed in the Performance
section of the System Properties window. To get there quickly, type **systemproper-
tiesadvanced** (all one word) at the Run prompt or in the Search tool. Then, under
Performance, click the **Settings** button. The Performance Options window appears.
Click the **Advanced** tab, and then, in the Virtual Memory section, click **Change**.
From there, you can modify how Windows uses virtual memory. We'll discuss this
more in the 220-1102 portion of the book.

On a different note, virtual RAM is a feature in some smartphones that allows a
system (such as Android) to run more applications in memory than the actual RAM
would normally allow. It does this by using the device's regular long-term storage as
additional RAM storage space. This is similar to Windows virtual memory.

For example, say that you have an Android-based smartphone with 4 GB of physical
RAM and 64 GB of long-term storage. Let's also say that you run a lot of resource-
hungry apps. The system can be configured to use a certain amount of the

long-term storage to act as additional RAM. For example, perhaps it was configured as 8 GB. That would mean you now have 4 GB of actual RAM, plus the ability to run 8 GB of additional applications. However, that will reduce the total amount of long-term storage that you can use for pictures, videos, and so on from 64 GB to 56 GB.

Remember that 8 GB isn't *actual* RAM; it's *virtual* RAM! The long-term storage (typically flash memory) used as virtual RAM will be much slower than actual RAM. So, Android will prioritize the applications that are running. More demanding applications such as video players and games will get a higher level of importance and will be the first applications to use actual RAM. Less demanding, and lesser used, applications (such as a calculator or note-taking program) will get a lower priority, and as the RAM fills up, those applications may be moved to virtual RAM.

In the past, this was a technique that could only be done if you "rooted" the phone (which is not recommended). However, today it is becoming more commonplace as a feature of the OS or through the use of special virtual RAM apps.

Cram Quiz

Answer these questions. The answers follow the last question. If you cannot answer these questions correctly, consider reading this chapter again until you can.

1. What is the transfer rate of DDR4-2133?

   ○ **A.** 17,066 MB/s

   ○ **B.** 19,200 MB/s

   ○ **C.** 21,333 MB/s

   ○ **D.** 25,600 MB/s

2. A technician attempts to install a DDR5 module into a motherboard, but it doesn't appear to fit. Which of the following are possible reasons for this? (Select the two best answers.)

   ○ **A.** The motherboard doesn't allow DDR5 memory.

   ○ **B.** Windows doesn't allow DDR5 memory.

   ○ **C.** The RAM stick is being installed backward.

   ○ **D.** The BIOS/UEFI hasn't been updated.

3. Which of the following technologies allows for a 256-bit-wide bus?

   ○ **A.** ECC

   ○ **B.** Quad-channel

   ○ **C.** Virtual RAM

   ○ **D.** Task Manager

4. A technician has just installed additional RAM into a Windows-based graphics-intensive workstation to meet software application requirements. What should the technician do next to ensure that the correct amount of RAM is installed and that it is working properly? (Select the two best answers.)

    ○ **A.** Increase the size of the paging file.

    ○ **B.** Test the RAM.

    ○ **C.** Go to Settings > System > About.

    ○ **D.** Press down with both thumbs until the ears lock.

5. A technician has installed dual-inline memory modules that each have 288-pins and use 1.1 V. What kind of RAM has the tech installed?

    ○ **A.** DDR4 DIMMs

    ○ **B.** DDR3 DIMMs

    ○ **C.** DDR4 SODIMMs

    ○ **D.** DDR5 DIMMs

Cram Quiz Answers

1. **A.** The transfer rate of DDR4-2133 is 17,066 MB/s. It is also known as PC4-17000. 19,200 MB/s is the speed of DDR4-2400 (PC4-19200). 21,333 MB/s is the speed of DDR4-2666 (PC4-21333). 25,600 MB/s is the speed of DDR4-3200 (PC4-25600).

2. **A and C.** It is possible that the technician is attempting to install DDR5 RAM into a motherboard that only accepts DDR4. Remember, DDR memory is not backward compatible, so you can't install DDR5 to a DDR4-based motherboard and vice versa. It's also possible that the RAM module simply needs to be turned around; always line up the notch on the RAM with the break in the RAM slot. A physical problem with the RAM wouldn't be caused by the operating system or the BIOS/UEFI.

3. **B.** The quad-channel memory architecture can allow for a 256-bit-wide bus (64-bit per channel). However, this will only be the case if all four channels have memory installed to them. ECC, which stands for error correction code, can detect and correct errors in RAM. Virtual RAM is used in smartphones to "extend" the amount of usable RAM to the phone's long-term storage. (It is known as virtual memory in Windows.) The Task Manager is a Windows program that is used to analyze the system.

4. **B and C.** The most important thing to do after installation is to test the RAM. Access the BIOS/UEFI and make sure the system recognizes the new RAM as the right type and speed. Next, view the RAM within the operating system. For example, in Windows, use the System window: Go to **Settings > System > About**. Virtual RAM or virtual memory, also known as the paging file, uses part of the storage drive to expand physical RAM. Pressing down with both thumbs is part of the installation process that, according to the scenario, has already been performed.

5. **D.** DDR5 dual-inline memory modules (DIMMs) have 288 pins and operate at 1.1 volts (V). Although DDR4 modules do have 288 pins, the architecture is different, and the voltage ranges between 1.2 and 1.35 V. DDR3 has 240 pins and common voltages of 1.2 or 1.5 V. Laptops use small-outline dual-inline memory modules (SODIMMs). Two common types of SODIMMs in laptops are DDR3 (which has 204 pins) and DDR4 (which has 260 pins).

Another chapter done. Fancy that! You are doing fantastic!

CHAPTER 15

Storage Drives

This chapter covers the following A+ 220-1101 exam objective:

▶ **3.3** – Given a scenario, select and install storage devices.

Everyone needs a place to store data. Whether it's business documents, audio/video files, or data backups, users must decide on the right storage medium. This can be solid-state media, magnetic media, or optical media. Devices include hard disk drives, solid-state drives, optical drives, and flash-based drives, among others. The media used depends on what is stored and how often and where it is needed. This chapter concentrates on the categories of media and how to identify, install, and troubleshoot them.

The two main types of internal storage drives are solid-state (which contains no disk) and magnetic (hard disk drive). These are the most common options for the location of the operating system. However, users also store frequently accessed data, such as documents, music, pictures, and so on. These could be stored on any of the media types mentioned so far. We'll discuss all of these media types in more depth, but first, let's take a look at a common standard for storage—SATA.

SATA

Serial AT Attachment (also known as Serial ATA, or just SATA) is a serial bus communication interface used to move data to and from storage drives. To transmit that data, the drive has a 7-pin data port, as shown in Figure 15.1. You use a SATA cable to connect that port to the motherboard or SATA adapter card of the computer.

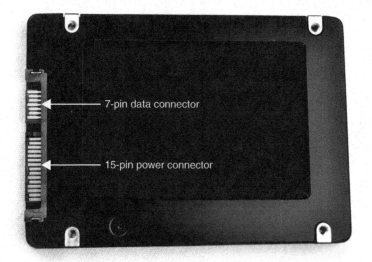

7-pin data connector

15-pin power connector

FIGURE 15.1 **SATA data and power connectors on a 2.5-inch SSD**

For power, a SATA drive utilizes a 15-pin power connector, as shown in Figure 15.1. The drive's connectors have vertical tabs in the center, making for easier orientation when connecting the cables. Power supplies send 3.3 V, 5 V, and 12 V to the SATA drive.

SATA technology is used by magnetic hard drives and solid-state drives. What has been described so far is SATA Revision 3.0. However, there is also SATA

Revision 3.2. It is less common than 3.0 and requires either a SATA Express port or an M.2 slot to operate. SATA Express ports are like triple connectors with 18 pins (7 pins + 7 pins + 4 pins). SATA Express isn't very common. Many people, including technicians, prefer other technologies over it, such as NVMe-based M.2 cards, which we'll discuss in a little bit. Table 15.1 shows these two SATA revisions.

TABLE 15.1 **Comparison of SATA 3.0 and 3.2**

Standard	Maximum Data	Transfer Rate
SATA Revision 3.0	6 Gb/s	600 MB/s
SATA Revision 3.2	16 Gb/s	1969 MB/s

ExamAlert

Know the maximum data transfer rates for SATA Revisions 3.0 and 3.2.

Note

You might also see some organizations refer to SATA measurements using the units Gbit/s or Gbps, instead of Gb/s, but they mean the same thing.

Note

Also listed in the objectives is mSATA (which is short for Mini-SATA). This is a type of connector that was used in laptops for SSDs. An mSATA drive has a single notch, as opposed to two notches on laptop-based M.2 devices that use the 2242 form factor. M.2, by the way, supersedes the mSATA specification.

Data Transfer Discrepancy

If you divided by 8 to determine rates for SATA Revision 3.0, the actual data written to the drive would be less than you would expect. This is due to overhead in the form of encoding. That brings Revision 3.0 down from 6.0 to 4.8 Gb/s (which equates to 600 MB/s). SATA 3.2 is not affected by this.

Magnetic Hard Drives

Magnetic hard drives, or *hard disk drives (HDDs)*, are the most common form of magnetic media. A hard disk drive contains one or more platters with a magnetic surface. As the platters rotate at high speed, read/write heads store and read information to and from the disk.

HDDs come in two main widths: 3.5 inch and 2.5 inch. 3.5-inch drives are used in desktop computers, network-attached storage (NAS), and other larger devices. 2.5-inch drives are used in laptops and other smaller devices. Generally, HDDs use the SATA communications interface. They are typically sold with data storage capacities of 500 GB, 1 TB, 2 TB, 4 TB, and beyond.

> **Note**
>
> A typical operating system such as Windows displays a 500 GB drive as having a capacity of 476 GB (or 465 GB or a similar number). This is due to a difference in numbering systems used to measure the drive. A hard drive manufacturer uses the base 10 system, whereas Windows uses the base 2 system, resulting in a slightly lower number. No actual space is lost during this conversion!
>
> I describe this phenomenon further at my website: https://dprocomputer.com/?p=1239.

HDDs are still somewhat common because they have been available for a long time and are generally cheaper than solid-state drives. However, there are a couple of things that set them apart, such as these specifications:

▶ **Rotational speed:** The platters in an HDD rotate at a certain speed. For example, 7200 revolutions per minute (RPM) is common; other typical speeds for hard drives include 5400 RPM (slower access time) and 10,000 RPM and 15,000 RPM (faster access times).

▶ **Latency:** Latency is the delay in time after a track has been reached by the read head and before a particular sector on the platter can be read. It is directly related to rotational speed and is usually half the time it takes for the disk to rotate once. For example, a 7200-RPM drive has an average latency of 4.2 ms (milliseconds), but a 10,000-RPM drive has an average latency of 3.0 ms.

Though you may still encounter HDDs, there are faster and more efficient technologies. Enter the SSD.

Solid-State Drives

A *solid-state drive (SSD)* is used to store operating systems and files, similar to a magnetic hard disk drive. However, SSDs don't use spinning disks or read/write heads; they instead write data to non-volatile microchips. Because of this, they are silent and more resistant to physical shock, and they have lower access time and less latency than magnetic hard drives. Because there are no moving parts, rotation speed is not an issue.

SATA-based SSDs normally measure 2.5 inches in width. Installation requires either a 2.5-inch internal bay, special screw holes drilled directly into the computer case, or an adapter kit for installation in a 3.5-inch internal bay.

However, there are other types of SSDs, such as the M.2-based SSD. These are small form factor cards that are installed directly into a motherboard or to an adapter card if the motherboard doesn't have an M.2 slot. Either way, the M.2 card is installed at a slight angle and then pressed flat against the board and screwed in. There are a variety of different M.2 card sizes. A common example is 2280, which means it is 22 mm wide by 80 mm long. M.2 cards are known to offer several times the data transfer rate of a typical 2.5-inch SATA 3.0 SSD. While the M.2 slot can be used with different types of technologies, the most common and fastest (as of the writing of this book) is Non-Volatile Memory Express (NVMe), which is a specification for accessing storage while using PCI Express. Essentially, the M.2 slot on a motherboard taps into the PCI Express bus (x4) and uses a portion of the total bandwidth associated with that bus. This usually results in the loss of one PCI Express version 3 slot, and depending on the type of CPU and motherboard, it could also mean a battle for bandwidth between the video card and the M.2 card (and possibly other devices). In addition, NVMe-based M.2 cards tend to run hot. So, careful planning is required before installing an M.2 card. There are also PCIe drives that exist as cards that you can plug directly into a PCIe slot. We'll discuss the PCI Express bus in more detail in Chapter 16, "Motherboards and Add-on Cards."

> **Note**
>
> I have an in-depth video/article on my website that demonstrates the installation of an NVMe M.2 SSD drive: https://dprocomputer.com/?p=2112. It also shows a slot-based PCIe drive being replaced with an M.2 drive.

> **Note**
>
> SSD technology can be combined with magnetic disk technology to form what is known as a hybrid drive. This could be accomplished in a drive that incorporates NAND flash memory (for caching of data and speed) and a magnetic disk (for increased capacity). There are also M.2-based caching cards that can be used in combination with a magnetic disk to increase performance.

Storage Drives Can Be a Bottleneck in a System

I often say that your computer is only as fast as its weakest link. A weak component can slow down your entire system, acting as a bottleneck when it comes to processing data, opening and running programs, and saving and rendering information. This can ultimately lead to decreased performance of the entire system. So, pay careful attention to the selection of storage drives when building or upgrading computers. If funds allow, make sure that you are taking full advantage of your system's capabilities.

RAID

Redundant array of independent (or inexpensive) disks (RAID) technologies are designed to either increase the speed of reading and writing data or to create one of several types of fault-tolerant volumes—or both. Fault tolerance is the capability of a storage drive system to continue working after there is a problem with one of the drives.

To create a RAID array, you need two or more drives. Then, you need to set up the array through either software or hardware. Some operating systems support the software option, but it is not usually recommended. Hardware-based RAID is more common, and it involves one of three things: either using the motherboard's built-in RAID support, if present; using a RAID adapter card; or using an external device such as network-attached storage (NAS) that has RAID capability.

The exam requires you to know RAID levels 0, 1, 5, and 10. Table 15.2 describes them.

TABLE 15.2 **RAID 0, 1, 5, and 10**

RAID Level	Description	Fault Tolerant?	Minimum Number of Disks
RAID 0	Striping. Data is striped across multiple disks in an effort to increase performance.	No	2

RAID Level	Description	Fault Tolerant?	Minimum Number of Disks
RAID 1	Mirroring. Data is copied to two identical disks. If one disk fails, the other continues to operate. When each disk is connected to a separate controller, this is known as disk duplexing. See Figure 15.2 for an illustration.	Yes	2 (and 2 only)
RAID 5	Striping with parity. Data is striped across multiple disks; the fault-tolerant parity data is also written to each disk. If one disk fails, the array can reconstruct the data from the parity information. See Figure 15.3 for an illustration.	Yes	3
RAID 10	Combines the advantages of RAID 1 and RAID 0. Requires a minimum of four or more disks. The system contains at least two mirrored disks that are then striped. Also known as "stripe of mirrors."	Yes	4

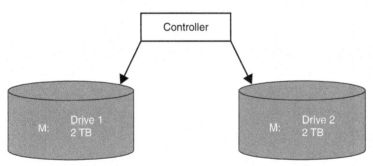

FIGURE 15.2 **RAID 1 example**

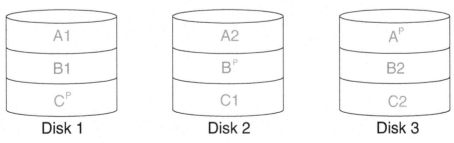

FIGURE 15.3 **RAID 5 example**

Figure 15.2 shows an illustration of RAID 1 (mirroring). You can see that data is written to both disks and that both disks collectively are known as the M: drive or M: volume. So, even though there are two 2 TB drives, this volume has a total capacity of only 2 TB.

Figure 15.3 shows an illustration of RAID 5 (striping with parity). In a RAID 5 array, blocks of data are distributed to the disks—A1 and A2 are a block, B1 and B2 are a block, and so on—and parity information is written for each block of data. It is written to each disk in an alternating fashion (Ap, Bp, and such) so that the parity is also distributed. If one disk fails, the parity information from the other disks will reconstruct the data. Some organizations prefer RAID 6, which requires four drives minimum and writes two sets of parity. This can work well for larger arrays—that is, arrays with more drives. In larger environments, *hot-swappable* capability is a must; this means drives can be removed and inserted while the system is on.

Figure 15.4 illustrates RAID 1+0 (pronounced RAID one plus zero), which is commonly known as RAID 10. RAID 10 is a type of nested, or hybrid, RAID that combines RAID 1 and RAID 0. In RAID 10, there are two or more mirrored drives that are then striped. The figure shows a RAID 1 mirror consisting of two drives: disk 0 and disk 1. Then, there is a second RAID 1 mirror with two more drives: disk 2 and disk 3. The two RAID 1 mirrors are then striped as RAID 0. Together, it becomes RAID 10. This makes for a more powerful version of mirroring that can use more drives.

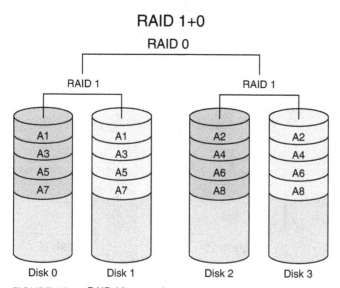

FIGURE 15.4 **RAID 10 example**

Remember that drive arrays should be built using identical drives. This means using a group of the same magnetic disk drives or a group of the same solid-state drives. Deviate from this suggestion at your own risk!

RAID can provide a type of fault tolerance. It is important to make the distinction between fault tolerance and backup. *Fault tolerance* means that the drives can continue to function (with little or no downtime) even if there is a problem with one of the drives; for example, RAID 1 and RAID 5 provide fault tolerance. *Backup* means copying the data (and possibly compressing it) to another location for archival in the event of a disaster. An example of a disaster would be if two drives in a RAID 5 array were to fail. Keep in mind that RAID 0 is *not* fault tolerant. It harnesses the power of multiple drives but cannot recover after a single drive failure.

> **ExamAlert**
>
> Know the differences between the various types of RAID: RAID 0 (striping), RAID 1 (mirroring), RAID 5 (striping with parity), and RAID 10 (stripe of mirrors).

Flash

Flash memory is used in all kinds of solid-state technologies. Most of these technologies use NAND-based flash memory. In this section, we'll focus on removable storage in the form of USB flash drives and Secure Digital cards.

USB Flash Drives

The USB flash drive is probably the most familiar of all flash media. Also known as USB thumb drives, these drives are often retractable and can be carried on a keychain.

When you plug in a USB flash drive on a Windows system, the drive shows up as a volume within File Explorer. Connecting the drive is easy: Just find an open USB port. But remember that you should eject the flash drive in the operating system before disconnecting the drive physically. Failing to do so can cause electrical irregularities that can damage the data on the drive. In Windows, right-click the **Safely Remove Hardware and Eject Media** icon in the notification area and then click **Eject** to shut down power to the selected USB device. Then you can safely remove it from the physical USB port. The icon appears as a USB cable connector with a check mark. If your USB device has a light, make sure that light is off before physically removing the device. You can also "eject" optical drives and virtual drives in this manner.

> **ExamAlert**
>
> Remember to *safely remove* USB flash drives in the operating system before physically disconnecting them.

> **Tip**
>
> Sometimes a USB or other flash-based solid-state device can't be removed with the Safely Remove Hardware option in Windows. If this happens, consider shutting down the computer before physically disconnecting the device to avoid data corruption or loss.

The advantages of a USB flash drive are obvious: quick and efficient moving of data—and a lot of data at that. However, such a drive is not meant for long-term storage in the way that a magnetic or solid-state drive is; it is meant for transferring data from one system to another. It can also be used to boot systems for installation purposes or for troubleshooting.

Let's talk about the type of memory used in this solid-state device. NAND flash memory is the core of a USB flash drive. This memory is divided into blocks that are generally between 16 KB and 512 KB. A USB flash drive's blocks can be written to only so many times before failures occur. With some flash drives, manufacturers estimate this limit is 1 million write/erase cycles, or 10 years of use. However, just as storage drives will never attain their maximum data transfer rate, it is doubtful that a flash drive will ever attain that maximum number of write/erase cycles. In addition, the number of years is subjective; it all depends on how often a user works with the flash drive. Basically, if you take the number given by the manufacturer and cut it in half, you should be in good shape, unless you are an extreme power user.

Now back to NAND flash failures: Because this type of memory incurs a small number of faults over time (as opposed to NOR flash, which should remain free of faults), a method known as Bad Block Management is implemented. Bad Block Management maintains a table of the faulty blocks within the USB flash device, making sure not to save data to those blocks. Blocks are divided into pages, which can be between 512 bytes and 4 KB. Each page has error detection and correction information associated with it. All this is done to prolong the life span of devices that use NAND memory.

Normally, USB flash drives are shipped in a formatted state (for example, FAT32). This enables the drive to be accessed by just about any computer on the market and makes for easy repair of corrupted files with Windows utilities. If the user so chooses, these drives can also be formatted as NTFS or other file systems, which may be necessary to interface with certain systems or perform particular installations. Sometimes NAND flash devices (such as USB flash drives) act up intermittently. Unless a device has failed completely, a quick reformat usually cures the flash drive of its woes. Just be sure to back up your data first! This method applies to other forms of solid-state, NAND-based media as well. After reformatting, test the drive by moving files to it and then opening them. Of course, after a certain point, the drive will fail and will need to be replaced. Periodically check USB flash drives for stability.

Some USB flash drives are preloaded with software that can restore data and possibly secure transferred data.

One problem with USB flash drives is that although they are small, they can't fit inside most digital cameras, smartphones, and other handheld devices. For that, you need something even smaller. Enter the SD card.

Secure Digital Cards

SD cards, for the most part, are technically the same type of device as a USB flash drive. They are solid-state drives, they use NAND memory, and they have most of the same pros and cons as a USB flash drive. However, SD technology can write and transfer data much faster. The other main difference is the form factor of the SD device; because of this, SDs are used differently. Instead of connecting an SD card to a USB port of a computer, you slide it into a memory card reader. As with USB flash drives, be sure to use the **Safely Remove Hardware and Eject Media** icon in Windows before physically removing an SD card. There are three sizes of SD cards, each smaller than the last: standard (32 mm × 24 mm), miniSD (21.5 mm × 20 mm), and microSD (15 mm × 11 mm). You can still find many standard-sized SD cards used in cameras and some other devices but note that most cell phones and smartphones use microSD cards for additional memory. Figure 15.5 shows a full-size SD card and a microSD card.

Write-Protect Tab

FIGURE 15.5 **A typical microSD card (left) and a standard SD card (right)**

Standard SD cards have capacities up to 4 GB. High-capacity (SDHC) cards range up to 32 GB. eXtended Capacity (SDXC) has a maximum capacity of 2 TB and supports up to 90 MB/s. Secure Digital Ultra Capacity (SDUC) supports up to 128 TB and 985 MB/s data transfer over the SD Express bus.

When it comes to data transfer rate, SD cards are divided into a variety of classes: SD 2, 4, 6, and 10 as well as UHS 1 through 3 and SD Express bus, each with a different range of speeds. For example, Class 10, required for Full HD video recording (1080p), has a minimum data writing speed of 10 MB/s. To record 4K video, you would need at least UHS 3, which has a minimum data writing speed of 30 MB/s. To simplify things a bit, SD cards are labeled with a video speed class rating. For example, V30 means that the card can write 30 MB/s minimum. Today's SD cards will often display their maximum transfer rate as well.

Optical Drives

The three main types of optical media in use today are compact discs (CDs), digital versatile discs (DVDs), and Blu-ray discs. These discs have a variety of functions, including audio, video, applications, data, and so on. Some discs can be read from, some can also be written to, and some can be rewritten to as well. It all depends on which media you use. Optical drives are usually 5.25 inches wide and use the SATA communications interface. With the advent of broadband Internet and USB flash drives, optical drives are not used nearly as much as they used to be, but they are available as internal drives or external add-ons. Let's briefly look at some of the optical media options.

▶ **Compact disc (CD):** A CD is a flat, round optical disc used to store music, sounds, or other data. Some computers use compact disc-read-only memory (CD-ROM) drives. A typical CD-ROM drive speed is 48x. The x equals 150 KB/s. So, to calculate a CD-ROM drive's maximum read speed, you multiply the number preceding the x by 150 KB. In this example, this would be 48 × 150 KB = 7.2 MB/s. A typical CD can hold up to 700 MB of data. Most optical drives that you can purchase for a computer have all three compact disc functions: They can read from CD-ROMs, write to CD-Rs, and write/rewrite to CD-RWs. Usually, the read speed and CD-R speed are the same.

▶ **Digital versatile disc (DVD):** For data, digital versatile discs, also known as digital video discs, have a much greater capacity than CDs. This is because the pits etched into the surface of a DVD are smaller than CD pits (.74 micrometers compared to 1.6 micrometers). Also, DVDs can be written to faster than CDs. There are read-only DVDs and writable DVDs. One typical example of a DVD is the single-sided, single-layer (SS, SL) DVD-5 technology, which can store 4.7 GB of data. But some DVDs can be written to two sides (known as dual-sided, or DS); simply flip the DVD to access the information on the other side. By using a combination of sides and layering, the DVD-18 technology can store up to 17 GB of data. A typical DVD drive reads a disc at 16x. However, the x in DVD speeds is different than the x in CD-ROM speeds. For DVDs, the x means approximately 1.32 MB/s, or about nine times the core CD speed. So, a typical 16x DVD is equal to 21 MB/s.

▶ **Blu-ray:** Currently, Blu-ray is *the* optical standard for high-definition video. It is used for high-def movies, with console games, and for storing data (up to 50 GB per disc, which is 10 times the amount of a typical DVD-5 disc). The standard disc is 12 cm (the same size as a standard DVD or CD), and the mini-disc is 8 cm. A typical Blu-ray disc can store between 25 GB and 128 GB of data. Drive speeds range from 1x to 16x. 1x is equal to 36 Mb/s, or 4.5 MB/s. At 16x, the speed would be 16 times the core amount, which comes to 576 Mb/s, or 72 MB/s; this is superior to other optical drive write speeds. If you want to record data to a Blu-ray disc, you can use one of two methods of "burning": Blu-ray Disc Recordable (BD-R), which can write to a disc once, and Blu-ray Disc Recordable Erasable (BD-RE), which can be erased and re-recorded multiple times.

Burning speed depends on the drive, but generally, you will see a typical data transfer rate of 50 MB/s when writing data to a Blu-ray disc.

> **ExamAlert**
>
> If an optical disc gets jammed in an optical drive tray, use a paper clip! It can be inserted into the small hole next to the tray. Add one to your PC toolkit!

Cram Quiz

Answer these questions. The answers follow the last question. If you cannot answer these questions correctly, consider reading this chapter again until you can.

1. How much data can a SATA Revision 3.0 drive transfer per second?
   - ○ **A.** 50 MB/s
   - ○ **B.** 90 MB/s
   - ○ **C.** 1969 MB/s
   - ○ **D.** 6 Gb/s
   - ○ **E.** 16 Gb/s

2. Which level of RAID stripes data and parity across three or more disks?
   - ○ **A.** RAID 0
   - ○ **B.** RAID 1
   - ○ **C.** RAID 5
   - ○ **D.** Striping
   - ○ **E.** RAID 10

3. A customer complains that an important disc is stuck in the system's Blu-ray drive. What should you recommend to the customer?
   - ○ **A.** Get a screwdriver and disassemble the drive.
   - ○ **B.** Format the disc.
   - ○ **C.** Use a paper clip to eject the tray.
   - ○ **D.** Dispose of the drive and replace the media.

4. Which of the following best describes a specification for accessing storage while using PCI Express?
   - ○ **A.** NVMe
   - ○ **B.** 7200 RPM
   - ○ **C.** Hot-swappable
   - ○ **D.** 3.5-inch and 2.5-inch

Cram Quiz Answers

1. **D.** SATA Revision 3.0 drives can transfer 6 Gb/s, which, after encoding, amounts to 600 MB/s. SATA Revision 3.2 is 16 Gb/s (1969 MB/s) but requires SATA Express or M.2. 50 MB/s is a typical write speed for Blu-ray discs and some flash media. 90 MB/s is a typical write speed for an SD card.

2. **C.** RAID 5 stripes data and parity across three or more disks. RAID 0 does not stripe parity; it stripes data only and can use two disks or more. RAID 1 uses two disks only. Striping is another name for RAID 0. RAID 10 contains two sets of mirrored disks that are then striped.

3. **C.** Tell the customer to use a paper clip (or mobile device tray pin) to eject the Blu-ray tray. Disassembling the drive is not necessary; the customer shouldn't be told to do this. If the disc is rewritable, formatting it would erase the contents, even if you could format in this scenario. Never tell a customer to dispose of optical drives. They rarely fail; and if one did, it should be recycled.

4. **A.** Non-Volatile Memory Express (NVMe) is a specification for accessing storage while using PCI Express. Essentially, the M.2 slot on a motherboard taps into the PCI Express bus x4) and uses a portion of the total bandwidth associated with that bus. The platters in a hard disk drive (HDD) rotate at a certain speed. For example, 7200 RPM is common; other typical speeds include 5400 RPM and 10,000 RPM. Hot-swappable capability means drives can be removed and inserted while the system is on. SATA-based drives come in two main widths: 3.5-inch and 2.5-inch. 3.5-inch drives are used in desktop computers, network-attached storage, and other larger devices. 2.5-inch drives are used in laptops and other smaller devices.

Time for a break. You've been storing a lot of facts and figures in your brain—the ultimate storage device—but it needs to rest now and then. Go and do something fun, regroup, and then come back and rock on!

CHAPTER 16

Motherboards and Add-on Cards

> **This chapter covers a portion of the following A+ 220-1101 exam objective:**
>
> ▶ **3.4** – Given a scenario, install and configure motherboards, central processing units (CPUs), and add-on cards.
>
> Without a doubt, the motherboard is the foundation of a computer. Everything connects to the motherboard, and all data is transferred through this matrix of circuitry.
>
> Over the years, I have found that if a student is going to lack knowledge in one area, it's quite often going to be the motherboard. This is one of the key elements in a computer system. It's the starting point for a quick and efficient computer. Because it connects to everything in the computer system, you need to know many concepts concerning it. Let's get right into it.

> **Note**
>
> Objective 3.4 covers a *lot*. That's why I broke it into two chapters. This chapter covers motherboards and add-on cards. The next chapter covers CPUs.

> **ExamAlert**
>
> This portion of **Objective 3.4** concentrates on the following concepts: motherboard form factors and connector types; motherboard compatibility; BIOS/UEFI settings; encryption; and expansion cards.

Motherboard Form Factors and Connector Types

A computer form factor specifies the physical dimensions of some of the components of a computer system. It pertains mainly to the motherboard but also specifies compatibility with the computer case and power supply. The form factor defines the size and layout of components on the motherboard. It also specifies the power outputs from the power supply to the motherboard. The form factors you need to know for the exam are ATX and ITX. Let's discuss them now.

ATX

Advanced Technology eXtended (ATX) was originally designed by Intel in the mid-1990s to overcome the limitations of the now-deprecated AT form factor. It has been the standard ever since. The motherboard shown in Figure 16.1 is ATX. This is the board used in the *AV-Editor* computer I created, which is the main workstation I'm using to demonstrate A+ hardware concepts. Full-size ATX motherboards measure 12 inches × 9.6 inches (305 mm × 244 mm). An ATX motherboard has an integrated port cluster and normally ships with an I/O plate that snaps into the back of the case, filling the gaps between ports and keeping airflow to a minimum.

FIGURE 16.1   **ATX motherboard and its components**

One identifying characteristic of ATX is that the RAM slots and expansion bus slots are perpendicular to each other. The ATX specification calls for the power supply to produce +3.3 V, +5 V, +12 V, and –12 V outputs and a 5 V standby output. These are known as "rails" (for example, the +12 V rail). The original ATX specification calls for a 20-pin power connector (often referred to as P1); the newer (and much more common) ATX12V version 2.x specification calls for a 24-pin power connector. You can test these voltages with a power supply tester, which typically comes with a 24-pin input as well as other inputs for SATA power, PCI Express 6-pin and 8-pin, and Molex.

ExamAlert

Know the voltages supplied to an ATX motherboard by a power supply: +3.3 V, +5 V, +12 V, and –12 V outputs and +5 V standby output.

An ATX motherboard is attached to the computer case with several screws. Before you screw it in, though, attach the I/O plate to the back of the case and dry fit the motherboard to see where the screws will attach to the case. Apply rubber standoffs, if required. Then attach the accepting screws to the case wall according to where the motherboard screws will be placed; be sure that the motherboard will be properly supported. Angle the motherboard slightly so that the port cluster fits into the I/O plate. Then line up the screw holes and attach the screws. Finally, connect the CPU, RAM, power connections, adapter cards, fans, and anything else necessary!

microATX

microATX (or mATX) was introduced as a smaller version of ATX; these motherboards can be a maximum size of 9.6 inches × 9.6 inches (244 mm × 244 mm) but can be as small as 6.75 inches × 6.75 inches (171.45 mm × 171.45 mm). microATX boards are usually square, whereas full-size ATX boards are rectangular. microATX is backward compatible with ATX, meaning that most microATX boards can be installed within an ATX form factor case, and they use the same power connectors as ATX. Often, they have the same chipsets as ATX as well. microATX works well for desktop cases, small rackmount servers, and home theater PCs (HTPCs).

ITX

Information Technology eXtended (ITX) is a group of form factors developed by VIA Technologies, Inc. between 2001 and today for use in small, low-power motherboards. The ITX group includes several versions, each smaller than the last:

- **Mini-ITX (6.7 × 6.7 inch/170 × 170 mm):** Smaller than microATX, but screw-compatible with it. Normally comes with one PCIe slot. Good for HTPCs and other small footprint systems. Of all the ITX systems, this is one that you might see more often.

- **Nano-ITX (4.7 × 4.7 inch/120 × 120 mm):** Designed for DVRs, media centers, and automotive PCs.

- **Pico-ITX (3.9 × 2.8 inch/100 × 72 mm):** Used in industrial automation, transportation, and thin client systems.

- **Mobile-ITX (2.4 × 2.4 inch/60 × 60 mm):** Designed for ultra-mobile personal computers (UMPCs) and smartphones. This board has no embedded ports, so it needs a separate I/O board to communicate with devices.

Next Unit of Computing (NUC)

Another small form factor you should know about is Intel's NUC. A NUC is actually a barebones kit that includes a case, a motherboard (typically 4 × 4 inch/10.16 × 10.16 cm), a fan, and an external power supply. If you are looking for a basic computer system with video, network, and USB ports that can fit in the palm of your hand, this is it.

Expansion Buses

There are two main expansion buses and their corresponding adapter card slots that you need to know for the exam, PCI Express and PCI. Let's discuss those now.

▶ **PCI Express (PCIe):** Currently the king of expansion buses, PCIe is the high-speed serial replacement for the older parallel PCI standard and the deprecated AGP standard. The most powerful PCIe slots—such as x16—connect directly to the processor (or northbridge). The lesser PCIe slots—such as x1—connect to the chipset. The PCIe expansion bus sends and receives data within *lanes*. These lanes can send and receive data simultaneously. There are several versions of PCIe, and their data rates are shown in Table 16.1. Commonly, PCIe video cards are x16 (pronounced "by 16"), which means they use 16 lanes, and usually require version 3 at a minimum. They can typically transfer 16 GB/s in each direction. Most other PCIe adapter cards are x1, but you might work with some x4 cards as well. Of course, compatibility is key. A x1 card can go in a x1 slot or larger, but a x16 card will fit only in a x16 slot—and nothing smaller. Figure 16.2 shows three x16 slots and one x1 slot.

TABLE 16.1 **Comparison of PCIe Versions and Data Transfer Rates**

PCIe Version	Frequency	Maximum Data Rate
Version 1.0	2.5 GHz*	2 Gb/s (250 MB/s) per lane
Version 2.0	5 GHz	4 Gb/s (500 MB/s) per lane
Version 3.0	8 GHz	8 Gb/s** (1 GB/s) per lane
Version 4.0	16 GHz	16 Gb/s** (2 GB/s) per lane
Version 5.0	32 GHz	32 Gb/s** (4 GB/s) per lane
Version 6.0	64 GHz	64 Gb/s** (8 GB/s) per lane

* This is also measured in transfers per second, referring to the number of operations that send and receive data per second. It is often closely related to frequency. For example, PCIe v1 is 2.5 gigatransfers per second (2.5 GT/s), and PCIe v4 is 16 GT/s.

** These numbers are approximate.

> **Note**
>
> Maximum data transfer rates are never attained, even in a lab environment. You can expect actual throughput to be substantially lower, but professionals use the maximum data rate as a point of reference and as a means of comparison.

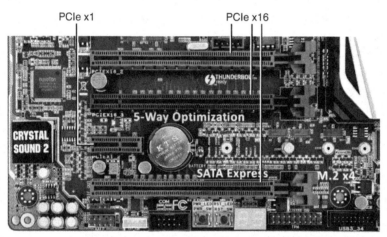

FIGURE 16.2 **PCIe x16 and PCIe x1**

> **ExamAlert**
>
> Make sure you can identify the PCIe x16 and x1 expansion slots for the exam.

▶ **PCI**: The Peripheral Component Interconnect (PCI) bus was developed in the 1990s by Intel as a faster, more compatible alternative to the deprecated ISA bus. It allows for connections to modems and to video, sound, and network adapters. This uncommon bus connects exclusively to the chipset (or southbridge). Because of this, other high-speed video alternatives were developed that could connect directly to the processor (or northbridge). PCI version 2.1 cards are rated at 66 MHz, and their corresponding PCI bus is 32 bits wide, allowing for a maximum data transfer rate of 266 MB/s. Derivatives of PCI include PCI-X, which was designed for servers using a 64-bit bus and rated for 133 MHz/266 MHz, and Mini PCI, which is used by older laptops. PCI slots are seldom found on today's motherboards. For the most part, they have been overtaken by PCIe technology.

> **Note**
>
> I've mentioned the *chipset* several times. The chipset connects all of the mother-board's secondary device interfaces together, such as USB, SATA 3.0, the network card, and more. The chipset then connects to the CPU, which has connections to the primary devices (RAM and video card). The motherboard displayed in Figure 16.1 uses the X99 chipset. To see a diagram of this chipset, and all of its connections, use the following link or search the Internet for "Intel X99 chipset diagram": https://www.intel.com/content/www/us/en/chipsets/performance-chipsets/x99-chipset-diagram.html.
>
> This is just one example. Most motherboard manufacturers have chipset diagrams available for you to view. Analyze them to understand how your system works!

Expansion Cards

If a motherboard does not have a necessary integrated component, you will have to add an expansion card to a PCIe slot. During the planning stage, you should make sure one is available and then determine the requirements of the card: the version of PCIe, bus width, and so on. There are plenty of different expansion cards that you might add, but the most common is probably the video card. Some computers come with integrated video cards (also known as on-board cards). In some cases (such as with some AMD systems), these cards use powerful processing that is built into the board, but many times the integrated video card is designed for basic computing and does not perform well enough for any high-end computing. In such cases, a video card is often necessary.

Installing Video Cards

A video card is like a little self-contained computer! It has a processor, known as a graphics processing unit (GPU), and a substantial amount of RAM. When choosing a video card, there are several things to consider, including the expansion bus that the card connects to, the card's GPU speed and amount of memory, the connectors it offers, whether there is an expansion slot available for it on the motherboard, whether the video card can fit in the case, and whether the case has adequate power and cooling capabilities for the card.

Video cards, like other adapter cards, are inserted into an expansion bus slot and then screwed into the chassis of the case to keep them in place. When deciding on a video card for a new system or a system to be upgraded, make sure it will fit in the computer case! The following steps describe how to install a PCIe video card:

1. **Check whether the card is compatible:** Verify that there is an open, compatible slot on the motherboard. Also make sure that the card is compatible with the operating system.

2. **Ready the computer:** Make sure that the computer is turned off and unplugged. Then implement ESD prevention measures (antistatic mat, antistatic wrist strap, and so on).

3. **Ready the video card:** Remove the card from the package and keep it in the antistatic bag until it is ready to be inserted. (Make sure the card is sealed when first opening it.)

4. **Document:** If the computer had a video card already, document how and where it was connected, either by taking a photo or by drawing a diagram. Otherwise, review the documentation that came with the motherboard and video card. Plan where to install the card and what cables need to be connected to the card and how they should be routed through the case.

5. **Prepare the slot:** Use a Phillips-head screwdriver to remove the slot cover (or covers) where the card will be installed. Bigger PCIe cards inhabit the space used by two slot covers. On most PCIe slots, there will be a thumb lever. Open this gently. When the card is inserted, the lever locks the card into place.

6. **Install the card to the slot:** Insert the card using both thumbs, applying equal pressure straight down into the slot. Try not to wiggle the card in any direction. Press down until the card snaps into place and you can't see any of the "gold" edge connectors. If it doesn't seem to be going in, don't force it. There might be something in the way (for example, one of the slot covers might not have been removed or the thumb lever might not be in the correct position).

7. **Connect cables:** A PCIe card needs its own power connection (or two). These cards use 6- or 8-pin PCIe power connectors. Most cases come with PCIe power connectors, but if yours does not, you can use a PCIe to Molex adapter (or two), which will work with older cases and power supplies. Next, make any Scalable Link Interface (SLI) bridge connections necessary if you have two or three video cards (which is less common but popular in high-end gaming systems). When complete, it should look similar to Figure 16.3.

Slot Cover Screws   6-pin PCIe Power Connectors
    SLI Connectors   S/PDIF Connector

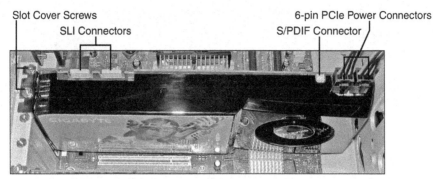

FIGURE 16.3 **An installed PCIe video card**

8. **Test:** Testing is simple: Plug in the monitor to the video card's port and boot the computer. If you don't get anything on the display, it's time to troubleshoot. Make sure the monitor is securely connected to the correct port. Then shut down the PC and make sure the card is seated properly and the power connections and any other connections are connected firmly. Listen for any beep codes that might be issued by the BIOS POST. Check whether the computer is booting without video; this can be done by watching the LED lights on the front of the case and listening for power supply fan and hard drive activity.

9. **Install the driver:** When the system boots properly, install the driver from the manufacturer's disc. If no disc was supplied with the device or if it is missing, or if you don't have an optical drive on the computer in question, go to the manufacturer's website and download the latest version of the driver for the exact model of the video card.

> **Note**
>
> You will find that sometimes the operating system installs a driver automatically. At times, this driver is good enough, but many times you will want the latest drive from the manufacturer.

10. **Test again:** Now that the driver is installed, test again. Verify whether the card is shown as the correct make and model in the Device Manager (**Run > devmgmt.msc**), under Display Adapters. Then make sure the monitor can output the desired resolution. Keep in mind that some video cards can output a higher resolution than a monitor can support. If the computer is used for graphics or gaming, open the appropriate application and verify that it works as expected. For example, check for fluidity, quick response, frame rate, and so on.

> **ExamAlert**
>
> Know how to install and test a video card.

> **Note**
>
> Check out this video of a step-by-step video card install/upgrade on my website: https://dprocomputer.com/?p=1699.

Challenge 2: Open and Analyze a Computer's Video Card

If you have a PC that you own or are allowed to open, open the case and analyze the system. Attempt to find out the following:

▶ The type of video card that is installed

▶ The type of motherboard you are using

You shouldn't have to actually disassemble anything to find out these things. Be sure to unplug the computer before opening it and employ antistatic prevention methods. If you are unsure about antistatic prevention, see Chapter 59, "Safety Procedures."

When you have booted up the computer again, do the following:

▶ Go to the Device Manager (if using Windows) and locate the name of the display adapter. Does it match with what you found?

▶ Check the manufacturer's motherboard documentation to find out what version of PCIe your video card is using.

The bottom line: It's one thing for me to tell you about computer technology, but it's another thing altogether for you to see it for yourself. Try to learn in a hands-on manner whenever possible; doing so will increase your overall knowledge greatly. If you don't have a PC, consider getting an older one to practice with. Ask family members and friends, check out yard sales, read the classifieds, and visit online auction sites to find something inexpensive to use for learning.

Sound Cards

A sound card is responsible for generating sound from the data sent to it by the operating system. Audio devices can be integrated into the motherboard, installed to PCIe slots, and connected to USB, but a sound card is typically installed to a PCIe slot on the motherboard.

Sound cards are not used as often as they once were. With the advent of USB 3.0 and beyond, many manufacturers choose to design their speakers and headphones with USB-only connectivity—or they are wireless. However, some still utilize connections that require a traditional sound card. And some audiophiles are concerned with the potential for USB latency or wireless interference and prefer the direct connectivity—and ports—that a sound card offers. Generally, the connections are 1/8 inch (3.5 mm).

Most sound card connections are color-coded. This color scheme is defined within the *PC System Design Guide*, version PC 2001—and the colors are still the same today. This guide specifies the following colors for the TRS 1/8 inch (3.5 mm) mini-jacks like the ones shown in Figure 16.4:

▶ **Light blue:** Line input. Sometimes this seconds as a microphone input.

▶ **Pink:** Microphone input.

▶ **Lime green:** Main output for stereo speakers or headphones. Can also act as a line out.

▶ **Black:** Output for surround sound speakers (rear speakers).

▶ **Silver/Brown:** Output for additional two speakers in a 7.1 system (middle surround speakers).

▶ **Orange:** Output for center speaker and subwoofer.

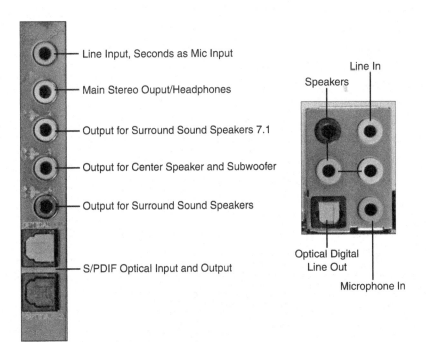

FIGURE 16.4 **A typical sound card's ports and integrated audio ports on a motherboard**

On the sound card shown in Figure 16.4, note the optical input and output. This is known as a Sony/Phillips Digital Interconnect Format (S/PDIF) port. This particular version of S/PDIF is called TOSLINK. It delivers high-quality digital sound over fiber optic cable. It is also known as a *digital optical port*.

Some users prefer to use an external audio interface that connects via USB but provides plenty of different connectivity options that are easily accessible on top of a person's desk. These interfaces usually offer high-fidelity sound (for example, 24-bit/192 kHz). They require USB 2.0 or higher, but for greater productivity and less latency, USB 3.0 or higher is often recommended.

Other Expansion Cards

There are expansion cards for just about anything you can think of. Many motherboards come with integrated network cards, USB ports, and so on. But sometimes a user simply needs a more powerful solution or more ports.

A motherboard usually has one RJ45 port for a wired Ethernet connection (the network interface card [NIC]). However, a system might require more. Network interface cards are available with one or more RJ45 ports that can be used for connections to other networks, or they can be "teamed" or "bonded" together to provide link aggregation (that is, to combine the bandwidth of the ports) or to offer redundancy in case one port fails. This feature is often used in Linux systems, especially servers.

Most motherboards have plenty of USB ports, but if you need more, USB hubs can be connected to a USB port in order to add devices. But what if the motherboard doesn't have the right *version* of USB? For example, what if your motherboard has USB 3.0 SuperSpeed ports, but you want to make use of a device that can run USB 3.2 SuperSpeed+ at 20 Gbps; in such a case, you would need to add a USB 3.2 expansion card.

There are also external SATA-based devices (eSATA). A few motherboards come with these ports, but if you need to connect to external storage drives that use eSATA, you might need an adapter card. Occasionally you might encounter Fibre Channel adapter cards. Such a card can be used to connect a PC to other Fibre Channel equipment (possibly within a SAN) by way of an LC connector or other fiber optic connection.

Don't forget about capture cards. These are adapter cards that can "capture," or record, video or audio, essentially turning the PC into a video or audio editing workstation. While professionals often use external devices, an internal adapter card can provide an easier, less expensive solution for small businesses and hobbyists.

All of these cards are installed in a similar way to a video card, but their installation is even easier. Simply unscrew the slot cover and insert the expansion card straight down into the slot. Try not to wiggle the card and only hold the card from the edges to avoid ESD or other damage. Then screw the card in. Check the card in the Device Manager (or similar tool in an OS other than Windows) to make sure it is seen properly; if it is not seen correctly, download the driver from the manufacturer and install it. Test the card to make sure it works properly and then pat yourself on the back for another tech job that's been well done!

> **ExamAlert**
>
> Know how to install, configure, and test sound, network, USB, and eSATA expansion cards.

More Ports and Connectors

The main type of drive technology on motherboards is Serial ATA (SATA). SATA supports the connection of storage/hard drives and optical drives. Most motherboards come equipped with several 7-pin SATA connectors and possibly one or more 18-pin SATA Express connectors. We talk more about drive technologies in Chapter 15, "Storage Drives."

You will find other ports as well, such as integrated audio ports, for use with an optical drive or sound card; internal USB ports, used with the front panel USB connections; and a variety of power connections that we will discuss further in Chapter 18, "Power."

Then there's the case connector group, which is usually on the edge of the motherboard and allows connectivity to the front panel connectors on a computer case. These wires start at the inside front of the case and have thin 2-, 3-, or 4-pin plugs on the other end. They are labeled with names such as POWER LED, POWER SW (for power switch), HDD LED, and so on. These plugs connect to *headers* on the motherboard, such as the Power button, reset button, and LED light headers.

A computer with limited motherboard space might come with a riser card. A *riser card* can provide for additional expansion slots, such as PCIe. It generally plugs into one of the expansion slots and typically allows for an additional two slots. This allows a person to take advantage of three-dimensional space, but it could decrease airflow, leading to increased heat. Riser cards are most common in small proprietary designs and with small form factor motherboards.

BIOS/UEFI Settings

Historically, the Basic Input/Output System (BIOS) has been the firmware loaded on most desktop and laptop computers. However, since 2005, the Unified Extensible Firmware Interface (UEFI) has gained popularity, and in 2014, it became the predominant type of firmware shipped with motherboards. But many technicians (and even some manufacturers) still just refer to it as "BIOS," or possibly as "BIOS/UEFI." For simplicity in this book, I often refer to a motherboard's firmware simply as BIOS.

UEFI communicates more effectively with the operating system, allows for a mouse-driven firmware-based setup program (instead of the menu-based BIOS setup program), and includes advanced system diagnosis (except for the worst of errors, such as the CPU failing). It also has a built-in Secure Boot mode, which prevents digitally unsigned drivers from being loaded and helps prevent rootkits from manifesting. It has faster startup times than the BIOS and supports more storage drive partitions.

The firmware is loaded onto a chip on the motherboard and can (and should) be updated, or "flashed," periodically to take advantage of the latest functionality and security updates. There are several ways to update the firmware, but generally you do it either from within Windows or by using some kind of bootable media (such as a USB flash drive) to boot the system and rewrite the firmware; this process is known as "flashing the BIOS."

This firmware stays resident in the computer after restarts. However, time and the individual settings that you select are stored elsewhere, such as in a complimentary metal-oxide semiconductor (CMOS). This chip is *volatile*, meaning that the settings could be lost if the computer is restarted. That's why the motherboard comes with a lithium battery (also known as a CMOS battery). That battery retains the individual settings and keeps time while the computer is shut down. A common battery used on motherboards is the CR2032, a nickel-sized battery that snaps into the motherboard and has a shelf life of anywhere from 2 to 10 years, depending on usage. The more you leave the computer on, the longer the battery lasts.

The BIOS is where you go to set a password, change boot options, configure time and date, configure devices, overclock the computer, and much more. Accessing the BIOS must be done before the operating system boots. For PCs and laptops, this can be accomplished by pressing a key on the keyboard (for example, F2 or Delete). Different manufacturers use different keys. The particular key should be displayed on the screen when your system boots—so watch carefully for it! For some mobile devices, you might need to press a button combination (such as the volume-up and power buttons). Here are a couple of examples of settings you might modify in the BIOS:

▶ **Boot options:** Also known as BIOS boot order or device priority, this setting enables you to select which media will be booted: hard drive, USB, optical drive, over the network, and so on. Usually, this should be set to hard drive first. But if you install an operating system (OS) from removable media, you will want to temporarily configure that removable media as first on the boot options list. For a secure and trouble-free system, it is recommended that you set this to hard drive first when you complete an installation of an OS, as shown in Figure 16.5. If you don't modify this setting, and removable media (such as a USB flash drive) is inserted, then it could cause the operating system to fail to load properly and could also pose a security risk. You'll note that the first boot device in the figure says Windows Boot Manager, P1, and the name of the device—a 250-GB Samsung solid-state drive. Windows Boot Manager is the primary boot file in Windows, and it is the first file on the hard drive that the BIOS looks for when it starts up. P1 means the first physical SATA port connection.

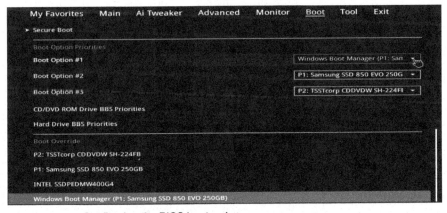

FIGURE 16.5 **Configuring the BIOS boot order**

ExamAlert

Know how to set the BIOS boot options! Also, if you boot a PC and see a black screen with a white blinking underscore on the top left, the issue could be the boot order.

▶ **Fan settings:** Some of today's motherboard BIOS programs have the ability to set whether case fans and CPU fans are turned on and at what speed they spin. In lieu of exact RPM settings for the fans, the BIOS might offer simplified settings, such as optimal, low, high, and so on. If any fans are not working and you don't know what to set them to, read the motherboard manual for best procedures or reset the BIOS to default settings. (Note that doing this will erase any other settings you might have configured previously.)

▶ **Passwords:** In most cases, two passwords are available on BIOS: user and administrator. The user password authenticates a user before it enables the operating system to boot; this is also known as a boot password. Most organizations do not use this password because it requires the user to know a second password. The administrator password authenticates a user to the BIOS Setup Utility itself. For a secure system, enter a strong administrator password. By strong, I'm talking about length and complexity, my friend!

▶ **More security settings:** *Secure Boot* is an option on UEFI-equipped systems. If enabled, it can potentially block rootkits and other malware from launching boot loaders that have been tampered with. Newer versions of Windows make use of a certificate stored in the UEFI that checks the boot loader for authenticity—meaning whether it has been digitally signed by Microsoft. If the drive's boot loader is not authentic, the computer will not boot to that drive. You can also create Secure Boot keys with a *hardware security module (HSM)*, which can come in several forms, including as an adapter card; however, it must be enabled properly within the BIOS. The HSM is a device that includes a cryptoprocessor that generates, stores, and manages digital keys and has the ability to perform performance-optimized cryptographic operations. To allow for drive encryption, some motherboards come with a *Trusted Platform Module (TPM)*, a chip that stores encryption keys and can be enabled in the BIOS. You can also set permissions for USB usage in the BIOS, such as whether USB can be utilized at all, disabling the ability to boot from USB drives, and so on. We'll discuss some of these computer security terms in more depth in the 220-1102 portion of the book.

ExamAlert

It is crucial to secure UEFI-equipped systems with Secure Boot and a TPM.

▶ **Virtualization support:** To support virtual computing, the BIOS must be configured properly. This setting is sometimes buried within the BIOS in a CPU submenu. For Intel CPUs, the Intel Virtualization Technology (Intel VT) option should be enabled. For AMD CPUs, enable AMD-V. We'll talk more about virtualization in upcoming chapters.

The POST

The power-on self-test (POST) is essentially a piece of code that the BIOS runs to find out which type of processor is on the motherboard and verify the amount of RAM. It also identifies buses on the motherboard (and other devices) as well as which devices are available for booting.

The BIOS indicates any system problems that the POST finds via either onscreen display codes, beep codes, or an integrated error code readout on the motherboard itself. The exact code(s) depends on the type of BIOS used. Your motherboard should come with documentation about any possible BIOS error codes. If not, the documentation can usually be downloaded from the manufacturer's website; you just need to know the model number of the board. In the case of a proprietary computer (Dell, HP, and such), you need the model number of the computer to download any necessary documentation from the manufacturer's website. We'll be discussing more computer trouble-shooting when we get to the chapters in Domain 5.0: Hardware and Network Troubleshooting.

> **ExamAlert**
>
> The POST is a built-in troubleshooting tool provided by the motherboard. Use it!

Cram Quiz

Answer these questions. The answers follow the last question. If you cannot answer these questions correctly, consider reading this chapter again until you can.

1. Which motherboard form factor measures 12 inches × 9.6 inches (305 mm × 244 mm)?

   ○ **A.** microATX

   ○ **B.** SATA

   ○ **C.** ATX

   ○ **D.** mITX

2. Which component supplies power to the CMOS when a computer is off?

   ○ **A.** Lithium battery

   ○ **B.** POST

   ○ **C.** Power supply

   ○ **D.** BIOS/UEFI

3. To implement a Secure Boot process, which device should be listed first in the Boot Device Priority screen?

   ○ **A.** Network

   ○ **B.** CD-ROM

   ○ **C.** USB

   ○ **D.** Hard drive

4. Which of the following connectors would you use to power a video card?

   ○ **A.** 24-pin power

   ○ **B.** 8-pin PCIe

   ○ **C.** Molex

   ○ **D.** 3.5-mm TRS

5. Which of the following is a chip that stores encryption keys?

   ○ **A.** Intel VT

   ○ **B.** Secure Boot

   ○ **C.** Firmware

   ○ **D.** TPM

6. Which of the following BIOS/UEFI settings are used to prevent USB drop attacks?

   ○ **A.** Boot password

   ○ **B.** BIOS time/date

   ○ **C.** Secure Boot

   ○ **D.** SAN settings

7. What do the POWER LED, POWER SW, and HDD LED plugs connect to on the motherboard?

   ○ **A.** Headers

   ○ **B.** SATA 7-pin

   ○ **C.** PCIe slots

   ○ **D.** 24-pin ATX port

Cram Quiz Answers

1. **C.** ATX boards measure 12 inches × 9.6 inches (305 mm × 244 mm). microATX boards are square and measure 9.6 × 9.6 inches (244 mm × 244 mm). SATA is a type of storage drive technology and the port used to connect drives to the motherboard. mITX (or Mini-ITX), also square, measures 6.7 × 6.7 inches (170 mm × 170 mm).

2. **A.** The lithium battery (or CMOS battery) supplies power to the CMOS when the computer is off. This is because the CMOS is volatile and would otherwise lose the stored settings when the computer is turned off.

3. **D.** To ensure that other users cannot boot the computer from removable media, set the first device in the Boot Device Priority screen to hard drive. (And consider Secure Boot and boot keys!)

4. **B.** A video card is normally powered by a 6-pin or 8-pin PCIe connector. Lesser cards are simply powered by the PCIe bus. The 24-pin power connector is the main connector that leads from the power supply to the motherboard. Molex is used for fans, older IDE drives, and other secondary devices. 3.5 mm (or 1/8 inch) TRS is an audio connection.

5. **D.** To perform drive encryption, some motherboards come with a Trusted Platform Module (TPM), a chip that stores encryption keys and can be enabled in the BIOS/UEFI. Intel Virtualization Technology (VT) is part of the firmware that supports the use of virtualization software such as Hyper-V and VMware. Secure Boot can block rootkits and other malware from launching boot loaders that have been tampered with. Firmware (such as a motherboard's BIOS/UEFI) should be updated, or "flashed," periodically to take advantage of the latest functionality and security updates.

6. **A.** Configure USB permissions to prevent USB drop attacks. In a USB drop attack, a malicious person leaves a USB drive lying around somewhere, in the hopes that someone will pick it up and plug it into their computer. The USB drive contains a virus or other malicious payload and subsequently infects the com-puter. By disabling USB altogether in the BIOS/UEFI, you can avoid these types of attacks. A boot password is a good idea also, so no one can modify your set-tings—once you have made them that is; you still have to configure USB securely first. The BIOS Time/Date settings allow you to modify the date and time for the system but won't prevent USB drives from being used and therefore won't pre-vent USB drop attacks. Storage area network (SAN) settings doesn't have any relationship to USB devices.

7. **A.** Power LED, Power switch, and storage drive LED case connectors plug into headers on the motherboard. The actual SATA drive connects to the motherboard's SATA port with a 7-pin data connector. PCIe slots are used for video, audio, and network cards (among other things). The main 24-pin power connection from the power supply connects to the 24-pin ATX port. Know your connections!

That is a pretty massive chapter with lots of details. Be sure to review carefully before moving on to the next chapter. You are doing great!

CHAPTER 17

CPUs

This chapter covers a portion of the following A+ 220-1101 exam objective:

▶ **3.4** – Given a scenario, install and configure motherboards, central processing units (CPUs), and add-on cards.

Here it is, the core of the desktop computer: the CPU. This is the second part of our coverage of Objective 3.4. Throughout this chapter, I often refer to the *AV-Editor* computer, which has a motherboard with an X99 chipset and a Core i7-5820K CPU. Refer to Chapter 16, Figure 16.1, and the supporting text, for more information about the motherboard. There's lots to do, so let's not waste any time!

CPU Architecture

The central processing unit (CPU) is quite often referred to as the "brain" of the computer. While that terminology may be debatable, the CPU is most definitely at the core of the computer—and it is fast. A typical CPU today runs between 2 and 4 GHz or higher. That CPU frequency is known as *speed* or, more accurately, *clock rate*.

Clock Rate

The clock rate is the frequency (or speed) of a component. It is rated in cycles per second and measured in hertz (Hz). For all practical purposes, the term *clock rate* is the same as the more commonly used term *clock speed*.

Components are sold to consumers with a *maximum* clock rate, but they don't always run at that maximum number. To explain, let me use a car analogy. The CPU is often called the "engine" of the computer, like a car engine. Well, your car's speedometer might go up to 120 MPH, but you'll probably never drive at that maximum—for a variety of reasons! When it comes to CPUs, the stated clock rate is the *maximum* clock rate, and the CPU usually runs at a speed less than that. In fact, it can run at any speed below the maximum, but there are only a few plateaus that it will usually hover around.

Now, we're all familiar with speeds such as 2.4 GHz, 3.0 GHz, or 3.5 GHz. But what is the basis of these speeds? Speed can be divided into two categories that are interrelated:

▶ **Motherboard bus speed:** This is the base clock of the motherboard and is often referred to simply as "bus speed." This is generated by a quartz oscillating crystal soldered directly to the motherboard. For example, the base clock of the motherboard in Chapter 16, Figure 16.1 is 100 MHz.

▶ **Internal clock speed:** This is the internal frequency of the CPU and is the well-known number that CPUs are associated with. For example, the Intel Core i7-5820K that I use with the motherboard in Figure 16.1

in Chapter 16 is rated at 3.3 GHz. The CPU uses an internal multiplier based on the motherboard base clock. The maximum multiplier for this particular CPU is 33. The math is as follows: Base clock × Multiplier = Internal clock speed. In this example, that would be 100 MHz × 33 = 3.3 GHz. However, as mentioned, the CPU can (and often does) run more slowly. Fewer open programs means a lower speed (for example, 1.2 GHz). As more programs are opened and more CPU power is required, the CPU throttles up—for example, to 2.4 GHz and, ultimately, 3.3 GHz. Like many boards, this motherboard can support faster and slower CPUs from a variety of CPU families, but the math works in the same way. To see the specifications for the i7-5820k CPU, or any Intel CPU, check out Intel's site: https://ark.intel.com.

> **ExamAlert**
>
> For today's CPUs, two of the most commonly used terms are *bus speed* (the base clock of the motherboard) and *clock speed* (the frequency of the CPU). These terms might not be completely accurate, technically, but you will see and hear them often, and you could see them on the exam as well.

Overclocking

Many motherboards allow for *overclocking*, which enables the user to increase the base clock within the BIOS, thereby increasing the clock speed of the CPU. For example, the Core i7-5820K CPU that I am using to write this book has a normal top speed of 3300 MHz (3.3 GHz). On this motherboard, increasing the base clock (BCLK) from 100 to 125 MHz results in an increase of the CPU top speed from 3300 MHz to 4000 MHz. As another example, the Core i9-9900K has a normal top speed of 3.6 GHz, but it can be overclocked safely to 5.0 GHz (with Turbo Boost) and unsafely far beyond that. You can also overclock RAM and some video cards independently of the CPU.

As you might guess, overclocking is risky; it increases the voltage, creates more heat, and could possibly cause system instability or even damage to the system—analogous to blowing the engine of a car when attempting to run a 10-second quarter mile. So, approach overclocking with extreme caution! Generally, if you find a system in the workplace that has been overclocked, overclocking should be disabled in the BIOS.

Types of CPUs

There are two types of CPUs you should know about for the A+ exams: x64/x86 and ARM. Let's discuss each briefly.

x64/x86

x64/x86 technology is typically found in PCs, laptops, and many servers. Simply stated, x64 means newer 64-bit CPUs, and x86 means older 32-bit CPUs. In computer architecture, 64-bit CPUs can handle exponentially higher amounts of data and larger RAM capacities than can 32-bit CPUs.

64-bit CPUs were introduced to the mainstream market around 2003. x64 technology is also referred to as Intel 64 (for Intel CPUs), amd64 (for AMD CPUs), and, more generically, x86-64 (which is how I refer to it throughout this book).

x86 32-bit CPUs were common in PCs from the 1980s to the early 2000s. The x in x86 is a variable; for example, the 80386 PC, shortened to 386, works with 32-bit versions of operating systems and software.

The older x86 CPU could only support up to 4 GB of RAM. In comparison, an x86-64 CPU can support 256 TB of RAM (that's terabytes, or trillions of bytes). Because many software programs are still written for the 32-bit platform, 64-bit CPUs are designed to be backward compatible, meaning they can run 64-bit *and* 32-bit software.

An example of an x86-64 Intel CPU is the Core i7-7700, which is a high-performance processor that can run between 3.6 and 4.2 GHz.

We'll discuss x86-64 and the differences between 64-bit and 32-bit software a little more when we get into the 220-1102 portion of this book.

ARM

Advanced RISC Machine (ARM) technology is typically found in smartphones, tablets, and other mobile devices. RISC stands for reduced instruction set computing, which essentially means small, highly optimized sets of instructions as compared to x64. ARM CPUs are designed to run cooler and more efficiently than their PC counterparts.

Like x64/x86, there have also been 32-bit and 64-bit versions of ARM CPUs, with 64-bit versions beginning around 2011. ARM CPUs are given version numbers, such as ARMv8 and ARMv9. An example of an ARMv8 CPU is the Cortex-A76 (released in 2018), which has a maximum clock rate between 3.0 and 3.3 GHz. ARM CPUs generally come with less cache memory than x64 CPUs. (More on cache in a little bit.)

So far, the concepts we have discussed can be applied to x86-64 or ARM. However, the examples in the rest of this chapter are geared more toward x86-64 technology.

> **Note**
>
> While not the only CPU architectures that exist, x86-64 and ARM architectures are by far the most common.

Multithreading and Multicore

Multithreading (for example, Intel's Hyper-Threading) enables a single CPU to accept and calculate two independent sets of instructions simultaneously, thereby simulating two CPUs. The technology was designed so that single CPUs could better compete with true multi-CPU systems for lower cost. In a multithreaded environment, only one CPU is present, but the operating system sees two virtual CPUs and divides the workload, or threads, between the two.

Whereas multithreading technology simulates multiple CPUs, *multicore* CPUs physically contain two or more actual processor cores in one CPU package that acts as a single entity. This enables more efficient processing of data and less generated heat.

A typical CPU combines multithreading and multicore technologies. For example, the Core i7-5820K CPU mentioned earlier has 6 cores, each of which can handle 2 threads at the same time, for a total of 12 threads. The Core i9-9900K mentioned previously has 8 cores, and so it can run 16 threads simultaneously. Most CPUs will handle 2 threads per core. In Windows, the total number of threads can be viewed within the Device Manager under Processors. In Linux, you can find this number in a terminal by running the **top** command and pressing **1**.

> **ExamAlert**
>
> Know the differences between multithreading and multicore technologies. *Multi-threading* enables a single-core CPU to calculate two instruction sets simultaneously, whereas *multicore* CPUs have two or more cores, each of which can use multithreading.

Cache Memory

Several types of cache are used in computers, but CPU cache is a special high-speed memory that reduces the time the CPU takes to access data. By using high-speed static RAM (SRAM) and because the cache is often located directly on—or even in—the CPU, using CPU cache can be faster than accessing information from dynamic RAM (DRAM) modules. However, it is limited in storage capacity compared to DRAM.

Cache is typically divided into three levels, which are accessed by the CPU sequentially: L1 (built into the CPU) and L2 and L3 (built onto the CPU). L1 and L2 cache are distributed to each core of the CPU, but L3 cache is shared by all of the CPU's cores. Generally, the more cache, the better. The less the CPU needs to access DRAM, the more quickly it can calculate data.

CPU Compatibility

CPU compatibility boils down to the socket available to you and the manufacturer you decide to use. Intel and AMD dominate the desktop and laptop market.

Intel and AMD

CPU manufacturers use the make/model system—for example, the Intel (make) Core i7-6700K (model) or the AMD (make) Ryzen 9 3900X (model). There are dozens of models of Intel and AMD CPUs. The A+ exam does not require you to know all of the individual models, but you should have a working knowledge of some of the basic makes and models available. Periodically visit the Intel and AMD websites for the latest and greatest CPUs.

A CPU might come with a built-in graphics processing unit (GPU). This means that with a compatible motherboard, no separate video card is necessary, and the monitor can be plugged directly into the video port on the mother-board. Both Intel and AMD have many CPUs with such *integrated GPUs*. AMD refers to this as the Accelerated Processing Unit (APU). Integrated GPUs have come a long way, but for power users (gamers, graphic designers, and so on), a separate video card is usually required for best functionality.

Intel and AMD are both good companies that make quality products, which leads to great competition. Which is better? In all honestly, it varies and depends on how you use the CPU. You can find advocates for both (albeit sub-jective advocates), and the scales are constantly tipping back and forth. On any given day, a specific Intel CPU might outperform AMD; three months later, a different AMD CPU might outperform an Intel. It's been that way for many years now. Whichever CPU you choose, make sure that you get a compatible motherboard. A couple of things to watch for are compatibility with the chipset and the socket type.

The chipset will either be Intel based or AMD based, depending on what type of motherboard you are using. It will only be compatible with a certain group of CPUs. For example, the motherboard in Chapter 16, Figure 16.1 uses the Intel X99 chipset. For Intel, the chipset is also known as a Platform Controller Hub (PCH). This particular chipset can work with Core i7 CPUs and Intel Xeon E5 CPUs. (Xeon CPUs are primarily used in servers.) Verify that the CPU make and model will be compatible with the chipset and, therefore, the motherboard. So, for instance, the motherboard shown in Figure 16.1 is an ASUS X99-A, and it accepts the Core i7-5820K, among others. The moth-erboard's socket type will also dictate compatibility, as we discuss in the next section.

Sockets

The *socket* is the electrical interface between the CPU and the motherboard. It attaches directly to the motherboard and houses the CPU. It also physically supports the CPU and heat sink and enables easy replacement of the CPU.

The socket is made of either plastic or metal and uses metal contacts for connectivity to each of the pins/lands of the CPU. One or more metal levers (retaining arms) lock the CPU in place. Figure 17.1 shows an example of an unlocked Land Grid Array (LGA) socket.

FIGURE 17.1   **An unlocked LGA 2011 socket**

Historically, the socket has been considered a ZIF, short for zero insertion force. This means that the CPU should connect easily into the socket, with no pressure or force involved during the installation. The socket will have many pin inserts, or lands, for the CPU to connect to. Pin 1 can be found in one of the corners and can be identified by either a white corner drawn on the motherboard or one or more missing pins or pinholes. This helps you to orient the CPU, which also has the arrow, or missing pin(s), in the corresponding corner. There are two types of sockets you should know for the exam:

▶ **PGA:** Pin Grid Array sockets accept CPUs that have pins covering the majority of their underside. The pins on the CPU are placed in the pinholes of the socket, and the CPU is locked into place by a retaining arm. Many AMD CPUs use PGA sockets.

▶ **LGA:** Land Grid Array sockets use lands that protrude out and touch the CPU's contact points. This newer type of socket (also known as Socket T) offers better power distribution and less chance to damage the CPU compared to PGA. LGA is commonly used today on Intel motherboards.

The CPU and socket must be compatible. For example, the X99-A motherboard used in the *AV-Editor* computer has an LGA 2011 socket, which is common but not the only socket that Intel uses on its motherboards. The Core i7-5820K CPU used on that motherboard is designed to fit into the LGA 2011 socket, and several other CPUs can fit into this socket as well. Other sockets from Intel include the 2066, 1155, and 1151. A few sockets from AMD include the AM3+, FM2+, and AM4.

Some computers have multiple sockets, allowing them to run more than one CPU at the same time. For example, a rackmount server found in a datacenter might have a multisocket configuration that runs two or more Intel Xeon CPUs at the same time.

> **ExamAlert**
>
> Compatibility is key! Find the correlation between sockets, chipsets, and CPUs by analyzing the motherboard and CPU documentation.

Power Consumption

Power consumption of CPUs is normally rated in watts. For example, the Core i7-5820K is rated as a 140 watt-hour CPU. This rating is known as *thermal design power (TDP)*, and it signifies the amount of heat generated by the CPU, which the cooling system is required to dissipate when operating with a complex workload. This number is usually displayed as the maximum; it could be less, depending on CPU usage, and does not take into account overclocking. The measurement should play into your decision when planning which power supply to use and which kind of cooling system. For more information on power supplies, see Chapter 18, "Power." Common TDP ratings for multicore CPUs range between 60 and 150 watts. That's comparable to a typical incandescent light bulb or 6 to 10 LED light bulbs!

While we are talking electricity, another important factor is voltage. CPUs are associated with a voltage range; for example, the Core i7-5820K runs at about 1 V by default. However, a CPU's voltage can increase as applications demand more processing power. The voltage that is received by the CPU can be monitored in the BIOS or, better yet, with applications within Windows. If the CPU goes beyond the specified voltage range for any extended length of time, it *will* damage the CPU. This becomes especially important for overclockers.

Cooling Mechanisms

Now that you know a CPU uses a good deal of electricity, you can understand why it gets so hot. Hundreds of millions of transistors are hammering away in these powerhouses, and you need to keep the CPU and other devices in the computer cool. This is done in a few ways, as outlined in this section.

Heat Sinks

A *heat sink* is a block of metal made to sit right on top of the CPU, with metal fins stretching away from the CPU. It uses conduction to direct heat away from the CPU and out through the fins. On secondary processors that use a passive heat sink, that's all there is to it; it dissipates heat and requires no moving parts; it is "fanless." But that's not enough for the main CPU in a typical PC. With an active heat sink, a fan is attached to the top of or on the side of the heat sink. The fan plugs into the motherboard for power. If installed on top, the fan blows air into the heat sink and toward the CPU, helping to dissipate heat through the heat sink fins. If installed on the side of a larger heat sink, it blows air sideways through the heat sink toward the case's exhaust fan. More powerful aftermarket CPU heat sinks/fans can be installed as well; just make sure that your power supply can handle the increased power requirements and that you have the space needed because some CPU heat sinks and fans are *big*.

In a PC-based motherboard, the chipset usually has a passive heat sink, but all new CPUs come with active heat sinks. Traditionally, heat sinks have been made of aluminum, but now you also see copper heat sinks used due to their superior conductivity. An important point about heat sinks: If they come loose, they could adversely affect the performance of the CPU or cause overheating, which could lead to random reboots. Make double sure that the heat sink is attached securely.

Thermal Paste

The CPU cap and the bottom of the heat sink will have slight imperfections in the metal. Surface area is key; the best heat dissipation from CPU to heat sink would occur if the metal faces on each were completely and perfectly straight and flat—but we live in the real world. To fill the tiny gaps and imperfections, thermal paste is used. (Thermal paste is also known as thermal compound or thermal interface material.) One example of thermal paste is Arctic Silver, available online and at various electronics stores.

In a new installation, thermal paste might not be needed. Some new CPUs' heat sinks have factory-applied thermal paste that spreads and fills the gaps automatically after you install the heat sink and boot the computer. However, if you need to remove the heat sink for any reason (for example, to clean it, or when upgrading, or if the CPU did not come with a heat sink), then thermal paste should be applied to the CPU cap before the heat sink is installed or upgraded.

To do this, first clean any old thermal paste off the CPU cap and the heat sink with thermal paste remover. Then apply new thermal paste to the CPU cap. The application method will vary depending on the CPU used, but it could require the traditional surface spread method (using an old, clean credit card for spreading), the middle dot method, or the increasingly common vertical line method (no credit card required!). There are other methods as well; review your CPU's documentation to find out which method is recommended. Finally, install the heat sink. Try to do so in one shot, without jostling the heat sink excessively.

> **ExamAlert**
>
> Reapply thermal paste whenever removing and reinstalling a heat sink.

Fans

Case fans are also needed to get the heat out of the case. The power supply has a built-in fan that is adequate for lesser systems. However, more powerful systems should have at least one extra exhaust fan mounted to the back of the case, and many cases today come with one for this purpose. An additional fan on the front of the case can be used as an intake for cool air. If you aren't sure which way the fan blows, connect its power cable to the computer but don't mount it; then hold a piece of paper against the fan. The side that pulls the paper toward it should be the side facing the front of the computer when it is mounted. Some cases come with fans that are mounted to the top, which is ingenious because heat rises.

Another thing to consider is where the heat goes after it leaves the case. If the computer is in an enclosed area, the heat has a hard time escaping and might end up back in the computer. Make sure there is an area for air flow around the computer case.

Of course, three or four fans can make a decent amount of noise, and they still might not be enough for the most powerful computers, especially the over-clocked ones, which leads us to our next option.

Liquid Cooling Systems

Although this method is not as common as the typical CPU/heat sink/fan combination found on a typical computer, you will see liquid-cooled systems used in high-end PCs. And newer water-cooling kits can be used not only to cool the CPU but to cool the chipset, storage drives, video cards, and more. A kit might come with a CPU water block, pump, radiator/fan, PVC tubing, and, of course, coolant; there are more simplified versions of liquid cooling systems as well. The advantages of such systems are improved heat dissipation (with proper installation), potential for higher overclocking rates, and support for the latest, hottest CPUs. Some of the disadvantages include the risk of a leak that can damage components; pumps becoming faulty over time; air being trapped in the lines, which can cause the system to overheat; and the need for maintenance in the form of inspecting the lines and replacing the coolant every few years. Due to the fact that most computers do not need this level of heat dissipation, and because of the complexity of some of these systems, liquid cooling is usually employed by enthusiasts (such as gamers). But you might see it in other CPU-intensive systems, such as virtualization computers and audio/video editing systems. Regardless of cost, installation complexity, and maintenance, liquid cooling systems can help dissipate heat the most efficiently.

> **ExamAlert**
>
> Of all PC cooling methods, liquid cooling systems can dissipate heat the most efficiently, but they are usually only necessary for the most powerful PCs.

Installing CPUs

As with most other computer components, installing a CPU is easy. But you must be careful because it can be damaged easily. Take it slow and employ proper safety measures. Let's break it down into some simple steps:

1. **Select a CPU:** If you build a new computer, the CPU needs to be compatible with the motherboard; consider the type of CPU, speed, and socket type. If you upgrade a CPU, be sure that it is on the motherboard's compatibility list (which can be found at the manufacturer's website).

   Power down the PC, disconnect the power cable (or turn off the kill switch), open the PC, and get your boxes of components ready!

2. **Employ ESD prevention methods:** Use an antistatic strap and mat. Remove the CPU and heat sink from the package, inspect them, and then place the CPU back in its plastic holder or inside an antistatic bag until you are ready to install it. (An antistatic bag usually comes with the motherboard, but you should have extra ones handy.) To prevent damage, make sure that the CPU's lands or pins are facing up if it is in an antistatic bag. Never touch the lands or pins of a CPU. Before touching any components, place both hands on an unpainted portion of the case chassis. For more information on ESD prevention measures, see Chapter 59, "Safety Procedures."

3. **Ready the motherboard:** Some technicians prefer to install the CPU into the motherboard and then install the motherboard into the case. If you do this, place the motherboard on the antistatic mat. (The mat should be on a hard, flat surface.) If you install the CPU directly into an already installed motherboard, clear away any cables or other equipment that might get in the way or that could possibly damage the CPU, heat sink, or fan.

4. **Install the CPU:** Be careful with the CPU! It is extremely delicate! Always touch the case chassis before picking up the CPU. Hold it by the edges and do not touch any pins, lands, or other circuitry on the CPU. Most of the time, a CPU will be installed to either an LGA socket or a PGA socket. The following two bullets show how to install a CPU into each type of socket. Be sure to refer to the installation guide that comes with your particular CPU and motherboard.

   ► If you install to an LGA socket, unlock the socket by releasing the retaining arm(s) and swinging it open as far as it can go. Open the socket hatch, unhook it if necessary, and remove any plastic cover. Next, place the CPU into the socket. One corner of the CPU has an arrow that should be oriented with either a white corner or other similar marking on the motherboard or the socket's missing pin(s); both of these corresponding corners indicate pin 1, as shown in Figure 17.2. Carefully place the CPU into the socket. If it is oriented correctly, the lands on the CPU match up with the lands on the socket. Make sure it is flush and flat within the socket. Close the cap and secure the retaining arm underneath the tab that is connected to the socket, thus securing the CPU. Install thermal paste if necessary. Next, install the heat sink/fan assembly. (If the heat sink came with the CPU, it might have thermal paste applied already.) LGA sockets usually have four plastic snap-in anchors. Carefully press each of these into and through the corresponding motherboard holes. Don't use too much force!

Then turn each of them to lock the heat sink in place. Make sure the heat sink is installed flush with the CPU by inspecting the assembly from the side. You want to be positive of this before turning on the computer because the thermal paste will begin to expand and fill the imperfections right away. Plug the fan into the appropriate motherboard power connector. (These connectors are usually labeled directly on the motherboard; if not, see your motherboard documentation for details on where to plug in the fan.) Install the entire motherboard assembly into the case (if that is your method of choice).

Pin 1

Pin 1

FIGURE 17.2   **Orientation markings on a CPU and LGA socket**

▶ If you install to a PGA socket, unlock the socket by moving the retaining arm(s) out and upward until it is open as far as it will go, without forcing it. Then gently place the CPU into the ZIF socket. There will be an arrow on one corner of the CPU that should correspond to a missing pin (or arrow) on the socket. Don't use force; slide the CPU around until it slips into the socket. Look at the CPU from the side and make sure it is flush with the socket. Lock down the retaining arm to keep the CPU in place. Then attach the heat sink/fan assembly to the metal clips that are on the sides of the socket. Make sure that the

heat sink is installed flush with the CPU by inspecting the assembly
from the side. You want to be positive of this before turning on the
computer because the thermal paste will begin to expand and fill the
imperfections right away. Attach the fan's power cable to the motherboard. (See your motherboard documentation for details on where to
plug in the fan.) Install the entire motherboard assembly into the case
(if that is your method of choice).

5. **Test the installation:** With the case still open, boot the computer to
make sure that the UEFI/BIOS POST recognizes the CPU as the right
type and speed. Enter the BIOS and view the CPU information to verify
this. If the BIOS doesn't recognize the CPU properly, check whether
a BIOS upgrade for the motherboard is necessary. Also make sure that
the CPU fan is functional. Then view the details of the CPU within the
BIOS. Be sure that the voltage reported by the BIOS is within tolerance.
Then access the operating system (after the OS is installed) and make
sure it boots correctly. Complete several full cycles and warm boots.
Finally, view the CPU(s) within Windows and/or third-party tools (such
as CPU-Z).

For example, check in the Device Manager to make sure the CPU is identified correctly. This can be accessed within Settings, the Control Panel,
within Computer Management, or by pressing Windows+R to open the
Run prompt and typing **devmgmt.msc** and pressing Enter. You should
see a category named Processors; expand it, and the CPU that is installed
should be listed. Remember, it will show up as multiple *logical* processors,
equal to the number of threads the CPU can run simultaneously.

Note

You can view basic CPU information in Windows at the System Information window,
which can be accessed by opening the Run prompt and typing **msinfo32**.

6. **Close the case and monitor the system:** Finally, if everything looks
okay, close the case and consider monitoring the clock rate, voltage, and
heat during the first few hours of operation. Voltage and heat can usually be monitored within the BIOS. All three can be monitored within
Windows and by using third-party applications or by using monitoring
utilities that accompany the motherboard. If all went well, congratulate
yourself on a job well done!

Cram Quiz

Answer these questions. The answers follow the last question. If you cannot answer these questions correctly, consider reading this chapter again until you can.

1. What does multithreading do?

   ○ **A.** It gives you multiple cores within the CPU.

   ○ **B.** It enables four simultaneous threads to be processed by one CPU core.

   ○ **C.** It enables two simultaneous threads to be processed by one CPU core.

   ○ **D.** It provides a high-speed connection from the CPU to RAM.

2. What seals the tiny gaps between the CPU cap and the heat sink?

   ○ **A.** Grape jelly

   ○ **B.** Plumber's putty

   ○ **C.** 3-in-1 house oil

   ○ **D.** Thermal paste

3. Which of the following can be defined as the amount of heat generated by the CPU, which the cooling system is required to dissipate?

   ○ **A.** GPU

   ○ **B.** TDP

   ○ **C.** PSU

   ○ **D.** 140 watts

4. When deciding on a CPU for use with a specific motherboard, what does it need to be compatible with?

   ○ **A.** Case

   ○ **B.** Socket

   ○ **C.** Wattage range

   ○ **D.** PCIe slots

5. Which kind of socket incorporates "lands" to ensure connectivity to a CPU?

   ○ **A.** PGA

   ○ **B.** Chipset

   ○ **C.** LGA

   ○ **D.** Copper

   ○ **E.** AM4

6. Which of the following enables the user to increase the base clock within the BIOS, thereby increasing the clock speed of the CPU?

   ○ **A.** Overclocking

   ○ **B.** L3 cache

   ○ **C.** Integrated GPU

   ○ **D.** Heat sink

7. Which of the following would you use if you needed a typical CPU for a PC that can access 16 GB of RAM?

   ○ **A.** ARM

   ○ **B.** x86-64

   ○ **C.** RISC

   ○ **D.** x86

8. A technician needs to install a new server system in a datacenter that can run more than one physical CPU at a time. Which configuration will support this requirement?

   ○ **A.** Single-core

   ○ **B.** Multi-core

   ○ **C.** Multithreading

   ○ **D.** Multisocket

Cram Quiz Answers

1. **C.** Multithreading allows for an operating system to send two simultaneous threads to be processed by a single CPU core. The OS views the CPU core as two virtual processors. Multiple cores would imply multicore technology, which means there are two physical processing cores within the CPU package. Hyper-Transport is a high-speed connection used by AMD from the CPU to RAM.

2. **D.** Thermal paste is used to seal the small gaps between the CPU and the heat sink. It is sometimes referred to as thermal gel or jelly (among a variety of other names), but not *grape* jelly. (Did I ever tell you about the time I found grape jelly inside a customer's computer? Fun times.) Note: Never use petroleum-based products (such as 3-in-1 oil or WD-40) inside a computer; the oils can damage the components over time.

3. **B.** TDP (thermal design power) is the amount of power required to cool a computer and is linked directly to the amount of heat a CPU creates. Some CPUs come with a built-in graphics processing unit (GPU). This means that with a compatible motherboard, no separate video card is necessary. PSU stands for power supply unit. 140 watts is a potential TDP rating but does not define what TDP is.

4. **B.** The CPU needs to be compatible with the socket of the motherboard. The case doesn't actually make much of a difference when it comes to the CPU. (Just make sure it's large enough!) There is no wattage range, but you should be concerned with the voltage range of the CPU. PCI Express (PCIe) slots don't actually play into this at all because there is no direct connectivity between the two.

5. **C.** LGA (Land Grid Array) is the type of socket that uses "lands" to connect the socket to the CPU. PGA (Pin Grid Array) sockets have pinholes that make for connectivity to the CPU's copper pins. AM4 is a PGA socket that accepts AMD CPUs such as the Ryzen 7.

6. **A.** Overclocking enables the user to increase the clock speed of the CPU within the BIOS. Level 3 (L3) cache comes in the largest capacities of the three types of cache and has the most latency; therefore, it is the slowest. If the CPU can't find what it needs in L1, it moves to L2 and then to L3. An integrated GPU is a video adapter that is built into the motherboard. The heat sink helps to dissipate heat from the CPU and is usually aided by a fan or liquid cooling system.

7. **B.** You would want an x86-64 CPU. This 64-bit CPU architecture can go beyond the 32-bit limitation of 4 GB of RAM and access as much as 256 TB of RAM (theoretically). Also, that is normally the type of CPU you would use in a PC. ARM-based CPUs are more often used with smartphones, tablets, and other mobile devices. Reduced instruction set computing (RISC) is a highly optimized technology used in ARM CPUs to make them more efficient. x86 is the older 32-bit version of PC-based CPUs. It is unlikely that you will see an x86 CPU, but you never know!

8. **D.** Some computers (such as servers) have multiple sockets, allowing them to run more than one CPU at the same time. Each of these physical CPUs will also incorporate multi-core and multithreading technologies. Get ready for 64 simultaneous threads or more! This is the kind of stuff that makes the cloud work.

Well, well, well, you completed the chapter! Excellent. We went pretty hardcore into CPUs there, so remember to review, take a break, and then continue on!

CHAPTER 18

Power

This chapter covers the following A+ 220-1101 exam objective:

▶ **3.5** – Given a scenario, install or replace the appropriate power supply.

Clean, well-planned power is imperative in a computer system. Power requirements should always be in the back of your mind when designing a computer. After the components of a computer have been selected—especially the CPU and GPU—the power supply needs to be chosen carefully. Not enough power, and the system might become unstable or might not work at all. Too much power, and it becomes expensive and wasteful. I can't tell you how much power plays into my decision-making process and how many power-related issues I have had to troubleshoot in the past.

The power supply unit (PSU) in a PC is in charge of converting the alternating current (AC) drawn from the wall outlet into direct current (DC) to be used internally by the computer. The power supply makes use of a transformer and a rectifier, working together to convert AC over to DC. The power supply feeds the motherboard, storage drives, optical drives, and any other devices inside the computer. Talk about a single point of failure! Many higher-end workstations and servers have redundant power supplies to protect against that single point of failure taking down the entire system. In this chapter, we focus on PC power supplies. For more information on power as it relates to laptops, see Chapter 1, "Laptop Hardware and Components."

You Have the Power!

By the way, for those of you starting to wonder about the sheer breadth of this tome and whether or not you can do this, I say: Yes! You most definitely can do this! And this is a shorter chapter, so let's get to it.

ExamAlert

Objective 3.5 focuses on the following: input 115 V vs. 220 V, output 3.3 V vs. 5 V vs. 12 V, 20-pin to 24-pin motherboard adapter, redundant power supply, modular power supply, and wattage rating.

Planning Which Power Supply to Use

It is important to use a reliable brand of power supply that is approved for use by organizations such as the International Electrotechnical Commission (IEC), Federal Communications Commission (FCC), UL, and so on, and that meets directives such as the Restriction of Hazardous Substances (RoHS). Adherence to appropriate standards reduces the risk of fire and allows for safer products in general.

You also must consider the following factors when planning which power supply to use in your computer:

▶ Type of power supply and compatibility

▶ Wattage and capacity requirements

▶ Number and type of connectors

Types of Power Supplies and Compatibility

The most common form factor used in PCs today is Advanced Technology Extended (ATX). Depending on the type of ATX, the main power connector to the motherboard will usually have 24 pins (or 20+4 pins), or 20 pins for much older ATX power supplies. Today's systems use power supplies that adhere to one of the ATX 12V 2.x standards which specify 24 pins. For backward compatibility with 20-pin connections, many power supplies' 24-pin connectors come with 4 pins that can be detached and moved out of the way. In case the power supply doesn't have this feature, there are also 20-pin to 24-pin adapters available.

The key here is compatibility. If a computer is proprietary, you can go to the computer manufacturer's website to find out the exact form factor and possibly get a replacement power supply for that model computer. Some third-party power supply manufacturers also offer replacement power supplies for proprietary systems. However, if a computer is custom built, you need to find out the form factor used by the motherboard and/or case, and you should open the computer to take a look at all the necessary power connections. Then you need to find a compatible power supply (according to those specifications) from a power supply manufacturer.

Most of today's motherboards have an additional 4-pin or 8-pin 12 V power port for the CPU (referred to as EATX12V). A typical power supply offers one or two 4-pin connectors or one 8-pin connector for this extra power. If the motherboard and power supply don't match up, there are 4- to 8-pin adapters available. Figure 18.1 shows an example of a 24-pin ATX connector and an example of an 8-pin CPU connector.

24-pin ATX
Connector

8-pin CPU
Connector

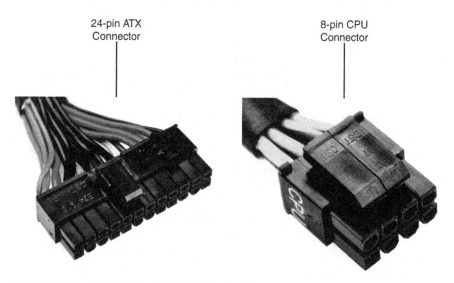

FIGURE 18.1 **24-pin ATX and EATX12V 8-pin CPU connectors**

> **ExamAlert**
>
> Be able to identify the main 24-pin power port/connector and the CPU's EATX12V 8-pin port/connector.

A quick word about rails. Remember that the ATX specification requires the power supply to produce +3.3 V, +5 V, +12 V, and −12 V outputs, as well as a 5 V standby output. These are known as "rails" (for example, the +12 V rail). You might have heard of dual-rail or multi-rail power supplies, such as multiple 12 V rails. This technology is important in systems that draw a lot of power. It is a way of monitoring power circuits individually instead of collectively (single-rail) and helps to prevent overheating and possibly fire by shutting down the PSU if a certain point is reached (for example, more than 18 amps on a single 12 V wire). If you plan to run a CPU-intensive system, such as a gaming system or multimedia system, you should look into a multi-rail PSU.

> **ExamAlert**
>
> The purpose of "dual-rail" PSUs is to separate and limit the current through each wire to avoid overheating.

Also, remember about case fans. If they have 4-pin connectors, they can connect directly to the motherboard. However, additional case fans may connect directly to the power supply feeds. What you use depends on how many fans you need and the configuration of the power connections.

Finally, case connectors for the Power button and the Reset button are usually located toward the front of the motherboard. When connecting these, the colored wire normally goes to positive (+), if necessary. Some case connectors can be connected either way, and it won't make a difference. But connectors like the power LED and the hard-drive activity LED need to be connected properly for the LEDs to display. Quite often, the motherboard will be color-coded; the fold-out instruction sheet (or manual) will show exactly where to plug in each case connector, and the case connectors themselves are normally labeled. Make sure you plug the case connectors into the correct motherboard headers and orient them properly.

Wattage and Capacity Requirements

Power supplies are usually rated in watts. They are rated at a maximum amount that they can draw from the wall outlet and pass on to the computer's devices.

Remember that the computer will not always use all that power. And the amount of power used depends on how many devices work and how much number crunching your processor does! In addition, when computers sleep or suspend, they use less electricity. What you need to be concerned with is the maximum amount of power all the devices need collectively. Most power-supply manufacturers today offer models that range from 300 watts all the way up to 1500 watts. Devices use a certain amount of power, defined in amps and/or watts. By adding together the power consumption of all the devices, you can get a clearer picture of the power supply you need. Consult the manufac-turer's web page of the device for exact requirements. Then consider using a power supply calculator on the Internet to find out how many watts you might need. Many desktop and tower computers can typically get away with using a power supply that is rated between 400 and 600 watts. But if you decide to add devices—especially video cards—you might find that the current power supply will not meet your needs anymore, and an upgrade will be necessary. So, plan for the future as well. (Apparently, technicians need to be prescient!)

ExamAlert

Remember that the PSU wattage rating refers to the maximum amount of power the PSU can output under 100% load capacity.

Number and Type of Power Connectors

It is important to know how many of each type of power connector you need when planning which power supply to use. You must be familiar with each type of power connector for the A+ exam. Be prepared to identify them by name and by sight. Table 18.1 defines the usage and voltages for some typical power con-nectors. Figure 18.2 shows these connectors.

TABLE 18.1 **Power Connectors**

Power Connector	Usage	Pins and Voltages
SATA	Serial ATA storage drives	15-pin, 3.3 V, 5 V, and 12 V
Molex	Case fans, IDE storage drives	4-pin, 5 V (red), 12 V (yellow), two ground wires
PCIe	PCI Express video cards	6-pin, 12 V (ATX12V version 2.1)
		8-pin, 12 V (ATX12V version 2.2 and higher)

FIGURE 18.2 **SATA, Molex, and PCIe power connectors**

ExamAlert

Be able to identify SATA, Molex, and PCIe power connectors, know their associated voltages, and know their number of pins.

Note

Don't confuse 8-pin PCIe power connectors with 8-pin CPU connectors! To tell the difference, look for the label! Also, the PCIe video connector will usually separate two of the pins so that you can use it in 6-pin or 8-pin scenarios.

Many PSUs still come with a Berg connector for backward compatibility. It's a smaller 4-pin connector used with the venerable 3.5-inch floppy drive.

Modular and Redundant PSUs

In older times, PSUs had all of the power cables coming out in a single bundle from the unit; a person had little control over the connections available. Newer PSUs fix this problem by being modular. To accomplish this, a modular PSU has a variety of ports that you can plug power cables into (some also come with a bundle of standard power connections). This modularity allows a person to add more connections as needed; for example, Molex to SATA power connections or PCIe connections for video. For added flexibility, go modular!

Redundant PSUs are very common on servers and some other high-end systems. To allow for true redundancy, the computer case must have two or more PSUs. (*Redundant* simply means more than one of a particular component.) When you have multiple PSUs, there is a separate IEC cable for each. For example, a rack-mount server might come with two power supplies. Each one requires an AC outlet. They both are powered on at all times. Typically, if one fails, the other is ready to take over the electric load without any downtime, because it is already running. In this case, it is not only redundant but able to tolerate a PSU failure (also known as *fault tolerant*). These power supplies are often removable, so if one fails, it can be slid out the back of the case and replaced. Some are even hot-swappable, meaning that you wouldn't even have to turn the server off to switch out the PSU; but always check the documentation first to be sure!

Installing the Power Supply

When the power supply arrives, you can install it. But first take a look at the back of the power supply to identify the components, which are shown in Figure 18.3.

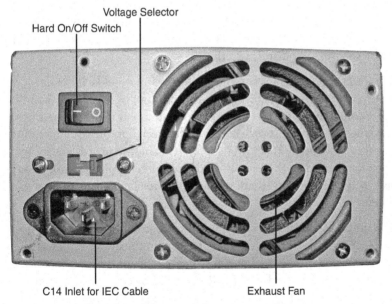

FIGURE 18.3 **Rear view of power supply**

In the top-left portion of Figure 18.3 is a hard on/off switch, sometimes referred to as a kill switch. This is a helpful feature when troubleshooting PCs. Instead of disconnecting the power cable, you can shut off this switch. It works effectively in emergencies as well. Below that, you see a (red) voltage selector switch. This indicates that this is a dual-voltage power supply. This should be set to 115 V in the United States. It also has a 230 V option to be used in other countries. (An additional adapter might be necessary for the different wall outlets you might encounter.) Always shut down the computer and disconnect the power cable before changing the voltage selector switch. Be sure to check this setting before initially using the power supply. This selector switch indicates an older, or atypical, power supply. Newer power supplies are equipped with a universal input, enabling you to connect the power supply to any AC outlet between 100 V and 240 V without having to set a voltage switch; the power supply "auto-detects" the voltage. To determine if a PSU without a voltage switch is truly dual-voltage, look for the phrase "100-240 V input" or something similar.

In Figure 18.3, below the voltage selector, you see the power cable inlet; this is known as a C14 inlet and is where you attach your power cord to the power supply. These inlets and the cables that connect to them are defined by the long-standing IEC 60320 specification and, because of this, some techs refer to the power cord as an "IEC cable." This cord actually has a standard three-prong connector suitable for an AC outlet on one end and a C13 line socket on the other to connect to the power supply. To the right, you see the power supply fan that is of great importance when troubleshooting power supplies. We'll discuss troubleshooting in Chapters 23 through 29.

Back to our power supply installation! For new computer builds, I usually install the power supply at the end. This may or may not be possible, depending on your configuration, but it is a good rule of thumb. If this is a repair or an upgrade, and there is a power supply currently connected to the computer, turn off the computer and unplug the power supply. ATX motherboards are always receiving 5 volts, even when they are off (if the computer is plugged in). Be sure that you use antistatic methods. Remove the old power supply and prepare to install the new one.

You might want to test the new power supply before installing it. This can be done by connecting a power supply tester, plugging in the power supply to the AC outlet, and turning on the hard on/off switch. (I'll show this in Chapter 24, "Troubleshooting Motherboards, CPUs, RAM, and Power.") Or you can test the power supply after it is installed by simply turning on the computer.

The power supply is placed inside the case and is often mounted with four standard screws that are screwed in from the back of the case. Make sure that there are no gaps between the power supply and the power supply opening in the case. Next, connect the main ATX 24-pin power connector to the motherboard. It can only be plugged in one way: a locking tab prevents a wrong connection and keeps the plug in place. Then, connect the 8-pin CPU power connector—again, tabbed for easy orientation. After that, attach the SATA and PCIe connectors as necessary to their corresponding devices. You might also have Molex connections to make for additional fans, monitoring devices, lights, or legacy devices. Most connectors are molded in such a way as to make it difficult to connect them backward or upside down. If you need a lot of strength to plug in the connector, make sure that it is oriented correctly. Don't force the connection. Afterward, remove any antistatic protection and, finally, plug in the power supply to the AC outlet, turn on the hard on/off switch (if the power supply has one), and turn on the computer. Check to see if the fan in the power supply is working and if the computer boots correctly. Do a final check of the CPU fan, case fans, internal/external indicator lights, and POST code read-out—if the motherboard has one. If all systems are go, then close up the case and chalk up one more successful install!

Cram Quiz

Answer these questions. The answers follow the last question. If you cannot answer these questions correctly, consider reading this chapter again until you can.

1. Which power connector should be used to connect directly to a SATA storage drive? (Select the best answer.)

   - **A.** Molex
   - **B.** 6-pin
   - **C.** 24-pin
   - **D.** 15-pin

2. Which voltages are supplied by a Molex power connector?

   - **A.** 12 V and 5 V
   - **B.** 5 V and 3.3 V
   - **C.** 3.3 V and 1.5 V
   - **D.** 24 V and 12 V

3. A company salesperson just returned to the United States after three months in Europe. Now the salesperson tells you that her PC, which worked fine in Europe, won't turn on. What is the best solution?

   - **A.** Install a new power supply.
   - **B.** The computer will not work in the United States due to European licensing.
   - **C.** Install a power inverter to the power supply.
   - **D.** Change the voltage from 230 to 115.

4. Which of the following can have 8 pins? (Select all that apply.)

- ○ **A.** PCIe
- ○ **B.** SATA
- ○ **C.** ATX main power
- ○ **D.** CPU
- ○ **E.** Molex

5. A gaming enthusiast is building a new system that requires a powerful power supply unit. Which of the following would most likely help the gamer purchase the correct PSU for the system? (Select three.)

- ○ **A.** Wattage rating
- ○ **B.** Manufacturer's website
- ○ **C.** Power supply calculator
- ○ **D.** Redundancy

Cram Quiz Answers

1. D. 15-pin connectors power SATA storage drives and other SATA devices (such as optical drives). That said, you might see a Molex power port on a modular PSU that can ultimately be connected to a SATA drive (with a Molex-to-SATA cable), but not directly; the SATA drive will have a 15-pin power connection on it. Molex connectors are also typically used for power fans, older IDE devices, and other secondary devices. 6-pin power connectors are used for video cards (as are 8-pin connectors). 24-pin refers to the main power connection for the motherboard.

2. A. Molex connectors provide 12 volts and 5 volts. There are four wires: if color-coded, yellow is 12 V, red is 5 V, and the two black wires are grounds.

3. D. Most likely, the voltage selector was set to 230 V so that it could function properly in Europe (for example, in the UK). It needs to be changed to 115 V so that the power supply can work properly in the United States. Make sure to do this while the computer is off and unplugged. Note: For shorter trips, a person will most likely use a laptop, which would require the right adapter to convert the voltage properly.

4. A and D. PCIe power can be 8-pin or 6-pin. CPU power (EATX12V) can be 8-pin or 4-pin. SATA power is 15-pin (and data is 7-pin). ATX main power is typically 24-pin. Molex is a 4-wire connector; it is sometimes also referred to as "peripheral."

5. **A, B, and C.** What the gamer needs to be concerned with is the maximum amount of power all the devices need collectively, especially the GPU (or GPUs), CPU, and RAM. The PSU wattage rating refers to the maximum amount of power the PSU can output under 100% load capacity. By adding all the devices' power consumption together, the gamer can get a clearer picture of how powerful a power supply is needed. The gamer should also consult the PSU manufacturer's website for exact requirements. A power supply calculator on the Internet can be used to find out how many watts the gamer might need. Redundant PSUs are very common on servers and some other high-end systems but not as often on gaming systems.

I told you that you could do it! Congratulations on completing another chapter. Carry on!

CHAPTER 19

Multifunction Devices/ Printers

This chapter covers the following A+ 220-1101 exam objective:

▶ **3.6** — Given a scenario, deploy and configure multifunction devices/ printers and settings.

A small office/home office (SOHO) multifunction device is usually a printer that can do other things, such as scan and save documents, copy documents, fax information, and more. However, for the A+ exam, the most important function of these multifunction devices is printing, so that is our main focus in this chapter.

Many printers connect via USB, but you will also encounter printers that connect directly to a network (via wires or wirelessly).

While there is a worldwide initiative to reduce the use of paper, printers are still an important part of the business world. Be ready to install and troubleshoot them.

ExamAlert

Objective 3.6 concentrates on the following concepts: properly unboxing a device, setup location considerations, use of appropriate drivers for a given OS, device connectivity, public/shared devices, configuration settings, security, network scan services, and automatic document feeder (ADF)/flatbed scanners.

Setup Considerations

New printers and multifunction devices should be given some consideration prior to installation and configuration. I often say: "It's all in the planning." And it's true; for most jobs, I spend more time on planning than I do on anything else. To ensure a smooth, easy printer or multifunction device installation, proper planning is imperative.

Before you purchase any equipment, it is important to define exactly what the equipment will be used for and by whom. Defining the amount of workload that you expect will help narrow down what type of printer to purchase and can save your organization money. Determine what client operating systems will be accessing the printer and what applications are being used by those clients.

For a printer, the "where" is also very important. You want a printer to be accessible to users, and you also want the printer to be able to access the network. If it is to be connected to a PC and shared, then some type of community area should be set up near the PC that it is to be connected to. However, it is more likely that a printer or a multifunction device will be connected directly to the network. If it is to be wired to the network, then it needs to be near a working RJ45 jack. If it will connect wirelessly, then you should do a wireless site survey to see if your desired printer location will be well within the Wi-Fi area.

Remember: safety first. When working on a printer, be sure to work in a secure area, away from any other employees. Also, use proper lifting techniques (bend at the legs and avoid straining the back), and don't move anything by yourself that requires two people. Finally, use proper safety protocols when working with tools. We'll discuss safety in more detail in Chapter 59, "Safety Procedures."

When unboxing a new printer, allow for some time and be sure to have your toolkit ready! A box cutter, screw gun, and work gloves are recommended. Some printers are shipped in protective wooden structure, and some are sent in hard foam. Either way, you will find that there are a lot of materials that have to be removed and/or disassembled. You may want to save the box and the materials just in case the device has been damaged and needs to be returned. Be kind to the environment and dispose of any cardboard, wood planks, and plastic wrapping according to proper waste and recycling regulations. Inspect the device for any signs of damage. Remove any blue security tape, safety bars, or other securing mechanisms. Install any paper trays, platens, or other physical devices that are part of the printer. Collect and properly store any manuals, extra toner, USB cables, Ethernet cables, software, power converters, and anything else that might come with the multifunction device. And, if time permits, READ THE MANUAL!

If the multifunction device passes inspection, you can verify functionality of the device in your test environment (if you have one). Be sure to check for any protective tape that would prevent the multifunction device from printing. Sometimes this will be in the device or come as part of a toner cartridge or other printer consumable. Some higher-end inkjet printers require that you fill all ink cartridges yourself, using a funnel and a syringe. Depending on the printer, printer unboxing and setup can be quite a time-consuming process, so plan wisely. For example, typically, people tend to print (and printers tend to fail) between 3 and 5 p.m. on workdays, so that might not be the best time to perform new installations.

Next on the list is to update firmware for the device (if necessary) and install the proper software driver. The driver might be software that came with the device in the form of an optical disc or a USB flash drive, or it might be software that you need to download from the Internet. Or, the device might be seen automatically by the operating system, and if you and your organization are okay with it, you can use that generic driver. Usually, I prefer using the correct latest driver from the manufacturer. Either way, it's important to understand the difference between PCL and PostScript drivers. For some printer models, there are separate drivers for each:

▶ **Printer Command Language (PCL) drivers:** These drivers are the more commonly used of the two. PCL is used for general office applications: printing typical documents, spreadsheets, and so on.

▶ **PostScript drivers:** These drivers are used for professional graphics and presentations. It is designed for higher-end printers but can be supported by lesser models as well.

When you install a driver, you might see whether it is PCL or PostScript within the name of the printer driver (for example, HP LaserJet 9065 PCL6 Class Driver) Be sure to use the correct driver type for your work environment.

> **ExamAlert**
>
> Know the differences between the printer driver types: PCL (more common, used for typical office printing) and PostScript (less common, used for professional graphics).

Next, run any multifunction device/printer self-tests that are required by the manufacturer. Color laser printers, inkjet printers, and multifunction printers might need to be calibrated before use. Calibration involves aligning the printing mechanism to the paper and verifying color output. Usually, the software that accompanies the printer guides you through this process. In some cases, these calibration tests can be done via the small display on the printer

Make sure that the device can successfully print, scan, copy, and perform any other jobs that you need it to. You can do this, for example, by using the Print a Test Page feature in Windows. If the device has a scanner—flatbed, automatic document feeder (ADF), or other—be sure to test whether the system can properly scan items and send them via email, store them to a Windows server share via the Server Message Block (SMB) protocol, route them to the cloud, or provide any other network scanning services necessary. At this time, you can also configure additional printer settings (which we'll cover in just a bit), and network settings (such as TCP/IP) from your test environment. When the device passes all tests, install it to the destination of your choice, test one more time, and celebrate another job well done!

Printer Configuration Settings

Configuration of printers can be done in one of three places:

- ▶ **The operator control panel (OCP):** These small displays are most common on laser printers. They are menu-driven displays and are usually user-friendly and intuitive.

- ▶ **The printer's web interface (for a network printer):** This is often accessed through a web browser.

- ▶ **Within Windows:** This is the option we'll focus on in this section. To open a printer in Windows, use **Settings > Devices** or **Control Panel > Devices and Printers**. If you work with printers often, consider placing a shortcut to the printer or printers on the desktop or pin it to the taskbar. Several items can be configured in Windows, including managing print jobs, setting the priority of the printer, configuring the print spooler, and managing permissions.

Basic Printer Configuration Settings

A typical print job is simple—one printed page, printed on one side, on 8.5-by 11-inch paper in portrait mode, and at the standard 600 DPI resolution. For example, you might print a typical document (such as a resume) this way. However, there are many occasions where the typical settings are not enough. There are some basic printer configuration settings you should know for the exams: duplexing, collating, orientation, tray settings, and print quality. They are generally found in the Printing preferences or Printer properties section of Windows. Let's briefly examine each one now.

Duplexing means printing on both sides of the paper, and it might simply be called "print on both sides." Some organizations require duplexing (for most print jobs) in their policies related to reducing paper consumption; however, most printers are not set to duplex by default. You might also see an option for duplexing on the main print screen when you go to perform a print job; it might be called "manual duplex."

If you print a single job, *collating* is not an issue. But when you print multiple copies of the same job, collating might become necessary. Historically, multiple copies of the same print job would print out all of page 1, then all of page 2, then all of page 3, and so on. It was up to the user to manually arrange, or collate, these pages. However, as printers became more sophisticated, they were equipped with the processing power to collate jobs, sorting them as page 1, page 2, page 3, and so on, and then moving on to the next copy of the entire job. This, of course, saves a lot of time for users. Some printers are set this way by default. Others have to be configured to collate.

Orientation is the method of positioning a printed page and is based on whether the page is going to be viewed vertically (portrait) or horizontally (landscape). This can be set permanently from the Printing preferences page, and it can also be set manually when you go to print a single document. Often, it will be found in the layout section. Most documents are printed in portrait mode (such as reports or resumes created in a word processor), but sometimes you need to print a spreadsheet or a slide presentation, which is best done in landscape mode.

Now on to *tray settings*. A printer's paper tray can be physically configured to work with the standard size paper mentioned before (8.5 × 11 inches) or other sizes, such as 8.5 × 14 inches. Or you might have more narrow guides that accept envelopes. More importantly, tray settings can be configured in the operating system. In Windows, this can also be done in Printing preferences, and most likely in the Advanced section. From there you can modify the default paper size to be used (for instance, standard letter size, legal size, or a particular envelope type). From Advanced, you can also specify the number of copies to be made, enable a built-in stapler (if the device has one), and configure several other options.

Finally, *quality* is the print resolution, which is measured in dots per inch (DPI). 600 DPI or higher is considered to be "letter quality" and acceptable for professional documents. But you might want an even better quality (1200 or 2400 DPI), especially for a document that includes graphics. A specific DPI setting can usually be configured within the Advanced section of the Printing preferences, but it can also be configured from the Print window, often using more generic terms (such as draft, normal, and best).

Take a look at your Printing preferences, Printer properties pages, and the main Print screen (when you go to print a document) and view the configuration settings just discussed. Even if you don't have a printer, you can set up a false printer on your system by adding the printer in the Devices and Printers window in the Control Panel. Typically, I suggest selecting any one of the newer HP laser printers from the list as a fake printer. You can then access its properties just as you would on a printer that is actually installed to the computer or network.

> **ExamAlert**
>
> Know the following printer configuration settings: duplex, collate, orientation, tray settings, and quality.

Sharing Printers and Managing Permissions

A printer that is connected to a Windows PC must first be *shared* before users of other computers can send print jobs to it. There are two steps involved in sharing printers in Windows. First, printer sharing in general must be enabled. To enable printer sharing in Windows, open the Network and Sharing Center. Then click the **Change advanced sharing settings** link. Click the down arrow for your network type and then select the radio button labeled **Turn on file and printer sharing**.

> **Note**
>
> You can also make a computer's devices visible when Windows is first installed. We'll discuss this and network discovery in the Windows networking section of this book.

Next, the individual printer needs to be shared. This can be done in the Sharing tab of the Printer properties window. Check the **Share This Printer** checkbox and give the printer a share name. Note that the share name does not need to be the same as the printer name. Click **OK**, and the printer should show up as shared in the Printers window.

Permissions can be set for a printer in the Security tab of the Printer properties window. Users and groups can be added in this window, and the appropriate permission can be assigned, including Print, Manage Printers, and Manage Documents. Standard users normally are assigned the Print permission, whereas administrators get all permissions, enabling them to pause the printer or cancel all documents (Manage Printers) and pause, cancel, and restart individual documents. For more information on permissions, see Chapter 47, "Windows Security Settings."

Local vs. Network Printers

A local printer is a printer that connects directly to a computer, normally by USB, or, on rare occasions, by RS-232 serial/parallel connections. When a user works at a computer, that computer is considered to be the local computer. So, when a printer is connected to that computer, it is known as the local printer.

A network printer is a printer that connects directly to the network (usually via Ethernet) or to a print server device. Network printers are shared by more than one user on the computer network. Usually, a network printer is given an IP address and becomes yet another *host* on the network. If a printer connects directly to the network, it is usually by way of a built-in RJ45 port on the printer, just as a computer's network card connects to the network. A print server could be a computer or a smaller black box device. Many SOHO routers offer integrated print server capabilities. With such devices, the printer connects via USB to the print server/router, and a special piece of software is installed on any client computers that want to print to that printer (that is, if the client OS doesn't automatically find the printer).

Network printing can also be accomplished wirelessly—via Wi-Fi or by Bluetooth—on most of today's printers. Remember that Wi-Fi typically has greater range than Bluetooth.

Then there is cloud-based printing. It is possible to harness the power of the cloud to print remotely. You might have a document you need printed to a printer in a network in another city. If your organization has implemented a cloud-based solution, you can print remotely simply by selecting the printer from a drop-down menu. We'll discuss cloud-based technologies further in Chapter 21, "Cloud Computing Concepts."

If a network printer is being controlled by Windows, you generally rely on direct TCP/IP connections. However, printers that are controlled by macOS might also make use of the networking service Bonjour and use AirPrint to automatically locate and download drivers for printers. Bonjour, which is a type of zero-configuration networking, enables automatic discovery of devices and services on a local network using industry-standard IP protocols. AirPrint is an Apple technology that helps you create full-quality printed output without the need to download or install drivers.

Basic Printer Security

Regardless of how a printer is connected and how a user connects to the printer, data privacy concerns should be addressed. An insecure printer can retain copies of information that could be accessible to anyone who has a little know-how. A printer might cache information to memory or to a print server's storage drive. This cache should be cleared at least every day and perhaps more often, depending on your organization's policy. A printer can also be audited—in Windows or elsewhere. Audit logs can show exactly who printed what, as well as when and where it was done. I say "can" because auditing normally needs to be enabled and configured properly. We discuss auditing briefly in Chapter 48, "Windows Best Practices."

As an administrator, you can also consider implementing user authentication for a printer or print server, ultimately requiring a person to present credentials of some kind. For example, in Windows, you can enable Secure Print, which requires the user to enter a passcode before printing to a printer. This is set up beforehand by the administrator within Printing preferences by changing the printer's default job type from Normal to Secure and setting a passcode. While this can help to secure a printer from unauthorized use, a single static passcode is somewhat unmanageable. A more effective and more manageable approach is to rely on networkwide multi-factor authentication—combining different factors such as username/password, biometrics, and an ID card or access badge that the user carries. We'll discuss authentication further in Chapters 43, "Physical Security," and 44, "Logical Security." For now, remember that personal and confidential data can be stored in many places and that those locations should be organized and secured accordingly.

> **ExamAlert**
>
> Printer security can be implemented through user authentication and policies, badging, and Secure Print. Audit logs can be used to see what was printed, where it was printed, and who printed it.

Cram Quiz

Answer these questions. The answers follow the last question. If you cannot answer these questions correctly, consider reading this chapter again until you can.

1. Where would you go in Windows to enable printer sharing?

   ○ **A.** Network Connections

   ○ **B.** Network and Sharing Center

   ○ **C.** The printer's OCP

   ○ **D.** Bonjour

2. Your printer supports printing to both sides of a piece of paper. What should you enable in the Printing preferences to print on both sides?

   ○ **A.** Collate

   ○ **B.** Orientation

   ○ **C.** Duplex

   ○ **D.** Quality

3. Which of the following address printer data privacy concerns? (Select the two best answers.)

   ○ **A.** Implementing user authentication on the device

   ○ **B.** PCL

   ○ **C.** AirPrint

   ○ **D.** Clearing the cache

4. When you are finished installing a new printer and print drivers, what should you do? (Select all that apply.)

    ○ **A.** Calibrate the printer.

    ○ **B.** Install the print drivers.

    ○ **C.** Check for compatibility.

    ○ **D.** Print a test page.

5. A technician is setting up a printer for a customer who prints professional graphics and presentations. Which print driver should be installed?

    ○ **A.** PCL

    ○ **B.** ADF

    ○ **C.** SMB

    ○ **D.** PostScript

6. A large company with several printers and Windows print servers located throughout the enterprise hires you to implement printer security measures. What industry-standard recommendations should you consider? (Select all that apply.)

    ○ **A.** Turn off all file and printer sharing

    ○ **B.** User authentication

    ○ **C.** Policies

    ○ **D.** Audit logs

Cram Quiz Answers

1. **B.** The Network and Sharing Center in Windows is where printer sharing is enabled. Network Connections is the window that shows the Ethernet and Wi-Fi connections that a system has to the network. Windows sharing has to be done in Windows; it can't be done from the printer's operator control panel (OCP). Bonjour is a macOS service that enables automatic discovery of devices on the LAN; it can also be run on Windows.

2. **C.** Duplexing (as it relates to printers) means printing on both sides of the paper. Collating means printing multiple copies of a document's pages in sequence instead of printing all of the copies of one page at a time. Orientation refers to how the print job is displayed on the paper; it could be portrait (vertical orientation—the default) or landscape (horizontal orientation). Quality refers to the clarity of the print job and is usually measured in dots per inch (DPI), where the higher the DPI setting, the better the quality.

3. **A and D.** Implementing user authentication for the printer or print server (PIN or password) and clearing the cache on the printer both address printer data privacy concerns. Printer Command Language (PCL) (sometimes referred to as Printer

Control Language) is a type of driver for printers typically used for standard office application printing. AirPrint is an Apple technology for macOS and iOS that is used to automatically locate and download drivers for printers.

4. **A and D.** After the printer is installed (meaning it has been connected and the drivers have been installed), you should calibrate the printer (if necessary) and print a test page. You should also consider updating the firmware for the printer. Before starting the installation, you should check for compatibility with operating systems, applications, and so on.

5. **D.** Know the difference between printer driver types: PostScript (less common, used for professional graphics and presentations) and PCL (more common, used for typical office printing). ADF, which stands for automatic document feeder, refers to a wonderful contraption that allows you to scan, copy, or fax multiple page documents without having to feed each page individually. SMB, which stands for Server Message Block, is a network file sharing protocol.

6. **B, C, and D.** Printer security can be implemented through user authentication and policies, badging, and Secure Print. Audit logs can be used to see what was printed, where it was printed, and who printed it. Turning off all file and printer sharing will most likely be counterproductive for an organization that has several printers that customers need to access. As you've seen, some questions have a "throw-away" answer. This is one of them.

Another chapter complete. Great work!

CHAPTER 20
Printer Consumables

This chapter covers the following A+ 220-1101 exam objective:

▶ **3.7** — Given a scenario, install and replace printer consumables.

Businesses use several types of printers. The most common business-oriented printer is the laser printer. Inkjet printers are more prevalent in homes due to their lower cost and their capability to print in color with excellent resolution. That said, high-end inkjet printers are sometimes used by organizations as well. A technician might also encounter thermal, impact, and 3D printers. This section describes those five types of printers, how they function, and the materials they consume.

> **ExamAlert**
>
> **Objective 3.7** focuses on the following: laser printers, inkjet printers, thermal printers, impact printers, and 3D printers.

Each type of printer has unique characteristics that affect how a technician installs, configures, and troubleshoots it. The most common type of printer used in businesses is the laser printer; this type of printer also happens to be the most complicated and difficult to troubleshoot. We'll discuss troubleshooting later in the book, but to be a good troubleshooter, you should know the technology well. Let's examine printer technology now.

Laser Printers

Laser printers can produce high-quality text and graphics on cut sheets of paper; printers that print to individual pieces of paper are known as *page printers*. The bulk of laser printers print in black, but there are also color laser printers (which, of course, are more expensive). Such printers are called laser printers because inside the printer is a laser beam that projects an image of the item to be printed onto an electrically charged drum; this image is later transferred to paper. Text and images that are shown on paper are created from electrically charged toner, which is a type of powder stored in a replaceable toner cartridge. The type of toner used can vary from one printer brand to the next, but they all work essentially the same way.

The laser printer drum, known also as a photoelectric or photosensitive drum, is at the center of the whole laser printing process, but there are a couple of other important components, including the primary corona wire, the transfer corona wire, the fuser assembly, and, of course, the laser itself. Figure 20.1 shows these components.

The laser printing process that a laser printer goes through is sometimes referred to as an imaging process (including in Objective 3.7). Knowledge of this process can help you when it comes time to troubleshoot and/or maintain a laser printer.

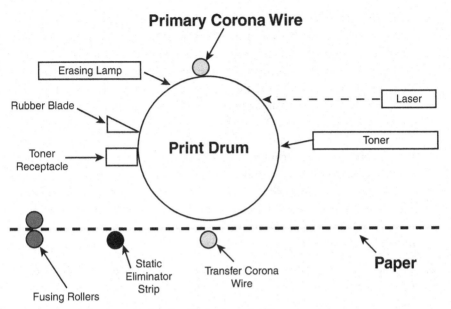

FIGURE 20.1   **Components involved in the laser printing process**

The following list describes the typical laser printing process:

1. **Processing:** The text or image to be printed is sent to the printer, where a processor recalculates it and stores it in RAM while the printer readies itself for the ordeal of laser printing. Additional processing may be done at the local computer that initiated the printing.

2. **Charging:** In this step, a negative charge is applied to the imaging drum by the primary corona wire, which is powered by a high-voltage power supply within the printer.

3. **Exposing:** In this step, the laser is activated and "writes" to the drum as it spins. Where the laser hits the drum, it dissipates the negative charge toward the center of the drum that is grounded. The "exposed" areas of the drum now have a lesser negative charge. (By the way, the drum is also known as an imaging drum.)

4. **Developing:** The surface of the drum that was previously exposed to the laser is now applied with negatively charged toner. This toner has a higher charge than the areas of the drum that were written to.

5. **Transferring:** The toner, and therefore the text or image, is transferred to paper as the drum rolls over it. The movement of the paper is assisted by pickup rollers (for feeding the paper) and transfer rollers (to move it through the rest of the printer). Separation pads are used to make sure only one page is picked up at a time. On many laser printers, the paper slides between the drum and a positively charged corona wire (known as the transfer corona wire). The transfer corona wire applies the positive charge to the paper. Because the paper now has a positive charge, and the toner particles on the drum have a negative charge, the toner is attracted to the paper. (For voltages, opposites attract.) In many printers, the paper passes by a static elimination device (often a strip), which removes excess charge from the paper. Some color laser printers use a transfer belt to apply the various layers of colors to the paper. Some printers use a duplexing assembly that allows the paper to be printed on both sides.

6. **Fusing:** The toner is fused to the paper. The paper passes through the fuser assembly, which includes pressurized rollers and a heating element that can reach approximately 400 degrees F (or about 200 degrees C).

7. **Cleaning:** A rubber blade removes excess toner from the drum as it spins. An erasing lamp removes any leftover charge on the drum, bringing it to zero volts. The printer is now ready for another print job.

> **ExamAlert**
>
> Know the steps of the laser printing process (also known as the imaging process).

> **ExamAlert**
>
> Know that laser printer components include the imaging drum, fuser assembly, transfer belt, transfer roller, pickup rollers, separation pads, and duplexing assembly.

In some laser printers, the drum, laser, and primary corona wire are contained within the toner cartridge. Issues that are caused by these components can usually be fixed just by replacing the toner cartridge.

> **Note**
>
> Toner cartridges are replaceable; they are known as *consumables*. Whatever material it is that actually prints onto paper is usually considered a consumable, regardless of the type of printer.

Laser printers have a couple advantages over other types of printers:

▶ **Speed:** A laser printer can print anywhere from 10 to 100 pages per minute (ppm), depending on the model and whether it is a color or black-and-white laser printer.

▶ **Print quality:** A laser printer commonly prints at 600 dots per inch (DPI), which is considered letter quality, but 1200 DPI and 2400 DPI printers are also available.

> **ExamAlert**
>
> Of all printer types, the laser printer is considered to have the lowest cost per page, making it an excellent long-term printer choice for businesses.

Maintenance of laser printers is vital. You should periodically inspect a laser printer and replace the toner cartridge if necessary. The toner cartridge usually slides into a compartment in the laser printer. Instructions on how to insert it accompany the cartridge. Be cautious of a couple of things:

▶ Toner can potentially spill or leak out of the cartridge—it's messy, and potentially hazardous. When you remove a cartridge, put it in a box or bag for transport to wherever it will be recycled. Carry it horizontally in the same position that it was taken out of the printer. Don't shake it!

▶ Remove the protective tape strip from the new toner cartridge. It is there to prevent toner spill, but the printer won't be able to print (and can even be damaged) if the tape is not removed.

Many laser printers have a counter that can be set to notify you when the printer has printed a particular number of pages, such as 50,000. Once the printer gets to that point, you should perform maintenance or, at the very least, carefully inspect the internals of the printer. Most laser printer manufacturers offer maintenance kits that include a variety of components, which we will discuss further in Chapter 28, "Troubleshooting Printers." If you do use the maintenance kit, reset the counter when you are finished. You will find that this is similar to the maintenance counter of a vehicle.

Another Automotive Parallel

A manufacturer will often set a relatively low number for the laser printer's counter, similar to how an automobile manufacturer will set the mileage maintenance counter to a number on the low end of the maintenance range. To put it nicely, the manufacturer is assuming the worst conditions for your printer. While this might be suitable for dirty environments, the average office printer can often last longer than the manufacturer's recommended time between maintenance. The beauty of this is that you can set the counter to a higher number if you think it is appropriate, which ultimately can save time and money for your organization. Keep a log of when printers were maintained and when failures occur. If failures occur earlier than expected on the whole, consider decreasing the counter once again.

During your maintenance of the printer, you should clean it up, including the outside cover, the trays, the bin where the cartridge sits, and possibly the rollers. After maintenance is complete, be sure to calibrate the printer. This is usually a subroutine that is built into the printer's firmware; you might also be able to initiate it from Windows. Calibration allows you to set the horizontal and vertical printing coordinates and margins so that text and images appear clear and straight.

> **ExamAlert**
>
> Remember that maintenance for laser printers includes replacing toner, applying a maintenance kit, calibration, and cleaning.

Inkjet Printers

Inkjet printers are common in small offices, home offices, and for personal use. They can print documents but more commonly print photographs and graphical information in color; most of the time, they connect to a computer by way of USB or Wi-Fi.

An inkjet printer works by propelling ink onto various sizes of paper. Many inkjet printers store ink in multiple ink cartridges that are consumable; they have to be replaced (or refilled) when empty. Some inkjet printers stop operating if just one of the ink cartridges is empty. Two common types of inkjet printers are the thermal inkjet and the piezoelectric inkjet:

> ▶ **Thermal inkjet printers:** These account for the bulk of consumer inkjets and are the more recognizable type of inkjet printer. To move the

ink to the paper, heat is sent through the ink cartridge, forming a bubble (known as a thermal bubble) that pushes the ink onto the paper; imme-diately afterward, another charge of ink is readied. The reservoir of ink is within the ink cartridge; this is where the heat transfer occurs. HP and Canon develop many models of thermal inkjet printers. Don't confuse thermal inkjets with thermal printers.

▶ **Piezoelectric inkjet printers:** These account for the bulk of commercial inkjets. The printing processes within a piezoelectric inkjet printer and a thermal inkjet printer are similar; however, a piezo inkjet printer applies current to the ink material, causing it to change shape and size and forc-ing the ink onto the paper. The reservoir of ink is in another area, outside where the current is applied. This process enables longer print head life than you get with thermal inkjet printers. Epson develops many models of piezoelectric inkjet printers. Piezoelectric inkjets can also be found in manufacturing assembly lines.

The inkjet print process is fairly simple:

1. The paper or other media is pulled or moved into position by a roller and feeder mechanism, or it's moved into position by an assembly line's con-veyor belt (as with some piezoelectric inkjets).

2. The print head, located on a mechanical arm, moves across the paper, assisted by a carriage and belt system. The print head delivers black and colored ink from the ink cartridges as directed by the print driver.

3. At the end of the line, the paper or media is advanced and the print head either reverses direction and continues to print (often referred to as Hi-Speed mode) or returns to the left margin before printing continues. In printers that allow for duplexing, a duplexing assembly refeeds the paper into the printer for printing on the other side.

4. When the page is complete, the paper or other media is ejected.

ExamAlert

Know that inkjet printer components include ink cartridge, print head, roller, feeder, duplexing assembly, carriage, and belt.

Maintenance of an inkjet printer is often much simpler than with a laser printer. Check the ink cartridges periodically by using the printer's onscreen display (OSD) or within Windows (if possible); you can also physically inspect them if necessary. If one or more cartridges are low, be prepared to replace them. Some higher-end inkjet printers require that you fill the cartridges using a syringe (and a funnel to protect against overspill). If you find that there is a buildup of residue on the print cartridge, clean it with a manufacturer-supplied solution or consider using a 50/50 mix of isopropyl alcohol and water. (A box of cotton swabs would be a handy addition to your toolkit!) Inkjet printers should periodically be calibrated so that horizontal and vertical imagery lines up properly and so colors are blended appropriately. Calibration should always be done after cartridges are removed and replaced. While inspecting and maintaining an inkjet printer, look for any bits of paper that might have been caught up in the rollers or feeder and remove them. Clear any paper jams that might have occurred.

> **ExamAlert**
>
> Remember that inkjet printer maintenance includes cleaning heads, replacing cartridges, and calibration.

Thermal Printers

Thermal printers produce text and images by heating specially coated thermal paper. It is typical to see thermal printers used in point-of-sale (POS) systems, gas station pumps, and so on. Thermal printers consist of the following parts:

▶ **Thermal head:** This generates the heat and takes care of printing to the paper.

▶ **Platen:** This is the rubber roller that feeds the paper past the print head.

▶ **Spring:** This applies pressure to the print head, which brings the print head into contact with the paper.

▶ **Circuit board:** This controls the mechanism that moves the print head.

To print, special thermal paper is run through the feed assembly and then inserted between the thermal head and the platen. The printer sends current to the thermal head (heating element), which, in turn, generates heat. The heat activates the thermosensitive coloring layer of the thermal paper, which becomes the image.

Maintenance of a thermal printer includes inspecting the paper tray and replacing the paper, cleaning the heating element, and removing any debris that can be left behind by the thermal printing process. It's also important to store any extra heat-sensitive paper away from direct sunlight and, of course, heat.

Impact Printers

Impact printers use force to transfer ink to paper (for example, a print head striking a ribbon with paper directly behind it—similar to an old typewriter). This type of printer is somewhat deprecated, although certain environments might still use it, such as auto repair centers, warehouses, and accounting departments.

One type of impact printer, the daisy wheel, uses a wheel with many petals, each of which has a letter form (an actual letter) at the tip of the petal. These strike against the ribbon, impressing ink upon the paper that is situated behind the ribbon. But by far the most common type of impact printer is the dot matrix.

Dot-matrix printers are also known as line printers because they print text one line at a time and can keep printing over a long roll of paper, as opposed to page printers, which print to cut sheets of paper. The paper is fed into the printer using a tractor-feed mechanism; many dot-matrix printers use paper that has an extra perforated space with holes on each side that allow the paper to be fed into the printer. Dot-matrix printers use a matrix of pins that work together to create characters, instead of using a form letter. The print head that contains these pins strikes the ribbon, which, in turn, places the ink on the paper. Print heads come with either 9 pins or 24 pins; the 24-pin version offers better quality, known as *near letter quality (NLQ)*. Dot-matrix printers are loud and slow but are inexpensive to maintain.

Maintenance of an impact printer includes replacing the ribbon, replacing the print head, replacing the paper, and checking for bits of the perforated paper along the tractor feed mechanism and elsewhere in the printer.

3D Printers

With 3D printing, various materials—often plastic—are joined together to build a three-dimensional object. It is done by designing the object on the computer (with CAD and slicing software) and, ultimately, exporting the appropriate files to the correct 3D printer. The technology is often used to create prototypes of products to be later manufactured in bulk. However, it can be used to actually create commercial products as well.

> **ExamAlert**
>
> Know that 3D printers use a special plastic filament or resin to create the 3D shapes.

3D printing can be accomplished by implementing one of a couple processes: fused deposition modeling (FDM) or laser sintering. FDM is an additive process in which materials are fed into an extruder, superheated, and then applied on top of a substrate, layer by layer, to create 3D shapes that harden immediately. Laser sintering uses a laser that compacts a piece of material—such as nylon—using heat and/or pressure and binds the materials to create the structure.

> **Note**
>
> 3D "printing" is not considered an accurate name by some, but the term is used widely. You will also see the name *additive manufacturing*, among others.

3D printers are made by several manufacturers. Some use proprietary processes and file types, and others use standardized processes and files. Either way, the device is usually of cuboid shape with one or more glass walls allowing the user to view the manufacturing process. The center of the device contains a print bed. Other names for the print bed include substrate, platform, and build plate. The print bed has open space above it for the item to be built, and an extruder moves about that area in three dimensions (the X, Y, and Z axes).

What's really important for an A+ tech is how to install, maintain, and troubleshoot 3D printers. Let's discuss installation and maintenance briefly; we will get to printer troubleshooting in Chapter 28.

Many 3D printers can connect via USB, Wi-Fi, and Ethernet. These printers are controlled by a computer running an operating system such as Windows 10 and higher or OS X 10.9 and higher. The computer itself should meet the recommended requirements for the various design software—such as CAD software and slicing software. Some manufacturers of 3D printers make their own software, and others use third-party programs. Be ready to install the different programs necessary and to even work with design templates, many of which are freely available on the Internet.

When first installing a 3D printer, and periodically afterward, be sure to update the firmware for the device. Next, periodically make sure the build plate is level; this is usually done via the LCD panel, but you could use an actual level tool. Then, lubricate, tighten, and re-align the rods and pulleys periodically. Finally, clean the device, including the extruder's drive gear, the build plate, and so on. Users *should* clean up after themselves when completing a 3D print job, but you and I know that this is a utopian concept, especially given the fast pace of engineering and prototyping work, so be ready to clean up excess resin from the device.

ExamAlert

3D printer maintenance includes updating firmware, ensuring that the print bed is level, and cleaning excess plastic from the print environment.

Cram Quiz

Answer these questions. The answers follow the last question. If you cannot answer these questions correctly, consider reading this chapter again until you can.

1. In which step of the laser printing/imaging process is the transfer corona wire involved?

   ○ **A.** Developing

   ○ **B.** Transferring

   ○ **C.** Fusing

   ○ **D.** Cleaning

2. Which stage of the laser printing/imaging process involves extreme heat?

   ○ **A.** Fusing

   ○ **B.** Transferring

   ○ **C.** Exposing

   ○ **D.** Writing

3. Which of the following is the proper order for the laser printing/imaging process?

   ○ **A.** Processing, charging, developing, exposing, fusing, transferring, cleaning

   ○ **B.** Developing, processing, charging, exposing, transferring, fusing, cleaning

   ○ **C.** Charging, exposing, developing, processing, transferring, fusing, cleaning

   ○ **D.** Processing, charging, exposing, developing, transferring, fusing, cleaning

4. Which of the following sets of parts is associated with inkjet printers?

   ○ **A.** Imaging drum, fuser assembly, transfer belt, transfer roller, pickup rollers, separation pads, duplexing assembly

   ○ **B.** Ink cartridge, print head, roller, feeder, duplexing assembly, carriage, and belt

   ○ **C.** Feed assembly, thermal heating unit, thermal paper

   ○ **D.** Print head, ribbon, tractor feed, impact paper

5. Which of the following consumables is used by a 3D printer?

   ○ **A.** Toner
   ○ **B.** Ink
   ○ **C.** Thermal paper
   ○ **D.** Ribbon
   ○ **E.** Resin

Cram Quiz Answers

1. B. The transfer corona wire gets involved in the laser printing/imaging process during the transferring step.

2. A. The fusing step uses heat (up to 400 degrees Fahrenheit/200 degrees Celsius) and pressure to fuse the toner permanently to the paper.

3. D. The proper order of the laser printing/imaging process is processing, charging, exposing, developing, transferring, fusing, cleaning.

4. B. Inkjet printer components include ink cartridge, print head, roller, feeder, duplexing assembly, carriage, and belt. Imaging drum, fuser assembly, transfer belt, transfer roller, pickup rollers, separation pads, and duplexing assembly are associated with laser printers. Feed assembly, thermal heating unit, and thermal paper are associated with thermal printers. Print head, ribbon, tractor feed, and impact paper are associated with impact printers.

5. **E.** The 3D printing process (or additive manufacturing process) requires that you use resin (plastic filament) or a similar consumable. This plastic is what the 3D structures are made of. Toner is used by laser printers. Ink is used by inkjet printers. Thermal paper is used by thermal printers. And a ribbon is used by an impact printer.

It's amazing how time flies when you're having fun! If you consider studying to be fun, then this chapter should have flown by. Great job! That closes out Domain 3.0: Hardware. Be sure to review the chapters in this domain before continuing.

Domain 4.0: Virtualization and Cloud Computing

CHAPTER 21

Cloud Computing Concepts

This chapter covers the following A+ 220-1101 exam objective:

▶ 4.1 – Summarize cloud-computing concepts.

Cloud computing and virtualization in general have grown by leaps and bounds in recent years. These technologies have become so popular for businesses, organizations, and home users that they are now common-place. You're not likely to go a day without connecting to some kind of cloud-based service or virtualized system.

Two chapters are not nearly enough to even scratch the surface of the cloud and virtualization. However, for the A+ exams, you need to know only the basics. Let's begin with an introduction to cloud computing.

> **ExamAlert**
>
> **Objective 4.1** concentrates on the following concepts: common cloud models, cloud characteristics, and desktop virtualization.

Introduction to Cloud Computing

Cloud computing can be defined as a way of offering on-demand services that extend the capabilities of a person's computer or an organization's network. These might be free services, such as browser-based email from providers such as Gmail and Yahoo!, and personal storage from providers such as Microsoft (OneDrive); they might also be offered on a pay-per-use basis, such as services that offer data access, data storage, infrastructure, and online gaming. A network connection of some sort is required to make the connection to the "cloud" and gain access to these services in real time.

Some benefits that cloud-based services provide for organizations include reduced costs, reduced administration and maintenance, greater reliability, increased scalability, and possibly increased performance. A basic example of a cloud-based service is browser-based email. A small business with few employees definitely needs email, but it might not be able to afford the costs of an email server and perhaps might not want to have its own hosted domain and face the costs and work that go along with that. By connecting to a free (or inexpensive) browser-based service, the small business can benefit from nearly unlimited email, contacts, and calendar solutions. However, keep in mind that with cloud computing, you lose administrative control, and there are some security concerns as well.

Common Cloud Models

Cloud computing services are generally broken down into a few categories of services, including

- ▶ **Software as a service (SaaS):** The most commonly used and recognized of the three categories is SaaS, in which users access applications provided by a third party over the Internet. The applications need not be installed on the local computer. In many cases, these applications are run within a web browser; in other cases, a user connects with a screen-sharing program or remote desktop program. A common example of this is webmail such as Gmail. Other examples include Dropbox and Microsoft Office 365. SaaS can potentially offer lower hardware, software, and maintenance costs because the provider houses the hardware and software.

▶ **Infrastructure as a service (IaaS):** IaaS is a service that offers computer networking, storage, load balancing, routing, and virtual machine (VM) hosting. The cloud provider hosts the network infrastructure hardware components that are normally present in a traditional on-premises data center. Through a subscription service, you access hardware only when you need it. The potential benefits include scalability, minimized hardware maintenance and support, and reduced downtime. Common examples of IaaS providers include Amazon Web Services (AWS) and Microsoft Azure. More and more organizations are seeing the benefits of offloading some of their networking infrastructure to the cloud.

▶ **Platform as a service (PaaS):** PaaS is a service that provides various software solutions to organizations, especially the ability to develop and test applications in a virtual environment without the cost or administration of a physical platform. It is also used on a subscription basis to reduce costs and increase collaboration. PaaS is used for easy-to-configure operating systems and on-demand computing. Often, PaaS users utilize IaaS as well for an underlying infrastructure to the platform. Cloud-based virtual desktop environments are often considered to be part of this type of service, but they can be part of IaaS as well. PaaS works well for *serverless* environments also—where the programmer/developer doesn't want or need a server to host applications or code. Examples of PaaS providers include the usual suspects: Azure, AWS (Lambda), and Google (App Engine). There are also private tools, such as OpenShift and Docker.

ExamAlert

Know what SaaS, IaaS, and PaaS are.

Organizations use different types of clouds: public, private, hybrid, and community. Let's discuss each briefly:

▶ **Public cloud:** A service provider offers applications and storage space to the general public over the Internet. A couple examples of this are free, web-based email services and pay-as-you-go business-class services. The main benefits of a public cloud include low (or zero) cost and scalability. Providers of public cloud space include Google, Microsoft, Rackspace, and Amazon.

▶ **Private cloud:** A private cloud is designed with the needs of an individual organization in mind. The security administrator has more control over the data and infrastructure than is the case with a public cloud. A limited number of people have access to a private cloud, and they usually must be located behind a firewall of some sort to gain access to the private cloud. Resources might be provided by a third party or could come from the security administrator's server room or data center. Some companies incorporate broad network access—meaning that resources are available to a wide range of devices, including PCs, Macs, laptops, tablets, smartphones, and so on. While a private cloud creates increased availability for clients, it also intensifies the level of security concerns.

▶ **Hybrid cloud:** A hybrid cloud is somewhere between public and private. Dedicated servers located within the organization and cloud servers from a third party form the collective network. In a hybrid scenario, confidential data is usually kept in-house.

▶ **Community cloud:** A community cloud is another mix of public and private, but multiple organizations can share the public portion. Community clouds appeal to organizations that usually share a common form of computing and way of storing data.

ExamAlert

Know what public, private, hybrid, and community clouds are.

Cloud Computing Characteristics

Cloud computing is all about shared resources—data, devices, and network resources that can be accessed from a remote location. Generally, if resources are stored internally within an organization, users will get faster and more efficient access to them; but this is not always true. Sometimes, externally stored resources can be just as effective, especially if they have a small footprint and don't use much in the way of networking and processing power. One example of this is off-site email and email applications. Email has been so streamlined over the years that it can now be accessed from almost any device from just about anywhere. Even an email application itself can be run in a way so as to tax the client less and the server more; this is the case with web-based email clients and email clients that run virtually—a form of virtual application streaming. Or perhaps the entire desktop, including the email application, is virtual, running either within a browser or from a thin client. In such a case, having externally shared resources is a viable option, although it might not integrate well with an organization's security policy. Also, for the enterprise environment, email technologies are often simply too immense and complex to be stored in any way except privately.

Another consideration is the type of applications that will be run from the cloud, the type of devices that will use them, and how they will synchronize. Basic email applications from major providers have one version for desktops/laptops and another version for mobile devices, such as smartphones and tablets. Complex applications are more difficult to port to more than one type of device, but you don't want to have a PC version of an application running on a mobile device such as a smartphone as it would put additional strain on the end user. However, the more versions of software you offer, and the more types of endpoint devices that connect to them, the greater the need for more resources within the cloud.

So, ultimately, the type of cloud an organization uses will be dictated by the organization's budget, the amount and type of resources to be supplied to users, the level of security the organization requires, and the amount of humanpower (or lack thereof) it has available to administer its resources. While a private cloud can be very appealing, it is often beyond the means of an organization, and the organization must instead use a public or community-based cloud. Whatever an organization chooses, the provider will measure the services supplied. *Measured services* means the provider monitors the services rendered in order to properly bill the customer and make sure the customer's use of services is being handled in the most efficient way. This can work in conjunction with a pay service called *metered utilization*, in which an organization has access to virtually unlimited resources and pays only for the resources that are used. This is also known as *metered services* or software metering. It should be measured carefully, and the details of the resources should be stated clearly every month.

ExamAlert

Know the difference between measured services and metered utilization.

There are some other cloud-based terms you should be familiar with for the A+ 220-1101 exam. For example, *rapid elasticity* is the ability to build or extend a cloud-based network quickly and efficiently. Choosing a provider that can provide you with a scalable model is important for an organization's growth. You also want to have *high availability (HA)* for any on-demand services; this means the cloud should be available in real time and whenever you need it (24/7); that is, it should be always on. In a community cloud scenario, the provider usually implements resource pooling, which is the grouping of servers and infrastructure for use by multiple customers but in a way that is on demand, highly available, and scalable. As you can imagine, *file synchronization* is of paramount importance when dealing with the cloud. This could mean something basic, such as email or basic document synchronization with SaaS, or something a little more in depth, such as database synchronization, or perhaps even more complex, such as synchronization of entire virtual desktops across the cloud with PaaS. Whatever the resource, synchronization methods should be monitored and tested periodically to make sure that end users are getting what they expect.

> **ExamAlert**
>
> Be familiar with these cloud-based concepts: rapid elasticity, high availability, and file synchronization.

Desktop Virtualization

Desktop virtualization, by definition, separates the desktop environment from any application software. However, there is a bit of a gray area when it comes to virtual desktop technology, and there is also some overlap, so be ready to accept different terminology from different vendors. The virtual desktop can act as part of a user's computing system, or it can be the only place where the user performs his or her work. It can be as simple as a browser window with a single application inside it, or it can include everything from a virtual OS to virtual hardware such as a virtual network interface card (virtual NIC) on down to all the required individual virtual applications.

When multiple virtual desktops for multiple users are hosted by a service (either in the cloud or on-premises), this is referred to as a *virtual desktop infrastructure (VDI)*. The idea with VDI is that a user can use any system to connect to their virtual desktop and applications via a browser window or third-party application. There are several companies that offer virtual desktops and VDI, including Citrix (Managed Desktops), VMware (Horizon Cloud), Microsoft (Windows Virtual Desktop), and AWS (Workspaces). Some of these are offered solely in the cloud, and others can be implemented on-premises. Most desktop virtualization technology is dependent on PaaS.

Here's a last thought for the chapter: All of this cloud technology might seem a bit beyond what an A+ technician will be routinely called upon to do. However, you should have a basic knowledge of cloud types, cloud technologies, cloud terminology, and desktop virtualization so that you can better facilitate users in your role as a help desk specialist or other tech support position. Later, if you decide to specialize in one of the cloud/virtualization providers, you will find that it really is a technology specialty all its own, with a lot of competition in the market and certifications to prove your worth.

Cram Quiz

Answer these questions. The answers follow the last question. If you cannot answer these questions correctly, consider reading this chapter again until you can.

1. Which of the following types of cloud services offers email through a web browser?

   ○ **A.** SaaS

   ○ **B.** IaaS

   ○ **C.** PaaS

   ○ **D.** Community cloud

2. Your organization requires more control over its data and infrastructure. Money is apparently not an issue. There are only 2 admins and about 30 users who will have access to the data in the cloud. Which of the following cloud types is the best option?

   ○ **A.** Public

   ○ **B.** Private

   ○ **C.** Hybrid

   ○ **D.** Community

3. You require the ability to quickly and efficiently add to your cloud-based network whenever necessary. What is the term for this?

   ○ **A.** Measured services

   ○ **B.** Metered utilization

   ○ **C.** Rapid elasticity

   ○ **D.** On-demand service

4. What is the term for multiple virtual desktops for multiple users being hosted by a service either in the cloud or on-premises?

   ○ **A.** High availability

   ○ **B.** Shared resources

   ○ **C.** File synchronization

   ○ **D.** Virtual desktop infrastructure (VDI)

Cram Quiz Answers

1. **A.** Software as a service (SaaS) is the most commonly recognized cloud service; it allows users to use applications to access data that is stored by a third party on the Internet. Infrastructure as a service (IaaS) is a service that offers computer networking, storage, load balancing, routing, and VM hosting. Platform as a

service (PaaS) is used for easy-to-configure operating systems and on-demand computing. A community cloud is a mix of public and private clouds, but one where multiple organizations can share the public portion.

2. **B.** The best option listed is a private cloud. This gives the most control over data and resources in an environment where there are limited users (and a healthy budget). These resources could be entirely internal, or a portion of them could also be provided by a third party. Public cloud technology is used for the general public to access applications over the Internet. Hybrid is a mixture of public and private, but it is not necessary in this situation because of the healthy budget and the limited number of users. Community cloud is similar to hybrid but is meant for multiple organizations that share data, which is not necessary in this scenario.

3. **C.** Rapid elasticity is the ability to build a cloud-based network or extend an existing one quickly and efficiently. Measured services refers to a provider monitoring a customer's service usage in order to properly bill the customer. Metered utilization (or metered services) refers to a customer being able to access as many resources as needed and be billed only for what was accessed. On-demand service means that the cloud service is available at all times. Also, it allows a user to store data to the cloud when necessary but remove that data from the cloud when space is freed up at the local system. The leaders of a successful organization don't care what it takes; they simply want high-speed, secure access to services 24/7.

4. **D.** With a virtual desktop infrastructure (VDI), multiple virtual desktops for multiple users are hosted by a service. High availability (HA) for any on-demand service means that the cloud should be available in real time and whenever needed. Shared resources are resources such as CPU, RAM, and drive storage resources that multiple customers use on a server in a cloud environment. File synchronization means that files that are stored in multiple different locations are kept up to date through the use of cloud services. The incorrect answers are important when planning and implementing a cloud-based service, but VDI can be hosted in the cloud or on-premises.

Continue on! You are doing just great!

CHAPTER 22

Client-Side Virtualization

This chapter covers the following A+ 220-1101 exam objective:

▶ **4.2** – Summarize aspects of client-side virtualization.

Virtualization is the creation of a virtual entity, as opposed to a true or actual entity. The most common type of entity created through virtualization is the virtual machine—usually housing an operating system.

Let's discuss the types of virtualization, identify their purposes, and define their requirements. We'll also talk about the types of hypervisors you should know for the exam. However, we will mostly focus on client-side virtualization in this chapter.

> **ExamAlert**
>
> **Objective 4.2** focuses on the following: purpose of virtual machines, resource requirements, and security requirements.

Purpose of Virtual Machines

Many types of virtualization exist, from network and storage to hardware and software. The CompTIA A+ exam focuses mostly on virtual machine (VM) software. The VMs created by this software run operating systems or individual applications. A virtual operating system—also known as a guest—is designed to run inside a real OS. So, the beauty of a VM is that you can run multiple various operating systems simultaneously from just one computer. This has great advantages for programmers, developers, and systems administrators, and it can facilitate an excellent testing environment. VMs can also be used to run legacy software and operating systems such as Windows 7 or older. Today, many VMs are also used in live production environments as servers (and possibly as clients).

Know this: Anything can be run virtually—from individual apps (in what is known as application virtualization) to complete operating systems—and in some cases, it can be hard to tell what's virtual and what's not. Today, anything that runs an OS virtually is generally referred to as a virtual machine, and that's what we will be focusing on the most during the rest of this chapter.

Virtualization vs. Emulation

The terms *virtualization* and *emulation* are often used interchangeably, but they are not quite the same. There are a couple of main differences between a virtual machine and an emulator. First, a VM is designed to create an isolated environment, whereas an emulator is designed to reproduce the behavior of some type of hardware and/or firmware. Second, VMs make use of a CPU's built-in virtualization capabilities, but emulators imitate hardware without relying on the CPU; they can even be coded to mimic an entire processor that is wholly different from the one in the programmer's computer. An example of an emulator is a SOHO router's firmware that you can access online for testing purposes. It doesn't really control a SOHO router, and it has no connectivity to anything. Another example is an emulated BIOS/UEFI that some motherboard manufacturers offer on their websites for testing purposes. An example of a VM is a virtualized Windows operating system that runs within your computer's main operating system, makes use of the hardware of that computer, and can connect to other systems internally or externally. Developing an emulator usually requires a programmer, whereas any tech can create a VM. Another way to differentiate between the two is that an emulator does not use a hypervisor, but a VM does.

Hypervisors

Have you ever wished that you had another two or three extra computers lying around so that you could test multiple versions of Windows, Linux, and possibly a Windows Server OS all at the same time? Well, with virtual software, you can do this by creating a virtual machine for each OS.

A virtualization system uses what is known as a *hypervisor*, which allows multiple virtual operating systems (guests) to run at the same time on a single computer (host). But there are two different kinds:

▶ **Type 1: Native:** This means that the hypervisor runs directly on the host computer's hardware. Because of this, it is also known as *bare metal*. Examples of type 1 hypervisors include VMware ESXi, Microsoft Hyper-V (for Windows Server), and KVM.

▶ **Type 2: Hosted:** This means that the hypervisor runs within (or "on top of") the operating system. Guest operating systems run within the hypervisor. Guests are one level removed from the hardware, and therefore a type 2 hypervisor runs less efficiently than a type 1 hypervisor. Examples of this type include VirtualBox, VMware Workstation, and Hyper-V for Windows 10/11.

Remember that a type 1 hypervisor is faster than a type 2 hypervisor, but it requires a proper server, requires more knowledgeable administration, and is sometimes costlier. The A+ exams focus mainly on type 2 hypervisors and the virtualization software that utilizes that technology. These can be run on typical client operating systems such as Windows. Table 22.1 reviews the two types of hypervisors.

TABLE 22.1 **Hypervisor Types**

Type	Description	Examples
Type 1 (native or bare metal)	The hypervisor runs directly on the host computer's hardware.	VMware ESXi, Microsoft Hyper-V (Windows Server), KVM
Type 2 (hosted)	The hypervisor runs within the operating system. Guest VMs are one step removed from the hardware.	VMware Workstation, VirtualBox, Hyper-V for Windows clients

ExamAlert

Know the difference between type 1 and type 2 hypervisors!

Examples of Virtual Machine Software

Let's look at a couple of examples of virtualization software that make use of a type 2 hypervisor on a typical Windows client computer. First on the list is Microsoft Hyper-V. For this to work, virtualization must first be enabled in the BIOS/UEFI (see Chapter 16, "Motherboards and Add-on Cards"). Then, Hyper-V needs to be turned on in Windows Features, as shown in Figure 22.1. You can get to Windows Features by navigating to **Control Panel > All Control Panel Items > Programs and Features** and clicking the **Turn Windows features on or off** link, or simply search for "Turn Windows features" with the search tool to go directly there.

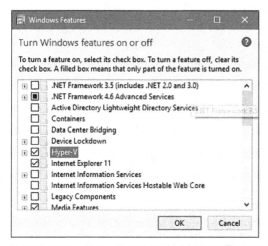

FIGURE 22.1　**Hyper-V enabled in Windows Features on a Windows system**

Enabling Hyper-V requires a restart, and it works only on certain editions of Windows. For example, it works on Windows 10 Pro and Enterprise but not Windows 10 Home Edition. If you are not sure whether Hyper-V will be compatible with your system, you can open the Command Prompt or the PowerShell and type **systeminfo**. At the bottom of the results, you will see the Hyper-V Requirements section and details.

Attention, PowerShell Users!

Skip the GUI! Enable Hyper-V directly within PowerShell (run as administrator) with the following command:

```
Enable-WindowsOptionalFeature -Online -FeatureName Microsoft-Hyper-V -All
```

To turn it off, change **Enable** to **Disable** and omit the **-All**.

Once you have performed those actions, you can create VMs in Hyper-V Manager. During the creation process, you will be prompted to create a virtual hard drive and install an operating system—which you will need to obtain in .iso format or in a virtual format. The virtual hardware for the VM can be configured in the Settings section. The networking connections can be configured in the Virtual Switch Manager. Figure 22.2 shows an example of a VM that was installed to Hyper-V Manager.

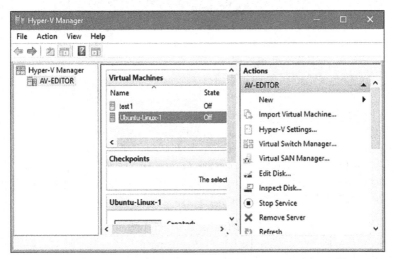

FIGURE 22.2   **An Ubuntu Linux virtual machine created in Hyper-V Manager**

Another popular type 2 hypervisor is VMware Workstation. For an example of that, see Figure 22.3. Note that it has a variety of virtual machines inside, such as Windows 10 Pro (running), Windows Server, and Ubuntu Linux.

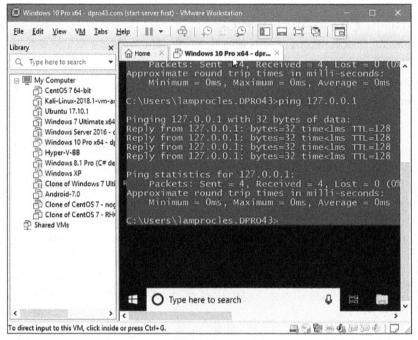

FIGURE 22.3 **VMware Workstation**

The concept is essentially the same across virtualization vendors, but of course navigation and names will be slightly different. One difference is the type of file extensions used. For example, VMware uses the .vmdk file extension for the virtual hard disk of a virtual machine, whereas Hyper-V uses the .vhdx extension. The two types of VMs are not compatible by default, meaning you can't run a VM from VMware in Hyper-V or vice versa.

A third well-liked offering is Oracle VirtualBox, which provides a free and easy way to test operating systems. Admins have been using it for years and years. Figure 22.4 shows an example of a VM that was created in VirtualBox. The default virtual storage file extension for VirtualBox VMs is .vdi; however, you can also use .vmdk for compatibility with VMware. That is the extension that was chosen for the VM shown in Figure 22.4.

FIGURE 22.4   A Kali Linux virtual machine created in VirtualBox

If at all possible, try out the different types of virtualization software so that you can learn more about them.

One more thing, and I can't stress this enough: Be sure to update your virtualization software! Bugs and vulnerabilities are constantly being found in all the major vendors' software, and updates are frequently available. Get in the habit of checking for updates!

Virtual Machine Requirements

There are a couple of requirements that you have to consider when installing a virtual machine: virtualization hosting software requirements and virtual machine requirements. Generally, most computers built in the past five years can run the latest version of virtualization software—as long as the BIOS/UEFI can support virtualization—but the VMs themselves can be very power hungry, especially with newer operating systems. For example, to install an operating system as a virtual machine, you will need to assign virtual resources—CPU, RAM, network connection, storage drive, and so on.

The CPU is the first of the virtual resources. The VM might run okay with one virtual processor (a single core, which is the default), but multiple cores are often recommended. Some virtualization platforms go by threads instead of cores. So, if you have a 6-core CPU, it will have 12 threads available. Be aware of this when selecting the virtual CPU usage for a VM. Also, be careful not to use more than 50% of the actual host's CPU power for a VM; doing so can cause the VM and the host to compete for the CPU. Ultimately, the amount of CPU resources you allocate will be dictated by the minimum requirements of the operating system you plan to install. And know this: Sometimes the minimum requirements for a VM installation can be higher than for a physical installation.

Commonly, a VM requires 2 GB of RAM, but again, more is suggested. The setting you select will depend on the physical hardware of the host. If you have a computer that is five years old with limited cores and RAM, then assigning more virtual RAM to the VM will simply bog down the main host system even more. But the beauty of the VM is that you can change the virtual resources at any time, as long as you shut down the VM first. You can test, tweak, and find the right balance.

For the network connection, you generally have three or four options. The following example is based on VMware:

▶ **Bridged networking:** This gives the VM (also known as the guest) direct access to the hosting computer's network connection. It allows external access, but in this case, the VM must have its own IP address on the external IP network. Because of the direct connectivity to the external network, this can be a security concern. In most cases, some type of NAT is preferred.

▶ **Network address translation (NAT):** Often the default, this gives the guest access to the external network, but by using NAT, the guest gets a separate IP address on a private network.

▶ **Host-only networking:** This creates a private virtual network for the guests, and they can communicate with each other but not with the external network.

▶ **No networking:** This option disables networking for the VM altogether, which might be required for users who are working on confidential systems, testbeds, applications, and so on.

ExamAlert

ExamAlert

Know the virtualization network connection options.

Networking is usually required for VMs. Just remember that any network connection (mapped network drive, browsing connection, and so on) can be a security concern. If there is a connection from the VM to the hosting OS, and the VM has a vulnerability that is exploited, the exploit could carry over to the host. Be ready to monitor for and disable any unused or unnecessary network connections between VMs and between the VMs and the host. Conversely, the host should be updated and secured vigilantly. If the hosting OS fails, then all guest VMs will go offline immediately.

ExamAlert

Because VM network connections can be security vulnerabilities, you will need to monitor and disable them as necessary, and in some cases you will have to disable networking altogether.

Different providers use different names for the types of networking connections, but they are similar; for example, Hyper-V uses external, internal, and private. You have the ability to create and configure virtual switches for the various VMs and to allow or disallow connectivity between them (and between the VMs and the host) as you see fit. It can get pretty complex, so it is wise to create network documentation that diagrams the various virtual machines and switches using software such as Microsoft Visio.

You can select different virtual storage drive connections such as SCSI, SATA, and IDE that emulate those technologies. Then you choose the size of virtual drive (for instance, 60 GB). A VM can be configured to use all of that space right from the beginning; this is a static configuration. Or it can be configured to use only what it needs; this is a dynamic configuration. The size of the virtual drive can grow, as needed, up to the maximum that was selected. This ultimately saves space on the host computer's drive.

Note

I built a Xeon-based virtualization server to house some of my test VMs. Ultimately, in the second video at this site, it runs a VMware ESXi server: https://dprocomputer.com/?p=2938.

I have mentioned security concerns a couple of times already. Take a look at Table 22.2 for some additional pointers and review of basic virtualization security. The first bullet says to configure the hosting computer securely. This is easily said but not so easily done! We'll discuss system security further in Chapter 47, "Windows Security Settings," and Chapter 48, "Windows Best Practices."

TABLE 22.2 **Virtualization Security Basics**

Best Practice	Methods
Updates	▶ Configure the hosting computer securely.
	▶ Update the virtualization platform software.
	▶ Update the VM operating system and applications.
	▶ Monitor common vulnerabilities and exposures (CVEs).
Disable unnecessary hardware in the VM's settings	▶ USB ports
	▶ Optical drives/floppy drives
	▶ Peripherals (mouse, tablet, and so on)
	▶ Extra storage drives and NICs
Secure networking connections	▶ Use appropriate network connectivity for VMs (such as NAT). Disable bridged connections if not used.
	▶ Remove unnecessary network shares between VMs and the host, as well as between VMs.
	▶ Consider secure VLANs.
Other security precautions	▶ Configure the virtual BIOS boot priority for hard drive first.
	▶ Limit the resources (CPU and RAM) used by a VM.
	▶ Protect and monitor VM files with permissions, logging, and auditing.
	▶ Secure VM files with encryption and digital signing.
	▶ Preserve the entire state of VMs with snapshots.
	▶ Use cross-platform virtualization management tools.

Cross-Platform Virtualization

Some organizations run multiple virtualization platforms. Studies show that an average company runs two different type 1 hypervisors in its data centers and at least two type 2 hypervisors across its various client systems. For example, some developers might work with VirtualBox, and others might work with VMware Workstation, while a third group might use Hyper-V.

This can lead to some problems, including application instability (when moving from one virtualization platform to the next) and incompatibilities between the virtualization systems on a resource level. It can also lead to VM sprawl, where the number of virtual machines on all systems goes beyond the control of the system owner or the administrator of the network.

Many organizations have some sort of cross-platform virtualization, so how do they make it run more smoothly? For one thing, they can attempt to use common file formats whenever possible. For example, let's say one developer is using VMware Workstation and another developer is using VirtualBox. The first developer saves VMs with the default file extension (.vmdk). The second developer could make sure that the VirtualBox VM is configured to use the same type of extension (instead of the default VirtualBox extension). To avoid application instability, both developers should have VMs that run the same OS at the same version level.

While those are good short-term options, a couple of long-term options are to have all developers use the cloud or to work in a container-based system. However, in a working environment, this is easier said than done due to cost, decision-making processes, and administrative overhead.

VM sprawl can be reduced by consolidating the hypervisors used as much as possible, creating an organized library of VM images (possibly with third-party software), and using a virtual machine life cycle management tool that can enforce how VMs are created, used, deployed, and archived.

In general, when it comes to working with virtual machines, proper type 1 hypervisors are the better option if at all possible. When these are combined with virtualization management software packages such as Microsoft System Center Virtual Machine Manager or VMware vCenter Server, an organization can better organize and secure its virtual machines.

Containers and Sandboxes

Let's discuss some more virtualization topics, including containers and sandboxes. You don't have to always run a full-blown virtual machine with a complete operating system and all the virtualized hardware. In some cases, especially for programming/developing, and even in production, you will want something much more trimmed down and simplified. Let's look at a couple of examples.

OS-Level Virtualization (Containers)

One type of operating system–level virtualization, known as containerization, allows you to run multiple isolated systems on a single OS kernel.

Now, a statement like that can cause some confusion, so let's put it into context and simplify it somewhat. A *container* is much simpler than a full virtual machine. First, it requires only a basic OS kernel. Second, it doesn't require much in the way of virtual hardware. Finally, in most container systems, you can run multiple containers on top of a single OS. Another important difference between a container and a virtual machine is usage. As mentioned previously, a virtual machine is used to run an entire operating system. A container is typically used to run a single application (and, less commonly, a couple of applications). Out of the box, container technology creates excellent isolation between applications.

Examples of container technology include Docker, Podman, and LXC. Docker is the most common of these. A Docker container is an open source software development platform. Its main benefit is that it packages applications in containers, allowing them to be portable from one system to another. A system such as Docker has to be installed on the host computer. Once it is installed, you can create containers and download very basic OS images that you can house in those containers. Ultimately, if a container is configured properly, it can be far less resource intensive than a virtual machine.

> **Note**
>
> Docker as a whole is a group of platform as a service (PaaS) products.

Let's compare two scenarios: one that requires a virtual machine and one that works just fine with a container.

In the first scenario, imagine that you need to run a server that will have multiple services running, including DHCP, DNS, a file server, and some monitoring software for those services. In this case, it would usually be better to have a full virtual machine, where you have access to a complete set of virtualized hardware and perform a complete installation of an operating system (such as Windows Server or Linux). When you are running multiple services that can be taxing, a more powerful virtual machine with a complete OS is usually the best solution.

In the second scenario, say that you need to run a single web server with an individual web application that is being developed in-house. In this case, a container would be a better option because you don't necessarily need a lot of power, access to virtualized hardware, or even a complete operating system.

The beauty of containers is that you can download premade OS kernels for them. These kernels are very basic, take up little space, and use very little processing and RAM power. They are simplified versions of operating systems.

In addition, containers can be run on just about any system, by anyone, and they are portable: You can move them to any other computer running the same containerization system. Finally, you can have one app that is being developed in one container, and another in a separate container, and so on, but they can all use the same OS kernel (or separate ones if you wish). This can be great for development, testing, training, and other purposes.

By now you should see the potential of containers. Containers are not specifically listed in the A+ objectives, but you should know what they are for the field. I highly recommend that you investigate container technology more (Docker in particular) and test it for yourself to see how it works.

Sandboxes

The term *sandbox* can be applied to software development and to computer security, and in both cases, virtualization can be involved. The term is somewhat open ended but, in this section, I'll be referring to it mostly from a software development perspective.

A sandbox can be any environment created for development, testing, or training that is isolated from any production servers and isolated from the rest of the operating system that the sandbox is running on.

Before we proceed any further, it's important to understand the difference between production and development. By "production server," I mean any server that is distributing applications and/or files to customers. Such servers are considered to be "live" and are critical to an organization's operations. A development server is a server that is used during the process of developing, programming, and testing software; it is not normally used by customers. To be safe, a development server shouldn't even be on the same network as a production server. Sandboxes should be run in a development environment, not in a production environment.

A sandbox could be run on a physical server, in a virtual machine, as a container, or as specially programmed software, depending on the scope of the project and the size and budget of the organization.

Many sandboxes are temporary. Every time a sandbox runs, it is pristine—meaning that it runs clean and new; any programming or testing that was done previously in the sandbox is discarded. You could say that the sand is smoothed out and the toys are removed after each use. This allows for a consistent environment every time a sandbox runs.

Let's consider an example. A developer designs a web-based application called *Asteroid Blaster*. It's a game where—yup, you guessed it—you blast asteroids to smithereens. After a time, the developer decides that the game is lacking in real physics and attempts to apply additional mathematics to make the game more real. However, the developer doesn't want to test it out on the live server where the website is hosted. So, the developer uses a sandbox. The developer can make slight modifications to the code, test them in the sandbox, and repeat until the outcome is what the developer wants. The developer could achieve this within third-party sandboxing software, a custom sandbox, a container, or a VM. As you can see, there are several options when it comes to sandboxing. The key is to make sure that the code or program is isolated from the rest of the system in a secure manner.

Revision Control

When multiple developers are working on a project, you need to incorporate revision control software. This allows the group of developers to keep a "stable" set of source code somewhere that is accessible to everyone involved. If one developer wants to propose a change, that person can download ("check out," or "pull") a copy of the source code. That developer would then make the necessary changes to the code within his or her own sandbox. After testing is complete, the code can be merged back ("checked in," or "pushed") to the original source code. Ideally, it would be placed in a "testing" source code section for other developers to look at first before it is merged with the stable code. One very common example of revision control software is Git, which tracks all changes made to the code. Developers can upload and download the code to and from a platform such as GitHub or GitLab and work in their own local sandboxes to keep their code isolated and tracked.

Also, for security purposes, a specific area of an operating system can be sandboxed (that is, isolated from the rest of the system) to allow the application to be isolated so that any malicious code can't travel from the application to the rest of the system. There are a variety of ways to do this in Windows and especially Linux systems. (Some sandboxing technologies are installed and running by default in Linux, such as SELinux and AppArmor.) In fact, just about anything can be sandboxed. So, as you can see, the term *sandbox* is somewhat ambiguous unless you know what the technician or developer is trying to accomplish. Ultimately, the best way to really understand a topic like this is to try it for yourself.

Challenge 3: Use a Sandbox

Try working with one or more sandboxes that are feely available on the Internet. Do a search for what you want to learn more about. Try any of the following Internet searches to locate a suitable sandbox: "Bash sandbox," "C++ sandbox," or "Linux sandbox" (for an entire Linux operating system). Make some changes to the code or system and then refresh the sandbox. You should see that it reverts back to its original state.

Also check out the Windows Sandbox feature (see https://docs.microsoft.com/en-us/windows/security/threat-protection/windows-sandbox/windows-sandbox-overview)—but note that it does not run on all editions of Windows.

Cram Quiz

Answer these questions. The answers follow the last question. If you cannot answer these questions correctly, consider reading this chapter again until you can.

1. Of the following listed technologies, which one should you select if you want to run an instance of Ubuntu Linux within your Windows 10/11 Pro workstation?

   ○ **A.** Type 1

   ○ **B.** Type 2

   ○ **C.** Bare metal

   ○ **D.** Cross-platform virtualization

2. Which of the following is the greatest risk with a virtual computer?

   ○ **A.** If a virtual computer fails, all other virtual computers immediately go offline.

   ○ **B.** If a virtual computer fails, the physical server goes offline.

   ○ **C.** If the physical server fails, all other physical servers immediately go offline.

   ○ **D.** If the physical server fails, all the virtual computers immediately go offline.

3. Which of the following file extensions is used by VMware by default?

   ○ **A.** .vmdk

   ○ **B.** .vdi

   ○ **C.** .vhdx

   ○ **D.** VT-x

4. Which of the following network connection types should be used to allow for connectivity to the external network but keep the VMs on a separate IP network?

    ○ **A.** Bridged

    ○ **B.** NAT

    ○ **C.** Private

    ○ **D.** No networking

5. A customer running Windows 10 Pro wishes to install a Linux VM in Hyper-V Manager. Which of the following requirements *must* be met in order for this to happen? (Select all that apply.)

    ○ **A.** Update and secure the host system.

    ○ **B.** Ensure that virtualization is enabled in the BIOS/UEFI.

    ○ **C.** Ensure that Hyper-V is turned on in Windows Features.

    ○ **D.** Restart the system.

6. A developer wants to test a custom web-based application in an isolated environment. Which of the following should be used?

    ○ **A.** Sandbox

    ○ **B.** Virtual machine

    ○ **C.** NAT

    ○ **D.** VirtualBox

Cram Quiz Answers

1. **B.** You would need to run virtualization software that includes a type 2 hypervisor such as Windows 10/11 Hyper-V, VMware Workstation, or VirtualBox. Type 1 hypervisors are used on servers; they are also known as *bare metal* because they allow virtual machines to access the computer hardware directly. With cross-platform virtualization, an organization uses multiple virtualization programs, such as VirtualBox and Hyper-V.

2. **D.** The biggest risk of running a virtual computer is that it will go offline immediately if the server that it is housed on fails. All other virtual computers on that particular server will also go offline immediately.

3. **A.** VMware uses the .vmdk file extension for the virtual hard drive file. VirtualBox uses .vdi by default (although it can use others). Hyper-V uses .vhdx. VT-x is the Intel virtualization extension that is incorporated into Intel-based systems and must be enabled in the BIOS/UEFI for virtualization software to work.

4. **B.** Network address translation (NAT)–based network connections are the most common default. NAT allows the VMs to have their own IP network but still connect to the external network and make use of the Internet. This is the same principle behind NAT used in a SOHO network. Bridged means that the VMs have access to the external network, but they must use IP addresses from that external network. Private means that multiple VMs within a host can communicate with each other but not beyond the host. The no networking option disables any type of networking connectivity for the VM in question.

5. **B, C, and D.** Virtualization must be enabled in the BIOS/UEFI. Then, Hyper-V needs to be turned on in Windows Features. Finally, the system needs to be restarted. Updating and securing the host system is recommended but is not a requirement.

6. **A.** The developer should run the custom application in a sandbox. A sandbox is designed to run code in an isolated way. It could possibly be done in a virtual machine, but the virtual machine is not secure by default; a container would usually be a better option. NAT stands for Network Address Translation, and while the sandbox could be located in a NAT network, that in itself is not enough. In addition, the developer might not want *any* network connectivity for the custom application. VirtualBox is a type of virtualization software. Again, the developer might choose VirtualBox as the tool to run a VM, but it has to be done in a secure way. A properly isolated sandbox would have to be set up within a VM on VirtualBox (which itself should be secured properly as well).

Phew! Lots of data here. Have you been taking notes? If you have, excellent. If your notes are lacking, remember that note taking is one of the best ways to retain information—either on paper or within your favorite note-taking program. I recommend that you review this chapter, review your notes, take a nice break, and then move on to the next domain. Terrific work so far!

CORE 1 (220-1101)

Domain 5.0: Hardware and Network Troubleshooting

CHAPTER 23

Computer Troubleshooting 101

This chapter covers the following A+ 220-1101 exam objective:

▶ **5.1** – Given a scenario, apply the best practice methodology to resolve problems.

Excellent troubleshooting ability is vital; it's probably the most important skill for a computer technician to possess. It's what we do—troubleshoot and repair problems! So, it makes sense that an ever-increasing number of questions about this subject are on the A+ exams. To be a good technician, and to pass the exams, you need to know how to troubleshoot hardware, software, and network-related issues. The key to troubleshooting is to do it methodically. One way to do that is to use a troubleshooting methodology or process. In this chapter, we will focus on the CompTIA A+ six-step troubleshooting methodology.

> **ExamAlert**
>
> **Objective 5.1** concentrates on the CompTIA A+ six-step troubleshooting methodology.

The CompTIA Six-Step Troubleshooting Process

It is necessary to approach computer problems from a logical standpoint, and to best do this, you can use a troubleshooting process. Several different troubleshooting methodologies are out there; this book focuses on the CompTIA A+ six-step troubleshooting methodology:

1. Identify the problem.

2. Establish a theory of probable cause. (Question the obvious.)

3. Test the theory to determine the cause.

4. Establish a plan of action to resolve the problem and implement the solution.

5. Verify full system functionality and, if applicable, implement preventive measures.

6. Document the findings, actions, and outcomes.

This six-step methodology included within the A+ objectives is designed to increase a computer technician's problem-solving ability. CompTIA expects a technician to take an organized, methodical route to a solution by memorizing and implementing these steps. Incorporate this six-step methodology into your line of thinking as you read this book and whenever you troubleshoot a desktop computer, mobile device, or networking issue.

> **ExamAlert**
>
> Always consider organizational and corporate policies, procedures, and impacts before implementing any changes.

Let's talk about each of the six steps in this methodology in a little more depth.

Step 1: Identify the Problem

In this first step, you already know that there is a problem, and you need to identify exactly what it is. This means gathering information. You do this in several ways:

▶ **Gather information from the user.** Ask the person who reported the problem detailed questions about the issue. You want to find out about symptoms, unusual behavior, and anything that the user might have done recently that could have inadvertently or directly caused the problem. Of course, do this without accusing the user. If the user cannot properly explain a computer's problem, ask simple questions to further identify the issue.

▶ **Identify any changes made to the computer.** Look at the computer. See if any new hardware has been installed or plugged in. Look around for anything that might seem out of place. Listen to the computer—and even smell it! For example, a hard drive might make a peculiar noise, or a power supply might smell like something is burning. Use all your senses to help identify what the problem is. Determine whether any new software has been installed or whether any system settings have been changed. In some cases, you might need to inspect the environment around the computer. Perhaps something has changed outside the computer that is related to the problem.

▶ **Review log files.** Review any and all log files that you have access to that can give you more information about the problem. For example, in Windows, use the Event Viewer to analyze the System and Application logs and perhaps the Security log. Figure 23.1 shows an example of the System log within the Event Viewer.

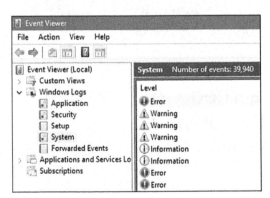

FIGURE 23.1   **The Event Viewer showing the System log in Windows**

▶ **Ask about any environmental or infrastructural changes.** Perhaps there was a change on the computer network, or a new authentication scheme has been put in place. Maybe the environment has changed in some way: higher temperatures, more or less humidity, or a user now working in a dustier/dirtier location. Perhaps there have been recent changes to the HVAC system or the electrical system. Changes such as these will often affect more than one computer, so be ready to extend your troubleshooting across multiple systems.

▶ **Review documentation.** The company might have electronic or written documentation that logs past problems and solutions. Perhaps the issue at hand has happened before. Or perhaps other related issues can aid you in finding out what is wrong. Maybe another technician listed in the documentation can be of assistance if he or she has seen the problem before. Perhaps the user has documentation about a specific process or has a manual concerning the computer, individual component, software, or other device that has failed. Documentation is important; the more technology there is, the more documentation that is created to support it. A good technician knows some details by heart, but a technician doesn't need to know every single specification; those can be looked up. A great technician needs to understand how to locate the right documentation, how to read it, and how to update it as necessary.

Keep in mind that you're not taking any direct action at this point to solve the problem. Instead, you are gleaning as much information as you can to help in your analysis. However, at this stage, it is important to back up any critical data before you do make any changes in the following steps.

> **ExamAlert**
>
> Perform backups before making changes!

Step 2: Establish a Theory of Probable Cause (Question the Obvious)

In step 2, you theorize about the most likely cause of the problem. Start with the most probable or obvious cause. For example, if a computer won't turn on, your theory of probable cause might be that the computer is not plugged in. This step differs from other troubleshooting steps in that you are not making a list of causes but instead are choosing one probable cause as a starting point. In this step, you also need to define whether it is a hardware- or software-related issue.

If necessary, conduct external or internal research based on symptoms. You might need to consult your organization's documentation (or your own personal documentation), research technical websites, and make calls or send emails to various tech support groups—depending on the severity of the situation. It also means that you might need to inspect the inside of a computer or the software of the computer more thoroughly than in the previous step.

The ultimate goal is to come up with a logical theory explaining the root of the problem.

Step 3: Test the Theory to Determine the Cause

In step 3, test your theory from step 2. For example, plug in the computer. If the computer starts, you know that your theory about the computer being unplugged has been confirmed. At this point, you can move on to step 4. But what if the computer *is* plugged in? Or what if you plug in the computer and it still doesn't start? An experienced troubleshooter can often figure out the problem with the first theory—but not always. If the first theory fails during testing, go back to step 2 to establish a new theory and continue until you have a theory that tests positive. If you can't figure out what the problem is from any of your theories, it's time to escalate. Bring the problem to your supervisor or team so that additional theories can be established.

Step 4: Establish a Plan of Action to Resolve the Problem and Implement the Solution

Step 4 might at first seem a bit redundant, but you need to delve a little further. When a theory has been tested and works, you can establish a plan of action. In the previous scenario, it's simple: Plug in the computer. However, in other situations, the plan of action will be more complicated; you might need to repair other issues that occurred due to the first issue. In other cases, an issue might affect multiple computers, and the plan of action would include repairing all those systems. Be sure to carefully analyze any applicable vendor guidance and documentation. Whatever the plan of action, after it is established, have the appropriate people sign off on it (if necessary) and then immediately implement it.

> **ExamAlert**
>
> Remember to refer to the vendor's instructions for guidance while implementing the solution in step 4.

Step 5: Verify Full System Functionality and, if Applicable, Implement Preventive Measures

During this step, you verify whether the computer works properly. This might require restarting once or twice, opening applications, accessing the Internet, or actually using a hardware device to prove that it works. As part of step 5, you want to prevent the problem from happening again, if possible. Yes, of course, you plugged in the computer, and it worked. But why was the computer unplugged? The computer being unplugged (or whatever was the particular issue) could be the result of a bigger problem that you would want to prevent in the future. You might need to reroute cables or, possibly, reposition the computer. Whatever your preventive measures, make sure they won't affect any other systems or policies; if they will, get permission for those measures first.

> **ExamAlert**
>
> Make sure the system works! Always remember to test and verify full system functionality.

Step 6: Document the Findings, Actions, and Outcomes

In this last step, you document what happened. Depending on the company you work for, you might have been documenting the entire time (for example, by using a trouble-ticketing system or other help desk software). In this step, finalize the documentation, including the issue, cause, solution, preventive measures, and any other steps taken.

Documentation is extremely important and helps in two ways. First, it provides you and the user with closure on the problem; it solidifies the problem and the solution, making you a better troubleshooter in the future. Second, if you or anyone else on your team encounters a similar issue in the future, the history of the issue will be at your fingertips. Most technicians don't remember specific solutions to problems that happened several months ago or more. Plus, having a written account of what transpired can help to protect all parties involved in the event that there is an investigation and/or legal proceeding.

So that's the six-step CompTIA A+ troubleshooting methodology. Try to incorporate this methodology into your thinking when covering the chapters in this book. In the upcoming chapters, apply it to hardware-, software-, and network-related issues.

> **Note**
>
> I have a video on my website that discusses this six-step process:
> https://dprocomputer.com/?p=2941.

Cram Quiz

Answer these questions. The answers follow the last question. If you cannot answer these questions correctly, consider reading this chapter again until you can.

1. What is the second step of the A+ troubleshooting methodology?

    ○ **A.** Identify the problem.

    ○ **B.** Establish a theory of probable cause. (Question the obvious.)

    ○ **C.** Test the theory to determine the cause.

    ○ **D.** Document the findings, actions, and outcomes.

2. When you run out of possible theories for the cause of a problem, what should you do?

    ○ **A.** Escalate the problem.

    ○ **B.** Document your actions so far.

    ○ **C.** Establish a plan of action.

    ○ **D.** Question the user.

3. What should you do before making any changes to a computer? (Select the best answer.)

    ○ **A.** Identify the problem.

    ○ **B.** Establish a plan of action.

    ○ **C.** Perform a backup.

    ○ **D.** Escalate the problem.

4. Which of the following is part of step 5 in the six-step troubleshooting methodology?

- ○ **A.** Identify the problem.
- ○ **B.** Document findings.
- ○ **C.** Establish a new theory.
- ○ **D.** Implement preventive measures.

5. What should you do next after testing the theory to determine cause?

- ○ **A.** Establish a plan of action to resolve the problem.
- ○ **B.** Verify full system functionality.
- ○ **C.** Document findings, actions, and outcomes.
- ○ **D.** Implement the solution.

6. There is a problem with the power supplied to a group of computers, and you do not know how to fix the problem. What should you do first?

- ○ **A.** Establish a theory about why you can't figure out the problem.
- ○ **B.** Contact the building supervisor or your manager.
- ○ **C.** Test the theory to determine cause.
- ○ **D.** Document findings, actions, and outcomes.

7. A technician has established a plan of action to resolve a problem that affects several users. What should the tech do before implementing any changes?

- ○ **A.** Refer to the vendor's instructions for guidance.
- ○ **B.** Ask about environmental or infrastructure changes.
- ○ **C.** Perform backups.
- ○ **D.** Consider corporate policies, procedures, and impacts.

Cram Quiz Answers

1. B. The second step is to establish a theory of probable cause. You need to look for the obvious or most probable cause of the problem. If necessary, conduct external or internal research based on symptoms.

2. A. If you can't figure out why a problem occurred, it's time to get someone else involved. Escalate the problem to your supervisor.

3. C. Always perform a backup of critical data before making any changes to the computer.

4. D. Implement preventive measures as part of step 5 to ensure that the problem will not happen again.

5. **A.** After testing the theory to determine cause (step 3), you should establish a plan of action to resolve the problem and implement the solution (step 4). Memorize the six-step troubleshooting methodology! You will use it often.

6. **B.** If you can't figure out a cause to a problem and have exhausted all possible theories, escalate the problem to the appropriate persons. It happens. No one knows everything, and sometimes we have to ask for help!

7. **D.** This one is a little tricky. Always consider corporate policies, procedures, and impacts before implementing changes! This is, in essence, "step zero," as it is listed *before* steps 1 through 6 in the official CompTIA A+ 220-1101 objectives. As such, it should always be on your mind, regardless of where in the troubleshooting process you are, especially if the solution will affect multiple users.

   In this scenario, the technician has already established a plan of action (step 4). The rest of the answers are things that should have already happened: "Refer to the vendor's instructions for guidance" is part of step 4. Establish a plan of action to resolve the problem and implement the solution. "Inquire regarding environmental or infrastructure changes" is part of step 1, and so is "perform backups before making changes." While these are all important, you must always consider policies, procedures, and impacts first *as well as* during each step of the troubleshooting methodology.

Yes! Great job! I can't stress enough how important this chapter is. Make sure you review it and your notes before continuing on.

CHAPTER 24

Troubleshooting Motherboards, CPUs, RAM, and Power

This chapter covers the following A+ 220-1101 exam objective:

▶ **5.2** – Given a scenario, troubleshoot problems related to motherboards, RAM, CPUs, and power.

Let's continue on our troubleshooting quest. This chapter gets into the guts of the PC. Sometimes it can be a bit difficult to figure out which component is causing a problem. In this chapter, I'll give some tips to help you identify whether a problem comes from the motherboard, the CPU, or the RAM or whether it is a power issue.

Always refer to the six-step CompTIA A+ troubleshooting methodology that we discussed in Chapter 23, "Computer Troubleshooting 101." This best practice methodology will help you think logically and clearly as you troubleshoot computer problems. If you are new to computers, I suggest reviewing the corresponding hardware chapters as well—mainly Chapters 14 through 18.

This chapter only refers to one exam objective, but it is a pretty massive one. We're basically talking about the entire core of a PC. We could fill a book on this subject, but alas, our time and space are limited. So, I've condensed as much as possible. Consider acquiring and breaking down older systems to help develop your troubleshooting skills.

> **ExamAlert**
>
> **Objective 5.2** concentrates on troubleshooting common symptoms related to motherboards, RAM, CPUs, and power, such as lack of power, proprietary crash screens, and POST beeps.

Troubleshooting Motherboards

It is uncommon to see a motherboard fail, but if it does, it may be due to a few different things. Let's discuss several of them now.

First and probably the most common of these rarities are UEFI/BIOS firmware issues. I'll refer to this as "BIOS" for simplicity. Remember that you might need to flash the motherboard's BIOS to the latest version. For example, a new CPU or RAM might not be recognized at the correct clock speeds. An adapter card might not be seen properly. Or perhaps the operating system isn't working as it should be with the hardware in the system. Updating the BIOS can fix many of these issues. On a separate note, you might encounter a PC that, instead of booting normally, accesses the BIOS. A drained or faulty CMOS battery could be the culprit. Change out the battery, and the system should boot normally. Often, this is a CR2032 lithium battery. If you are not sure whether the battery is discharged, you test it with a multimeter. CR2032 batteries normally have an output of 3 volts. Such a battery is only usable down to 2 V, so if it measures 2.5 V or less, it should be replaced. Also, if the battery is discharged, then the time and date of the system will revert to a default (such as January 1, 2012). Also, any other settings you configured will be lost. After a new battery is installed, the time/date and any other required settings will have to be reconfigured or imported from a backup.

> **ExamAlert**
>
> If the time and date on a system have reset, there is a good chance that the rest of the settings have also reset to defaults. Review the BIOS configuration settings, compare them with your organization's documentation, and make any modifications necessary. Remember to save your work!

> **Note**
>
> A multimeter is a measuring device used to test electrical properties, including resistance (ohms), current (amps), and voltage (volts). You should have a multimeter in your toolkit!

If the system attempts to boot to an incorrect device, then it could be because the intended boot device is new; again, a BIOS flash could fix the problem. Of course, it could also be due to a configuration error. You should know how to change the BIOS boot order and many other settings in the BIOS. You should also know where to go in the BIOS to view log entries and error messages. The BIOS log can help describe various system problems (though it might require a bit of translation, with the aid of the motherboard manual). We discuss the BIOS further in Chapter 16, "Motherboards and Add-on Cards."

Electrostatic discharge (ESD) and other electrical issues might present inter-mittently. If you find some intermittent issues (for example, the computer reboots out of nowhere) or you receive random proprietary crash screens, such as blue screens of death (BSODs) in Windows or the spinning pinwheel in macOS, ESD could be the culprit. Or a power surge could cause the problem. A particular wire, circuit, or capacitor on the motherboard could have been damaged. Document when failures occur. Swap out the motherboard with a known good one to see if the issue happens again when running through the same processes. If the issue doesn't recur, chances are the original motherboard is headed for the bit bucket (meaning it is to be disposed of). There are lots of circuits on a motherboard; electrical damage to any one circuit could cause the system to behave "irrationally" at best and trigger intermittent device failure. Beyond this, electrical damage can go right through the power supply to the motherboard, disabling it permanently. Be sure to use a surge suppressor or an uninterruptible power supply (UPS) to protect your equipment and, of course, implement antistatic measures whenever you work inside a system.

Note

Antistatic measures such as using an antistatic wrist strap and mat are crucial when working on systems. I cover these measures in depth in Chapter 59, "Safety Procedures."

Another issue is component failures. It is possible for a single component of the motherboard (for example, the SATA controller) to fail and for the rest of the motherboard to work fine. This can be verified by doing a power-on self-test (POST) analysis. The POST process starts when the computer first boots. It can result in visible codes or *audible beeps*. The visible codes could be on the screen or could be part of a two-digit digital readout that is incorporated into the motherboard. Either way, the visible codes or the beep codes can be deciphered with the help of the motherboard manual.

> **Note**
>
> Keep in mind that different BIOS manufacturers (AMI BIOS, Award BIOS, and Dell) have different beep codes. For example, two or three beeps sounded by a motherboard with AMI BIOS means a memory issue.

To fix a problem such as a SATA controller failure, a separate PCIe SATA controller card can be purchased. Then you can connect the hard drives to the new controller and disable the original integrated SATA controller in the BIOS. A good bench or lab will have extra controller cards of all kinds so that you can test these types of problems. In some cases, a failed controller can be symptomatic of a bigger problem; the entire motherboard might need to be replaced. Some component failures can cause system lockups, where the OS freezes and the keyboard and mouse become nonfunctional. Such failures could be due to controller issues, chipset issues, or faulty hard drives. Check all connections and consider flashing the BIOS. Worst-case scenario: Replace the motherboard. We'll discuss hard drive troubleshooting in Chapter 25, "Troubleshooting Hard Drives and RAID Arrays."

Finally, manufacturing defects and failed motherboard components often occur. Printed circuit boards (PCBs), such as motherboards, are mass-produced at high speed. Problems might be found immediately when receiving a motherboard. In general, defects are uncommon but can occur due to mechanical problems in the machinery or due to engineering errors. If you suspect a manufacturing defect, you should return the motherboard.

Motherboard component failure can also manifest over time. For example, a distended capacitor is a capacitor that becomes swollen and possibly leaks electrolytic material; this bulging can cause the system to unexpectedly restart or shut down, cause BSOD, or cause other errors. If possible, the affected capacitor(s) should be replaced right away. If that does not work, the motherboard should be replaced. In the early 2000s, capacitor swelling, or "swollen caps," was somewhat prevalent due to raw material issues—the problem was even dubbed the "capacitor plague." However, the problem is much less common today. In fact, motherboards that are received in a DOA (dead-on-arrival) state are uncommon with reputable manufacturers. To give you an idea of just how uncommon they are, I have built more than 1000 systems and have only had to return 1 motherboard—and I'm fairly sure that the board failure was due to poor shipping and handling.

Troubleshooting CPUs

The most common issue with a CPU is when it isn't installed properly or securely. This could possibly cause a complete failure when you try to turn on the system. This failure might be accompanied by a series of beeps from the POST. If this happens, always check the power first, just in case. Then check the main power connections and then the 8- or 4-pin CPU power connection. Another possibility is that the system might turn on and power might be supplied to the system, but nothing else happens: no POST, no display (meaning a blank or black screen), and no drive activity. In any of these situations, after checking power, make sure of the following:

▶ **Ensure that the fan is connected and functional:** Some motherboards have a safeguard that disables booting if the fan is defective or not plugged in. Or you might get a message on the screen or another type of warning, depending on the motherboard. Be sure that the fan is plugged into the correct power connector on the motherboard (or elsewhere) and verify whether it turns on when the computer is on. If the fan has failed, purchase a replacement fan; just make sure that the new fan is compatible with the heat sink and motherboard.

▶ **Check other major components:** Remember that the CPU is a part of a bigger system—one in which other components are more likely to be the cause of many problems. These components include the video card, RAM, and motherboard. Be sure to check these other components for simple connectivity problems, which could be the actual culprit. Always check connections first before taking apart the CPU assembly.

▶ **Make sure the heat sink is connected properly:** Make sure that the heat sink is flush with the CPU cap and that it is securely fastened to the motherboard (or socket housing).

▶ **Ensure that the CPU is installed properly:** Make sure it was installed flush into the socket and that it was oriented correctly. Of course, this means removing the heat sink. If you do so, you should clean off excess thermal compound and reapply thermal compound to the CPU cap before reinstalling the heat sink.

ExamAlert

When troubleshooting the CPU, be sure to first check all connections and then make sure the fan, heat sink, and CPU are secure and installed properly.

Following are a few more possible symptoms of a failing CPU:

▶ Unexplained crashes (shutdowns) occur during bootup or during use.

▶ The system locks after only a short time of use.

▶ Voltage is near, at, or above the top end of the allowable range.

Sometimes a CPU is just plain defective. It could have been received this way, or maybe it overheated. Perhaps there was a surge that damaged it, or maybe someone overclocked it too far, and it was a victim of overvoltage (and subsequent overheating). Regardless of the culprit, the CPU needs to be replaced. Now, by default, CPUs come with a heat sink and fan, and you can install the CPU as you normally would. But in some cases, you can save money by purchasing only the CPU and using the existing heat sink. In this case, remember to clean excess thermal compound and then reapply thermal compound; but reapply it to the CPU cap and not to the heat sink. If the CPU was installed properly, users don't usually have many problems with it (unless they are overclockers). Keep this in mind when troubleshooting the CPU or when troubleshooting an issue that *appears* to be a CPU issue but that might actually be something else altogether.

On a lighter note, sometimes you might get reports from customers about strange noises coming from inside a PC—a buzzing of sorts (or perhaps even a grinding noise). The noise could be caused by a wire or cable that is brushing up against the CPU fan (or other case fan). Be sure to reroute cables inside the computer so that they are clear of the CPU and any other devices. This will also aid with airflow in the PC and keep the PC cooler. The CPU fan might also make noise due to being clogged with dust, especially in dirtier environmental conditions. If the fan is still functional, you can use compressed air to clean it out. But be careful because too much air movement could cause a static discharge. For example, if the CPU fan (or case fans) is moved due to the air flow of a compressor, it could cause ESD. Use a piece of foam or other plastic stopper to keep the fan(s) in place while you use compressed air. Keep a computer vacuum handy to clean up the mess, if necessary; I've seen computers that had so much dust and dirt inside it could fill a garden! But be careful with computer vacuums and air compressors. Use a plastic nozzle or tip (never metal) and don't actually touch any of the components.

Troubleshooting RAM

It's not common, but RAM modules can cause intermittent issues, or they can fail altogether. Always make sure that the RAM is fully seated within the RAM slot and that the plastic ears are locking the RAM into place. An unstable system can be caused by several components, including RAM. Remember to check other components in the system as well, including the video card, motherboard, and CPU.

A lot of the issues you see occur because a user has purchased and installed a memory stick that is not compatible, or is semi-compatible, with the motherboard: wrong speed, incorrect capacity, improper configuration, and so on. Be ready for this; check the RAM compatibility against the motherboard, even if the user swears it has been checked already. Remember, a good technician has documentation available, has access to the Internet, and knows how to use both.

> **ExamAlert**
>
> Verify compatibility of RAM with the motherboard when troubleshooting!

Perhaps there was some kind of surge inside the computer; maybe the computer is not protected by a surge suppressor or UPS. Another possibility is that the RAM was damaged by ESD, and this damage manifests in intermittent problems. There are expensive hardware-based RAM testers that can tell you if the RAM is electrically sound and if it can process data correctly. If your company owns one, or if you can get your hands on one for a short time, you might narrow the problem. However, I have rarely needed to use these.

Here are some possible symptoms of a RAM issue and corresponding troubleshooting techniques:

▶ **Computer will not boot/intermittently shuts down:** If there is no RAM in the computer, or if the RAM is damaged or is not installed securely, it can prevent the computer from doing anything at all (aside from draining electricity from your AC outlet). For example, the power supply fan turns but nothing else happens—no beeps and no displays. First, if the RAM was just installed, make sure that the RAM is compatible. Next, and in general, try reseating the RAM before you attempt to troubleshoot a CPU or motherboard. Add RAM if none exists. (Sounds silly, but I've seen this!) If you suspect faulty RAM, corroded contacts, or a faulty RAM slot, you can try taking the RAM out, cleaning the RAM and RAM slot, and putting the RAM back in, being sure to seat the memory module properly. (For cleaning, use contact cleaner on the RAM contacts and use compressed air on the slot.) Next, try moving memory modules to different slots; check your motherboard documentation for proper orientation. As mentioned, a POST analysis can be helpful in these situations as well. If necessary, replace the memory module with an identical one (if you have an extra one handy) or purchase a new one if you have identified the memory module as the source of the problem. In some cases, RAM can overheat and cause intermittent shutdowns. To prevent this, purchase a heat sink for RAM. These are made of aluminum or copper, just like CPU heat sinks, and are sometimes referred to as heat spreaders. You can also purchase RAM with heat sinks preinstalled. This type of RAM might be necessary for high-end systems.

▶ **BIOS indicates a memory error:** The BIOS can indicate a memory error through a message on the screen and a flashing cursor or by beeping. If it beeps, you need to reference the motherboard documentation for the specific beep codes. Sometimes a BIOS setting can be incorrect. If the computer has a saved version of the BIOS settings, you can try reverting to them, or you can try loading the BIOS defaults; I can't tell you how many times this has worked for me! Sometimes the BIOS indicates the wrong amount of RAM. If this is the case, check the RAM, as explained in the first bullet. Finally, a BIOS update can be the cure; perhaps the BIOS just doesn't have the programming necessary to identify the latest type of RAM that was installed.

▶ **An application crashes:** If an application crashes, it could be due to faulty RAM (or, uncommonly, a CPU issue). Make sure that the RAM is compatible with the motherboard and use memory testing programs to verify if there is any damage to the RAM. (More on memory testing in just a bit.)

▶ **A stop error, aka BSOD (blue screen of death), occurs:** This is a critical system error that causes the operating system to shut down. Most of the time, these errors are due to device driver errors (poor code), but they can be associated with physical faults in memory. One example of this would be a non-maskable interrupt (NMI). An NMI can interrupt the processor to gain its attention regarding nonrecoverable hardware errors, resulting in a BSOD. The BSOD usually dumps the contents of memory to a file (for later analysis) and restarts the computer. If you don't encounter another BSOD, it's probably not much to worry about. But if the BSOD happens repeatedly, you should write down the information you see on the screen and cross-reference it to the Microsoft Support website, at https://support.microsoft.com. Again, if you suspect faulty RAM, try the troubleshooting methods in the first bullet.

> **Note**
>
> BSODs are covered in more depth in Chapter 53, "Troubleshooting Microsoft Windows."

Chances are you won't need them often, but memory testing programs such as MemTest86 (https://www.memtest86.com) are available online. In fact, a whole slew of testing and benchmarking software is freely available to you. Search around! Plus, you can use the Windows Memory Diagnostics Tool, which can be accessed by typing **mdsched.exe** in the Run prompt or from the Windows Recovery Environment (more on that in Chapter 53). These steps can help diagnose whether a memory module needs to be replaced. But in general, trust in your senses. Look at and listen to the computer as you try to diagnose any RAM issues that might occur.

Troubleshooting Power Supply Issues

Many types of power problems can happen. We discuss power in general in Chapter 18, "Power," and Chapter 60, "Environmental Controls," but for now we focus on power issues related to the power supply within a computer.

Many issues that occur with power supplies are intermittent. This makes the troubleshooting process a little tougher. Your best friends when troubleshooting power supplies are a power supply tester and your eyes and ears.

Of course, always make sure that the power supply cable connects from the power supply to a properly wired AC outlet properly before troubleshooting further. Next, check all of the internal power connections. Make sure they are connected firmly. To *test* these connections, use a power supply tester.

A power supply tester (or PSU tester) is a tool every computer tech should have in their toolkit. Figure 24.1 shows an example of a PSU tester. These testing devices normally test for 12 V, 5 V, and 3.3 V for most of the connections within the computer, including the main 24-pin ATX power connector, 8- and 4-pin CPU connector, PCI Express 8-pin and 6-pin connectors, SATA power connector, and Molex power connector. If there are error readings, error lights, no lights, or missing lights for specific voltages on the tester, you should consider replacing the power supply; or if it is modular, you should replace that particular power cable. If all the lights and indicators are normal, then the issue resides somewhere else.

FIGURE 24.1 **PSU tester testing a 24-pin ATX power connector**

Here are several of the issues you might encounter with power supplies:

▶ Fan failure

▶ Fuse failure

▶ Quick death

▶ Slow death

Fan failure can be due to the fact that the power supply is old, the fan is extremely clogged with dirt, or the fan was of a cheaper design (without ball bearings). However, for the A+ exam, it doesn't make a difference. As far as the A+ exam is concerned, if the fan fails, the power supply needs to be replaced (and that strategy makes sense). Chances are, if the fan has failed, other components of the power supply are on their way out also. It is more cost-effective to a company to simply replace the power supply than to have a technician spend time opening it and trying to repair it. More importantly, although it is possible to remove and replace the fan by opening the power supply, this can be a dangerous venture because the power supply holds an electric charge. So, the A+ rule is to never open the power supply.

ExamAlert

Do not open a power supply! If it has failed, replace it with a working unit.

Fan failure can sometimes cause a loud noise to emanate from the power supply; it might even sound like it is coming from inside the computer. Any fan in the computer (power supply fan, case fan, or CPU fan) can make strange noises over time. If a customer reports a loud noise coming from the inside a PC, consider the power supply fan as a suspect.

On the other hand, sometimes the fans spin but no other devices receive power, and the computer doesn't boot. This could be due to improper installation (or failure) of the motherboard, CPU, or RAM.

Fuse failure can occur due to an overload or due to the power supply malfunctioning. Either way, the proper course of action is to replace the power supply. Do not attempt to replace the fuse. If the fuse is blown, chances are that the power supply is faulty.

If the power supply dies a quick death and provides no power, it might be for several reasons, ranging from an electrical spike to hardware malfunction. First, make sure that the IEC power cable is connected properly to the power supply and to the AC outlet. Sometimes it can be difficult to tell whether the power supply has failed or whether the problem is something else inside or outside the computer system. You should check the AC outlet with your trusty receptacle tester, make sure that a circuit hasn't tripped, and verify that any surge protectors and/or UPS devices work properly. Depending on what you sense about the problem, you might decide to just swap out the power supply with a known good one.

A power supply that is dying a slow death may cause intermittent errors or frequent failure of hard drives and other devices, and this can be tough to troubleshoot. If you suspect intermittent issues, first make sure the power cord is connected securely and then try swapping out the power supply with a known good one. Boot the computer and watch it for a while to see if the same errors continue to occur.

Note

If a system was recently upgraded, the power supply could cause the system to reboot intermittently because the new components are causing too much power drain. When upgrading components, be sure to check whether you need to upgrade the power supply as well!

Remember that connections sometimes can be jarred loose inside and outside a computer. Check the IEC cord on both ends and all power connections inside the computer, including the main motherboard connector as well as the CPU, Molex, SATA, and PCIe connectors. Any single loose connector can have "interesting" results on the computer!

Heating and Cooling

Another thing to watch for is system overheating. This can happen for several reasons:

▶ Power supply fan failure

▶ Auxiliary case fan failure

▶ Inadequate number of fans

▶ Missing or open slot covers

▶ Case not being tightly closed and screwed in

▶ Location of the computer

Air flow is important on today's personal computers because their processors can often operate at hundreds of billions of instructions per second or more (referred to as 100 giga-instructions per second [GIPS]). They typically use 50 to 150 watts of power, and that creates a lot of heat! Add to that the video card and other cards that have their own on-board processors, and you quickly realize it can get *hot* inside the computer case. Plus, environmental factors and higher-temperature areas (such as warehouses and cafeterias) can cause heat to be trapped in the case, producing intermittent shutdowns. Circulation is the key here. Air should flow in the case from the front and should be exhausted out the back. Any openings in the case or missing slot covers can cause circulation to diminish. If you have a computer that has a lot of devices, does a lot of processing, or runs hot for any other reason, your best bet is to install a case fan in the front of the case (which pulls air into the case) and a second case fan in the back of the case (which, with the power supply fan, helps exhaust hot air out the back). Standard sizes for case fans are 80 and 120 mm. Also, try to keep the computer in a relatively cool area and leave space for the computer to expel its hot air! Of course, there are other special considerations and options, such as liquid cooling and special processor cooling methods, such as oversized tower heat sinks; however, for typical workstations, these options will most likely not be feasible.

You should also train your nose for smells and watch for smoke. If a power supply starts to emit a burning smell, or if you see any smoke emanating from it, you should turn off the computer and disconnect the power right away. The power supply is probably about to fail, and it could short out, trip the circuit, or, worse yet, start a fire. Be sure to replace it. In some cases, a power supply has a burn-in period of 24 to 48 hours, during which time you might smell some oils burning off, but it's best to be safe and check/test the power supply if you smell something that seems wrong.

Troubleshooting Questions in the A+ Exams

Hardware and software troubleshooting make up at least a quarter of the A+ exam objectives. For bench techs, help desk people, and other tech support personnel, it makes up a much larger percentage of work. When it really comes down to it, we technicians are here to solve problems, and troubleshooting is a key component of problem solving. So, I have included a lot more cram quiz questions for these troubleshooting chapters than for other chapters. It seemed the proper way.

Cram Quiz

Answer these questions. The answers follow the last question. If you cannot answer these questions correctly, consider reading this chapter again until you can.

1. What is the best way to tell if a CR2032 lithium battery has been discharged?

   - ○ **A.** Use a power supply tester.
   - ○ **B.** Check within Windows.
   - ○ **C.** Use a multimeter.
   - ○ **D.** Plug it into another motherboard.

2. A PC reboots without any warning. You rule out any chance of viruses. When you look at the motherboard, you see that some of the capacitors are swelling and appear distended and out of shape. What should you do?

   - ○ **A.** Replace the motherboard.
   - ○ **B.** Replace the hard drive.
   - ○ **C.** Remove and replace the capacitors.
   - ○ **D.** Reconfigure the BIOS.

3. A computer you are troubleshooting won't boot properly. When you power on the computer, the video display is blank, and you hear a series of beeps. What should you do?

- ○ **A.** Check power supply connections.
- ○ **B.** Consult the vendor documentation for the motherboard.
- ○ **C.** Remove all memory and replace it.
- ○ **D.** Unplug the speakers because they are causing a conflict.

4. You are troubleshooting a CPU and have already cut power, disconnected the power cable, opened the case, and put on your antistatic strap. What should you do next?

- ○ **A.** Check the BIOS.
- ○ **B.** Check connections.
- ○ **C.** Remove the CPU.
- ○ **D.** Test the motherboard with a multimeter.

5. What is a possible symptom of a failing CPU?

- ○ **A.** CPU is beyond the recommended voltage range.
- ○ **B.** Computer won't boot.
- ○ **C.** BIOS reports low temperatures within the case.
- ○ **D.** Spyware is installed in the browser.

6. You are repairing a computer that has been used in a warehouse for several years. You suspect a problem with a memory module. What should you do first?

- ○ **A.** Replace the module with a new one.
- ○ **B.** Install more RAM.
- ○ **C.** Clean the RAM slot.
- ○ **D.** Install RAM heat sinks.

7. You are investigating a computer that is suffering from intermittent shutdowns. You note that the RAM modules are overheating. What is the best solution?

- ○ **A.** Install a heat sink on the memory controller.
- ○ **B.** Install more CPU fans.
- ○ **C.** Install heat sinks on the RAM modules.
- ○ **D.** Install a heat sink on the chipset.

8. You just installed new, compatible RAM into a motherboard, but when you boot the computer, it does not recognize the memory. What should you do?

   ○ **A.** Flash the BIOS.

   ○ **B.** Replace the RAM.

   ○ **C.** Upgrade the CPU.

   ○ **D.** Add more RAM.

9. You are troubleshooting a computer that won't power on. You have already checked the AC outlet and the power cord, which appear to be functioning properly. What should you do next?

   ○ **A.** Test the computer with a PSU tester.

   ○ **B.** Plug the computer into a different outlet.

   ○ **C.** Check that the RAM is seated correctly.

   ○ **D.** Install a UPS.

10. A computer you are troubleshooting shuts down without warning. After a few minutes, it boots back up, but after running for a short time, it shuts down again. Which of the following components could be the cause? (Select the two best answers.)

    ○ **A.** Power supply

    ○ **B.** SATA hard drive

    ○ **C.** RAM

    ○ **D.** CPU fan

    ○ **E.** Video card

Cram Quiz Answers

1. **C.** Although there might be a Windows application that monitors the battery, the surefire way is to test the voltage of the lithium battery with a multimeter. A CR2032 lithium battery is designed to run at 3 volts (and they often ship at approximately 3.3 volts). Some UEFI/BIOS programs can also monitor the voltage of the battery.

2. **A.** You should replace the motherboard if it is damaged. It would be much too time-consuming to even attempt replacing the capacitors and probably not cost-effective.

3. **B.** You should check the BIOS version and consult the documentation that accompanies the motherboard. You might need to go online for this information. You can also try performing a POST analysis to discern the problem. The issue could be video based, or RAM based, but the beep code should help identify the problem.

4. **B.** Check connections first as they are a common culprit.

5. **A.** If the CPU is running beyond the recommended voltage range for extended periods of time, it can be a sign of a failing CPU. If the computer won't boot at all, another problem might have occurred, or the CPU might have already failed. Low case temperatures are a good thing (as long as they aren't below freezing). Spyware is unrelated in this case.

6. **C.** Because the computer is being used in a warehouse (and a warehouse is often a fairly dirty environment), you should use compressed air on the RAM slot and clean the memory module with contact cleaner. Clean out all of the dust bunnies within the entire computer. Using MemTest86 or another memory diagnostic tool is another good answer.

7. **C.** The best thing to do in this situation is to install heat sinks on the RAM modules. On older computers, the memory controller in a northbridge doesn't usually overheat because it already has a heat sink; on newer computers, it is within the CPU. A CPU can have only one fan. You can't install more (although an additional case fan might help). The chipset also usually has a heat sink.

8. **A.** If you are sure that the RAM is compatible and the system doesn't recognize it during POST, try flashing the UEFI/BIOS. It could be that the RAM is so new that the motherboard doesn't have the required firmware to identify the new RAM.

9. **A.** You should test the computer with a PSU tester. This can tell you whether the power supply functions properly. You already know that the AC outlet is functional, so there is no reason to use another outlet. The computer would still turn on if the RAM wasn't seated properly. A UPS won't help the situation because it is part of the power flow before the power supply.

10. **A and D.** The two components that could cause the system to shut down are the power supply and the CPU fan. Check the CPU fan settings and temperature in the BIOS first before opening the computer. If those are fine, you most likely need to replace the power supply. The RAM, video card, and hard drive should not cause the system to suddenly shut down.

Now we are getting deep into troubleshooting. This was a longer chapter (for this book at least), and I recommend that you review it carefully. Great work so far!

CHAPTER 25

Troubleshooting Storage Drives and RAID Arrays

This chapter covers the following A+ 220-1101 exam objective:

▶ **5.3** – Given a scenario, troubleshoot and diagnose problems with storage drives and RAID arrays.

Storage drives contain the data that we need, so we depend on our drives and RAID arrays to run efficiently every day. For this to happen, the drives need to be healthy. We can keep our drives healthy by carrying out a variety of precautionary measures. But sometimes, our systems can be affected by powers outside our control and beyond our planning. Then, they can potentially fail—and then, we have to troubleshoot.

Preventive Maintenance and Troubleshooting of Storage Drives

Storage drives will fail. It's not a matter of if; it's a matter of when, especially when it comes to mechanical drives. The moving parts are bound to fail at some point. Storage drives have an average warranty of three years, as is the case with the SATA drives used in the examples in this book. But many of us want our drives to last longer than that. So, to quote Benjamin Franklin, "an ounce of prevention is worth a pound of cure" or, for those of you using the metric system, 29 grams and .45 kg—but that just doesn't seem to roll off the tongue quite so well! Either way, by implementing good practices, you can extend the life span of a storage drive. So, before we get into troubleshooting storage drives, let's consider some examples of prevention.

Storage Drive Preventive Maintenance

Always the pessimist, I'm constantly on the lookout for ways to *prevent* problems before they happen. By taking preventive measures, a technician can reduce the risk of catastrophic failure. Here are a couple of ways to prevent storage drive issues.

▶ **Turn off a computer when not in use:** This can help increase the life span of a magnetic-based drive (or hard disk drive). Turning off the computer tells the hard disk drive to spin down and enter a "parked" state. It's kind of like parking a car or placing a record player's arm on its holder. Turning off a computer when not in use increases the life span of just about all its devices (except for the lithium battery). You can also set the computer to hibernate, sleep, or standby, or you can simply set your operating system's power scheme to turn off hard disks after a certain amount of inactivity, such as five minutes. The less the drive is in motion, the longer the life span it will have. Of course, if you want to take the moving parts out of the equation, you can opt for a solid-state drive, as discussed later in this chapter.

▶ **Clean up the disk:** Use a storage drive cleanup program to remove temporary files, clean out the Recycle Bin, and so on. Microsoft includes the Disk Cleanup program in Windows. And there are free cleanup programs available on the Internet. (Just be careful what you download.) When you remove the "junk" from the drive, there is less data that the drive must sift through, which makes it easier on the drive when it is time to defragment.

▶ **Defragment the drive:** Defragmenting, also known as *defragging*, rearranges the data on a partition or volume so that it is laid out in a contiguous, orderly fashion. Defragmentation is most commonly performed on a hard disk drive. Consider defragmenting the disk every couple months or perhaps more often if you are a power user. Don't worry: The operating system tells you if defragging is not necessary during the analysis stage. Over time, data is written to the drive and subsequently erased, over and over again, leaving gaps in the drive space. New data is sometimes written to multiple areas of the drive, in a broken or fragmented fashion, filling in any blank areas the drive can find. When this happens, the drive has to work much harder to find the data it needs. Logically, data access time is increased. Physically, the drive spins more, and it starts and stops more; in general, there is more mechanical movement. It's kind of like changing gears excessively with the automatic transmission in your car. The more the drive has to access this fragmented data, the shorter its life span becomes due to mechanical wear and tear. But before the drive fails altogether, fragmentation can cause intermittent read/write failures. Defragmenting the drive can be done with Microsoft's Disk Defragmenter, with the command **defrag**, or with other third-party programs. If using the Disk Defragmenter program, you need 15% free space on the volume you want to defrag. If you have less than that, you need to use the command-line option **defrag -f**. To summarize, the more contiguous the data, the less the drive has to work to access that data, thus decreasing the data access time and increasing the life span of the drive. While defragmenting works best on magnetic drives, it can also help with solid-state drives, but not to the same extent or in the same way because of the design differences between the two types of drives.

> **Note**
>
> Be careful with defragging; it can wear out a drive if it is done too much, especially when performed on SSDs.

> **ExamAlert**
>
> Know how to troubleshoot failures such as read/write errors using tools such as Optimize Drives/Disk Defragmenter and the **defrag** command.

▶ **Leave at least 10% of the drive free:** If you use up all the space on a drive, its performance and life span will decrease greatly. Consider leaving between 10% and 25% of the space on a drive free of data. Some manufacturers add a 10% buffer by design, and some companies have a policy that states drives should never go past 50% or 60% of capacity. This preventive measure applies to HDDs and SSDs.

▶ **Make sure that high-performance drives have good airflow:** NVMe drives (such as M.2 and PCIe-based drives), as well as RAID arrays, can generate a lot of heat. Be sure to have good airflow and adequate cooling, and if at all possible, don't cramp the drives too much.

▶ **Scan the drive with anti-malware:** Make sure the computer has an anti-malware program installed. Also known as an endpoint protection platform, this program should include antivirus and anti-spyware at the very least. Verify that the software is scheduled to scan the drive at least twice a week. (The manufacturer default is usually every day.) The quicker the software finds and quarantines threats, the lower the chance of physical damage to the drive.

Preventive techniques will save you time, save your users some heartache, and save your organization money. But as I said, storage drives will fail. When failures happen, you troubleshoot.

Storage Drive Troubleshooting

Now, let's get into some of the problems you might encounter concerning storage drives:

▶ **Bootable device not found:** If the UEFI/BIOS doesn't recognize the drive you have installed, you can check a few things. First, make sure the power cable is firmly connected and oriented properly. Next, make sure SATA data cables are fully seated in the ports and weren't accidentally installed upside down; if you find one that was, consider replacing it because it might be damaged due to incorrect installation. An "OS Not Found" error message or another boot failure could also be caused by improperly connected drives or an erroneous BIOS boot order. Finally, check if there is a motherboard BIOS update; sometimes newer drives require new BIOS code to access the drive.

▶ **Windows does not "see" a second drive:** There are several reasons Windows might not see a second drive. Maybe a driver needs to be installed for the drive or for its controller. This is more common with newer drive technologies. Perhaps the secondary drive needs to be initialized within Disk Management. Or it could be that the drive was not partitioned or formatted. Also try the methods listed in the first bullet.

▶ **Slow reaction time:** If a drive is suffering from longer read/write times than usual, it could be due to several things. Perhaps the drive is full, or has become fragmented, or has been infected with malware. Sometimes it could be the fault of torrent-based software. Or perhaps there are bad sectors, indicating a damaged drive. In any of these cases, it is common to see that the drive's LED status indicator on the front of the computer is blinking more than usual, telling you that the drive is working harder than it normally would. Check for (and remove) undesirable software such as bit torrent clients, P2P software, and so on. Check the drive's properties in the OS; if it is full or nearly full, start offloading data. If it is not full, analyze and defragment the drive. If it is heavily fragmented, the drive can take longer to access the data needed, resulting in slow reaction time. You might be amazed at the difference in performance! If you think the drive might be infected, scan the disk with your anti-malware program to quarantine any possible threats. It's wise to schedule deep scans of the drive periodically as well. You will learn more about viruses, spyware, and other malicious software in Chapter 45, "Wireless Security and Malware."

After you have worked on the drive, check it with some type of benchmarking software (CrystalDiskMark, ATTO, or similar program). These programs can measure the data transfer capabilities of your storage drive, either in megabytes per second (MB/s) or in input/output operations per second (IOPS). Either of these measurements can be compared to the vendor's documentation for the drive to see if the drive is working within specifications. Note that vendor tests are usually done in an optimal environment and show the *maximums* for the drive. Your results will often be 10% to 20% lower, which is usually okay. However, if your results are 25% or more below the vendor's numbers, you should investigate the drive further.

In extreme cases, you might want to move all the data from the affected drive to another drive, being sure to verify the data that was moved. Then format the affected drive and, finally, move the data back. This is common in audio/video environments and when dealing with data drives, but it should not be done to a system drive (that is, a drive that contains the operating system).

▶ **Missing files at startup:** If you get a message such as "BOOTMGR Is Missing," the file needs to be written back to the drive. For more on how to do this, see Chapter 53, "Troubleshooting Microsoft Windows." In severe cases, this can mean that the drive is physically damaged and needs to be replaced. If this happens, the drive needs to be removed from the computer, and the data must be copied from the damaged drive to a known good drive (which might require a third-party program). Then, a new drive must be installed to the affected computer. Afterward, the recovered data can be copied on the new drive.

▶ **Missing or corrupted files:** Missing or corrupted files could result from drive failure, operating system failure, malware infection, user error, and so on. If data corruption happens, be sure to back up the rest of the data on the drive and then use the preventive methods mentioned previously, especially defragmenting and scanning for malware. (Ultimately, you may have to replace the drive.) You can also analyze the drive's S.M.A.R.T. data. S.M.A.R.T., which stands for Self-Monitoring, Analysis, and Reporting Technology, is a monitoring system included with almost all drives that creates reporting data which, when enabled in the BIOS, can be accessed within the operating system. You can easily view some basic S.M.A.R.T.-based information in the Windows Command Prompt by using the command **wmic diskdrive get status**. Each (S.M.A.R.T.-enabled) drive will be analyzed; the message "OK" means that Windows didn't find any issues. The message of "Bad," "Unknown," or "Caution" should convince you to initiate more analysis. There are also plenty of third-party tools available that can be downloaded from the Internet and are very easy to use. The problem with S.M.A.R.T. data is that it can be unreliable at times due to lack of hardware and driver support within the third-party S.M.A.R.T. application, lack of common interpretation, and incorrectly diagnosed data. Also, a drive might be diagnosed as a failing drive when in reality the problem is power surges or another issue.

Note

If a file is written during a power surge (whether the surge originates internally or externally), that file will most likely be placed on the drive in a corrupted fashion—with the associated sector being affected by the power surge. In this case, you should find out two things: 1, if the power supply has the right capacity for the equipment in the computer, and 2, if the proper power suppressing/conditioning equipment is being used. If a drive is making clicking sounds or other strange noises, analysis with S.M.A.R.T. data is not recommended. See the following bullet for more information.

▶ **Noisy drive/lockups:** Watch out for clicking and grinding sounds! If your SATA magnetic disk drive starts getting noisy, it's a sure sign of impending drive failure. You might also hear a scratching or grating sound, akin to a record being scratched with a record player needle. Or the drive might intermittently just stop or lock up, with one or more loud audible clicks. You can't wait in these situations; you need to connect the drive to another computer immediately and copy the data to a good drive. Even then, it might be too late. However, there are some third-party programs available on the Internet that might help you recover the data.

> **Note**
>
> Storage drive issues can also result in proprietary crash screens: either a Windows blue screen of death (BSOD) or a macOS spinning pinwheel. Fixing these issues often requires using recovery environment tools and/or restoring the system to an earlier point in time. If these issues happen often and drive repair methods do not work, consider either a new installation of Windows or a new drive. We cover how to troubleshoot these problems further in the Core 2 (220-1102) portion of the book.

As mentioned, storage drives *will* fail, so it is important to make backups of your data. The backup media of choice will vary depending on the organization. It could be the cloud, tape backup, a secondary system, optical discs, or USB flash drives, depending on the scenario. Know this: RAID arrays are not considered to be backups. They are fault-tolerant ways of storing data. Because they consist of storage drives, it stands to reason that you will have to troubleshoot them, too.

Troubleshooting RAID Arrays

Sometimes, hardware RAID arrays fail. They might stop working, or the OS could have trouble finding them. If you see an issue like this, check whether the storage drives are securely connected to the controller and ensure that the controller (if an adapter card) is securely connected to the motherboard. Also, if you use a RAID adapter card or an external enclosure and the motherboard also has built-in RAID functionality of its own, make sure you disable the motherboard RAID within the BIOS as it could cause a conflict. Verify that the driver for the RAID device is installed and updated. Finally, check whether any of the drives or the RAID controller has failed. If a RAID controller built into a motherboard fails, you will either have to purchase a new motherboard or a RAID adapter card.

Intel-based RAID setups are common as part of server and workstation motherboards and as separate RAID adapter cards. To configure Intel RAID, a technician needs to press Ctrl+I when the system first boots up. From there, the RAID array can be configured as shown in Figure 25.1.

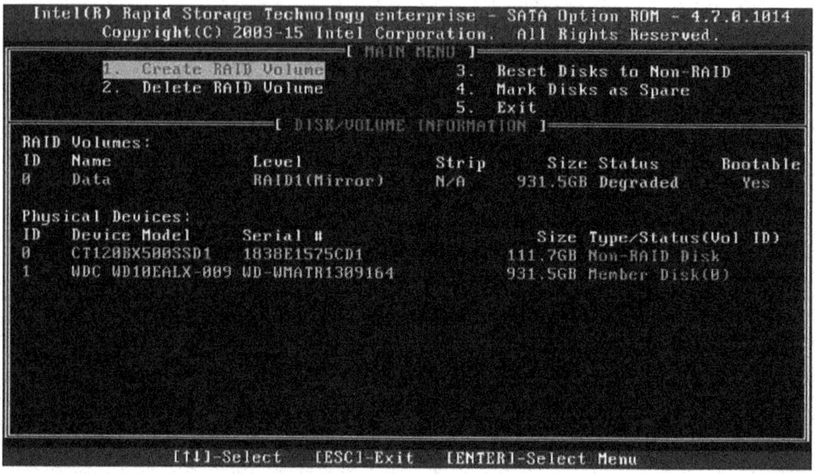

FIGURE 25.1   Intel RAID configuration screen

In Figure 25.1 you can see that there is a RAID 1 mirror, but that the status is "Degraded." This means the array has failed or has been deconstructed in some way. The listed drive is part of a RAID 1 volume called Data, but the second drive of the mirror is missing, so the mirror is broken. (That's because I removed it from the system to show this very error.) Look in the listed physical devices for the drive that is 931.5 GB; you can see that it is listed as Member Disk, meaning that it is part of an array. A degraded RAID 0, 1, 5, or 10 array can result in either a loss of access to data or—if the OS is installed to the array—failure of the OS to boot. Either way, the array would have to be repaired, or the data would have to be recovered from backup and placed on a new array. Repairing a RAID array could be as simple as reconnecting the physical drives, but it could also mean reconfiguring the array within the RAID utility. Some organizations have a rule that if a RAID array fails and it is more than three years old, the organization should downgrade the array, create a new array with new drives, and recover the data from backup.

Now, let's say that that RAID functionality is indeed built into your motherboard, as it is on the system shown in Figure 25.1. In order to configure a RAID array, you first have to enable RAID in the BIOS. Quite often, that is done by accessing the SATA configuration screen and changing from AHCI to RAID. If you don't do this, you won't be able to access the RAID utility at bootup. Take it to the next level: If someone resets the BIOS to defaults, then that SATA setting will revert to AHCI, rendering the RAID array useless and non-bootable—ultimately leading to various error messages. This could also happen after a BIOS flash update. Yet another reason to know the BIOS of your systems!

> **Note**
>
> AHCI stands for Advanced Host Configuration Interface, which is the default setting for SATA drives in many BIOS programs.

One way to check the status of a RAID array is to use S.M.A.R.T. For example, in Figure 25.2, you can see the S.M.A.R.T. information screen for one of the disks in a RAID 1 mirror of a network-attached storage (NAS) device. This screen gives some meaningful data that requires some analysis, but for quick peace of mind, just check the Status column. OKs are good; anything else requires further attention and could be a precursor to a RAID failure. Also note in the figure the S.M.A.R.T. Test page, where you can do additional testing of the drive, drives, or array. Just be sure to run tests of this nature off-hours!

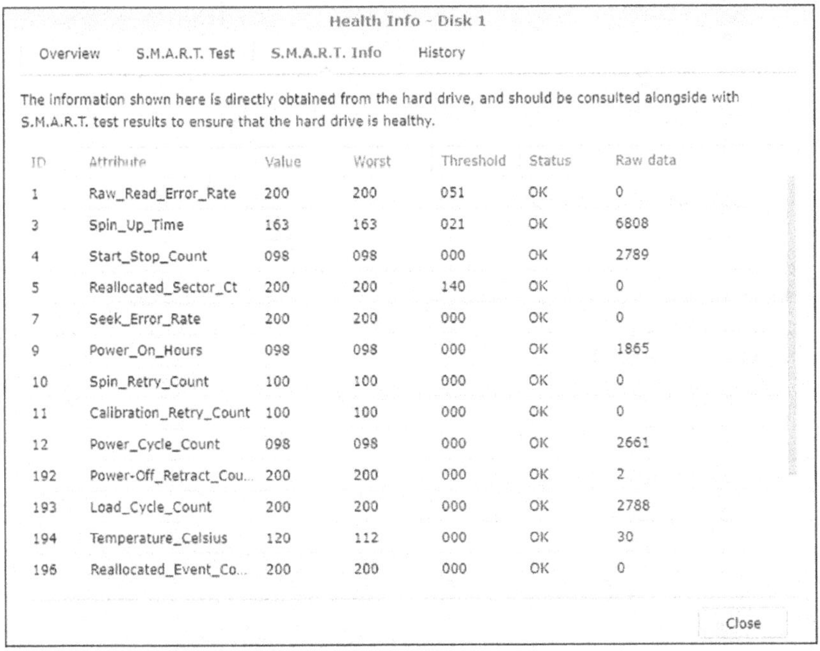

Health Info - Disk 1

Overview   S.M.A.R.T. Test   S.M.A.R.T. Info   History

The information shown here is directly obtained from the hard drive, and should be consulted alongside with S.M.A.R.T. test results to ensure that the hard drive is healthy.

ID	Attribute	Value	Worst	Threshold	Status	Raw data
1	Raw_Read_Error_Rate	200	200	051	OK	0
3	Spin_Up_Time	163	163	021	OK	6808
4	Start_Stop_Count	098	098	000	OK	2789
5	Reallocated_Sector_Ct	200	200	140	OK	0
7	Seek_Error_Rate	200	200	000	OK	0
9	Power_On_Hours	098	098	000	OK	1865
10	Spin_Retry_Count	100	100	000	OK	0
11	Calibration_Retry_Count	100	100	000	OK	0
12	Power_Cycle_Count	098	098	000	OK	2661
192	Power-Off_Retract_Cou...	200	200	000	OK	2
193	Load_Cycle_Count	200	200	000	OK	2788
194	Temperature_Celsius	120	112	000	OK	30
196	Reallocated_Event_Co...	200	200	000	OK	0

Close

FIGURE 25.2   **S.M.A.R.T. information and status of a NAS drive**

RAID Is Not Backup!

Remember, in the workplace, RAID is generally used for fault tolerance; it is not a backup of data, even if you are using RAID 1 (mirroring). A RAID array's data should be properly backed up to a *separate* system, according to your organization's procedures. The backup should be tested thoroughly and documented.

Cram Quiz

Answer these questions. The answers follow the last question. If you cannot answer these questions correctly, consider reading this chapter again until you can.

1. What should you do first to repair a drive that is acting sluggish?
   - ○ **A.** Remove the drive and recover the data.
   - ○ **B.** Run Disk Cleanup.
   - ○ **C.** Run Disk Defragmenter.
   - ○ **D.** Scan for viruses.

2. Which of the following are possible symptoms of storage drive failure? (Select the two best answers.)
   - ○ **A.** System lockup.
   - ○ **B.** Antivirus alerts.
   - ○ **C.** Failing bootup files.
   - ○ **D.** Network drive errors.
   - ○ **E.** BIOS doesn't recognize the drive.

3. You just replaced a SATA drive that you suspect failed. You also replaced the data cable between the drive and the motherboard. When you reboot the computer, you notice that the SATA drive is not recognized by the BIOS. What most likely happened to cause this?
   - ○ **A.** The drive has not been formatted yet.
   - ○ **B.** The BIOS does not support SATA.
   - ○ **C.** The SATA port is faulty.
   - ○ **D.** The drive is not jumpered properly.

4. You are troubleshooting a SATA drive that doesn't function on a PC. When you try it on another computer, it works fine. You suspect a power issue and decide to take voltage readings from the SATA power connector coming from the power supply. Which of the following readings should you find?

   ○ **A.** 5 V and 12 V

   ○ **B.** 5 V, 12 V, and 24 V

   ○ **C.** 3.3 V, 5 V, and 12 V

   ○ **D.** 3.3 V and 12 V

5. You are troubleshooting a Windows server that normally boots from a SATA-based RAID 0 array. The message you receive is "missing operating system." As it turns out, another technician has been updating the BIOS on several of the servers in your organization, including this one. What configured setting needs to be changed? (Select the best answer.)

   ○ **A.** RAID 1

   ○ **B.** AHCI

   ○ **C.** S.M.A.R.T.

   ○ **D.** NVMe

6. What should you do *first* if your SATA magnetic disk begins to make loud clicking or grinding noises? (Select the best answer.)

   ○ **A.** Copy the data to another drive.

   ○ **B.** Replace with a new SATA drive.

   ○ **C.** Update the UEFI/BIOS.

   ○ **D.** Replace the SATA power cable

7. Which are performance measurements for storage drives that measure data transfer capabilities every second? (Select two.)

   ○ **A.** wmic

   ○ **B.** MB/s

   ○ **C.** RAID

   ○ **D.** IOPS

Cram Quiz Answers

1. **C.** Attempt to defragment the disk. If defragmentation is not necessary, Windows lets you know. Then you can move to other options, such as scanning the drive for viruses.

2. **A and C.** System lockups and failing bootup files or other failing file operations are possible symptoms of storage drive failure. Antivirus alerts tell you that the

operating system has been compromised, viruses should be quarantined, and a full scan should be initiated. Sometimes drives fail due to heavy virus activity, but usually if the malware is caught quickly enough, the drive should survive. Network drives are separate from the local drive; inability to connect to a network drive suggests a network configuration issue. If the BIOS doesn't recognize a drive, consider a BIOS update.

3. **C.** Most likely, the SATA port is faulty. It might have been damaged during the upgrade. To test the theory, you would plug the SATA data cable into another port on the motherboard. You can't format the drive until it has been recognized by the BIOS, which, by the way, should recognize SATA drives if the motherboard has SATA ports! SATA drives don't use jumpers unless they need to coexist with older IDE drives. Most of today's drives do not come with jumpers.

4. **C.** If you test a SATA power cable, you should find 3.3 V (orange wire), 5 V (red wire), and 12 V (yellow wire). If any of these doesn't test properly, try another SATA power connector.

5. **B.** When the BIOS was updated, the SATA setting in the BIOS probably reverted to AHCI. That caused the RAID 0 array to be ignored, and so the OS would not boot because it is stored on that array. The setting should be changed from AHCI to RAID (or similar name). Now, if this was a RAID 1 mirror, a copy of the OS would be on each drive, and it *might* still boot (though you would probably receive a message about the state of the mirror being degraded or broken). But with RAID 0, the OS is *striped* across two or more drives; all drives need to be present and accessed via RAID in order for the OS to boot. That's one of the reasons the golden rule for many years was to "mirror the OS and stripe the data." Phew! Anyway, on to the incorrect answers. RAID 1 is incorrect because there would be no option to set this; this scenario uses RAID 0. S.M.A.R.T. is the monitoring system included in HDDs and SSDs. NVMe (Non-Volatile Memory Express) is the specification for non-volatile storage used by M.2 drives, PCIe card–based drives, and so on. Remember to back up any and all BIOS configurations!

6. **A.** Don't hesitate! Copy the data to another drive. Afterward, update the UEFI/BIOS, replace the drive with a new one, and consider getting a new SATA cable while you are at it.

7. **B and D.** Megabytes per second (MB/s) and input/output operations per second (IOPS) are performance measurements for storage drives that measure data transfer capabilities every second. The **wmic** command enables you to view basic S.M.A.R.T.-based information in the Windows Command Prompt. Redundant array of inexpensive disks (RAID) is an array of storage drives; you can measure the performance of these in addition to individual drives.

Fantastic! Another chapter complete. You are getting closer to the halfway point of this book. Take a break, clear the mechanism, and continue.

CHAPTER 26

Troubleshooting Video Issues

This chapter covers the following A+ 220-1101 exam objective:

▶ **5.4** – Given a scenario, troubleshoot video, projector, and display issues.

Video is a technology that you will troubleshoot often. Video issues could be hardware based or software based. There are many types of video connectors, standards, and different output devices, and so there is plenty of work for techs. Be sure to refer to Chapter 13, "Cables and Connectors," for more information on video connections.

> **ExamAlert**
>
> **Objective 5.4** concentrates on troubleshooting common symptoms of video issues, such as incorrect data source, physical cabling issues, burned-out bulb, fuzzy image, display burn-in, dead pixels, flashing screen, incorrect color display, audio issues, dim image, and intermittent projector shutdown.

PC Video Troubleshooting

Several parts, both hardware and software, make up a video system: GPUs, monitors, cables and connections, video drivers, video settings, and so on. So, there is plenty to troubleshoot when it comes to video. I like to look at it as a system within the computer system, and I tend to follow the path of video when troubleshooting; for example, from the software, to the operating system and driver, to the video card itself, through the cables and connectors, and out to the display (or displays, whatever they might be). And let's not forget power: Many video cards require a power connection, and the monitor does as well. Also remember the types of video connections: HDMI, DVI, DisplayPort, and so on. Keep all these things in the back of your mind as you are trouble-shooting video—and remember to write out your process. Document and write down (or type) as much as possible about what you see and what you try: include pictures and illustrations to help in the troubleshooting process.

When troubleshooting video issues, there are a number of things to check, including the following:

- ▶ **Connections:** If nothing is showing up on the display, first make sure the monitor is plugged into the video card properly (and to the correct video port) and then verify whether the monitor is connected to the AC outlet and is powered on. Poor connectivity of cables can also cause screen flicker. Inspect for damage along the length of cables and the plugs. Wear and tear can cause physical cable issues over time, which could lead to flicker, fuzziness, and other eye-straining issues.

- ▶ **Check the data source:** By "data source," I mean what type of video connection the monitor is using. For example, if a PC is connected to a monitor by way of DisplayPort, and the monitor's onscreen display (OSD) is set to HDMI, the monitor won't receive any signal; the moni-tor will simply display a black screen. Always check which video port the monitor is configured to use by accessing the OSD with the appropriate button on the monitor.

> **ExamAlert**
>
> When troubleshooting video issues, check the data source (HDMI, DisplayPort, DVI, USB-C, VGA) within the OSD of the monitor!

▶ **Power cycle the computer, display, and any power protection equipment:** Power cycling the equipment can fix all kinds of problems and is an easy solution to implement. Problems such as video memory (image retention) and stuck pixels might be easily repaired by a power cycle of the display, the computer, and any surge suppressor that the equipment is plugged into. You might also need to leave a display off for a couple of hours to fix a video memory problem, such as the video memory/image retention issue that is sometimes referred to as burn-in. But burn-in is actually a *symptom* of the problem that occurs in the older (but still used) cathode ray tube (CRT) type of monitor. While image retention and flickering image issues are more common with CRTs, you might still see them with flat-panel monitors as well. If you use a KVM (keyboard, video, mouse) switch, power cycle that as well. Many KVMs need to be turned on first (and left on for 10 seconds or so) before a connecting computer can be turned on; otherwise, that computer won't display through the KVM properly.

▶ **Check for an onboard video setting in the UEFI/BIOS:** If you install a new video card in a computer that previously used onboard video, check that the onboard video setting is disabled in the UEFI or BIOS. It can conflict with the new video card. And, of course, be sure to plug the monitor into the new video card—not the old onboard connection.

▶ **Resolution and refresh settings:** If the resolution was set too high or was set to a resolution not supported by the monitor, you might get a distorted image, a fuzzy image, or no image at all. In Windows, boot into low-resolution VGA mode or Safe Mode. This starts the computer with a resolution of 640×480. Then modify the resolution setting in the Screen Resolution window. Lower resolutions will result in oversized icons and images that might be preferable to some but will make it difficult for the typical user to view all the information required on one screen (for example, within a spreadsheet or A/V editing program). Simply increase the resolution to "resolve" the problem! For CRT monitors, an incorrect resolution setting could cause distorted geometry—where the image doesn't fit the display properly—although this might also be caused by poor horizontal or vertical settings on the monitor itself. The refresh rate can also cause issues if it is not set correctly (for example, screen flicker, flashing screen, or no display at all). The refresh rate is the number of times that the screen image is refreshed per second; a common number is 60 Hz. The number it is set to should coincide with the monitor's capability. You'll learn more about resolution and refresh rate in Chapter 35, "Windows Control Panel Utilities."

▶ **Check the driver:** Maybe the driver failed, or perhaps the wrong driver was installed. Maybe an update is necessary, or perhaps an update to the driver is causing the problem. If there is nothing on the display, or if the image is distorted, or if the monitor only displays a lower resolution, boot into low-res mode or Safe Mode and update the driver from within Device Manager (in Windows) or consider "rolling back" the driver, which means reverting to the older driver that was installed previously. Driver failures can also be the cause of blue screens of death (BSODs).

▶ **Check the version of DirectX:** DirectX is a Windows technology that includes video, animation, and sound components. It helps a computer get more performance out of multimedia, games, and movies. The DirectX Diagnostic Tool (DxDiag) helps troubleshoot DirectX-related issues. This tool provides information about the installed version of DirectX and whether it is operating correctly, among other things. The DirectX Diagnostic Tool can be started by opening the Run prompt and typing **dxdiag**. By default, Windows 10/11 uses DirectX 12. However, it can be updated to newer versions if necessary.

> **Note**
>
> I've mentioned Windows several times in this chapter. We'll be covering DirectX and other Windows utilities in depth in Chapters 33 through 36.

▶ **Check the temperature threshold of the video card:** High-end video cards are intensely used by gamers and designers, and such a card can be the hottest component in a computer. If the temperature surpasses the safeguards in place, it might cause the card to throttle back the GPU speed, or it might cause an overheat shutdown, where the video card might stop working altogether, causing the current application to close or, at worst, the display to go blank. If this happens more than once or twice, consider additional cooling fans or a liquid cooling system.

▶ **Use software to check and repair stuck or dead pixels:** When a single pixel fails, it can be irritating. But there are third-party software programs that can be used to identify stuck pixels and possible dead pixels and attempt to fix them. (Search "LCD repair," "dead pixel repair," or similar terms.) Try power-cycling the device as well. If you can't repair a stuck or dead pixel, you might have to send the display to the manufacturer or an authorized repair center for repair or for replacement. If it is a laptop, replace the screen yourself!

▶ **Calibrate the monitor:** If you see artifacts (image distortions) or notice incorrect color patterns being displayed, or if the display just doesn't seem to look quite as good as it used to, try calibrating the monitor either by resetting it with the OSD or by adjusting the contrast, brightness, and color levels. Also try adjusting the color depth in Windows and check the screen resolution. You can also try using the built-in Windows Display Color Calibration tool, which can be accessed by going to Search and typing **color calibration** or by going to Run and typing **dccw**. Try to limit reflections on the screen. If you are using an older CRT monitor and the artifacts still appear, consider upgrading to an LCD display. Dim images could also be caused by misconfigured brightness and contrast. Always configure the brightness first, and once the optimal brightness level has been found, configure the contrast.

▶ **Use a filter on the monitor:** Sometimes a user will complain of eye strain. This might not be a video issue at all; it could be due to glare. Consider using an antiglare filter. Companies make these filters specifically for individual monitor models. They help reduce glare from fluorescent lights, sunlight, and so on. In a more secure environment, consider also using privacy filters. These reduce the viewing angle of the screen—so that only the person sitting directly in front of the screen can read it—and help reduce the chance of shoulder surfing. Privacy filters often reduce glare as well.

▶ **Check for newly installed applications:** New applications could cause the display to malfunction or stop working altogether. Check the application manufacturer's website for any known hardware compatibility issues.

▶ **Check inside the computer:** Unless I have a sneaking suspicion that one of the connections inside the computer is loose, I usually leave this for last because it is time-consuming to open the system. If you decide to check inside the computer, check whether the video card is seated properly. In areas in which the temperature and humidity change quickly, the card could be unseated due to thermal expansion and contraction. (Some refer to this as chip creep or card creep.) Also, if the computer was moved recently, it could cause the card to come out of the slot slightly. Verify that the power connections and other cables are not loose. Check all other connections inside the PC to make sure it isn't a video problem. For example, if the system uses an onboard video controller and you start seeing garbled images, strange colors, or cursor trails, you might have defective RAM (or maybe you have been working on computers too long). Remember that onboard video controllers rely on the sticks of RAM in the motherboard, whereas individual video cards have their own RAM.

Again, verify that it is actually a video problem. Don't forget about the other major components of a computer system. When you can't see anything on the display and you know the computer is receiving power, you can narrow down the issue to video, RAM, processor, or the motherboard (what I sometimes refer to as the "big four"). But if the system appears to boot, and you can see storage drive activity from the LED light on the front of the case, and/or hear the drive accessing data, then it is most likely a video problem. Go back to the basics: Check power and connections. Check the data source at the OSD of the monitor. Try substituting a known good monitor in place of the current one. When it comes to video, as with most other things in life, the simple answers are usually the most common.

External Laptop Monitors and Projectors

We discussed laptops in the beginning of the book, but we should also include them here since we are talking about video troubleshooting. And you'll probably get your hands dirty with projectors as well. Let's briefly consider some usage and troubleshooting techniques for those now.

External Laptop Monitors

Most laptops have the capability of sending video signals to an external monitor. Some people refer to this technology as *screen switching* and/or extending the display.

Almost all laptops come with an external connection (for example, HDMI or DisplayPort) for a second monitor or for a projector. When such a monitor is plugged in, it can be enabled by pressing the display toggle key (otherwise known as the secondary monitor button). On some laptops, this can be done by pressing Fn+F4 simultaneously. However, on other brands of laptops, this key might be a different key than F4. The icon on the key often looks like an open laptop with a monitor to its right. Normally, you have several options: Display the desktop to the laptop, display the desktop to the external monitor, display a copy of the desktop to both screens, or "extend" the desktop across both monitors. These last two options are also known as using *dual displays*. In addition to using the display toggle key, you can configure your video for any of these scenarios in Windows, macOS, or Linux, which we'll discuss later in the book.

If an external monitor won't display anything, make sure that the cable is firmly connected to the external port, verify that the external monitor is plugged in and is turned on, and then try cycling through the various video options by pressing the button several times, waiting a few seconds each time. Make sure you are holding down the Fn key while doing so. Finally, restart the computer if necessary.

By the way, HDMI and DisplayPort connections and cables have the ability to transmit video *and* audio. However, DVI does not. Understand this if you need to transmit audio over the video cable to an external monitor. Verify that the external monitor is set to the correct video standard and that audio is enabled (if necessary, within the OSD). You might need an adapter to change from one video standard to another—for example, if a laptop has a DisplayPort connection but the external monitor only has HDMI. In this scenario, DisplayPort can support video and audio transfer with the use of a proper adapter.

Also, know how to set the audio output from a laptop or PC so that it will output through the HDMI or DisplayPort cable properly. For example, in Windows, you can go to **Settings > System > Sound** or simply right-click the speaker icon in the notification area and select **Open Sound Settings**. (Or, for the Control Panel option, go to Run and type **mmsys.cpl**.) From there, you can select the output device to use. Think about it: You don't want to display video on a 60-inch TV and have weak, tinny audio coming from a laptop somewhere else in the room, right? The attendees' focus should be on the display and the presenter. You might also need to adjust the volume for that connection with the volume mixer, which you can also get to by right-clicking the speaker icon. For a presentation to be great, you need audio!

ExamAlert

Know how to configure Windows to output sound to an external monitor via HDMI or DisplayPort!

Projectors

We haven't covered projectors yet, so let's talk about them briefly.

A video projector can be plugged into a computer's external video port to project the computer's video display to a projection screen. An extremely bright bulb is necessary to project this image to the screen. The light output is measured in *lumens*. A typical high-def projector might output 2000 to 3000 lumens. This is *really* bright, and you should never allow a person to look into the projector's lamp! Increased lumens are necessary for locations with higher amounts of ambient light (that is, existing light in the room).

Projectors are used for presentations and for teaching and are common in conference rooms and training centers. However, some schools and companies opt to use large, flat-screen TVs instead of projectors, even though projectors can usually project a larger image. Projectors are available in LCD, LED, and Digital Light Processing (DLP) versions. The LCD type works in a similar fashion to the monitor technology of the same name, whereas DLP uses light valves with rotating color wheels. Common high-definition display resolutions used by projectors include 1080p and 4K; the price of the projector increases with the resolution standard and with other characteristics, such as the brightness, contrast, and noise. You can use a video projector with a laptop by using the display toggle button, or you can use a projector with a computer that has a video card with dual outputs.

Troubleshooting can get a little tricky when you are using a projector as the second display. A projector might need time to warm up or might need to be configured via its own OSD. You might also need a video adapter if your laptop's ports and projector's ports don't match up. Identify the projector's ports and consult the projector's documentation for more details.

Bulbs fail, and you should be prepared to encounter burned-out bulbs in projectors now and again. A failed bulb is evident because no light comes from the projector at all. (The device might even flash a message on an OSD.) Be sure to replace a bulb with the exact type for the model of projector in question; it's also wise to go with manufacturer bulbs or manufacturer-suggested bulbs as they usually work better out of the box and last longer. Before replacing a bulb, make sure to power down the unit and unplug it. Many projectors are mounted to the ceiling; so have a step ladder ready. A projector's bulb is usually behind an access panel. Watch the orientation of the bulb and consider taking a picture of it so you know how to orient the new bulb. Make sure the bulb makes full contact inside the projector. Then, close the access panel securely, plug in the projector, and power it on. If all goes well, there should be light! Reset the lamp counter to zero hours. This counter can be found in one of the menus in the OSD of the projector.

You might also encounter intermittent projector shutdown. This could be due to several things, including environmental factors, poor installation (such as the projector not having any space to exhaust heat properly), or a faulty bulb. It usually means that the projector has overheated. Check for good airflow and check the bulb. As mentioned, bulb issues are less common if you use manufacturer-recommended bulbs. Also, ensure that the cooling fan is working and replace it if necessary.

Another intermittent issue is screen flicker or random display shutoff, which could be due to a faulty cable. (In fact, I see this often.) Use a quality cable, and make sure the plugs are intact and haven't been damaged. Also make sure that you are not exceeding the maximum length for any particular video standard. For example, as a rule of thumb, a practical limit for HDMI cables that are transferring 1080p signal is 25 feet (7.6 meters); higher resolutions allow shorter distances. HDMI cables are usually rated based on the number of feet they can transmit signal. A cable rated for longer distance is usually a thicker, stronger cable. Use the right one for the resolution being passed by the laptop or other device. If you are in a situation where you don't know where a cable came from, try to decipher the writing on the cable to find out what it is rated for or simply replace it with the proper cable if it doesn't appear to work properly.

ExamAlert

Use quality cables that are rated for the distance you need and the resolution at which you wish to transmit!

If extenders are being used, make sure they are of good quality; it's recommended to use an active extender (meaning one that plugs into an AC outlet) as opposed to a passive one.

One last thought: *When troubleshooting, write it down.* A quick sketch or diagram can work wonders for your thought process, especially when you have a chain of devices, cables, and equipment to troubleshoot. This technique can also be helpful when you take the A+ exams.

Cram Quiz

Answer these questions. The answers follow the last question. If you cannot answer these questions correctly, consider reading this chapter again until you can.

1. A user set the resolution in Windows too high, resulting in a scrambled, distorted display. What should you do to fix the problem? (Select the best answer.)

   ○ **A.** Upgrade the video driver.

   ○ **B.** Boot into low-resolution mode.

   ○ **C.** Press the monitor toggle key.

   ○ **D.** Check the video connections.

2. You are troubleshooting a video issue. Which utility should you use?

   ○ **A.** Regedit

   ○ **B.** Msconfig

   ○ **C.** DxDiag

   ○ **D.** Task Manager

3. You receive a very basic computer that has a broken onboard DVI connector. What should you attempt first?

   ○ **A.** Replace the motherboard.

   ○ **B.** Replace the DVI connector.

   ○ **C.** Install a video card.

   ○ **D.** Use an adapter.

4. You just replaced a video card in a PC with another card from a different manufacturer. However, the driver installation does not complete. What should you do first?

   ○ **A.** Install the driver again.

   ○ **B.** Locate the latest version of the driver.

   ○ **C.** Roll back the driver.

   ○ **D.** Install the original video card.

5. You are helping a project manager with a presentation using a laptop that feeds video to a projector. During your tests, the projector's image begins to flicker. The laptop's display does not have any problems. You attempt to change the resolution on the laptop, but the issue continues. Which of the following should you do next?

   ○ **A.** Change the projector settings.

   ○ **B.** Check the connectivity of the video cable.

   ○ **C.** Change the aspect ratio of the laptop.

   ○ **D.** Check the connectivity of the power cable.

6. A user needs to transmit video and audio to an external monitor. Which of the following technologies allows this? (Select two.)

  ○ **A.** OSD

  ○ **B.** HDMI

  ○ **C.** DisplayPort

  ○ **D.** DVI

  ○ **E.** VGA

Cram Quiz Answers

1. **B.** Boot into a low-resolution mode. In Windows, this is called Enable Low-Resolution Video. Safe Mode is another valid option, but keep in mind that Safe Mode loads Windows with a minimal set of drivers, and you can't access the Internet. Depending on the display configuration, pressing the monitor toggle key might actually fix the problem temporarily by displaying the screen on a secondary monitor, but it doesn't solve the root cause of the problem.

2. **C.** You should use DxDiag to troubleshoot video issues. The other three answers are not used to troubleshoot video. Regedit is used to perform advanced configurations in the registry. Msconfig is used to change how the system boots and to enable/disable services. The Task Manager is used to see the performance of the computer and view applications and processes that are running. We'll discuss the rest of those tools in more depth in the Windows portion of this book.

3. **C.** Try installing a video card first to see if the system will still work. Unless it is a specialized system, the video card should be less expensive than the motherboard. (In addition, it will take a lot less time to install.) PC techs usually do not replace connectors, and this step should be further down your troubleshooting list. An adapter cannot help if the DVI port is broken.

4. **C.** If the driver installation doesn't complete, you should roll back the driver. It could be that you have attempted to install the incorrect driver. After you roll back the faulty installation, find the correct latest version of the video driver from the manufacturer's website. Installing the driver again will most likely have the same result. Only reinstall the original video card temporarily if you cannot find a proper solution right away.

5. **B.** Check the connectivity of the video cable. If it is flickering, chances are that the cable is loose, or the cable's quality is lacking. Screen flicker is more common with older VGA cables, but it can happen with just about any connection, depending on the age and quality of the cable. Remember, always check the basic stuff first: connectivity, power, and so on. It is unlikely that the projector settings will make a difference in this particular case. You cannot change the aspect ratio by itself on most laptops; however, when you change the resolution (which was already done, according to the question), you might be changing the aspect ratio as well, depending on the resolution selected. A loose or damaged power cable would probably result in more than just screen flicker; the projector might power off and power back on, which would prevent the image from being displayed for at least several seconds while the projector powers back up.

6. **B and C.** HDMI and DisplayPort connections and cables have the ability to transmit video *and* audio. However, DVI and VGA do not. An onscreen display (OSD) is a computer monitor control panel that allows you to adjust horizontal/vertical positioning, contrast, brightness, and other monitor settings. On a side note, keep in mind that USB-C can also transfer video, audio, *and* data.

I hope this chapter has been enlightening and that I have projected some of my experience on to your brain. Dad jokes aside, great work so far! Review your notes, take a short break, and continue!

CHAPTER 27

Troubleshooting Mobile Devices

This chapter covers the following A+ 220-1101 exam objective:

▶ **5.5** – Given a scenario, troubleshoot common issues with mobile devices.

It's time to think portable and mobile. Fixing mobile devices can be a life-long career. Just look at the abundance of mobile device repair shops: There seems to be no end to cracked screens, missing displays, overheated devices, and battery issues to sustain all these shops. And most mobile devices can be difficult to open and work on because of their small size.

There is some overlap between this objective and 220-1102 Objective 3.4. Some of the content (mostly hardware based) I cover here, while the rest (mostly software based) I cover in Chapter 55, "Troubleshooting Mobile Operating Systems and Application Issues."

ExamAlert

Objective 5.5 focuses on troubleshooting common symptoms of mobile device issues, such as poor battery health, swollen batteries, broken screens, improper charging, poor/no connectivity, liquid damage, overheating, digitizer issues, physically damaged ports, malware, and cursor drift/touch calibration.

Mobile Device Display Troubleshooting

The display is the cause of many user headaches. Lots of things can go wrong with it. Sometimes devices fail, but more often than not, such issues are due to user error or, more accurately, user ignorance.

For example, the display might look dim. This could be because the brightness level is too low in the display settings. Or it could be that automatic brightness was enabled, and perhaps it doesn't react well in highly lit areas. Or perhaps auto-brightness isn't calibrated properly; perhaps it was initially enabled in a very bright (or very dark) environment. To recalibrate the device's light sensor, turn off auto-brightness and then go to an unlit room and set the brightness to the lowest setting. Finally, turn auto-brightness back on and leave the unlit room. The device should now make better use of its light sensors, and auto-brightness should function better.

You might also encounter a situation in which there is no display whatsoever or in which there appears to be no display. It could simply be that the device is in sleep mode or turned off. Always check the simple solutions first; they work more often than you might expect! Another issue could be that the brightness (once again) is at the lowest setting and the user is working in a bright area. When taking a device out of sleep mode, the user might not be able to tell that the display is working because it might be barely visible. Take the device to a dark area to fix it or hold it under a desk or table so you can see the screen until it is fixed. The brightness might have been turned down by accident, the user might have turned it down the night before (because it was dark out), or a virus could be affecting the slider that controls the brightness.

Brightness is definitely a common culprit. Let's just thank our lucky stars that there is no contrast setting on the majority of mobile devices! However, no display or a nonresponsive display could also mean that the device is turned off or that the battery has been discharged. It could also be that the display needs to be calibrated. Finally, the display connection might be loose, or the display might be damaged. In these last two scenarios, the device will have to be opened to repair/replace the display. If your organization uses an authorized repair center to perform these duties, and the device is under warranty, document what the problem is and pack it securely to be shipped out right away. For disassembly tips, see the last section of this chapter, "Disassembling Processes."

Mobile Device Overheating

How many times have you heard a user say that a mobile device is running hot? How many times has your own device run hot? It's common. Overheating can be caused by a number of things: poorly written applications, excessive use of applications, excessive browsing, old batteries, damaged batteries, and, of course, the simple fact that the device is very small, and there is an inherent lack of ventilation.

Some applications use a lot of power (CPU-wise and battery-wise). These applications tend to slow down a mobile device, eat up battery reserves, cause power drain, and make a device run hot. Certain GPS programs, games, and streaming media apps are among the top offenders, but just about any app could cause such issues. And then you have the aging effect; newer apps don't run very well on older devices because of the lack of resources, and they can overheat the device. Unfortunately, there isn't too much the user can do about this other than remove apps suspected to be the cause of the problem and disabling unnecessary functionality on the device. Does the user need that live wallpaper? Has that user collected enough "coins" in that game? You know what I mean. Let's not forget about mobile OS updates; they can make a device feel like it was in an oven. This is normal, and the device should be plugged in and placed in a cool area, away from sunlight, while an update proceeds.

A device's battery can get hot simply because it is old (or damaged). Battery manufacturers use the term "charging cycle" to refer to the process of charging a mobile device that is completely discharged up to 100%. Most battery manufacturers say that a typical battery can handle a maximum of several hundred charge cycles. This essentially means that a typical smartphone battery has a shelf life of about three to five years because most people charge their phone every day. Tablets usually last much longer because of the greater battery capacity and the fact that they aren't charged as often. So, it's mobile phones that we are most concerned with. A user can do the following to increase the life span of their battery:

▶ **Avoid draining the battery:** Charge the device often, before it gets too low. The more the battery is discharged below 50%, and especially below 10%, the less shelf life it will have in general.

▶ **Conserve power:** Set sleep mode to 1 minute or less. Decrease brightness. Disable or remove unnecessary functions and apps. Restart the phone at least once a day to stop any running apps. (This is a big power saver.) Consider putting the device into airplane mode at night.

▶ **Keep the device away from heat sources:** For example, if the device is mounted near a vehicle's air vent during the dead of winter, it's bound to run hot. Sarcasm aside, this can actually cause battery wear and damage over time. Keep it out of direct sunlight, too, if at all possible.

▶ **Turn off the mobile device when not in use:** Some people simply cannot do this, but I thought I'd mention it anyway!

▶ **Don't bang or throw the device:** It might seem crazy that I would have to say this, but it's good advice. Dropping, throwing, or banging a device can break the device completely, damage the battery and cause it to overheat, reduce the life span of the battery, or cause a battery leak, which is a toxic mess that you don't want to be a part of.

▶ **Select protective cases carefully:** Using a protective case is a very good idea (especially for a user who is prone to actions in the previous bullet) but make sure it has good airflow. Sometimes these cases can envelop the battery, causing it to overheat.

ExamAlert

Know how to increase the life span of a mobile device's battery.

More Mobile Device Troubleshooting

When it comes to mobile devices, batteries—and power in general—tend to account for a lot of troubleshooting.

For many users, mobile devices need to be charged daily. As you have probably experienced, charging issues are common. A mobile device not charging or charging improperly could be due to many things, but the cable is the first thing to check and is usually the culprit. Inspect the charging cable for rips, bends, or cuts. Check the cable—especially the connector ends—for any discoloration or burn marks. If any of these things are identified, it's time for a new charging cable. Check the device's charging port for dust and debris. Clear it out with compressed air and clean it as well (following the cleaning recommendations below). Unfortunately, if the port(s) is damaged, the entire device may need to be replaced.

No power or failure to charge could be a sign that the battery needs to be replaced—either because it is simply too old and won't hold a charge anymore or because it is damaged. Battery damage can manifest internally (which can't be seen with the naked eye), or it could show up as a visibly swollen battery. As mentioned previously in the book, watch out for swollen batteries; they could be caused by damaging, overcharging, overvoltage, or a manufacturing problem. A damaged battery should be removed (if possible); use great care if you are the one handling the battery and make sure it is stored in a cool, dark place until it can be recycled. If it can't be removed, the device should be taken to an authorized repair center.

Be sure to clean your device. Every month or so, turn off the device, take it out of the case, and clean it (as well as the inside of the case) with a mix of half isopropyl alcohol and half water (applied to a dry, lint-free cloth). Take extra care when cleaning the charging port: Use a cotton swab and/or toothpick. This really works in situations when the device is not charging properly. Use that solution sparingly, though; a little goes a long way.

A battery issue could also cause a system to "freeze," or lock up, rendering it useless; however, a frozen system could also be caused by faulty applications or a problem with the mobile OS or a driver. If a system freezes up, it might require you to force stop an application, perform a battery pull (if possible), or, more likely, a soft reset (again, if possible). You might need to initiate a hard reset, which you normally want to avoid if you can because it will wipe the system. We'll discuss force stops and resets in Chapter 55.

If a mobile device is the victim of liquid damage, remove the device from the liquid immediately. Turn off the device and leave it off until cleanup is complete. Remove any protective case and remove any microSD cards, SIM cards, and batteries (if possible). Use a clean cloth to dry the device as much as you can. If the liquid in question was not water, you can later attempt to clean the screen and charging port with the isopropyl alcohol solution mentioned previously. After the device is completely dry, return any microSD cards, the case, and so on, and see if it will boot. Because many devices are IP68 (or IP65) compliant, the device may still work because it has a certain level of protection against water and dust.

Sometimes the touchscreen (or digitizer) of a mobile device may become nonresponsive. There are several potential reasons for this:

▶ An application or the OS has failed.

▶ The system froze up.

▶ The display connection is loose.

▶ The display needs to be replaced.

▶ User error has occurred.

This last one should always be on your mind. A person might be wearing gloves that prohibit proper touchscreen response. Or perhaps the person is using the wrong type of stylus or the touchscreen doesn't accept stylus input. Perhaps the touchscreen needs to be calibrated; this is not very common with today's devices, but it is possible. Be ready for a variety of issues!

No sound from the speaker? Start with the easy stuff, such as checking whether the volume is muted or turned down. It is not always easy for some users to figure out sound issues because of the built-in mixer in most of today's smartphones: There are separate volumes for voice calls, media, notifications, and so on. So even though one volume might be up, another might be down. Or perhaps the speaker has been blocked by a protective case that doesn't quite fit right. Or maybe an app simply isn't registering sound correctly or has its own volume or mute option. It's unlikely, but another possibility is that the speaker connection is loose, or the speaker has failed. For such issues, a tech needs to open the device or send it out for repair.

Keep an open mind. When you are dealing with technology that can potentially fail often, combined with users who might not have been trained to use devices properly, you can expect to do *lots* of troubleshooting.

Disassembling Processes

You should try to disassemble mobile devices in a logical manner, so that when it comes time to put them back together, you will not be confused and can reduce the chance of making mistakes. The first and best way to do this is to document what you do. Just as with bigger computers such as PCs, you should write down as much as you can. Take notes and make little illustrations—even if your artwork is a bunch of chicken scratch like mine! Organize any parts that have been removed. Document and label wires and cables and where they are supposed to connect. Record what type of screws go where and store the screws temporarily in an organized manner. Some people put them all in a bowl or can. My preference is to use a large weekly pill box (which many healthcare organizations give away for free). In your documentation, mark which screws are where; for example, Monday has the #6-32 thumbscrews, and Tuesday has the T4 Torx screws, and so on. Chances are that you won't see both thumbscrews and Torx screws on the same device as they are for different devices (PCs and phones and similar devices, respectively). Take photos with your smartphone or another digital camera during the disassembly process. These are just some examples! Remember that good documentation aids in efficient planning, proper testing, and insightful troubleshooting.

Make use of manufacturer resources, such as tech support via phone, email, or website; help forums; downloadable manuals in PDF format; and information on removable media.

> **ExamAlert**
>
> Use manufacturer-supplied resources such as manuals, tech support, and forums to help troubleshoot issues.

Use appropriate hand tools when working with mobile devices. Of course, first make sure you are protecting against ESD—which means using proper anti-static equipment. Also, have your tools at the ready: miniature screwdrivers, shims, spudgers, magnifying glass, mini-flashlight, multimeter and other testing gear, SD and microSD card reader, and various USB, Lightning, and other cables and adapters for hooking up the mobile device to a testing PC or laptop. Take a look at Figure 27.1 for an example of some of the hand tools I use on mobile devices. The list goes on, and there are several manufacturers of mobile device toolkits that can help you on your way toward mobile device repair. Make sure that you are not using magnetically charged tools, and again, implement ESD prevention procedures before you start working.

FIGURE 27.1 **Mobile device hand tools**

Cram Quiz

Answer these questions. The answers follow the last question. If you cannot answer these questions correctly, consider reading this chapter again until you can.

1. A user's mobile device is overheating. Which of the following could be the problem? (Select the two best answers.)
   - ○ **A.** A damaged battery.
   - ○ **B.** The brightness setting is too low.
   - ○ **C.** Excessive gaming.
   - ○ **D.** The device is not in a case.
   - ○ **E.** The charging cable is defective.

2. You are troubleshooting a user's smartphone. The user informs you that he can't see anything on the screen. Of the following, what should you do first?
   - ○ **A.** Disassemble the device for proper reassembly.
   - ○ **B.** Check the volume mixer sliders.
   - ○ **C.** Verify the brightness setting.
   - ○ **D.** Calibrate the screen.
   - ○ **E.** Restart the phone.

3. When disassembling a mobile device, what should you *not* do?
   - ○ **A.** Document everything you see.
   - ○ **B.** Store screws in a logical manner.
   - ○ **C.** Make use of manuals.
   - ○ **D.** Implement antistatic procedures.
   - ○ **E.** Use magnetic-tip screwdrivers.
   - ○ **F.** Label cables.

4. Which of the following are common reasons that a mobile device might not charge properly? (Select three.)
   - ○ **A.** Airplane mode is activated.
   - ○ **B.** A cable is ripped or bent.
   - ○ **C.** A port is dirty.
   - ○ **D.** A port is damaged.
   - ○ **E.** The user installed *Asteroid Blaster*.

5. What can cause a digitizer to become nonresponsive? (Select three.)

   ○ **A.** Application failure

   ○ **B.** Defective charging cable

   ○ **C.** Loose display connection

   ○ **D.** User error

   ○ **E.** Disabled audio

Cram Quiz Answers

1. **A and C.** The best answers listed are a damaged battery and excessive gaming. If the brightness setting is low, the device should use less power and run cooler. If the device is not in a case, it should not overheat; however, a poorly manufactured case could cause the device to overheat. A defective charging cable usually does not cause a device to overheat; if it is defective, it is likely not even charging the device.

2. **C.** Check the brightness slider first! Chances are that the brightness is turned all the way down, and in a bright environment, it might appear that nothing is on the screen. Or the device might simply need to be woken up, so use the side button or the home button or double-tap the screen to wake up the device. If these measures are not successful, restart the device. Screen calibration has nothing to do with brightness, but on some rare mobile devices, it might be necessary. The volume sliders are not part of the problem. Don't open the device until you have exhausted every other known option—and do so only if you are qualified to work on this type of device; otherwise, send it to an authorized repair center.

3. **E.** Stay away from magnetically charged tools such as screwdrivers and bits. These can potentially damage circuitry and components. All of the other answers are valid procedures—things you *should* do when working on mobile devices, and computers in general.

4. **B, C, and D.** A mobile device not charging or charging improperly could be due to many things, but the cable is the first thing to check and is usually the culprit. Inspect the charging cable for rips, bends, or cuts or damage to the connector. Check the device's charging port for dust and debris and use compressed air to clear it out. Unfortunately, if the port(s) is damaged, the entire device probably needs to be replaced. Placing the device in airplane mode actually conserves battery power and won't normally have an impact on the device's ability to charge properly. Installing apps on a mobile device will usually not have an effect on the device's ability to charge properly (unless a virus was unknowingly downloaded with the app). However, many apps (especially games) can drain the battery quickly.

5. **A, C, and D.** There are several potential reasons a digitizer might be nonresponsive, including failure of an application or the OS, a frozen system, a loose display connection, a failed display, and user error. For example, something might be interfering with the touchscreen; perhaps the user is wearing gloves that prohibit proper touchscreen response. A bad charging cable and disabled audio are not likely to cause a digitizer to become nonresponsive.

Chapter done. You're getting very close to the end of the 220-1101 material. Great job!

CHAPTER 28

Troubleshooting Printers

This chapter covers the following A+ 220-1101 exam objective:

▶ **5.6** – Given a scenario, troubleshoot and resolve printer issues.

This chapter delves into a variety of common printer issues that you will face. They can happen in large organizations and small offices alike. A printer is a mechanical device, but it is controlled by embedded firmware and by computers that manage it. Be ready to get your hands dirty (perhaps literally) as you fix printer problems, and be ready to work in the operating system as well.

ExamAlert

Objective 5.6 focuses on troubleshooting common symptoms in printers, such as unwanted lines, garbled print, paper jams, faded print, paper failing to feed, and more.

Troubleshooting Printers

If a printer will not print or prints incorrectly, it has to be fixed. Sometimes companies hire paid consultants to manage all their printers and copiers, and sometimes the care of these devices is the job of the in-house IT technician. Even if your company pays consultants, it is a good idea to know some of the basic issues that can occur with printers and how to troubleshoot them. Table 28.1 describes some of these issues and possible solutions. Some of these problems (for example, paper jams and resulting error codes) might be displayed on a printer's operator control panel (OCP).

TABLE 28.1 **Printer Problems and Solutions**

Printer Issue	Possible Solutions
Paper jams or creased paper	1. Turn the printer on and off in the hope that the printer will clear the jam. This is known as power-cycling the printer. If this doesn't work, turn the printer off and unplug it and then open it.
	2. Remove paper trays and inspect them for crumpled papers that can be removed by firmly grabbing both ends of the paper and pulling or rotating the rollers to remove it. In general, clear the paper path.
	3. Verify that the right paper type is in the printer. Paper that is too thin or thick might cause a paper jam. Also, watch for paper that has been exposed to humidity.
	4. Check for dirty or cracked feed rollers. A temporary fix for dirty rubber rollers is to clean them using isopropyl alcohol. A permanent fix is to replace the rollers.
	5. Check whether the fusing assembly has overheated. Sometimes a printer just needs time to cool or perhaps it is not in a sufficiently ventilated area. In uncommon cases, the fuser might have to be replaced. Be sure to unplug the printer and let the printer sit for an hour or so before doing so, due to the high temperatures of the fuser. The fusing assembly can usually be removed by removing a few screws.
	6. Check the entire paper path. Duplexing printers (those that print on both sides of the paper) have more complicated and longer paper paths, providing more chances for paper to get jammed.

Printer Issue	Possible Solutions
Blank pages printing	▶ Determine whether the toner cartridge is empty or has failed, and if so, install a new one. Toner cartridge failures may be associated with the developing and transferring stages of the laser printing process, with the developing stage being more common. ▶ Determine whether the toner cartridge was installed without the sealing tape still in place. If it was, remove the tape. ▶ Check whether the transfer corona wire has failed. If the transfer corona wire fails, there will be no positive (opposite) voltage to pull the toner to the paper. Replace the wire.
Paper not feeding	Check the type and condition of the paper. Check the rollers (and raise the humidity if possible). Clean the rollers. Reset the printer. Consider using a maintenance kit.
Multiple pages fed in at once (that is, multipage misfeed)	Check whether the separation pad is getting enough traction; it might need to be cleaned. Also check whether the paper is too thin; 20 lb. or heavier paper is usually recommended.
Error codes	If a specific error is shown on the printer's OCP, read it. It might tell you exactly what the error is and how to fix it (or at least what the error is). On some printers, it displays error numbers. Check your printer's documentation to find out what an error code means.
Out-of-memory or low-memory error message	Check whether the user's computer is spooling documents. The setting with the least chance of this error is the Start Printing Immediately spool setting. You might also need to restart the Print Spooling service. A user who tries to print a large image might need to change settings in the application in which the image was made. In some cases, the printer's RAM might need to be upgraded. Whenever installing RAM to a printer, take all the same precautions you would when working on a PC.
No image on printer display (OCP)	Check whether the printer is in sleep mode (or off altogether). Verify that the printer is plugged in. In rare cases, the internal connector that powers the display might be loose.
Vertical lines on page, streaks, smearing, speckling, toner failing to fuse to paper	Black lines or streaks (and sometimes faded print) can be caused by a scratch in the laser printer drum or a dirty primary corona wire. Usually, the toner cartridge needs to be replaced. White lines could be caused by a dirty transfer corona wire; this can be cleaned or replaced. Wide white vertical lines can occur when something is stuck to the drum. Smearing can occur if the fusing assembly has failed; in this case, you might also notice toner coming off of the paper easily. If it is an inkjet, one or more ink cartridges might need to be replaced or the printer might need to be calibrated. If toner is not fusing to the paper correctly, the fuser rollers might not be heating properly, likely due to mechanical fuser failure.

Printer Issue	Possible Solutions
Faded prints	Replace ink or toner. Clean ink cartridge head. Also, check the fuser and increase the humidity, if necessary.
Garbage printout or garbled characters on paper	This can occur due to an incorrect driver. Some technicians like to try "close" drivers. This is not a good idea. Use the exact driver for the exact model of the printer that corresponds to the appropriate version of the operating system. A bad formatter board or printer interface can also cause garbage printouts. These can usually be replaced easily by removing two screws and a cover.
Ghosted image	Ghosted images or blurry marks can be a sign that the drum has some kind of imperfection or is dirty, especially if the image reappears at equal intervals. Replace the drum (or toner cartridge). Another possibility is that the fuser assembly has been damaged and needs to be replaced.
Double/echo images	The toner cartridge/print heads might be misaligned, or the drum or fuser unit may be faulty. The printer driver and even printer firmware might need to be reinstalled or updated. Administer printer maintenance according to the manufacturer's documentation.
Grinding noise	Grinding or similar noises emitting from a printer could relate to a defective toner cartridge. (Always have backup cartridges near the printer!) The noise could also be due to a paper jam or carriage stall.
No connectivity	Check the following: ▶ The printer is plugged in to an AC outlet and is online. ▶ The printer is securely connected to the local computer or to the network. ▶ The computer has the correct print driver installed. ▶ The printer is shared to the network. ▶ The printer has a properly configured IP address. (This can be checked on the OCP of most networkable laser printers.) ▶ Remote computers have a proper connection over the network to the printer. ▶ The printer is set up as the default printer, if necessary.
Access denied	If an Access Denied message appears on the screen while attempting to print, the user doesn't have permission to use the printer. You (or the network administrator) will have to give the user account permissions for that particular printer. This message might also be displayed when a person attempts to install a printer without the proper administrative rights.

Printer Issue	Possible Solutions
Multiple prints pending in the print queue	If the printer window shows several documents listed in the queue, but the printer is not currently printing anything, a document might have stalled and may need to be restarted. Also, the print spooler might need to be restarted in the Services console window, in the Task Manager, or in the Command Prompt. In less common cases, you might need to reinstall the printer driver.
Color printouts are a different (wrong) color than shown on the screen or incorrect chroma display	A printout will always be *slightly* different from the screen. But if the difference is very noticeable, check the ink or toner cartridges and make sure none of the colors are empty. Run the calibration tool for the printer. Verify that the printer is a PostScript-capable printer that can do raster image processing (RIP). If this functionality is not built into the printer, look for it as a separate software solution.
Finishing issues such as staple jams or hole punches	Some printers can perform finishing tasks on print jobs, such as stapling and hole punching. Sometimes a printer might not staple all pages or might hole punch everything at once. Ensure the following: ▶ Paper guides are in the proper place and paper is being stacked properly by the printer. ▶ The printer has a supply of *quality* staples. ▶ The correct printer driver is installed. ▶ The stapler/punching settings in the OS or printing application or on the printer's OCP are correct. ▶ The tray settings are correct. ▶ The punch hole tray is not full.
Incorrect paper size or page orientation	Make sure the correct paper is in the printer. Then check the Windows settings for paper size (or envelope size) and orientation. We discuss these topics further in Chapter 19, "Multifunction Devices/Printers."
Multiple failed jobs in logs	Reset the printer, analyze the controlling operating system or print server, clear the print queue, and reconfigure the spooler.
Unable to install printer	Check whether the printer is properly connected to the computer or network physically. Check whether it is getting an IP address. In Windows, start the Print Spooler service and update the driver. (Advanced: Define new printer keys in the registry.) More on the spooler and how to start it appears later in this chapter.

ExamAlert

Study the printer troubleshooting methods in Table 28.1.

In general, when working with printers, keep them clean and use printer maintenance kits and always refer to manufacturers' instructions. As a car needs its oil changed periodically, printers also need maintenance. HP and other manufacturers offer maintenance kits that include items such as fusers, rollers, separation pads, and instructions on how to replace all these items. Manufacturers recommend that maintenance be done every once in a while (for example, every 200,000 pages printed). When you finish installing a maintenance kit, be sure to reset the maintenance count. You should also have a toner vacuum available for toner spills. A can of compressed air can be helpful when you need to clean out toner from the inside a laser printer; remember to do this job outdoors.

Vacuum any leftover residue. Printer maintenance can be broken down into the following basic categories:

▶ **Laser:** Replace toner, apply maintenance kit, calibrate, clean.

▶ **Inkjet:** Clean heads, replace cartridges, calibrate, clear jams.

▶ **Thermal:** Replace paper, clean heating element, remove debris.

▶ **Impact:** Replace ribbon, replace print head, replace paper.

▶ **3D printer:** Clean the filament nozzle, resin reservoir, and anywhere there is a supply or distribution of plastic/resin. Also check the platform (print bed), check whether fans are working, and check the axis and gear movement.

When troubleshooting printers, don't forget to RTM (read the manual)! Most printers come with manuals, and these manuals often include troubleshooting sections. In some cases, the manual is in PDF format on the Internet, or on the disc that accompanied the printer. In addition, manufacturers usually have manuals on their websites as well as support systems for customers. Use them!

Remember to check the printer's display, which is referred to as the operator control panel (OCP). Back in the day, messages were sometimes obscure—for instance, the famous "PC LOAD LETTER" error—but today they are much more human readable. Get to know your way around the OCP and use the displayed information in conjunction with the printer manual to troubleshoot issues.

Keep in mind that many products come with warranties, and customers sometimes purchase extended warranties. I once had to do some troubleshooting on two color-laser printers that were only two weeks old when they failed. When I described to the manufacturer the error code that was flashing on the printers' displays, the representative didn't need to hear anything else and simply sent out a tech the next day because the devices were under warranty. Let the manufacturer help you. It can save you a lot of time and aggravation, and it might not cost you or your company anything.

Print Jobs and the Print Spooler

It's a good idea to know how to work with printers in Windows. You should know how to manage printers and print jobs, and you should be able to configure the print spooler. Let's talk about those two concepts now.

Managing Printers and Print Jobs

To manage a printer or an individual print job in Windows, just double-click the printer to which the job was sent. This might open a proprietary screen designed by the printer manufacturer or a Microsoft window similar to the one in Figure 28.1.

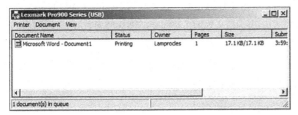

FIGURE 28.1   **A typical printer window showing one print job**

Figure 28.1 shows one print job, called Document1, listed. The job went to the printer properly; you can tell because it says Printing in the Status column. Any other message would mean that the job was either spooled, queued, stopped, or failed altogether. You can pause, restart, or stop a job completely if it is not printing properly. This can be done by right-clicking on the job in the window or by clicking the Document menu. Keep in mind that larger documents might take longer to spool before they start printing. (We'll discuss that topic in a little bit.) In addition, all documents can be paused or cancelled, or the entire printer can be taken offline from the Printer menu. Use these tools to help troubleshoot printing issues.

The Windows Print Spooler

Spooling is page-by-page processing that is done at the local system before a print job goes to the printer.

Whenever a job goes to print, there are three options:

▶ **Print directly to the printer:** This means the print job goes right to the printer, without any delays. How well this works depends solely on the amount of memory in the printer (which can be increased, just as with computers). Of course, if the print job is larger than the amount of RAM in the printer, the job will probably fail. Usually, a better solution is to spool the document.

▶ **Start printing immediately:** This is the first of two spooling options. When this setting is selected, the document will be *spooled* to the storage drive one page at a time. When an entire page has been spooled, it is sent to the printer for printing. This repeats until all the pages of the document have been spooled and, ultimately, printed. This is the default setting in Windows and is usually the best option because it prints faster than other spooling options. Figure 28.2 shows an example of this.

▶ **Start printing after last page is spooled:** This means the entire document will be spooled to the storage drive and then pages will be sent to the printer for printing. This is usually slower than the Start printing immediately option but might have fewer issues, such as stalls or other printing failures.

FIGURE 28.2 **Printer spooling options in Windows**

The print spooler is controlled by the Print Spooler service, which processes print requests and sends them to the printer. Not only can you experience issues in which print jobs or printers stop working, the Print Spooler service can fail. This service can be started, stopped, and restarted from the GUI and from the Command Prompt:

▶ **Adjusting the Print Spooler service in the Services window:** Open the Run prompt and type **services.msc** to open the Services console window. Scroll until you find the Print Spooler service. To start a stopped service, right-click it and click **Start**. Alternatively, you can click the Start button or other buttons on the toolbar. Also, you can double-click the Print Spooler service to see its properties, where you can start and stop the service and make additional configurations (see Figure 28.3).

FIGURE 28.3 **The Print Spooler service Properties window**

▶ **Adjusting the Print Spooler service in Task Manager:** Open the Task Manager from the taskbar or Power User menu by pressing Ctrl+Shift+Esc or by going to Run and typing **taskmgr.exe**. Under the Services tab, right-click the **Spooler** service and select **Start, Stop, or Restart service**.

▶ **Adjusting the Print Spooler service in the PowerShell/Command Prompt:** When you open PowerShell or the Command Prompt (as an administrator), you can start the Print Spooler service by typing **net start spooler**. Typing **net stop spooler** stops the service. (This is a good one. I've actually heard of several companies asking how to do this during an interview!)

ExamAlert

Know how to configure spooling and how to start and stop the Print Spooler service within the services console window, the Task Manager, and especially in PowerShell.

Cram Quiz

Answer these questions. The answers follow the last question. If you cannot answer these questions correctly, consider reading this chapter again until you can.

1. How can a paper jam be resolved? (Select all that apply.)

    ○ **A.** Clear the paper path.

    ○ **B.** Use the right type of paper.

    ○ **C.** Check for, and replace, damaged rollers.

    ○ **D.** Check the OCP.

2. A user informs you that color printouts are noticeably different from what appears on their screen (incorrect chroma display). What actions should you take? (Select two.)

    ○ **A.** Ensure that ink/toner cartridges aren't empty.

    ○ **B.** Make sure the separation pad is getting enough traction.

    ○ **C.** Ensure that the paper is not too thin.

    ○ **D.** Run the printer calibration tool.

3. A technician is troubleshooting finishing issues with the company laser printer. Which of the following actions should the tech perform? (Select all that apply.)

    ○ **A.** Clean the filament nozzle and platform (print bed).

    ○ **B.** Make sure the staple cartridge is full and free of jams.

    ○ **C.** Ensure that the hole punch tray is not full.

    ○ **D.** Change out the toner cartridge.

    ○ **E.** Ensure that the proper paper tray is specified in the printer settings.

    ○ **F.** Verify proper paper orientation.

4. Which of the following are usually included in a laser printer maintenance kit? (Select the two best answers.)

    ○ **A.** Rollers

    ○ **B.** Image drum

    ○ **C.** Toner

    ○ **D.** Duplexer

    ○ **E.** Fuser

5. One of your customers is connected to a standalone printer. The customer gets an "out of memory" error when printing large graphic files. What should you do?

○ **A.** Upgrade the storage drive on the computer.

○ **B.** Upgrade the RAM on the printer.

○ **C.** Upgrade the RAM on the computer.

○ **D.** Reinstall the printer drivers.

6. What should you do first when removing a paper jam?

○ **A.** Take the printer offline.

○ **B.** Clear the print queue.

○ **C.** Open all the doors of the printer.

○ **D.** Turn off the printer.

7. You have been called to a customer site to perform maintenance on an impact printer. Which should you consider?

○ **A.** Replacing paper, cleaning heating element, and removing debris

○ **B.** Replacing toner, applying maintenance kit, calibrating, and cleaning

○ **C.** Replacing ribbon, replacing print head, and replacing paper

○ **D.** Cleaning heads, replacing cartridges, calibrating, and clearing jams

8. Which is the faster option for spooling documents?

○ **A.** Print directly to the printer

○ **B.** Start printing immediately

○ **C.** Start printing after last page is spooled

○ **D.** Start printing after the separator page

9. How can you immediately stop the Print Spooler service? (Select the three best answers.)

○ **A.** Start printing immediately.

○ **B.** Type **sc config spooler start= disabled** in the Command Prompt.

○ **C.** Print directly to the printer.

○ **D.** Type **net stop spooler** in the Command Prompt.

○ **E.** Open the Services console window, right-click **Print Spooler** and select **Stop**.

○ **F.** Open the Task Manager, click the **Services** tab, right-click **Spooler** and select **Stop**.

Cram Quiz Answers

1. **A, B, and C.** There are several possible reasons a paper jam might occur. The paper could be stuck somewhere in the paper path, the paper could be too thick, or the rollers could be damaged. However, just checking the operator control panel (OCP) will not resolve anything. It will hopefully clue you in to why the paper jam has happened, though.

2. **A and D.** The printout will always be slightly different from what is shown on the screen, but if the difference is very noticeable, check the ink or toner cartridges and make sure none of the colors are empty. Run the calibration tool for the printer to adjust color output as necessary. Checking whether the separation pad is getting enough traction and whether the paper is too thin are proactive actions related to multipage misfeeds, not color issues.

3. **B, C, E, and F.** For finishing issues (such as stapling and hole punching), check the staple cartridge, hole punch tray, tray settings, and paper orientation. Cleaning the filament nozzle and platform are measures to take with 3D printers, not laser printers. The toner cartridge is very important for printing on a laser printer, but it is not important for finishing processes such as stapling and hole punching.

4. **A and E.** Maintenance kits usually include things like paper pickup rollers, transfer rollers, and a fuser. The duplexer, image drum, and toner are parts of the printer and/or toner cartridges. Toner cartridges are not included in maintenance kits.

5. **B.** You should upgrade the RAM on the printer. Large graphics files need a lot of memory (in both on the PC and the printer). But if the PC can send the file to the printer, it has enough RAM and storage drive space. Printer drivers will not cause an "out of memory" error to display on the printer.

6. **D.** Turn off the printer before you start working inside it. You want to make sure it is off and unplugged before you put your hands inside it. Taking it offline is not enough in this case.

7. **C.** Impact printer maintenance procedures include replacing the ribbon, replacing the print head, and replacing paper. Laser printer maintenance includes replacing toner, applying a maintenance kit, calibrating, and cleaning. Thermal printer maintenance includes replacing paper, cleaning the heating element, and removing debris. Inkjet printer maintenance includes cleaning the heads, replacing cartridges, calibrating, and clearing jams.

8. **B.** The Start printing immediately option is faster than the Start printing after last page is spooled option when spooling documents. The Print directly to the printer option doesn't use the spooling feature. There is no option called Start printing after the separator page.

9. **D, E, and F.** To immediately stop (or turn off) the Print Spooler service, you have several options. You can stop it in the Command Prompt with the **net stop spooler** command or the **sc stop spooler** command. You can also do it in the Services console window or in the Task Manager. (By the way, the answers listed are based on Windows 10 Pro.) Note that in Services you look for "Print Spooler," and in the Task Manager you look for "Spooler."

   The answers Start printing immediately and Print directly to the printer are options for how (or whether) documents will be spooled. While printing directly

to the printer does not use the spooler, it doesn't turn it off either. Finally, **sc config spooler start = disabled** *disables* the service, but it doesn't turn it off—immediately, that is. However, it won't start the next time the computer is restarted. Try that command and then the **net stop spooler** command to see what I mean. Then, to set everything back to run as normal, type the following:

```
sc config spooler start= auto
net start spooler
```

Yes, we went there. Chapter over.

CHAPTER 29

Troubleshooting Wired and Wireless Network Problems

This chapter covers the following A+ 220-1101 exam objective:

▶ **5.7** – Given a scenario, troubleshoot problems with wired and wireless networks.

You've made it to the last of the 220-1101 troubleshooting chapters. In this chapter we'll discuss troubleshooting of network connectivity issues. Because you will have users who connect in a wired fashion and other users who connect in a wireless fashion—and some connecting both ways—you have to be ready to support a variety of network connectivity. The goal of this chapter is to explain some basic troubleshooting techniques in a generic sense and ensure you have the right troubleshooting mindset.

To perform their work, users need access to resources, and network connectivity enables this access. Network connectivity is crucial. A faulty network connection means little to no available resources and, consequently, little to no work getting done.

ExamAlert

Objective 5.7 concentrates on troubleshooting common symptoms of wired and wireless network problems, such as intermittent wireless connectivity, slow network speeds, limited connectivity, jitter, poor VoIP quality, port flapping, high latency, and external interference.

Troubleshooting Common Symptoms

Network troubleshooting? Oh yes, it could be one of the best ways to learn how networks operate. First, I recommend reviewing the CompTIA troubleshooting methodology in Chapter 23, "Computer Troubleshooting 101." Second, I suggest a quick review of the networking chapters in this book (Chapters 5 through 12). And, most importantly for successful troubleshooting, remember to check the simple and obvious first. For example, physical power connections and network connections or disabled wireless connections are common culprits for network problems.

When you think about network troubleshooting, you should consider access to resources. If a resource—be it a data share, a printer, or something else—is unavailable, users won't be able to get their work done. Efficiency decreases, and the organization loses money.

Resources can be broken down into two types—local resources (those on the LAN) and remote resources (those beyond the LAN, possibly on the Internet or another external network):

▶ **Local resources:** You might find that a user can't browse the network or map network drives to network shares, or connect to network printers, or access an email server on the LAN. There are lots of examples, but the bottom line is that if a user can't access local resources, you need to troubleshoot the network connection. That's the bulk of what we discuss in this chapter. If multiple users can't access resources, you may be looking at a more centralized problem. For example, if a server is down, perhaps a DHCP server is not properly handing out IP addresses to clients or a domain controller has failed, and users cannot be authenticated to resources. This type of issue might go beyond the scope of your work as a technician with the A+ certification, so be prepared to escalate the problem if necessary.

▶ **Internet-based resources:** If remote resources—for example, websites, VPN connections, and streaming media services—are not available to a user, it could be that the IP configuration (especially the gateway and

DNS settings) needs to be inspected and possibly reconfigured. If multiple users are having connectivity problems, it could be that the gateway itself or the DNS server (among other things) needs to be fixed. Again, escalate the problem if necessary.

All of the following bullet points list symptoms you might encounter that could lead to unavailable resources, either locally or on the Internet, as well as how to troubleshoot the underlying problems:

▶ **No connectivity:** If a user complains of a problem connecting to the network and you verify that there is indeed a problem, check the patch cable first and verify that there is a link light. Make sure the user's computer is actually connected to the network. If it appears to be a cable issue, use a patch cable tester or cable certifier to test the cable. If it isn't a cable problem, make sure the network adapter is enabled. If it's a laptop (or other mobile device) and the user has a wireless problem, check the Wi-Fi switch or button. Next, run **ipconfig /all** and check the settings. Afterward, ping the local computer to see if TCP/IP works. If you haven't resolved the problem by now (and you probably will have), access the Network and Sharing Center in Windows and view the graphical connections to see if there is a red X anywhere, denoting a problem. Search for and use the network troubleshooter if necessary. You can also right-click the **Network** icon in the Notification Area and select **Troubleshoot problems**. This brings up the Windows Network Diagnostics program; follow the steps for a possible resolution. Don't forget to check for the latest drivers for the network adapter. You can also try rebooting the computer to find out if any programs were recently installed or updated. Sometimes anti-malware software or firewall updates can cause connectivity issues. Some switches and routers have the capability to enable/disable specific ports; make sure the port in question is enabled in the firmware.

If it's a network-wide problem, power down the network equipment (SOHO routers, cable modems, and so on); then disconnect the network and power cables and wait 10 seconds. Finally, reboot the network equipment. If users cannot find the wireless network that they need to connect to using Windows or the wireless adapter's software, find a good third-party Wi-Fi locator program that you can download for free. Such programs can locate all wireless networks in the vicinity and display information such as SSID, signal quality, distance, and channel used (as long as the wireless network adapter is functional). If an SSID does not show up in Windows *or* in third-party software, you should enter the SSID manually.

▶ **Limited and intermittent connectivity:** If the problem is limited connectivity, attempt some pings. First, ping the localhost (**ping 127.0.0.1**) to see if TCP/IP is functioning. If that works, ping the router or another system on the network. If that fails, the user only has local area network connectivity. Run **ipconfig /all** and check the rest of the IP settings. If pinging the router *does* work, try pinging a website by domain name. If that fails, the DNS server address is probably not configured properly. Check it with **ipconfig /all** and modify it in the IP Properties dialog box, if necessary. Run **ipconfig /release** and **ipconfig /renew** if you suspect an issue with obtaining an address from a DHCP server. Intermittent connectivity could be caused by a faulty patch cable, a wireless network adapter that is too far away from the WAP, or a router that needs to be reset. In a larger environment, if a person can access some networks but not others, you might want to try using **tracert** with inaccessible networks to see where the problem lies. This type of network troubleshooting gets a bit more in depth, but the **tracert** program basically shows which router between you and the final destination has failed. We'll cover that command and more networking commands in the 220-1102 portion of this book.

▶ **Low RF signal:** A low radio frequency signal spells doom for wireless users. The first thing to check is the distance of the computer from the WAP. Make sure the computer is within the appropriate range. Take advantage of the network's potential! For instance, if the WAP uses 802.11ax and the wireless adapter is 802.11n, consider upgrading to an 802.11ax adapter. Update the software on the wireless adapter and WAP as well. Placement of the router is important; it should be central to all users and away from sources of EMI. Try different antenna placement on the router and the wireless adapter. Normally, a 90-degree angle is best, but a little tweaking can go a long way. Also, some routers can boost their wireless signals. Check for this setting in the firmware.

▶ **Slow network transfer speeds:** The type of Internet connection is the biggest contributor to speed. For example, if a user has dial-up and complains about slow transfer speeds, it's time to upgrade! Even though dial-up can be tweaked for speed, it's simply easier to move up to DSL, cable, or fiber-based services. Slow transfer speeds could also be related to network equipment, patch cables, and network adapters. The newer and faster the equipment and cables, the better the data transfer rate. Of course, slow speeds could also be caused by network-wide congestion. What exactly is running on the network? A detailed analysis of captured packets (via a tool such as Wireshark) can be very telling. Check the router as well. See what kind of traffic is passing through it. Update everything, clear all cache, and power cycle all equipment (off-hours), and you just might see an improvement. If necessary, invest in a newer, faster router.

It could also be that the user simply has too many open network connections. Run **netstat -a** to see which types of connections the local computer has to the Internet. If you see dozens of established connections, the computer might be compromised by malware or might be part of a botnet. Or perhaps the user runs torrent software or just goes to a lot of websites for various reasons. Advise the user to close any unnecessary programs and limit the number of streams of data.

▶ **High latency:** Latency is the typical amount of time that it takes for packets of data to travel from one computer to the next. The higher the latency, the worse the experience when it comes to real-time video conferencing, webinars, gaming, and so on. (Another term used to describe latency is "lag.") To reduce latency, use the techniques mentioned in the previous bullet, especially the part about closing any other programs and connections that are running. The most bandwidth-intensive culprits are video sharing websites and movie-streaming sites and applications.

▶ **Jitter:** Network congestion can cause *jitter*, which is an irregular time delay in the sending of certain data packets. Jitter is similar to latency, but the delay that is involved is inconsistent; you might call it "inconsistent latency." The connection might be good one minute and bad the next. This is a problem that can affect voice over IP (VoIP) and streaming video and audio connections, which may lose quality for a period of time (or get "jittery"). Jitter may be more common with wireless connections. If using wireless, consider moving closer to the WAP. Also consider the wireless channel being used and check for external interference from neighbors or electrical equipment. Next, configure quality of service (QoS). QoS is a feature that attempts to prioritize data for specific computers or for specific programs. Configure it at the router to prioritize the packets that are more important to the users (for example, VoIP or other packets). In addition, you might opt for a jitter buffer, which is a shared data area where voice packets are collected and sent out smoothly during times of network congestion. Consider also that wireless connections are still in many cases slower than wired connections and break out that trusty old Ethernet cable (if at all possible). Finally, see the earlier bullet about slow transfer speeds for additional techniques to reduce jitter and network congestion in general.

ExamAlert

Know the difference: Latency is the typical time it takes for packets to travel from source to destination; jitter is irregular latency that often affects VoIP connections.

▶ **Port flapping:** Port flapping (also known as link flapping) is an issue where a communications link periodically changes between up and down states. For example, a computer that is wired to a switch might experience a network connection that alternates between a working state and a non-working state. You can check this by viewing the LED light on the switch's port that corresponds to the affected computer. You could also run a continuous **ping** command (for example, **ping -t example.com**) to see if some of the packets are being dropped. Flapping could be caused by a bad patch cable, improper duplex settings, or power-saving features. Test cables and check settings!

ExamAlert

Port flapping involves a communications link alternating between up and down states.

▶ **IP conflict:** An IP conflict message will pop up on the displays of both Windows computers that are causing the conflict. Usually, the first computer that used the IP address will continue to function, and the second computer will not be able to access the network. The second computer will have to be reconfigured to a different IP address and rebooted. Reboot the first computer for good measure. IP conflicts usually happen only when static IP addresses are being used. Consider using DHCP for all client computers.

▶ **Link-local/APIPA address:** If a computer is showing an IPv4 link-local address such as 169.254.49.26 when you type **ipconfig /all**, it generally means that the computer is attempting to obtain an IP address from a DHCP server but is failing to do so. IPv4 link-local addresses always start with 169.254. Microsoft also uses the name Automatic Private IP Addressing (APIPA). Usually, a link-local address is assigned internally, so the real problem could be that the computer is not getting connectivity to the network. Check everything in the first bullet point. Also, consider using **ipconfig /release** and **/renew**. Finally, if these measures do not work, check the DHCP server to make sure it is functional and available.

> **ExamAlert**
>
> In Windows, use **ipconfig /all** to check whether a system is using an APIPA address on the 169.254.0.0 network.

▶ **Cannot connect to Internet websites:** There could be a DNS issue. Consider flushing the DNS cache. This can be done by issuing the command **ipconfig /flushdns**. Or you could reset the TCP/IP stack with the **netsh int ip** command. Resetting the TCP/IP stack and flushing the DNS cache can also be helpful if a client computer cannot connect to a network path by name on the LAN.

> **ExamAlert**
>
> Double-study your networking troubleshooting techniques and common symptoms in this chapter! It's all about troubleshooting!

Cram Quiz

Answer these questions. The answers follow the last question. If you cannot answer these questions correctly, consider reading this chapter again until you can.

1. A user complains that the computer is not connecting to the network. Which of the following should be done first?

   ○ **A.** Use **ipconfig /all**.

   ○ **B.** Ping the router.

   ○ **C.** Check the patch cable.

   ○ **D.** Check the network drivers.

2. One of your customers received the following error message while trying to connect to a shared drive on the network at \\server1\datashare:

   ```
   Network Path was Not Found
   ```

   Which of the following should you perform to resolve the issue? (Select two.)

   ○ **A.** Reset the TCP/IP stack.

   ○ **B.** Configure the network interface card to full duplex.

   ○ **C.** Disable the Ethernet adapter.

   ○ **D.** Use static IP addressing instead of DHCP.

   ○ **E.** Flush the DNS cache.

   ○ **F.** Disable the local firewall.

3. One of your customers no longer has access to a frequently accessed website. You ping another computer and the router on the network successfully. Which of the following should be done next?

   ○ **A.** Check the IP configuration.
   ○ **B.** Ping the website.
   ○ **C.** Update the OS.
   ○ **D.** Update the AV software.

4. A user moves a laptop from one office to another. The patch cable and the network adapter do not appear to be working properly at the new office. The cable is plugged in correctly and tests okay when checked with a patch tester. Which of the following should be done first?

   ○ **A.** Check whether the port on the switch is enabled.
   ○ **B.** Update the network adapter driver.
   ○ **C.** Replace the patch cable with a crossover cable.
   ○ **D.** Make sure the network adapter is compatible with the OS.

5. A computer is experiencing a problem in which the network connection alternates between a working state and non-working state. It affects all applications. What is most likely occurring in this scenario?

   ○ **A.** Jitter
   ○ **B.** Network congestion
   ○ **C.** Port flapping
   ○ **D.** High latency

6. A user is experiencing slow network transfer speeds. You suspect that the user's system has too many open network connections to the Internet. Which of the following commands should you run to see which connections the user's system has to the Internet?

   ○ **A.** netstat -a
   ○ **B.** tracert
   ○ **C.** ipconfig /release
   ○ **D.** ipconfig /renew

7. What is the first thing you should check for when experiencing low RF and intermittent wireless connectivity issues?

   ○ **A.** APIPA address
   ○ **B.** Configure QoS
   ○ **C.** The distance of the computer from the WAP
   ○ **D.** Outdated equipment and cables

Cram Quiz Answers

1. **C.** Check the super-obvious first: Make sure the computer has a physical cabled connection to the network. Then attempt things such as **ipconfig**, **ping**, and network driver updates.

2. **A and E.** The issue here is most likely related to name resolution (which means DNS). Try resetting the TCP/IP stack or flushing the DNS cache. You can reset the TCP/IP stack in PowerShell or the Command Prompt by typing **netsh int ip**. Or you can disable *and* enable the Ethernet adapter in Windows (as disabling alone is not enough). The DNS cache can be flushed by issuing the **ipconfig /flushdns** command. Configuring the network interface to full duplex would allow it to send and receive data simultaneously. Chances are that this is not the problem in the scenario. Assigning a static IP address probably won't help as this issue is usually a name-based problem, and DNS is probably not functioning properly. Disabling the local firewall is a bad idea from a security standpoint as it would allow people to access the local computer. However, it wouldn't help in this scenario anyway because a firewall normally wouldn't stop the local system from connecting to a remote data share.

3. **B.** This is the concept of pinging outward. Start by pinging the localhost, then a computer, and then the router on the network. Then ping a domain name or website. If you can ping a website but the browser cannot get through, the browser might have been compromised. If you cannot ping the website, you should check the IP configuration; the DNS server address might be incorrectly configured. You should update the OS and AV software right away if you suspect that the browser has been compromised.

4. **A.** Some routers and switches can disable physical ports (which is a smart security measure). Check that first. Later, you can check whether the network adapter is compatible with the OS and update it if necessary. Do not replace the cable with a crossover cable; this type of cable is used to connect one computer to another.

5. **C.** It is most likely port flapping (aka link flapping), which involves a communications link alternating between on and off states, back and forth. Jitter is an irregular time delay for particular packets (such as VoIP packets). It can be caused by network congestion, which simply means there is too much traffic on the network! High latency means data packets take longer to travel between a client computer and another system, and it occurs all the time.

6. **A.** Run **netstat -a** to see which types of connections the local computer has to the Internet currently. Advise the user to close any unnecessary programs and limit the number of streams of data. The **tracert** command in Windows is used to determine the route or path taken to a destination. The **ipconfig /release** and **ipconfig /renew** commands release and renew the DHCP-obtained IP address on a Windows system.

7. **C.** The first thing to check is the distance of the computer from the WAP. Also consider the wireless channel being used and check for external interference. An APIPA address is a self-assigned IP address in Windows (for example, 169.254.49.26). Configuring quality of service (QoS) on a router prioritizes the packets that are more important to the users. Outdated equipment is a potential culprit; perhaps the organization needs a new WAP. However, "outdated cables" is not correct because this is a wireless scenario!

220-1101 Wrap-up

Congratulations! This is the end of the 220-1101 chapters of this book. Following, you will find a practice exam that is designed to test your knowledge of the 220-1101 objectives. Good luck!

If you are planning on taking the actual CompTIA A+ 220-1101 exam, be sure to go through the 220-1101 checklist in "Introduction to Core 1 (220-1101)," just before Chapter 1. However, keep in mind that I recommend going through this *entire* book before attempting either of the A+ exams.

A+ Core 1 (220-1101) Practice Exam

The 80 multiple-choice questions provided here help you to determine how prepared you are for the actual exam and which topics you need to review further. Write down your answers on a separate sheet of paper so that you can take this exam again if necessary. Compare your answers against the answer key that follows this exam. Read through the explanations and also the incorrect answers very carefully. If there are any concepts that you don't understand, go back and study them more.

Exam Questions

1. Which of the following components can be considered the "brains" of a computer?

   - ○ **A.** RAM
   - ○ **B.** Storage drive
   - ○ **C.** CPU
   - ○ **D.** Motherboard

2. You are attempting to load an operating system from a USB flash drive at computer startup. Which of the following settings should you modify in the BIOS?

   - ○ **A.** Enable a BIOS password
   - ○ **B.** Boot sequence
   - ○ **C.** Enable TPM
   - ○ **D.** Disable TPM

3. Which of the following is the most common type of networking connector used in a PC's network interface card?

   - ○ **A.** RJ11
   - ○ **B.** F-connector
   - ○ **C.** ST
   - ○ **D.** RJ45

4. Which of the following is the bus width of quad-channel RAM?

   - ○ **A.** 64-bit
   - ○ **B.** 128-bit
   - ○ **C.** 288-pin
   - ○ **D.** 256-bit

5. Which of the following should be reset during normal printer maintenance?

   ○ **A.** Page count

   ○ **B.** Job queue

   ○ **C.** Print job cache

   ○ **D.** Tray settings

6. You are a technician for an accounting company. You are helping a user who is unable to access websites and is reporting connectivity issues as well as pop-ups on the screen. You discover and remove malware. After rebooting the system, you are able to ping the gateway and access the Internet.

   Which of the following next steps should you take while troubleshooting this issue? (Select the two best answers.)

   ☐ **A.** Reboot the computer and verify that it works.

   ☐ **B.** Research the problem based on the symptoms you found.

   ☐ **C.** Perform a virus scan.

   ☐ **D.** Verify TCP/IP settings with ipconfig.

   ☐ **E.** Document findings, actions, and outcomes.

   ☐ **F.** Reconnect the system to the network.

7. A laptop's battery fails to charge. Which of the following should be checked first?

   ○ **A.** DC-in jack

   ○ **B.** AC-in jack

   ○ **C.** CMOS battery

   ○ **D.** AC circuit breaker

8. One of your co-workers has opened a trouble ticket concerning paper jams on a laser printer. The paper jams have become more frequent as of late. You decide to attempt to re-create the problem and then check the printer log for more information. Which of the following are the most likely solutions to the problem? (Select the two best answers.)

   ☐ **A.** Clean and inspect the entire paper path.

   ☐ **B.** Clean the fuser roller and verify fuser operation.

   ☐ **C.** Clean and replace the paper out sensor.

   ☐ **D.** Use a printer maintenance kit to replace parts.

   ☐ **E.** Replace the paper exit assembly switch.

   ☐ **F.** Clean and inspect the print drum.

9. What should you do after you have located a device for pairing during the Bluetooth connection process?

   ○ **A.** Test the connection.

   ○ **B.** Turn both devices off and then back on.

   ○ **C.** Enter the PIN code.

   ○ **D.** Enable Bluetooth on both devices.

10. The power supply fan and case fans spin, but there is no power to other devices. Which of the following is the most likely cause of this?

○ **A.** Failed boot drive

○ **B.** Improper connectivity

○ **C.** Drive not recognized

○ **D.** Failed RAM

11. One of the desktop computers at a customer site is randomly rebooting several times per day. You have checked for overheating issues, but everything seems okay with the case fans, CPU fan, and power supply. What should you check next?

○ **A.** Make sure the integrated network adapter has the latest drivers.

○ **B.** Ensure that the storage drive is defragmented.

○ **C.** Check the motherboard for signs of swollen capacitors.

○ **D.** Check the RAM and confirm that it is the right type.

12. Which of the following cable types should be used to connect a cable modem to a SOHO router?

○ **A.** Coaxial

○ **B.** Ethernet

○ **C.** USB

○ **D.** Thunderbolt

○ **E.** SATA

13. Which of the following is an example of a MAC address?

○ **A.** 10.1.1.255

○ **B.** 4410:FF11:AAB3::0012

○ **C.** https://dprocomputer.com

○ **D.** 00-1C-C0-A1-55-21

14. Your client has three business locations within the city limits. All three locations need to be networked. The vendor's network requirements for all three locations include a minimum data transfer rate of 1 Gbps. Which of the following network types should you most likely use for the internal office communications and the office-to-office network communications? (Select the two best answers.)

☐ **A.** SAN

☐ **B.** WAN

☐ **C.** LAN

☐ **D.** MAN

☐ **E.** PAN

15. Which of the following best describes the most likely reason for connecting a tone generator to an RJ45 cable drop?

- ○ **A.** To confirm continuity of the conductors
- ○ **B.** To locate the position of the cable on a patch panel
- ○ **C.** To test the transmission quality of the connection
- ○ **D.** To validate proper wiring of the network jack

16. When a mobile device is put into airplane mode, which of the following features are typically disabled? (Select the two best answers.)

- ☐ **A.** Cellular data
- ☐ **B.** Wi-Fi
- ☐ **C.** Multitouch capability
- ☐ **D.** Data encryption
- ☐ **E.** Camera

17. One of your co-workers has asked for a cable for an Apple mobile device that can charge it and transfer data to and from it. Which of the following connection types would meet the customer's requirements?

- ○ **A.** Lightning
- ○ **B.** Micro-USB
- ○ **C.** Molex
- ○ **D.** Mini-USB

18. A client is having a problem printing a specific type of document. The main network printer OCP shows that the printer is online and that there are no errors. No other users are having issues printing to that printer. You ask the person to send the same document to another printer, and the document prints fine. Which of the following should you do first when troubleshooting this problem?

- ○ **A.** Stop and start the print spooler service.
- ○ **B.** Stop and start the print server queues and have the user resend the document.
- ○ **C.** Verify that the user is sending the document to the correct printer queue.
- ○ **D.** Have all users send the same document to the correct printer queue.

19. A desktop computer (named workstation22) can't connect to the network. A network card was purchased without documentation or driver discs. Which of the following is the best way to install the network card driver?

- ○ **A.** Purchase the disc online and install the drivers.
- ○ **B.** Run Windows Update to install the driver.
- ○ **C.** From the desktop computer (workstation22), download and install the driver.
- ○ **D.** Copy the driver to a flash drive and install it.

20. You are working in a command line and see the following results:

```
example.com = 93.184.216.34
```

Which of the following server types has most likely helped supply this information to you?

- ○ **A.** DHCP server
- ○ **B.** DNS server
- ○ **C.** Authentication server
- ○ **D.** Syslog server
- ○ **E.** Print server

21. Which of the following features allows users to store files in cloud-based storage when needed but can be removed when space is freed up locally?

- ○ **A.** Shared resources
- ○ **B.** Metered utilization
- ○ **C.** On-demand
- ○ **D.** Resource pooling

22. You are the systems administrator for a medium-sized enterprise organization. You configure a server to host several virtual machines (VMs). Now, you are ready to begin provisioning the VMs. Which of the following should you implement to perform this task?

- ○ **A.** Remote Desktop Services
- ○ **B.** Hypervisor
- ○ **C.** Virtual LAN
- ○ **D.** Disk Management
- ○ **E.** Device Manager

23. You are part of a team that has decided to make use of a cloud provider for some of your organization's technology needs. Your top priority is to offload some of your networking, storage, and VM hosting to the cloud. Which of the following services best suits your needs?

- ○ **A.** SaaS
- ○ **B.** IaaS
- ○ **C.** PaaS
- ○ **D.** Hybrid cloud

24. Your guest virtual machines get direct access to the hosting computer's network connection. What is another name for this?

- ○ **A.** NAT
- ○ **B.** Private virtual network
- ○ **C.** Host-only networking
- ○ **D.** Bridged networking

25. Your office printer was working earlier in the day but is no longer printing any documents. Preexisting workstations are manually configured to print to the printer directly over the network. You begin troubleshooting the problem and determine that the printer is still visible when browsing the network directory. You also verify, at the physical printer, that the printer can print test pages successfully. Which of the following is the most likely cause of the problem?

○ **A.** The print spooler was restarted.

○ **B.** Two users sent print jobs at the same time, and a collision occurred.

○ **C.** The printer's IP address has changed.

○ **D.** The message "perform printer maintenance" is displayed on the printer's display panel.

26. Which of the following is an advantage of UDP over TCP?

○ **A.** It uses flow control.

○ **B.** It transfers packets faster.

○ **C.** It uses connection handshakes.

○ **D.** It is connection based.

27. John is a PC technician for an organization that has a computer network with 12 computers. All the computers contain vital information, so they use static IP addresses (on the 192.168.50.0 network). John just finished troubleshooting a Windows computer that could not access the network. He ascertained (correctly) that the computer needed a new network card. He purchased a plug-and-play card and physically installed the card. He then turned on the computer and noted that the network card's LED link was lit and that there was activity. He then rebooted the computer to Windows and documented the whole process. Later, his boss tells him that the user is complaining that there is no Internet access. Which step of the A+ troubleshooting methodology did John forget to perform?

○ **A.** Identify the problem.

○ **B.** Establish a theory of probable cause.

○ **C.** Test the theory to determine cause.

○ **D.** Establish a plan of action to resolve the problem.

○ **E.** Verify full system functionality.

○ **F.** Document findings, actions, and outcomes.

28. On your server, two drives of a RAID 5 array have failed. What should you do?

○ **A.** Replace one of the drives and run RAID repair.

○ **B.** Replace the failed drives and format the RAID array using the quick option.

○ **C.** Replace one of the failed drives and repair the RAID array using system utilities.

○ **D.** Replace the failed drives and restore the data from tape backup to the repaired RAID array.

29. Which of the following could be used for two-factor authentication?

    ○ **A.** IMEI and IMSI

    ○ **B.** Password plus biometric

    ○ **C.** GPS and location services

    ○ **D.** PRL and baseband updates

30. Which of the following types of printers requires a maintenance kit that contains a fuser, a transfer roller, and pickup rollers?

    ○ **A.** Thermal

    ○ **B.** Laser

    ○ **C.** Inkjet

    ○ **D.** Impact

31. You are tasked with fixing a laptop that is not booting. You have analyzed the system and can't see any system lights or display, and you can't hear any sounds when the Power button is pressed. Which of the following should be attempted first when troubleshooting the problem?

    ○ **A.** Boot the system from a flash drive.

    ○ **B.** Disconnect the AC and the battery and press and hold the Power button for several seconds.

    ○ **C.** Remove storage drives and optical drives, RAM, and USB devices from the laptop.

    ○ **D.** Connect an external monitor to the laptop to determine if the LCD has failed.

32. You are planning to build a computer that will be used at trade shows on several different continents. Part of your planning includes specifications such as maximum RAM and a typical video card, CPU, and storage drive. Which of the following specifications is the most important for you to consider when you select a power supply unit?

    ○ **A.** Efficiency

    ○ **B.** 12 V rail amperage

    ○ **C.** Input voltage

    ○ **D.** Number of SATA connectors

33. You are a technician for a small organization of 50 employees. You are tasked with replacing a damaged LED screen on a mobile computer. After installing a new LED screen, you find that the OS can be seen on the screen, but the touchscreen is not working. Which of the following are the most probable root causes of this failure? (Select the three best answers.)

    ☐ **A.** The touchscreen needs to be calibrated after replacement.

    ☐ **B.** Touchscreen drivers must be installed.

    ☐ **C.** The hardware replacement in the scenario is not touchscreen capable.

    ☐ **D.** A grounding screw is not attached securely.

   ☐ **E.** The digitizer cable is not attached to the motherboard properly.

   ☐ **F.** The LCD panel firmware should be updated.

34. A monitor's onscreen display (OSD) indicates that the proper video source has been selected, yet no image is displayed. Which of the following are the most likely causes? (Select the two best answers.)

   ☐ **A.** The monitor's brightness setting is too low.

   ☐ **B.** The monitor's backlight has failed.

   ☐ **C.** There is no device sending video.

   ☐ **D.** The source cable has been disconnected.

   ☐ **E.** The monitor's contrast setting is too high.

35. A computer you are working on randomly reboots. Which of the following should be checked first when troubleshooting the computer? (Select the two best answers.)

   ☐ **A.** Memory integrity

   ☐ **B.** Video card integrity

   ☐ **C.** CMOS battery

   ☐ **D.** PSU integrity

   ☐ **E.** Optical drive integrity

36. One of your customers has signed up for a mobile pay service to be used on a first-generation smartphone. However, the smartphone does not work at any location that supports mobile pay service. Which of the following is missing from the customer's smartphone?

   ○ **A.** IMSI

   ○ **B.** NFC

   ○ **C.** RFID

   ○ **D.** Bluetooth

37. You are setting up a network for a small office with 30 computers and 1 server. The server will be used as a file sharing device and a print server, and it will act as the domain controller. What kind of addresses should you assign to the server? (Select the two best answers.)

   ☐ **A.** DHCP

   ☐ **B.** MAC

   ☐ **C.** Static IP

   ☐ **D.** Dynamic IP

   ☐ **E.** Subnet mask

   ☐ **F.** FTP

38. Which protocol does Active Directory rely on most? (Select the best answer.)

   ○ **A.** SMB

   ○ **B.** HTTPS

○ **C.** LDAP

○ **D.** DHCP

39. As you are building a new PC, you notice that the motherboard has eight DIMM sockets that are labeled 0 through 7. Four of them are gray, and the other four are a darker shade of gray. Which of the following should be performed first?

    ○ **A.** Install the memory into the gray slots.

    ○ **B.** Install the memory into the dark gray slots.

    ○ **C.** Install the memory into slots 0 through 3.

    ○ **D.** Fill all the slots with memory.

    ○ **E.** Consult the motherboard documentation.

40. Which of the following printer technologies uses piezoelectric pressure pads to produce small bubbles that are moved to the paper?

    ○ **A.** Laser

    ○ **B.** Inkjet

    ○ **C.** Thermal

    ○ **D.** Impact

41. You need to describe RAID to a nontechnical customer. Which of the following is the best description to use for this customer?

    ○ **A.** RAID stands for redundant array of independent disks.

    ○ **B.** RAID utilizes multiple disks to increase performance and/or enable protection against data loss.

    ○ **C.** RAID is a dynamic disk management system.

    ○ **D.** RAID uses striping to reduce the amount of storage drive write time and utilizes parity bits to reconstruct the data from a failed drive.

42. You just completed a CPU installation. When you turn on the computer, the POST sounds a series of beeps, and the system won't boot. What is the most likely cause?

    ○ **A.** The mouse is not plugged in.

    ○ **B.** The operating system is corrupted.

    ○ **C.** The CPU is not properly seated.

    ○ **D.** The fan is running too fast.

43. Which of the following devices should be configured to block specific ports on a network?

    ○ **A.** Firewall

    ○ **B.** Gateway

    ○ **C.** Router

    ○ **D.** Bridge

    ○ **E.** Access point

44. Which connector is necessary to supply power to a graphics expansion card? (Select the best answer.)

- ○ **A.** 8-pin EATX12V
- ○ **B.** PCIe 8-pin
- ○ **C.** 24-pin ATX
- ○ **D.** SATA 15-pin

45. Which of the following monitor types provide for the widest viewing angle, along with rich colors and consistent backlighting? (Select the two best answers.)

- ☐ **A.** VA
- ☐ **B.** TN
- ☐ **C.** IPS
- ☐ **D.** LED

46. You replaced a bad internal WLAN card in a Windows laptop. You completed the installation and verified that the new WLAN card is listed in the Device Manager as enabled. What should you do next to actually use the card?

- ○ **A.** Type the security passphrase.
- ○ **B.** Update the firmware of the WLAN card.
- ○ **C.** Configure encryption on the router.
- ○ **D.** Add the SSID of the network to the connection.

47. You need to connect external peripherals to a typical PC. Which of the following connector types will allow you to do this? (Select the two best answers.)

- ☐ **A.** SATA
- ☐ **B.** SAS
- ☐ **C.** EIDE
- ☐ **D.** eSATA
- ☐ **E.** USB 3.0

48. Look at the following list of wires. What wiring standard is being used here?

```
1. White/orange 2. Orange 3. White/green 4. Blue
5. White/blue   6. Green   7. White/brown 8. Brown
```

- ○ **A.** RJ45
- ○ **B.** T568B
- ○ **C.** T568A
- ○ **D.** TIA

49. You need to make a patch cable to connect a computer to an RJ45 wall jack. Which of the following tools should be used to attach the RJ45 plugs to the patch cable?

- ○ **A.** Crimper
- ○ **B.** Punchdown tool

   ○ **C.** Loopback plug

   ○ **D.** Cable tester

50. Four people share a connection to a SOHO router that connects to the Internet. When a single user starts streaming media over the Internet, browsing slows down for the rest of the users. Which setting should be configured to alleviate the problem?

   ○ **A.** QoS

   ○ **B.** DSL

   ○ **C.** WAN

   ○ **D.** VPN

51. A user with an inkjet printer states that all color printouts are missing red ink. The printer has cartridges for each of the CMYK colors, and the user has recently replaced the magenta cartridge. Which of the following steps should be performed next?

   ○ **A.** Verify that the printer cables are connected.

   ○ **B.** Perform printer head cleaning.

   ○ **C.** Purchase a maintenance kit.

   ○ **D.** Use paper of a different weight.

52. A user calls you and says that his computer won't boot and that there is a faint smell of something burning. Which tool should be used to identify the problem?

   ○ **A.** Loopback plug

   ○ **B.** Cable tester

   ○ **C.** PSU tester

   ○ **D.** ESD strap

53. Which of the following describes the function of a switch in a network?

   ○ **A.** Converts a packet for transmission from one network to another network

   ○ **B.** Transmits packets it receives to specific connections

   ○ **C.** Broadcasts packets it receives to all connections

   ○ **D.** Determines whether a packet belongs on an internal or an external network

54. You are troubleshooting a user's system that connects to the network and disconnects from the network in an alternating fashion. The system is connected via an Ethernet cable. Which of the following is the most likely cause?

   ○ **A.** Port flapping

   ○ **B.** High latency

   ○ **C.** Jitter

   ○ **D.** External interference

55. Which of the following cable types is prone to EMI?

   ○ **A.** Fiber optic

   ○ **B.** STP

   ○ **C.** UTP

   ○ **D.** Multimode

56. You are troubleshooting a projector in a conference room. The training manager tells you that it flickers during presentations. As you investigate the problem, you verify the flicker on the projector screen but notice that the laptop display does not yield the same issue. You modify the resolution on the laptop, but the issue continues. Which of the following is the next step that you should take to fix the problem?

   ○ **A.** Check power cable connectivity.

   ○ **B.** Check video cable connectivity.

   ○ **C.** Modify settings on the projector.

   ○ **D.** Change the aspect ratio on the laptop.

57. A workgroup of five PCs uses a shared printer. A customer says she cannot print to the printer but can access shares on another PC used for common files. The printer appears to be powered on. Which of the following would be the most likely cause?

   ○ **A.** The PC with the connected printer is off the network.

   ○ **B.** The printer needs to be restarted.

   ○ **C.** The printer is low on toner.

   ○ **D.** Device drivers are corrupted.

58. What is the term for devices that have an integrated CPU and RAM and are part of the Internet of Things (IoT), such as smart security systems and fire alarms, medical sensors, and appliances?

   ○ **A.** Embedded systems

   ○ **B.** Syslog servers

   ○ **C.** Web servers

   ○ **D.** IDS/IPS systems

59. You just set up a printer in the company training room. The trainer wants to be able to print multiple copies of the training documentation for class, and to comply with the company's new green policy, she needs to conserve paper by printing on both sides of the documents. To comply with the policy, which feature should she be primarily concerned about?

   ○ **A.** Orientation

   ○ **B.** Print quality

   ○ **C.** Duplexing

   ○ **D.** Sharing

   ○ **E.** ADF

60. Which of the following voltages are normally supplied by a PSU's rails? (Select the two best answers.)

- ☐ **A.** 1.5 V
- ☐ **B.** 3.3 V
- ☐ **C.** 5 V
- ☐ **D.** 9 V

61. You are troubleshooting a printer. Which of the following are common symptoms of printer failure or other printer issues? (Select the three best answers.)

- ☐ **A.** Vertical lines down the printed pages
- ☐ **B.** Garbled print
- ☐ **C.** Faded print
- ☐ **D.** Failure to document screw and cable locations

62. Which of the following cable types would most likely experience degraded video signal quality over long distances?

- ◯ **A.** VGA
- ◯ **B.** HDMI
- ◯ **C.** DVI
- ◯ **D.** DisplayPort

63. You are building a high-performance workstation. You are required to select a boot drive with the highest performance available. Which of the following is the best option?

- ◯ **A.** NVMe
- ◯ **B.** 15K rpm HDD
- ◯ **C.** MicroSD
- ◯ **D.** USB flash

64. You are tasked with fixing a client's PC that hasn't booted after the latest test of the building's backup generator. As you analyze the computer, you notice that once it is powered on, there is no display and there are no beep codes. After 15 seconds, the fans inside the computer start spinning faster and making more noise. The computer was working fine before the test, and you verify that no one has opened the computer. Which of the following is most likely the problem?

- ◯ **A.** The RAM was damaged by ESD.
- ◯ **B.** The motherboard was damaged by the power test.
- ◯ **C.** The storage drive was erased due to the power test.
- ◯ **D.** The power supply was damaged and is nonfunctional.

65. Which of the following memory technologies enables protection against random inconsistencies when storing data?

- ◯ **A.** Quad-channel
- ◯ **B.** Parity
- ◯ **C.** Dual-channel

○ **D.** ECC

○ **E.** RAID 5

Note

You may have heard of unbuffered memory and buffered memory. While these terms are not in the A+ objectives, as a tech, you should know what they mean: Unbuffered memory is standard RAM that you would install to a typical PC. Buffered memory (also known as registered memory) places less electrical load on the memory controller, making a system that has a lot of sticks of RAM more stable. It is sometimes found in servers.

---

66. You are servicing a small office's network. One PC's network adapter has a link light that is lit, but the PC can't access internal network resources located on other PCs on the LAN. Which of the following is the most likely cause of the issue?

    ○ **A.** IP address conflict

    ○ **B.** High latency

    ○ **C.** Jitter

    ○ **D.** Limited connectivity

    ○ **E.** APIPA

    ○ **F.** Slow network transfer speed

67. A workstation fails to boot. The POST found an error, and the computer beeps twice. This happens again and again. Which of the following is the most likely issue?

    ○ **A.** Power supply failure

    ○ **B.** Video adapter failure

    ○ **C.** Memory failure

    ○ **D.** CPU failure

68. You are attempting to install Hyper-V on a Windows computer. However, you receive an error saying that the software cannot be installed. Which of the following CPU characteristics should be checked?

    ○ **A.** Number of cores

    ○ **B.** Virtualization support

    ○ **C.** Hyper-Threading

    ○ **D.** Cache size

69. You are a technician working on a problem with a projector. While investigating, you find that the lamp turns off for brief periods during longer demonstrations. You replace the lamp, but the problem continues, and now you get a message that appears just before the lamp turns off. Which of the following should you perform? (Select the two best answers.)

    ☐ **A.** Replace the cooling fan

    ☐ **B.** Change the video resolution

☐ **C.** Install a more powerful lamp

☐ **D.** Adjust the brightness

☐ **E.** Reset the lamp counter

☐ **F.** Update the laptop's video driver

70. Which of the following are found in electrical power grids, water treatment plants, gas/oil pipelines, hydroelectric systems, sewage systems, and traffic systems and must be heavily secured because they are often used in protected environments and infrastructures?

○ **A.** SCADA systems

○ **B.** Routers

○ **C.** Load balancers

○ **D.** Spam gateways

71. Which of the following ports can be used for audio, video, and storage?

○ **A.** Thunderbolt

○ **B.** DisplayPort

○ **C.** HDMI

○ **D.** DVI

72. Which RAID configuration is displayed in the figure?

○ **A.** RAID 0

○ **B.** RAID 1

○ **C.** RAID 5

○ **D.** RAID 10

73. Which of the following protocols is used to perform file sharing between Apple computers running macOS and PCs running Windows on a LAN?

○ **A.** RDP

○ **B.** SSH

○ **C.** POP3

○ **D.** SMB

74. You have been hired to install a network cable in a crawl space that runs the length of a hallway. You are required to meet fire code specifications. Which of the following types of cable should you run?

   ○ **A.** Shielded

   ○ **B.** Coaxial

   ○ **C.** Fiber

   ○ **D.** Plenum

75. You replace a failed storage drive with a new one. You then boot to a special pre-installation environment disc so that you can install a custom operating system build that is meant for deployment to the network. The storage drive is recognized in the UEFI/BIOS, but once you have booted to the preinstallation environment, the storage drive is not recognized, the process fails, and the drive can't be imaged. Which of the following statements best describes the most likely problem?

   ○ **A.** The PC's power supply cannot provide enough power for the new drive.

   ○ **B.** The boot media has failed and needs to be replaced.

   ○ **C.** The storage drive has not been partitioned correctly.

   ○ **D.** The storage drive must be configured in the UEFI/BIOS.

76. Which of the following LAN hosts would most likely provide the services needed to allow multiple clients access to cached Internet web pages?

   ○ **A.** File server

   ○ **B.** Proxy server

   ○ **C.** Web server

   ○ **D.** DNS server

77. Your organization has paid access to virtually unlimited cloud resources but pays only for the resources that are used. What is this called?

   ○ **A.** Rapid elasticity

   ○ **B.** Community cloud

   ○ **C.** Metered services

   ○ **D.** High availability

78. One of the workstations at your organization was just moved to a new work location in the same building. The new location does not have a surge suppressor. The workstation was working the day before, but today the system will not power up, the fans do not spin, and there are no other signs of activity. Which of the following should you do first?

   ○ **A.** Check the voltage of the PSU with a multimeter.

   ○ **B.** Check for swollen capacitors.

   ○ **C.** Check the voltage switch on the PSU.

   ○ **D.** Check the power cable connection.

79. You are planning a secure screened subnet (DMZ) that will incorporate several servers, including a web server, an FTP server, and a mail server. Which inbound ports will need to be opened at the firewall so that the servers can securely communicate with users on the Internet? (Select the four best answers.)

   ☐ **A.** 21
   ☐ **B.** 22
   ☐ **C.** 23
   ☐ **D.** 53
   ☐ **E.** 80
   ☐ **F.** 110
   ☐ **G.** 143
   ☐ **H.** 443
   ☐ **I.** 587
   ☐ **J.** 995
   ☐ **K.** 3389

80. You need to run a diagnostic program by booting to a USB flash drive on a laptop running Windows. You modify the boot order in the UEFI/BIOS and set it to the flash drive first. However, the laptop still boots into Windows. What do you need to adjust to boot to the USB flash drive?

   ○ **A.** Secure Boot
   ○ **B.** TPM
   ○ **C.** UEFI/BIOS password
   ○ **D.** Virtualization

Answers at a Glance

   1. C
   2. B
   3. D
   4. D
   5. A
   6. C, E
   7. A
   8. A, D
   9. C
   10. B
   11. C
   12. B

13. D

14. C, D

15. B

16. A, B

17. A

18. C

19. D

20. B

21. C

22. B

23. B

24. D

25. C

26. B

27. E

28. D

29. B

30. B

31. B

32. C

33. B, C, E

34. C, D

35. A, D

36. B

37. C, E

38. C

39. E

40. B

41. B

42. C

43. A

44. B

45. C, D

46. D

47. D, E

48. B

49. A

50. A

51. B

52. C

53. B

54. A

55. C

56. B

57. A

58. A

59. C

60. B, C

61. A, B, C

62. A

63. A

64. B

65. D

66. A

67. C

68. B

69. A, E

70. A

71. A

72. A

73. D

74. D

75. C

76. B

77. C

78. D

79. B, H, I, J

80. A

Answer Explanations

1. Answer: **C**. The central processing unit (CPU), otherwise known as the processor, is often considered to be the "brains" of the computer because it performs the bulk of the calculations for the system. See Chapter 17, "CPUs," for more information.

   Incorrect answers: Random access memory (RAM) stores calculated data over the short term; it is often called volatile memory because its contents are lost when the computer is shut down. A storage drive stores data over the long term; it is often called non-volatile memory, or simply "storage," because it retains data when the computer is shut down. The motherboard is the central connecting point for all components and connections within the computer, including the CPU, RAM, and storage drive.

2. Answer: **B**. Most of the time a computer's BIOS (or UEFI) is configured to boot to the storage drive first. To boot from a USB flash drive, an optical disc, or other removable media, you might need to change the boot sequence—also known as the boot order or boot priority—and place the removable media first. However, if the drive is brand new and blank, you still might be able to boot from the removable media, even if it is not first on the list. This will depend on the system, but essentially, the BIOS will see that the drive is blank and move on to the next boot media on the list. Keep in mind that you might boot to removable media with an operating system for other reasons than installing the OS (for example, recovering an existing system). See Chapter 16, "Motherboards and Add-on Cards," for more information.

   Incorrect answers: Enabling a password is not necessary, but there should be a password. If there is, you need to know it to access the BIOS. If there is not a password, you should create one while you are there. TPM (Trusted Platform Module) deals with the encryption of data on the storage drive and should be enabled or disabled before an operating system is installed; it won't have any bearing on the boot sequence.

3. Answer: **D**. The RJ45 connector is the most common type of networking connector. It is used in twisted pair networks. See Chapter 13, "Cables and Connectors," for more information.

   Incorrect answers: RJ11 is the connector used by landline-based phones (POTS connections) and DSL connections in households. The F-connector is a type of coaxial connector used for cable TV and cable Internet connections. ST stands for straight tip, and it is a type of fiber optic connector that is not common on a PC's network interface card.

4. Answer: **D**. The data channel (bus width) of quad-channel RAM is 256-bit. In this environment, you can have four separate modules of RAM (or possibly eight or more) working together. See Chapter 14, "RAM," for more information.

   Incorrect answers: Single-channel is 64-bit wide, dual-channel is 128-bit. Triple-channel is 192-bit. 288-pin is different; it refers to the connection type for DDR4 and DDR5 RAM (though they are not compatible with each other).

5. Answer: **A**. The page count counter should be reset whenever you perform normal, scheduled printer maintenance. For example, a laser printer can print about 200,000 pages before it needs scheduled maintenance. By resetting the page count after a successful maintenance, you will know when the next maintenance should occur. This is reset on the printer itself. See Chapter 20, "Printer Consumables," for more information.

Incorrect answers: The job queue and cache should reset automatically; this is because you would normally turn the printer off before maintaining it. Any print queue located on a computer is not reset automatically, but jobs in the queue will probably have to be re-sent. The tray settings do not have to be reset.

6. Answers: **C and E**. You should perform a virus scan and then document findings, actions, and outcomes. Remember the six-step CompTIA A+ troubleshooting methodology. The virus scan (almost certainly a second scan) is performed as part of step 5 (verify full system functionality and, if applicable, implement preventive measures). Then, in step 6, you document findings, actions, and outcomes. See Chapter 23, "Computer Troubleshooting 101," for more information.

Incorrect answers: The computer was already rebooted in the scenario, and you already verified that it can now access the Internet. While that is part of step 5, it was already accomplished. Researching the problem based on the symptoms you found would be part of step 2 (establish a theory of probable cause). If you can ping the gateway (router) and access the Internet, then the TCP/IP settings should be fine, and using **ipconfig** isn't necessary. If you can connect to the Internet, then the system was already reconnected to the network previously. However, it is important to note that any system that you are troubleshooting for malware should indeed be taken off the network right away until the malware is removed.

Note

Yes, be ready for questions that might traverse the 220-1101 *and* 220-1102 objectives. This question covers virus scans, which aren't covered until the 220-1102 portion of this book. Also, while the A+ troubleshooting methodology is listed in the 220-1101 objectives, you will need to apply it during the 220-1102 exam as well. That's why I suggest going through this entire book before attempting either of the exams. Read the whole book and then revisit the concepts and objectives for each exam—and take one exam at a time.

Also, be sure to read the entire question. Questions such as these are much more in-depth than questions 1–5. Not all the questions you see will be this wordy (or have as many potential answers), but you need to be prepared for the tougher ones. In addition, when you see questions that require multiple answers, you will see checkboxes instead of the typical radio buttons. Use the process of elimination when you encounter these and any other questions.

7. Answer: **A**. Of the listed answers, you should check the DC-in jack on the laptop first. However, the **very** first thing you should do is check the basics: See if the power brick is connected to the AC outlet and to the DC-in jack and verify that the battery is connected properly. See Chapter 1, "Laptop Hardware Components," for more information.

   Incorrect answers: Laptops don't have an AC-in jack; the power adapter takes care of converting AC power to DC power for the laptop to use. Of course, you should always check the laptop battery first, to ensure that it is not missing and make sure it is connected properly. Next, make sure the power adapter is plugged into the DC-in jack and that the jack is not damaged. A damaged DC-in jack can also cause the laptop to occasionally shut off. Users often damage the DC-in jack because they leave the power adapter plugged in while they are in transit. On most laptops, a new one has to be soldered on to the board. The CMOS battery is inside the laptop. It retains UEFI/BIOS settings and has nothing to do with charging the main laptop battery. The AC circuit breaker might have tripped, but this is less likely than the previously listed reasons. Also, a good indication of a failed AC circuit is that all of the devices on that circuit stop working.

8. Answers: **A and D**. You should clean and inspect the entire paper path first. This costs nothing; plus, by clearing out any papers in the path, you will often solve the problem, at least temporarily and perhaps permanently. Also, use the correct printer maintenance kit to replace worn parts. The parts from these kits should be installed every 100,000 to 200,000 pages printed (depending on the printer). Older worn parts can often lead to paper jamming, especially if the problem has been getting worse lately. See Chapter 28, "Troubleshooting Printers," for more information.

   Incorrect answers: Paper jams don't usually occur in the fusing assembly, but it is a possibility. Of course, you should wait 10 to 15 minutes for the fuser to cool before cleaning or replacing it. (Don't forget to make sure the printer is turned off and unplugged.) Replacing other components such as sensors and switches (if they exist) is less common. It is also uncommon to clean and inspect the print drum; instead, you simply replace the toner cartridge. However, this concerns problems such as streaking, marks, and ghosting more than it does paper jams.

9. Answer: **C**. CompTIA lists the Bluetooth connection process in the following order: Enable Bluetooth, enable pairing, find a device for pairing, enter the appropriate PIN code, and, finally, test connectivity. See Chapter 4, "Mobile Device Network Connectivity and Application Support," for more information.

   Incorrect answers: Testing connectivity is the final step and should be completed after you have entered the appropriate PIN code. You don't have to turn the connecting devices off and then back on during the connection process. Enabling Bluetooth is the recommended first step in the Bluetooth connection process.

10. Answer: **B**. If the power supply fan and the case fans are spinning but there is no power to other devices, chances are that the main 24-pin power connection was not made from the power supply to the motherboard. In this scenario, the case fans would have been connected by way of Molex power connectors directly to the power supply. Although it's usually better to connect case fans to the motherboard, if they are connected to the motherboard, they do not spin because the motherboard is not receiving power. If this scenario were to occur, no other

devices would get power, including the CPU, RAM, motherboard, storage drives, optical drives, and so on. See Chapter 18, "Power," for more information.

Incorrect answers: If the boot drive fails, the operating system will fail to boot up. If the drive cannot be repaired, it will have to be removed and replaced. If the drive is not recognized, again, the OS will not boot. It would have to be reconnected properly, configured in the UEFI/BIOS, or partitioned and formatted properly in Windows, depending on the specific situation. Failed RAM could cause a boot failure and will definitely be registered by the POST, but it doesn't necessarily mean that the RAM (or any other device) is not receiving power.

11. Answer: **C**. The best answer listed is to check the motherboard for swollen capacitors. A swollen (or distended) capacitor could cause the system to reboot intermittently. The capacitor (or entire motherboard) needs to be replaced. See Chapter 24, "Troubleshooting Motherboards, CPUs, RAM, and Power," for more information.

Incorrect answers: It is unlikely that the network adapter or fragmented storage drive would cause the system to sporadically reboot, but you should check for the latest drivers and firmware for the network adapter anyway and analyze whether the storage drive has been defragmented of late (especially for magnetic disks). RAM could cause the system to periodically reboot, mainly if the RAM is overheating. (RAM heat sinks could fix that.) But the wrong type of RAM will usually result in a POST failure instead.

12. Answer: **B**. Use an Ethernet patch cable to connect a cable modem to a SOHO router. Consider Cat 5e, Cat 6, or better. This is the same kind of patch cable that is used to connect a computer to an RJ45 jack, as well as connect a patch panel port to a switch port. This is a shorter question (and perhaps a bit easier than the last few) but could still be a little tricky if you are not reading carefully. See Chapter 13, "Cables and Connectors," for more information.

Incorrect answers: Use an RG-6 coaxial cable to connect the cable modem to the coaxial jack. USB cables can be used to connect a plethora of devices to PCs, laptops, and mobile devices or can be used to charge devices (depending on the type of USB cable). Thunderbolt can be used to transmit data to devices or video to displays. SATA cables are used to connect storage drives to a motherboard.

13. Answer: **D**. The only answer listed that is an example of a MAC address is 00-1C-C0-A1-55-21. The MAC address is the address burned into the ROM chip of a network adapter that uniquely identifies it. This address is composed of six hexadecimal numbers, each between 00 and FF. The decimal equivalent of this is 0 through 255. The first three numbers are the OUI (organizationally unique identifier); 00-1C-C0 is an Intel OUI. The last three numbers are the individual address of the particular network adapter. You might also encounter MAC addresses separated by colons instead of hyphens. See Chapter 6, "Network Devices," for more information.

Incorrect answers: 10.1.1.255 is an IPv4 address. 4410:FF11:AAB3::0012 is a truncated IPv6 address. https://dprocomputer.com is a web address (or URL). It includes the protocol used (HTTPS) and the domain name (dprocomputer.com).

14. Answers: **C and D**. You would most likely use LAN (local area network) and MAN (metropolitan area network) network types. The LAN is for internal office communications, and the MAN is for office-to-office network communications (which will require a data communications provider). Both of these can handle 1 Gbps network communications. See Chapter 11, "Network Types," for more information.

Incorrect answers: A SAN (storage area network) is used to connect NAS devices and RAID arrays at high speed. A WAN (wide area network) is used to connect multiple LANs but over large geographic distances—and perhaps at speeds lower than 1 Gbps. A PAN (personal area network) is used to connect Bluetooth devices in an ad hoc manner.

15. Answer: **B**. A tone generator is often used to locate cables, especially if there are a bunch of them in a small area. In the scenario, the technician is connecting the tone generator to an RJ45 port, perhaps near a person's desk. Then the technician uses the probe (an inductive amplifier) to locate the other end of that cable at the patch panel either in a wiring closet or in the server room. Collectively, the two tools are known as a tone and probe kit, or toner probe. See Chapter 12, "Networking Tools," for more information.

Incorrect answers: The other answers require a cable tester/cable certifier. Although a cable tester can often act as a tone generator, a tone generator is not a cable tester; it can only generate a tone across the cable. Cable certifiers are used to confirm continuity, validate proper wiring, and test the transmission quality of a given connection.

16. Answers: **A and B**. Cellular connections are disabled when a mobile device enters airplane mode, and so are other wireless connections, such as Wi-Fi, Bluetooth, GPS, and NFC. However, on some devices, some of these other wireless technologies can be turned on individually after the device has been placed in airplane mode. See Chapter 4, "Mobile Device Network Connectivity and Application Support," for more information.

Incorrect answers: The display's multitouch capabilities will work as normal, but web browsers, email programs, and other apps that require Internet access will appear not to function properly when tapped on and navigated through— because, indeed, they are not functioning at all due to airplane mode. Data encryption will still function, though you won't be able to send that encrypted data anywhere. The camera will work, but posting images and video to a remote source will not function.

17. Answer: **A**. The Lightning connector is a proprietary connector used by Apple mobile devices. However, keep in mind that some Apple devices use USB-C. See Chapter 3, "Mobile Device Accessories and Ports," for more information.

Incorrect answers: Apple devices do not use Micro-USB or Mini-USB, although adapters may be available depending on the device used. Micro-USB is common on Android-based devices. Molex is a power connection found inside PCs.

18. Answer: **C**. Verify that the user is sending the document to the correct printer (printer queue). When there are multiple printers on a network, it's easy to mistake one name for another. Remember that OCP stands for operator control panel, which is the display on the printer. See Chapter 28, "Troubleshooting Printers," for more information.

Incorrect answers: You should not need to stop and start the print spooler service (which would undoubtedly be at the user's PC) because the user is able to print exactly the same document to other printers. Stopping and starting the printer queues could cause some angst among employees and won't do anything to help the problem either. It's never wise to ask *all* employees of an organization to do anything—in this case, sending the same document to the printer—especially when you already know that the other users can print to the printer in question.

19. Answer: **D**. You need to go to another computer, download the driver from the manufacturer's website, copy that to a flash drive, and bring it back to the affected computer. See Chapter 29, "Troubleshooting Wired and Wireless Network Problems," for more information. "What's a disc?" you say? For that, you will need to review Chapter 15, "Storage Drives."

    Incorrect answers: If you have access to another computer, it would be silly to wait for a disc from the manufacturer. And any manufacturer that charges for drivers (or a driver disc) should be ashamed, as should the user who actually purchases the disc! You can't run Windows Update or download drivers from the computer in question because the computer has no network connection; and remember, Windows Update is used to download Microsoft drivers, not other vendors' drivers.

20. Answer: **B**. The Domain Name System (DNS) server is the server that is in charge of resolving domain names (such as example.com) to their corresponding IP addresses (such as 93.184.216.34 or another IP address). So, in other words, it maps user-friendly names to network resources. The DNS server can supply this information to you when you make use of various commands at the command line, such as **ping**, **tracert**, **nslookup**, and **dig**. See Chapter 8, "Networked Hosts," and Chapter 10, "Network Configuration Concepts," for more information.

    Incorrect answers: A DHCP server takes care of handing out IP addresses to client computers automatically. An authentication server—such as a domain controller running LDAP—is in charge of verifying the identity of users who attempt to log in. A syslog server is used to gather the logs from network devices and present the information in a manageable way to an admin's workstation. A print server is a computer that is in charge of one or more printers on the network.

21. Answer: **C**. On-demand means a cloud service is available when the user needs it, 24/7. It allows a user to store data to the cloud, when necessary, but can be removed when space is freed up at the local system. See Chapter 21, "Cloud Computing Concepts," for more information.

    Incorrect answers: Shared resources means that different customers share server space, infrastructure, and so on in a public cloud setting. With metered utilization, an organization has virtually unlimited cloud resources but only pays for what is needed. Resource pooling is the grouping of servers used by customers in a highly available and scalable way.

22. Answer: **B**. Use a hypervisor! This is the software that hosts virtual machines (for example, VirtualBox, which is a type 2 hypervisor). However, if you are working for a medium-sized enterprise organization, you might want to consider a type

1 hypervisor, such as ESXi or Hyper-V for Windows Server. See Chapter 22, "Client-Side Virtualization," for more information.

Incorrect answers: Remote Desktop Services is a Microsoft utility that lets you connect to and remotely control other Windows systems or use applications from those systems. (It is also known by its older name: Terminal Services.) A virtual LAN allows you to regroup systems virtually within a LAN; it is done at the switch or with special software. A virtual LAN is not required to have *virtual* machines. Disk Management is a Windows utility used to configure storage drives. Device Manager is a Windows utility used to configure the various devices on a PC or laptop.

23. Answer: **B**. The best answer listed is infrastructure as a service (IaaS). This allows for networking services, storage, load balancing, routing, VM hosting, and more. See Chapter 21, "Cloud Computing Concepts," for more information.

    Incorrect answers: Software as a service (SaaS) provides common applications such as Gmail or Microsoft Office 365 to clients over the Internet. Platform as a service (PaaS) provides software solutions such as the ability to develop and test applications within the cloud. A hybrid cloud is a mixture of public and private clouds that combines dedicated on-premises servers with servers from a cloud service provider.

24. Answer: **D**. With bridged networking, virtual machines can get *direct* access to the hosting computer's network connection and access other systems on the LAN and the Internet. You might also see this referred to as "external," or "public." See Chapter 22, "Client-Side Virtualization," for more information.

    Incorrect answers: With network address translation (NAT), the guest can access the external network but not directly. Instead, the guests using NAT get IP addresses on a separate private IP network. Host-only networking creates a private virtual network for the guests, and they can communicate with each other, but not out to the external network or Internet.

25. Answer: **C**. In this scenario, it is possible that the printer's IP address has been changed, and it is the best choice of the listed answers. The workstations were manually configured (most likely via IP address), which means that an IP address change on the printer would cause any print jobs from those workstations to fail. The IP address could have been configured manually by another tech, or if it was set to DHCP, the printer might have received a new address from the DHCP server. Because of this exact scenario, it is always a good idea to configure a static IP address at the printer itself (within the LCD display). Remember, in the scenario, the printer can be seen in the network directory, which usually searches by printer *name* as opposed to printer IP address. Also, test pages are printing successfully. All these are clues that point to a potential IP problem. See Chapter 28, "Troubleshooting Printers," for more information.

    Incorrect answers: Restarting the print spooler service is a troubleshooting technique used when the spooler service is hung up for some reason. It generally doesn't cause problems but can fix a lot of spooling issues. Two print jobs can't be sent at the same time; collisions are a concept related to networking. It is possible that packets or frames can collide, but not the actual print jobs. The print jobs are placed into a queue either at the printer or at the print server. The need to perform printer maintenance doesn't usually cause print failures, but if you see that message, you should attend to it right away.

26. Answer: **B**. The main advantage of UDP (User Datagram Protocol) over TCP (Transmission Control Protocol) is that it can transfer data packets faster. Because it is a connectionless protocol, it doesn't require the synchronization or sequencing that TCP does. This makes it a faster option for streaming services, VoIP, and so on. See Chapter 5, "TCP and UDP Ports and Protocols," for more information.

Incorrect answers: UDP does not have an option for flow control. Also, it does not use a handshaking process. (TCP uses the three-way handshake: SYN, SYN-ACK, ACK.) As mentioned, UDP is connectionless, whereas TCP is connection based. However, even though UDP can transmit packets faster, you will find that TCP is used for most services and applications you will deal with.

27. Answer: **E**. John forgot to verify full system functionality. I can't stress it enough: Always *test!* And by "*test*," I mean verify functionality—make sure it works—not "test the theory." With a default installation of a plug-and-play network card, the card will, by default, be set to obtain an IP address automatically. If the computers need to be configured for static IP addresses, this will most likely cause a problem. There might not even be a device or server that is handing out IP addresses on the network. If that is the case, the Windows computer would attempt to self-assign an IP address (an APIPA address starting with 169.254). If that happens, the computer will most definitely not be able to communicate with the gateway—or the Internet, for that matter. And even if there is a DHCP server on the network, the chances are very slim that it is handing out addresses on the 192.168.50.0 network. Most SOHO routers will hand out addresses on the 192.168.0.0 or 192.168.1.0 networks, and that is only if DHCP is enabled.

John should have logged in to Windows, checked the system with **ipconfig /all**, run a ping test, tried to connect to websites with one or more browsers, and so on. Verifying full functionality is very important. Always remember to test every repair thoroughly. See Chapter 23, "Computer Troubleshooting 101," for more information.

Incorrect answers: All the steps of the A+ troubleshooting methodology are listed in the answers. John performed each step except for verifying full system functionality.

ExamAlert

Know the A+ troubleshooting methodology like the back of your hand for both exams!

---

28. Answer: **D**. You will need to replace both failed drives (which causes a total RAID 5 array failure, by the way) and restore the entire set of data from tape backup, from the cloud, or elsewhere. See Chapter 15, "Storage Drives," and Chapter 25, "Troubleshooting Storage Drives and RAID Arrays," for more information.

Incorrect answers: In a RAID 5 array, one drive can fail, and you can still recover from the issue without tape backup (using the RAID parity information), but no more than one drive can fail. If more than one drive fails—as in the question's scenario—you need to restore all data from a previous backup. However, in RAID 6, two drives can fail, and it can still recover. Formatting the RAID array is a good idea if you have to recover from backup but not a good idea otherwise because it will make the current data inaccessible. However, the term "quick option" is a Windows term, implying that the RAID array was created in Windows and is therefore a software-based array. It is recommended that you create hardware-based arrays that connect to a RAID adapter card (or RAID-enabled mother-board). In a hardware-based system such as this, you could repair the array with the system utilities, but again, in this scenario (with RAID 5), only if one drive has failed.

29. Answer: **B**. Using a password and some kind of biometrics is an example of two-factor authentication, or 2FA. See Chapter 4, "Mobile Device Network Connectivity and Application Support," for more information.

Incorrect answers: The rest of the answers do not deal with authentication directly. Some deal with identification, but none offer two-factor authentication solutions. The IMEI identifies a mobile device, and the IMSI is used to identify the user of a device. GPS technology is a mobile tracking service that can help a user navigate while driving (among other things). PRL updates help you get better coverage by keeping your device on preferred networks. Baseband updates are necessary to communicate properly with GSM cell towers.

30. Answer: **B**. The laser printer is the one that is most associated with maintenance kits. Common components of a laser printer maintenance kit include a fuser assembly, a transfer roller, and pickup rollers. See Chapter 28, "Troubleshooting Printers," for more information.

Incorrect answers: Common components of a thermal printer include the feed assembly and heating element. The inkjet printer normally includes the ink cartridge, print head, roller, feeder, duplexing assembly, carriage, and belt. An impact printer's components include the print head, ribbon, and tractor feed.

31. Answer: **B**. Although you could try several things, the best of the listed answers is to disconnect the AC connection and the battery and press and hold the Power button for several seconds. This effectively discharges the laptop (capaci-tors and such) and may also clear the BIOS, either one of which could potentially fix the problem. Exactly what happens will depend on the model of laptop, and the length of time you will need to hold down the Power button will vary (it could be up to 30 seconds). Afterward, reconnect the battery and AC connection and continue troubleshooting from there, if necessary. The key in this question is that you cannot hear or see anything happening. In most cases, something will hap-pen, but in this case, the laptop may have had a voltage overload or other similar problem. Discharging it in this fashion can fix the problem, but you might have to reconfigure your BIOS. See Chapter 1, "Laptop Hardware Components," for more information.

Incorrect answers: Booting the system to a flash drive will probably result in noth-ing. If you can't see or hear anything, you need to take stronger measures than that. Sometimes, removing drives and USB devices can help when troubleshooting, but again, in this scenario, where you can see and hear nothing, it probably won't help. Connecting an external monitor is a good idea if you can see LED lights blinking when you press the Power button but get no main display. In this case, the result will probably be no image on both displays.

32. Answer: **C**. One of your most important considerations should be the input voltage. For example, in the United States (and some other countries), this is 120 volts. However, in many other countries, it is 240 volts. (These are also represented as 115 V and 230 V.) It's better to avoid voltage converters if at all possible, so you will need a power supply unit (PSU) that can handle both. That means one of two things: an auto-selecting PSU or a PSU with a voltage switch. The former is preferable, so that the person setting up the computer at trade shows does not need to remember to check the switch. However, keep in mind that you might still need an adapter for the actual three-prong connection used in other countries. See Chapter 18, "Power," for more information.

Incorrect answers: The efficiency rating tells you how effectively the PSU uses energy. For example, the 80 Plus program promotes energy efficiency of more than 80%. While this is important for most computers—because we all want to conserve energy, right?—it is not as important for this particular system because the PC will be relying on power that is provided by the trade show venues. Rail amperage is important for resource-intensive computers such as gaming PCs, design systems, and so on, where an individual rail (such as the 12 V) can overheat if driven too hard. Of course, we don't want our devices (such as GPUs) to draw too much current from the PSU (which generally can max out at about 30 amps or so); however, the system is using typical components, so current should not be a factor. As long as the PSU meets the wattage requirements, it should be okay. Maximizing the RAM shouldn't cause the computer to go beyond the maximum current or wattage (as long as you don't overclock it—but even then, it is unlikely). Almost all PSUs come with several SATA power connectors, and you are only using one storage drive, so that should not be a factor either.

33. Answers: **B, C, and E**. Potential root causes include the following: The touchscreen drivers need to be installed; the hardware replacement is not touchscreen capable; and the digitizer cable is not attached to the motherboard. Always make sure you install drivers, or the functionality on the system will be limited. Be sure to get the exact model screen that you need. And always verify that cable and connections are secure before closing up a system. See Chapter 2, "Mobile Device Display Components," for more information.

Incorrect answers: There's nothing to calibrate yet because the touchscreen is not working at all. If it were working, and if the cursor (or touch sensitivity and positioning) were a little bit off, then calibration would be a good idea. A missing or insecure grounding screw shouldn't affect the touchscreen capabilities *only*; however, it might cause the entire system to fail to boot. You normally wouldn't have to update the panel's firmware (it should be done at the manufacturer), and also, the panel in question is an LED panel, not an LCD panel—splitting hairs, I know—but it is always important to purchase the correct replacement parts.

34. Answers: **C and D**. The most likely answers here are that there is no device (such as a video card) sending video or that the source cable has been disconnected (for example, from the computer's video card to the monitor). Always check the

connections on both ends and make sure that the computer (the video source) is on and booting properly. See Chapter 26, "Troubleshooting Video Issues," for more information.

Incorrect answers: The brightness and contrast settings are not likely to cause a no-image issue. On most monitors, you can reduce the brightness to 0 but still see the image on the screen. Likewise, you can increase the contrast to 100 (or whatever maximum number is used) and still see the image on the screen. It is not possible for the monitor's backlight to have failed because you can see in the OSD that the proper video source has been selected. The OSD would not be visible (or would only be barely visible with a flashlight) if the backlight had failed. Again, it is much more likely that there is a connectivity or source video problem. Always check the connections first!

35. Answers: **A and D**. Check the memory and the power supply unit (PSU) first. Both of these can fail intermittently, causing random reboots. Try reseating and cleaning RAM (and replacing it, if necessary). Test the PSU with a PSU tester or multimeter and replace it if necessary. The PSU can also cause the computer to quickly shut down immediately after it was started. See Chapter 24, "Troubleshooting Motherboards, CPUs, RAM, and Power," for more information.

Incorrect answers: If the video card fails, the computer simply won't display to the monitor. If the CMOS battery fails (or discharges), the time and date will reset to an earlier date (for example, to January 1, 20XX.) Other settings in the BIOS will be lost as well. If the optical drive fails, you won't be able to read CDs and DVDs, but the optical drive should not cause the computer to reboot.

36. Answer: **B**. Near-field communication (NFC) is missing from the smartphone. Older (first-generation) smartphones do not have NFC. Always check the minimum requirements of any software or service that you are planning to use with a smartphone, a tablet, or another computer. Make sure that the mobile device in question meets the minimum requirements. See Chapter 3, "Mobile Device Accessories and Ports," for more information.

Incorrect answers: IMSI, which stands for International Mobile Subscriber Identity, is a unique 64-bit field used to identify the user of a cellular network. By the way, don't confuse IMSI with IMEI. IMEI, which stands for International Mobile Station Equipment Identity, identifies the phone. RFID stands for radio-frequency identification, a technology that uses tags and radio-frequency scanning to identify those tags. Bluetooth is a technology primarily used to allow for peripherals' access to a computer, such as using a Bluetooth headset with a smartphone.

37. Answers: **C and E**. Unless a company has a lot of servers, the servers will usually be assigned static IP addresses, as opposed to having them dynamically assigned by a DHCP server. When you manually configure the TCP/IP properties of a computer, you are required to enter the IP address and a subnet mask (for example, IP address 192.168.1.100 and subnet mask 255.255.255.0). Often, you will also configure a gateway address and a DNS server address, although they might not be required. The great thing about the static IP address is that you know what it is because you assigned it; you can enter it into your network documentation, knowing that it will not change. DHCP-assigned addresses can

change from time to time, depending on how the DHCP scope was configured. See Chapter 9, "SOHO Network Configuration," for more information.

> **Note**
>
> There is one glaring issue in this question's scenario. Ever heard of the phrase "Don't put all your eggs in one basket"? That's exactly what is happening here. The server is doing everything: It's a domain controller, a file server, a print server, and who knows what else. Talk about a single point of failure! While small companies sometimes have to make do with the resources at hand, it would be wise to separate one or more of these services and either place them on a second server or use virtual machines or containers to achieve that goal.

Incorrect answers: Dynamic Host Configuration Protocol (DHCP) is not typically used for servers in a small company. Dynamic IP addresses are handed out by the DHCP server to client computers. The MAC address is the hexadecimal address that is programmed into the firmware of the network adapter at the manufacturing plant; it is not (normally) set by the administrator. A File Transfer Protocol (FTP) address is rather vague. Does that mean an IP address or a name? Either way, the scenario doesn't mention anything about FTP.

38. Answer: **C**. Of the listed answers, Lightweight Directory Access Protocol (LDAP) is relied upon most by Active Directory. LDAP deals with directory lists (such as the users within a Microsoft Active Directory domain) or the users' email addresses listed within a Microsoft Exchange server. See Chapter 5, "TCP and UDP Ports and Protocols," for more information.

Incorrect answers: Server Message Block (SMB) is a protocol that allows shared access to files; it is important to any computer running Windows, not just computers that are in charge of, or connect to, a Microsoft Active Directory domain. SMB is also known as the Common Internet File System (CIFS). HTTPS (Hypertext Transfer Protocol Secure) is used to transfer data from a web server to a client computer's web browser. DHCP (Dynamic Host Configuration Protocol) is used to provide IP address information to clients automatically.

39. Answer: **E**. Always check the motherboard documentation before you begin installing components. You need to know what type of memory you should be using, what type of channel configuration (most likely dual- or quad-channel) to use, and where the sticks of RAM should be installed, depending on the configuration you will use. The motherboard documentation will have a table or matrix explaining all the different possibilities. A single motherboard might allow one stick of RAM, plus configurations for dual-channel, tri-channel, and quad-channel. You need to know what is allowed and plan for the right type of RAM before you purchase it. In this scenario, there are eight slots in total (0–7). If you install the memory into all the gray slots, then you are probably setting up the system for a multichannel configuration, but you must get the correct RAM. Note that the colors of the slots can be different, depending on the manufacturer; for example, they might be blue and black, and the first slots you should use are the blue ones. Check documentation! See Chapter 14, "RAM," for more information.

Incorrect answers: Installing the memory to the dark gray slots might work, but it might not if those are the secondary slots for each channel. Going by the first four numbers might not be correct either, depending on the motherboard. In fact, a motherboard often uses the numbering system A1, A2, B1, B2, C1, C2, D1, D2, with each letter corresponding to a different channel. Filling all the slots might work, perhaps if you get quad-channel-compliant memory (and a lot of it), but it is not the recommended choice because it can be expensive and probably is not necessary. The main lesson here is that there are a lot of possibilities, depending on the motherboard and depending on what you as the user wish to accomplish. So always RTM (read the manual) and plan your purchases wisely.

40. Answer: **B**. The inkjet printer uses piezoelectric pressure pads to produce small bubbles that are moved to the paper. See Chapter 19, "Multifunction Devices/Printers," for more information.

Incorrect answers: The laser printer applies toner to the paper in the electro-photographic imaging process. A thermal printer uses heat to create text and images on specially coated paper. Impact printers use a print head to hammer the letters through a ribbon and on to the paper.

41. Answer: **B**. RAID uses multiple disks to increase performance and/or enable protection from data loss. RAID 0 and 5 can be used to increase read performance, while RAID 1, 5, and 10 can be used to enable protection from data loss. See Chapter 15, "Storage Drives," for more information.

Incorrect answers: Telling a customer that RAID stands for redundant array of independent (or inexpensive) disks is technical jargon that you should try to avoid. RAID is not a dynamic disk management system. However, in Microsoft operating systems, you need to set disks to dynamic in the Disk Management utility if you wish to add them to RAID arrays. Regardless, this is more information that the customer does not need to know. Finally, the statement "RAID uses striping to reduce the amount of storage drive write time and utilizes parity bits to reconstruct the data from a failed storage drive" is not altogether correct. RAID can also be mirroring. In addition, not all versions of RAID can use parity bits to reconstruct data from a failed storage drive. RAID 0, 1, and 10 do not. However, RAID 5 and 6 do. Remember that the customer needs to know how the technology will make their business more efficient; they do not need to know the technical details or jargon.

42. Answer: **C**. Of the listed answers, the most likely cause is that the CPU needs to be reseated. This will result in a series of beeps from the power-on self-test (POST) as the BIOS searches for the CPU and can't find it. If a computer were being built in this scenario, then it's also possible that the RAM was not seated properly or there is some RAM compatibility issue. See Chapter 24, "Troubleshooting Motherboards, CPUs, RAM, and Power," for more information.

Incorrect answers: No other answer choice would cause the POST to issue a series of beeps. The mouse would not, but a lack of a keyboard would result in beeps. (Always make sure the keyboard is securely connected!) Also, the POST doesn't look for operating system corruption; it is relegated to hardware only. However, it can display messages such as "no operating system found" if the storage drive is missing, not formatted, or not in the correct location in the BIOS boot order. "The fan is running too fast" is subjective; regardless, its maximum speed is usually governed by the BIOS and shouldn't affect how the system boots.

43. Answer: **A**. The firewall is the device that prevents outside intrusion by blocking ports and protocols. In many networks it is the first line of defense. See Chapter 6, "Network Devices," for more information.

Incorrect answers: A gateway (usually a router) is a device that allows multiple clients on one network access to another network (for example, computers on the LAN that want to gain access to the Internet). A router connects two networks together. A bridge separates a LAN into two distinct network sections. An access point allows wireless connectivity to the network for Wi-Fi-enabled computers.

44. Answer: **B**. PCIe 8-pin is the best answer. Don't confuse this with 8-pin CPU power connectors. 6-pin PCIe power connectors are also common. See Chapter 18, "Power," for more information.

Incorrect answers: The EATX12V 8-pin connector is used for CPUs. 24-pin ATX refers to the main power connection from the PSU to the motherboard. SATA power connectors are 15-pin and are used for storage drives and optical drives.

45. Answers: **C and D**. IPS (in-plane switching) monitor technology offers the widest viewing angle, and LED (light-emitting diode) monitors offer rich colors and consistent backlighting. See Chapter 2, "Mobile Device Display Components," for more information.

Incorrect answers: Vertical alignment (VA) screens are significantly better than TN screens but not quite as good as IPS for viewing angle. TN (twisted-nematic) monitors are less expensive monitors that do not have as good of a viewing angle as IPS. Note that LED also performs well when it comes to use in an area with a lot of natural light.

46. Answer: **D**. The next thing you need to do is connect to a wireless network, the first step of which is to scan for network names (SSIDs) or to add them manually. See Chapter 29, "Troubleshooting Wired and Wireless Network Problems," for more information.

Incorrect answers: You won't type the security passphrase until you connect to a wireless network. Updating the firmware and/or drivers for the WLAN card (Wi-Fi adapter) should be done as part of the installation of that card. If the router is set up to accept wireless connections, encryption should have already been configured on that router as well.

47. Answers: **D and E**. External SATA (eSATA) is a SATA port that is meant for use with external devices. It is sometimes found as a port on the back of a PC or can be added with an adapter card. Of course, USB (3.0, 2.0, and so on) is another external port that is used to connect to audio and video equipment as well as external storage drives. See Chapter 13, "Cables and Connectors," for more information.

Incorrect answers: Normally, SATA (without the *e* preceding It) is used for internal devices, not external devices. Serial Attached SCSI (SAS) is a type of storage drive technology that is used in servers and power workstations rather than in typical PCs. Enhanced IDE (EIDE, also known as Parallel ATA) is an older storage drive standard that you won't see often—unless you are recovering data!—and it is internal by default.

48. Answer: **B**. White/orange, orange, white/green, blue, white/blue, green, white/brown, brown is the correct wiring sequence for the T568B wiring standard. You might also see this shown as WO, O, WG, B, WB, G, WBr, Br. It's the same thing, just abbreviated. See Chapter 13, "Cables and Connectors," for more information.

Incorrect answers: The T568A standard, which switches the orange and green pins, is the older standard that was replaced by T568B. But to stay within electrical code and municipal guidelines, use the wiring scheme defined by the T568B standard on each end for straight-through cables. To create a crossover cable, use T568B on one end and T568A on the other. RJ45 is a type of plug (or jack) that network cards, switches, and network jacks use. TIA (Telecommunications Industry Association) developed the T568 standards and other wiring standards.

49. Answer: **A**. Use an RJ45 crimper to crimp those RJ45 plugs on the ends of a patch cable. See Chapter 12, "Networking Tools," for more information.

Incorrect answers: Use a punchdown tool to terminate individual wires to the RJ45 wall jack and to patch panels. Use a loopback plug to test a network adapter by plugging it into the card's RJ45 port. Use a cable tester to test patch cables or longer LAN cable connections.

50. Answer: **A**. Quality of service (QoS) refers to the performance of user connections over the network, particularly connections to the Internet. On some small office/home office (SOHO) routers, QoS can be configured to allow for equal data transfers among all users, or it can be used to configure special traffic (such as streaming media) to transfer faster. See Chapter 29, "Troubleshooting Wired and Wireless Network Problems," for more information.

Incorrect answers: DSL (Digital Subscriber Line) is a family of technologies used to transfer data over the Internet. A WAN (wide area network) is a network that spans a large geographic area and connects two or more LANs. A VPN (virtual private network) allows for secure (tunneled) connections over the Internet.

51. Answer: **B**. You should clean the print head! Most printers come with an onscreen utility that will do this, or you can manually clean the print head (delicately!). Similarly, printers might need to be calibrated if colors are slightly off. See Chapter 28, "Troubleshooting Printers," and Chapter 20, "Printer Consumables," for more information.

Incorrect answers: If the printer cables weren't connected, the printer wouldn't print anything at all. Maintenance kits are used more often for laser printers and are unnecessary in this case. The weight of the paper will not affect what colors are printed by an inkjet printer.

52. Answer: **C**. Use a power supply unit (PSU) tester to check whether the power supply is malfunctioning. If you ever smell something burning, even if it is a faint smell, turn off the power to any associated computers or devices and disconnect them from the AC outlet. Then test the affected PSU. Sometimes there is a burn-in period for new PSUs, and there might be a very faint smell for the first 24 to

48 hours. This is possible if the PSU was newly installed, but you should still test and monitor the PSU until the smell goes away. However, if the computer was working previously but suddenly doesn't work anymore, and you smell something burning, then you should most likely replace the PSU after testing it. Only test the PSU in your lab and make sure you have all the necessary fire prevention tools and technologies available. See Chapter 24, "Troubleshooting Motherboards, CPUs, RAM, and Power," for more information.

Incorrect answers: A loopback plug is used to test a switch port or the RJ45 port on a computer. There are many cable testers, but the term is often associated with network cabling, such as cable certifiers for Cat 6 cable. An ESD strap, or, more accurately, antistatic strap, is used to protect components from electrostatic discharge (ESD).

53. Answer: **B**. A switch is a network device that transmits packets it receives to specific connections. It does this by mapping systems' MAC addresses to physical ports on the switch. See Chapter 6, "Network Devices," for more information.

Incorrect answers: A router converts a packet for transmission from one network to another network. It also determines whether a packet belongs on an internal or an external network, though this process can be augmented by other devices. A hub broadcasts packets it receives to all connections.

54. Answer: **A**. With port flapping, a communication link alternates between on and off states. See Chapter 29, "Troubleshooting Wired and Wireless Network Problems," for more information.

Incorrect answers: High latency means that the typical time for packets to get from the local computer to a remote source is higher than you desire (for example, an average ping of 130 ms instead of 50 ms). Jitter is inconsistent latency and often associated with VoIP. External interference could cause issues with connectivity on a wireless connection (which could appear similar to port flapping if the issue is severe), but the scenario implies a wired connection when it says the system "is connected via an Ethernet cable."

55. Answer: **C**. Unshielded twisted pair (UTP) cable is prone to electromagnetic interference (EMI). See Chapter 13, "Cables and Connectors," for more information.

Incorrect answers: Fiber optic cable is not prone to EMI because it uses light as the medium instead of electricity. Multimode cable is a type of optical fiber. STP stands for shielded twisted pair, and as the name indicates, it incorporates an aluminum shield around the wires to prevent EMI.

56. Answer: **B**. The best answer listed is to check the video cable connectivity. A loose connection or an older or damaged cable could cause the projected video to flicker. This is especially the case with VGA connections. Use a quality cable and make sure it is properly secured to the projector and the laptop. See Chapter 26, "Troubleshooting Video Issues," for more information.

Incorrect answers: The power cable wouldn't cause video flicker, but it could cause the projector to randomly shut down if it isn't connected securely. There aren't any projector settings that should produce flicker, so modifying them probably won't help. Changing the aspect ratio is along the lines of changing the resolution (which the scenario says was already performed). For example, a 16:9 aspect ratio is used for HD video (such as a 1920×1080 resolution).

A 16:10 aspect ratio (such as 1920×1200 resolution) might be used by graphics workstations.

57. Answer: **A**. The most likely listed cause is that the PC to which the printer is connected is currently off the network. It would appear from this scenario that the printer is connected to a PC by way of USB and is shared at the PC itself, which is offline. If the customer can connect to other shares on other PCs, you know that that particular computer is functional on the network. Another possibility in this scenario is that the Share this Printer checkbox in Printer properties in Windows is unchecked. See Chapter 19, "Multifunction Devices/Printers," for more information.

> ## Note
>
> In this scenario, the user is accessing shared files from another PC. Remember that this is a *shared printer*. That means that the printer is connected to another PC on the network, not directly to the network. The answer "PC is off the network" means the PC that has the printer connected to it.
>
> The key here is that the customer can access shares on other PCs, which indicates that there is an issue with the computer that has the printer connected to it.

Incorrect answers: The printer is on, and restarting a printer can fix some issues, but it will most likely return the printer to the same state it was in previously. The printer being low on toner should have no effect on whether it can be accessed. But a message would probably appear on one of the computer's screens, stating that the toner cartridge should be changed soon. If device drivers are corrupted, the printer should still be accessible and might print, but it will probably print garbled information.

58. Answer: **A**. *Embedded systems* are devices that have integrated CPU and RAM and can process information internally without the need for a controlling system. They are commonly found in home appliances, office automation, thin clients, security systems, telecommunications, automotive, medical, assembly systems, and much more. They make up a large percentage of that nutty Internet of Things! See Chapter 8, "Networked Hosts," for more information.

Incorrect answers: Syslog is a protocol that can take logged event information from a router or other network device and send it to a logging server—also known as a *Syslog server*. The *web server* is the server that houses the website of an organization. An *intrusion detection system (IDS)* can determine whether an unauthorized person has attempted to access the network and then alert the systems administrator of its findings. Building on this concept, an *intrusion prevention system (IPS)* not only detects unauthorized access to the network but attempts to thwart it, making the admin's job somewhat easier.

59. Answer: **C**. The functionality that the trainer desires is duplexing, which means printing on both sides of the paper. Some organizations require this (for most print jobs) in their policies related to reducing paper consumption; however, most printers are not set to duplex by default. See Chapter 19, "Multifunction Devices/Printers," for more information.

Incorrect answers: Orientation is the method of positioning a printed page and is based on whether the page is going to be viewed vertically (portrait) or horizontally (landscape). Print quality is the print resolution, which is measured as dots per inch (DPI). A printer that is connected to a Windows PC must first be *shared* before other users at other computers can send print jobs to it. An ADF (automatic document feeder) is a wonderful contraption allows you to scan, copy, and fax multiple-page documents without having to feed each page individually. Although this may be an important feature for the trainer, she should first be concerned about the duplex settings!

60. Answers: **B and C**. The voltages a power supply unit (PSU) typically supplies include 3.3 V, 5 V, and 12 V (as well as their negatives) to components in the computer. See the section "Power Supplies" in Chapter 18, "Power," for more information.

   Incorrect answers: 1.5 is a common voltage for DDR3 RAM (and for AA and AAA batteries). 9 V is usually associated with batteries used by handheld devices such as power supply testers and multimeters. PSUs do not supply a 9 V rail or a 1.5 V rail.

61. Answers: **A, B, and C**. A common symptom of printer trouble is vertical lines on the page, which would indicate a print drum issue, likely fixed by a toner cartridge replacement or inkjet cartridge calibration. Garbled print can occur due to an incorrect driver. Some technicians like to try "close" drivers. This is not a good idea. Use the exact driver for the exact model of the printer that corresponds to the appropriate version of the operating system. For faded print, replace ink or toner. Clean the ink cartridge head. Also, check the fuser and increase the humidity, if necessary. See Chapter 28, "Troubleshooting Printers," for more information.

   Incorrect answers: Failure to document cable and screw locations and failure to organize parts could make reassembly of a printer or laptop difficult. These failures could possibly even be reasons the printer or laptop fails, but they wouldn't be symptoms of the problem. When troubleshooting, be sure to understand the difference between a symptom of a problem and a cause of a problem. And, of course, think carefully about the best solution to the problem!

62. Answer: **A**. VGA is an older standard that outputs analog signals to a monitor. Of the listed answers, it is the most susceptible to signal degradation. See Chapter 13, "Cables and Connectors," for more information.

   Incorrect answers: HDMI, DVI, and DisplayPort are designed to work by sending digital signals and can send them over longer distances than can analog cables (such as VGA). Digital is inherently better in terms of distance and signal quality.

63. Answer: **A**. The best answer listed is NVMe (Non-Volatile Memory Express)—for example, an M.2 drive. This technology can transfer the most data and provides the highest performance of the listed answers. See Chapter 15, "Storage Drives," for more information.

   Incorrect answers: A 15K rpm HDD means a hard disk drive (or magnetic-disk drive) that can revolve 15,000 times per minute. While that is one of the fastest speeds of an HDD, it will be lucky to move one-quarter as much of the data as an NVMe drive. A MicroSD card is meant for mobile devices as a means of secondary storage (for photos, videos, music, and so on); it is not a good candidate for a boot drive. Neither is a USB flash drive, unless you are testing a new operating system or troubleshooting an existing system.

64. Answer: **B**. The most likely option of the listed answers is that the motherboard was damaged by the power test. This causes a failure to power-on self-test (POST) and causes the fans to function improperly. There was probably some kind of surge or spike of electricity, which could have overloaded the motherboard in a variety of ways. Perhaps a capacitor burst, or maybe one of the circuits burned out. You might be able to repair it, but chances are you will need to replace the motherboard. You should notify your manager or your building facilities department about the issue. Also, to protect systems against this kind of problem in the future, consider upgrading the surge suppressor, installing a new one, or using a line conditioner or an uninterruptible power supply, or UPS (depending on the type of system). See Chapter 24, "Troubleshooting Motherboards, CPUs, RAM, and Power," for more information.

Incorrect answers: If no one opened the computer, then it is unlikely that the RAM was damaged by electrostatic discharge (ESD). Internal components are usually affected by ESD only when someone handles them improperly. You don't know yet, but the storage drive could experience data corruption or be erased due to a power surge. But that isn't the cause of the problem in the scenario; it is simply another potential result. It's another reason to have good protective power equipment to plug the computer into. If the power supply were damaged and nonfunctional, the fans wouldn't spin at all. However, the power supply might also be partially damaged. You need to do a lot of testing of the computer to make sure it is fully functional before putting it back into its normal work environment.

65. Answer: **D**. ECC (error correction code) memory can detect and correct common types of data corruption. It is often used in servers. It is not typically installed in desktops but might be used if data corruption cannot be tolerated. It provides for error correction and, therefore, protection while storing data in RAM. See Chapter 14, "RAM," for more information.

Incorrect answers: Quad-channel means that the RAM can send data over four 64-bit channels at the same time—and four sticks of RAM are required to take advantage of that. Parity support in RAM means that the memory can *detect* errors, but it cannot correct them the way ECC does. Dual-channel RAM uses two 64-bit data channels at the same time. RAID 5 is not a memory technology; rather, it is a redundant storage drive array technology. While RAID 5 does use parity, it is not the same type of parity that RAM might use.

Note

You may have heard of unbuffered memory and buffered memory. While these terms are not in the A+ objectives, as a tech, you should know what they mean: Unbuffered memory is standard RAM that you would install to a typical PC. Buffered memory (also known as registered memory) places less electrical load on the memory controller, making a system that has a lot of sticks of RAM more stable. It is sometimes found in servers.

66. Answer: **A**. An IP address conflict is a possible cause of the problem. This happens when two computers are assigned the same IP address (usually when at least one was configured statically). When this happens, the link light on the network adapter will still work as usual because the system has a physical link to a central connecting device such as a switch, and bits (and frames) of data are still being sent back and forth between that computer and that switch. It's the IP layer that is nonfunctional due to the IP conflict. IP conflicts are most common in smaller networks where the clients might use static IP addresses, but they are not common in larger enterprise networks that use DHCP. See Chapter 29, "Troubleshooting Wired and Wireless Network Problems," for more information.

Incorrect answers: Latency is the typical amount of time that it takes for packets of data to travel from one computer to the next. The higher the latency, the worse the experience.

Network congestion can cause *jitter*, which is an irregular time delay in the sending of certain data packets. Jitter is similar to latency, but the delay that is involved is inconsistent; you might call it "inconsistent latency."

Limited connectivity means that a system can connect some of the time. This is different from what you would see with an IP conflict in that the system will have periodic connectivity.

APIPA (Automatic Private IP Addressing) is a type of link-local addressing. The OS gives itself (self-assigns) an IP address, such as an address on the 169.254.0.0 network. If that happens, the system will probably not be able to access network resources. However, this is just a symptom and not a cause of the problem. In a typical network, an APIPA address usually occurs because there is no DHCP server to obtain proper IP addresses from.

Although slow transfer speeds could cause the system to take a while to connect, the system should still connect at some point to internal network resources. You can tell if the system has sent or received data in the current session by going to the network icon in the notification area or by running the **netstat -e** command in the Command Prompt (in Windows); this shows packets that were transceived (that is, transmitted and received).

67. Answer: **C**. The most likely cause is a memory failure. Two beeps often means a problem with memory. Of course, this depends on the type of BIOS or UEFI. For example, two beeps in some Dell systems means that no memory has been detected, causing a RAM failure. Two short beeps in AMI BIOS systems means a memory parity error. See Chapter 24, "Troubleshooting Motherboards, CPUs, RAM, and Power," for more information.

Incorrect answers: If the power supply were to fail, the system wouldn't even POST because the motherboard doesn't receive power. If the video adapter failed, you would get a different set of beeps. For example, in Award BIOS systems, one long and two short beeps (or three short beeps) means some kind of video error. In some Dell systems, six beeps means a video card failure. Read the motherboard documentation to find out what the beep codes mean. If the CPU fails, the system will not boot or go through the power-on self-test (POST).

68. Answer: **B**. You need to check whether the CPU has virtualization support enabled in the UEFI/BIOS. If it is not enabled, Windows will not allow the installation of Hyper-V to continue. You may receive an error message, or Windows might simply have a grayed out area where you want to select Hyper-V in Programs and Features. See Chapter 16, "Motherboards and Add-on Cards," and Chapter 22, "Client-Side Virtualization," for more information.

Incorrect answers: The number of cores, Hyper-Threading, and cache size will not cause an error in Windows. However, you should make sure that the system meets the minimum requirements to run Hyper-V. In most cases, if a system can run Windows, then it *should* be able to run Hyper-V. According to Microsoft, the general requirements to run Hyper-V are a 64-bit processor with second-level translation (SAT), at least 4 GB RAM (though more is better!), and virtualization support turned on in the UEFI/BIOS.

69. Answers: **A and E**. The scenario most likely is depicting an overheating issue. This is causing the lamp to turn off periodically until the projector cools down. Perhaps the cooling fan failed and needs to be replaced. The message that appears is most likely about resetting the lamp life counter to zero because the system "sees" that a new lamp was involved. See Chapter 26, "Troubleshooting Video Issues," for more information.

Incorrect answers: Because this is most likely an overheating issue (which is common), changing the resolution or brightness won't help. Neither will updating the laptop's video driver. The scenario doesn't even mention what kind of system is being used, but it is *usually* a laptop (or another mobile device). A more powerful lamp might not even work in the projector and would probably worsen the problem because it would require more power and therefore create more heat.

70. Answer: **A**. Supervisory control and data acquisition (SCADA) systems are found in electrical power grids, water treatment plants, gas/oil pipelines, hydroelectric systems, sewage systems, traffic systems, building controls, and so on. Compared to typical home offices and small offices, SCADA solutions must be heavily secured because they are often used in protected environments and infrastructures. See Chapter 8, "Networked Hosts," for more information.

Incorrect answers: A router is a device that allows access from one network to another. A load balancer is a hardware or software solution that monitors the servers in question and routes client requests to servers in a uniform fashion, making sure that no servers are overloaded and that no servers are idle. A spam gateway is a software solution that is either incorporated into an email server or installed as a virtual appliance—generally, just behind an organization's firewall to protect the network to a certain extent from spam email.

71. Answer: **A**. Thunderbolt is the only answer listed that can be used for audio, video, and storage. See Chapter 13, "Cables and Connectors," for more information.

Incorrect answers: DisplayPort and HDMI can transfer audio and video data but are not used for storage. DVI is used for video only.

72. Answer: **A**. RAID 10 combines the advantages of RAID 1 and RAID 0. It requires a minimum of four or more disks. The system contains at least two mirrored disks that are then striped; it is also known as "stripe of mirrors." See Chapter 15, "Storage Drives," for more information.

Incorrect answers: RAID 0 is striping. It is not fault tolerant and does not incorporate mirroring. RAID 1 is mirroring and does not use striping the way RAID 10 does. RAID 5 is striping with parity. Data is striped across multiple disks. It does not include mirroring the way RAID 10 does.

73. Answer: **D**. SMB (Server Message Block) can be used to facilitate file sharing between Windows computers and computers running macOS. It is sometimes referred to by its older name, CIFS (Common Internet File System). See Chapter 5, "TCP and UDP Ports and Protocols," for more information.

Incorrect answers: RDP (Remote Desktop Protocol) is used to view or take control of remote computers from a central workstation. SSH (Secure Shell) is a protocol used to make secure connections to other systems; it replaces protocols such as Telnet. POP3 (Post Office Protocol version 3) is used for downloading email.

74. Answer: **D**. You should run plenum-rated cable, which has a special outer covering that will not burn (or will not burn as quickly as other cable) in a fire. It should be used in areas that cannot be accessed by a fire suppression system. (In some cases, it needs to be used throughout a municipal installation.) See Chapter 13, "Cables and Connectors," for more information.

Incorrect answers: Shielded cable (for example, shielded twisted pair, or STP) is used to reduce electromagnetic interference (EMI). It does not meet fire code for plenum areas. Unless specified as plenum rated, coaxial cable will not work, especially because you are running a network cable (which implies twisted pair cable). Fiber optic cable is a high-speed cable but by default is not rated for plenums.

75. Answer: **C**. Of the listed answers, the most likely problem is that the storage drive has not been partitioned correctly. In this scenario, the point of the preinstallation environment (PE)—which is often located on removable media such as a USB flash drive or boot disc—is to boot the system and partition the storage drive, readying it for the image to be obtained over the network. If the drive is not partitioned properly, the process will fail because the image will expect to be installed to a specific partition. See Chapter 25, "Troubleshooting Storage Drives and RAID Arrays," for more information.

Note

In some scenarios, a drive can be fully unpartitioned, and you can have the image install properly. This depends on several factors, including the local system hardware, what type of network installation is being done, and what software is being used for the imaging process.

Incorrect answers: Storage drives don't vary much from one to the next in regard to power, so the power supply should provide plenty of power. If it didn't, you wouldn't see the drive in the UEFI/BIOS. The boot media has not failed; the scenario says that you have accessed the preinstallation environment, and that is only possible if the PE boot media was booted to successfully. Today, it is uncommon for a drive to be configured in the BIOS or UEFI (unless it is part of a RAID array, which is controlled by the motherboard). Normally, the drive is either seen or not. If not, you might need to perform a flash of the BIOS or UEFI.

76. Answer: **B**. A proxy server provides the services needed for multiple clients to access Internet web pages. It is a server that is normally located on the LAN, or the internal computer network, and as such is known as a LAN host or a network host. See Chapter 8, "Networked Hosts," for more information.

Incorrect answers: A web server does provide web pages, but the web server is not normally on the LAN. Web servers normally exist on the Internet, on an intranet, or in a DMZ or screened subnet, so they cannot be considered network hosts or LAN hosts. File servers simply store files for multiple clients to access; Word documents and Excel spreadsheets are examples. A DNS server is used to resolve hosts' domain names to their corresponding IP addresses. They are very common on the Internet, though they can exist on a LAN as well. However, they don't deal with *cached* web pages the way that a proxy server does.

77. Answer: **C**. With metered services, an organization has access to virtually unlimited resources but pays only for the resources that are used. This is also known as metered utilization. See Chapter 21, "Cloud Computing Concepts," for more information.

Incorrect answers: With rapid elasticity, a provider offers a scalable cloud-based network that can grow as the organization needs it to. On-demand is the ability for customers to gain access to resources 24 hours a day, 7 days a week. A community cloud is a mix of public and private where multiple organizations can share the public portion. High availability (HA) means the cloud should be available in real time and whenever needed (24/7); it should be "always on."

78. Answer: **D**. You should first check the power cable connection. Remember to check the simple stuff first! If there are no signs of life from the computer at all, then it's most likely a power problem. Make sure the cable is connected securely to the PSU and to the AC outlet. See Chapter 18, "Power," for more information.

Incorrect answers: Checking the voltage of the PSU means opening the system. Try to avoid doing that until after you have checked the obvious and easy things first. Also, while you can use a multimeter, consider using a proper PSU tester. Checking for distended capacitors can be risky business. It requires opening the PSU, which is not recommended. Checking for capacitor issues on the motherboard shouldn't be necessary in this scenario. If the PSU has a voltage switch, it is something that you could check (after checking the power cable). However, it should not have been changed if the system was moved within the office.

79. Answers: **B, H, I, and J**. In this scenario, the screened subnet/DMZ needs to have several inbound ports open to the servers. To do this in a secure way, one possibility would be to use SFTP on port 22, HTTPS on port 443, SMTP on port 587 (for outbound mail), and POP3 on port 995 (for inbound mail). That would meet the requirements for the secure FTP server, web server, and mail server. Besides SFTP—which rides on Secure Shell (SSH)—the rest of the secure solutions use SSL/TLS by default. See Chapter 5, "TCP and UDP Ports and Protocols," for more information.

Incorrect answers: While you can use any port and secure it with the appropriate protocols, there are default security port numbers that you will usually work with. For example, when configuring FTP, you use SFTP (port 22) or FTPS (ports 989/990) but not port 21, which is used with standard FTP. As for the rest of the incorrect answers: Port 23 is used with Telnet (which is considered insecure). Port 53 is used by DNS, which can be secured in a variety of ways, but the scenario does not require a DNS server. Port 80 is HTTP (which is rarely seen today). Port 110 is POP3 without security. Port 143 is IMAP without security. Port 3389 is used by Remote Desktop Protocol (RDP). By the way, you probably won't get a question with 11 possible answers, but I'm just trying to stress that you should know your ports and protocols!

80. Answer: **A**. You need to adjust the Secure Boot setting. Secure Boot uses encryption in conjunction with operating systems such as Windows to make sure that only a particular operating system will boot. Secure Boot blocks devices from booting from external media such as bootable USB sticks or optical discs. In this scenario, to boot off the flash drive, you not only need to change the UEFI/BIOS boot order but most likely also need to disable Secure Boot. See Chapter 16, "Motherboards and Add-on Cards," for more information.

Incorrect answers: TPM, which stands for Trusted Platform Module (and is located on the motherboard), is used to encrypt an entire storage drive. The UEFI/BIOS password most likely refers to the administrator password of the UEFI/BIOS. You already knew this password; otherwise, you would not have been able to modify the boot order. Virtualization refers to the ability for the CPU to work with virtual machine software (such as Windows Hyper-V). It has to be enabled for Hyper-V and other virtualization machine managers to work properly.

A Final Word About the 220-1101 Exam

After taking this practice exam, if you are unsure or unconfident in any way, I urge you to step back and continue studying the 220-1101 objectives before attempting the real exam. And don't forget, if you purchased the print version of this book, you have a bonus practice exam waiting for you on the companion website (as well as other bonus materials). See the Introduction of this book for details. For even more practice questions, check out the A+ Exam Cram *Practice Questions* book.

Be ready for anything! I can't tell you *exactly* what will be on the exam because that would violate the CompTIA NDA and, more importantly, the questions can change at any time! But the bottom line is this: If you know the concepts, you can pass any test. Use the official CompTIA A+ objectives as your guide. Review this book thoroughly. Finally, I challenge you to study in a hands-on manner on real computers and investigate all the concepts to the best of your ability. This will help you not only for the exam but also for the real world!

PART II

Introduction to Core 2 (220-1102)

Welcome to the Core 2 (220-1102) section of this book. This portion of the CompTIA A+ certification focuses on operating systems, computer and network security, software troubleshooting, and operational procedures. Sound like a lot? It is—but you can do it. Study hard, stay confident, and you will prevail.

The Core 2 content of this book comprises Chapters 30 through 64. For the most part, I've written the content to match the order of the objectives. This way, you can follow along with the official CompTIA A+ objectives and mark them up as you wish while you progress through the book. After Chapter 64, you will find a practice exam that is designed to test your knowledge of the 220-1102 objectives.

Core 2 (220-1102) Domains

The CompTIA A+ Core 2 exam objectives are broken down into four domains:

▶ 1.0—Operating Systems

▶ 2.0—Security

▶ 3.0—Software Troubleshooting

▶ 4.0—Operational Procedures

After this introduction, we'll address these objectives in order, starting with Chapter 30, "Comparing Windows Editions." Be sure to study each of the domains! To do so effectively, I recommend studying in a hands-on manner. If at all possible, get your hands on some operating systems such as Windows, Linux, macOS, Android, and iOS. Work with as many of these systems as possible so that you can learn how the software really works. Then apply that knowledge to the objectives and the content in this book.

Core 2 (220-1102) Checklist

You must be fully prepared for the exam, so I created a checklist that you can use to make sure you are covering all the bases as you study. Take a look at the table below and make sure you check off each item before attempting the 220-1102 exam. Historically, my readers and students have benefited greatly from this type of checklist. Use the table as a guide for ordering your studies. I suggest you bookmark this page and refer to it as you complete each item.

Exam Preparation Checklist

Step	Item	Details	220-1102 Status
1.	Read the Core 2 (220-1102) content.	Thoroughly read through Chapters 30 through 64.	
2.	Review the Exam Alerts.	The little boxes with Exam Alerts are interspersed throughout the book. Review them and make sure you understand every one.	
3.	Review the Cram Quizzes.	Cram Quizzes are categorized by exam. You can review them in the text or on the companion website.[1]	
4.	Complete the practice exam in the book.	Directly after Chapter 64 is a 220-1101 practice exam. Your goal should be to get at least 90% correct on the exam on the first try. (100% would be preferable!) If you score less than 90%, go back and study more!	
5.	Study the Core 2 Real-World Scenarios.	These can be found on the companion website. Complete them by reading and answering the scenarios and questions within the PDFs and accessing the corresponding videos and simulations.	
6.	Create your own cheat sheet.	Although there is a Cram Sheet in the beginning of this book, you should also create your own. The act of writing down important details helps commit them to memory. Keep in mind that you will not be allowed to take your own cheat sheet or the Cram Sheet into the actual testing room.	

Step	Item	Details	220-1102 Status
7.	Register for the exam.	Do not register until you have completed the previous steps; you shouldn't register until you are fully prepared. When you are ready, schedule the exam to commence within a couple days so that you won't forget what you have learned! Registration can be done online. Register at Pearson Vue (https://home.pearsonvue.com/). It accepts payment by major credit cards for the exam fee. You need to create an account to sign up for exams.	
8.	Read the test-taking tips.	These can be found in the last chapter of the book and on the companion website.	
9.	Study the Cram Sheet and cheat sheet.	The Cram Sheet is a fold-out in the beginning of this book. It is also on the companion website. Study from the Core 2 portion of the Cram Sheet and your cheat sheet during the last 24 hours before the exam. (If your exam is delayed for any reason, go back to step 3 and retake the Cram Quizzes and practice exam 24 hours prior to your test date.)	
10.	Take the exam!	When you pass, place that final check mark in the box! Good luck!	

[1] Some electronic editions do not have access to the practice test software.

ExamAlert

Do not register for the exam until you are thoroughly prepared. Meticulously complete items 1 through 6 in the checklist before you register.

CORE 2 (220-1102)

Domain 1.0: Operating Systems

CHAPTER 30
Comparing Windows Editions

This chapter covers the following A+ 220-1102 exam objective:

▶ **1.1** – Identify basic features of Microsoft Windows editions.

Welcome to the first chapter of the 220-1102 section of this book. Until now, we have been talking about hardware for the most part. But without software, hardware is fairly useless. So now we'll be digging into the software side of things.

In this chapter, we'll discuss Windows 10 editions (such as Windows 10 Home and Windows 10 Pro), Windows features that are available in each edition, and ways to upgrade to the various editions of Windows 10. We'll also cover the basic components of a Windows operating system. Let's go!

Note

Don't forget, a complete list of the Core 2 (220-1002) objectives can be found on the companion website of this book (see the introduction for details) and on CompTIA's website: https://www.comptia.org/certifications/a.

Windows 10 Editions and Feature Differences

Windows 10 is a group of operating system (OS) editions including Home, Pro, Pro for Workstations, and Enterprise. There have been more derivatives of Windows 10, but to align ourselves with the CompTIA A+ objectives, we'll focus on those four. As a technician, you should be less interested in cosmetic differences than in technical differences between editions. Take a look at Table 30.1 for a basic comparison of the technical differences between these editions.

TABLE 30.1 **Comparison of Windows 10 Editions**

Component	Windows 10 Home	Windows 10 Pro	Windows 10 Pro for Workstations	Windows 10 Enterprise
RAM limitation	128 GB	2 TB	6 TB	6 TB
Physical CPU Support	1	2	4	4
Remote Desktop Protocol (RDP)	✓ but client only	✓ client and server	✓ client and server	✓ client and server
Domain access	—	✓	✓	✓
EFS and BitLocker	—	✓	✓	✓
Hyper-V	—	✓	✓	✓
Group Policy Editor (gpedit.msc)	—	✓	✓	✓

> **ExamAlert**
>
> Windows 10 editions RAM limits: Home = 128 GB, Pro = 2 TB, Pro for Workstations/ Enterprise = 6 TB.

> **Note**
>
> See the following site for more about Windows features:
> https://www.microsoft.com/en-us/WindowsForBusiness/Compare

You might wonder, "What would I do with 6 TB of RAM?" Well, you might not need that much, but it's the ability to go beyond the Windows 10 Home limitation of 128 GB that is important. There are plenty of software packages that can only run with more RAM, and those software packages might require Windows 10 Pro. In addition, for people such as CAD professionals, data scientists, and graphic designers who use software that is *incredibly* resource intensive, Windows 10 Pro for Workstations provides the "server-grade" experience that might be required. Always check the minimum requirements of the software you plan to install. We'll discuss this concept further in Chapter 38, "Application Installation and Configuration Concepts."

You have probably noticed that the Home edition is missing most of the features in the table, but this makes sense. A typical home user doesn't need them. For example, a home user usually doesn't need to connect to and log on to a domain, or use virtual machines, so those features are omitted from that edition. But business users will be more sophisticated when it comes to features. Their needs might include domain access, virtualization, encryption, remote access, and so on. We'll discuss each of these features in more depth as we continue through the book.

> **Note**
>
> Regardless of what edition you run, it's important to make sure that your system has the resources required to run Windows. For example, on a 64-bit system, the Windows 10 minimum requirements include 1 GHz CPU, 2 GB of RAM, and 20 GB of free storage space (32 GB for virtual machines).

Windows Desktop/User Interface and Components

The essence of Windows is the graphical user interface (GUI), which allows users to interact with Windows. Normally, a keyboard, a mouse, a touchpad, or a touchscreen is used to input information to the operating system's GUI, and that input is shown on the screen. Basically, everything you see on the display (including windows, icons, menus, and other visual indicators) is part of the GUI, but remember that the GUI also governs how the user interacts with the OS.

The Windows GUI has many parts, including the desktop with all its pieces; applications such as File Explorer, Settings, and the Control Panel; and administrative tools such as Computer Management and the Device Manager. To grasp Windows, you need to learn how to navigate quickly through the GUI to the application or tool that you need. But the system is pretty deep and can be a bit confusing at times. Quick tip: Know how to navigate the system, but especially know how to use the Search and Run components of Windows. More on those in a little bit.

What do you see when you start Windows? Some of the components that make up Windows include the following:

▶ **Desktop:** In Windows, the desktop environment is basically what you see on the screen—essentially, it *is* Windows, from a cosmetic standpoint. An example of the Windows 10 desktop is shown in Figure 30.1, which shows the Start menu in the open position. The desktop is a key component of the GUI; it includes icons, wallpapers, windows, toolbars, and so on. It is meant to take the place of a person's physical desktop, at least to a certain extent, replacing calculators, calendars, notepads, and so on. Spend a minute looking at Figure 30.1, and then we'll talk about the various elements of the desktop.

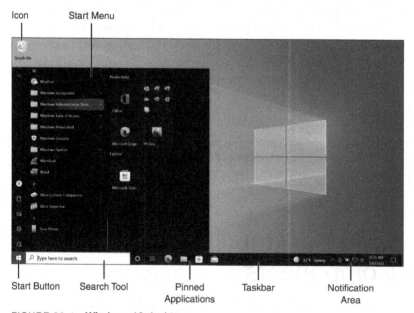

FIGURE 30.1 **Windows 10 desktop**

▶ **Icons:** Icons are the little clickable pictures you see on the desktop. They can be entire programs that run directly from the desktop, files that are stored directly on the desktop, or *shortcuts* that redirect to a program or file that is stored elsewhere in Windows. You can often tell that something is a shortcut because it has a little arrow in the lower-left corner of the icon. Shortcuts are small, usually around 1 KB to 4 KB in size, and store well on the desktop. However, storing actual files and programs on the desktop is not recommended because it can adversely affect the performance of the computer—and can quickly get really unorganized!

▶ **Start menu:** This is the main menu that is launched from the Start button. It contains a listing of all the tools within Windows and any Microsoft or third-party applications. From here, you can search for files and access the Control Panel. You can get anywhere in Windows from the Start menu. This menu shows who is currently logged on to the system and also enables you to log off, restart, shut down, or place the computer in sleep mode.

▶ **Taskbar:** This bar spans the bottom of the desktop. It houses the Start button, Quick Launch, any open applications, and the notification area (where applicable). It can be moved to the top or to any side of the desktop and can be resized. The taskbar and Start menu can be customized to just about any user's liking. To make modifications to these, right-click the taskbar and select Taskbar settings. From here, you can unlock/lock the taskbar, auto-hide it, and so on.

▶ **Search tool:** The Search tool is where you can search for files and applications. Use it! To open it, click in the search field area, click the magnifying glass, or press the Windows key and Q on the keyboard at the same time. (I'll be referring to this shortcut simply as Windows+Q.) Then type whatever search you desire. You will also note a circle to the right of the search field. That is Cortana, the built-in Windows virtual assistant search tool, which you can communicate with by typing or speaking.

▶ **Pinned applications:** Windows gives you the ability to "pin" applications or files to various locations in the GUI. You then have shortcuts to the applications and files. In the figure, the pinned applications exist on the taskbar. The beauty of pinned applications is that, by default, they are always visible, whereas shortcuts on the desktop background are covered up by open applications—if you have not hidden the Start menu, that is!

▶ **Notification area:** To the far right of the taskbar is the notification area, which houses the clock, volume control, network icon, battery power indicator, and so on. Also, if you click the show hidden icons symbol (^), it shows the icons of applications that are running in the background. The more icons you see in the notification area, the more resources are used (in the form of memory and CPU power), possibly making the computer less responsive. You can modify the notification area in the taskbar settings or by right-clicking the clock.

ExamAlert

Be able to identify Windows 10's icons, Start button, Start menu, taskbar, search tool, pinned applications, and notification area.

Today's versions of Windows can run side-by-side apps with the use of Snap technology. This means you can drag an application to an edge of the screen, and it will snap into place to inhabit that half of the display. A second application can be dragged in the same manner to the other side of the screen. This is an easy way to run two apps on the same screen without having to resize them manually. It becomes a bit more complex when you have multiple monitors, but, essentially, only the outer edges of the collective group of monitors can be used with Snap.

To actually do anything in Windows, you have to open a program (such as Calculator or WordPad) or a configuration window. Technicians are most concerned with the configuration windows. Be ready to work in Windows Settings, the Control Panel, and a variety of dialog boxes. For example, Figure 30.2 shows the Computer Name/Domain Changes dialog box, which was opened from System Properties. System Properties (not shown) runs as a process, and the Computer Name dialog box is just part of that overall process. A dialog box prompts a user for information—in this case, the name of the computer and the name of the network of which the computer is a member. You'll note that the network can be a workgroup (in a small office/home office) or a domain (in an enterprise business). This is just one example of many in Windows where you will configure the system.

FIGURE 30.2 **The Computer Name/Domain Changes dialog box**

We have covered a lot of stuff in just a few pages. If you are not already familiar with Windows, I highly recommend that you practice navigating through the operating system and become accustomed to the desktop and all of its components.

Settings vs. the Control Panel

There are two main places in Windows that you can go to configure the system: Settings and the Control Panel. Over the past several years, Microsoft has been leaning toward using Settings by default over the venerable Control Panel. However, you will need to use each of them. Which one you use depends on the scenario but be ready to work in both. To open Settings, simply click the **Start** button and then click the **Settings** gear, or use the Windows+I shortcut on the keyboard. There are several ways to open the Control Panel. One great way is to open the **Run** prompt and type **control**. By the way, to open the Run prompt, right-click the **Start** button and select **Run**, or use the Windows+R shortcut.

You will find that with both Settings and the Control Panel, it can at times be challenging to find what you want. A potentially faster solution is to use the Search tool or the Run prompt to go directly where you want without all the navigation. For example, if you want to add the Hyper-V feature to Windows 10 Pro, open the Search tool and type **Turn on Windows features** (or just **turn**), and you will see that it searches for and finds **Turn Windows features on or off**, which you can just click to open it. Alternatively, you could open the **Run** prompt and type **optionalfeatures**, which will bring you directly to the same place.

We'll be working in both Settings and the Control Panel and will discuss them further as we progress through the book.

Windows 10 Upgrade Paths

It's important for you to know which Windows operating systems can be upgraded to Windows 10, just in case you encounter an older system. Let's look at two scenarios and then summarize the various upgrade paths in a table (see Table 30.2).

In the first scenario, say that you work for an organization with a lot of older laptops running Windows 8.1 Pro. To be in alignment with organizational policy, all client systems should use Windows 10 Enterprise. As luck would have it, Windows 8.1 Pro can indeed be upgraded to Windows 10 Enterprise. However, whenever doing upgrades, you need to make sure to back up all data (and applications) and be ready to supply a license/key for the software.

In the second scenario, say that you have a home user with a PC that has Windows 7 Home Basic installed; it's due for an upgrade. The user heard that the Enterprise edition of Windows 10 has lots of great features and asks you to upgrade to that edition. There's no "luck" here. Windows 7 Home Basic cannot be upgraded to Windows 10 Enterprise. That would require a *fresh* installation, but as a reputable tech, you should discourage this path; chances are that the user does not need any of the features of Enterprise. The good news is that Windows 7 Home Basic can be upgraded to Windows 10 Pro, which is almost as good, especially for a home user. Or, you could convince the user to simply use Windows 10 Home. Always try to select an OS (and edition) with the consumer's best interests and needs in mind. And again, back up everything before you do any type of upgrade!

TABLE 30.2 **Windows 10 Upgrade Paths**

		Windows 10 Home	Windows 10 Pro	Windows 10 Enterprise
Windows 7	Home Basic	✓	✓	—
	Home Premium	✓	✓	—
	Professional/ Ultimate	D	✓	✓
	Enterprise	—	—	✓

		Windows 10 Home	Windows 10 Pro	Windows 10 Enterprise
Windows 8.1	Connected (Core)	✓	✓	—
	Pro	D	✓	✓
	Enterprise	—	—	✓
Windows 10	Home	N/A	✓	—
	Pro	D	N/A	✓

✓ = Full upgrade is supported, including personal data, settings, and applications.

— = Cannot upgrade to that edition.

D = Edition downgrade; personal data is maintained; applications and settings are removed.

> **Note**
>
> To save space in this book, I've listed some common upgrade paths, but the table is not complete. For more information about upgrade paths and *all* the possibilities, see https://docs.microsoft.com/en-us/windows/deployment/upgrade/windows-10-upgrade-paths.

Now, as you can see in the table, Windows 10 can also be upgraded to…yup, Windows 10! I am writing this book on a Core i5 laptop that was running Windows 10 Home but is now running Windows 10 Pro. The "upgrade" took about 15 minutes, and all files were kept intact—though you better believe I backed them up!

> **Note**
>
> You might have noticed the table says "N/A" in a couple of locations, such as for an upgrade from Windows 10 Home to Windows 10 Home. N/A means not applicable, and in this case, it is because it is the same edition of the same operating system. However, there is a case when you would perform such an upgrade. This is known as an *in-place upgrade*, and is usually done to fix issues with the operating system. We'll talk about this further as we move through the Windows chapters of this book.

Windows 11

As of the writing of this book, Windows 11 was recently released, and a note about it was just added to the CompTIA A+ objectives. While the objectives focus on Windows 10, we should make mention of Windows 11 as well.

Cosmetically, Windows 11 looks different from Windows 10, as shown in
Figure 30.3.

FIGURE 30.3   **Windows 11 Desktop**

In the figure, the Start button was clicked, displaying the centered Start menu
(as opposed to the left-hand Windows 10 Start menu). By default, this shows
the "pinned" applications, which are meant to be the most commonly used
apps. For example, you can click on the Settings gear to open the Settings
app, where you can make the necessary changes to Windows 11. (You'll note
that Settings has been redesigned in Windows 11.) If you look at the taskbar,
you'll see that the pinned apps are centered. These are the kinds of cosmetic
differences that you will find in Windows 11.

However, for the most part, Windows 11 behaves in the same manner as
Windows 10 when it comes to applications, Settings, the Control Panel, the
Search tool, the Run prompt, PowerShell, and so on. And these are the things
that are important for the exam.

Windows 11 editions are similar to Windows 10 editions (Home, Pro,
Enterprise, etc.), and Windows 10 can be upgraded to Windows 11 easily.
However, the minimum requirements are a bit more stringent for Windows 11,
so you need to make sure your computer can handle it before upgrading. As
of the writing of this book, a typical 64-bit Windows 11 installation requires a
1 GHz CPU, 4 GB of RAM, 64 GB of storage, a secure-boot capable UEFI (and
Trusted Platform Module), and a display with a resolution of 720p or greater.

Windows 10 will be supported until 2025 and will be heavily used for some time, but going forward, Windows 11 will be Microsoft's focus. Be ready to support the cosmetically different but architecturally similar Windows 11 in the field!

Cram Quiz

Answer these questions. The answers follow the last question. If you cannot answer these questions correctly, consider reading this chapter again until you can.

1. Which editions of Windows 10 offer Hyper-V? (Select the three best answers.)

    ◯ **A.** Windows 10 Home

    ◯ **B.** Windows 10 Pro

    ◯ **C.** Windows 10 Pro for Workstations

    ◯ **D.** Windows 10 Enterprise

2. Where should you go to find out what applications are running in the background in Windows 10?

    ◯ **A.** Taskbar

    ◯ **B.** Start menu

    ◯ **C.** Quick Launch

    ◯ **D.** Notification area

    ◯ **E.** Cortana

3. A customer requires a current operating system that can utilize 512 GB of RAM that is installed to a PC. Which of the following should you suggest? (Select two.)

    ◯ **A.** Windows 10 Home

    ◯ **B.** Windows 10 Pro

    ◯ **C.** Windows 7 Pro

    ◯ **D.** Windows 10 Enterprise

Cram Quiz Answers

1. **B, C, and D.** Of the listed answers, Windows 10 Pro, Pro for Workstations, and Enterprise offer Hyper-V virtualization functionality. Windows 10 Home does not. Remember that just because Hyper-V is included as a feature doesn't mean it will work. The motherboard of the computer has to support virtualization; in addition, virtualization must be enabled in the BIOS/UEFI, and Hyper-V has to be enabled (turned on) within Programs and Features.

2. **D.** Go to the notification area to find out what applications are running in the background. (Another way is to use the Task Manager.) In Windows 10, click the arrow that points up to show hidden icons. In other versions of Windows, the applications might actually appear in the notification area itself.

3. **B and D.** You should suggest Windows 10 Pro or Enterprise to take advantage of the PC's 512 GB of RAM. Windows 10 Pro can access up to 2 TB of RAM, and Enterprise can access up to 6 TB (so you could say there is plenty of headroom here). However, Windows 10 Home can only access 128 GB of RAM—and that is not enough! And Windows 7 Pro can only access 192 GB of RAM. That wasn't mentioned in the chapter, but it doesn't matter because Windows 7 is not **current**. Support for Windows 7 ended in January 2020.

There you go! The first chapter of the 220-1102 section is complete. Great job! I suggest you review the chapter and make sure you have a Windows system of some sort to practice on.

CHAPTER 31

Microsoft Command-Line Tools, Part I

This chapter covers a portion of the following A+ 220-1102 exam objective:

▶ **1.2** – Given a scenario, use the appropriate Microsoft command-line tool.

The command line is where the real technicians live. Anything you can do in a GUI-based system, you can also do in the command line—and sometimes you can do more at the command line. Get to know it. For Microsoft Windows, you should become fluent in PowerShell, the Command Prompt, and the newer Windows Terminal, and you should know as many commands as you can.

The command line is so important that I spread out this objective over two chapters. There are a lot of commands in this chapter, and I suggest you take a break after each group of commands. We'll begin with the types of command-line tools available in Windows. Then we'll cover how to navigate folders and files within the Command Prompt. (By the way, when working in the command-line interface, the original name for folders was *directories*, so I will be using that term often.) Next, we'll discuss some of the commands that can be used to analyze and configure the storage drive and file system. Finally, we'll cover a couple advanced tools.

Once you get the hang of the command line, you'll see that it's a blast. The great thing about the command line is that it hasn't changed much over time. It has certainly not changed nearly as much as the GUI in Windows. Plus, many companies desire technicians who have good command-line skills, which can ultimately translate to job security. Enough said.

> **ExamAlert**
>
> **Objective 1.2** focuses on navigational commands such as **cd**, **dir**, **md**, and **rmdir**; as well as command-line tools such as **chkdsk**, **sfc**, **format**, and **robocopy**.

Microsoft Command-Line Basics

Microsoft has three command-line options: the Command Prompt, PowerShell, and Windows Terminal. The first two are text-based interfaces where you can issue commands to the operating system. The last one acts as a launching point for the other two tools. Let's discuss each of them now.

Command Prompt

The Command Prompt is the original Windows command-line interface (CLI). You can use this program to issue commands concerning files and directories (folders), networking, services, and so on. In Windows 10, you can open it in several ways, including the following:

▶ Open the Search tool and type **cmd** (or search for a variety of words/ phrases associated with the Command Prompt).

▶ Press Windows+R to open the Run prompt and type **cmd** (my personal favorite).

▶ Click **Start** and then, on the programs list, scroll down to **Windows System > Command Prompt**.

▶ Right-click the **Start** button and select **Command Prompt**.

In Windows, some commands need to be run as an administrator. To open the Command Prompt as an administrator, do one of the following options (and type the password for the administrator account if necessary):

▶ Go to the **Start > Windows System**, right-click **Command Prompt**, click **More**, and select **Run as administrator**.

▶ Open the Search tool and type **cmd** in the Search field; then right-click **Command Prompt** and select **Run as administrator** (or press Ctrl+Shift+Enter).

▶ Right-click the **Start** button and select **Command Prompt (Admin)**.

> **Note**
>
> In Windows 11, right-clicking on the Start button shows Terminal instead of Command Prompt by default.

PowerShell

You will want to use PowerShell more often than the Command Prompt. PowerShell is a combination of the Command Prompt and a scripting language. It enables administrators to use typical commands and also to perform administrative tasks that integrate scripts and executables. You can open PowerShell in the following ways:

▶ Open the **Search** tool and type **powershell**. (Or press Windows+Q.)

▶ Go to the **Run** prompt and type **powershell.exe**.

▶ Navigate to **Start > Windows PowerShell > Windows PowerShell**.

▶ Right-click **Start** and click **Windows PowerShell**. By the way, another great keyboard shortcut is Windows+X. This is the same as right-clicking the **Start** button.

> **Note**
>
> The option in the last bullet might not be set up by default in Windows 10. To change the option from Command Prompt to PowerShell, you have to go to **Settings > Personalization > Taskbar** and toggle the **Replace Command Prompt with PowerShell** option. In Windows 11, this option is not available because the system defaults to Windows Terminal.

> **ExamAlert**
>
> Know how to open PowerShell from the Search tool, from the Start menu, and from the Run prompt.

You need to open PowerShell as an administrator to run advanced procedures. This can be performed in the following ways:

▶ Open the Search tool and type **powershell** in the Search field; then right-click **PowerShell** and select **Run as administrator** (or press Ctrl+Shift+Enter).

▶ Go to the **Start > Windows PowerShell**, right-click on **Windows PowerShell**, and select **Run as administrator**.

▶ Right-click any pinned shortcut to PowerShell and select **Run as administrator**. Pinned shortcuts might be placed on the taskbar, the Desktop, or elsewhere. Very handy!

▶ Right-click **Start** and click **Windows PowerShell (Admin)** (if configured).

Running PowerShell as an administrator is also known as running it in *elevated mode*. You will be using PowerShell in elevated mode often. We'll discuss PowerShell further in Chapter 62, "Basic Scripting, Part I," and Chapter 63, "Basic Scripting, Part II."

> **Note**
>
> Administrators who write scripts often are likely to use Visual Studio Code (known as VSC or VSCode). This is an integrated development environment (IDE) that can be used to build PowerShell scripts and scripts in other programming languages (such as Python). It has a built-in command line as well—often defaulting to PowerShell—that you can use to test your scripts. It's free and open source as of the writing of this book. Also, it's cross-platform—meaning you can run it on other systems as well, such as Linux. I highly suggest checking it out: https://code.visualstudio.com.

Windows Terminal

Windows Terminal is another place to run commands. It is multi-tabbed, meaning you can run multiple sessions within the same program. You can run any Windows command-line tool or shell within the tabs, such as PowerShell, the Command Prompt, and so on.

By default, Windows Terminal starts a PowerShell session when you open it. So, in actuality, the command-line tool is PowerShell, and Windows Terminal *houses* that command-line tool.

Taking it further, you can also run an Azure Cloud Shell in Windows Terminal. Or, if you have the Windows Subsystem for Linux (WSL) installed, you can run various distributions of Linux in different tabs.

Windows Terminal is included in newer versions of Windows 10 (and in Windows 11), but if for some reason you don't have it, you can download it from the Microsoft Store. This tool is designed to be an efficient and productive terminal application for developers and systems administrators. As of the writing of this book, Windows Terminal is not specifically listed in the CompTIA A+ objectives, but I highly recommend that you check it out because it is used pretty extensively in the field.

Ask for Help!

If you are ever stumped about a particular command, read the help file associated with it. The naming convention for this is

```
[command name] /?
```

which means whatever command you want to learn more about followed by the **/?** characters. For example, for more information about the **ping** command, you can type **ping /?**. In some cases, you can also type **help** and then the command (for instance, **help dir**), but **/?** is the best all-around way to do it because this option encompasses all the commands available. You can also find out more about Microsoft commands at https://docs.microsoft.com/en-us/ windows-server/administration/windows-commands/windows-commands.

Challenge 4: Access Each of the Microsoft Command-Line Tools

Go forth and use the command line! Try to access the Command Prompt, PowerShell, and the Windows Terminal (which you might need to install). Then try to run each of them as an administrator. Type the command **help** in both the Command Prompt and PowerShell and browse through the help files for each. Think about some of the scenarios where you might use the command line. For example, you might want to build a script, or run multiple tabs, or just navigate through the directories. Which tool would fit best in each of those scenarios?

Navigating in the Command Line

Have I mentioned yet that just about anything you can do in the Windows GUI you can also do by using the command line? It's true. And sometimes using the command line is faster than using the GUI—if you can type quickly!

> **Note**
>
> As a reminder, *directory* is the original name for *folder*. The more accurate names are *directory* when working in any command line and *folder* when working in the GUI, but the two terms are sometimes used interchangeably.

There are three main commands used to work with directories in the command line: **cd**, **md**, and **rd**. Feel free to use PowerShell or the Command Prompt for these three commands:

▶ **cd:** Change directory. This command enables you to move from one directory to another. Actually, you can go from any one directory to any other by using just one **cd** command. Two simple commands that you can issue are **cd ..** and **cd **. The **cd ..** command moves you up one directory; it takes you from the current directory to the parent directory. The **cd ** command takes you directly to the top (root) of the volume that you are working in.

▶ **md:** Make directory. This command creates directories.

▶ **rd:** Remove directory. This command enables you to remove directories. You can also remove directories that contain files by using the **/S** switch.

> **Note**
>
> The older versions of **md** and **rd** are **mkdir** and **rmdir**, respectively.

All of these commands can be used such that their functions affect any directory you choose within the directory structure (which used to be known as the *DOS tree*, but I digress). Figure 31.1 provides a sample directory structure.

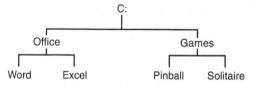

FIGURE 31.1 **A sample directory structure**

For example, let's say that your current position is C:\Office. From here or any other location, you can do anything to any directory in the entire directory tree. Let's consider a couple examples:

▶ To change the current position to the Pinball directory, the command would be either **cd c:\games\pinball** or just **cd \games\pinball**.

▶ To make a directory called **documents** within Word, the command would be **md c:\office\word\documents**.

▶ To delete the directory **excel**, the command would be **rd c:\office\excel**.

ExamAlert

Know how to use the **cd**, **cd ..**, and **cd ** commands in PowerShell or the Command Prompt.

So far, we've been working in the C: drive. In Windows land, we use the terms *volumes* or *drives* when referring to storage drive areas that are assigned letters. Chances are that you will have multiple volumes, and you will sometimes want to change from one volume to another. For example, maybe your operating system is installed in the C: drive, and you have data stored in the F: drive. To change from one to the other, you use drive navigation inputs. Simply type the name of the drive, such as **F:**.

A quick way to find out what volumes you have on your system is to issue the **wmic logicaldisk get name** command, as in this example:

```
PS C:\Data> wmic logicaldisk get name
Name
C:
F:
PS C:\Data> F:
PS F:\> C:
PS C:\Data>
```

In this example, I issued the **wmic logicaldisk get name** command, and Windows told me I have a C: drive and an F: drive. I then switched to the F: drive and back to the C: drive.

You'll note that the system remembers the last directory you were working in for each drive that you access. The PS means that you are working in PowerShell. (Another good option for learning what volumes are available is **get-volume**, but it works only in PowerShell.)

As you can guess, you can apply the **cd**, **md**, and **rd** commands mentioned previously to any drive letter. For example, if you were working in the C: drive and needed to get into the test1 directory in the F: drive, you would issue the command **cd F:\test1**, like this:

```
PS C:\Data> cd F:\test1
PS F:\test1>
```

Finally, you might see the *x*:\ drive letter in documentation. When you see this, *x* is a variable, and it can take the place of whatever drive letter is required. For example, you might install a program from a USB flash drive, but the program's creator will not know what drive letter your USB drive will be assigned by the operating system. Yours might be D:, and another user's might be F:, and so on. So, we use *x* as a catch-all. Fun!

Working with Directories and Files

Some other commands you might use when working with directories and files include **dir**, **tree**, **copy**, **xcopy**, **robocopy**, and **del**:

▶ **dir:** This is the directory command. When used alone, it displays the contents of the current directory. But it can be configured to show information in any other directory. For example, **dir \office\excel** shows the contents of the excel directory, regardless of what directory you are currently in. You can also use the **dir** command to customize how content is listed. For example, **/p** shows information by the page, **/w** is wide list format, and so on. To find out more about the **dir** command (or any other command, for that matter), type **dir /?**. **/?** is the switch that tells the Command Prompt to display the help file for that command. It can be placed on the end of any valid command in the Command Prompt.

▶ **tree:** This command shows all the directories and subdirectories at your current position. Be careful where you run this command because it could list information for quite a while and cause some stress on the storage drive. For example, avoid using it in big directories, such as the root, which is C:\, \Windows, and \Windows\System32.

▶ **copy:** This command allows you to copy one or more files to another location. If you wanted to copy a file named test.txt from the office directory to the excel directory, you would type **copy \office\test.txt \office\excel**. Now the original file is in \office, and the copy is in \excel. There are more powerful versions of this command—**xcopy** and **robocopy**—that we talk about next.

▶ **xcopy:** The **xcopy** command is meant to copy large amounts of data from one location to another; it even makes exact copies of entire directory trees. For more information about **xcopy**, type **xcopy /?**.

▶ **robocopy:** Robust File Copy is a directory replication tool. It is meant to copy directories that contain lots of data, and it can even mirror complete directory trees from one computer to another. **robocopy** is the successor to **xcopy**. Some of the advantages of this tool are that it can tolerate network interruptions, skip past junctions (such as the \Documents and Settings to \Users junction), and preserve data attributes and timestamps. **robocopy** does not copy individual files; it copies only directories. For example, **robocopy c:\office c:\games** copies all the information within the \office directory to the \games directory. This command also gives in-depth results of its actions. You can also use **robocopy** to copy information to other computers by using ***computername**share***, which is Microsoft's Universal (or Uniform) Naming Convention (UNC).

▶ **del:** When you are done with a file and are ready to delete it, use **del**. For example, if you want to delete the test.txt file that you just copied to the excel directory, type **del \office\excel\test.txt**.

Note

You can create a file such as test.txt within Notepad, which is available via the Search tool or by going to **Run** and typing **notepad**. Notepad is the default graphical text editor in Windows, and you can use it for editing text files and scripts. However, you might opt to use another editor, especially if you plan on doing any scripting or coding. (Some alternatives include Notepad++, Sublime Text, Atom, and my favorite—though it is not graphical—Vim.)

ExamAlert

Understand how to use **dir**, **copy**, **xcopy**, and **robocopy** for the exam.

Partitioning and File System–Based Commands

There are a slew of commands that you can use to make changes to your storage drive's partitions and file systems and to check the integrity of your storage drive and file system. These are a few of the commands that you should know for the exam:

▶ **diskpart:** This utility is the command-line counterpart of the Windows Disk Management program. This program needs to be run by typing **diskpart** before any of the **diskpart** actions can be implemented. This brings you into the DISKPART> prompt. From here, you can create, delete, and extend volumes; assign drive letters; make a partition active; and so on. Essentially, everything that you can do in the Disk

Management graphical utility can be done with **diskpart**. When you are in the DISKPART> prompt, you can enter a question mark (?) to learn about the various options within the Diskpart program. When you finish using **diskpart**, type **exit** to return to the standard Command Prompt.

▶ **format:** You use this command to format storage media to a particular file system, such as NTFS, FAT, or FAT32. An example of formatting a USB flash drive at the command line would be **format F:**. You can specify the type of file system that the media will be formatted to with the switch **/FS:***filesystem*, where *filesystem* equals NTFS, FAT, and so on.

▶ **defrag:** This is the command-line version of Disk Defragmenter. To analyze a drive, type **defrag -a**. If a volume needs to be defragmented but has less than 15% free space, use the **-f** parameter.

chkdsk and sfc

A good technician uses commands to analyze and possibly repair a storage drive and its system files. Two commands that can aid in this endeavor are **chkdsk** and **sfc**.

chkdsk

chkdsk checks a drive, fixes basic issues like lost files, and displays a status report; it can also fix some errors on the drive with the addition of the **/F** switch.

One issue that plagues users is the infamous "Missing Operating System" message. This message usually means that the drive has a few small errors. But even though the system won't boot, you can still run **chkdsk** to find and fix problems on the drive. Boot to the repair environment (if possible) or boot to the Windows media, access Windows RE, and then open the Command Prompt. From there, run **chkdsk** with either the **/F** switch (which fixes errors on the drive) or the **/R** switch (which locates bad sectors and recovers data)—or run both. This procedure can also help with "Invalid Boot Disk" errors. (Of course, first check that the BIOS/UEFI is booting to the correct drive in the boot priority menu.) If you can fix the drive, it is recommended to back up files right away, as there could be subsequent drive failure.

SFC

System File Checker (SFC) is a Windows utility that checks protected system files. It replaces incorrect versions or missing files with the correct files. SFC can be used to fix problems with Edge/Internet Explorer and other Windows applications. To run SFC, open the Command Prompt and type **sfc** with the appropriate switch. A typical option is **sfc /scannow**, which scans all protected files immediately and repairs files. During this procedure, SFC writes the details of each repair to a file called CBS.log, located in %systemroot%\Logs\ CBS, which can be used to further analyze the system and the integrity of files. Another option is **sfc /verifyonly**, which scans the integrity of files but does not perform a repair. If SFC finds that some files are missing, you might be prompted to reinsert the original operating system disc so the files can be copied to the DLL cache.

> **Note**
>
> %systemroot% is the folder where Windows was installed; by default, it is C:\Windows.

> **ExamAlert**
>
> Know the basic switches for **chkdsk** and **sfc**, such as **chkdsk /F** and **sfc /scannow**.

winver and shutdown

The **winver** command brings up a window that tells you what operating system you are running, the edition, and the build number. It also displays trademark and licensing information. This is one of those commands that you can run from anywhere: at the command line, in the Run prompt, in the Search tool, and so on. An example of the **winver** command is shown in Figure 31.2.

FIGURE 31.2   **An example of the winver command**

The figure shows that this system is running Windows 10 Pro version 21H1, which began to be rolled out in May 2021. However, the availability of a new version doesn't mean that all devices get it at the same time; there might be a delay when receiving an update to Windows (for a variety of reasons). If you so desire, you can attempt to force an update by going to **Windows Settings > Update & Security > Windows Update** and clicking the **Check for updates** button.

In Figure 31.2, you can also see the build number (19043.1288) which is what developers sometimes go by when working deep in Windows. In this case, Windows 10 is also referred to as version 10.0.19043.1288, which is what you would see if you typed the **ver** command in the Command Prompt or the **$psversiontable** command in PowerShell. Try all three! Note that your build number will most likely be different from the one shown here.

> ### Note
>
> Here's an example of a Windows 11 version and build number displayed by using the **winver** command:
>
> ```
> Version 21H2 (OS Build 22000.376)
> ```

shutdown

The **shutdown** command is used to turn off a computer, restart it, send it to hibernate mode, log a person off, and so on. For example, if you want to shut down a computer after a short delay, you can type **shutdown /s**. For an immediate shutdown, you can type **shutdown /p**. The command can also be used programmatically to shut down systems at specific times and provide a pop-up window explaining the reason for the shutdown. This just scratches the surface of the command. Remember that you can get more information about a specific command by using the help system. In this case, by typing **shutdown /?** you can see all of the possible options for the command.

Advanced Commands: gpupdate and gpresult

Let's now look at two advanced commands: **gpupdate** and **gpresult**.

Windows uses a set of policies to define rules that users and computers are effectively forced to follow. These policies can be viewed within the Local Group Policy Editor (**Run > gpedit.msc**) and a subset of that, the Local Security Policy (**Run > secpol.msc**). To properly work with these policies and tools, you should be running Windows Pro edition or higher.

You can also use commands to view and analyze that information. For example, the **gpresult** command displays the Resultant Set of Policy (RSoP) information for a user and computer. (It is designed for remote users/computers.) You can use **gpresult /R** to get some basic information about the local computer, the user, and what policies are running. You can view this information for remote computers and users by using the **/S** switch and the name of the remote system. For example:

```
gpresult /S computername /R
```

where *computername* is whatever the target system's name is. To save the reported information, use the **/x** (for XML) or **/h** (for HTML) parameters.

In many cases, policy changes that were made in the Local Group Policy Editor or Local Security Policy won't take effect until the admin logs off and logs back on. Enter the **gpupdate** command, which can be used by itself or by specifying a remote system. When run, it updates all policies that have been modified on the target computer, without requiring the administrator to log off and log back on.

These commands can be run on Windows workstations or servers. But be very careful when using them. You have to be sure your policy changes are allowed, and you should consider scheduling them to run after work hours.

> **Note**
>
> For more information on **gpresult** and **gpupdate**, see the following sites:
>
> https://docs.microsoft.com/en-us/windows-server/administration/windows-commands/gpresult
>
> https://docs.microsoft.com/en-us/windows-server/administration/windows-commands/gpupdate

> **Note**
>
> I know I just hit you with a lot of commands, but you should try to memorize as many of them as you can! Try them on your computer and write them down to force those little gray cells into action.

Cram Quiz

Answer these questions. The answers follow the last question. If you cannot answer these questions correctly, consider reading this chapter again until you can.

1. Which command can copy multiple files and entire directory trees?
   - ○ **A. copy**
   - ○ **B. cut**
   - ○ **C. paste**
   - ○ **D. robocopy**

2. Which command determines whether protected system files have been overwritten and replaces those files with the original version?
   - ○ **A. chkdsk**
   - ○ **B. md**
   - ○ **C. sfc**
   - ○ **D. xcopy**

3. You need to assign drive letters and make a partition active from the Command Prompt. What of the following will allow you to perform these activities?

- ○ **A.** Disk Management
- ○ **B. format**
- ○ **C. defrag**
- ○ **D. diskpart**

4. You have been tasked with bringing the policies of a Windows 10 computer up to date. You won't be able to log off and back on, and you must use the Command Prompt. Which of the following tools should you use?

- ○ **A. shutdown**
- ○ **B. rd**
- ○ **C. gpupdate**
- ○ **D.** Local Security Policy
- ○ **E. winver**

Cram Quiz Answers

1. **D. robocopy** can copy an entire drive of information with just one command (including switches). **xcopy** could also do the job, but **robocopy** takes its place.

2. **C. sfc** determines whether system files have been overwritten and replaces those files with the original versions. **chkdsk** can check for errors and fix some errors, but it cannot work with system files. **md** is the command used to make a directory. **xcopy** is used to copy large amounts of data to a new location.

3. **D. diskpart** is the command-line counterpart of Disk Management. From the DISKPART> prompt, you can create, delete, and extend volumes; assign drive letters; make a partition active; and so on. The **format** command is used to format storage media to a particular file system, such as NTFS, FAT, or FAT32. **defrag** is the command-line version of the Disk Defragmenter; these tools help make the files on a drive contiguous instead of fragmented.

4. **C.** You should use **gpupdate** to bring the Windows policies up to date without requiring the admin to log off and on again. The **shutdown** command is used to turn off or restart a computer. **rd** is used to remove directories. The Local Security Policy is where you can go to modify many policy settings (such as the password policy), but it is a graphical tool. To enforce the changes made in the Local Security Policy, use the **gpupdate** command. **winver** is used to find out what operating system version you are running.

Oh yeah! Now we're really starting to cook. The command line is what it's all about here. If you are new to the command line, I strongly urge you to review this chapter very carefully before you continue.

CHAPTER 32

Microsoft Command-Line Tools, Part II

This chapter covers a portion of the following A+ 220-1102 exam objective:

▶ **1.2** – Given a scenario, use the appropriate Microsoft command-line tool.

The command-line interface (also known as the CLI) is just so much fun I had to write another chapter about it. So, let's get into the networking side of commands. Now.

Networking Commands

There are many command-line tools that you can use in Windows to help analyze and troubleshoot a computer's network connection; in this section, we delve into several of them. I recommend that you try all the variations of these commands on your computer. Some commands require that you open the PowerShell or Command Prompt as an administrator (elevated mode).

The most commonly used command for analyzing a computer's networking configuration is **ipconfig**. Let's start with that.

ipconfig

The Internet Protocol configuration command, **ipconfig**, displays current TCP/IP network configuration values. This is one of the first tools you should use when troubleshooting network connectivity. When you type **ipconfig**, you get results similar to the following:

```
Windows IP Configuration

Ethernet adapter Local Area Connection:

Connection-specific DNS Suffix . :

Link-Local IPv6 Address. . . . . : fe80::404b:e781:b150:b91a%11

IPv4 Address. . . . . . . . . . . : 192.168.0.100

Subnet Mask . . . . . . . . . . . : 255.255.255.0

Default Gateway . . . . . . . . . : 192.168.0.1
```

ipconfig combined with the **/all** option shows more information, including whether or not DHCP is being used, the DNS server's IP address, and the MAC address. The MAC address is the hexadecimal address that is burned into the ROM of the network adapter. It is a set of six hexadecimal numbers (for example, 00-03-FF-A0-55-16).

> **ExamAlert**
>
> To view additional IP configuration information, such as DNS servers and MAC addresses, use the **ipconfig /all** command.

> **Note**
>
> The **ipconfig** command (and most other commands, for that matter) can also be run from the Search tool or the Run prompt. Just open one of these tools and type **cmd /k ipconfig** to open up a shell and display the results of the command.

The **ipconfig /all** command can offer a lot of information that can help you troubleshoot a problem. For example, if a user cannot connect to any Internet resources, it could be because the gateway address is improperly configured. Remember that the gateway address must be on the same network number as the IP address of the client computer. If a user can't connect to any websites but can connect to other computers on the LAN, it could be that the DNS server address is incorrectly configured. **ipconfig** also tells you whether the client computer's IP address is obtained from a DHCP server or assigned via APIPA and whether it is a private or public address.

ipconfig can also be used to release and renew IP addresses. Sometimes this needs to be done if a computer's IP address is not working properly and you want to obtain a new address from a DHCP server. To release the current IP address, type **ipconfig /release**; to renew, type **ipconfig /renew**.

Finally, if you are having DNS issues (for example, problems connecting to web-sites), you can erase the DNS cache by typing **ipconfig /flushdns**. Check out the various **ipconfig** options by opening the Command Prompt and typing the **ipconfig /?** command. You should try this with every command in this section.

> **Note**
>
> Another way to flush the DNS cache is to issue the command **netsh int ip** in PowerShell. But beware: This completely resets the TCP/IP connection for the network adapter.

ping

ping tests whether another host is available over the network. Using this com-mand is an easy way to see if another host is "alive." Let's say your gateway's IP address is 192.168.0.1. To ping that computer, you would type **ping 192.168.0.1** (as an example) and hopefully get the following output:

```
Pinging 192.168.0.1: with 32 bytes of data:
Reply from 192.168.0.1: bytes=32 time<1ms TTL=64
Reply from 192.168.0.1: bytes=32 time<1ms TTL=64
Reply from 192.168.0.1: bytes=32 time<1ms TTL=64
Reply from 192.168.0.1: bytes=32 time<1ms TTL=64
Ping statistics for 192.168.0.1:
Packets: Sent = 4, Received = 4, Lost = 0 (0% loss),
Approximate round trip times in milli-seconds:
Minimum = 0ms, Maximum = 0ms, Average = 0ms
```

The replies in this case indicate that the host is alive and can be communicated with on the network. Any other message would indicate a problem (for example, a "Request Timed Out" or "Destination Host Unreachable" messages would require further troubleshooting). Keep in mind that if the local computer is configured incorrectly, you might not be able to ping anything! Also watch for the amount of time the ping takes to reply. A longer latency time could indicate network congestion.

> **Note**
>
> *Latency* is the time it takes for sent data packets to be received by a remote computer. Latency increases with distance, type of network connection used, and network congestion. For example, a ping to a computer on the LAN should have very low latency—perhaps less than 1 millisecond (ms). But a ping initiated from a computer in New York City to a computer in Los Angeles over a cable Internet connection might have a latency of 25 ms. This can be a very enlightening piece of the ping results.

You can also use **ping** to test whether a computer has TCP/IP installed properly, even if it isn't wired to the network! To do this, use the **ping 127.0.0.1** command for IPv4 and **ping ::1** for IPv6. These IP addresses, known as *loopback addresses*, are used for testing and are available on every host that has TCP/IP installed. They differ from the IP addresses we talked about previously (for example, 192.168.0.100) in that they work internally. Loopback **ping** commands essentially enable you to ping yourself, meaning you can test the local computer's network connection without a valid IP configuration and without a physical connection to the network. Replies are simulated within the local computer; they prove whether the network adapter and TCP/IP have been installed properly. However, they do not prove whether TCP/IP has been *configured* properly for a particular network.

> **Note**
>
> You can also use the **ping loopback** and **ping localhost** commands, adding **-4** for IPv4 and **-6** for IPv6. However, for testing, pinging the IP address is usually recommended.

> **ExamAlert**
>
> Know how to ping the local loopback IPv4 and IPv6 addresses.

You can also modify the way that **ping** works with options (also known as switches). Six that you should know for the exam are **-t, -n, -l, -a, -4**, and **-6**:

▶ **ping -t:** This pings the host until the command is stopped. Remember that a host is any device or computer that has an IP address. An example of this would be **ping -t 192.168.0.1**. The option can go before or after the IP address. You will keep getting replies (or timeouts) until you stop the command by pressing Ctrl+C or by closing the Command Prompt. This is a great way to test cable connections. After running the command, you can plug and unplug cables and watch the screen to see which cables or ports are live. You can also use this option to monitor a connection over a period of time to discern whether there are many packet drops or whether the connection slows down at certain times.

▶ **ping -n:** This pings a host a specific number of times. For example, the command **ping -n 20 192.168.0.1** would ping that host 20 times and then display the results. This can be a good baselining tool that you can run every day against a router or server and compare the results. (You would probably want to use a higher number than 20.)

▶ **ping -l:** This pings the host, but you can specify the number of bytes per packet to be sent. If you look at the previous ping results, you can see that the default number of bytes is 32, but this can be increased to simulate real data. For example, **ping -l 1500 192.168.0.1** would send four 1500-byte packets to the other host. This can also be beneficial when testing how a server, a router, or another device reacts to larger packet sizes.

▶ **ping -a:** This resolves addresses to hostnames. When pinging an IP address with **-a**, you also see the hostname associated with the IP address.

▶ **ping -4:** This forces the use of IPv4 and results in IPv4-based data. For example, in Windows, if you are running both IPv4 and IPv6 and type a command such as **ping loopback**, your results will by default be IPv6 based and might result in a reply from ::1 (that is, if your system is working properly). But by adding the **-4** option, you force the use of IPv4, so the command **ping -4 loopback** can result in a reply from 127.0.0.1. Try it!

▶ **ping -6:** This forces the use of IPv6 and results in IPv6-based data. For example, a **ping -6 loopback** will result in a reply from ::1.

ExamAlert

Know how to use the **-t, -n, -l, -a, -4**, and **-6** options with **ping**.

These options can be combined as well; for example, **ping -n 450 -l 1500 192.168.0.1** would send 450 pings, each 1500 bytes in size. To create a baseline, you could use this command at a specific time every month, store the results, and then compare them to find possible deficiencies in performance of a server, router, and so on.

tracert and pathping

tracert, short for *traceroute*, builds on **ping** in that it sends packets to destinations beyond the local computer's network. It pings each router along the way between you and the final destination. If you ran the command **tracert example.com**, you would get output like this:

```
PS C:\Windows\System32> tracert example.com
Tracing route to example.com [93.184.216.34] over a maximum of 30
hops:

  1    <1 ms    <1 ms    <1 ms   gateway.localdomain [192.168.0.1]
  2     7 ms    17 ms     8 ms   10.42.13.1
  3     8 ms     8 ms     6 ms   router1.dpro42.net [208.58.XXX.XXX]
  4    11 ms    12 ms    12 ms   router2.dpro42.net [207.17.XXX.XXX]
  5    10 ms     9 ms    11 ms   router3.dpro42.net [207.17.XXX.XXX]
  6    20 ms    11 ms    11 ms   207.17.XXX.XXX
  7    10 ms    10 ms    11 ms   93.184.216.34
Trace complete.
```

> **ExamAlert**
>
> Be able to recognize the output of a **tracert** command!

Some of the names and IP addresses have been changed to remain anonymous. Note in this example that there are three pings per line item, measured in milliseconds (ms). Also note that every line item (hop) contains a router name and IP address. **tracert** starts by sailing through the various routers in the fictitious ISP, dpro42.net. It ends at a server simply named 93.184.216.34, but it could just as easily be a domain name. Try using **tracert** on example.com (or another domain of your choice) to see results based on your location and ISP. Keep in mind that some traces will take longer and will go through additional hops.

If you see any asterisks in the place of the millisecond amounts, you might question whether the router is functioning properly. If **tracert** stops altogether before giving the message Trace Complete, you should check your network documentation to find out which router it stopped at and/or have the appropriate personnel troubleshoot the router. As with **ping**, the **-4** and the **-6** options force IPv4 and IPv6, respectively.

The **tracert /d** command does not resolve IP addresses to hostnames. All names along the way (such as dpro42.net and gateway.localdomain) are shown as their corresponding IP addresses only. Running numeric versions of commands can be faster because there is no name resolution to get in the way. Connecting directly by IP address will always be faster than connecting by name.

Another command similar to **tracert** is **pathping**. One of the differences is that it does not show the three individual pings per hop initially; it instead computes the statistics of the pathping at the end. (You can specify the number of individual pings with the **-q** option, though.) Sometimes, this command might freeze (or *hang*), requiring you to press the Ctrl+C shortcut to break out of the process.

hostname

The **hostname** command simply displays the name of the local computer. Try typing the command **hostname** at the command line, and you will see the name of the system displayed. This is the same hostname that is shown in the Computer Name/Domain Changes dialog box (refer to Figure 30.2 in Chapter 30, "Comparing Windows Editions"). However, you can't *change* the hostname at the command line with the **hostname** command; you have to do it in the GUI either in the Computer Name/Domain Changes dialog box or by going to **Windows Settings > System > About** and clicking on **Rename this PC**. Now, you might say, "Dave! This is a chapter about doing things at the command line! How do I do it?" Okay, since you asked, open PowerShell and type this:

```
rename-computer -newname "name here"
```

Then you need to restart the computer for the changes to take effect. (Or simply add **-restart** to the end of the command to do a restart automatically.)

> **Note**
>
> Programmatically, the hostname is referred to as the %COMPUTERNAME% variable in any Windows system. Developers can use this variable to specify the system's name without knowing the actual hostname! Try the following command:
>
> **echo %COMPUTERNAME%**
>
> in the Command Prompt, and you will see the hostname displayed once again—only this time it's all uppercase characters. We will be covering variables further in Chapter 62, "Basic Scripting, Part I," and Chapter 63, "Basic Scripting, Part II."

As you read the next section, see if you can locate the hostname of the local computer.

netstat

netstat shows the network statistics for the local computer. The default command displays sessions to remote computers. In the following example, I connected to google.com and ran the **netstat** command:

```
Active Connections
TCP Music-Box:1395 8.15.228.165:https ESTABLISHED
TCP Music-Box:1396 he-in-f101.google.com:https ESTABLISHED
```

> **ExamAlert**
>
> Be able to recognize the output of a **netstat** command!

This output shows that there are two established TCP sessions (which are actually to the same website) to google.com. In the local address column, you see the computer's name (Music-Box) and the outbound ports it uses to access the website (1395 and 1396). In the foreign address column, you see an IP address and the protocol used (https); in the second session, you see a hostname followed by the protocol (again https). The protocol used by google.com corresponds to port 443.

This command can tell you a lot about your sessions (for example, whether a session times out or whether it closes completely). To see this information numerically, try using the **-n** option. To see TCP and UDP sessions, use the **-a** option. To see TCP *and* UDP in numeric format, use the **-an** option. To include the executable name for each session shown, use the **-nab** option.

Note that if you said *Music-Box* is the hostname of the local computer in the example above, you are correct!

> **Note**
>
> There are plenty of other **netstat** options. For example, **netstat -e** shows Ethernet statistics. For more information on **netstat**, see https://docs.microsoft.com/en-us/windows-server/administration/windows-commands/netstat.

nslookup

nslookup queries DNS servers to discover DNS details, including the IP addresses of hosts. For example, to find the IP address of example.com, you would type **nslookup example.com**. The resulting output should look something like this:

```
Non-authoritative answer:

Name: example.com

Addresses: 93.184.216.34

 2606:2800:220:1:248:1893:25c8:1946
```

From this output, you now know the IP addresses that correspond to the domain name example.com. The results show an IPv4 address (93.184.216.34) and an IPv6 address (2606:2800 etc.).

nslookup means *name server lookup* and can aid in finding DNS servers and DNS records in a domain as well. If the command **nslookup** is typed by itself, it brings the user into the **nslookup** shell. From here, several commands can be used. To find out more about these commands, type **?** and press Enter. To exit the **nslookup** shell, type **exit**, press Ctrl+C, or press Ctrl+Break. The Linux equivalent of this is **dig**, which can also be installed in Windows as part of the BIND DNS tools (see https://www.isc.org/downloads/). I strongly suggest that you use **dig** whenever possible. You will learn more about **dig** in Chapter 42, "Linux."

net

The **net** command is actually a collection of commands. You can use the **net stop** command to stop a service and the **net start** command to start a service from the command line. In networking, you might use the **net view** command to see which computers are currently available on the network or the **net share** command to share folders for other users to view.

For the exam, you should know the types of **net** commands that enable you to view or create mapped network drives. To view any currently mapped network drives, simply type **net use**. To create a mapped network drive, use the following syntax:

```
net use x: \\computername\sharename
```

where *x*: is the drive letter. (In this case, *x* is a variable; you can use whatever drive letter you want, if it's available, including x!) *computername* is the name of the remote host you want to connect to, and *sharename* is the share that was created on that remote host. You can connect to whatever share you want, as long as you have permissions to do so.

You can even connect to hidden shares—denoted with a $ at the end of the share name. For example, there is a network share on another computer on my network called c$. The following example shows the command to connect to it and the resulting output:

```
net use f: \\Music-Box\c$
The command completed successfully.
```

This example uses f: as the drive letter; the computer connected to is called Music-Box, and the share is c$ (the default hidden share).

For more information on the **net** command, type **net /?**. For more information on the **net use** command, type **net use /?**.

> **ExamAlert**
>
> Know how and why to use the **net use** command!

> **Note**
>
> See the following link for a video demonstrating how to use **net share** and **net use** between two systems: https://dprocomputer.com/?p=864.

Another **net** command listed in the A+ objectives is **net user**. When typed by itself, this command lists the user accounts on the local computer. You can also create accounts from here with the **net user /add %username%** command, where **%username%** is a variable. For example, to create the user account dadams, you would type **net user /add dadams**. This creates a standard user account. In addition, you can activate or deactivate user accounts with the **/active** option or delete accounts with the **/delete** option. There is lots more; check out the command with **/?** for more information or go to the following link: https://docs.microsoft.com/en-us/previous-versions/windows/it-pro/windows-xp/bb490718(v%3dtechnet.10).

Bonus Command: arp

The **arp** command is not listed in the bulleted objectives for the exam, but it is in the acronym list, so let's briefly touch on it. Address Resolution Protocol (ARP) resolves between IP addresses and MAC addresses so that data communications can flow from the operating system to the physical network adapter. Every computer that runs TCP/IP has an ARP table, which is a cache of information including the IP address and MAC address of every other computer that the local system has been in contact with. The **arp** command can be used to display or modify those ARP entries. If you type **arp -a**, you might get results similar to the following:

```
Interface: 192.168.41.202 --- 0x19
  Internet Address       Physical Address       Type
   192.168.41.1          30-b5-c2-b2-59-e6      dynamic
   192.168.41.103        e8-4e-06-69-1a-99      dynamic
   192.168.41.104        00-e0-4c-68-00-e9      dynamic
   192.168.41.201        38-60-77-59-68-58      dynamic
   192.168.41.255        ff-ff-ff-ff-ff-ff      static
   224.0.0.2             01-00-5e-00-00-02      static
```

The local system in this case is 192.168.41.202. Every computer that it has connected to in the recent past is shown. For example, you can see that there has been a connection to 192.168.41.103; that computer's corresponding MAC address is displayed as well. It is shown as a dynamic connection, meaning that it will time out at a specific point, usually when the computer restarts. However, you can have static connections as well, and they won't time out. Default broadcasts are set up this way automatically. Individual static connections can be added to the ARP table with the **-s** parameter. I personally use static connections for connections to servers to reduce the amount of IP-to-MAC resolutions that are done from my system to the systems I administer the most.

Cram Quiz

Answer these questions. The answers follow the last question. If you cannot answer these questions correctly, consider reading this chapter again until you can.

1. Which command shows the path of routers between your computer and a web server?

    ○ **A. ping**

    ○ **B. ipconfig**

    ○ **C. tracert**

    ○ **D. nbtstat**

2. You need to map a network drive to a share named data1 on a computer named Jupiter-Server. You want to use the J: drive letter. Which syntax should you use to do this in the Command Prompt?

    ○ **A. net use J: \\Jupiter-Server\data1**

    ○ **B. net use J \Jupiter-Server\data1**

    ○ **C. net use Jupiter-Server\J\data1**

    ○ **D. net use J: \Jupiter-Server\data1**

3. A user's computer is powered on and appears to work properly. However, the user cannot access any wired network resources, printers, or shared drives. In addition, the user cannot access the Internet. Which of the following commands should you use to troubleshoot the problem?

- ○ **A. netstat**
- ○ **B. net use**
- ○ **C. ping**
- ○ **D. nslookup**

4. A customer is unable to access a network share. However, the customer can access email. You analyze the system and confirm that the customer has the correct permissions to access the share. Which command should you use first to troubleshoot the problem?

- ○ **A. nslookup**
- ○ **B. net use**
- ○ **C. ipconfig**
- ○ **D. ping**

Cram Quiz Answers

1. **C. tracert** is used to run a trace between the local system and a remote destination. It shows all routers along the way. **ping** is used to test connectivity to another system directly. **ipconfig** displays the Internet Protocol configuration of the local computer. **nbtstat** shows the name table cache and services running on the system.

2. **A.** You should use the command **net use J: \\Jupiter-Server\Data1**. All the other answers are incorrect. The Universal Naming Convention (UNC) is \\computername\sharename.

3. **C.** Of the listed answers, the best one is the **ping** command. It will help you to decipher what the problem is. However, consider using **ipconfig /all** before running **ping**. The **netstat** command shows a list of current connections (among other things). Chances are that there are none currently in the scenario. The **net use** command displays and makes connections to remote shares. The **nslookup** command does name resolution between domain names and IP addresses.

4. **B.** Implement the **net use** command so that you can make the connection to the network share. (Of course, you could also do this in File Explorer, but this chapter is about the command line!) Use **nslookup** to resolve domain names to IP addresses or to modify DNS servers. Use **ipconfig** to analyze the system. Use **ping** to test whether another system is "alive" on the network.

That's it for the Windows command line—for now. But keep practicing! Chances are you'll be called on to use it.

CHAPTER 33

Microsoft Operating System Features and Tools, Part I

This chapter covers a portion of the following A+ 220-1102 exam objective:

▶ **1.3** – Given a scenario, use features and tools of the Microsoft Windows 10 operating system (OS).

Now let's move into the graphical side of things. The Windows GUI is popular because users are familiar with it, and for many people, its usage is intuitive—meaning it comes naturally. However, there are a lot of utilities, tools, and features for an administrator to know. In fact, there are so many utilities that I split coverage of this objective into two chapters. In this chapter, we'll be covering the Task Manager and a bunch of administrative tools that you can incorporate into the Microsoft Management Console (MMC). This is super important stuff for the exam, so let's not waste any time.

Task Manager

One simple and effective tool to use when analyzing a computer is the Task Manager. Besides using the Search tool, there are several other ways to open the Task Manager, including

▶ Right-click the taskbar (or Start) and select **Task Manager**.

▶ Press Ctrl+Alt+Del and select **Task Manager**.

▶ Open the **Run** prompt and type **taskmgr**.

▶ Press Ctrl+Shift+Esc. (I'm a keyboard shortcut hound, and this is my favorite way to open the Task Manager.)

The Task Manager enables you to analyze a computer's processor and memory performance in real time; this can be done from the Performance tab, as shown on the left in Figure 33.1, and the Processes tab, shown on the right. You can see on the Performance tab that the CPU usage fluctuates and is currently at 10%. More importantly, the Processes tab shows that the Firefox and Chrome browsers are using the bulk of the memory on that system.

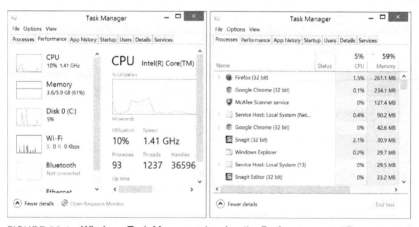

FIGURE 33.1   Windows Task Manager, showing the Performance and Processes tabs

Optimizing a system can be as simple as shutting down programs. This can be done in the Processes tab. But sometimes you need to shut down underlying processes. For example, the Processes tab in Figure 33.1 shows all the processes that are running and the amount of CPU and RAM resources they are using individually. You can stop a process that is hoarding resources by right-clicking it and then selecting **End Task**. (You can also stop processes in the Details tab.) Keep in mind that this method shuts down the process or application only temporarily. If the process or application is designed to do so, it will turn back on when the computer is rebooted.

> **ExamAlert**
>
> Understand how to open the Task Manager, how to read its Performance tab, and how to end processes and applications.

The Task Manager has several other tabs, including Users, Startup, Services, and App History. Let's briefly discuss each of them.

The Users tab shows the resources being used by each user. Normally, on a Windows client computer, it shows only the user who is currently logged in. However, if another user is listed, and that account is using resources, then that user can be signed off from here (by right-clicking the username and selecting **Sign off**). This way, the resources are freed up. For example, if a remote user was connected previously and chose to disconnect instead of logging off, this tab shows that user as "Disconnected," but the user might still be using memory resources if some programs were opened before the user disconnected. This is common with Remote Desktop sessions. There is a difference between *disconnecting* and *logging off*. When you disconnect, the programs and resources are left open, allowing you to reconnect later and continue where you left off; when you log off, the programs are closed, and the resources are freed up.

The Startup tab shows applications in Windows, their status, and their startup impact. "Status" means whether the application is enabled or disabled. If it is enabled, then it will start every time the computer starts. If it is disabled, it won't. You can enable or disable the applications by right-clicking on them. "Startup impact" means how much of the system's resources are being used during the startup process. For example, you might see that Windows Explorer has a low impact, which means it won't use too many resources on that system.

The Services tab displays any services that are available in Windows. Services are underlying programs used by applications and by Windows. There are a great many of them, but you don't need to know them all for the exam. You do need to know how to start and stop them, though. Some run automatically, and others do not. Take the Spooler service (Print Spooler), for instance. This runs when Windows starts up, but in some cases, you might need to stop this service. Simply right-click the service to stop it. From there, you can also start it (run it), or you can do both successively by clicking Restart. This tab shows the process IDs (PIDs), which are numbers associated with the services that are running. (You'll learn more on PIDs later, in Chapters 53 through 56.) While you can start and stop services here, you cannot enable or disable them. To start or stop a service, you need to right-click the service and select **Open Services**. That takes you to the Services console window, where you can start, stop, enable, disable, and more. You can get to the Services console window directly by going to **Run** and typing **services.msc**. (You'll learn more on this later in this chapter.)

The App History tab shows the applications that have run and the CPU and network resources used by each application. This differs from the Processes tab in that it shows cumulatively used resources, not real-time resources.

> **Note**
>
> Work with the Task Manager on your system and get to know the program. You will be using it often.

The MMC and Administrative Tools

An administrator (that's you) can access the Windows administrative tools in a variety of ways:

▶ Use the Microsoft Management Console (MMC), which is the console that houses all the other console windows. It's super-customizable. You'll learn more on the MMC in just a bit.

▶ Select **Start > Windows Administrative Tools**.

▶ Select **Control Panel > All Control Panel Items > Administrative Tools**.

▶ Go to **Run** and type **control admintools**.

> **Note**
>
> For a table of the Run window commands covered in this book (and more), see https://dprocomputer.com/?p=3010.

The MMC

Console windows such as the Device Manager, Event Viewer, and Performance Monitor can be grouped into one super console window known as the Microsoft Management Console (MMC). The MMC acts as a shell for these other console windows. You can also use it to control remote computers in addition to the local computer. And you can control what particular users see by changing the Console Mode. Finally, part of the beauty of the MMC is that it saves everything you add and remembers the last place you worked. To create an MMC window, open the Run prompt or Search tool, type **MMC**, and press Enter. By default, the MMC window is empty.

> **Note**
>
> You will learn quickly that administrative functions should be carried out only by users who have administrative privileges. Even if you have administrative privileges, a pop-up User Account Control (UAC) window appears every time you try to access tools such as the MMC. Simply click **Yes** or **Continue** to open the program. Users who don't have administrative capabilities will either be blocked altogether or won't be able to continue when the UAC window pops up.

To add consoles (known as snap-ins), do the following:

1. On the Menu bar, click **File** and then click **Add/Remove Snap-in**. The Add or Remove Snap-ins window appears.

2. Select the components you want from the left by highlighting them one at a time and clicking the **Add** button. In some cases, you will need to select the local computer or a remote computer. Click **OK** when finished. These snap-ins should now be shown inside the Console Root. Figure 33.2 shows an example of the MMC.

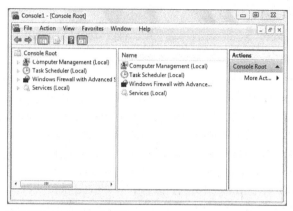

FIGURE 33.2   **The MMC**

3. Save the MMC. By default, this window prompts you to save to the Windows Administrative Tools folder of the user who is currently logged on. For easier retrieval of the MMC, consider saving it to a more accessible folder.

You can now access the console you created by navigating to the folder where you saved it in. I suggest adding a shortcut to it within the Quick Launch for easy access. Or, once again, go to Run, Search, or the command line and type **MMC**. Click **File**, and you should see your console in the history list. Or you can open the specific MMC file directly from Run. For example, if you saved the file as console1.msc in the root of the C: drive, then you type

```
mmc C:\console1.msc
```

The administrative tools discussed in this chapter can be added to the MMC. I suggest you practice using the MMC. It will help your workflow and can be a real time-saver.

Event Viewer

Applications are both a boon and a bane. They serve a purpose, but sometimes they are prone to failure. The operating system itself can cause you grief as well by underperforming, locking up, or causing other intermittent issues. One good tool for analyzing applications and the operating system is the Event Viewer.

The Event Viewer tells a technician a lot about the status of the operating system and programs. It notifies of any informational events or audits, warns about possible issues, and displays errors as they occur. Aside from accessing it from the Administrative Tools folder, you can also access it by typing **eventvwr.msc** in the Run or Search prompts or by right-clicking the **Start** button. Try opening it on your system!

> **Note**
>
> The extension .msc is used for a Microsoft Management console snap-in control file, also known as a Microsoft console window. As mentioned, this and many of the other tools we'll discuss in this chapter can be added to the MMC as snap-ins. I recommend that you add them to your MMC so that you can get to them easily while you are studying.

Figure 33.3 shows an example of the Event Viewer. You can see that this console is a three-pane window. The left pane shows all of the places you might navigate to in the Event Viewer, including Custom Views and Windows Logs. The middle pane shows the details of whatever you click in the left pane. The right pane provides additional actions, which are also available on the menu bar. Many of the console windows use this three-pane design.

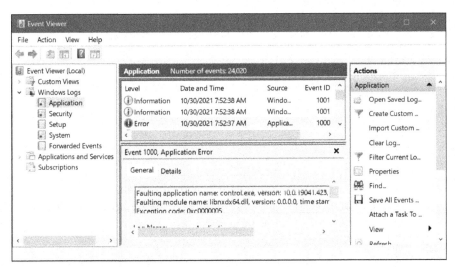

FIGURE 33.3 **The Event Viewer**

In the Event Viewer, information entries, auditing entries, warnings, and errors are stored in several log files within the Windows Logs folder. There are three main log files that you should know for the exam:

▶ **System:** The System log contains information, warnings, and errors about hardware, device drivers, system files, and so on. This log deals primarily with the operating system.

▶ **Application:** The Application log contains events about programs that are built into Windows, such as the Command Prompt and File Explorer, and might contain information about applications that have been loaded since the operating system was installed.

▶ **Security:** The Security log holds information gathered for auditing and security purposes; for example, it might log who logged on to the computer or who tried to gain access to a particular file.

You can view an event listed in a log file by double-clicking it. Events are organized into four categories:

▶ **Information:** These entries, indicated by a letter *i* in a circle, give you basic information about a service starting or an application that ran successfully. The log files are usually chock-full of these entries as part of the normal operation of the system.

▶ **Warning:** These entries, indicated by an exclamation point (!) within a yellow triangle, might be messages telling you an installation did not complete or a service timed out. You should check for these entries now and again and investigate them if nothing else is pressing.

▶ **Error:** These entries, indicated by an exclamation point (!) in a red circle, mean that something failed or has been corrupted, a service failed to start, and so on. Errors should be investigated right away.

▶ **Audit success:** These entries, indicated by a gold-colored key, are located within the Security log file. They track what a user attempts to accomplish within the operating system. For example, if auditing was turned on for a specific folder and a person attempted to access that folder, a security event would be written to the log, especially if the person was denied access. Auditing entries are maintained by organizations so that they can trace what happened to deleted or modified data.

In Figure 33.3, you can see that the Application log is open. In the middle pane, you can see a highlighted application error. It tells you that that there was a faulting application named control.exe. It gives the event ID 1000. Essentially, this means the Windows Control Panel crashed. If this happens once in a while, it might not be a big deal, but if it happens often, you need to troubleshoot the problem further. (You'll see this type of troubleshooting in Chapter 53, "Troubleshooting Microsoft Windows.")

You can find more information about a specific error code by either typing the code number for the event or typing the description into Microsoft Help and Support: https://support.microsoft.com. You never know when an error might occur, so you should review the Event Viewer logs regularly. You can erase an entire log by right-clicking the log file (for example, System) and selecting **Clear Log**. The program asks if you want to save the log for future viewing. By right-clicking a log and selecting **Properties**, you can modify the maximum size of the log and disable logging altogether.

> **ExamAlert**
>
> Be able to describe the Event Viewer's System, Application, and Security log files as well as the information, warning, error, and audit success events.

Task Scheduler

The Task Scheduler can run particular programs, send emails, or display messages at scheduled times designated by the user. You can open it from the Administrative Tools folder or the Search tool, and you can also open it by going to **Run** and typing **taskschd.msc**.

Once in the Task Scheduler, you can set up basic scheduling, specify certain conditions and triggers that cause tasks to run, and tell the Task Scheduler which actions to take when a task starts. Plus, there are a bunch of built-in preprogrammed tasks in the Task Scheduler Library—from memory diagnostics to registry backups. Instead of re-creating the wheel, consider using one of these tasks to automate processes. Some of these built-in tasks are enabled by default. Try creating some tasks yourself, such as memory diagnostic, registry backup, and time synchronization.

Device Manager

A computer probably has a dozen or more devices that all need love and attention. Taking care of a computer means managing these devices. The primary tool a technician uses to manage devices is the Device Manager.

There are a few ways to open the Device Manager:

▶ Use the Administrative Tools folder or the Search tool.

▶ Select **Settings > System > About** (and other locations in Settings).

▶ Use the Control Panel (in icons mode).

▶ Right-click **Start** and select **Device Manager**.

▶ Open the **Run** prompt and type **devmgmt.msc**.

When the Device Manager opens, as shown in Figure 33.4, notice that there are categories for each type of device. By expanding any one of these categories, you can see the specific devices that reside in your computer.

FIGURE 33.4   **Device Manager**

By right-clicking a specific device, you can update its driver; enable or disable it; uninstall it altogether; check for any hardware changes; or access additional properties, such as the driver details and resources used by the device. Figure 33.4 shows the menu that appears when you right-click a network adapter. These are the standard options, but you might have more or fewer options, depending on the device you right-click.

ExamAlert

Know how to access the properties of a device, install drivers, and enable/disable devices in the Device Manager.

Some drivers are installed/updated through .exe files that are downloaded from manufacturer websites. Others are installed from within the Device Manager;

it can search for drivers automatically, or you can manually install a driver by browsing for the correct file (often a file with an .inf extension). Windows attempts to install drivers automatically when it recognizes that a device has been added to the system. Usually, however, it is recommended that you use the media that came with the device or that you download the latest version of the driver from the manufacturer's website, especially when dealing with video, audio, and storage controller drivers.

> **Note**
>
> Device Manager troubleshooting is covered in Chapter 53.

Certificate Manager

The Certificate Manager displays all security certificates that are installed in Windows. Certificates help secure your applications and connections to websites. You can open the Certificate Manager from the Administrative Tools folder or by going to **Run** and typing **certmgr.msc**. We'll discuss this tool further in Chapter 43, "Physical Security," and Chapter 44, "Logical Security."

Local Users and Groups

You can access the Local Users and Groups utility from the Administrative Tools folder or by going to **Run** and typing **lusrmgr.msc**.

While you can add users within Settings or the Control Panel, Local Users and Groups is where you go if you want to take more control of user account management. From here, you can add users, change passwords, group users together, or take advantage of built-in Windows groups such as Backup Operators and Performance Monitor Users. We'll look at Local Users and Groups in Chapter 47, "Windows Security Settings."

Performance Monitor

There are several tools you can use to track the performance of a Windows-based computer. Performance Monitor is an extensive program that can track how much your devices are utilized, such as the percentage of the processor that is used or how much RAM is currently being accessed. Performance Monitor uses real-time graphs to track usage and can log the information for later viewing. It can be accessed from the Administrative Tools folder or by going to **Run** and typing **perfmon.msc**. Figure 33.5 shows an example.

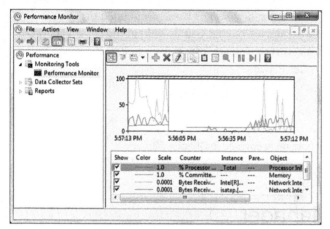

FIGURE 33.5 **Performance Monitor in Windows**

By working with Performance Monitor, you can track the usage of any device in a computer (known as an *object*) using a variety of measurements (known as *counters*). By default, this screen tracks only the CPU. By clicking the + sign toward the top of the window, you can add devices to track. Figure 33.5 shows that I added the default counters for memory and the network adapter card. The highest spikes are from the network adapter, which is sending and receiving a lot of data over the Internet. The second-highest levels are from the processor, which is running seven real-time applications simultaneously.

Information can be viewed in different formats, such as line charts and histograms, and can also be viewed and saved in Report view. Information can be exported as well. Any objects that are added in this program are not saved when you close the window, but you can configure the program so that it saves your additions. To do so, just add the Performance Monitor snap-in to your MMC. The MMC saves its contents and remembers the last place you were working. This works great if you will be analyzing the same things day in and day out.

Performance Monitor (and similar Windows applications) can tell you a lot about the functionality of your computer. When troubleshooting why a certain piece of hardware isn't living up to its promise, Performance Monitor can be invaluable.

> **Note**
>
> Other tools that can be used to track resource usage include the Resource Monitor
> (**Run > resmon.exe**) and the Performance tab of the Task Manager, though these
> are not as thorough as Performance Monitor, nor do they have the ability to save the
> tracked resource usage.

Group Policy Editor and Local Security Policy

The Group Policy Editor is where you make the rules—or configure the rules put forth by your organization. The Group Policy Editor is used to configure rules for a computer system and its users. You can access it by going to **Run** and typing **gpedit.msc**. When it opens, the title bar of the console should read Local Group Policy Editor.

> **Note**
>
> If you want to add the Group Policy Editor to your MMC, go to **File > Add/Remove
> Snap-in**, and then click **Group Policy Object Editor** and click **Add**. For the Group
> Policy Object, you will see Local Computer. Leave that as is and click **Finish**.

When you open the Group Policy Editor, you see Local Computer Policy, which has two main sections—Computer Configuration and User Configuration—each with Software Settings, Windows Settings, and Administrative Templates. As you can imagine, there are hundreds of settings here.

One section that you will probably use often is Local Security Policy. You can access this section in three ways:

▶ In the Group Policy Editor, navigate to **Computer Configuration > Windows Settings > Security Settings**.

▶ Open it from the Administrative Tools folder.

▶ Access **Run** and type **secpol.msc**.

In Local Security Policy, you can configure policies for passwords, account lockout, encryption keys, software restriction, and much, much more. I use Local Security Policy so much that I usually add it as a snap-in to the MMC.

But remember, the content within the Local Security Policy is only a subset of the entire Local Group Policy Editor content. We'll be revisiting both of these in the security section of this book.

Services

The Services console window is another place where you can go to start, stop, and restart services such as the Print Spooler or Windows Defender Firewall. You can access it directly from the Administrative Tools folder and from **Run > services.msc**. For example, if the Windows Defender Firewall service is interfering with another application, you can stop the service from the Services console window and see if that fixes the problem (at least temporarily). In the Services console, it's known as Windows Defender Firewall. You can also stop the service in the Task Manager, as mentioned earlier. In that case, you can search for Windows Defender Firewall (shown in the second column) or mpssvc (shown in the first column).

You can also configure a service's startup type to be automatic, manual, or disabled. This configuration is persistent—meaning the startup type will remain every time the system reboots. It's important to understand the difference between starting/stopping services and enabling/disabling services. Essentially, starting/stopping is not persistent, whereas enabling/disabling is persistent (for the most part). You'll work with the Services console window more in the Windows troubleshooting section of the book.

Bonus Tool: Computer Management

We have already discussed a lot of tools. One tool that groups many of them together is Computer Management. It has many utilities loaded into one nice little console window, including the Task Scheduler, Event Viewer, Local Users and Groups, Device Manager, Services, and Disk Management. If you plan on using more than one of these tools on a consistent basis, consider using the Computer Management console window.

There are a few ways to open this window:

- ► Use the Administrative Tools folder.
- ► Open the **Run** prompt and type **compmgmt.msc**.
- ► Right-click **Start** and then click **Computer Management**.

You can also add Computer Management to your MMC. It's one of the first things I do with a new Windows system. By using Computer Management and the MMC, you can increase your productivity when working in Windows.

This chapter does not cover all of the administrative tools yet, but you will learn about more of them as you progress through the book.

Cram Quiz

Answer these questions. The answers follow the last question. If you cannot answer these questions correctly, consider reading this chapter again until you can.

1. Which of the following do you type in the Run prompt to open the Device Manager?

   ○ **A. mmc**

   ○ **B. secpol.msc**

   ○ **C. cmd**

   ○ **D. devmgmt.msc**

2. Which of the following would you use to track the percentage of resources being used?

   ○ **A. devmgmt.msc**

   ○ **B. eventvwr.msc**

   ○ **C. compmgmt.msc**

   ○ **D. perfmon.msc**

3. Where can a user go to start and stop services In WIndows? (Select all that apply.)

   ○ **A. gpedit.msc**

   ○ **B.** Task Manager

   ○ **C. services.msc**

   ○ **D.** Command Prompt

4. Which log file in the Event Viewer contains information concerning auditing?

   ○ **A.** System

   ○ **B.** Application

   ○ **C.** Local Users and Groups

   ○ **D.** Security

5. Which tool can run particular programs at times designated by the user?

   - ○ **A.** Services
   - ○ **B.** Task Scheduler
   - ○ **C.** Event Viewer
   - ○ **D.** Task Manager

Cram Quiz Answers

1. **D. devmgmt.msc** is the Microsoft console window known as Device Manager. **mmc** opens up a new blank Microsoft Management Console. **secpol.msc** opens the Local Security Policy window. **cmd** opens the Command Prompt.

2. **D. perfmon.msc** (or **perfmon.exe**) opens the Performance Monitor utility, which is used to graphically track the resources that are being used on a computer, such as CPU, RAM, and so on. You could also use **Task Manager > Performance** to track resource usage (but without the ability to save the data), as well as the Resource Monitor. **devmgmt.msc** opens the Device Manager. **eventvwr.msc** opens the Event Viewer. **compmgmt.msc** opens the Computer Management console window.

3. **B, C, and D.** You can start/stop services in **Task Manager > Services**; in the Services console window (services.msc); and in the PowerShell/Command Prompt by using the **net start**, **net stop**, **sc start**, and **sc stop** commands. **gpedit.msc** brings up the Group Policy Editor in Windows.

4. **D.** The Security log contains information about auditing and other security events. The System log contains information about the OS and system files. The Application log contains information about built-in Windows programs and some third-party programs. Local Users and Groups is an administrative tool you can use to add people and systems to the local computer.

5. **B.** The Task Scheduler can run particular programs at scheduled times designated by the user. The Services console window is where you go to start, stop, and restart services. The Event Viewer is used to find messages about the system, applications, and security developments. The Task Manager is used to analyze the performance of a system and view the applications and services that are running.

Marvelous! This is a pretty power-packed chapter. You are doing very well. Be sure to review your notes, take a break, and then continue on!

CHAPTER 34

Microsoft Operating System Features and Tools, Part II

This chapter covers a portion of the following A+ 220-1102 exam objective:

▶ **1.3** – Given a scenario, use features and tools of the Microsoft Windows 10 operating system (OS).

There is much to discuss when it comes to Windows features and tools. That's why I split coverage of this objective into two chapters. In this chapter, we'll complete the objective by covering Disk Management and a whole bunch of system utilities. Onward!

> **ExamAlert**
>
> This portion of **Objective 1.3** concentrates on Disk Management and additional tools (such as Resource Monitor, System Configuration, and Regedit).

Disk Management

The information in this section applies to working with new drives that are designated for operating system installation, as well as drives that have already been installed to. Either way, the concepts of partitioning and formatting remain the same. Regardless of what you are doing with a drive, the proper order for drive preparation is to partition the drive, format it, and then copy files to your heart's delight. However, sometimes you might also need to initialize additional drives within Windows; this would be done before partitioning. All of these things can be done within the Disk Management program.

The Disk Management Utility

The Disk Management utility is a GUI-based application for analyzing and configuring storage drives. You access it from **Run > diskmgmt.msc** or from within Computer Management. You can do a lot with this tool, including the following:

▶ **Initialize a new drive:** A secondary drive installed in a computer might not be seen by File Explorer immediately. To make it accessible, locate the drive (for example, it might be referred to as Disk 1), right-click on the name of the disk, and then select **Initialize Disk**. When you install an OS to the only drive in the system, it is initialized automatically.

▶ **Create a volume:** Windows generally uses the term *volume*, but you will also see the terms *partition* and *logical drive*. To create a volume, right-click the area with the black header (which identifies it as unallocated), as shown in Figure 34.1.

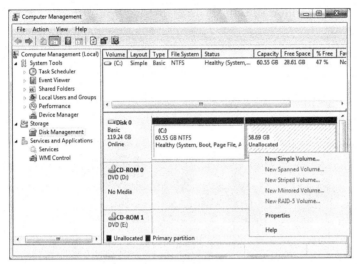

FIGURE 34.1 **Creating a volume within unallocated disk space**

▶ **Format a volume:** When formatting a volume, select the file system (usually NTFS) and whether to do a quick format. Remember that quick format is usually the way to go, but if you leave this option unchecked (for a full format), it will take much longer and could reduce the life span of the drive. When you format a partition, you must select a drive letter, such as C: or E: or F:. You can change drive letters in the future, but it's a good idea to plan them early on. You can use up to Z:, but you probably won't need to; regardless, keep a few drive letters open in the case that you need to map a network drive in the future.

> **Note**
>
> WARNING: ALL DATA WILL BE ERASED during the format procedure.

▶ **Make a partition active:** A partition needs to be set to active if you want to install an operating system to it.

▶ **Convert a basic disk to dynamic:** Basic disks can have only simple volumes or regular partitions/logical drives. If you want to create a spanned, striped, mirrored, or RAID 5 volume, you need to convert the disk to dynamic. This is done by right-clicking the drive where it says Disk 0 or Disk 1, for example, and selecting **Convert to Dynamic Disk**. It's highly recommended that you back up your data before attempting this configuration.

▶ **Extend, shrink, or split a volume:** You can extend, shrink, or split a volume if you have converted it to a dynamic disk. Just about any volume can be shrunk or split, but to extend a volume, you need available unallocated space on the drive. By shrinking a volume that takes up the entire drive, you can also ultimately split that partition into two pieces, which gives you a way to better organize where the OS is stored and where the data files are stored.

ExamAlert

There is, technically, a difference between a partition and a volume. A partition is a logical division of a drive. A volume is any space among one *or more* drives that receives a drive letter.

You can also see the drive at the top of the window shown in Figure 34.1, along with its status. For example, the C: partition is healthy. You also see that it is a System partition, which tells you that the OS is housed there. It also shows the capacity of the drive, the free space, and the percentage of the drive used. What's more, this section tells you if the drive is basic or dynamic or if it has failed. In some cases, you might see "foreign" status. This means that a dynamic disk has been moved from another computer (with another Windows operating system) to the local computer, and it cannot be accessed properly. To fix this and access the drive, add the drive to your computer's system configuration. This is done by right-clicking the drive and then clicking **Import Foreign Disks**. Any existing volumes on the foreign drive become visible and accessible when you import the drive.

Mount Points and Mounting a Drive

You can "mount" drives in Disk Management. A *mounted drive* is a drive that is mapped to an empty folder within a volume that has been formatted as NTFS. Instead of using drive letters, mounted drives use drive paths. This is a good solution when you need to work with disc or OS images. It's also helpful in the uncommon case that you need more than 26 drives in your computer (because you are not limited to the letters in the alphabet). Mounted drives can also provide more space for temporary files and can allow you to move folders to different drives if space runs low on the current drive. To mount a drive:

1. Right-click the partition or volume you want to mount and select **Change Drive Letters and Paths**.

2. In the displayed window, click **Add**.

3. Browse to the *empty* folder you want to mount the volume to and click **OK** for both windows.

To remove the mount point, just go back to Disk Management, right-click the mounted volume, select **Change Drive Letters and Paths**, and then select **Remove**.

Remember that the folder you want to use as a mount point must be empty, and it must be within an NTFS volume.

Storage Spaces

Storage Spaces enables a Windows user to virtualize storage by grouping physical drives into storage pools and then creating virtual drives called *storage spaces* from the available capacity in the storage pools. The physical drives (or arrays of drives) need to be SATA or Serial Attached SCSI (SAS). The Storage Spaces tool can be accessed by typing **spaces** in the Search field or by going to **Control Panel > System and Security > Storage Spaces**. From here, multiple drives can be selected and used collectively as a "pool." From within a pool, you can then create a storage space. There are four main types of storage spaces that can be selected:

▶ **Simple:** This is similar to RAID 0 and has no fault tolerance.

▶ **Two-way mirror:** This is similar to RAID 1 mirroring.

▶ **Three-way mirror:** This is similar to RAID 10.

▶ **Parity:** This is similar to RAID 5.

The concept is similar to RAID in that you are looking to either increase performance or, more likely, fault tolerance. But remember: A hardware-based RAID solution is usually the more effective option, but it depends on your environment. If you use Storage Spaces, consider downloading the DISKSPD utility (or finding a similar tool), which can test the speed and efficiency of the storage space array. This can help you to verify quantitatively whether your array is working at peak performance. You can find instructions for how to install and run DISKSPD at https://docs.microsoft.com/en-us/azure-stack/hci/manage/diskspd-overview.

Disk Cleanup

The Disk Cleanup program is used to remove temporary Internet files, downloaded program files, the Recycle Bin, and more. It is located within the Administrative Tools folder and can be opened from the Run prompt by typing **cleanmgr.exe**. Simply select the drive you want to clean up and then select the items you want to remove (permanently) from the computer by checking them. You can also remove cached system files—by clicking the button of the same name—including Windows Update cleanup (which can be substantial), Microsoft Defender Antivirus files, and Windows upgrade log files. A disk cleanup should be performed according to your organization's policies—which could specify once per week or once per month, for example. Note that the newer Storage Spaces is intended as the replacement for Disk Cleanup; you'll learn more about it in Chapter 36, "Windows Settings."

Optimize Drives/Disk Defragmenter

When it comes to hard disk drives (HDDs), data can easily get jumbled. Over time, data is written to a drive and subsequently erased, over and over again, and gaps are left in the drive space. New data will sometimes be written to multiple areas of a drive in a broken or fragmented fashion by filling in any blank areas. When this happens, the drive must work much harder to find the data it needs—spinning more and starting and stopping more (in general, more mechanical movement). The more a drive has to access this fragmented data, the shorter its life span becomes due to mechanical wear and tear. Also, the computer will run more slowly and will continue to get worse until the problem is fixed. A common indicator of this is a drive LED constantly showing activity. When this happens, you need to rearrange the file sectors so that they are contiguous—that is, you need to defragment!

Defragmenting a drive can be done with Microsoft's Optimize Drives utility, via the command-line utility **defrag.exe**, or with third-party programs. The Optimize Drives utility is actually listed within the Administrative Tools folder in Windows as Defragment and Optimize Drives, but when it opens, the title simply says Optimize Drives. You can also search for the utility by typing **defragment** in the Search field or open it directly via **Run > dfrgui.exe**.

This program can be used to analyze your drives for fragmentation, remove fragmentation, and schedule periodic examinations. You can also access this utility by right-clicking a volume in File Explorer, selecting **Properties**, clicking the **Tools** tab, and finally clicking **Optimize**. The ultimate goal with this tool is to make the data contiguous—to move and reorganize it so that it is not fragmented—or at least not *as* fragmented.

If you are using the Disk Defragmenter program, you need 15% free space on the volume you want to defrag. If you have less than that, you need to force the operation by using the command-line option **defrag -f**.

> **ExamAlert**
>
> Know how to access the Optimize Drives/Disk Defragmenter utility in Windows and know the **defrag** command in the Command Prompt.

When you initiate a defrag, it can take a while, so it's best to do this off-hours. After it completes, a restart is recommended.

Additional Windows Tools

There are more tools and programs in Windows than you can shake a stick at. In this section, we'll cover some of the important ones for the exam. But remember, don't be a sheep! Use the right tool for the job, even if it might be a different one than everyone else is using.

System Information/msinfo32

The System Information tool is used for system and device analysis. You can access it by opening the Run prompt and typing **msinfo32.exe**. (Typing **.exe** actually isn't necessary by default.) Using this tool, you can view and analyze information about the hardware components, the software environment, and the hardware resources used, but you cannot make any changes. You can view this information for the local computer and for remote computers as well by typing the name or IP address of the system you want to analyze.

Resource Monitor

The Resource Monitor tool is a handy tool that displays information about the hardware on a system and how the OS and software are using that hardware. It gives more information than the Task Manager but is not as complicated as Performance Monitor. Everything you commonly want to see is summarized nicely in the Overview tab, as shown in Figure 34.2. You can access the Resource Monitor from the Administrative Tools folder or by selecting **Run > resmon.exe**. You can also open it from the Performance tab of the Task Manager.

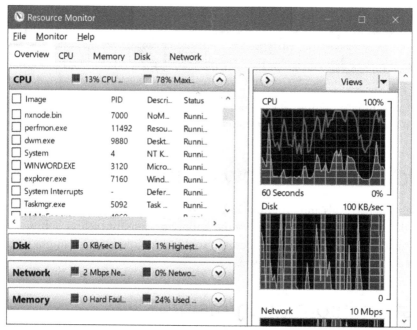

FIGURE 34.2 **The Resource Monitor tool**

In the figure, you can see that the Overview tab displays the CPU information by default. This includes processes that are running such as WINWORD.EXE (Microsoft Word, which I'm using to write this chapter), perfmon.exe (the Performance Monitor utility, which I also have open), and explorer.exe (the Windows GUI itself). It also shows the process ID (PID) and the status of each process. Similar displays are listed under Disk, Network, and Memory. On the right in the figure are graphical charts for CPU, Disk, Network, and Memory. So, you can see that the Resource Monitor gives you a lot of information in a nice, condensed space. Try it out.

System Configuration/MSConfig

MSConfig is the commonly used name for the System Configuration tool. It can help you analyze and troubleshoot various things, from operating system startup issues to application and service problems. Open MSConfig from the Administrative Tools folder or by selecting **Run** > **msconfig**.

System Configuration is an excellent troubleshooting tool that has multiple tabs:

- ▶ **General:** You can use this tab to configure the system for diagnostic or selective startup. This helps you troubleshoot devices or services that are failing.

- ▶ **Boot:** You can use this tab to modify OS bootup settings (such as using Safe boot), log the boot process, and boot without video. If you have multiple operating systems, you can change the order and choose which one to set as the default. Also, clicking the **Advanced options** button lets you choose things such as how much memory you want to use and what port to use if you need to output debugging information.

- ▶ **Services:** This tab lists the services and the current status of each one. You can enable or disable them from this tab (it requires a computer restart). However, you can't start or stop them. To do that, you need to go to the Task Manager or the Services console window, or you can do it from within the PowerShell/Command Prompt. The beauty of this tab is that it allows you to much more quickly enable/disable services than you can by using other options in Windows.

- ▶ **Startup:** In Windows 10/11, the Startup tab still exists but displays "To manage Startup items, use the Startup section of Task Manager" and provides a link to open the Task Manager.

- ▶ **Tools:** This tab lists a lot of the common utilities you might use in Windows and allows you to launch them. As a launching point for programs you use a lot (Task Manager, PowerShell, System Properties, Command Prompt, and so on), this tab can be a real time saver.

MSConfig is a time saver when you're changing boot settings, working with services, and troubleshooting the system. One caution: Be sure to reset MSConfig to the regular settings when you finish using it. For example, if a user complains about a system starting in Safe boot every time or other similar problems in which the user doesn't have full access to the system, MSConfig might need to be reconfigured to Normal startup on the General tab.

ExamAlert

Be able to open MSConfig and identify what each of the tabs is used for.

The Windows Registry

Left this one for last! The Windows registry is a database that stores the settings for Windows. It contains hardware and software information and user settings. If you cannot make the modifications that you want in the Windows GUI and don't want to use the command line, the registry is the place to go. To modify settings in the registry, use the Registry Editor, which can be opened from the Administrative Tools folder or by typing **regedit.exe** at the Run prompt. This displays a window like the one shown in Figure 34.3.

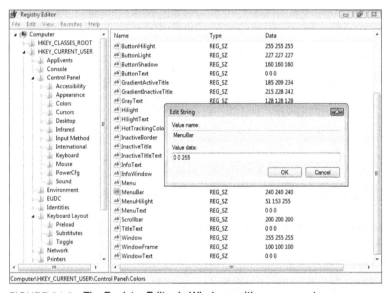

FIGURE 34.3   **The Registry Editor in Windows with an open entry**

The registry is divided into several sections, known as *hives*, each of which begins with the letters HKEY. Table 34.1 describes the five visible hives in the Registry Editor.

TABLE 34.1   **Description of Registry Hives in Windows**

Registry Hive	Description
HKEY_CLASSES_ROOT	Stores information about applications' file associations and Object Linking and Embedding (OLE).
HKEY_CURRENT_USER	Stores settings that concern the currently logged-on user. It is common to make changes in this hive.
HKEY_LOCAL_MACHINE	Stores hardware and software settings that are specific to the computer. This is where the bulk of a PC technician's registry edits are made. One example of data stored here is the programs that run when the OS starts.
HKEY_USERS	Stores data corresponding to all users who have ever logged on to the computer.
HKEY_CURRENT_CONFIG	Contains information that is gathered every time the computer starts up.

Hives are also known as keys, and they contain other keys and subkeys. This forms the organizational system for the registry. It is similar to folders and subfolders within File Explorer. However, the registry does not store actual data files; it stores settings. Inside the keys and subkeys are registration entries that contain the actual settings. These can be edited, or new entries can be created. The types of entries include

▶ String values, which are used for decimal numbers

▶ Binary values, which are used for binary entries

▶ DWORD and QWORD entries, which are used for binary and hexadecimal entries

▶ Multistring values, which can contain a variety of information

Registry hive data is stored in \%systemroot%\System32\Config. For example, a complete copy of the HKEY_CURRENT_CONFIG hive data is stored as the SYSTEM file (with no extension.)

Many users fear the registry, but a technician need not. Just follow a couple simple rules: Back up the registry before making changes and don't make modifications or additions until you have a thorough understanding of the entry you are trying to modify or add.

> **Note**
>
> Don't forget, I made a table of Run commands for you, which you can find at https://dprocomputer.com/?p=3010. For example, **regedit.exe** opens the Registry Editor.

Cram Quiz

Answer these questions. The answers follow the last question. If you cannot answer these questions correctly, consider reading this chapter again until you can.

1. You are preparing to troubleshoot a system that is having some driver issues. Which of the following tools should you use to configure the system to boot safely?

   ○ **A.** Event Viewer

   ○ **B.** Resource Monitor

   ○ **C. msinfo32**

   ○ **D.** System Configuration

2. You have been tasked with repairing a magnetic-based hard drive that is running sluggishly. Which of the following tools should you use to fix the problem? (Select the best answer.)

   ○ **A.** Disk Management

   ○ **B.** Optimize Drives

   ○ **C.** Storage Spaces

   ○ **D.** Mount point

3. What is HKEY_LOCAL_MACHINE considered to be?

   ○ **A.** A registry entry

   ○ **B.** A subkey

   ○ **C.** A string value

   ○ **D.** A hive

4. What must you do first to a basic disk to create spanned, striped, mirrored, or RAID 5 volumes in Disk Management?

   ○ **A.** Extend it

   ○ **B.** Shrink it

   ○ **C.** Split it

   ○ **D.** Initialize it

   ○ **E.** Convert it to dynamic

Cram Quiz Answers

1. **D.** Use the System Configuration utility (MSConfig) to configure the system to boot safely by going to the **Boot** tab and checking the **Safe boot** option, as shown in Figure 34.4. In the figure, it is configured as Minimal (the default), meaning that the system will boot with a minimal set of drivers and programs; however, there are several other options listed there. Make sure you go through the Windows utilities and all the tabs. Know what everything does!

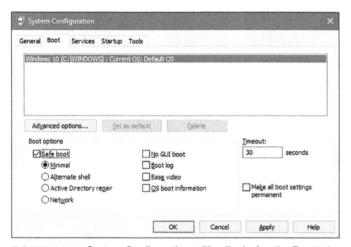

FIGURE 34.4 **System Configuration utility displaying the Boot tab**

The Event Viewer is a tool you can use to review Windows logs, including informational entries, warnings, and errors. The Resource Monitor is an analysis tool for hardware on your system; it's more detailed than the Task Manager but less detailed (and easier to use) than Performance Monitor. The System Information tool (msinfo32) provides non-configurable information about hardware components and the software environment.

2. **B.** Use the Optimize Drives (Disk Defragmenter) utility. This utility attempts to defragment the drive and place the files in a contiguous order so that the hard disk drive (HDD) doesn't behave so sluggishly. Of course, there could be other causes for the poor hard drive performance, such as too many applications at startup, malware, capacity issues, and so on. Disk Management is where you go to configure the storage drive but not to repair it—at least not directly. Storage Spaces is used to build software-based drive arrays. A mount point is a drive that is mapped to an empty folder; it is not a utility.

3. **D.** HKEY_LOCAL_MACHINE is one of the five visible hives that can be modified from within the Registry Editor. This hive stores hardware and software settings that are specific to the computer (for example TCP/IP settings).

4. **E.** Convert the disk to dynamic. Once this is done, the volume can be extended, shrunk, or split. You initialize a drive if it is not recognized by Windows immediately—for example, if it is a new or foreign drive that has been installed to a computer that already had Windows functioning.

Absolutely fantastic. It's important to take your time so that the concepts can sink in properly. In essence, go slowly…but efficiently. Review and take a break before you move on to the next chapter. Great work so far!

CHAPTER 35

Windows Control Panel Utilities

This chapter covers the following A+ 220-1102 exam objective:

▶ **1.4** – Given a scenario, use the appropriate Microsoft Windows 10 Control Panel utility.

In Windows 10 there are two main configuration areas: the Control Panel and the newer Settings (covered in Chapter 36, "Windows Settings"). Over time, Microsoft has been moving away from the Control Panel and more toward Settings; however, the Control Panel is still a valid place for administrators to configure some things in Windows.

In this chapter, we'll be discussing some of the utilities that are stored in the Windows Control Panel, and we'll be digging through a bunch of dialog boxes and other utility windows. Take some time to look at your Windows system's Control Panel and familiarize yourself with the various icons that are displayed—in Category mode and in icons mode. Let us begin.

> **Note**
>
> Some of the items listed in this CompTIA A+ objective are covered elsewhere in the book.
>
> As always, I highly recommend opening and working on programs and utilities within a virtual machine or on a system that is located on an isolated test network (or both!).

> **ExamAlert**
>
> **Objective 1.4** concentrates on the following Control Panel utilities: Internet Options, Devices and Printers, Programs and Features, Network and Sharing Center, System, Windows Defender Firewall, Mail, Sound, User Accounts, Device Manager, Indexing Options, Administrative Tools, File Explorer Options, Power Options, and Ease of Access.

Opening and Viewing the Control Panel Utilities

The Control Panel is where an administrator can go to make system configuration changes, such as making connections to networks, installing, or modifying new hardware, and so on. The Control Panel can be opened in a variety of ways, including

- ▶ Navigate to **Start > Windows System > Control Panel**.
- ▶ Type **control** in the Search field or Run prompt.

By default, the Control Panel shows up in Category view. For example, in Windows 10, System and Security is a category. To see all the individual Control Panel icons, click the drop-down arrow next to **View by: Category**, and then select either **Large icons** or **Small icons**. By doing so, you change the path to **Control Panel > All Control Panel Items**, which you will be using for the rest of this chapter.

Get used to working in the Control Panel but keep in mind that for Windows 10, some of the icons and configurations have been moved to the Settings area. Be ready to operate these tools—for the exam and for the real world.

ExamAlert

The CompTIA A+ exams expect you to know the individual icons in the Control Panel. In Windows, this is also referred to as All Control Panel Items. Study them!

You will see a few dozen items within the Control Panel when you open it as All Control Panel Items, otherwise known as icons mode. Let's cover some of them now.

Internet Options

Internet Options is where you go if you want to make configuration changes for Internet Explorer (IE); however, Internet Explorer has been replaced by Edge (which, for the most part, has its own settings), and many organizations use other browsers. It's on the CompTIA objectives though, so let's cover it at least briefly.

If you open the Internet Options applet in the Windows Control Panel, it brings up the Internet Properties dialog box. You can also open it by going to **Run** and typing **inetcpl.cpl**. Here you see seven tabs: General, Security, Privacy, Content, Connections, Programs, and Advanced. If you need to configure Internet Explorer to open a certain home page or use a specific certificate, these tabs are where you need to go. Another example is special network connections, such as proxy-based connections, which you can configure in the Connections tab. But remember that these settings are specific to the Internet Explorer browser, which is end-of-life (EOL) in June 2022.

Note

To configure settings in the newer Edge browser, open the browser and type **edge://settings** in the address bar.

These are the tabs in Internet Options:

▶ **General:** In this tab, you can set the home page (or pages), configure how pages are displayed, delete the browsing history, and change the appearance of the browser.

▶ **Security:** Here you can create and modify security zones—including the Internet—and change the security levels for each zone.

▶ **Privacy:** In this tab, you can block or allow specific websites (domains) and enable/configure the pop-up blocker.

▶ **Content:** Use this tab to find out what security certificates have been installed that the browser can use and to import new certificates. You can get more in-depth information about certificates in the Certificate Manager (certmgr.msc). In this tab, you can also change the setting for AutoComplete, which suggests full words and phrases based on the first several letters that you type into the URL bar and text fields.

▶ **Connections:** Here you can set up different connections to the Internet, including broadband and dial-up, and manage LAN settings, including the ability to connect to websites via a proxy server.

▶ **Programs:** Use this tab to select how links will be opened, manage add-ons, use an HTML editor, and set programs and associations with Internet Explorer/Edge.

▶ **Advanced:** This tab is the catch-all for the rest of the settings that don't fit in the other tabs, as well as advanced settings such as international, multimedia, and security settings. You may have to access this tab from time to time, and you will see an example later in the book. Take a minute to scroll through the different options that are listed here.

Devices and Printers

Devices and Printers is where you can add, configure, troubleshoot, and remove printers and other devices, such as monitors, UPSs, wireless devices, mice, and audio/multimedia devices. Most technicians use Devices and Printers for printers, and if you do, you'll find that it can be a good launching point for the configuration of other devices on the system. We discuss this Control Panel utility further in Chapter 19, "Multifunction Devices/Printers," and elsewhere in the book.

> **Note**
>
> We discuss the Network and Sharing Center, another Control Panel utility listed under Objective 1.4, in Chapter 37, "Windows Networking."

Programs and Features

You use Programs and Features to modify Windows applications and features, as well as third-party applications and features, and to repair them or uninstall them.

You can get to the list of options under Programs and Features from the Control Panel by selecting **Programs** (this time in Category view). You can then see options to uninstall programs, turn Windows features on or off, view the installed updates for Windows and other programs, and run programs made for previous versions of Windows. Except for that last one, these options are also available if you go to **Control Panel > All Control Panel Items > Programs and Features**. (Or you can go directly there by accessing **Run** and typing **appwiz.cpl**.)

If you need to uninstall or repair a program, or if you need to add features (such as Hyper-V or the .NET Framework), use Programs and Features.

ExamAlert

Know how to access Programs and Features to uninstall programs or turn Windows features on or off.

Program Compatibility

Most applications run properly on Windows. However, some applications that were designed for older versions of Windows might not run properly on your version of Windows. To make applications written for older versions of Windows compatible with a newer version of Windows, use the Program Compatibility utility or the Compatibility tab of a program file's Properties window.

To start the wizard in Windows, open the Control Panel and then click the **Programs** icon (in Category view). Then, under Programs and Features, click the link **Run programs made for previous versions of Windows**. This brings up the Program Compatibility Troubleshooter, which asks you which program you want to make compatible, asks which OS it should be compatible with, and (depending on the version) inquires as to the resolution and colors that the program should run in. Windows will attempt to "fix" programs automatically, if possible. You can also run the Program Compatibility Troubleshooter from the Compatibility tab of an individual program's Properties window.

To use the Compatibility tab, in File Explorer, right-click the program you want to make compatible and then click **Properties**. From there, click the **Compatibility** tab. You can select which OS compatibility mode you want to run the program in and define settings such as resolution, colors, and so on.

Compatibility mode can be helpful if a system has undergone an upgrade—such as an in-place upgrade—and older applications cease to function after the upgrade is complete. For security and impact reasons, it's a best practice to remove any programs that run in Compatibility mode after they are used.

Windows incorporates the Program Compatibility Assistant (PCA), which automatically attempts to help end users run applications that were designed for earlier versions of Windows. If for some reason this assistant causes a program to fail, you can disable it in services.msc or in the Group Policy Editor.

> **ExamAlert**
>
> Know how to use the Program Compatibility utility and the Compatibility tab in a program's Properties window. Understand that Compatibility mode can be helpful if a system has undergone an upgrade but the running program might be a security risk.

> **Note**
>
> Opening the System icon in the Control Panel automatically redirects to Settings. We'll cover this further in Chapter 36.

Windows Defender Firewall

The Windows Defender Firewall is Microsoft's built-in software that can protect a system from unwanted inbound connections. To make sure it is on, simply click the Control Panel icon and view the status of the private and public networks. Remember that green is good, and red is bad. To enable or disable the firewall, click **Turn Windows Defender Firewall on or off** and then modify the firewall as necessary. You can also access it by going to **Run > firewall.cpl**. We'll discuss this tool further in Chapter 36 and in the security portion of this book.

Mail

The Mail icon opens up a control panel that allows you to create one or more email profiles that work with Microsoft Outlook. To create a new profile, you need to know your email address, password, and server types. For more information on email client configuration, see Chapter 4, "Mobile Device Network Connectivity and Application Support."

Sound

Audio takes a back seat in the A+ certification somewhat, but in some environments—such as in my line of work—it is crucial. To troubleshoot audio problems, click the Sound icon to open the Sound dialog box, as shown in Figure 35.1. You can also get to this dialog box by right-clicking the sound icon in the notification area and selecting **Sounds** or by going to **Run** and typing **mmsys.cpl**.

FIGURE 35.1   **Sound dialog box in Windows**

You can use this dialog box to modify which audio devices are used for playback and recording and to select specific sound themes for Windows. You can also modify what happens with the volume of Windows and programs when communications are detected (for example, video chatting or webinars).

In Figure 35.1, notice that the device simply called Speakers is checked; this means it is the default device that will be used for the playback of audio. On my system, that happens to be a USB headset. In addition, there is a Focusrite USB device whose status is Ready. To output audio from that device, you could right-click its icon and select **Set as default device**. The same process is necessary in the Recording tab if you are using multiple microphones and recording devices. For people such as technicians, educators, presenters, and video bloggers who want to incorporate better microphones than the ones that are included with a system, the Recording tab of the Sound Control Panel is critical. However, if you have a custom audio processor with its own software, you might have to access that instead of the Sound dialog box to get full functionality—or, possibly, to have any functionality at all.

> **ExamAlert**
>
> Know how to enable and disable audio devices in the Playback and Recording tabs of the Sound dialog box.

User Accounts

When you open User Accounts, you can change your account name and account type (for example, administrator or standard user), and you can manage other accounts. You can also manage credentials and file encryption certificates, modify User Account Control (UAC) settings, and configure advanced user profile settings. However, to create new accounts, you either need to be redirected to the Settings area or use Local Users and Groups (which is the preferred method for administrators) by accessing **Run** and typing **lusrmgr.msc**. We'll be discussing user accounts further (especially user security) as we move through the book.

> **Note**
>
> We cover the Device Manager in Chapter 33, "Microsoft Operating System Features and Tools, Part I."

Indexing Options

Indexing is the cataloging of file information. It helps you find results faster when you search your files for names or keywords. Indexing runs automatically on Windows 10 and constantly tracks any changes to indexed areas. The index can take up as much as 10% of the size of the indexed files—so this is something to keep in mind when working with Windows systems.

When you open the Indexing Options control panel, you see a list of indexed locations such as Users and Microsoft OneNote. If you click the Modify button, you can change what locations are indexed—but be careful! If you select an entire drive (for example, C:), you could really slow down the performance of the system. If you click the Advanced button, you will see options to rebuild the index, change the index storage location, and change the file types that will be indexed.

File Explorer Options

You can use the File Explorer Options icon to modify how folders display information, whether or not certain data is visible, and how indexes are searched. Once the File Explorer Options control panel is open, you see a few tabs. Let's discuss them now.

The General tab gives you the option to change how folders are browsed. By default, folders are opened in the same window, but you could modify this so that each clicked folder opens in a separate window; just be careful because clicking folders could result in a lot of open windows and confusion. You can also choose whether to single-click or double-click to open items as a preference. You can also increase privacy by deselecting the two options for showing recently used files and folders in the Quick access areas.

The View tab allows you to apply a *view*, which is a way of organizing all folders. So, for example, if you were viewing a current folder in File Explorer in Details view, you could set that view to all folders in the system by clicking **Apply to Folders**. Note that this works only if you are currently in File Explorer and have a folder open. It doesn't work if you open File Explorer Options from the Control Panel.

Importantly, the View tab offers some more specific options (see Figure 35.2).

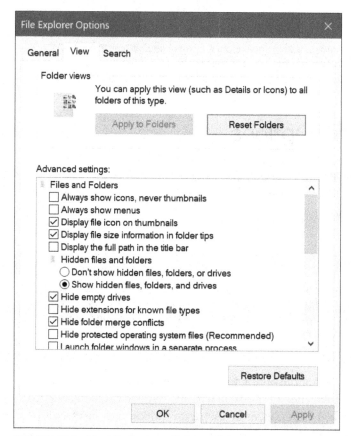

FIGURE 35.2   The File Explorer Options dialog box, opened to the View tab

For example, hidden files are not displayed by default. But if you select the
Show hidden files, folders, and drives radio button, hidden files will be
displayed in File Explorer. Another option a couple of lines below that is
Hide protected operating system files (Recommended). This is checked
by default, but if you were to deselect it, system files would become visible to
you. If you were to do both of these things, then files such as bootmgr and
pagefile.sys would become visible in the root of C:. You can also deselect the
Hide extensions for known file types checkbox so that you can see all the
extensions associated with files. All these are great options for an administrator, but they are not set up by default so that typical users don't get any more
information than they need. Spend a little time configuring the various File
Explorer options in the View tab and consider what would be best for the
typical user and what would be best for the admin.

The Search tab allows you to turn off indexing. Doing this might result in slower searches, but it's something that you might need to do when trouble-shooting a system if you suspect an issue with the indexing system.

Power Management

Optimizing an operating system involves managing power wisely. You can manage power for storage drives, the display, and other devices; you can even manage power for the entire operating system.

Some configurations can be done from the Power Options icon (which can be accessed directly from **Run > powercfg.cpl**). You can select what the Power button does and what closing the lid of a laptop does. For both of these, you can select from Do nothing, Sleep, Hibernate (if enabled), Shut down, and Turn off the display. You can also display the Sleep and Hibernate options in the Power menu, and you can turn on fast startup, which helps restart the computer faster after a full shutdown.

You might also want to turn off devices in Windows after a specified amount of time. From the Power Options initial screen, you can create or select a power plan such as Balanced, Eco, Power Saver, or High Performance, depending on the computer. Proprietary computers (such as Dell, HP, and so on), especially laptops, have their own preferred plans that balance power and performance according to the laptop's hardware.

There are a lot of settings within these power plans. For example, you can select **Balanced** and click **Change plan settings**, and you see that the display is set to turn off after a certain amount of time; you can set it to anywhere from 1 minute to 5 hours, or you can set it to never.

Going a little further, if you click the **Change advanced power settings** link, the Power Options dialog box appears, as shown in Figure 35.3. Using this dialog box, you can specify how long before the storage drive turns off and set power savings for devices such as the processor, wireless, PCI Express, and so on.

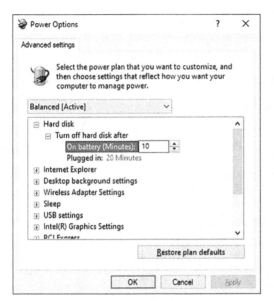

FIGURE 35.3   **Windows Power Options dialog box**

Another option is USB Selective Suspend. It is enabled by default, and it effectively reduces the power to USB devices that have been inactive for a period of time. It is a great power saver for laptops. Take a few minutes to look through the options in the Power Options dialog box.

Let's go a bit beyond the Control Panel. Some users confuse the terms *standby* and *hibernate*, but the two terms have different meanings:

▶ **Standby:** This means that the computer goes into a low-power mode, shutting off the display and storage drives. Information that you were working on, and the state of the computer are stored in RAM. The processor still functions but has been throttled down and uses less power. Taking the computer out of standby mode is a quick process; it usually requires the user to press the Power button or a key on the keyboard. It takes only a few seconds for the CPU to process the standby information in RAM and return the computer to the previous working state. Storage drives and other peripherals might take a few more seconds to get up to speed. Keep in mind that when there is a loss of power, the computer will turn off, and the contents of RAM will be erased unless there is a built-in battery (as in a laptop) or the computer is connected to a UPS; but either way, uptime will be limited. Note that some laptops still use a fair amount of power when in standby mode.

▶ **Hibernate:** This is different from standby in that it effectively shuts down the computer. Hibernation consumes the least amount of power of any power state except for when the computer is turned off. All data that was worked on is stored to the C: drive, in a file called hiberfil.sys. This is usually a large file. Because RAM is volatile and the storage drive is not, hibernate is a safer option when it comes to protecting the data and the session that you were working on, especially if you plan to leave the computer on for an extended period of time. However, because the drive is so much slower than RAM, coming out of hibernation takes longer than coming out of standby mode. Hibernation has also been known to fail in some cases and cause various issues in Windows.

Standby is known as Sleep in Windows and is accessible in the same location as the Shutdown or sign out options. Either use the **Start** button (click or right-click) or press Alt+F4 (after all other programs have been closed).

Before you can use hibernation, you might need to turn it on. This requires some doing, so hold on to your hats! To enable hibernation in Windows, do the following:

1. If you have the Power Options dialog box open, close it.

2. Open the PowerShell/Command Prompt as an administrator. Then type **powercfg.exe /hibernate on**.

3. Open the Power Options dialog box. You now see the Hibernate after option this dialog box.

4. Expand **Sleep** and expand the **Hibernate after** option and set it to the number of minutes you desire. The system is now set to automatically go into hibernation mode after the number of minutes of inactivity that you selected.

5. Finally, you can display the Hibernate option in the power menu. Go to **All Control Panel Items > Power Options** and click either **Choose what the power buttons do** or **Choose what closing the lid does**. From there, you can click the **Hibernate** checkbox so that it will show in the power menu. (If the checkbox is grayed out, click the **Change settings that are currently available** link above so that you can modify the setting.) Save your settings.

6. Check the Start menu again, and you should see the Hibernate option there, just below Sleep.

To disable hibernation, deselect the settings you chose in steps 4 and 5 and run the command **powercfg.exe /hibernate off**.

> **ExamAlert**
>
> Know the differences between standby, sleep, and hibernate and understand how to set up hibernation in Windows.

Ease of Access Center

The Ease of Access Center allows a user to turn on a variety of tools: the magnifier to view small objects more easily, the narrator for voice prompts while working in Windows, the onscreen keyboard, and high contrast.

There are several other options available to make Windows easier to use, including making the display easier to see, using the computer without a keyboard or mouse, making the keyboard and mouse easier to use, and so on. There is also an Ease of Access Center available in Settings (which is accessible via the keyboard shortcut Windows+U).

Cram Quiz

Answer these questions. The answers follow the last question. If you cannot answer these questions correctly, consider reading this chapter again until you can.

1. Which power management mode stores data on a storage drive?
   - A. Sleep
   - B. Hibernate
   - C. Standby
   - D. Pillow.exe

2. What tool can assist a user who needs to find results faster when searching for files on a storage drive?
   - A. firewall.cpl
   - B. Internet Options
   - C. appwiz.cpl
   - D. Indexing

3. You are about to start troubleshooting a Windows system. You need to be able to view the bootmgr file in the C: root of the storage drive. Which of the following should you configure to make this file visible? (Select the two best answers.)

- ○ **A.** Hidden files and folders
- ○ **B.** Extensions for known file types
- ○ **C.** Encrypted or compressed NTFS files in color
- ○ **D.** Protected operating system files

4. A customer wants you to set up the system to scale images at 200%. Which Control Panel icon should you access to configure this?

- ○ **A.** Programs and Features
- ○ **B.** Mail
- ○ **C.** Sound
- ○ **D.** Ease of Access Center
- ○ **E.** Devices and Printers

Cram Quiz Answers

1. B. When a computer hibernates, all the information in RAM is written to a file called hiberfil.sys in the root of C: within the storage drive.

2. D. Indexing helps you find results faster when you search your files for names or keywords. Indexing runs automatically on Windows 10 and constantly tracks any changes to indexed areas. **firewall.cpl**, when issued in the Run prompt or at the command line, opens Windows Defender Firewall. The Internet Options dialog box (**inetcpl.cpl**) is used to configure settings for the Internet Explorer web browser. **appwiz.cpl** opens the Programs and Features window, where you can uninstall or change programs and turn Windows features on and off.

3. A and D. In **File Explorer Options** > **View**, configure hidden files and folders and set it to **Show hidden files, folders, and drives**, and configure protected operating system files by deselecting the check mark for the setting **Hide protected operating system files**. Files such as bootmgr are hidden and protected by default; you need to unhide them in both ways to see them.

4. D. Use the Ease of Access Center to turn on the magnifier and increase the view of the display to 200%. You can also operate the magnifier with keyboard short-cuts: Windows + Plus (+) to turn it on or to increase scaling; Windows + Minus (-) to reduce scaling; and Windows+Esc to turn off the program. Programs and Features is used to add and remove programs and add specific features to Windows. Mail and Sound are self-explanatory: they allow you to configure email and sound profiles, respectively. Devices and Printers is where you go to configure printers, keyboards, and multimedia devices.

Tremendous! Review your notes, take a short break, and then continue!

CHAPTER 36

Windows Settings

This chapter covers the following A+ 220-1102 exam objective:

▶ **1.5** – Given a scenario, use the appropriate Windows settings.

The Windows Settings utility is designed to be the replacement for the Control Panel. Keep this in mind as you work in both configuration systems. Windows Settings is set up to be easy for typical users to navigate and to search for the options they require.

This chapter starts calmly enough, but it gets a little deep as it progresses. Be sure to take notes and practice the configurations on a test installation of Windows 10. Most of this chapter focuses on Windows 10, but if any differences exist in Windows 11, I show them as well. Let's get into Settings now.

ExamAlert

Objective 1.5 concentrates on the following Windows settings: Time & Language, Update & Security, Personalization, Apps, Privacy, System, Devices, Network & Internet, Gaming, and Accounts.

How to Access Settings

The typical way to get to Windows Settings is to click **Start** and click the **Settings** gear; however, there are many other options. Here are some alternatives for you:

▶ Right-click **Start** and select **Settings**.

▶ Open the **Search** tool and type **Settings**.

▶ Press the Windows+I keyboard shortcut.

▶ Open **Run** and type the **ms-settings:** command.

▶ Open PowerShell or the Command Prompt and type **start ms-settings:**.

▶ Open it from File Explorer or from the Action Center.

▶ Create a shortcut by right-clicking on the desktop and going to **New > Shortcut**. Then, in the Location field, type **ms-settings:** and complete the creation of the shortcut.

Note

To enhance the ms-settings command in the Run window, try **ms-settings:display**, which should open the Settings program directly to the Display portion of Settings. You can run similar commands for uniform resource identifiers (URIs) such as sound, printers, taskbar, USB, and so on. For a list of the URIs for ms-settings:, see https://docs.microsoft.com/en-us/windows/uwp/launch-resume/launch-settings-app.

Open Settings now and take a minute to look over the categories that are listed. You can see that each category is identified with a different icon and that there is a short description for each one. Note that the CompTIA A+ objectives list them in a different order than you see onscreen. We'll cover them in the order of the objectives for easier studying. Let's get into the various Settings options now.

Time & Language

You can use the Time & Language category to modify time/date settings, regional and language information, and speech options for microphone-based speech recognition.

Here's one scenario where you would use Time & Language. Say that you don't want to have Windows set the time automatically for you (which it does by default). If that's the case, you can navigate to the **Date & time** page under Time & Language, disable the **Set time automatically** slider, and then click the **Change** button to set the date and time manually. However, most organizations want their computers' time to be synchronized to a time server (such as time.windows.com).

Remember that there is always more than one way to get to a particular setting in Windows. For instance, if you right-click on the clock in the lower-right corner of your screen and click **Adjust date/time**, Windows will take you to the same Settings window.

> **Note**
>
> I use the term *right-click* quite often in this book. However, if you are using a touch-screen (or another device), the right-click procedure might be different. For example, on a Microsoft Surface device, you would long press the screen to activate a context (or right-click) menu. On other devices, you could use a two-finger tap on the touch-pad. It will differ from one device to the next, but for ease of reading, I simply refer to the process as right-clicking.

Take a few minutes to look through the Time & Language settings—and do this for each of the Settings categories covered in this chapter. If you make any changes, be sure to put everything back as it was when you are finished.

> **Note**
>
> As you progress deeper through the Settings options, you may find that a link will actually open a Control Panel dialog box or even a Control Panel window. Be ready for it!

Update & Security

The Update & Security category includes the Windows Update system; Windows Security, including anti-malware and firewall features; backup and recovery options; troubleshooting tools; Windows activation options; and advanced developer options. We'll be discussing the security side of Update & Security, as well as backup, recovery, and troubleshooting, later in the book. For now, let's briefly cover Windows Update and Windows Defender Firewall a little more.

Windows Update

Like any other OS, Windows should be updated regularly. Microsoft recognizes deficiencies in the OS—and possible exploits that could occur—and releases patches to increase OS performance and protect the system. These patches can be downloaded and installed automatically or manually, depending on the user's needs or the organization's needs, and they are controlled via the Windows Update program.

Windows Update can be accessed in Windows 10 by going to **Settings > Update and Security > Windows Update** and in Windows 11 by going to **Settings > Windows Update**. Or, you can search for "windows update" or go to **Run > ms-settings:windowsupdate**. You can also update the system from PowerShell, if necessary. Once you open the Windows Update window, you can see if your system is up to date, and you have the option to check for updates and install them.

From within Windows Update, you can decide how updates will be delivered and installed. In Windows 10, you can only defer updates temporarily—unless you do one of the following: stop and disable the Windows Update service in the Services console window (or from the command line); disable it with the Group Policy Editor; disable it within the registry; or otherwise turn it off programmatically. Sometimes, larger organizations do this—in a more enterprise manner—so that Windows is not randomly updating computers on the network and causing functionality issues between systems.

Troubleshooting Windows Update Program Issues

At times, individual Windows updates or the Windows Update program itself can fail. To troubleshoot an issue, use the Windows Update Troubleshooter program or check the logs manually.

To access the Windows Update Troubleshooter program in Windows 10, go to **Settings > Update & Security > Troubleshoot > Additional Troubleshooters** and under Windows Update, click **Run the troubleshooter.** (In Windows 11, go to **Settings > System > Troubleshoot > Other Troubleshooters > Windows Update > Run**.)

Want to check the logs manually? The Windowsupdate.log files are located in C:\Windows\Logs\WindowsUpdate, but they are not readable until you run the command **Get-WindowsUpdateLog** in PowerShell (as an administrator). Once you run this command, Windows converts the files to a readable WindowsUpdate.log file and places it on your desktop. For more information about Windows Update log files, see https://docs.microsoft.com/en-US/windows/deployment/update/windows-update-logs.

For more information about Windows Update troubleshooting and a list of error codes, visit these sites:

https://docs.microsoft.com/en-us/windows/deployment/update/windows-update-troubleshooting

https://docs.microsoft.com/en-us/windows/deployment/update/windows-update-error-reference

ExamAlert

Know how to run and troubleshoot Windows Update.

Windows Defender Firewall

Windows Defender Firewall is a built-in software-based firewall in Windows. We mentioned it in Chapter 35, "Windows Control Panel Utilities," when we discussed the Control Panel icon, but it has a different look in Settings. To access it, go to **Settings > Update & Security > Windows Security** (or **Run > ms-settings:windowsdefender**) and click **Firewall & network protection**. (In Windows 11, Update & Security is called Privacy & Security.)

From here you can turn on/off the firewalls for the domain and for private and public networks. You can also allow individual programs through the firewall (known as exceptions). Finally, you can run Windows Defender Firewall with Advanced Security by clicking the **Advanced Settings** link (or directly with **Run > wf.msc**). The main difference between this and the basic Windows Defender Firewall is the ability to create rules for incoming and outgoing traffic. We'll be discussing both in more depth in the security section of this book.

Personalization

Finally, a place to have some fun with the system! The Personalization section is where you can style your Windows computer the way you want. You can add custom backgrounds, modify colors, choose fonts, and modify how the Start menu and taskbar behave. I'll let you play around in the settings here without further discourse.

Apps

The Apps category opens up the Apps & features section of Settings, where you can see a list of what applications are loaded on the system and how much space they take up. You can also uninstall them here, if necessary, and see a list of optional features and add ones that are not installed by default. For example, you might decide to use the OpenSSH Client program to make secure connections to servers using open source software. Or maybe you need to add a font type for another language. You can also modify the default apps that are used on the system. For example, you can change from Microsoft Edge as the default web browser to another browser, or you can change which video player to use. There are also settings for map storage, apps for websites, video playback features, and startup. For instance, if you want to stop Cortana from starting up when the computer boots, go to **Startup** and drag the slider for Cortana to the off position.

Privacy

Individuals as well as organizations are very concerned with privacy—now more than ever before. Many operating systems and applications gather data about users. The Privacy portion of Settings is where you can enable—and, more importantly—*disable* data collection services. Know this: Most systems (including Windows) set these options to enabled when you first install the operating system.

Components of Privacy include the following:

► **General data collection:** This component is related to website-provided locally relevant data, application launch tracking, advertisement-based data, and suggested content.

▶ **Speech:** This means collected data based on any dictation a user might do. Many people talk to their computers and don't realize that what they say could be stored somewhere.

▶ **Inking & typing:** Typing history and handwriting patterns can be stored so that Windows can shape a more efficient personal dictionary for you.

▶ **Diagnostic data:** By default, Windows sends required diagnostic data, though there is a setting for optional and additional diagnostic data. This can't be completely disabled—here. More on this in a moment.

▶ **Activity history:** This is where Windows stores data about the websites you browse to and how you use programs.

Some individuals benefit from sharing data with Windows (and, ultimately, Microsoft). Others consider this type of sharing to be an invasion of privacy. In fact, some organizations have policies saying that all these settings must be disabled. You as the technician, though, are tasked with setting up the system the way the customer wants. However, you should discuss privacy with the customer and make sure there is an understanding of what data Windows will collect if these options are enabled.

Further Disabling Data Collection and Telemetry

You might wish to go a little further with your "disabling" of data collection. There are plenty of methods to do this, including within services.msc, in the registry, with the Task Scheduler, and with Group Policy. But I caution you! Be wary of third-party websites and their step-by-step procedures. Stick to Microsoft documentation if at all possible. Also, be sure to back up your settings, and don't use your personal computer for testing. Instead, perform these types of configurations on a virtual machine first to make sure they work as intended.

System

The System category is where you as a technician will spend a lot of time. The settings here govern your display, sound, notifications, power, storage, and more. That's a ton of stuff. Let's spend some time detailing some of the options.

Display

The Display section of System is where you can modify how your monitor outputs the image of the OS. You can modify the brightness, change the size of items, calibrate color, project to other screens, and so on. Most of these options are pretty straightforward settings, but there are a few concepts that require a little more discussion, including resolution, refresh rate, and color space.

Resolution

Display resolution is the number of pixels (or picture elements) on a screen. It is measured horizontally by vertically (*HxV*). The more pixels that can be used on the screen, the bigger the desktop and the more windows a user can fit on the display. The word *resolution* is somewhat of a misnomer and might also be referred to as *pixel dimensions*. A typical high-definition resolution is 1920x1080. A typical 4K resolution is 3840x2160. In the Display page, you can modify the resolution by clicking the **Display resolution** drop-down menu and making a selection (see Figure 36.1).

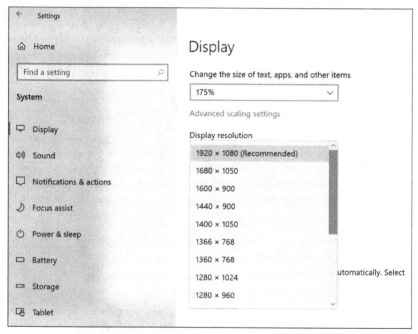

FIGURE 36.1   **Modifying the resolution in Windows 10**

Display resolutions continue to get larger. Keep in mind, however, that the maximum resolution of a monitor can be achieved only if the video card and cable can support it.

Another related concept is video scaling. Windows allows for scaling, which makes icons, text, and images appear bigger on the screen without requiring any adjustment to the resolution. For example, Windows 10 allows custom scaling between 100% and 500% of the original. This can be very helpful for educators and presenters, for people with poor vision, or for technicians who remotely control systems that have very high resolutions. In Figure 36.1, you can see that the Scale and Layout section is set to 175%. This is 75% larger than normal and allows me to see and present my screen with larger elements.

> **ExamAlert**
>
> Know where and how to modify display resolution and scaling in Settings.

Refresh Rate

Refresh rate is the number of times a display is "painted" per second. It is more specifically known as *vertical refresh rate*. For example, on an LCD panel, the liquid-crystal material is illuminated at a specific frequency. This is usually set to 60 Hz and may not be configurable. However, there are some computer monitors (such as LED and OLED screens) that can go to 120 Hz, 144 Hz, 240 Hz, and beyond. If it *can* be configured, you can click the **Advanced display settings** link, click the **Refresh rate** drop-down menu, and select the refresh rate that best matches your monitor—that is, if it wasn't selected for you automatically.

Color Space

Color space in Windows refers to the dynamic range of color intensity and luminance and how colors are represented on the display. Many devices—such as the 2017 laptop that I am writing this book on—use standard dynamic range (SDR). However, more advanced monitors support high dynamic range (HDR), which displays brighter and more detailed highlights and darker and more detailed shadows, with more intense colors overall compared to SDR. HDR is not something you would notice in the Windows GUI, but you would see the difference when gaming or watching HD or 4K video.

You can find out if your system is running HDR by going to **Settings > System > Display** and then clicking either **Windows HD Color Settings** or **Advanced display settings**. In either place, you can see whether your monitor is SDR or HDR.

> **Note**
>
> *Color depth* is different from color space. This refers to the number of colors that the Windows desktop uses. In the old days, you could have 8-bit color, 16-bit color, and other options. However, in Windows 10/11, the default option is 32-bit, which means 4,294,967,296 colors. Because of this, you might have difficulty displaying older programs properly. With older programs, you can use the Program Compatibility tool (discussed in Chapter 35) to run the programs at a lower color depth. You might also accomplish this within the Advanced Display settings or by using a virtual machine.

Power & Sleep

Power & Sleep is where you can set how long the screen turns off or how long the system waits until the system is put to sleep. If you have a laptop or another device that can run on a battery, you can configure settings for when the device is plugged in and when it is running on battery power.

The **Additional power settings** link opens up the Power Options portion of the Control Panel (as of the writing of this book). You can create customized power plans and configure advanced power settings in the Power Options dialog box. We cover that in more depth in Chapter 35.

Storage

The Storage portion of System Settings gives you the ability to view file storage and choose how and where files and applications are stored. It also includes the Storage Sense tool, which is the intended replacement for Disk Cleanup. It is enabled by default, but it is designed to run only when the computer is running low on storage space—unless you manually tell it to run. In that case, items in locations such as the Downloads folder will be deleted if they are older than 30 days.

There are also advanced links that enable you to manage storage spaces and optimize drives. You can learn more about those two options as well as Disk Cleanup in Chapter 34, "Microsoft Operating System Features and Tools, Part II."

About and System Properties

If you do a little digging, you'll see that there's more to the System category than meets the eye. I'm talking about advanced system properties. You might have noticed that we never talked about the System *icon* during Chapter 35's foray into the Control Panel. That's because if you click it, it brings you directly to **Windows Settings > System > About**. And that's where I want us to focus for a moment.

In the About page, you can view (and copy) the basic details of your system, including the CPU and RAM, device ID, system type, device name, and Windows specifications (which are essentially the same ones you see with the **winver** command). The copy option is handy when a user needs to give information about the system to a technician who is attempting to troubleshoot it. You can also rename a device here if you so desire, as well as change the product key or upgrade the edition of Windows.

The additional links at the end of this section are especially interesting. Many of them lead to the System Properties dialog box, which is a Control Panel dialog box. For example, if you click the **Advanced system settings** link in Windows 10, the System Properties dialog box opens, with the Advanced tab showing (see Figure 36.2).

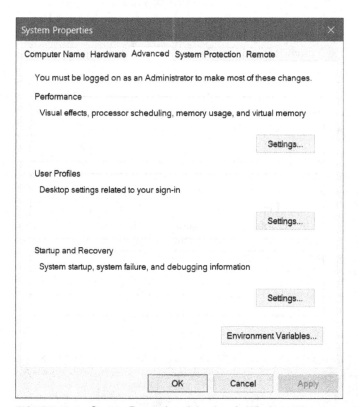

FIGURE 36.2   **System Properties dialog box in Windows 10**

> **Note**
>
> Is this the only way to access the System Properties dialog box? Of course not. **Run > sysdm.cpl** opens the dialog box but with the Computer Name tab open. In addition, you can type **sysdm.cpl ,3** to open System Properties directly with the Advanced tab showing. You just change the number for the tab that you want. Or you could use the *systemproperties(tabname)* naming convention—for example, **systempropertiesadvanced**. For the Computer Name tab, there is no space, and for the System Protection tab, it is simply **systempropertiesprotection**. Quick tip: Press Ctrl+Tab to quickly switch between tabs.

There are many more things to discuss in System Properties than we can fit in a cram book, but let's briefly talk about each tab:

▶ **Hardware:** The Device Manager and Device Installation settings are available on this tab. To learn more about the Device Manager, refer to Chapter 33, "Microsoft Operating System Features and Tools, Part I."

▶ **Advanced:** Given its name, you can guess that this tab is handy for a technician. As shown in Figure 36.2, it includes Performance, User Profiles, and Startup and Recovery. You will learn more about Performance (specifically virtual memory) in a little bit.

▶ **System Protection:** You can use this tab to configure System Restore points so that you can revert your computer to an earlier state. We'll discuss how to do this and when you would want to use System Restore points in Chapter 53, "Troubleshooting Microsoft Windows."

▶ **Remote:** You can use this tab to configure the Remote Assistance and Remote Desktop programs so that a user can request remote help and so you can remotely control systems, if necessary. Remote Desktop Connection is a Microsoft tool used to control and work on remote Windows systems. It displays the remote OS in a window on the desktop. It works as a client and a host in Windows Pro and higher editions and only as a client in Home editions. The executable name is **mstsc**, and you can use this in the Run prompt or at the command line to open the program and connect directly to systems. We'll discuss this tool further in Chapter 64, "Remote Access Technologies."

> **ExamAlert**
>
> Know the tabs of the System Properties dialog box.

Let's expand on one concept that can be handled within the System Properties dialog box: virtual memory.

Virtual Memory

Bear with me for moment here. In Chapter 14, "RAM," you learned that virtual memory (aka virtual RAM) allows you to go beyond the physical RAM storage of a system by making use of some kind of storage drive. Let's take that concept further and then tie it in with the System Properties dialog box.

Virtual memory makes a program think that it has contiguous address space, when in reality the address space can be fragmented and often spills over to a storage drive. RAM is a limited resource, whereas virtual memory is, for most practical purposes, unlimited.

There can be a large number of processes, each with its own virtual address space. When the memory in use by all the existing processes exceeds the amount of RAM available, the operating system moves pages of information to the computer's storage drive, freeing RAM for other uses. In Windows, virtual memory is known as the *paging file* (specifically, pagefile.sys), and it exists in the root of C:. To view this file, you need to unhide it. As previously mentioned, this can be done within the File Explorer Options dialog box in the View tab. Select the **Show hidden files, folders, and drives** radio button and then, a few lines below, deselect the **Hide protected operating system files** checkbox. While you're at it, deselect **Hide extensions for known file types**. This allows you to see not only the filename but the three-letter extension as well. Finally, pagefile.sys should now show up in the root, C:, where pagefile is the filename and .sys is the extension. Take a look at the size of your page file and write down what you find.

Now let's tie it in with the System Properties dialog box. The Virtual Memory dialog box is where you configure the size of the paging file. It is buried deep within System Properties. To access it, do the following:

1. Open the System Properties dialog box to the **Advanced** tab.

2. Click the **Settings** button in the Performance box; this brings up the Performance Options window.

3. Click the **Advanced** tab and then click **Change** in the Virtual memory section. This opens the Virtual Memory dialog box. A customized example is shown in Figure 36.3.

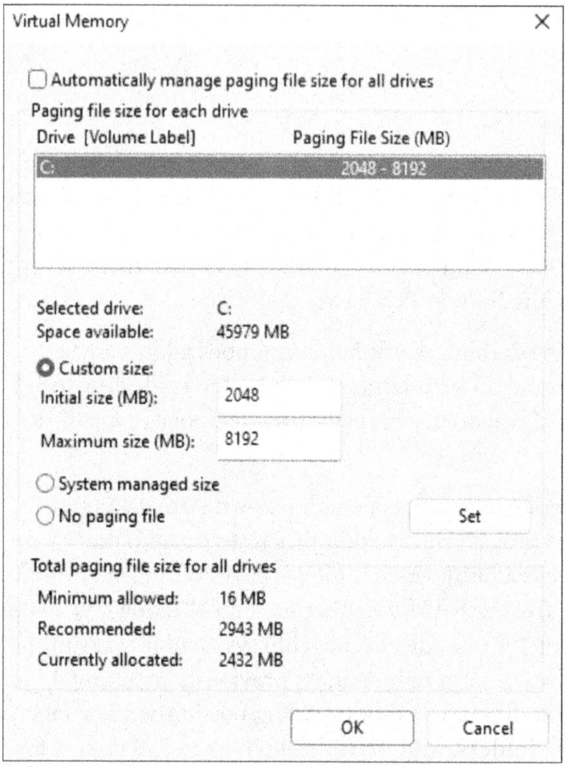

FIGURE 36.3 Customized Virtual Memory Dialog Box in Windows

4. Configure virtual memory. By default, Windows is configured to automatically manage the size of the paging file. However, you can select a custom size for the paging file (or select no paging file at all). To use a custom size for the paging file, deselect the **Automatically manage paging file size for all drives** checkbox, select the **Custom size** radio button, click the **Set** button, and click **OK**. In Figure 36.3, the paging file has a maximum size of 8192 MB.

The paging file has the capability to increase in size as needed. If a user runs a lot of programs simultaneously, then increasing the page file size might resolve performance issues. Another option would be to move the page file to another volume on the drive or to another drive altogether. It is also possible to create multiple paging files or stripe a paging file across multiple drives to increase performance. Of course, nothing beats adding physical RAM to a computer, but when this is not an option—possibly because the motherboard has reached its capacity for RAM—optimizing the page file might be the solution.

Will a typical user need to do this? Not often, but be sure to watch the Resource Monitor (or Performance Monitor) memory chart. If a power user or developer consistently has a measurement at the top of the chart, then it might be time to increase the size of the page file.

ExamAlert

Know where to configure virtual memory and know the location of pagefile.sys.

That wraps up the System category of Windows Settings (for now). Remember that the About section (including the System Properties dialog box), as well as the Storage, Power & Sleep, Sound, and Display sections, are all part of the System category. As you can see, this category is pretty massive, and we've only scratched the surface. You'll be spending some time there, so get to know it well.

Devices

The Devices category is where you configure your keyboard, mouse, touchpad, Bluetooth devices, and printers. You can also configure typing settings (such as auto correction), handwriting/inking options, and enable/disable AutoPlay, and you can use this category to have Windows notify you if there are any issues with USB devices.

Note

Windows Ink Workspace is a tool for people who want a whiteboard to draw on or a quality snipping tool. You can access it by pressing Windows+W. When you do, you see the whiteboard and fullscreen snip options. If you click the fullscreen snip portion, Windows takes a screenshot and opens the Snip & Sketch tool (which you can also annotate). Or you can open the Snip & Sketch tool directly at any time with the Windows+Shift+S keyboard shortcut, which gives you additional screen capture options.

One example of a configuration you might perform in Devices is modifying the scroll rate for the mouse wheel. Some people like to scroll through documents one or two lines at a time; others like to scroll entire pages at a time. You can change this from multiple lines at a time to pages at a time from the drop-down menu in the Mouse section. If it is set to lines, you can modify the exact number of lines per mouse wheel movement.

For an A+ technician, this is a bit of an easier Settings section. Nevertheless, familiarize yourself with some of the configurations, such as adding Bluetooth devices and adding printers.

Network & Internet

Another important category that you will be working in quite often is Network & Internet. Get to know the different sections of this category.

For example, in Status, you can quickly view whether the system is connected to the Internet and see the total data transfer over the past 30 days. There are some advanced network settings that you can access, such as Data usage and Change adapter options (which is More network adapter options in Windows 11). By the way, clicking **Change adapter options** has the same effect as going to **Run > ncpa.cpl**. For more information on how to configure an Ethernet adapter (especially with TCP/IP), see Chapter 9, "SOHO Network Configuration."

You can also create or modify Wi-Fi, Ethernet (wired), and VPN connections and set up mobile hotspots and proxy connections, as well as enable/disable airplane mode in this category.

We'll be discussing this category and its concepts further in Chapter 37.

Gaming

The Gaming section focuses in on Xbox usage: the game bar, keyboard shortcuts, screen and video captures, optimizing the computer for game play with Game Mode, and Xbox networking. Absolute fun for sure, but it probably won't show up on the exam much.

Accounts

This section is about user accounts. In it, you can manage an existing account or add new ones. By default, Microsoft attempts to have you sign up for a Microsoft account, but other accounts are allowed as well, including work and school accounts. (This requirement becomes more stringent in the Enterprise version of Windows.) Work and school resources are available in this section as well. Additional email accounts can be created also.

You can also modify the security factors used for authentication to Windows, including the Windows Hello Face, fingerprint, PIN, security key, password, and picture password.

The Family & other users section allows you to set up family members and specify the access levels for those accounts. For example, kids are often given less access by an adult creating an account. In this section, you can add local accounts for people who only want to sign in to Windows without using a Microsoft account.

The Sync your settings section allows you to synchronize settings and passwords across multiple Windows devices. Any other Windows devices that use the same account—and have sync enabled—will automatically get the syncing options you selected.

> **Note**
>
> You can also work with synchronization by going to **Control Panel > All Control Panel Items > Sync Center**.

We'll be discussing user accounts (especially user security) further as we progress through the book.

> **Note**
>
> Windows is constantly being improved. This means lots of updates and changes over time. Be sure to work on the latest versions of any software to keep *yourself* up to date.

Cram Quiz

Answer these questions. The answers follow the last question. If you cannot answer these questions correctly, consider reading this chapter again until you can.

1. Which of the following sections of Windows Settings allows a user to copy important information about a PC and possibly send it to a technician for troubleshooting purposes?

   ○ **A.** System > About

   ○ **B.** Network & Internet > Ethernet

   ○ **C.** Ease of Access > Narrator

   ○ **D.** Privacy > Diagnostics & Feedback

2. Which window would you navigate to in order to modify the virtual memory settings in Windows? (Select the best answer.)

   ○ **A.** Network & Internet

   ○ **B.** Performance Options

   ○ **C.** Devices

   ○ **D.** Device Manager

   ○ **E.** Display

3. Where can a technician create rules for inbound and outbound network traffic? (Select the two best answers.)

   ○ **A.** Windows Defender Firewall with Advanced Security

   ○ **B.** Windows Defender Firewall

   ○ **C.** Apps & Features

   ○ **D.** wf.msc

4. What should you modify if you need to change the number of pixels that are displayed horizontally and vertically on the screen?

   ○ **A.** Color space

   ○ **B.** Refresh rate

   ○ **C.** Resolution

   ○ **D.** Scaling

Cram Quiz Answers

1. **A.** Navigate to **Windows Settings** > **System** > **About**. Here you can copy device and Windows specifications and paste them into an email or to another location.

2. **B.** Navigate to the Performance Options dialog box and then click the **Advanced** tab to modify virtual memory in Windows. To access that window from the System Properties dialog box, click the **Advanced** tab, select the **Performance** section, and then click the **Settings** button.

3. **A and D.** The main difference between Windows Defender Firewall with Advanced Security and the basic Windows Defender Firewall is the ability to create rules for incoming and outgoing traffic. You can run Windows Defender Firewall with Advanced Security directly with **Run > wf.msc**. While the standard Windows Defender Firewall can allow apps through, it can't make specific rules. The Apps category opens up the Apps & features section of Settings, where you can see a list of what applications are loaded on the system and how much space they take up and uninstall them if necessary.

4. **C.** Modify the screen resolution to change how many pixels are displayed on the screen (*HxV*). For example, change from 1280x720 to 1920x1080 or vice versa. Scaling is similar in that it makes text and images appear larger or smaller, depending on how you set it, but it doesn't actually change the number of pixels that are displayed on the screen.

As mentioned, Windows is a morphing system—it is changing constantly. Be ready for this. Know the Control Panel and especially know Windows Settings for the exam, since that is the direction that Microsoft has moved. What's the best way to hedge your bets as you prepare to work in the IT field? Know the command line the most. It changes far less rapidly than does the GUI—and it rules. Continue.

CHAPTER 37

Windows Networking

This chapter covers the following A+ 220-1102 exam objective:

▶ **1.6** – Given a scenario, configure Microsoft Windows networking features on a client/desktop.

To a certain extent, Windows networking is automated. In a lot of scenarios, the technician doesn't have to configure very much. However, the larger and/or more complicated a network becomes, the more configuration is usually required.

This chapter goes over some of the basics of Windows networking, including network types, sharing and connecting to data, establishing different networking connections, and modifying additional networking settings. It might seem like a lot, but the great thing about TCP/IP—and computer networking in general—is that it works in essentially the same manner across the board, regardless of the operating system that is installed on the computer. So, the more you learn about networking, the easier it becomes to network *any* operating systems together.

Let's continue on our quest toward the A+ certification.

ExamAlert

Objective 1.6 focuses on workgroup vs. domain setup, local OS firewall settings, client network configuration, establishing network connections, proxy settings, public networks vs. private networks, File Explorer navigation and network paths, and metered connections and limitations.

Workgroup vs. Domain Setup

After you have configured a network adapter, you are ready to join a network. There are only a couple of choices: either workgroup or domain.

Workgroups and domains are logical groupings of computers. A *workgroup* (sometimes also referred to as peer-to-peer) is usually a small group of computers that share the same network name. No single computer controls the network, and all systems are considered equal. One of the disadvantages is that a computer storing data can be accessed only by a maximum of 20 other systems simultaneously. A *domain* (sometimes also referred to as a client/server network) builds on this by having one or more computers (servers) that are in control of the network. This enables more computers, more simultaneous access, and centralized administration. A domain also gets a name, such as dprocomputer.com. You can select whether your computers will be part of a workgroup or a domain by opening the **System Properties** dialog box and selecting the **Computer Name** tab. (Remember, you can also go to **Run** and type either **sysdm.cpl ,1** or **systempropertiescomputername**.) Then click the **Change** button. This displays the Computer Name/Domain Changes dialog box, as shown in Figure 37.1.

You can use this dialog box to join a workgroup (which is the default, by the way) or attempt to join a domain. Your SOHO network will probably not have a domain; domains are more commonly found in larger organizations. A domain is controlled by a Microsoft server known as a *domain controller*. To connect to the domain from a client computer, you need to know the domain name (for instance, dpro42.com) and the DNS server IP address for that domain. You also need an account on the domain and need to log on to that domain with a username and password assigned to you by the systems administrator. It's also a good idea to make sure that the workstation's time and server's time are synchronized.

FIGURE 37.1   **Computer Name/Domain Changes dialog box**

ExamAlert

Be able to define the differences between a workgroup and a domain and know where to change from one to the other (System Properties dialog box > Computer Name tab).

Sharing Resources and Making Network Connections

Before anyone can view the amazing things you have to offer on your computer, you need to *share* them. Let's discuss the sharing of data and then the sharing of printers.

Data Sharing and Access

First, sharing needs to be turned on. To do this, go to **Control Panel > All Control Panel Items > Network and Sharing Center**. Then click the **Change advanced sharing settings** link. The Advanced sharing settings window appears.

> **Note**
>
> You can quickly get to the Advanced sharing settings window by opening the Search tool and typing **sharing**.

In the Advanced sharing settings window, you can turn on folder and printer sharing for private networks only, guest or public networks only, or all networks. You can also enable or disable password-protected sharing. What you select depends on your environment, the kind of network you have, and the security level you desire. You do not need to be overly concerned with these settings in a domain environment (other than turning off sharing for the client computers), but in a workgroup environment, you might opt to have sharing enabled on one or more network types. Some small offices turn off password-protected sharing to make it easier to share resources with other users on other computers, but there is a potential security risk in doing this.

> **Note**
>
> Some companies with small networks avoid Windows sharing altogether and instead install a network-attached storage (NAS) device that also has print server capabilities.

After sharing has been configured for the computer that will host the data, sharing can then be enabled for *individual* resources. For example, let's say you have a folder named data, and you want to share the contents of that folder to other users and computers. You would need to locate the folder, right-click it, and either select **Give Access To** or select **Properties** and then click the **Sharing** tab. Figure 37.2 shows the Sharing tab of a folder's Properties page. You can use this tab to share the folder; plus, you can use this tab to enable Advanced Sharing and set custom permissions for users.

You can also create hidden shares, which can be seen by administrators but not by typical users. To do this, add a dollar sign ($) to the end of a share name. Drive letters are automatically shared as administrative shares (for example, C$). An example of a built-in Windows administrative share is admin$, which is the share name for C:\Windows. We discuss administrative shares further in Chapter 47, "Windows Security Settings."

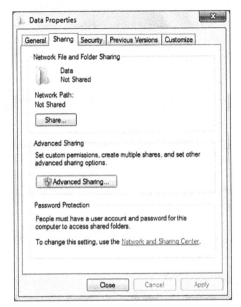

FIGURE 37.2   **The Sharing tab of the Data folder Properties window**

Now, if you want to access shares on another computer, you can do it in a couple of ways. First is browsing the network, which is done in File Explorer. Simply click **Network** in the left pane; you might have to wait while the computer refreshes the information before other systems and devices show up. Click to open a remote computer, and its shares (if any) should show up there.

Another way to access shares is to map a network drive. This means making a permanent connection to a shared folder using File Explorer and assigning it a drive letter. These network drives are mapped according to Microsoft's universal naming convention (UNC), which is *computername\sharename*.

To map a drive, follow these steps:

1. Locate the Map Network Drive window.

   ▶ **In Windows 10:** Open **File Explorer**, select **This PC** in the left pane, click **Computer** on the menu bar, click the **Map network drive** drop-down, and again click **Map Network Drive**.

   ▶ **In Windows 11:** Open **File Explorer**, select **This PC** in the left pane, click the three-dot button on the toolbar, and select **Map Network Drive**.

2. Select a drive letter (for example, F:).

3. Type the entire path to the share you want to map to. Use one of the following naming conventions:

`\\servername\sharename`

`\\IPaddress\sharename`

4. Click **Finish**.

Figure 37.3 shows an example. Note that the computer name in this example is nasbox1, and the share name is datashare. In this case, I mapped a drive to a NAS device instead of to a Windows computer, but it works the same way. In the figure, I used Y:. Some organizations like to use F: or M: or Z:, but it's really just a matter of a preference. The key is to be consistent. If 10 computers are going to map a drive to the same resource, consider using the same letter to do so; this makes it easier for the administrator to recognize where mapped drives are connecting.

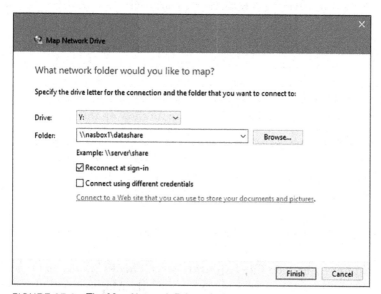

FIGURE 37.3   **The Map Network Drive window**

Note that **Reconnect at sign-in** is checked. When this option is selected, users won't have to reconnect and supply credentials every time they want the data. Always check this setting if you are troubleshooting a share/mapped network drive that isn't working after a system is rebooted.

The option **Connect using different credentials** may be necessary if the remote share, or network policy, requires it. If it is selected, the system will prompt a user to enter a username and password.

Mapping network drives can also be done in PowerShell and the Command Prompt with the **net use** command. For example, to map the same drive as shown in Figure 37.3, the command would be **net use y: \\nasbox1\datashare**. We discuss this further in Chapter 32, "Microsoft Command-Line Tools, Part II."

Printer Sharing and Access

To share a printer, you need to first make sure that printer sharing has been enabled in the Network and Sharing Center (click the **Change advanced sharing settings** link and select either the Private, Guest, or Public profile drop-down). Then, you can share the individual printer. Go to **Devices and Printers**, right-click the printer you want to share, select **Printer properties**, and access the **Sharing** tab. From there, check **Share this printer** and give it an easy-to-remember share name, preferably without spaces.

To connect to the printer from a remote computer, users can attempt to browse for it or add the printer by using its name (and network path). To do this, once again go to **Devices and Printers** (this time on the remote system) and click **Add a printer**. If Windows doesn't find the printer on the network automatically, click **The printer that I want isn't listed**. You then have some options. First, you can select the shared printer by name—for example, \\av-editor\hp-printer1, where the printer share name is hp-printer1, and the computer it is connected to is AV-Editor. Figure 37.4 shows this configuration screen. HTTP and HTTPS connections can also be made if the computer that is controlling the printer supports this.

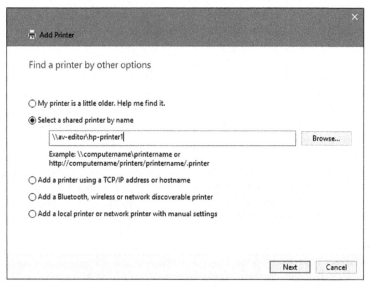

FIGURE 37.4 **The Add Printer window**

You can also connect via TCP/IP by clicking the **Add a printer using a TCP/IP address or hostname** radio button. You can then connect to a standalone network printer by IP address directly or use Web Services for Devices (WSD) to connect to a printer. WSD is a Microsoft API that is used to enable programming connections to web service–enabled devices, such as printers, scanners, and file shares.

ExamAlert

Know how to connect (map) to a network printer by printer share name or IP address.

Note

The "Local OS firewall settings" portion of Objective 1.6 is covered in Chapter 47. The "Client network configuration" portion is covered in Chapter 9, "SOHO Network Configuration."

Establishing Networking Connections

From within Windows, a user can connect to a variety of networks. There are two main ways to do this:

- ▶ Navigate to **Settings > Network & Internet**.

- ▶ Navigate to the Network and Sharing Center and click the link **Set up a new connection or network** to display the window shown in Figure 37.5.

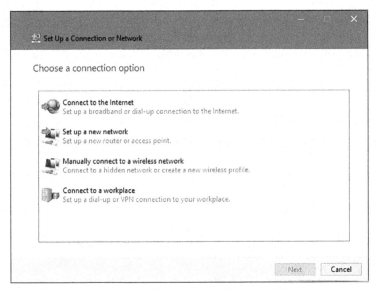

FIGURE 37.5   **The Set Up a Connection or Network window**

From these locations, you can connect to wireless networks, wired Ethernet networks, virtual private networks (VPNs), dial-up networks, wireless wide area networks (WWAN), and, of course, the Internet.

From the window shown in Figure 37.5, you can do several things. First, you can make Internet connections via broadband or dial-up. You can also create a new network by configuring a SOHO router (if available). In addition, you can manually connect to a wireless network, which might be necessary if the AP is not broadcasting the SSID. You can also connect to the workplace via direct dial-up (which is uncommon) or virtual private network (VPN). To establish a wireless wide area network (WWAN)/cellular connection, you usually rely on third-party software that comes with the WWAN adapter. You can also configure metered connections for VPNs and hotspots. This means you have control over your data cap (if you have one). Windows looks at a typical Ethernet or Wi-Fi connection as unlimited, but a user might have a service that is not unlimited. By setting up a metered connection, you can watch over your data limitations and get notifications when you approach those limits.

Usually, what you need to know is the IP address (or name) of the gateway or server that you need to connect to, as well as the appropriate passwords to get into the network and, possibly, to establish encrypted networking sessions.

In general, whenever you establish a new networking connection, you are asked to provide a *network location*. Windows asks you whether you want it to be private or public. A private profile means that network discovery is turned on (and that the system is searchable on the network) and file and printer sharing is enabled. Private is good for home connections and when connecting to a workplace where you trust the systems that you are connecting to (and their surrounding systems). A public profile means that network discovery and file/print sharing is turned off; this connection is good for when you need to connect to public networks that you don't trust because you don't know what computers will be on those networks.

Proxy Settings

Some organizations use proxy servers to cache HTTPS, FTP, and other information. To connect to the Internet in this scenario, the client workstations must have the Proxy server setting configured. This allows the client to access the proxy server, which then forwards requests out to the Internet and to the corresponding web servers, or other types of servers.

The Proxy setting is located in different places, depending on the web browser you use:

▶ **Microsoft Edge:** Navigate to **Settings > Network & Internet > Proxy** or search for "proxy" in the Edge browser settings (**edge://settings**).

▶ **Internet Explorer:** Open the Internet Properties window, which can be opened from the browser, or go to **Control Panel > Internet Options**. From there, access the **Connections** tab, click the **LAN settings** button, and click the **Proxy server** checkbox.

You can have Windows attempt to set up a proxy connection automatically, and you can use a script to aid in the process. Otherwise, you have to manually set up the proxy connection. Essentially, that means you need to know the IP address and the port used for the proxy server. For example, 172.18.0.105:443 would mean that the IP address of the proxy server is 172.18.0.105, and the server's listening port is 443. You can also exclude particular addresses that you don't want to go through the proxy; for example, sometimes websites and services don't allow a user access if that user is using a proxy. In addition, you can disable the use of the proxy server for local addresses (on the LAN or an intranet). We discuss proxy servers further in Chapter 8, "Networked Hosts."

> **ExamAlert**
>
> Know how to navigate to and configure the proxy settings in Windows!

Cram Quiz

Answer these questions. The answers follow the last question. If you cannot answer these questions correctly, consider reading this chapter again until you can.

1. Which of the following are administrative share names? (Select the two best answers.)
   - ○ **A.** C$
   - ○ **B.** C:\Windows
   - ○ **C.** ADMIN$
   - ○ **D.** System32
   - ○ **E.** $print

2. You need to design a local area network for 10 computers with very limited data sharing. Which of the following network types is the best option?
   - ○ **A.** Workgroup
   - ○ **B.** Client/server
   - ○ **C.** VPN
   - ○ **D.** Domain

3. You want to connect to a share on \\server1\data-share. Which of the following should be used to accomplish this?
   - ○ **A.** Use a proxy server.
   - ○ **B.** Right-click the folder and select **Share with**.
   - ○ **C.** Use **ipconfig**.
   - ○ **D.** Use **net use**.

4. You have been tasked with setting up a client Windows computer. It needs to gain access to the Internet, but all web traffic is cached and filtered by a go-between server on the LAN. What should you configure to enable Internet access for the Windows client?

   ○ **A.** VPN

   ○ **B.** Proxy server

   ○ **C.** Domain

   ○ **D.** Workgroup

5. In Windows 10, which network location profile setting should you choose if you are not sure what computers will be on the network or if you can trust them?

   ○ **A.** Private

   ○ **B.** VPN

   ○ **C.** Metered connection

   ○ **D.** Public

Cram Quiz Answers

1. **A and C.** Every volume gets an administrative share by default, including the C: drive, which is assigned C$. ADMIN$ is another administrative share; it is the share name for C:\Windows. System32 is simply a folder name within C:\Windows. $print is not an administrative share, but it could be used as a share name. An actual administrative share is print$, with the $ at the end of the share name. By the way, the print$ share is used to deliver print drivers from the print server to the client computer.

2. **A.** The best listed option is the workgroup. In Microsoft environments, it works well for 20 or fewer computers. Client/server networks such as Microsoft Active Directory domains are designed for more computers, often in an enterprise setting. A VPN is usually implemented for users who need secure connections to other networks or the Internet.

3. **D.** The **net use** command can connect to shares such as \\server1\data-share or any other share on the network. Of course, you could also do this by mapping a network drive in File Explorer. A proxy server is used to filter and cache client connectivity to the Internet. Right-clicking the folder and selecting **Share with** allows you to share the folder but doesn't make a connection to the share. **ipconfig** is used in the command line to learn the IP configuration of the network adapter.

4. **B.** Configure a proxy server by entering the IP address of the proxy server and the port to be used. A VPN allows secure connectivity to the Internet. A domain is a large network of computer systems that are centrally administered. A workgroup is a small group of networked systems.

5. D. A public profile means that network discovery and file/print sharing is turned off; this connection is good when you need to connect to public networks that you don't trust because you don't know what computers will be on those networks. Private is good for networks where you trust the systems. While a VPN is private and secure (hopefully), it is not one of the "network location profiles" in Windows but rather a network connection type. A metered connection should be used for hotspots, VPNs, and other connection types that may have data caps.

We could go on and on about Windows networking. Be sure to explore Windows and the various configuration locations mentioned in this chapter. Review your notes, take a break, and then continue on. Great work!

CHAPTER 38

Application Installation and Configuration Concepts

This chapter covers the following A+ 220-1102 exam objective:

▶ **1.7** – Given a scenario, apply application installation and configuration concepts.

Let's briefly cover some application installation and configuration concepts and a couple of best practices. This is a shorter chapter, but it is important for the exam and for the IT field. There are a lot of numbers and specifications in this chapter, so it might be a bit more of a difficult read. Take your time, and it will all be fine.

32-Bit vs. 64-Bit

We should start this chapter by discussing the difference between 32-bit and 64-bit. We touched on this from a hardware perspective in Chapter 17, "CPUs." Let's review what we covered in that chapter and then dig a bit deeper into this concept from a software perspective.

Almost all of today's PC-based CPUs are 64-bit; this is a type of CPU architecture that incorporates registers that are 64 bits wide. These registers, or temporary storage areas, allow the CPU to work with and process 64-bit data types and provide support for address space in the terabytes. 64-bit CPUs have been available for PCs since 2003.

A little history: The predecessor to the 64-bit CPU was the 32-bit CPU. Intel started developing well-known 32-bit CPUs as early as 1985 with the 386DX CPU (which ran at a whopping 33 MHz!), and AMD did likewise in 1991 with the Am386. A 32-bit CPU can't support nearly as much address space as a 64-bit CPU; 32-bit is limited to 4 GB.

You might hear of the terms x86 and x64. x86 refers to older CPU names that ended in an 86—for example, the 80386 (shortened to just 386), 486, 586, and so on. Generally, when people use the term x86, they refer to 32-bit CPUs that enable 4 GB of address space. On the other hand, x64 (or x86-64) refers to newer 64-bit CPUs that are a superset of the x86 architecture. This technology has a wider data path to handle program execution; it can run 64-bit software and 32-bit software and can address a default maximum of 256 terabytes (TB) of RAM. It's actually more than 256 TB, but the real limitation right now is the operating system, and that's the focus here. For example, Windows 10 Home can access up to 128 GB of RAM, while Windows 10 Pro can use 2 TB, and Windows 10 Pro for Workstations as well as Enterprise can use up to 6 TB. To put this into perspective, the motherboard of the *AV-Editor* computer—which I discuss earlier in the book—supports a maximum of only 64 GB of RAM (which is typical). This is far less than Windows 10 can handle, which in itself is just a tiny slice of what a 64-bit CPU can address.

ExamAlert

Know the differences between 32-bit and 64-bit architectures. For example, remember that 32-bit CPUs can only address a maximum of 4 GB of RAM, and 64-bit CPUs can address many terabytes of RAM.

Prior to Windows 10 version 2004, Windows came in 64-bit (x64) and 32-bit (x86) versions so that users from both generations of computers could run software efficiently. But since Windows 10 version 2004, Microsoft has abandoned new 32-bit releases. However, 64-bit versions of Windows are backward compatible—meaning that they can run 32-bit Windows applications as well as 64-bit applications. The 64-bit system files and apps are stored in C:\Windows\System32, and the 32-bit system files and apps are stored in C:\Windows\SysWOW64.

Note

Yes, the pathnames are sort of backward from what you would expect, but that is due to how Windows developed over time and how it progressed from a 32-bit system to a 64-bit system.

In addition, you will find that some applications are still written for the 32-bit platform. And so, there are also two locations for programs in Windows: 64-bit programs are stored in C:\Program Files, and 32-bit programs are stored in C:\Program Files (x86). This makes sense because x86 means 32-bit. But keep in mind that it is preferable to use 64-bit applications if at all possible. Because of this, you will spend more time in the 64-bit areas of Windows, including C:\Program Files and C:\Windows\System32.

ExamAlert

Know the locations for 64-bit and 32-bit system files and program files in Windows.

System and OS Requirements for Applications

You might find yourself involved with designing a system, or systems, to use a certain type of program, such as virtualization, programming, graphic design,

CAD, A/V editing, gaming, and so on. If so, it is important to carefully analyze the main program that will be used and plan carefully for its installation and configuration—making sure that it will run properly within your hardware configuration and the operating system that is running. As with most other things in technology, planning is vital.

First, you have to plan the system and OS requirements for the application. Some applications have versions for Windows and for Mac, but it's important to think about platform compatibility regarding the main application you want to use. Many applications have a set of minimum requirements and also have a set of *recommended* requirements. With any specific applications that will be resource intensive, I suggest you go with the recommended requirements (or more); otherwise, you could experience slow performance.

Let's consider a couple of scenarios. First, we'll take a look at a powerful video editing program and its requirements. Then we'll look at a commonly used developer program.

Scenario 1: Video Editing Program

A powerful video editing application might *require* Windows 10/11 Pro or higher, 10 GB of storage drive space, a dedicated Windows-compatible audio device and speakers, a display resolution of at least 1920×1080, and an external USB drive (acting as a hardware token) that needs to be plugged into the computer for the application to work. But those are just the minimum requirements.

The application could *recommend* more, such as a 2.8 GHz quad-core CPU, 16 GB of RAM, and a discrete PCIe video card that can be used for hardware acceleration. The program might even require a video card with a specific amount of onboard video RAM (VRAM), such as 4 GB or more. Remember that a discrete (or dedicated) video card is one that connects to a PCI Express slot on the motherboard, whereas an integrated video card is *part* of the motherboard—and is usually far less powerful. For any custom applications that rely on video, you'll probably want a dedicated card! So, the recommended requirements can become somewhat costly.

One last thought: Sometimes even the recommended requirements might not be quite enough, depending on the system and environment. Keep this in mind as you build systems.

Scenario 2: Developer Program

Compared to a video editing program, a typical integrated development environment (IDE) program might have far less stringent *requirements*, such as Windows 10/11 (any edition) and 500 MB of storage drive space. This means that it can run on just about anything! The *recommendations* might also be less than the ones in Scenario 1—for example, a 1.6 GHz processor and 1 GB of RAM (the actual recommended specifications for Visual Studio Code as of 2021; see https://code.visualstudio.com/docs/supporting/requirements). As of the writing of this book, Visual Studio Code (VSC) is also available for Mac (OS version 10.11 and higher), Windows 7 (with .NET 4.5.2) or higher, and Linux (Red Hat, Ubuntu, and Debian), so you can see that it does run on almost anything. Not your toaster yet, but it's solidly cross-platform.

> **Note**
>
> Recommended requirements change over time, and new versions of applications are always being released, usually consuming more resources and requiring newer operating systems. Be ready!

> **ExamAlert**
>
> Understand minimum requirements categories for software, including CPU, RAM, GPU (and VRAM), storage space, and OS type and edition.

Remember: Compatibility is key. And, when planning a system, you have to over-engineer. Make sure you have plenty of resources (and then some) based on the *recommended* requirements of an application. Otherwise, the productivity of your users will be less than optimal.

Distribution Methods

Many applications are simply downloaded and run through the installer for Windows, macOS, or Linux. But in some cases, the application you wish to install might be stored on physical, removable media, such as a USB flash drive or possibly even an optical disc. Perhaps it is located somewhere on the network. You might have to connect to a mapped network drive or an FTP server, and you might possibly have to extract the content from a .zip file or another compressed group of files.

How an application will be installed should play into your planning. Be ready for multiple installation and deployment types. For instance, in the case of a program such as Microsoft Office, you might use a server to deploy the program (or a new version of the program) to multiple clients at once. Finally, know where you are installing the program. If you are using Windows, for example, a 32-bit version of the program will go to C:\Program Files (x86), and a 64-bit version of the program will be installed to C:\Program Files. In essence, you need to know the source and also the target.

Some applications (and especially operating systems) can be downloaded in .iso format. An ISO image is an optical disc image. It is a single file that is a complete representation of all the files that would be placed on an optical disc. This is the standard format for downloading operating systems from the Internet. An ISO image can download quickly because it is a single file. Once downloaded, it can be mounted to an area of a storage drive or USB flash drive as the original complete set of files to ultimately be installed to a computer. Besides using Disk Management for mounting, you could use third-party programs such as PowerISO and Rufus. (See Chapter 34, "Microsoft Operating System Features and Tools, Part II," for more information on mounting in Disk Management.)

> **ExamAlert**
>
> An ISO image (.iso file) is a single file that represents a complete set of files that would be placed on an optical disc. It's commonly used for operating systems and large applications.

An ISO image can also be useful for implementing over-the-network installations, and it can be used directly by a virtualization program (such as Virtual-Box) to install virtual operating systems. Finally, an ISO image can be burned to an optical disc if necessary.

Other Considerations for New Applications

Answer me these questions three: How will an application impact your computers and network? How will it impact business operations? And how should you consider security as it pertains to new applications? Let's look at the answers to these questions together now.

Application Impact

Any application that is installed will have an impact on the device or computer. Every running application—and every running process, for that matter—uses precious CPU and RAM resources.

You can see the resources being used if you view an application in the Task Manager, Resource Monitor, or Performance Monitor in Windows; the Activity Monitor in macOS; or the top program in Linux. Some applications run quietly in the background, and others might use more resources than you would like, even when they are inactive. It's important to know how to remove applications from the startup process if necessary so that resources can be freed up on the local system.

As a basic example, in Windows, if you click the up arrow in the notification area, you will see what basic apps are running in the background, such as video card configuration programs and Bluetooth. This area is also known as the system tray (or just "tray"), and you can disable programs from there temporarily by right-clicking them and selecting **Exit**. However, they will start back up when the system is restarted. To remove them from the startup process altogether, you need to go to **Settings > Apps > Startup**. They might also be listed in the Task Scheduler, so look there as well.

Don't forget that applications also take up space on the storage drive. Contrary to popular belief, *storage space is not infinite!* Periodically, you will need to remove apps that are not being used. You can do so from **Settings > Apps > Apps & features**.

In many cases, an application will impact the network as well. Imagine a video-telephony program or any type of application that deals with the streaming of video to the desktop. Such applications have a big impact on an individual computer's network connection and possibly the entire network—potentially slowing down other users. Can your network handle multiple users running video chat? Are your switches up to the task? A typical video chat can use between 1 and 5 Mbps. A typical high-definition video stream can use up to 20 Mbps. Multiply that by 50, and your 1 Gbps switch will be in trouble. Make sure that your network's bandwidth meets the requirements of your applications, given the number of users who will be working with those apps. Implement quality of service (QoS) tweaking and set thresholds for your users either at the switch or router or locally at the computer system.

A multi-user application can also impact a business in general: its operations, productivity, and continuity—from a networking standpoint and from a security standpoint. For example, video chat programs and social media programs are known for having security and privacy issues. And let's not even mention gaming. New applications that are not coded properly can bring down systems and even entire networks, resulting in lost productivity that translates to lost revenue—and that usually means someone is headed for the unemployment line. Who? The person who installed the application. Don't be that person. Thoroughly test your potential new applications on testing systems in an isolated network before deploying them.

Safe deployment of applications also hinges on user permissions and some other security considerations. Let's briefly discuss those now.

User Permissions

When you install an application in Windows, Windows usually asks who you want to have access to the program. Quite often, the options are the user who is installing the application only or everyone on the computer. That can be somewhat limiting, especially if you have several users that share the system. Later, you can assign permissions to users/groups on the folder that contains the application's executable file. Be ready to navigate to C:\Program Files (x86) and C:\Program Files to do this for 32-bit and 64-bit applications, respectively.

As an administrator, you might be called upon to install a special application to a user's computer, where only that user may use the application—and even you aren't allowed to use it, regardless of the fact that you are an admin. In such a case, you have to change permissions appropriately or give the user permissions to install the application. Be ready to be called upon to make changes to ownership and permissions in Windows. We'll discuss these topics further in Chapter 47, "Windows Security Settings," and Chapter 48, "Windows Best Practices."

Security Considerations

I'd like you to consider this: Every installed application increases the target surface of an operating system. An application could open up networking connections, or open ports on the firewall, or create backdoors, all of which can be inviting to attackers. Plus, the availability of the rest of the system could be reduced by some applications that are not coded well.

Remember: Consider running evaluation versions of software on a testbed (that is, an isolated network or a VM network) before installing to live clients. Test the security of an application by scanning the system for malware, scanning for open ports, and running the application side-by-side with other applications to find out if there will be any conflicts. Then, check how the application updates. You may or may not want it to auto-update. If it does not auto-update, you should periodically check for updates that will address security vulnerabilities and increase the functionality of the program. Depending on your organization's policies, that could be every six months or less. The installation of the program and the program's updates could also affect the network. The larger the program, the more the network will be affected. So, after you have tested an application thoroughly, be sure to run installations and upgrades off-hours unless they are absolutely necessary!

Cram Quiz

Answer these questions. The answers follow the last question. If you cannot answer these questions correctly, consider reading this chapter again until you can.

1. Which of the following are important considerations when planning the installation of a new application? (Select the three best answers.)

   ○ **A.** CPU speed

   ○ **B.** Windows location

   ○ **C.** Program Files location

   ○ **D.** User permissions

   ○ **E.** Warranty

2. What is the name of the folder where Windows stores 64-bit system files?

   ○ **A.** Systemroot

   ○ **B.** System32

   ○ **C.** SysWOW64

   ○ **D.** Program Files (x86)

3. One of the users at your company attempts to install an application and receives the following error:

   `Not enough disk space to install...`

   Which of the following was overlooked by the user?

   ○ **A.** Operating system compatibility

   ○ **B.** Installation method

   ○ **C.** File permissions

   ○ **D.** System requirements

4. A customer submits a request for a technician to install a new application on a computer. The computer has the following specifications:

CPU	Quad core (x86-64)
RAM	16 GB DDR4
Storage drive	1 TB (900 GB used)
Network	1000 Mbps Ethernet

The new application has the following minimum requirements: quad-core processor, 64-bit operating system, 8 GB of RAM, 120 GB of free space, and 1 Gbps network connection.

Which of the following will result when the technician installs the software?

- ○ **A.** Insufficient RAM
- ○ **B.** Network connection is too slow
- ○ **C.** Insufficient storage
- ○ **D.** Unknown CPU
- ○ **E.** Incompatible system architecture

Cram Quiz Answers

1. A, C, and D. When installing a new application, you should consider the CPU speed (and other minimum/recommended hardware requirements), the Program Files location (64-bit or 32-bit), and user permissions. The Windows location isn't really important; by default, it will be C:\Windows, but its location doesn't really impact the installation of the application. The warranty (if there is one) can be important if there is a failure, but it doesn't play into the installation of the software.

2. B. System32 is the folder used by Windows to store 64-bit system files. Systemroot is a variable used for the main Windows folder. More accurately, it is written as %systemroot%. It usually equals C:\Windows. SysWOW64 is actually the location of 32-bit system files. Program Files (x86) is where 32-bit versions of programs are stored.

3. D. The user did not pay attention to the *minimum* system requirements. Perhaps the application needed 10 GB of storage drive space, and there was only 8 GB left on the partition. (Close is not good enough!) It appears that the installation started well enough, so the OS should be compatible, and the installation method is most likely correct. As long as the user has rights to run executable files, which is likely, there shouldn't be any file permissions issues.

4. **C.** The system has insufficient storage space. If the system has a 1 TB drive that has 900 GB used, that leaves 100 GB free, which is not enough for an application that requires 120 GB. The technician would first have to free up space by going to **Settings > Apps > Apps & features** and removing some unused applications. There is plenty of RAM on the system, and the network connection is fine (1000 Mbps is the same as 1 Gbps). A quad-core CPU is very common, be it Intel or AMD. Any application should be able to install to it. The system architecture should be adequate: The software requires a 64-bit system, and today's quad-core CPUs are 64-bit. The table says x86-64, which means 64-bit.

Well, that wraps up this chapter. Excellent work. Review, break, and then continue on!

CHAPTER 39

Common Operating Systems

This chapter covers the following A+ 220-1102 exam objective:

▶ **1.8** – Explain common OS types and their purposes.

What type of operating system do you run at home? What do you run at work? What do other people you know use? Think about these questions for a moment. The answers usually depend on the type of computer a person has: desktop, laptop, handheld, and so on. They also depend on a person's preference, or a company's preference. Often, the choice is based on *need*. Always consider what kind of work a user needs to perform. The answer will, in part, dictate what type of operating system—and ultimately the type of computer—a user requires. Let's discuss the most common operating systems now.

> **ExamAlert**
>
> **Objective 1.8** focuses on workstation operating systems, cell phone/tablet operating systems, various file system types, vendor life-cycle limitations, and compatibility concerns between operating systems.

Workstation Operating Systems

Workstation operating systems include Microsoft Windows, Apple macOS, Linux, and Chrome OS. In this case, "workstation" means a desktop or laptop computer that a user sits at to perform work—so we are not including servers in this section.

By far the most common workstation OS in the workplace is Microsoft Windows, and Windows is the main focus of the rest of this book. For the exam, you need to be able to work with Windows 10, but be ready for newer (and possibly older) versions in the field! The good thing about different Windows versions is that they are quite similar architecturally and from a user standpoint. Most of the built-in programs work in the same manner, though the names and navigation might be slightly different. Also, the command line hasn't changed too much in the past 10 years. Most of the exam questions you will come upon and most of the Windows problems you will face can be approached in the same manner, regardless of the *version* of Windows.

Next on the list is macOS, previously known as OS X. It is the proprietary operating system used by Apple for its Macintosh desktop computers and MacBook Pro and Air laptop computers. This operating system (and the Mac computer in general) has been a favorite of multimedia designers, developers, graphic artists, and musicians since the 1990s. macOS has used version numbers since its inception, such as macOS 10.14 (codenamed Mojave) and version 12 (Monterey). Apple used the name "OS X" through version 10.11 (El Capitan) but changed to the name macOS at version 10.12 (Sierra).

Although some Macintosh computers may have Intel processors, they are not PCs. Likewise, macOS is not compatible with PC add-on hardware. Conversely, PC-based operating systems, such as Windows and Linux, do not normally run on Macintosh computers—though it can be done in the case of Windows (for example, with Boot Camp, as described in Chapter 41, "macOS").

Linux is an ever-expanding group of operating systems that are designed to run on PCs, servers, gaming consoles, DVRs, mobile phones, IoT devices, and many other devices. Originally, Linux was designed as an alternative operating system to Windows; however, it has been estimated that no more than 3% of the U.S. market uses Linux on PCs. Linux does, however, have a much larger market share when it comes to servers, penetration-testing laptops, and other computer devices, and in those markets, the percentage is growing rapidly. Linux was originally written by Linus Torvalds (thus the name) and can be freely downloaded by anyone. Several organizations and companies emerged and developed this free code (or a variant of the free code) into their own versions of Linux, which are referred to as *distributions* (often abbreviated as *distros*). Some examples of Linux distributions include Red Hat, Fedora, Debian, Ubuntu, and Kali, each of which uses its own version number scheme. Although Linux is free to download, it is licensed under a General Public License (GPL), which states that derived works can be distributed only under the same license terms as the software itself.

The Chrome operating system (Chrome OS) is designed by Google to act as a workstation that uses mostly web-based applications. Chrome OS can run on a variety of devices but is best known for being loaded on Chromebooks, which are a favorite among grade schools and some home users. While Chrome OS is based on Android, and ultimately based on Linux, and it can access many apps from the Google Play Store, it is still considered to be a separate operating system because it has been so heavily modified to work with Chromebook hardware. However, Chrome OS is designed in such a way that a user could accomplish everything he or she needs to do from within the Chrome browser.

> **Note**
>
> If you have access to Windows, macOS, Linux, and Chrome OS, I recommend that you attempt to locate the following for each: Settings, the command line, and the built-in Internet browser. This will get you started on your way to becoming familiar with each interface. Quick tip: The Chrome OS command line (called Crosh) is not important for the exam, but you can access it by pressing Ctrl+Alt+T, which launches the Terminal in a new browser tab.

Smartphone and Tablet Operating Systems

The world of mobile device operating systems consists of four main players: Android, iOS/iPadOS, Chrome OS, and Windows. But when it comes to actual smartphones and tablets, Android and iOS/iPadOS are the primary players. So, we'll focus on them in this section.

Mobile device software comes in one of two forms: open source, which is effectively free to download and modify, and closed source, otherwise known as commercial or vendor-specific, which cannot be modified without express permission and licensing. There are benefits and drawbacks to each type of system. Because you will see both in the field, you should know each one equally. Let's consider examples of these types, using Android and iOS.

Android

Android is an example of open source software. It is a Linux-based operating system used mostly on smartphones and tablet computers and is developed by the Open Handset Alliance, a group directed by Google. Google releases Android code as open source, allowing developers to modify it and freely create applications for it. Google also commissioned the Android Open Source Project (AOSP), whose mission is to maintain and further develop Android. You know you are dealing with the Android open source OS and related applications when you see the little robot caricature, usually in green.

Android versions were referred to by such sweet names as Lollipop, Marshmallow, Nougat, Oreo, and Pie (versions 5 through 9, respectively), until version 10, when the delectables were discontinued. To find out what version you are currently running, start at the Home screen, which is the main screen that boots up by default. Access the Settings screen (often by swiping down from the top and clicking the Settings gear). Locate the About page (within General or a similar section) and tap it. The version should be listed there.

Suppose a company wants to create a custom version of Android for a handheld computer that it is developing. According to the license, the company would be allowed to do this and customize the OS to its specific hardware and applications. This is exactly what smartphone manufacturers do, and it's what differentiates those devices' software packages from each other. Such companies all design their own types of launcher software. The launcher is the part of the graphical user interface (GUI) in Android where a user can customize the Home screen.

Manufacturers of Android-based devices (as well as the general public) can create their own applications for Android as well. To do this, a developer needs to download the Android application package (APK), which is a package file format used by Android for distribution and installation of application software and middleware.

iOS

Apple's iOS is an example of closed source software. It is found on iPhones and older iPads. To learn what version of iOS you are running, go to the Home screen and then tap **Settings**. Tap **General** and then tap **About**. You'll see the version number. For example, if you saw Version 11.3.1 (15E302), then 11 is the version, .3.1 is the point release, and 15E302 is the build number.

Unlike Android, iOS is not open source and is not available for download to developers. Only Apple hardware uses this operating system. This is an example of vendor-specific software. However, if developers want to create an application for iOS, they can download the iOS software development kit (SDK). Apple license fees are required when a developer is ready to go live with an application.

iPadOS

iPadOS is a variant of iOS developed specifically for iPad tablet computers. iPads previously used the iOS operating system through version 12; however, at version 13, iPads starting using iPadOS.

iPadOS has a different design and orientation than iOS, taking advantage of the additional real estate of a tablet compared to a smartphone. A user can open more than one instance of an application and can take advantage of additional multitasking that might not be available on iOS. With iPadOS, you can also use an iPad as a secondary monitor/drawing tablet when connected to a Mac.

Keep in mind that there are many similarities between iPadOS and iOS, including the fact that iPadOS is closed source (but with open-source components).

Understand the difference between open source and closed source.

Note

We don't cover the basic usage of Android, iOS, iPadOS, or Chrome OS in this book. It is considered prerequisite knowledge to the CompTIA A+ exams. We do cover mobile OS troubleshooting later in the book, but if you are new to Android or iOS, consider getting your hands on a device or two and practicing with the OS!

File System Types and Formatting

Once you have chosen your partition scheme and created a partition, you then need to format the partition so that it will be ready to accept data. To do this, you must select a file system, which enables the storage and reading of data to and from the drive.

Windows File System Basics

When formatting a storage drive in a Windows environment, you have the option to format it as NTFS (recommended), FAT32, or FAT. NTFS is a more secure and stable platform and can support larger volume sizes. It also supports encryption with the Encrypting File System (EFS) and works better with backups. FAT32 and FAT should be used only to interact with older versions of Windows and to format devices such as USB flash drives. Depending on the cluster size used, NTFS can support partitions up to 16 TB (4 KB clusters) or 256 TB (64 KB clusters), but some systems are limited to 2 TB due to the limitations of partition tables on MBR-based drives. This hardware limitation applies to maximum FAT32 partition sizes of 2 TB as well (aside from the installation maximum of 32 GB). To go beyond this, a set of striped or spanned dynamic drives would have to be used, creating a multidrive volume.

Another file system introduced by Microsoft, called the Extended File Allocation Table (exFAT), is suited specifically for USB flash drives but addresses the needs of many other mobile storage solutions. The successor to FAT32, it can handle large file sizes and can format media that is larger than 32 GB with a single partition. In fact, exFAT (also known as FAT64) has a recommended maximum of 512 TB for partitions, with a theoretical maximum of 64 ZB (zettabytes). The file size limit when using exFAT is 16 EB (exabytes). This file system can be used in many versions of Windows. If NTFS is not a plausible solution and the partition size needed is larger than 32 GB, exFAT might be the best option.

As of the writing of this book, exFAT is not used for internal SATA storage drives; it is used for flash memory storage and other external storage devices. exFAT is considered to be a more efficient file system than NTFS when it comes to flash memory storage; it experiences less fragmentation, leading to more possible read/write cycles over the life of the flash memory device.

> **ExamAlert**
>
> Know the differences between NTFS, FAT32, and exFAT.

Regardless of the file system used, in Windows you can opt for a quick format or a full format (which is also known as a *normal format*). In Windows, a quick format removes *access* to files on the partition or drive; a full format writes zeros to the entire partition and also scans the partition or drive for bad sectors, which can be quite time-consuming. Generally, technicians should avoid the full format. However, if a drive is brand new and has never been formatted, or if a drive has been acquired from another source and you are concerned with its integrity, you should consider running a full format. But be careful with full formats because they put a lot of stress on the drive, which can reduce its life span, especially in the case of magnetic-based hard drives. If you are concerned that a partition was "quick" formatted and possibly has bad sectors, you can run the **chkdsk /r** command to find out for sure.

> **Note**
>
> Quick and full formats are *not* considered secure solutions for drives that will be repurposed or that have been obtained from other parties. More secure solutions that do *multiple* passes (zeroing out the data) are required. We'll discuss this further in Chapter 50, "Data Destruction and Disposal."

Linux File System Basics

Linux supports many file systems, including the ext family, FAT32, and NTFS. It also supports Network File System (NFS), a distributed file system that allows a client computer to access files over the network. It was designed especially for Linux and Unix systems, but other systems such as Windows can use it as well.

> **Note**
>
> In the following two paragraphs, I'll be discussing commands that you can type in Linux. This is done in the Terminal, which is the command-line tool used in Linux and macOS. It is similar to the PowerShell/Command Prompt used in Windows. It can be opened by searching **terminal**.

However, the most common file systems used on the local system are ext3 and ext4. ext4 is the Fourth Extended file system, which can support volume sizes of up to 1 exabyte (EB). You can discern the type of file system used in Linux by typing the **df -T** command. On systems commonly used during the writing of this book (in 2021), /dev/sda1 (where the Linux OS is installed) is usually ext4.

In /dev/sda1, /dev refers to the file system representation of devices. There can be more than one storage drive within the /dev path. Originally, sd stood for SCSI devices, but now it also includes SATA drives. Instead of calling each disk "disk 0," "disk 1," and so on (as Windows does), Linux refers to them as "a," "b," "c," and so on, and the number at the end of the path is the number of the partition. Linux is normally installed to partition 1, the full path being /dev/sda1; this is known as the *boot partition*. The second partition listed is an extended partition, similar to the Windows extended partition in that it can be used to create additional partitions for data, such as /dev/sda2 or /dev/sda3 and beyond. You might find that a particular partition (for example, /dev/sda5) is used by the OS as a swap file (that is, a paging file) between the memory and the storage drive. You can find a list of the partitions available on most Linux systems by opening the command line (Terminal) and typing **lsblk**, which is short for *list block devices*.

The following is an example of a Debian Linux system with two storage drives:

```
sda          8:0    0 465.8G  0 disk
├─sda1       8:1    0 433.9G  0 part /
├─sda2       8:2    0    1K   0 part
└─sda5       8:5    0  31.9G  0 part [SWAP]
sdb          8:16   0 111.8G  0 disk
```

In this example, there are two solid-state drives: sda (465 GB) and sdb (111 GB). sda is divided into three visible partitions: sda1, where the OS is installed; sda2, which is a startup partition; and sda5, the swap partition. Is **lsblk** the only command you could use? No. In Linux, there are always more commands, but **lsblk** is a good one.

> **Note**
>
> There are a variety of other file systems used by Linux, so be prepared for lots of different acronyms. For example, btrfs is another Linux-based file system used by some network-attached storage (NAS) devices.

As you can see, Linux makes use of a *swap partition*, also known as swap space. The swap partition acts as an overflow for RAM. If the RAM fills up, any subsequently opened applications will run inside the swap partition on the storage drive until some RAM space is cleared up. This is somewhat similar to the Windows pagefile concept, but the Linux swap space exists on a separate partition, whereas the Windows page file exists on C:\ by default.

We'll discuss Linux further in Chapter 42, "Linux."

macOS File System Basics

As of the writing of this book, and since macOS version 10.13, Apple has used the Apple File System (APFS). It is the successor to Hierarchical File System Plus (HFS+). These file systems work in a similar fashion to Linux-based file systems (it's all Unix-based by the way) and can be analyzed in a similar way in the Terminal. For example, to see a list of the partitions, type **df -t** (lowercase *t* here) or use the macOS command **diskutil list**. macOS also uses a set of swap files in a similar manner to Linux. They are stored in /private/var/vm. They can be displayed with the Disk Utility program, or in the Terminal using the **ls -lh /private/var/vm/swapfile*** command.

We'll discuss macOS further in Chapter 41.

Vendor Life-Cycle Limitations

Today, most computing devices and their operating systems have limited life spans. Some manufacturers of hardware and software decide on an end-of-life (EOL) date as part of the original design of a system. This can mean a couple of things, including the discontinuation of updates and the ending of support for software/hardware. It's all part of the life-cycle policy.

Typically, a device's software support can be expected to last between three and five years before EOL—and that's it. Think that over for a moment. It means that your organization needs to continually plan what will happen to the multitude of devices and operating systems that it supports. The more types of devices and operating systems, the more complex the work. It can be daunting. That is why most organizations implement complete life-cycle planning—from initial installation to decommissioning.

Table 39.1 gives some examples of support end dates (as of the writing of this book). While EOL dates are not set in stone, manufacturers usually adhere to them once they have published them. The Windows dates listed in this table are "end of *extended* support" dates, which are the important dates to know. Depending on when you are reading this book, you will note that Windows 8.1 end-of-support is right around the corner or has already happened!

TABLE 39.1 **End-of-Life/End-of-Support**

Product	Ending Date
Windows 8.1	January 2023
Windows 10 (21H1)	December 2022
Windows 10 (20H2)	May 2023
macOS 10.15 (Catalina)	October 2022
macOS 11.0 (Big Sur)	October 2023
Chromebook (3400)	June 2025
Ubuntu 20.04 LTS	April 2025

What does all this mean? You need to be cognizant of the fact that all hardware and software has a limited life span. When the end-of-support date comes, then no more updates—most importantly, security updates—will be available. Being without security updates is a risk that most companies are not willing to take. So, in many cases, a company needs to upgrade software (and potentially hardware) every couple of years—and more often if the company uses several different platforms.

Windows 10 takes a bit of a different approach compared to previous Windows platforms. With Windows 10, there are different "versions" of Windows, such as Windows 10 version 20H2 and Windows 10 21H1. Windows 10 uses this numbering convention instead of the commonly used *point release* numbering convention, but it is similar conceptually. While the published end of extended support for 21H1 is December 2022, chances are the system will attempt to auto-update to the next version; if you run Windows 10 Home or Pro, and if not configured properly, the update could happen at an inopportune time! Companies that run Windows 10 Enterprise (and other select editions) often disable auto-update and/or defer updates until they can be tested. In addition, the Windows 10 Enterprise LTSC extended support end date is pushed out much further. To find out the version of Windows you are running, go to the **Run** prompt and type **winver**.

> **Note**
>
> For more about the Windows life-cycle and extended support end dates, see https://docs.microsoft.com/en-us/lifecycle/faq/windows.

> **ExamAlert**
>
> Remember that a software version has an end-of-support date, also known as an end-of-life date. Be ready to have an upgrade plan well before that date!

Some companies don't publish end-of-support dates until they stop supporting a version. But you can take a good guess as to when this will happen, based on historical data. For example, Android 6.0, released in late 2015, was discontinued in late 2018, and Google stopped updating security patches for it at that point—a three-year span. This is typical. Another example: Typically, Apple only supports MacBooks that were built in the past five years or so. What it boils down to is this: You can expect a device to be supported for x amount of time before security patches stop. Plan for it!

Compatibility Concerns Between Operating Systems

In a computer network that has multiple platforms, there is definite concern about how the different operating systems will work with each other. That's why some organizations opt to become single-shop houses—meaning they only use one manufacturer, such as Microsoft. But that isn't always possible (or preferable), so operating systems often have to interoperate. That means cross-platform compatibility for apps, file sharing compatibility, and the process of different systems logging into each other—for example, a Linux computer connecting to a Microsoft domain or an Apple Mac system interacting with Chrome OS. As we progress through the book, we'll be discussing different ways to approach compatibility between different systems.

Furthermore, even if two systems *are* compatible, it doesn't mean that every *version* of each of those systems is compatible. An older version of Android might have no chance of connecting to a newer Windows domain controller. Or an older version of Windows (such as Windows 7) won't be able to interact properly with a newer version of a Linux server—not to mention that Windows 7 is not supported anymore and is a security risk. As I said, we'll get into compatibility issues more as we progress through the book.

The bottom line is this: The more platforms and systems you introduce to your infrastructure, the more complex things get, and the more you need to think about how these systems will all interact from networking, security, and usability standpoints.

Cram Quiz

Answer these questions. The answers follow the last question. If you cannot answer these questions correctly, consider reading this chapter again until you can.

1. Which of the following operating systems is a free download with no evaluation period limitations?

   ○ **A.** Windows

   ○ **B.** Ubuntu

   ○ **C.** macOS

   ○ **D.** iOS

2. Which of the following is used on iPads newer than 2019?

   ○ **A.** Chrome OS

   ○ **B.** Windows 10

   ○ **C.** iPadOS

   ○ **D.** Android

   ○ **E.** iOS

3. Scenario: It's the summer of 2024. Your company has many types of technologies running — and many of them interact with each other. Of the following operating systems that are used in your company's infrastructure, which is *not* a major security concern?

   ○ **A.** Windows 8.1

   ○ **B.** Windows 10 (21H1)

   ○ **C.** Ubuntu 20.04 LTS

   ○ **D.** macOS 11.0

4. Which of the following statements is true?

   ○ **A.** Android is an example of closed source software.

   ○ **B.** 32-bit CPUs can only address a maximum of 256 GB of RAM.

   ○ **C.** Chrome OS is designed by Apple to use mostly desktop applications.

   ○ **D.** 64-bit versions of Windows can run 32-bit apps as well as 64-bit apps.

5. Which of the following does macOS use that works in a similar fashion to Linux-based file systems?

   ○ **A.** APFS

   ○ **B.** EOL

   ○ **C.** ext4

   ○ **D.** exFAT

Cram Quiz Answers

1. B. Ubuntu (regardless of the version) is a free download. While you can download some versions of Windows, they are only for evaluation periods of time. Apple-based operating systems, such as macOS and iOS, are not free downloads.

2. C. iPadOS is the operating system used on iPads that were built after 2019. iOS is used on iPhones. Chrome OS is used on a group of devices, most notably Chromebooks. Windows 10 is used on PCs, laptops, and Microsoft Surface devices. Android is used by several manufacturers of smartphones and tablets; it is the main competitor of iOS.

3. C. The only one of the listed answers that is not a *major* security concern is Ubuntu 20.04 LTS, which has an EOL of April 2025. The rest have EOL dates before the summer of 2024, and if they are not updated to something newer before that, they will cease to receive security updates — and that's when it can get scary. But really now, this is a bit of a trick question. All of them are security concerns! Every OS and device on a network should be a security concern, regardless of age. Consider that.

4. **D.** The only true statement is that 64-bit versions of Windows can run 32-bit apps as well as 64-bit apps. 32-bit CPUs enable 4 GB of address space (RAM) maximum. On the other hand, 64-bit CPUs have a wider data path and can address a default maximum of 256 terabytes (TB) of RAM. For the A+ exam, remember that Android and Linux are examples of open source software, while Windows, macOS, and iOS are examples of closed source commercial software. Chrome OS is designed by Google to act as a workstation that uses mostly web-based applications.

5. **A.** Apple uses the Apple File System (APFS) on macOS and some other Apple-based devices. It works in a similar fashion to Linux-based file systems. End-of-life (EOL) is the discontinuation of updates and the ending of support for software/hardware. ext4 is the Fourth Extended file system in Linux. exFAT is the successor to FAT32 in Windows, it can handle large file sizes and can format media larger than 32 GB.

Wow! We just ran the gamut of operating systems, so to speak. If you can build a knowledge base for each of the operating systems in this chapter, then you can be a powerhouse technician! Great work. Continue!

CHAPTER 40

Operating System Installations and Upgrades

This chapter covers the following A+ 220-1102 exam objective:

▶ **1.9** – Given a scenario, perform OS installations and upgrades in a diverse OS environment.

A technician may be called upon to install or reinstall an operating system to a new computer, an older computer, or a virtual machine. A smart technician knows the various ways to boot from an installation source, which may be removable media, a source that is internal to the computer, or a source that is stored on the network. Professional technicians will ask questions such as what type of installation is it? How will we partition and format the drive? are there any special considerations during setup? Always consider these questions as part of your planning for an installation or upgrade.

When working in a small environment, clean installations are typical; when working in a larger environment, network installs, unattended installations, imaging, and repairs are much more common. This chapter covers the basics when it comes to operating system considerations. When you are done here, you should understand how to install any OS (Windows, Linux, macOS, and so on) from any source and to any destination drive. Let us begin.

ExamAlert

Objective 1.9 focuses on boot methods, types of installations, partitioning, drive format, upgrade considerations, and feature updates.

Boot Methods

To install an operating system to a computer, you first have to boot the system to the installation media. There are several types of boot methods you should know for the exam:

▶ **Local installation from an external drive/flash drive:** The most common type of local installation is via USB flash drive. To do this, download the operating system .ISO file (or similar file type) from the OS developer's website. Make the USB flash drive bootable and extract the contents of the .ISO file to the drive. There are free programs available that can speed up the process by making the drive bootable, formatting it, and extracting the .ISO all at once (for instance, Rufus, Yumi, and the Windows USB/DVD Download Tool). Once the flash drive is set up, insert the flash drive to the target system, boot the computer, change the BIOS/UEFI boot order to USB flash drive first, and get installing! Often this will be quick and painless. Less commonly, you might install from a hot-swappable drive within a USB drive enclosure or perhaps from an eSATA drive.

Note

Try downloading an .ISO image of Linux or Windows (evaluation) and extract the contents to a USB flash drive. Then, install the OS to a physical computer so that you can see the installation process. You can also run through the installation process with virtual machines by accessing the .ISO file directly.

▶ **Local installation from an optical disc:** This means that you insert the disc into the optical drive of the computer you are sitting at, known as the local computer. Generally, the type of optical disc used is a DVD-ROM, although this option is not used often anymore because it is a slow process, and there are other faster methods; in addition, most machines today do not have optical drives.

> **Note**
>
> By the way, when you sit at a computer and answer all the questions it asks you, step-by-step, it is known as an *attended* installation; you are attending to the computer as the installation progresses.

▶ **Network boot (PXE) installation:** You can install an OS to a client by booting to the network and using a Windows server and the Windows Deployment Services (WDS) and/or Microsoft Endpoint Configuration Manager (MECM) or by accessing any Windows or Linux server acting as a repository for the Windows installation files. (Those servers will also operate as DHCP and TFTP servers.) If you do need to perform an over-the-network installation, be sure that the target computer has a Preboot Execution Environment (PXE)–compliant network adapter. This allows the computer to boot to the network and locate the DHCP server and, ultimately, perform the installation (as long as the server is configured properly). We'll discuss a couple of those options in an upcoming section.

▶ **Internal drive installation:** You can install from fixed media inside a computer; however, usually the source of the media should not be stored in the same location as the target area for the OS. There are two options here: Install from a separate partition of a storage drive or install from a separate drive altogether. As usual, I am using the term "storage drive" loosely. It could be a magnetic-based disk, an SSD, an NVMe-based drive, or even a USB flash drive if the motherboard has an internal USB port (with a USB drive inserted). Some power workstations and server motherboards come with these, for installation purposes, or even to run the OS! In any case, the installation media will have to have the .ISO or another image of the operating system to be installed.

▶ **Internet-based installation:** Operating systems can also come directly from the Internet, either in part or completely. For example, Ubuntu Server has options for automated server provisioning in bare-metal cloud environments and instant operating systems that are ready for virtualization platforms such as VirtualBox, Hyper-V, and KVM. Just go to the website, click, and start installing. Going further, you might also do installations of software, or even install entire operating systems, by using Microsoft's task sequencer. An example might be a Windows in-place upgrade using MECM—most likely within the Azure cloud. For more information, see https://docs.microsoft.com/en-us/mem/configmgr/osd/deploy-use/deploy-task-sequence-over-internet.

> **ExamAlert**
>
> Know these boot methods for OS installation and upgrades: optical disc, external/flash drive, network boot (PXE), internal drive, and Internet based.

Whatever method you choose, be sure to select that method as the first boot option in the BIOS/UEFI of the computer. Other configurations might also be necessary. When you are finished, reset the BIOS/UEFI boot priority to storage drive first and, if necessary, disable any removable media options in the BIOS/UEFI.

Types of Installations

Along with the boot method, you should be prepared for the type of installation you require. There are several types of OS installation

▶ **Clean install:** With a clean installation, the OS is installed to a blank partition. It could be a new storage drive or a drive/partition that was wiped clean of data. Generally, a clean install is attended to by the technician, who interacts step-by-step with the OS as it is installing. Newer hardware might not be seen correctly by some operating systems, so be ready to supply third-party drivers for hardware (such as storage drives or video).

▶ **Upgrade:** With an upgrade installation, the target storage drive (or partition) already has an operating system installed and is upgraded to a newer version of that operating system—for example, from Windows 8.1 to Windows 10 or from Windows 10 to Windows 11. Another example is an in-place upgrade (often used for repairs), in which the OS is effectively reinstalled but without losing files or applications. The repair in-place upgrade and other similar repair-based installations are usually last-resort options for fixing individual systems. Remember that upgrades may or *may not* retain a user's data. Regardless of the upgrade type, you should always back up the data and the user preferences/profile before initiating the upgrade. Also, be sure that current applications will function on the new OS and that any older hardware will have an applicable driver for the newer OS before upgrading.

▶ **Unattended installation:** This type of installation requires an answer file that has been created in advance. Also, it normally requires a specific service. For instance, to automate the process of installing Windows, you can use WDS. This server-based program works with the Windows System Image Manager program in Windows. It can be used to create the answer file that is used during an unattended installation. The answer file provides the responses needed for the installation, eliminating the need for user intervention. In Windows, there is a single XML-based answer file called Unattend.xml.

Note

The Windows System Image Manager (SIM) is part of the Windows Assessment and Deployment Kit (ADK) for Windows 10, which can be downloaded from Microsoft's website.

For more information about Windows 10 deployment with the ADK, visit https://docs.microsoft.com/en-us/windows/deployment/windows-deployment-scenarios-and-tools.

▶ **Image deployment:** Images can be made and deployed in a variety of ways, such as by cloning the entire drive image of another installation. This can be done by using programs such as Acronis True Image or Ghost. When cloning a drive image, both computers must be identical, or as close to identical as possible. The drive of the target for a cloned installation must be at least as large as the original system. To avoid security identifier (SID) conflicts, use the Sysprep utility. The Sysprep utility for Windows is installed with the operating system and can be found in C:\Windows\System32\Sysprep\. Sysprep uses an answer file created with the SIM. It creates a unique SID and makes other changes as needed to the network configuration of the system. You can also "image" the computer with a *premade* OS image. Do this with the Microsoft Deployment Toolkit or with third-party tools such as Ghost. In addition, you can install from a recovery disc/drive that you created or that was supplied by the vendor of the computer.

▶ **Remote network installation:** A remote network installation can be initiated while the target computer is booted to a preexisting OS or by booting a PXE-compliant computer to the network and specifying the server (where the OS installation files are located) to access from the BIOS/UEFI. Once again, WDS and the Microsoft Deployment Toolkit are key components if you are remotely deploying Windows.

▶ **Reset/restore:** These are options for troubleshooting problems with a Windows system. In Windows 10, for example, **Reset your PC** enables the user to clear everything or keep personal files. Restoring the PC means undoing recent changes. Windows can also be installed from a previously made System Restore image. For more information on System Restore and troubleshooting Microsoft Windows in general, see Chapter 53, "Troubleshooting Microsoft Windows."

▶ **Installing from a recovery partition or disc:** Computers with Windows preinstalled use a recovery disc, a hidden partition, or both. This disc and/or partition contains a factory image of Windows. The purpose is to enable users to return their computers back to their state when they were first received. This means that the system partition (usually the C: drive) will be properly formatted and reimaged with Windows. This works well in a two-partition system, in which the operating system is on C: and data is stored on D: or another drive letter. In this scenario, when the operating system fails and cannot be repaired, the computer can be returned to its original "factory" state, but the data won't be compromised (and neither will applications if they were installed to the other partition!). When you buy a computer from a company such as HP, Dell, and so on, make sure it offers some kind of factory recovery partition, recovery disc (or flash drive), or other recovery option.

ExamAlert

Know the difference between local, network, drive image, and recovery partition installations.

Multiboots

Since the 1990s, technicians have been setting up two or more operating systems on the same drive; this is known as dual-booting, tri-booting, and so on. The process is easier today than it used to be back in the 1990s; now you can usually get away with using built-in tools in Windows or Linux. For example, if you have Windows 10 installed, you can modify the partition structure with Disk Management, create an additional partition, and install another OS to that new partition. This requires a bit of planning, but if successful, both operating systems display in a menu when the computer is booted. The information pertaining to these operating systems is stored in the Boot Configuration Data (BCD) store in Windows and in GRUB (GRand Unified Bootloader) in Linux.

Partitioning

Partitioning is the act of dividing a storage drive into sections. It's kind of like a floor plan for your drive, with "walls" that separate your formatted areas for data. You don't have to have any walls, so to speak; you can have a single partition, or you can have more than one. The design is up to you. Let's talk about the basic partitioning terms you should know for the exam.

Primary and Extended Partitions and Logical Drives

The first partition that the OS is installed to is called a *primary partition*. Many systems have a single primary partition, which is inhabited by the OS and also stores the data. In Windows, it is usually known as the C: drive. However, it is a good practice when first partitioning a drive to create two partitions: one for the OS, and one for the data (perhaps C: and D: or C: and F:). This keeps the data *safer* in the event of an OS crash and subsequent repair or reinstall of the OS. In a typical Windows system, the storage drive is limited to four partitions. Those can be four primary partitions or three primary partitions and one extended partition. The extended partition can be further broken up into logical drives, allowing a person to have as many sections as there are letters in the alphabet—which is usually enough!

Letter assignments (C:, F:, G:, and so on) are also referred to as *volumes*. A volume can be a single partition or logical drive, or it can span different drives or even different systems. We discuss this further in Chapter 34, "Microsoft Operating System Features and Tools, Part II."

Basic and Dynamic Drives

A typical installation of an OS such as Windows normally results in a basic drive. This is a storage drive that has finite-sized partitions and volumes. Those partitions cannot be resized unless you convert the drive to a dynamic drive. This is a process done in Windows with the Disk Management program or at the command line with the **diskpart** utility. Once converted, partitions and volumes can be resized as the user sees fit—as long as there is space available on the drive. There is risk involved with using this process, and data should be backed up prior to initiating the conversion. It's a fairly easy process that we detail in Chapter 34.

GPT vs. MBR

There are two partitioning schemes that you should know for the exam: GPT and MBR. These schemes define the maximum number of partitions that a drive can have as well as the maximum size of each partition. Which partitioning scheme will you use? You will usually make use of the globally unique identifier (GUID) Partition Table (GPT) instead of the older Master Boot Record (MBR). GPT is a newer standard and has, for the most part, replaced MBR; it is not limited in the way that MBR is. With GPT, you can have up to 128 partitions, and no extended partition is necessary. Also, you are not limited to the MBR's maximum partition size of 2 TB. In addition, the GPT is stored in multiple locations, so it is harder to corrupt the partition table data.

Note

Use of the term "master" is ONLY in association with the official terminology used in industry specifications and standards, and in no way diminishes Pearson's commitment to promoting diversity, equity, and inclusion, and challenging, countering and/or combating bias and stereotyping in the global population of the learners we serve.

GPT is used heavily in Linux systems, and Windows has supported it since 2005. It forms a part of the UEFI standard, and your system needs to have a UEFI-compliant motherboard. It uses globally unique identifiers (secure 128-bit numbers) to reference partitions, making it virtually impossible for any two computers to have two partitions with the same ID.

In essence, GPT was designed to replace MBR, and it is strongly linked to how the UEFI is designed to replace (or augment) the BIOS. It's important to remember that you might need to select either GPT or MBR when you first add a new drive or start an installation. You can convert a drive from MBR to GPT, but the drive will be wiped when you do this. For more information on how to do this conversion, visit https://docs.microsoft.com/en-us/windows-server/storage/disk-management/change-an-mbr-disk-into-a-gpt-disk.

Most systems today are UEFI compliant, so if you perform a fresh installation of Windows, it should automatically seek to use GPT, as long as UEFI is enabled.

> **ExamAlert**
>
> Know the differences between GPT and MBR! GPT is newer and better, has 128 partitions, and can go far beyond the 2 TB MBR maximum partition size.

More OS Installation and Upgrade Considerations

There are plenty of other considerations to make before and during an OS installation, including the following:

▶ **Load alternate third-party drivers when necessary:** For example, if you are installing Windows to a newer and less common storage drive (perhaps a brand-new-model NVMe), you might have to supply the manufacturer's drivers if Windows doesn't recognize the drive.

▶ **Workgroup vs. domain setup:** If a Windows computer will be stand-alone or used in a small office, chances are it will be set up to connect in workgroup mode. In a larger environment that is controlled by a Windows server, you might have to select "domain." Before this, however, you will need to make sure that the network adapter is properly configured with the IP address of the DNS server on the network or has obtained that information properly from a DHCP server.

▶ **Time/date/region/language settings:** During the installation, you will be prompted to enter basic information such as the time, date, time zone (and/or region of the world), and language you will be using. For the rest of this book, we will focus on English as the main language (out of personal preference as well as a necessity)!

▶ **Driver installation, software, and Windows updates:** You might be prompted to load additional drivers for storage, video, and network devices—especially network interface cards so that the system can access the Internet. Have these ready for beforehand.

▶ **Properly formatted boot drive with the correct partitions/format:**
If you install Windows and decide to customize the partitions, you have
to be sure to use the right formatting and build out at least one recovery partition. The unwritten rule is to use the NTFS file system for the
main primary partition where the OS will be housed, and the written
rule is to make it 32 GB or more (for Windows 10). The minimum size
of the recovery partition will depend on the version of Windows, but, for
example, Windows 10 will often use 450 MB. A recovery partition is created automatically if you do a default installation of Windows and if you
select the default partition layout. After the installation is complete, you
can view the partitions in Disk Management or with the **diskpart** utility
in the Command Prompt. For example, type **diskpart** to enter the utility,
type **select disk 0** (where 0 is the first drive), and then type **list partition**. Figure 40.1 shows an example of this. In this example, Partition 4
is 145 GB. That is the C: drive, and it is where I installed Windows 10. I
store the data separately on Partition 7, which is 86 GB. Also, there are
three recovery partitions in this case, ranging between 300 and 450 MB.
The Disk Management equivalent is shown in Figure 40.2, though this
does not display Partition 3 "Reserved." Keep in mind that your default
installation of Windows will probably have fewer partitions; for example,
you might see a recovery partition, an EFI system partition, and the OS
partition.

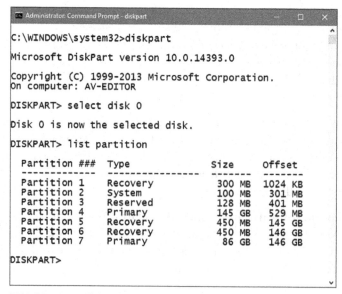

FIGURE 40.1 **diskpart utility, showing the partitions of a Windows boot drive**

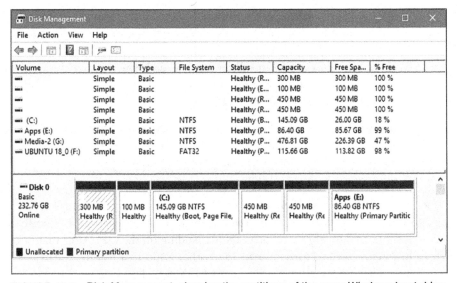

FIGURE 40.2 **Disk Management, showing the partitions of the same Windows boot drive as in Figure 40.1**

ExamAlert

Know how to use the Disk Management and diskpart utilities!

▶ **Factory recovery partition:** If you buy a computer from a manufacturer, the software may be preloaded. In that case, there will usually be one or more recovery partitions on the storage drive that are separate from the system partition. These are generally less than 1 GB each and can be used to repair the system and recover from any errors that occur.

▶ **Prerequisites/hardware compatibility:** As mentioned earlier, you have to make sure that your physical computer (or virtual machine) will meet the minimum requirements as set by Microsoft or another OS developer. Before installing, you should also check the hardware compatibility list for the particular OS and make sure that the motherboard, CPU, video card, audio card, network adapter, and storage drives will work with that OS.

▶ **Application compatibility:** This all stems from the original question: What are you going to use the computer for? If it's going to be used to run Logic (audio software), then you need a Mac. If you are running Pro

Tools, then you need to decide whether you will use Windows or Mac. Or maybe you want to build a Hyper-V virtualization system using Windows. If so, it will run on any edition except Home. Know what you are doing with the computer before installing the OS and know whether the applications will run on the computer's hardware and within the version and edition of the OS you wish to install.

▶ **OS compatibility/upgrade path:** If you are upgrading from one OS to another and wish to save the data/settings, you have to make sure that the upgrade path is valid. We discuss upgrade paths further in Chapter 30, "Comparing Windows Editions."

▶ **Product life cycle:** Remember to keep in mind any operating system or application life cycle. For example, once an OS is released, it typically is supported for three to five years (depending on the OS). After that, it won't receive security updates (and other important feature updates) unless it is upgraded to a new version of the OS. For instance, support will end for all versions of Windows 10 Home and Pro on October 14, 2025 (see https://docs.microsoft.com/en-us/lifecycle/products/windows-10-home-and-pro). Well before the end of the product life cycle, you and your team will need to decide what will become of the device and its software.

Planning Is Crucial!

There is a lot to consider in this chapter. I always say that *planning is key*. Clean and sharp planning helps you avoid problems and saves time in the long run. Planning is extremely important when dealing with all things technology.

Cram Quiz

Answer these questions. The answers follow the last question. If you cannot answer these questions correctly, consider reading this chapter again until you can.

1. Which of the following installation types would require PXE compliance?

   ○ **A.** Local

   ○ **B.** Network

   ○ **C.** Internal

   ○ **D.** USB flash drive

2. To avoid SID conflicts when drive imaging, which program should you use in Windows?

○ **A.** Sysprep

○ **B. diskpart**

○ **C.** SIM

○ **D.** Windows Deployment Services

3. You are tasked with installing Windows with the standard configuration. It needs to support a storage drive with a single 8 TB partition. Which of the following should you configure the system to use?

○ **A.** GPT

○ **B.** FAT32

○ **C.** MBR

○ **D.** ext4

4. Which of the following uses an answer file to provide responses and eliminates the need for user intervention?

○ **A.** Factory recovery partition

○ **B.** Clean installation

○ **C.** Unattended installation

○ **D.** Reset your PC

5. What should a technician consider first when planning to install Windows to a newer, less common storage drive? (Select the best answer.)

○ **A.** Alternate third-party drivers

○ **B.** A repair installation

○ **C.** Recovery partition

○ **D.** The product life cycle

Cram Quiz Answers

1. **B.** A network-based installation requires that the network card be PXE compliant so that it can boot to the network and locate a DHCP server and deployment server. Local installations, such as those using a USB flash drive or optical disc, do not need the network adapter. Internal installations, such as those that are done from a secondary internal drive, also do not need a PXE-compliant network card.

2. **A.** Sysprep can modify unattended installations so that every computer gets a unique SID (and other unique information). Windows SIM creates the answer files for unattended installations. **diskpart** is used to view and configure partitions from the Command Prompt in Windows. Windows Deployment Services (WDS) is run on Windows Server and is used to deploy operating systems across the network.

3. **A.** Use GPT as your partitioning scheme (instead of MBR) and follow that up by using NTFS as your file system for the partition. That is the typical setup when installing Windows. In this scenario, GPT and NTFS can support 16 TB partitions. FAT32 is an older file system that you could use, but it would not support the 8 TB partition that is required. ext4 is a Linux-based file system not used in Windows. Know your file systems for the exam!

4. **C.** An unattended installation uses an answer file that provides the responses needed for the installation. A factory recovery partition is preloaded by the computer manufacturer. A clean installation means that the OS is installed to a blank partition or new drive. Reset your PC is an option in Windows that allows a user to repair a computer by reinstalling the OS with one of two options: wiping all data or keeping user files.

5. **A.** If you are installing Windows to a newer and less common storage drive, you might have to supply the manufacturer's drivers (or third-party drivers) if Windows doesn't recognize the drive. A repair in-place upgrade and other similar repair-based installations are usually last-resort attempts to fix individual systems. The purpose of a recovery partition is to enable users to return their computers back to their state when they were first received. A product's life cycle is everything that happens from purchase to installation to end-of-life (EOL) and recycling/disposal. Support is the important thing here when it comes to software. For example, once an OS is released, it is typically supported for three to five years (depending on the OS).

As your "tech coach," I have to say, you are doing great! Keep going!

CHAPTER 41

macOS

This chapter covers the following A+ 220-1102 exam objective:

▶ **1.10** – Identify common features and tools of the macOS/ desktop OS.

Although Windows has the largest market share of the desktop and laptop market, there are other operating systems you can choose from as well. macOS is a favorite with users who need to manipulate audio and video media. It's also commonly used by engineers and developers. Plus, some people just plain prefer macOS to Windows and favor the Apple MacBook Air and/or MacBook Pro over Windows-based PCs. This chapter discusses some basic features and tools of the macOS operating system.

ExamAlert

Objective 1.10 focuses on macOS: the installation and uninstallation of applications, Apple ID and corporate restrictions, best practices, system preferences, features, Disk Utility, FileVault, Terminal, and Force Quit.

macOS Basics

macOS is closed source. That means that the code is *not* released to the public; you cannot download it. Essentially, macOS is originally based on Unix source code. The type of Unix code is Berkeley Software Distribution (BSD). The original BSD was discontinued long ago, but it became the basis for a lot of software, including operating systems such as FreeBSD, OpenBSD, and NetBSD (which are open source), as well as macOS and iOS.

ExamAlert

macOS is closed source and is based on BSD (Unix).

Apple is credited with making the original graphical user interface (GUI) that people manipulate with a mouse and keyboard—the mainstream way of working with a computer. macOS uses control panels (windows with icons) to configure, troubleshoot, and maintain the computer. Collectively, these are known as System Preferences. This is similar to the Microsoft Windows Control Panel, though different functions have varying names and locations. Some applications are ported for macOS (for example, Microsoft Office for Mac); however, macOS uses its own web browser (Safari) as opposed to Windows' Microsoft Edge. Web browsers such as Chrome and Firefox can be run on macOS as well.

An example of the macOS GUI is shown in Figure 41.1. macOS's desktop has a user-friendly design that includes a basic menu bar at the top, which includes the Apple menu, the currently opened application (in this case, Terminal), and standard options (such as Edit, View, and so on). There are icons on the bottom (in the "Dock") used for commonly used applications, such as Safari, Mission Control, Mail, and FaceTime. The *Dock* is a major feature of the macOS GUI used to launch common applications and switch between running apps.

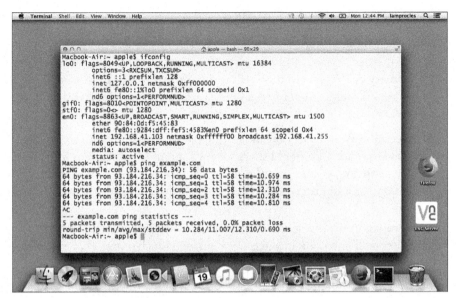

FIGURE 41.1   **Example of the macOS GUI**

ExamAlert

Use the Dock to open common applications and switch between running apps.

In Figure 41.1 you can see that the Terminal program is open. Two commands were run: the **ifconfig** command, which shows information about the network interface, including the IP address (192.168.41.103), and the **ping** command, showing 64-byte ping replies from example.com. The Terminal works in a similar fashion to the Linux Terminal.

System Preferences

System Preferences is where you can go to configure macOS. It is similar to the Control Panel and Settings in Windows and Settings in Linux. There are many options here, including the following:

▶ **Displays:** Here you can modify the look of the display, change the resolution, and modify the brightness and color scheme.

▶ **Networks:** In this section you can modify wired networks, wireless connections, and USB Ethernet connections. You can also configure advanced TCP/IP settings.

▶ **Printers & Scanners:** Here you add or remove printers or scanning devices, work with the print queue, share printers, and modify printer options.

▶ **Security & Privacy:** In this section you can change your password, enable FileVault, configure the firewall, and enable/disable location services.

▶ **Accessibility:** This section allows you make the system more accessible by incorporating keyboard shortcuts for zooming in and out of the display, setting up gestures via the keyboard, turning on dictation, enabling captions, and additional keyboard, mouse, video, and audio options.

System Preferences is the home to many other configurable options for the Dock, Mission Control, audio, energy savings, and much more. There are also programs that you can work with, including the Time Machine, which we'll discuss later in the chapter.

macOS Features

There are many features in macOS that make it a user-friendly environment. The CompTIA 220-1102 exam focuses on a small group of them, which we'll discuss now.

The best way to open applications or files is to use *Finder*, a program similar to File Explorer but designed to make finding applications easy. Finder is available on the menu bar as well as within the Dock. Applications and files can also be stored on the Dock and anywhere on the desktop, but if you don't see the application or file you want, you can use the Finder program. If you still can't find what you are looking for or if you aren't even sure if it is on your computer, use the *Spotlight* search tool. This is displayed as a spyglass in the menu bar on the top right of the desktop and can also be accessed by pressing and holding the Command and Spacebar keys simultaneously on the keyboard. (The Command key is similar to the Windows key on a PC keyboard.) This search tool searches through files, emails, apps, songs, printers, and so on. It can also search other computers on the network (which it discovers using Bonjour—a networking technology used by macOS to locate networked computers and devices). Plus, it looks through external sources such as Wikipedia, Bing, and iTunes, to name a few. The goal is to receive a media-rich, definitive set of results to your query.

ExamAlert

Understand what the Finder and Spotlight programs are in macOS.

Let's get into what you see on a Mac and how it is displayed. First, you can modify how the desktop is displayed or you can set up *multiple desktops*. This is done within *Mission Control*. Mission Control zooms away from the desktop, giving you a larger perspective of apps, "spaces," and virtual desktops. It acts as an application switcher and window manager. Mission Control can be launched in a variety of ways, including by swiping up on the Trackpad with three fingers, double-tapping the Magic Mouse (which is an Apple mouse that allows for special clicking and gesturing, making it easier to navigate through macOS), clicking the Mission Control icon on the Dock, or pressing the Mission Control key on the keyboard. Now you can have multiple desktops by dragging windows to the upper-right corner, or you can add windows to already existing desktops by dragging them to the appropriate desktop at the top of the window. The Dashboard is available here as well; it has some default functions, such as the clock, calendar, and calculator. You can also add special programs to the Dashboard by clicking the + sign. This technology has great implications for researchers, students, programmers, A/V editors, and so on. It allows a user to highly customize the user interface. But be careful because too many desktops and too many open applications will cause the system to run sluggishly. Also, users sometimes forget that they have applications open in other desktops; a quick, three-finger swipe up will reveal anything that is currently running.

Speaking of three-finger swipes, there are all kinds of *gestures* and multitouch gestures that can make you a more efficient macOS user. If you have the supporting hardware (such as a Magic Trackpad or Magic Mouse), you can make use of things such as tapping, scrolling, pinching, and swiping, similar to the same functions on a mobile device. For example, a two-finger swipe up or down will scroll content; a two-finger double-tap will perform a smart zoom, and you can do it again to return; and, of course, there is the pinch out to zoom. The list goes on and on. For a complete list of available multitouch gestures, visit https://support.apple.com/en-us/HT204895.

You can also allow users on other Macs to view your screen and even take control of your computer with a tool called *Screen Sharing* (similar to Windows Remote Desktop). To enable this, go to the **Apple** menu > **System Preferences**, click **Sharing**, then select **Screen Sharing**. For a step-by-step procedure on how to do this and how to connect from another system, visit https://support.apple.com/guide/mac-help/share-the-screen-of-another-mac-mh14066/mac. Things get a little more complicated when you want a Windows computer to control (or just see) a Mac. Third-party Virtual Network Computing (VNC) software (such as RealVNC) can help with this. VNC works cross-platform between Windows, macOS, Linux, and mobile OS versions. VNC can also be used to view a Mac that has Screen Sharing enabled. In Figure 41.1, you can tell that there is VNC server software installed by the icon in the lower-right corner.

> **Note**
>
> Sometimes you might need to share the screen with a second display or to a projector. Many Mac computers come with a secondary DisplayPort (DP) port to enable duplication of the screen.

> **ExamAlert**
>
> Know how to configure multiple desktops, Screen Sharing, and the replication of the display to a secondary monitor.

Ah, the dual-booters! It's amazing how many people want to run Windows on their Mac. Apple offers a utility called *Boot Camp* that allows you to do just this with Windows 7 and later (64-bit versions). However, more powerful Mac hardware is required for newer versions of Windows. After the Windows OS is installed, you can reboot the computer to switch from one OS to the other.

Boot Camp can be found in **Finder > Applications > Utilities > Boot Camp Assistant**. You then need to download the supporting software, create a partition (to be used by Windows), and preferably install the OS from a disk image (ISO). This image can be created with third-party programs such as PowerISO. Then follow the Boot Camp prompts, complete the installation of Windows, and reboot the system. You can switch from macOS to Windows by making use of the Startup Disk preference pane or you can switch from Windows to macOS by accessing the Boot Camp icon in the notification area. For more details on how to install Windows on a Mac with Boot Camp, visit https://support.apple.com/en-us/HT201468.

As you can imagine, there are some security concerns when it comes to dual-booting. Dual-booting potentially opens a computer to attacks on both macOS *and* Windows sides. Both operating systems (but especially Windows) should be carefully secured if you are a Mac owner with a dual-boot system.

Speaking of security, passwords need to be protected in macOS just as they are in any other OS. Apple provides the *Keychain Access* utility, a password management system that can contain not only passwords but private keys and certificates. Keys and certificates are cryptographic methods for storing (and transmitting) secrets; they are generally considered to be more secure than passwords. Keychain Access, which can be accessed from **Finder** > **Applications** > **Keychain Access**, enables a user to automatically populate passwords in applications and save passwords to the cloud (for example, to an iCloud account).

ExamAlert

Consider configuring the Keychain utility to save passwords to an iCloud account. This will enable password population even if a user switches to a replacement macOS device.

Managing and Maintaining macOS

Once again, for the location and management of files and running applications, macOS uses Finder. Finder will open up automatically whenever you access a drive or file listing. From Finder, you can create files, copy and paste files, access favorites (such as Applications, Downloads, and so on), access removable drives, and tag files/applications with various colors. You can also manipulate files at the command line. As mentioned, macOS has a shell utility called *Terminal* that allows you to manipulate data and make configuration changes similar to the PowerShell or Command Prompt in Windows. However, the syntax is different and is similar to that of BSD and Linux. To open the Terminal, go to **Finder** > **Applications** > **Utilities** > **Terminal**. You can also open an application by using the Spotlight tool and simply typing the name of the application.

In addition to viewing locally stored data, you can view remote discs on other Mac computers by sharing them in the System Preferences, and you can view them from the local computer by selecting the **Remote Disc** option in **Finder** > **Devices**. Data can also be stored on the cloud; Apple's version is called *iCloud*. To back up data to iCloud, go to the **Apple** menu > **System Preferences**, click **Apple ID**, and click **iCloud**.

For backing up the state of the computer, macOS utilizes the *Time Machine* backup program. To enable it, go to the **Apple** menu and select **System**

Preferences. Then select the **Time Machine** icon and turn it on to enable automatic backup of any drive. From here, you can back up drives locally or to iCloud. Restoring data also happens from this program. Essentially, you can select the point to which you want to restore—be it a day ago or a year ago. To do this, simply select the desired snapshot from a timeline in the program. This is similar to Windows System Restore. Because the program saves multiple states of files over time, a separate backup method (such as a USB flash drive or other external media) is also recommended for important files.

Although Macs are known for their resilience, their drives should still be maintained. The built-in *Disk Utility* is used for verifying and repairing the storage drive, repairing drive permissions, and possibly booting from the recovery partition (which all Macs have). Disk Utility can also be used to create an image or to recover a system from that image. Note that macOS version 10.14 and higher require the GPT partitioning type.

You can also encrypt the contents of the main storage drive on a Mac with *FileVault*. This program uses the Advanced Encryption Standard (AES) at 128-bit security (as of the writing of this book) to encrypt the entire contents of the drive and prevent unauthorized access to the data stored there. To enable it, go to the Apple menu and click **System Preferences > Security & Privacy**. Then, click the **FileVault** tab, enter the administrator name and password, and click **Turn On FileVault**.

Sometimes you might encounter the *spinning pinwheel*, also known as the spinning pinwheel of death (SPOD). This multicolored spinning wheel is a variation of the mouse pointer arrow; it appears when an application either becomes temporarily unresponsive or enters an infinite loop and cannot recover. If an application freezes or is otherwise not responding properly, you can force that app to close by using the *Force Quit* application. This is located on the Apple menu; after you open Force Quit, you can select the application you want to force to close. This is similar to using the Task Manager in Windows. You can also use the keyboard combination Command+Option+Esc, which is similar to Ctrl+Alt+Del on a Windows PC. However, be ready to troubleshoot further; launching the application again may result in another SPOD.

> **ExamAlert**
>
> Know how to use the Time Machine, Disk Utility, and Force Quit tools in macOS.

General system maintenance includes system updates, anti-malware updates, driver updates, and firmware updates. macOS can be updated by going to the **Apple** menu and selecting **Software Update**. It can also be updated from the App Store. Anti-malware updates should of course be done within the third-party application you are using; we discuss malware in more depth in Chapter 45, "Wireless Security and Malware." The video driver is built into macOS, and it can only be updated by upgrading to a new version of the operating system. Keyboards, mice, and many other devices need to be approved for use with Mac computers; if you buy an Apple-approved device, it should work with macOS. Unfortunately, if a device requires a higher version of macOS, you'll have to upgrade. Most printers work with macOS also, and if a printer driver needs to be downloaded, macOS will automatically run the AirPrint program to locate and download the driver. In general, macOS is designed to simplify the process of installing devices. Finally, firmware updates are usually done automatically when you upgrade to a newer version of macOS.

Installation and Uninstallation of Applications

Because Apple devices are designed to be extremely user friendly, the installation and uninstallation of applications is usually very easy.

A typical way to get apps is to simply go to the App Store. From here, it's a breeze to search for, install, and update applications. However, while that process is very intuitive, sometimes you might need to go a little further. For example, you might need to download a program from the Internet that is not in the App Store. Usually, this is still a pretty straightforward installation: Once an application is downloaded to the Downloads folder, you double-click the package (or disk image) and follow the installer's onscreen instructions.

Here are the file types that you should know for the exam:

- ▶ **.dmg:** These are mountable disk image files that are intended for distribution of software to macOS systems. This format is commonly used by developers to build and distribute applications for macOS. These files can be validated during installation to make sure they have not been tampered with during transit. When a user double-clicks a package, it is opened by the Disk Image Mounter utility, which mounts a virtual disk in Finder (and possibly on the desktop) that appears similar to a USB flash drive.

The user may then find one or more program icons (APP files) which can be run from that location or dragged to another location such as the Applications folder.

▶ **.app:** Also known as APP files, these are application bundles that are designed to run under the macOS system. They run when they are double-clicked, in a similar fashion to .exe files in Windows. They are often found within .dmg software packages. While entire APP files can be moved to another location and run, individual files within an APP file should not be moved away from the rest of the files in the package.

▶ **.pkg:** These are packages of software and other files that can be installed to macOS and iOS devices. In some cases, a .pkg file is a file saved as plaintext; if that's the case, it can be opened with any text editor in macOS. The extension is also used by several other types of systems and may be developed by more insidious persons. macOS provides an automatic security safeguard related to these files, and a user might encounter a situation where the .pkg file can't be opened because it is from an unidentified developer. It's not recommended to install programs that give messages like this.

ExamAlert

Know the differences between .dmg, .app, and .pkg. For example, you can't install from a .dmg file on Windows because that file type is not compatible with Windows; it is designed for macOS.

Uninstalling applications can be done within **Finder > Applications**. Generally, you want to use an uninstaller program. Open the application's folder and check for an uninstaller. If one exists, double-click it and follow the onscreen instructions to remove the application. If an uninstaller program does not exist, drag the application from the Applications folder to Trash (located at the end of the Dock by default). You can uninstall applications that came from the App Store by using the Launchpad program. In Launchpad, click and hold on the application that you wish to remove until all the applications start to jiggle and then click the application's delete button.

In a corporate environment that uses Managed Apple IDs, the user will not be able to install or uninstall applications. You'll learn more about Managed Apple IDs in the next section.

Apple ID

To sign in to Apple services and use iCloud for storage, Apple devices use the Apple ID, which identifies a user.

The Apple ID is designed to keep settings and services up to date across all Apple devices. If a person uses an iPad, an iPhone, and a MacBook, then things such as passwords, apps, documents, and configurations can all be synchronized among these devices.

By default, an Apple ID starts with an email address and a password. However, it can be augmented with two-factor authentication to allow connections only from trusted devices and only if the user knows the required multi-digit verification code in addition to the password. This is designed to prevent unauthorized logins.

For example, if an iPad requires a user to sign in with his or her Apple ID, that user would have to type the password, and then most likely access an iPhone (or other smartphone) to get the verification code requested on the iPad. As of the writing of this book, the secondary code is optional, but many technology companies are planning on making two-factor authentication mandatory for users. Typically, this is a more secure way of authenticating users, so be ready for it!

A company can also create Apple IDs to be assigned to users for business purposes. These are known as *Managed* Apple IDs. They are separate from a user's personal Apple ID and are assigned by the administrator at the company. However, a user can have the same email address and phone number for both a Managed Apple ID and a personal Apple ID. To protect the company, there are several restrictions for Managed Apple IDs. For example, these IDs cannot make purchases, and certain features are disabled. To get access to something, a typical user might have to contact the administrator at the company. Effectively, the company owns the Managed Apple ID user accounts.

> **Note**
>
> Apple provides extremely concise instructions on how to do just about anything on an Apple device at https://support.apple.com.

Cram Quiz

Answer these questions. The answers follow the last question. If you cannot answer these questions correctly, consider reading this chapter again until you can.

1. Which of the following is the built-in web browser for macOS?

   ○ **A.** Safari

   ○ **B.** Chrome

   ○ **C.** Firefox

   ○ **D.** Edge

2. Which program should you use to access Utilities in macOS? (Select the two best answers.)

   ○ **A.** Mission Control

   ○ **B.** Finder

   ○ **C.** Spotlight

   ○ **D.** Keychain

3. Which of the following should be enabled when you want a user at another Mac to take control of your computer?

   ○ **A.** Remote Desktop

   ○ **B.** Remote Assistance

   ○ **C.** Screen Sharing

   ○ **D.** Screen Mirroring

4. Which utility allows a Mac user to dual-boot macOS and Windows?

   ○ **A.** Ubuntu

   ○ **B.** **apt-get**

   ○ **C.** **bootrec**

   ○ **D.** Boot Camp

5. You want to save the state of a Mac running macOS. Which tool should be used?

   ○ **A.** System Restore

   ○ **B.** Time Machine

   ○ **C.** Force Quit

   ○ **D.** Disk Utility

6. Due to recent corporate espionage attempts, a technician needs to secure the contents of the main storage drive on the CEO's Mac. Which macOS utility will allow the tech to encrypt the drive? (Select the best answer.)

   ○ **A.** Terminal

   ○ **B.** FileVault

   ○ **C.** App Store

   ○ **D.** 128-bit encryption

7. Which program handles installing a printer's driver automatically in macOS? (Select the best answer.)

   ○ **A.** Bonjour

   ○ **B.** Magic Mouse

   ○ **C.** AirPrint

   ○ **D.** iCloud

8. You need to download an application that is not available on the App Store. It needs to be mounted as an image. Which of the following extensions should you use?

   ○ **A.** .pkg

   ○ **B.** .app

   ○ **C.** .dmg

   ○ **D.** Finder

9. A customer reports that a spinning wheel appears on her screen whenever she tries to run a specific application. What does this spinning wheel represent? (Select the best answer.)

   ○ **A.** A failing CPU

   ○ **B.** An Apple macOS proprietary crash screen

   ○ **C.** A Microsoft Windows proprietary crash screen

   ○ **D.** A Linux proprietary crash screen

Cram Quiz Answers

1. **A.** Safari is Apple's web browser. It is used in macOS and iOS. Chrome is developed by Google and can be added to macOS. Firefox (Mozilla) can also be added to macOS. Microsoft Edge is the built-in browser that Windows uses.

2. **B and C.** Finder is the application to use when looking for applications and files. Utilities is located in **Finder** > **Applications**. Spotlight can be used to locate just about anything on a Mac, including Utilities. Mission Control allows you to modify

the desktop (and run multiple desktops). Apple provides the Keychain Access utility, a password management system that can contain not only passwords but private keys and certificates.

3. **C.** Use Screen Sharing in macOS to allow another user to view and take control of your Mac. (The remote user could also use VNC.) Remote Desktop and Remote Assistance are similar programs used in Windows. Screen mirroring is a technology (common in mobile devices) that allows the display to be mirrored to a TV or to another computer.

4. **D.** Use the Boot Camp Assistant to dual-boot macOS and Windows on a Mac. Ubuntu is a distribution of Linux. **apt-get** is a command run in Linux to install, uninstall, and upgrade applications. **bootrec** is a command used in Windows to troubleshoot Boot Manager and data store issues.

5. **B.** Use the Time Machine to save the state of the computer or to restore to that computer's earlier state. This is similar to the Windows System Restore utility. Force Quit is a utility in macOS that closes a nonresponsive application. Disk Utility is used to verify and repair macOS drives.

6. **B.** The tech can encrypt the contents of the main storage drive on a Mac with FileVault. Terminal allows you to enter commands, manipulate data, and make configuration changes and is similar to the PowerShell or Command Prompt in Windows. A typical way to get macOS apps (with a valid Apple ID) is to simply go to the App Store. Although FileVault implements AES 128-bit encryption to encrypt the entire contents of a drive, 128-bit encryption by itself is not a macOS utility.

7. **C.** AirPrint is the technology used to install a printer automatically in macOS (as long as the printer is compatible with macOS). Bonjour is a networking technology used by macOS to locate networked computers and devices. The Magic Mouse is an Apple mouse that allows for special clicking and gesturing, making it easier to navigate through macOS. iCloud is Apple's cloud infrastructure, where a Mac user can store and back up data. While AirPrint might locate the printer driver on iCloud, iCloud is not the best answer.

8. **C.** Download the .dmg file format. This provides a mountable image that is opened by the Disk Image Mounter utility when double-clicked. It then mounts a virtual disk in Finder, but Finder is a program, not an extension. The .pkg and .app file types do not mount an image the way that a .dmg does. However, an .app might exist inside a .dmg!

9. **B.** A pinwheel, also known as a spinning pinwheel of death (SPOD), is an Apple macOS proprietary crash screen. An example of a Microsoft Windows proprietary crash screen is the blue screen of death (BSOD). Linux is an open source operating system. Although there are crash screens in Linux, they are not considered proprietary. A spinning wheel could possibly be *caused* by a failing CPU, but it is more likely caused by a stalled or frozen application.

Your learning of macOS has been massively magnificent—to the max! Review the chapter and your notes, take a break to drink your favorite beverage, and then continue!

CHAPTER 42

Linux

This chapter covers the following A+ 220-1102 exam objective:

▶ **1.11** – Identify common features and tools of the Linux client/desktop OS.

On the desktop side, Linux is used mostly by enthusiasts and techies—such as systems administrators, developers, engineers, gamers, and so forth. Linux on the desktop side has a smaller business market share than Windows, but even its small share of the market still represents a substantial number of computers. It's worth covering Linux for that reason alone.

On the server side, IT infrastructure is dominated by Linux. Couple this with the fact that any Linux system (desktop or not) can act as a server, and you see that it is important to cover some server-side content as well within this chapter.

Supporting Linux is a valued skill in today's job market. We won't go too deep, but you should come away from this chapter with a basic understanding of how to manipulate any Linux system, especially from the command line.

Linux Basics

Linux is open source. The code for Linux can be downloaded and used/modified by anyone, which means anyone can build their own version of Linux. You might have heard of several (or more) different distributions of Linux. In no particular order, some common examples include Debian, Ubuntu, Fedora, Red Hat, Kali Linux, and Arch Linux. But the list goes on and on. These distributions are community supported, and some have client-side and server-side versions (for example, Ubuntu Desktop and Ubuntu Server). There are so many Linux distributions that we could fill a book describing them, and more are being released every week. This is the beauty of the General Public License (GPL) for Linux: It basically states that Linux is free to use and to develop. People at home can make their very own versions of Linux if they so desire.

On the client side, Linux users have the option of using one of several desktop environments (GUIs). One popular desktop environment is GNOME, which stands for GNU Network Object Model Environment. A GUI that runs on top of the Linux operating system, GNOME consists solely of free and open source software. Its emphasis is on simplicity and accessibility and endeavoring to use a low amount of resources.

A number of programs available for Linux are fairly equivalent to Microsoft applications. For example, LibreOffice is a group of free software applications that can be used to create word processing documents, spreadsheets, slide shows, and so on. Files can be saved in LibreOffice with the same extensions used in Microsoft Office, and therefore they can be opened in either application.

The command-line functionality in most Linux distributions is in depth and well documented, allowing a user to configure and troubleshoot just about anything from within the "shell," or command line. To help you learn more about any commands, the operating system usually has built-in manual (or man) pages that are accessible online.

Linux Desktop Distributions

The most common types of Linux by far include Android (for mobile devices), Google Chrome OS, and various derivatives of Linux used by gaming consoles. However, this section concentrates on desktop computers and the types of Linux that can be loaded on them.

There are literally hundreds of Linux desktop distributions. Most are used by PC enthusiasts and gamers, as well as by some programmers and engineers (and the number is growing). One popular distribution (or "distro") is Ubuntu. Ubuntu is commonly used for a variety of purposes. Figure 42.1 shows an example of Ubuntu Desktop (a client-side version of Linux).

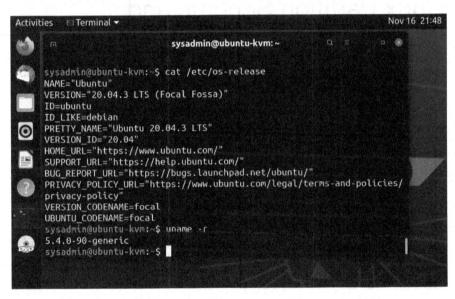

FIGURE 42.1 **Ubuntu Desktop**

In the figure, you can see a column of icons on the left that allow a user to open programs such as the web browser (Firefox), mail, files, and more. On the top is a basic information bar that shows the active window that is running—in this case, Terminal. The Terminal program is the command-line program included in most distributions of Linux. In this Terminal window, you can see that I have run a couple of commands. The first one, **cat /etc/os-release**, results in the version number of Ubuntu that I am running (20.04.3 LTS). The second one, **uname -r**, indicates the Linux kernel version (5.4.0-90). Commands such as these work on most distributions of Linux.

> **Note**
>
> For practice with Ubuntu, consider creating an Ubuntu bootable USB stick within Windows; see https://ubuntu.com/tutorials/create-a-usb-stick-on-windows#1-overview. An Ubuntu bootable USB stick enables you to boot Linux from the flash drive and practice Linux commands using the built-in Terminal application. You might also consider downloading the latest version of Ubuntu and installing it on a virtual machine. Or, if you are using Windows, consider using the Windows Subsystem for Linux (WSL). Ubuntu Desktop can be downloaded from https://www.ubuntu.com/download/desktop.

Linux Partition Scheme and File System

Linux uses the GUID Partition Table (GPT) to list and control the partitions on the systems. GPT supports UEFI, 128 partitions, and partition sizes beyond 2 TB, and it is stored in multiple locations, making it superior to MBR technology. Linux most commonly uses the ext4 file system, which allows a user to resize partitions at will—if there is additional space available on the drive.

> **ExamAlert**
>
> Most Linux systems use the ext4 file system and GPT by default.

Linux Command Line

For the typical Linux user, the command line is not a necessity. Today's Linux desktop interfaces (such as GNOME) offer most of the configuration settings that a standard user needs. However, for power users, sysadmins, and typical geeks, it's all about the command line. Use it.

The command line in Linux is normally referred to as "Terminal," and you access it by using the search tool or by opening the list of applications. The search tool can be accessed by pressing the Superuser key (which is the Windows key on most keyboards). Then just type **terminal**. Or press Superuser+A (in the GNOME environment) to see the list of applications and select **Terminal** from there. In Ubuntu (and some other distributions), you can press Ctrl+Alt+T to open Terminal.

When you open Terminal, Linux places you in a *shell*, which is a command processor that runs within a command-line tool (usually Terminal). One of the most commonly used shells is the Bash shell. From a shell, you can enter commands and execute scripts. Everything we discuss in this chapter is based on the Bash shell.

> **Note**
>
> If you work on a proper Linux server, it is command line only, and there is no desktop. Be ready!

There are hundreds of Linux commands. The CompTIA A+ exam only requires you to know a couple dozen of them. Table 42.1 describes the commands you should know for the exam as well as some commands that are useful in real-world Linux administration.

Know that when working in the Linux directory structure, you always use a slash (/) to separate directory levels. (In Windows, you use a backslash [\].) So, you might have a path such as **/Downloads/pdfs**. If there is ever any confusion as to which is the slash and which is the backslash on the keyboard, remember that the backslash (\) is the one near the backspace key (on U.S. keyboards). Use the slash (/) for Linux, which usually shares the key with the question mark.

TABLE 42.1 **List of Linux-Based Commands**

Command	Description
ls	Lists directory contents. Similar to **dir** in Windows.
cd	Changes the directory. Similar to the Windows **cd** command. Try typing **cd /etc** and look at the contents of the /etc directory.
pwd	Displays the full path/filename of the working directory. Don't confuse this command with **passwd**!
mv	Moves (or renames) files. Similar to the Windows **move** command.
cp	Copies files and directories. Similar to the Windows **copy** command.
rm	Removes files or directories. Similar to the Windows **del** and **rd** commands.
find	Searches for files (or directories) in a directory hierarchy.
cat	Displays the contents of text files (and configuration files) within Terminal.

Command	Description
grep	A filtering command that searches for matching information in specified files and displays that information. The general syntax for **grep** is **grep [*options*] *pattern* [*file*...]**. For example, to locate any lines that include the word "root" in the passwd file, you could type the **grep root /etc/passwd** command. That will normally display one line item: `root:x:0:0:root:/root:/bin/bash` Various options can also be used, including **-i:** Makes the search case insensitive **-d:** Can specify how to handle directories **-w:** Finds exact matches of whole words **-c:** Counts the number of matches found in a particular pattern **-n:** Searches for line number matches Type **grep --help** or **man grep** for more information about **grep** options. **grep** can also be used to filter the results of another command. For example, **ip a | grep inet** will show all IP addresses associated with all network interfaces on the system.
df	Reports file system disk space usage. The command **df -T** includes the file system used by each partition.
chmod	Modifies the read and write permissions for a file or directory.
chown	Changes ownership for files and directories.
ps	Displays information about a process/list running processes. For example, **ps -aux | grep firefox** lists all processes concerning the Firefox web browser that are running. The **kill** command can be used to terminate unwanted processes that are discovered with the **ps** command.
apt or **apt-get**	Used to handle packages (installing, updating, or upgrading) in Debian, Ubuntu, and other Debian derivatives.
dnf or **yum**	Used to handle packages (installing, updating, or upgrading) in Red Hat, Fedora, and similar distributions.
su	Lets you run the shell/Terminal session as another user (root or any other user). Originally short for *superuser*, it is also used to mean *substitute user*. An example of this is shown after this table.
sudo	Allows a user to execute a single command as another user (such as a root). By default, a user with **sudo** privileges can do anything on the system.
passwd	Used to update a user's password.

Command	Description
ip	A group of commands, including **ip address**, **ip link**, **ip route**, and so on. For example, typing the **ip address** command (**ip a** for short) shows the TCP/IP properties of all network connections. An example of this is shown after this table.
iwconfig	Shows the TCP/IP properties of the wireless network connections and can be used to configure them.
dig	Used to find information about DNS.
top	An analysis program that displays the running Linux processes and the CPU and RAM usage for each.
nano	A text editor that can be run from Terminal. Included in most versions of Linux.
vi	Another text editor but more cryptic than Nano. We'll discuss vi (and VIM) in Chapter 62, "Basic Scripting, Part I," and Chapter 63, "Basic Scripting, Part II."
shutdown or **poweroff**	Brings the system down but can be modified in a variety of ways to gracefully shut down the system, notify users, and many more options. To restart the system, type **reboot**.
man	Opens the manual page for any command. For example, **man dig** opens the manual page for the **dig** command. Manual pages give *lots* of information about the command in question. To exit the manual page, press **q** (for quit). A slimmed-down help file is also available for most commands. For example, type **dig --help** for basic information about the **dig** command. The help information is displayed directly in Terminal.

Challenge 5: Use Linux Tools

I say unto you: Go forth and use the command line! Try now to access Terminal in Linux and practice the commands listed in Table 42.1. Remember that the only way to really get to know these commands is to run them in a working Linux environment. Good luck!

Let's look at how to use a few commands. The following example includes two **ip** commands and the **su** command. Take a close look at the results:

```
sysadmin@ubuntu-kvm:/etc$ ip a

2: enp1s0: <BROADCAST,MULTICAST,UP,LOWER_UP> mtu 1500 qdisc fq_codel
state UP group default qlen 1000
```

```
    link/ether 52:54:00:f6:4c:1e brd ff:ff:ff:ff:ff:ff
    inet 10.42.0.53/16 brd 10.42.255.255 scope global enp1s0
        valid_lft forever preferred_lft forever
    inet6 fe80::5054:ff:fef6:4c1e/64 scope link
        valid_lft forever preferred_lft forever
sysadmin@ubuntu-kvm:/etc$ ip r
default via 10.42.0.1 dev enp1s0 proto static
10.42.0.0/16 dev enp1s0 proto kernel scope link src 10.42.0.53
192.168.122.0/24 dev virbr0 proto kernel scope link src 192.168.122.1
linkdown
sysadmin@ubuntu-kvm:/etc$ su - user
Password:
user@ubuntu-kvm:~$
```

In the first line, you can see that I am working using a user account called *sysadmin*. You also see that the name of the Linux system is *ubuntu-kvm*. In addition, I am currently located in the **/etc** directory. Finally, the first command issued is **ip a** (short for **ip address**). Normally, you would see more information if you ran this command, but I truncated the results and am only displaying the main Ethernet network interface here. Among other things, it shows you the name of the network interface *enp1s0*, and the IP address (10.42.0.53/16). Another command you can run to find this information on this system—and many others—is the **nmcli** command. This command is not on the A+ exam objectives (yet), but it is very commonly used.

The second command is the **ip r** command (short for **ip route**). This command displays the default gateway (10.42.0.1) and any network routes available to the network interfaces.

The third command is **su - user**. Remember that the **su** command allows you to log in as someone else; in this case, it is used for the user account, but you can use it this way only if you know the password for the account! I know the password and typed it (although you can't see it, of course), and the system logged me in as *user@ubuntu-kvm*. Good stuff!

When you are finished working in another account, you can end the login session by simply typing **exit** (or pressing Ctrl+D). In the example above, that would return me to the sysadmin login (which was always running).

The default administrative account in most versions of Linux is *root*. You can access this account by typing the **su** command. Linux will ask for the root password, and if you can supply it, you'll have full access to the system. But it's always a good idea to create a separate working administrative account and keeping the root account as a backup; you should also make sure that both accounts have lengthy, complex passwords. However, know this: If you want to take administrative action when logged in as any account (other than root), you need two things: The account has to be added as an administrator of the system, *and* you have to prepend every administrative command with the **sudo** command.

For example, let's say I am logged in as sysadmin, and I want to change the password for the dprowse account. I would type **sudo passwd dprowse**. The **sudo** command gives sysadmin the ability to run administrative commands. The **passwd** command is used to change the password of the currently logged-in account or other accounts. And *dprowse* is the account for which the password will be changed.

> ### ExamAlert
> Know your Linux commands! Practice them on a distribution such as Ubuntu or Fedora.

This command-line information is accessible and available in most versions of Linux. Remember that you can learn more about most of these commands by accessing the help files or the manual pages. The manual pages are also available in several locations on the Internet.

> ### Note
> Another operating system, called FreeBSD, is a common Unix-like OS that has a variety of uses. For example, pfSense uses it for its open source firewalling software. FreeBSD is similar to Linux (yet is not Linux), and is a derivative of Berkeley Software Distribution (BSD). Many commands work in the same manner on Linux and FreeBSD because both are, ultimately, Unix based.

Samba

Samba is a group of programs designed to make Linux interoperate with Windows better. It provides file and print connectivity by making use of the SMB (Server Message Block)/CIFS (Common Internet File System) protocol. (You can find more information on SMB in Chapter 5, "TCP and UDP Ports and Protocols.")

Samba is used in the IT field to integrate Linux systems with Microsoft Active Directory environments. Samba can even operate as an Active Directory domain controller. You can download Samba for Linux from https://www.samba.org/samba/.

In essence, with Samba, you can have Linux clients map drives to Windows servers, and, more importantly, you can have Windows systems map drives to Linux servers (the way they normally would: **net use** *x:* and so on). This way, you can leverage powerful Linux servers to store data and connect to those servers easily from Linux clients *and* Windows clients. Ultimately, those Linux servers can be joined to an Active Directory domain or can become domain controllers themselves.

Linux Best Practices

It's important to make sure that a Linux system is updated and secured, just like any other system. Let's discuss those concepts and some best practices that you can implement on Linux.

Updates and Patches

If a system isn't up to date, it's vulnerable to attack. It's been documented that more than 50% of successful attacks on Linux servers are due to the fact that the Linux system wasn't up to date. Enough said.

So, how do you update Linux? It depends on the distribution and whether you have a desktop environment. Let's discuss the latter first.

If you have a desktop environment, such as GNOME, you usually go to the applications list and then **Software**—or a similar name, such as Software & Updates, or the Software Updater; which one you use depends on the distribution that you are using. With these programs, you can install updates for the operating system and for other software. In addition, many Linux distros tell you when updates have become available to the system and provide painless procedures to perform updates.

In addition, to work at the command line, there are a few commands you can use for updating, as shown in Table 42.2.

TABLE 42.2   **Linux Updating in the Command Line**

OS Distribution	Command	Description
Debian/Ubuntu	**apt update**	Finds out if there are any updates available for the system
	apt upgrade	Actually downloads and installs the updates
	apt install *<program>*	Installs (or upgrades) one or more applications
Fedora/RHEL	**dnf update**	Looks for updates, and if agreed to, downloads and installs them
	dnf install *<program>*	Installs (or upgrades) one or more applications

Keep in mind that you can also use the older **apt-get** command for Debian and Ubuntu and the older **yum** command for Fedora, RHEL, and RHEL clones—and in some scenarios you may *need* to, so know both. In case you were wondering, RHEL (pronounced *rell*) stands for Red Hat Enterprise Linux.

For example, let's say you want to update everything on an Ubuntu system all at once on a single command line. Using the root account, you could use something like this:

```
apt update && apt upgrade -y
```

The double ampersand allows you to string two or more commands together to be run in succession. In this case, the Ubuntu system would look for updates and then install any that are available. The -y means you are saying "yes" to the upgrade (as normally Linux asks you for permission before installing). However, this command is not quite secure—especially for servers. You should always check what is upgradable first before blindly running full upgrades. You can do so with this command:

```
apt list --upgradeable
```

When you use this command, you might find that you only want (or need) to patch one or more files. Perhaps the Firefox browser needs to be patched, but you don't want to do any other upgrades. You could do this with a command similar to the following:

```
apt install firefox-esr.<version_number>
```

This will install the latest version of Firefox for Linux.

As a best practice, at the very least, make sure that all *operating system* updates are installed and check them often (or have an automated system check for you). Operating system updates include security updates, and that's what you really want. But you should also be concerned with applications, especially web browsers, because they are primary targets for attackers as well.

As mentioned, you might install updates individually. Generally, however, Linux systems such as Ubuntu, Debian, and Fedora are very careful about what updates are released; updates are tested thoroughly. So, chances are that if you run full updates of all software, the system will be more secure and will most likely behave as it should.

> **ExamAlert**
>
> Understand how to update Linux systems with **apt update** and **apt upgrade** or **dnf update**.

Backups

One thing about Linux that you might not know is that everything that makes up Linux is a file. There are no databases (by default), there is no registry (as is the case with Windows), and even devices are looked at as files. So, if you want to back up Linux, it's as easy as copying files with the **cp** command. You can also use the **scp** or **rsync** commands to securely copy data to other systems. Of course, there are specific GUI-based backup utilities for Linux as well. For example, Ubuntu has the Backups program, which can back up entire directories (folders) of information to a specified storage location and schedule those backups. Also, most distributions of Linux have the Disks program. Aside from partitioning and formatting, this program can create and restore disk images. In addition, there are plenty of free third-party programs that you can download for backing up Linux, such as Déjà Dup and Grsync. That's the beauty of Linux: Anyone can create these programs, and they are usually open source and free.

A best practice for Linux backup is to schedule your backups to run periodically. You can do this with a lot of third-party programs (and some built-in backup programs), and you can also use a command-line scheduler program such as **cron**, **at**, **systemd**, or **anacron**. FYI: These schedulers are not just for backing up; they can also be used to schedule just about anything you want to happen in Linux.

Anti-malware

In the old days, Linux wasn't targeted by viruses and other malware. That is not the case today. While it is not targeted the way Windows and macOS are, Linux is still a target. Infected Linux systems are not common, but many organizations still require some kind of malware protection. My personal favorite over the years has been ClamAV, but other options include Sophos, Firetools, Rootkit Hunter, and plenty of others, each with unique strengths.

One argument for using anti-malware programs on Linux is to avoid the spread of malware to other systems, such as Windows or macOS, in a multi-platform environment. For example, a Linux system might not be affected by malware stored in a locally run SFTP server, but those files could be transferred to other systems on the network—systems that could be affected. So, a best practice is to have zero trust and to protect all endpoints as much as possible. The concept of zero trust is one that many organizations have been adopting over the past decade. Essentially, it means that the organization accepts the fact that attacks could come from inside or outside and that no system is 100% secure. Convinced?

> **Note**
>
> In a way, Linux goes above and beyond malware protection with Linux kernel security modules, such as AppArmor (Ubuntu/Debian) and SELinux (Fedora/RHEL). These modules restrict the capabilities of programs on the system, and they do it at the kernel level. They are very powerful if used correctly.

In Closing

It's important to keep in mind that Linux changes fast. The core concepts of Linux remain the same (for the most part), but new Linux kernels, security releases, and updates to Linux distributions are constantly emerging. In essence, if you want to work with Linux, you have to be ready to roll with the changes!

Finally, one of the great things about Linux is that many of the distributions are incredibly well documented on the Internet—by very talented people. Support pages, wikis, and forums are available for most distros. Use these resources! Chances are the error you are encountering has been seen before, described online, and *solved*.

> **Note**
>
> If you would like to learn more about how I use Linux, check out my website https://prowse.tech.

Cram Quiz

Answer these questions. The answers follow the last question. If you cannot answer these questions correctly, consider reading this chapter again until you can.

1. Which command in Linux shows the contents of a directory?
   - ○ **A. ls**
   - ○ **B. pwd**
   - ○ **C. cd**
   - ○ **D. mv**

2. Which command should be used to change the permissions of a file?
   - ○ **A. ps**
   - ○ **B. chown**
   - ○ **C. NTFS**
   - ○ **D. chmod**

3. You are working as a junior administrator at a midsized company. You are tasked with updating Linux system software. Which command should be used to gain the necessary permissions to update the software?
   - ○ **A. grep**
   - ○ **B. sudo**
   - ○ **C. chmod**
   - ○ **D. pwd**

4. One of your customers is trying to install a 3 TB storage drive to a Linux system. The customer wishes to use half of the drive capacity for one partition now and wants to have the option to increase the partition size later on. Which file system should you recommend?
   - ○ **A. NTFS**
   - ○ **B. FAT32**
   - ○ **C. ext4**
   - ○ **D. APFS**

5. You are troubleshooting a network connectivity problem on a Linux computer. Which of the following commands will display information about the network interface?

- ○ **A. ip a**
- ○ **B. grep -i**
- ○ **C. sudo**
- ○ **D. netsh**

6. One of your customers tells you that an application in Linux will not open and gives this error:

Only one instance of the program can be run at any time.

You log in to the system as root and open Terminal. Which of the following commands should you run to ensure that no other instances of the program are open?

- ○ **A. cp** and **rm**
- ○ **B. ls** and **chown**
- ○ **C. ps** and **kill**
- ○ **D. pwd** and **chmod**
- ○ **E. sudo** and **nano**

7. An administrator logs in to a Linux computer and runs the following command:

```
ps -aux | grep firefox
```

Of the following, which best describes the functionality of this command?

- ○ **A.** It locates and lists the processes used to run the Firefox web browser.
- ○ **B.** It kills any running programs that start with the word *firefox*.
- ○ **C.** It opens directories that start with the word *firefox*.
- ○ **D.** It creates a new tab for filtering in Firefox.

Cram Quiz Answers

1. **A. ls** will list the directory contents in Linux and macOS. It is similar to the **dir** command in Windows (which can also be used in Linux). **pwd** is used to display the full path of the working directory (for example, /home/root). **cd** is used to change directories. It is very similar to the Windows command of the same name. **mv** is used to move files.

2. **D.** Use the **chmod** command to change permissions in Linux and macOS. **ps** displays information about a given process. **chown** changes ownership of a file. NTFS is the file system used by Windows that allows for file-level security assigned by a user or group.

3. **B.** Use the **sudo** command before other commands that require administrative permissions. For example, you might type:

```
sudo apt upgrade
```

CramQuiz

Linux Best Practices

This will initiate an upgrade on a Debian-based system. Without the **sudo** command, it will not work for any user other than root. Don't forget, you can also use **apt-get** instead of **apt**. **grep** is used to search for matching information in specified files or to filter the results of a command being run. **chmod** is used to change permissions. **pwd** shows the current path that you are located in (**pwd** stands for print working directory).

4. **C.** Recommend ext4. It is the default on most Linux systems, and it has the ability to be resized at a later date. NTFS is a Windows file system, and it doesn't function well with Linux, though it does allow for dynamic resizing of disks in Windows. FAT32 can be used in Linux, and it works well for drives that need to be accessed by Linux *and* Windows systems, but it doesn't allow for resizing. APFS is the Apple File System, and it works only on macOS.

5. **A.** Use the **ip a** command (short for **ip address**) to find information about the network interface. **grep** is a search and filtering tool. If used with the -i option, it ignores case distinctions (meaning uppercase and lowercase). **sudo** needs to be issued before any administrative commands. **netsh** (short for network shell) is actually a Windows command that you would run in PowerShell or the Command Prompt—tricky!

6. **C.** Use the **ps** command to see what processes are running and the **kill** command to terminate the processes as necessary. **cp** is used to copy files, and **rm** is used to remove them. **ls** lists the contents of a directory, and **chown** changes ownership of files and directories. **pwd** shows the current path, and **chmod** changes permissions on files and directories. **sudo** is used before administrative commands, and **nano** opens the built-in text editor.

7. **A.** The command will list the processes used by the Firefox web browser. To show this, you would need to have Firefox running when you type the command. You can break it down like this: The **ps** command reports a snapshot of the current running processes. It can be used with a variety of options. In this case, you use -aux, which will see every single process. The pipe symbol (|) is used to make a modification to the **ps** command. The **grep** command filters the results of the **ps** command, asking the system to display only results that include the word *firefox*. **ps -aux** is commonly used but is a somewhat older option. A simpler way to display process IDs for a particular program would be to use the -e option. For more information, visit the manual page for **ps**. As for the incorrect answers: to "kill," or terminate, programs or processes, you need the **kill** command. To open, or access, a directory, use the **cd** command. Creating new tabs in Firefox is best done in the browser itself!

That last question went a bit above and beyond what I think you need to know for the A+ certification, but you might see a question like this! Even if you don't need to know this for the exam, it's good knowledge for the IT field.

That ends this chapter. Excellent work! I can guarantee that you will see questions about Linux on the A+ exams, so review this chapter *carefully*. That closes out this domain as well. Be sure to study your notes for the entire domain. Then take a nice break; you deserve it!

CORE 2 (220-1102)

Domain 2.0: Security

CHAPTER 43

Physical Security

This chapter covers a portion of the following A+ 220-1102 exam objective:

▶ **2.1** – Summarize various security measures and their purposes.

Welcome to the first chapter on security. Everyone should have some basic knowledge of information security. Computers and computer networks are constantly at risk, and new risks are always rearing their ugly heads.

An attacker might try to break into a facility physically or hack into a system logically. This chapter and the next one cover these two concepts. Here, I use the terms "break" and "hack" loosely; the methods used to accomplish those ends can vary. The goal of this chapter is to present some basic options for securing against a person who would attempt to unlawfully enter a building or another location.

Know this: *Nothing is 100% secure*. It is impossible to completely secure something. Attackers and hackers are always finding ways to get around security solutions; it just takes time and persistence. So, what we are interested in is solutions that are *relatively* secure. We need powerful security methods that are within budget but not so cumbersome that they will bring our computers and networks to a crawl. That's the essence of a good security plan.

To repeat, nothing is 100% secure. Keep that in mind as you progress through the security chapters.

> **ExamAlert**
>
> This portion of **Objective 2.1** concentrates on physical security and physical security for staff.

> **Note**
>
> Remember that the CompTIA A+ certification is not a security certification. However, because security is such an important part of the IT world, it accounts for a substantial percentage of the exam. We therefore spend quite a few chapters of this book on security topics.

Physical security has to do with tangible, visible, and hands-on methods of preventing access to a home, building, server room, datacenter, or any other location. There are lots of ways to accomplish an acceptable level of physical security. Let's start with one of the most important—yet often overlooked—methods: using locks.

Physical Locks

The physical door lock and key is one of the oldest security methods used as a deterrent against unlawful entry. In addition to locking main entrances, you should always lock server rooms, wiring closets, labs, and other technical rooms when not in use. An organization should document who has the keys to server rooms, datacenters, and wiring closets. Locks should be changed out and rotated with other locks every so often. This keeps things dynamic and harder to guess. Another type of lock, a cipher lock, requires a punch code to unlock the door. These physical methods might be used by themselves or combined with an electronic system.

It's important to use a lock for the room that the servers are in, and the servers themselves can also be locked up. Consider placing them in a well-ventilated, lockable cabinet. Special cable locks can also be installed for PCs, laptops, and servers. Some PC cases come with built-in locks. Configure the BIOS/UEFI to log when someone opens the case of the computer. This is logged as a chassis intrusion notification. Use a USB lock to stop people from removing USB devices or to block the physical ports.

Entry Systems

The most common electronic entry system is a key card system. Such a system uses proximity-based door access cards that you simply press against, or near, a transmitter next to the door handle. They are often RFID based. Although these systems are common, they are not the most secure option. (Smart cards can be more secure, as we will discuss in a moment.) But because they are less expensive than other systems, you might see them more often. Other electronic systems use key cards that incorporate a photo ID (such as a worker's badge). Such a card can contain information about the identity of the user, which in combination with a *badge reader* ultimately authenticates the user. While cards are common for entry systems, they can also come in smaller form factors, such as *key fobs*—similar to a vehicle's key fob—which can be attached to a user's keychain. These systems sometimes offer entry control, limiting someone's ability to enter or exit during certain times of the day and identifying and checking names against an authenticated roster, or an *entry control roster*.

Moving on to the next level of security, let's talk briefly about smart cards. A smart card is a card that has a nano-processor and can actually communicate with the authentication system. Examples of these cards include the Personal Identity Verification (PIV) card used by U.S. government employees and contractors and the Common Access Card (CAC) used by Department of Defense (DoD) personnel. Such a card identifies the owner, authenticates them to areas of the building and to computers, and can digitally sign and encrypt files and email with the RSA encryption algorithm (using an RSA token) or another algorithm. Because these are physical items a user carries to gain access to specific systems, they are known as *hardware-based tokens*. A token might also display a code that changes, say, every minute or so; these are known as one-time password (OTP) tokens. When a person wants access to a particular system, such as the accounting system or another confidential system, that person must type the current code that is shown on the token into the computer. This is a powerful method of authentication but can be expensive.

An organization may use an *access control vestibule* (aka *mantrap*), which is an area with two locking doors. A person might get past a first door by following someone else in (tailgating/piggybacking) but might have difficulty getting past the second door, especially if there is a security guard in between the two doors. If the person doesn't have proper authentication, he or she will be stranded in the access control vestibule until authorities arrive.

> **ExamAlert**
>
> An access control vestibule (mantrap) is used to stop and monitor people during the identification process.

Biometrics

Biometrics is the science of recognizing humans based on one or more physical characteristics. Biometrics is used as a form of authentication and access control. It is also used to identify persons who might be under surveillance.

Biometrics falls into the category of "something a person is." Examples of bodily characteristics that are measured include fingerprints, palmprints, retinal patterns, iris patterns, and even bone structure. Biometric readers (for example, fingerprint scanners) are becoming more common in door-access systems and can be found integrated with mobile devices or used as external USB devices that connect to computers. Biometric information can also be combined with smart card technology. An example of a biometric door-access system is Suprema, which has various levels of access systems, including some that incorporate smart cards and biometrics, together forming a multi-factor authentication system. There are also less expensive consumer-grade biometric locks that often include a fingerprint reader as well as a key code or a key lock. One example of biometric hardware for a local computer is a USB-based fingerprint scanner, which is used to authenticate users during the login process.

Movies and TV shows often portray biometric systems as infallible. However, some biometric systems are easily compromised. It has only been recently that readily available biometric systems have started to live up to their potential. Thorough investigation and testing of a biometric system is necessary before purchase and installation. In addition, a biometric system should be used in a multi-factor authentication scheme. The more factors, the better, as long as your users can handle it. (You would be surprised what a little bit of training can do.) Voice recognition software has made great leaps and bounds since the turn of the millennium. A combination of biometrics, voice recognition, and PIN access would make for an excellent three-factor authentication system—if you can get it through budgeting!

Other Physical Security Precautions

There are myriad ways to increase security from a physical perspective. You can use, for example, fences, bollards, alarm systems, video surveillance, and security guards.

Protecting an organization's building is an important step in general security. The more security a building has, the less you have to depend on your authentication system. A building's perimeter should be surveyed for possible breaches—including all doors, windows, loading docks, and even the roof. The area around the building should be scanned for hiding places; if there are any, they should be eliminated. The area surrounding a building should be well lit at night. I can't stress enough the need for good lighting; it's an excellent deterrent. Some companies may opt to use security guards and guard dogs. It is important that they be trained properly; usually an organization enlists the services of a third-party security company for training.

Video surveillance can also be used to track individuals' movements. Video cameras should be placed on the exterior perimeter of a building in areas that are hard to access (for example, 12 feet or higher with no lateral or climbing access). The better the cameras are hidden, the better. Video cameras can also be placed inside a building, especially in secure areas such as executive offices, wiring closets, server rooms, datacenters, and research and development areas. Many organizations use closed-circuit television (CCTV), but some opt for wired/wireless IP-based solutions. In any case, the video stream may be watched and recorded, but it should not be broadcast (especially to the Internet, unless absolutely necessary). Video cameras provide an excellent way of tracking user identities. However, proper lighting is necessary inside and outside in order for the cameras to capture images well. Also, video cameras must be properly secured as they are prime targets for reverse-engineering techniques where the attacker attempts to gain access to the pan-tilt-zoom (PTZ) controls and redirect the video feed.

Alarm systems are commonplace in most buildings today. Such a system sounds a siren and alerts a central monitoring service in the event of an intrusion or a break-in. The placement of door and window sensors and motion detectors is part of a total alarm system, and should be planned out carefully. Motion sensors are often infrared based (set off by heat) or ultrasonic based (set off by certain higher frequencies).

An organization might opt for *fencing* around parking lots or perhaps around specific areas of a building, such as the waste disposal/recycling area or any HVAC units installed on concrete pads outside. Perhaps an entire building is fenced in and has an entry gate (staffed with security guards). Another related option is bollards. A *bollard* is a short vertical post that blocks access to vehicles or protects a building or walkway. Retractable bollards are available, to allow temporary access to an area. *Magnetometers* (metal detectors) can be implemented at entry points to a building to detect metal objects, such as concealed weapons.

One great security technique is to have an employee (or a third party) attempt to access every portion of an organization's property and buildings during the day and at night as well. Monitor and track the user step-by-step to see what the person is able to do and what is accessible. This can be an eye-opening experience. Document what happened carefully and adjust the security plan as needed. An organization can hire third-party companies to do just this—but contracts and agreements must be judiciously carried out beforehand.

The level at which an organization implements these security methods will depend on the organization's security mindset and budget. We could go on and on about general building security, but I think you get the idea. If your organization is extremely concerned about building security and doubts that it has the knowledge to protect the building and its contents properly, consider hiring a professional.

Protecting Data Physically

Confidential documents should never be left sitting out in the open. They should either be properly filed in a locking cabinet or shredded and disposed of when they are no longer needed. Passwords should not be written down and definitely should not be left on a desk or taped to a monitor where they can be seen. Many organizations implement a clean desk policy that states each user must remove all papers from his or her desk before leaving for lunch, breaks, or at the end of the day. Anything that shows on the computer screen can be protected in a variety of ways. To protect data while a person is working, you can use a privacy screen or install a privacy filter, which is a transparent cover for a PC monitor or laptop display. It reduces the cone of vision, usually to about 30 degrees, so that only the person in front of the screen can see the content shown on the screen. Many of these filters are also antiglare, helping to reduce eye stress for the user. Also, users should lock their computers whenever they leave their workstations. Windows can also be automatically set to lock after a certain amount of time, to protect a machine even if a user forgets to do so manually.

Cram Quiz

Answer these questions. The answers follow the last question. If you cannot answer these questions correctly, consider reading this chapter again until you can.

1. Which of the following is the science of recognizing humans based on physical characteristics?
   - ○ **A.** Mantraps
   - ○ **B.** Biometrics
   - ○ **C.** Tailgating
   - ○ **D.** CAC

2. You have been tasked with preventing unwanted removal of a webcam. Which of the following tools should you implement?
   - ○ **A.** Smart card
   - ○ **B.** USB fingerprint scanner
   - ○ **C.** USB lock
   - ○ **D.** Privacy filter

3. You want to know if there is any intrusion to your organization's building. Which of the following should you implement? (Select the two best answers.)
   - ○ **A.** Video surveillance
   - ○ **B.** Magnetometer
   - ○ **C.** Alarm system
   - ○ **D.** Standard door lock
   - ○ **E.** Proper lighting
   - ○ **F.** Access control vestibule

Cram Quiz Answers

1. **B.** Biometrics is the science of recognizing humans based on physical characteristics. In the authentication world, it falls into the category of "something a person is." Access control vestibules (also known as mantraps) are implemented to stop tailgating. CAC, which stands for Common Access Card, is a card used by defense personnel such as DoD employees.

2. **C.** Use a USB lock to prevent the removal of USB-based devices such as external USB storage drives, keyboards, mice, and webcams. Smart cards and USB-based fingerprint scanners are ways to authenticate a user to the computer or network. A privacy filter is used to prevent shoulder surfing—in which a person attempts to watch what a user is typing/performing in a system—by reducing the viewing angle.

3. **A and C.** Video surveillance and alarm systems can help to let you know if an intrusion occurs. However, they differ in that a video surveillance is often passive in design. It usually requires a person to actively monitor it. An alarm system, on the other hand, will trigger an alarm and then send an alert to a monitoring company, which will in turn notify the appropriate personnel at the organization that has been intruded upon. A magnetometer (metal detector) is used to detect metal objects on a person. A standard door lock is an excellent security precaution, but if it is bypassed, the lock itself won't notify you of an intrusion. Proper lighting is also a magnificent idea, but it is passive as well and won't notify of any wrongdoing unless additional sensors (or special types of lighting with sensors) are put in place. An access control vestibule (or mantrap) is used to detain people in an area with two doors—usually for authentication purposes. This by itself won't alert anyone, but access control vestibules are often equipped with video surveillance and possibly security guards (both of which could alert the organization of any wrongdoing).

Good work! This was a shorter chapter that covers just the basics you need to know for the A+ exam. Even so, as usual, be sure to review, take a break, and then continue on.

CHAPTER 44
Logical Security

This chapter covers a portion of the following A+ 220-1102 exam objective:

▶ **2.1** – Summarize various security measures and their purposes.

As an A+ technician, you will probably be more concerned with logical security than physical security. This chapter is therefore a little longer than the last one—and also more in-depth. The goal of this chapter is to present some options for securing against a person who would attempt to unlawfully gain access to a computer network and individual systems. Big task? You bet! However, if we stick to the fundamentals and cover just what you need to know for the CompTIA A+, everything will be just fine. Let's go.

Logical security has to do with operating systems, programs, and data. It is less tangible than physical security. When logical and physical security are used together and implemented properly, they can provide for a high level of security. A lot of what we will discuss in this chapter is within the realm of authentication. Let's start with that.

Authentication

Unauthorized access can be prevented through the use of authentication, which is the verification of a person's identity. It is a preventive measure that can be broken down as the following categories:

▶ Something the user knows (for example, a password or PIN). These factors are known as *knowledge factors*.

▶ Something the user has (for example, a smart card or another security token). These factors are known as *possession factors*.

▶ Something the user is (for example, the biometric reading of a fingerprint or retina scan). These factors are known as *inherence factors*.

▶ Something the user does (for example, a signature or speaking words). These factors are known as *behavioral factors*.

▶ Some*where* the user is (for example, at work or at home). These factors are known as *location-based factors*.

There are more categories, but this bulleted list is a good starting point for you. The first three categories (or factors) are the most common. A powerful security methodology is to combine two or more of these factors together. When this is done, it is known as *multi-factor authentication (MFA)*. An example of this is the combination of a password (knowledge factor) and a smart card (possession factor). Another example is a combination of a fingerprint (inherence factor) with a software token that has been installed to a user's smartphone (possession factor). Both of these are two-factor authentication schemes that you might see in the field. The beauty of MFA is that if one factor is defeated or compromised by a malicious person, the second factor still stands. Think about it for a couple of minutes. Imagine some scenarios where two-factor authentication can help prevent security breaches. Of course, efficient and effective multi-factor user authentication works well only if it is strong—using complex passwords, powerful biometric systems, and updated smart card systems.

> **ExamAlert**
>
> When two or more authentication factors are combined, such as a password and a physical token, the result is multi-factor authentication (MFA).

Principle of Least Privilege

The principle of least privilege says that a user should have access to only what is required. If a user needs to update spreadsheet files and browse the Internet, that user should not be given administrative access. You might think of this as common sense, but it should not be taken lightly. When user accounts are created locally on a computer and especially on a domain, great care should be taken when assigning users to groups. Also, as programs are installed, they request who can use and make modifications to the program; quite often, the default is All Users. Some technicians just click Next when hastily installing a program, without realizing that a user now has full control of the program—control that the user possibly should not have. Remember: Keep users on a need-to-know basis; give them access only to what they specifically need to do their job.

One example of a Microsoft technology that is based on this principle is User Account Control (UAC). UAC is a security component of Windows that keeps every user (besides the administrator account) in standard user mode instead of as an administrator with full administrative rights—even if the user is a member of the administrators group. It is meant to prevent unauthorized access and user error in the form of accidental changes. With UAC enabled, users perform common tasks as non-administrators and, when necessary, as administrators, without having to switch users, log off, or use Run As.

Basically, UAC was created with two goals in mind: first, to eliminate unnecessary requests for excessive administrative-level access to Windows resources, and second, to reduce the risk of malicious software using the administrator's access control to infect operating system files. When a standard end user requires administrator privileges to perform certain tasks (such as installing an application), a small pop-up UAC window appears, notifying the user that an administrator credential is necessary. If the user has administrative rights and clicks Continue, the task will be carried out; if the user does *not* have sufficient rights (and can't provide an administrative password), the attempt fails. Note that these pop-up UAC windows do not appear if a person is logged on with the administrator account.

MDM Policies

For large organizations that have many mobile devices, a *mobile device management (MDM)* suite can be implemented. An MDM solution can take care of pushing updates and configuring hundreds of mobile devices from a central location. Decent-quality MDM software secures, monitors, manages, and supports multiple different types of mobile devices across an enterprise.

Don't forget that Windows runs on many mobile devices, and they can be administered from a centralized MDM solution such as Microsoft Intune, VMware AirWatch, Cisco Meraki, and SOTI MobiControl. Elements that you might administer and enforce include device setup, policy acceptance, profile distribution, device tracking, roaming mitigation, remote lock, remote wipe, and so on. We'll discuss MDM further in Chapter 49, "Mobile Device Security."

Active Directory

We don't cover too much concerning servers in this book, but this section is an exception. Get ready for a crash course on Active Directory!

A Microsoft *domain* is a network of Windows computers that is controlled by a Windows Server which has Active Directory installed—that server is a *domain controller*. Active Directory (AD) is a Microsoft directory service that centralizes the management of user accounts, computer accounts, and so on for a domain.

> **ExamAlert**
>
> Know that a domain is Microsoft's implementation of a client/server network. It centralizes the management of users and computers.

For a user to log on to the domain, that person must have a user account on the domain controller, and the user must know the username, password, and the domain to be logged on to (for example, dpro42.com). In addition, the Windows client computer must have been previously configured to connect to the domain.

The user account is stored within the domain in one of two places: within the Users folder (which is the default) or within an organizational unit that the administrator has created. Take a moment to analyze Figure 44.1.

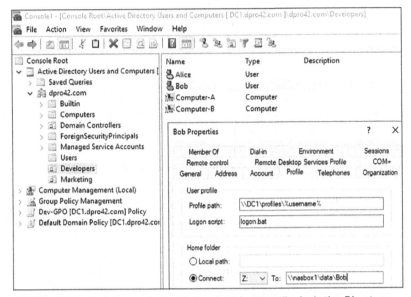

FIGURE 44.1   **User account stored on a domain controller in Active Directory**

I packed a lot of stuff into Figure 44.1. Here you see a Windows server that is acting as a domain controller (which means it has AD installed). It shows Active Directory Users and Computers, which, as the name implies, is where you would go to add, remove, and configure user accounts and computer accounts. (I actually added it to an MMC along with a few other snap-ins.)

By default, users are created within the Users folder, which you can find by following the path **Active Directory Users and Computers >** *Domain Name >* **Users**. dpro42.com is the domain name I chose for this Microsoft network (I own the domain as well). The Users folder has lots of built-in users and groups for you to work with. However, as mentioned, you can also add users to an *organizational unit (OU),* which is a container that you can use to categorize users and computers. Also, you can apply separate group policies for different OUs. This allows you to configure different rules for each set of users, groups, and computers, from one OU to the next. There's a *lot* more to it, but this should suffice for the A+ exam.

Generally, I set up OUs to mimic an organization's departments. So, Figure 44.1 shows that I've created two OUs: Developers and Marketing. The Developers OU is selected, and on the right you can see that there are two users and two computers within that OU: Alice, Bob, Computer-A, and Computer-B (all of which I created).

Furthermore, the user account Bob is selected, and you can see that I have opened the Properties dialog box for Bob. In this figure, you can see the Profile tab. This is where you can set up a profile path, logon script, and home folder for the account. Let's discuss each of these briefly.

User Profiles

Every user account gets a profile, which is a group of folders and settings based on how the user configures his or her desktop environment: Start menu options, desktop icons, background color, and so on. By default, when a user first logs on to a computer, a *local* profile is created and stored on that computer. For example, in Windows 10, this profile is stored in C:\Users\%*userprofile*%, where %*userprofile*% is a variable for whichever user is currently logged on. You can get to the currently logged-on user's profile folder by going to **Run** and typing **%userprofile%** or **%homepath%**. Windows displays the profile folders and—if you are showing hidden files—the NTUSER. DAT file, which is what Windows actually uses to store the profile data.

Now, if you would like a user's profile to follow the user from one computer to the next on a domain, you want a *roaming* profile. That's a profile that is stored on a server. And that's where the Profile path field in Figure 44.1 comes in. The figure shows the location of this user's roaming profile configured as \\DC1\profiles\%username%. *DC1* is the computer where the profile is stored. In this case, it is the domain controller that is being used, but it might be stored somewhere else, and it's probably a good idea to store it elsewhere. *profiles* is the share name for the folder where all the user profiles are stored. %*username*% is another variable, which takes the place of the account name. (I could have used Bob if I'd wanted to, with the same result, but you can appreciate the power of a variable, especially if you will be working with a lot of accounts.) As long as the path to the profile is valid, the domain controller will store it there, and the user can log on to various computers on the network, and the profile will follow the user around.

Logon Script

A logon script is used to assign tasks that are executed when the user logs on to the domain. It could assign tasks like running programs, mapping network drives, setting variables, updating anti-malware applications, running commands, and calling other scripts. The idea is to automate the configuration process for a user's environment and workflow so that the user can simply sit down, log on, and start working. In Figure 44.1, the script is called logon.bat. Who knows, maybe some command-line functionality is included in the script; for example, perhaps a particular program such as Excel is opened up, or maybe the user receives a welcome message when logging on. Imagine the power of scripting! In the figure logon.bat is the name, which means it is a batch file, but you often use PowerShell to create scripts, too. (PowerShell scripts use the .ps1 extension.) Whatever you use, the file has to be stored—either in the default location on the server (NETLOGON) or elsewhere, in which case the path to the file location must be entered into the field in addition to the filename.

Home Folder

The home folder is where a user stores documents by default. Look again at Figure 44.1. If you select the **Local path** option, stored documents will end up at the local computer that the user is sitting at. However, the idea behind having a Microsoft domain is that it enables you to centrally store files. So, in many cases, you will select **Connect:** and use a mapped network drive (such as Z:) to a path. This is known as *folder redirection*.

In Figure 44.1, Z: is mapped to *nasbox1*, which has a share called *data*, and finally to a folder named *Bob*. This way, regardless of what computer Bob logs on to, data will be stored to the Z: drive.

Note

The last three concepts (profile, logon script, and home folder) can be used on a local Windows system as well. Just go to **Local Users and Groups > Users**, right-click the user in question, and select **Properties**, and then go to the **Profile** tab. The same options are there, but they are limited when there is no domain in use. The whole concept here is that having a domain allows you to centralize data, profiles, and home folders; everything is more organized and more easily monitored, and that *usually* equates to more security. By the way, Local Users and Groups can be added to an MMC or can be accessed from Computer Management.

Group Policy

Group policies are part of Windows, whether you are working at a local system or within a domain. They house all of the rules that users must abide by within the OS—for example, what programs they can use, and when passwords have to be changed. There are hundreds of policies that can be modified to secure a system. In a domain environment, there is a default domain policy, which is stored on the domain controller; it affects all typical users that are created. However, you can create separate policies for users that are organized into OUs. In Figure 44.1 you can see in the left pane a policy named Dev-GPO [DC1.dpro42.com] Policy. That is a policy that I created just for the Developers OU, with its two users and two computers. It could be that I want those users to have even longer passwords than the rest of the users on the domain. I can ensure that by modifying the Dev-GPO Policy.

On the local system, you can modify the group policy by going to **Run** and typing **gpedit.msc**, which opens the Local Group Policy Editor. Two of the policies that you will most commonly modify are the Password Policy and Account Lockout Policy. These can be accessed quickly by going to **Run** and typing **secpol.msc**, which brings you to the Local Security Policy console window, a subset of the entire Group Policy. Figure 44.2 shows an example of this window on a Windows 10 Pro computer, with the Password Policy opened. Policy modification is essentially the same, regardless of whether the policy is stored on a local Windows client or on a Windows domain controller.

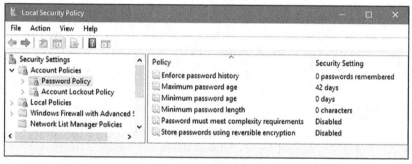

FIGURE 44.2 **Local Security Policy opened to the Password Policy**

ExamAlert

Know how to access and configure the Group Policy Editor (**gpedit.msc**) and the Local Security Policy (**secpol.msc**).

Some changes take effect immediately, but some require further action. So, when you are finished configuring group policy, you should either log off and back on or restart the computer or, better yet, run the **gpupdate** command, so that the group policy entries are updated in the operating system.

Security Groups

Security groups in Active Directory provide an efficient way to set permissions and assign access to resources in a Windows domain.

You can build custom security groups, but to leverage Active Directory out of the box, you use the built-in security groups. One example of a built-in security group is the Domain Admins group. This group is created automatically when you create a Windows domain by installing Active Directory on a Windows server. Members of the Domain Admins group have full control of the Windows domain but do not have full control over local Windows computer systems. (That responsibility lies with the administrator account locally on each computer.)

Another example is the Backup Operators group. Members of this security group can perform backup operations on domain controllers but are quite limited in other respects within the domain.

There are a lot of other default security groups in Active Directory, including Account Operators, DNSAdmins, Enterprise Admins, and Domain Users. Each of these security groups has different levels of built-in permissions to resources. For example, the Domain Users group is designed to house the bulk of your typical users, who intentionally have very little access to programs, data, and the domain. In fact, if you were to create a user in Active Directory, that user account would be assigned to the Domain Users group by default. If none of the plethora of built-in groups have the level of security you want, you (as a domain admin) can then create new security groups for the domain. For more information on security groups, see https:// docs.microsoft.com/en-us/windows/security/identity-protection/ access-control/active-directory-security-groups.

A Quick Word About AD

This is just the tip of the iceberg when it comes to Active Directory, and there are loads of Microsoft certifications dealing with Windows Server. What you have learned here should be enough for the A+ exam, but if you are interested in learning more, then I recommend that you check out the following links:

▶ **Getting Started with Windows Server:** https://docs.microsoft.com/en-us/ windows-server/get-started/get-started-with-windows-server

▶ **Windows Server Free Trial:** https://www.microsoft.com/en-us/windows-server/ trial

More Logical Security Concepts

There are several more concepts packed into Objective 2.1. This section acts as a catch-all for the rest of the logical security concepts that we haven't gotten to yet, including authenticator applications, access control lists, tokens, email, and SMS.

Authenticator Applications

An authenticator application is often used as a second level of security. It provides a secondary verification mechanism that is simple to use.

One example is the Google Authenticator app, which has to be installed to a person's smartphone or other mobile device running Android or iOS. Once the app is installed, the user enables two-step verification in their account. Afterward, all affected connections will require two steps of authentication. For example, a user logs in to a service/website with a username and password. The service then sends a verification code through to the Google Authenticator app on the mobile device. Only the person who possesses the mobile device will see the code and be able to type it in the appropriate security field to gain access to the website or service.

There are plenty of other authenticator apps out there for mobile devices. However, an organization might just opt to use standard two-step verification by way of SMS text, phone call, or email. Most websites and services that deal with any kind of personally identifiable information (PII) or transfer of currency require this—or, at the very least, provide it as an optional feature for a person's account.

Know this: Two-step verification is *not* two-factor authentication because both steps require the same factor: knowledge. In the example above, it would be two pieces of knowledge (password and code), but still, it's only one *factor* of authentication. Is security improved with two-step verification? Yes. And you could argue that a person *has* a smartphone or other mobile device. But a proper two-factor authentication scheme such as password and biometric or password and a hardware-based token, such as a smart card, is more secure.

> **ExamAlert**
>
> An authenticator app uses a passcode to achieve two-step verification.

Hard Tokens vs. Soft Tokens

You will find that the term *token* is used in a lot of ways and can have several meanings. For the A+ certification, tokens are considered to be hardware- or software-based ways of providing secondary authentication codes.

Hardware-based security tokens are small, physical devices given to authorized users to help with authentication. Such a device might be attached to a keychain or might be part of a card system. Hardware-based tokens might be used as part of a door access system or as something that gives access to an individual computer or networks. For example, RSA tokens carry and generate rolling one-time passwords (OTPs), each valid for only one login session or transaction.

Software-based tokens are virtual and are installed to mobile devices and other computers. These tokens are also used to generate single-use codes when accessing various platforms (for example, the previously mentioned two-step authentication process). In comparison to hardware-based tokens, software-based tokens are more easily accessible and cheaper, there are no batteries to deal with, and they don't have to be physically carried. However, users need to access them on mobile devices or desktop computers.

Software-based tokens are not as secure as hardware-based tokens because they can be duplicated more easily. Hardware-based tokens cannot be duplicated unless they are stolen, and even then duplication would be a difficult task.

> **Note**
>
> As mentioned, the term *token* can be used in different ways. For example, a crypto token is a virtual currency token that represents a tradable asset within a blockchain. The token can be used by the owner for investment purposes. Though not covered in the A+ objectives, I recommend learning about blockchain technologies, which are being used in many ways in the technology world.

Access Control Lists

Access control lists (ACLs) are lists of permissions attached to an object specifying the levels of access that users or groups have to that object.

There is a little bit of confusion when talking about ACLs because they can be applied to firewalls and to operating systems. But in both cases, an ACL is a set of instructions for a computer system to follow. When dealing with firewalls, an ACL is a set of rules that applies to a list of network names, IP addresses, and port numbers. Permissions in an ACL might allow access or deny access, depending on what systems are required to have access.

The focus of this chapter is on operating systems. When dealing with operating systems, an ACL specifies the permissions—such as file and printer access—that can be assigned to individual users or groups. Permissions include read, write, modify, full control, and so on. We'll discuss these permission types further in Chapter 47, "Windows Security Settings."

ACLs are also known as file system access control lists (FACLs or FSACLs). An ACL is a list of permissions attached to an object. In a Windows environment, ACLs are broken down into individual access control entries (ACEs); for example, the user JohnT might have read access to the marketing folder. Also, Microsoft uses the term discretionary access control list (DACL) to refer to an ACL that identifies trustees who are allowed or denied access to an object. It uses the term system access control list (SACL) to refer to an ACL that enables admins to log attempts to access a secured object.

SMS

The messaging app is a particularly devious gateway for attackers. Short Message Service (SMS) and Multimedia Messaging Service (MMS) are vulnerable to malware. Unwary users of mobile devices are especially susceptible to Trojans and phishing via SMS texts.

One way to prevent SMS-related attacks is to install mobile anti-malware in the form of a mobile security suite. This endpoint protection platform needs to be updated and is best controlled using a mobile device management (MDM) solution. Another way is to use encrypted messaging apps. Yet another is to block messaging apps altogether or to use company-approved messaging apps that are deemed to be more secure. The option chosen depends on what type of mobile environment you are allowing. It will work for some mobile environments where the IT department has more control over devices but might not work for "bring our own device" (BYOD) environments.

Email Security

Email security is a specialty all its own. You may have heard of the various attacks on email servers over the years; such attacks can filter down to each of the users in an email domain—and it can get ugly. As an A+ technician, you are not expected to secure email servers, but you should have some basic knowledge about email clients.

First, email client software should be updated as often as possible to get access to the latest security fixes. Next, educate your users about how to recognize, avoid, and quarantine malicious emails. These two things are very important! Between updates and user awareness, half the security battle is already done.

Then, it's all about security controls. For example, use encryption and digital signatures. Encryption modifies the contents of an email message, making it difficult (or even impossible) for an attacker to decipher. Digital signatures, on the other hand, use cryptographic hashing to "sign" the email, allowing a user to verify who the email came from. Also, make sure that email clients are using secure servers and ports. (Remember that they are POP3 on port 995, IMAP on port 993, and SMTP on port 465.)

Finally, think of the entire path of email. It's impossible to secure everything, but you might consider using a secure VPN for network access and ensuring that the client OS is updated and has anti-malware protection.

ExamAlert

Protect email communications with encryption, digital signatures, secure ports, VPNs, and, especially, updates, and user education.

Note

It's important to prevent spam email. Some methods include using spam filters, strong passwords, allow and deny lists, and user education!

Cram Quiz

Answer these questions. The answers follow the last question. If you cannot answer these questions correctly, consider reading this chapter again until you can.

1. When is a Windows computer completely secure?

   ○ **A.** When you have updated to the latest version

   ○ **B.** When you have locked down the Local Security Policy

   ○ **C.** When Microsoft releases the latest update

   ○ **D.** Never

2. Which of the following is a built-in security component of Windows?

   ○ **A.** UAC

   ○ **B.** Firefox

   ○ **C.** Active Directory

   ○ **D.** MFA

3. You have been tasked with configuring a user account so that its folders and settings will follow the user to whatever computer the user logs on to within the domain. Which of the following should you configure?

   ○ **A.** OU

   ○ **B.** Roaming profile

   ○ **C.** Logon script

   ○ **D.** Home folder mapped to a network drive

4. You need to block users from installing programs in Windows. Of the following, what tool should you use?

   ○ **A.** **wf.msc**

   ○ **B.** Principle of least privilege

   ○ **C.** Digital signature

   ○ **D.** **gpedit.msc**

5. You are moving up in the world and have been tasked with securing a server room. Your manager tells you to design a system that will implement two-factor authentication. Which of the following should you use as your solution to provide the best level of security for the server room?

   ○ **A.** A security guard and an entry control roster

   ○ **B.** A biometric lock and hardware tokens

   ○ **C.** A door lock and an access control vestibule

   ○ **D.** A server cabinet lock and badge readers

Cram Quiz Answers

1. **D.** Neither Windows nor any other technology is ever completely secure. Complete security is impossible. But you can reduce risk to a certain extent by configuring a system properly and by using technology wisely—ultimately providing *relative* security. Updating to the latest version is often a good idea (if done according to organization policy), but you can't rely on software updates alone. Using the Local Security Policy can help to "lock down" the system to a certain extent, but again, it is only one method. A combination of security updates, security configurations, and user education should be part of an overall security plan.

2. **A.** User Account Control (UAC) adds a layer of security to Windows to protect against malware and user error. Firefox is considered by many to be a secure web browser, but it is not included in Windows, nor can it be called a "security component"; it is a browser. Active Directory runs on Windows Server (though it can be accessed remotely from a Windows client); while it can increase the security of an organization's Windows network, it isn't a security component per se. With multi-factor authentication (MFA), two or more types of identification are required for a user to be authenticated to a system, network, or facility. MFA is not a built-in security component of Windows, but it can be accomplished on a Windows sys-tem—for example, by using the default username/password scheme (something the person knows), adding a USB-based fingerprint scanner (something the per-son is), and configuring them to both be used during logon to Windows.

3. **B.** Configure a roaming profile for the user. The roaming profile is configured at the domain controller and allows the user to move from one computer to the next, and the user profile follows—as long as the user is logging on with the same user-name and password and logging on to the domain. Refer to Figure 44.1 for the paths and naming conventions. OUs (organizational units) provide a way of orga-nizing users, computers, and policies. A logon script is designed to execute pro-grams, features, and actions when a user logs on. As long as a user logs on to the domain, this script will be initiated. The home folder is the default location where a user will save and download files; it can be either local or mapped to a network drive, the latter of which is preferred on a domain.

4. **D.** Use the Group Policy Editor (**Run** > **gpedit.msc**) to make modifications to how (and whether) programs are installed to Windows. (There are a variety of other ways as well.) **Run** > **wf.msc** brings up Windows Defender Firewall with Advanced Security. The principle of least privilege is not a tool but a concept, which states that a user (or program) should only be given the access required to complete a task—and no more. Digital signatures are used to cryptographi-cally "sign" emails so that users can verify that the emails came from known good sources.

5. **B.** The most secure solution listed is the biometric lock and hardware tokens. This solution combines two factors of authentication: biometrics (something you are) and hardware tokens (something you have). While the other answers are good security methods, they do not incorporate two factors of authentication, and so they do not provide enough security for today's typical organization. Remember the phrase *defense in depth*, which means layered security. The more layers you have (within reason), the more secure your environment will be.

Yowza, that was a lot of content. Great job so far!

CHAPTER 45

Wireless Security and Malware

This chapter covers the following A+ 220-1102 exam objectives:

▶ **2.2** – Compare and contrast wireless security protocols and authentication methods.

▶ **2.3** – Given a scenario, detect, remove, and prevent malware using the appropriate tools and methods.

You can't get enough security! That's because, as mentioned earlier in the book, nothing is ever 100% secure. However, you need to temper your vigilance and security aggressiveness by using prioritization. Always be thinking in terms of the most urgent threats and vulnerabilities to your organization and continue the list of risks from there. Secure them accordingly, starting from the top.

This chapter continues the security journey by discussing wireless security and authentication and how to prevent malware. It's a bit of a catch-all chapter due to the number of varying concepts covered, but I'll try to make it as pleasant as possible by breaking it up into manageable sections. Let's go!

Comparing/Contrasting Wireless Security Protocols and Authentication Methods

> **ExamAlert**
>
> **Objective 2.2** concentrates on the following: protocols and encryption (WPA2, WPA3, TKIP, and AES) and authentication (RADIUS, TACACS+, Kerberos).

Wi-Fi connections are used by PCs, laptops, tablets, smartphones, industrial devices, and the list goes on. However, with ease of use comes additional security considerations. The plain truth is that a signal traveling in the air is going to be more insecure than a signal traversing a cable. So, you need to use proper wireless protocols and encryption protocols. Let's talk about some of them now.

Wireless and Encryption Protocols

We discussed wireless encryption protocols a little bit in Chapter 7, "Wireless Protocols." Let's review those protocols now. Table 45.1 shows the protocols you should know for the exam.

TABLE 45.1 **Wireless Encryption Methods**

Wireless Protocol	Description	Encryption Level
WPA2	Wi-Fi Protected Access version 2	128-bit
WPA3	Wi-Fi Protected Access version 3	192-bit
TKIP	Temporal Key Integrity Protocol (deprecated encryption protocol used with WEP or WPA)	128-bit
AES	Advanced Encryption Standard (encryption protocol used with WPA2/WPA3)	128-, 192-, and 256-bit

> **ExamAlert**
>
> Know the differences between WPA2, WPA3, TKIP, and AES.

At the writing of this book (2021), the best option is to go with WPA3 for wireless connectivity—if it is available—and AES for data encryption over that wireless connection. In fact, AES may be your only option, depending on the client used. For example, in Windows 10 Pro, if you select WPA2 (Personal or Enterprise), you will be forced to use AES. Figure 45.1 shows an example of this.

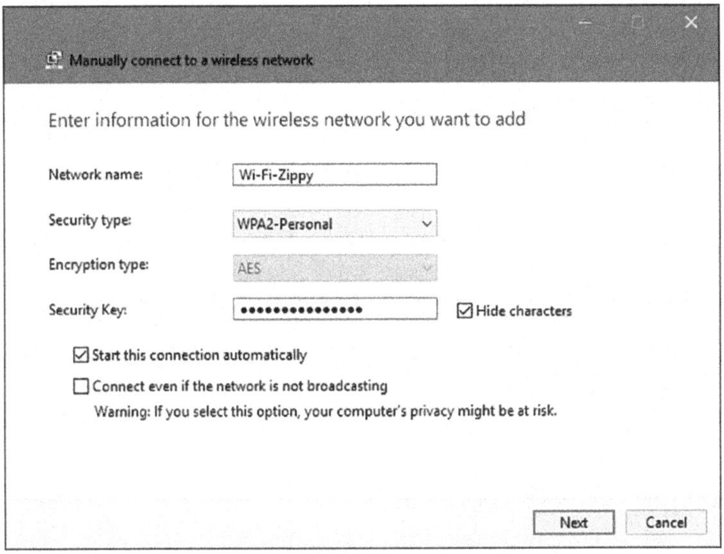

FIGURE 45.1   Manual wireless network connection in Windows

> **Note**
>
> You can get to the window shown in Figure 45.1 by navigating to the **Network and Sharing Center** and clicking the **Set up a new connection or network** link.

The Encryption type field is grayed out, and while you could modify that in the Group Policy Editor or in the Registry Editor, doing so is usually not wise. What would be wise is to check the **Hide characters** checkbox for the Security Key; by default on some systems the box is not checked, and the Security Key field displays what is typed.

In the figure, the security type specified is WPA2-Personal. This means that we are connecting to a basic Wi-Fi access point, and there is a pre-shared key (PSK) that allows access. The PSK is stored on the access point. However, there are other options—some less secure and some more secure. The no authentication (Open) option has no key and no security, but you might use it to temporarily make a network connection and download the required software. Many larger organizations disable this option so that users and admins cannot connect without encryption. WEP may also be listed; WEP is generally not recommended because it can be compromised.

The more secure options include WPA2-Enterprise and 802.1X. WPA2-Enterprise, as the name implies, is designed for larger networks—ones that use an authentication server of some sort. That could be a RADIUS server or a Terminal Access Controller Access-Control System Plus (TACACS+) server, which we'll discuss more in just a bit. These can be used as centralized authentication platforms for wireless connections and a variety of other authentication purposes, and they can be used as single sign-on (SSO) servers as well.

> **ExamAlert**
>
> RADIUS servers can be used to provide secure SSO access for Wi-Fi and network resources.

RADIUS and TACACS+

Remote Authentication Dial-In User Service (RADIUS) provides centralized administration of dial-up, VPN, and wireless authentication and can be used with 802.1X as well. It uses ports 1812 and 1813 by default, and when connecting to a RADIUS server from a wireless client, you often need to enter the port (1812) and the IP address of the server. Figure 45.2 shows an example of an access point that has been configured to redirect authentication requests to a RADIUS server using the IP address 172.18.0.13 on the default port 1812.

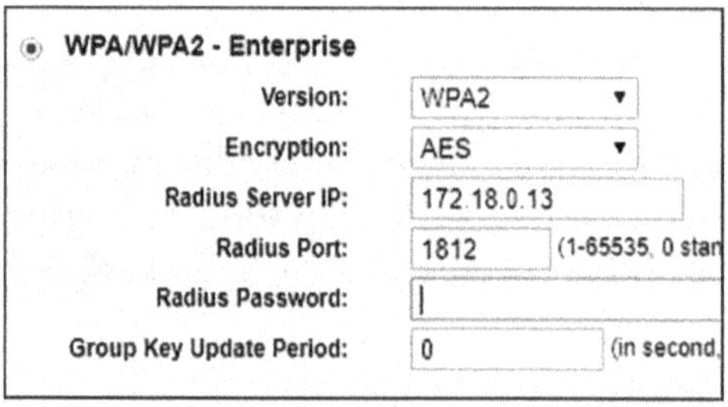

⊙ WPA/WPA2 - Enterprise		
Version:	WPA2 ▾	
Encryption:	AES ▾	
Radius Server IP:	172.18.0.13	
Radius Port:	1812	(1-65535, 0 star
Radius Password:		
Group Key Update Period:	0	(in second

FIGURE 45.2 **WPA2-Enterprise configuration on an AP**

> **ExamAlert**
>
> Know how to connect a wireless client to a RADIUS server using WPA2-Enterprise and port 1812.

RADIUS can be run on a variety of devices and servers, including Windows Server devices. RADIUS can also be used as a multi-factor authentication (MFA) tool or as part of an MFA scheme. This can be much more secure than using a single-factor authentication scheme such as a typical WPA2-PSK connection.

> **Note**
>
> 802.1X is an IEEE standard that defines port-based network access control (PNAC). Not to be confused with 802.11x WLAN standards, 802.1X is an authentication technology used to connect hosts to a LAN or WLAN. 802.1X allows you to apply a security control that ties physical ports to end-device MAC addresses and prevents additional devices from being connected to the network. It is a good way of implementing port security—better than simply setting up MAC address filtering.

TACACS+ (pronounced "tack-ax plus") is really the pinnacle of confusing computer acronyms. TACACS+ is developed by Cisco and uses inbound port 49; however, it uses TCP as the transport mechanism instead of UDP.

There are a few differences between RADIUS and TACACS+. Whereas RADIUS uses UDP as its transport layer protocol, TACACS+ uses TCP as its transport layer protocol, and TCP is usually seen as a more reliable transport protocol than UDP (though each has its own unique set of advantages). Also, RADIUS combines the authentication and authorization functions when dealing with users; however, TACACS+ separates these two functions into two separate operations—introducing another layer of security. This means that you can run separate commands on a Cisco device for the individual authentication and authorization functions. TACACS+ also separates the accounting function into its own operation. Finally, TACACS+ provides for more types of authentication requests than does RADIUS.

ExamAlert

RADIUS uses port 1812 and UDP. TACACS+ uses port 49 and TCP.

Note

Authentication, authorization, and accounting are collectively known as AAA. RADIUS and TACACS+ servers are often referred to as AAA servers.

Kerberos

Kerberos is an authentication protocol designed at MIT that enables computers to prove their identity to each other in a secure manner. It is used most often in client/server environments, where the client and the server both verify each other's identity. This is known as two-way authentication, or mutual authentication. Often, Kerberos protects a network server from illegitimate login attempts; it is named after Cerberus, the mythological three-headed guard dog who guards Hades.

A common implementation of Kerberos occurs when a user logs on to a Microsoft domain. (Note: I am not implying that Microsoft domains are analogous to Hades!) The domain controller in the Microsoft domain is known as the key distribution center (KDC). This server works with tickets that prove the identity of users. The KDC is composed of two logical parts: the authentication server and the ticket-granting server. Basically, a client computer attempts to authenticate itself to the authentication server portion of the KDC. When it does so successfully, the client receives a ticket. This is actually a ticket to get other tickets—known as a ticket-granting ticket (TGT). The client uses this preliminary ticket to demonstrate its identity to a ticket-granting server in the hopes of ultimately getting access to a service—for example, making a connection to Active Directory on a domain controller. The domain controller running Kerberos will have inbound port 88 open to the service logon requests from clients. Kerberos goes hand in hand with the modified LDAP service used by Active Directory (which, by the way, uses port 389 by default and port 636 for secure LDAP).

Know this: Active Directory is the most commonly used directory services solution, but it's not the only game in town. Kerberos can be used with any directory services solution, including the open source FreeIPA and its cousin

Red Hat Identity Management. However, the A+ exam will most likely focus on Active Directory.

ExamAlert

Kerberos uses mutual authentication to provide security for clients attempting to connect to Active Directory domain controllers. It uses inbound port 88.

Cram Quiz

Answer these questions. The answers follow the last question. If you cannot answer these questions correctly, consider reading this chapter again until you can.

1. Which of the following is the strongest form of wireless encryption?

   ○ **A.** WPA3

   ○ **B.** WPA

   ○ **C.** AES

   ○ **D.** TKIP

2. You have been tasked with connecting wireless clients to a server that supports SSO and 802.1X. Which of the following technologies should you implement? (Select the two best answers.)

   ○ **A.** WPA2-PSK

   ○ **B.** WPA2-ENT

   ○ **C.** WEP

   ○ **D.** TKIP

   ○ **E.** RADIUS

   ○ **F.** Kerberos

Cram Quiz Answers

1. **C.** Of the list of options, Advanced Encryption Standard (AES) is the strongest form of wireless encryption. WPA is a wireless encryption protocol, but it is deprecated; WPA2 or WPA3 is recommended. TKIP is deprecated and has been compromised; it should be avoided. Use TKIP, WEP, or the no authentication only option if you are temporarily connecting a device to a Wi-Fi network in an attempt to update it to a newer protocol or if you are initiating testing. Even then, use extreme caution!

2. **B and E.** To take advantage of single sign-on (SSO) and 802.1X, you would need a special authentication system (such as RADIUS) on the server side and WPA2-Enterprise on the client side (sometimes abbreviated as WPA2-ENT). And what port does RADIUS use by default? Do you remember?

   WPA2-PSK uses a pre-shared key that is stored on the AP, and it doesn't support the other technologies. WEP and TKIP are outdated and should be avoided. Kerberos is a mutual authentication protocol used by Active Directory and other directory services programs.

Detecting, Removing, and Preventing Malware Using the Appropriate Tools and Methods

ExamAlert

Objective 2.3 focuses on malware (Trojans, rootkits, viruses, spyware, ransomware, keyloggers, boot sector viruses, and cryptominers) and the tools and methods used to mitigate malware issues (recovery console, antivirus, anti-malware, software firewalls, anti-phishing training, user education regarding common threats, and OS reinstallation).

Malicious software, or *malware*, is software designed to infiltrate a computer system and possibly damage it without the user's knowledge or consent. Malware is a broad term used by computer professionals to include viruses, Trojan horses, spyware, ransomware, rootkits, keyloggers, and other types of undesirable software.

Malicious Software Types

Of course, we don't want malware to infect our computer systems, but to defend against it, we first need to define it and categorize it. Then we can put preventive measures into place. It's also important to locate and remove/quarantine malware from a computer system in the event that it shows up. Table 45.2 summarizes the various malware threats you should know for the exam.

TABLE 45.2 **Malware Types**

Malware Threat	Definition
Virus	Code that runs on a computer without the user's knowledge; it infects the computer when the code is accessed and executed. Sometimes also called a worm. A *boot sector virus* infects the portion of the storage drive that contains the OS boot information. This type of virus can cause boot failures and other issues.
Trojan horse	Malicious software that appears to perform desired functions but is actually performing malicious functions behind the scenes.
Spyware	Malicious software either downloaded unwittingly from a website or installed along with some other third-party software that spies on the user's work.
Rootkit	Software designed to gain administrator-level control over a computer system without being detected.
Ransomware	Malicious software that restricts access to a computer system or locks the system until a ransom is paid. Ransomware is often propagated by Trojans, and it uses RSA encryption keys to "lock" the files.
Keylogger	A program or device that captures all the keystrokes made by a user on a computer keyboard. A software-based keylogger may be loaded into a computer knowingly or without the user's knowledge using a Trojan. A hardware-based keylogger may be connected physically to a keyboard's cable so it can store data and possibly transmit it wirelessly.
Cryptominer	Hardware or software that is designed to "mine" for cryptocurrencies and can be legitimate or illegitimate. An illegitimately placed software-based cryptominer uses up the resources of a computer. The computer is also compromised because the existence of the cryptominer proves that someone has gained access to the system in some way.

ExamAlert

Know the difference between viruses, Trojan horses, spyware, rootkits, ransomware, keyloggers, and cryptominers.

Malware can be spread in a variety of ways, including via removable media, email attachments, downloaded programs, malicious hyperlinks, and the dreaded botnet. A *botnet* is a group of compromised computers that are controlled by a main computer (somewhere) that directs them to attack particular servers and routers on the Internet. It is called a botnet because it is a network of computers—robots, or bots for short—that work as a collective. Usually, the computer is infected with a Trojan that contains the code to connect the system to the botnet. Unless the anti-malware program detects it, the user has no knowledge of it happening; it all occurs behind the scenes. You'll learn more about botnets in Chapter 46, "Social Engineering."

Preventing Malicious Software

Now that you know the types of malware, let's talk about how to stop them before they happen.

In a nutshell, prevention of malware infection can be performed by using anti-malware programs, updating the OS and apps, scanning the system, implementing policies, and educating users. But that's just in a nutshell. Let's dive a little deeper.

Preventing Viruses and Trojans

There is some confusion about the differences between viruses, worms, and Trojans; even some hackers and antivirus software developers are confused about the differences. That's because there are literally thousands of strains of malware (and possibly many more), and they can be quite difficult to classify. To a certain extent, the distinction doesn't matter. The bottom line is that for the most part, prevention is the same for viruses, worms, and Trojans.

You can do several things to protect a computer system from these types of malware. First, every computer should have antivirus (AV) software running on it. Companies that provide antivirus and anti-malware solutions often call them *endpoint protection platforms*. Second, that software should be updated. If AV software is bundled with the OS—for example, Windows Security (previously known as Defender Antivirus)—then OS updates will also update the AV software. Third-party AV software requires a current license and must be renewed yearly with most providers. Or if it is free AV software, you need to periodically check if it is still a full version of the software. If it isn't already set to auto-update, set the AV software to automatically update at periodic intervals (for example, every day or every week). It's a good idea to schedule regular full scans of the system within the AV software or within the Windows Task Scheduler.

As long as the definitions have been updated, antivirus systems will usually locate viruses along with worms and Trojans. However, these systems usually do not locate rootkit activity. Keep in mind that AV software is important, but it is not a cure-all.

You also need to make sure a computer has the latest updates available. This goes for the operating system and applications such as Microsoft Office. Backdoors into operating systems and other applications are not uncommon, and OS manufacturers often release fixes for these breaches of security. For example, Windows offers the Windows Update program. It should be enabled, and by default it will update your system automatically; however, you should manually verify that the system is up to date and that updates are turned on. It might be that your organization has rules governing how Windows Update will function. If so, configure Automatic Updates according to your company's policy.

It's also important to consider boot sector viruses. When it comes to boot sector viruses, your AV software is still the best bet. The AV software might use a bootable USB flash drive to accomplish scanning of the boot sector, or it might have boot shielding built in. Some BIOS/UEFI programs have the capability to scan the boot sector of the storage drive at startup; this might need to be enabled in the BIOS setup first. You can also use recovery environments and the command line to repair the boot sector. We'll discuss recovery environments in Chapter 53, "Troubleshooting Microsoft Windows." Another possibility is to use freely downloadable Linux-based tools and Live Linux technologies such as Knoppix, which can be used to boot and repair a computer.

It's vital to make sure that a firewall is available, enabled, and updated. A firewall closes all the inbound ports to your computer (or network) in an attempt to block intruders. Windows Defender Firewall is a built-in feature of Windows, and you might also have a SOHO router with a built-in firewall. By using both, you have two layers of protection from viruses and other attacks. You can access Windows Defender Firewall by going to **Run** > **firewall.cpl**. Keep in mind that you might need to set exceptions for programs that need to access the Internet. You might do this based on the program or the port used by the protocol, enabling specific applications to communicate through the firewall while keeping the rest of the ports closed.

> **Note**
>
> Another good technique when trying to prevent viruses (and just about any other malware) is to disable AutoPlay/AutoRun for USB-connected devices and optical drives. Plus, remember to disable these devices in the BIOS/UEFI! We'll discuss this more in Chapter 48, "Windows Best Practices."

From a more generalized perspective, preventing malware is done through the use of a concept called *defense in depth*, or layering of security, and through monitoring the system and end-user education.

Educate users about how viruses can infect a system. Consider implementing an anti-phishing educational campaign. By using simulations, you can help users know how to identify phishing attacks. (You'll learn more about phishing in Chapter 46.) Instruct users on how to screen (or filter) their emails, text messages, and other communications, and tell them not to open unknown attachments. Show them how to scan removable media before copying files to their computers or set up the computers to scan removable media automatically. Sometimes user education works; sometimes it doesn't. One way to make user education more effective is to have a technical trainer educate your users instead of doing it yourself. This can provide for a more engaging learning environment. During this training, you might opt to define an organization's acceptable use policy (AUP). This is a document that stipulates constraints and practices that a user must agree to before being granted access to a corporate network or the Internet. Sometimes an AUP can be a bit difficult for the average non-techie to understand. However, an AUP is usually designed to not only stipulate constraints but educate the user, so it is in the user's best interest to learn what policies are covered in the AUP.

By using these methods, virus infection can be severely reduced. However, if a computer is infected by a virus, you want to know what to do to troubleshoot the problem. We'll get into that as well as the CompTIA A+ malware removal process in Chapter 54, "Troubleshooting PC Security Issues."

You can prevent and troubleshoot Trojans in much the same manner as viruses. There are scanners for Trojans as well (for example, Microsoft's Malicious Software Removal Tool). In some cases, AV software scans for worms and Trojans in addition to viruses. Both of these tools can easily detect *known* Trojans, regardless of whether it is the actual attacker's application or any .exe files that are part of the application and are used at the victim computer. However, if a Trojan or worm is brand new, a hot fix or an individual scanner might become available from your anti-malware provider. New Trojans and variants of Trojans are created every day. Until the anti-malware provider finds out about them, they are known as zero-day attacks (as discussed in more detail in Chapter 46). The only way to prevent these attacks is to stick to the fundamentals discussed throughout this section.

Preventing and Troubleshooting Spyware

Preventing spyware works in much the same manner as preventing viruses in that spyware prevention includes updating the operating system and using a firewall. Also, because spyware has become much more common, antivirus companies have begun adding anti-spyware components to their software. Here are a few more things you can do to protect your computer in the hopes of preventing spyware:

▶ Download and install anti-spyware protection software (which might be included in your anti-malware suite). Be sure to keep the anti-spyware software updated.

▶ If you are using Windows, consider enabling SmartScreen for Microsoft Edge, which checks web content and protects against malicious sites and downloads.

▶ Adjust web browser security settings in the following ways:

  ▶ Enable a phishing filter if you have one and turn on automatic website checking.

  ▶ Enable checking of certificates. If a certificate (that is, a secure encrypted connection on the web) has been revoked or is otherwise invalid, you want to know about it; a message such as "invalid certificate (trusted root CA)" will only be received when the browser is checking for it. If the browser is not protecting you in this way, you could inadvertently stumble onto a disreputable website.

  ▶ Check for unwanted proxy connections. (For more information on proxy connections, see Chapter 37, "Windows Networking.")

▶ Uninstall unnecessary applications and turn off superfluous services (for example, Telnet and FTP if they are not used).

▶ Educate users on how to surf the Web safely. Remember: User education is the number-one method of preventing malware!

▶ Consider technologies that discourage spyware. For example, use a browser that is less susceptible to spyware.

Preventing Rootkits

A successfully installed rootkit enables unauthorized users to gain access to a system, acting as the root or administrator user. A rootkit is copied to a computer as a binary file; this binary file can be detected by signature-based and heuristic-based antivirus programs. However, after a rootkit is executed, it can be difficult to detect. This is because most rootkits are collections of programs working together that can make many modifications to the system. When subversion of the operating system takes place, the OS can't be trusted, and it is difficult to tell whether your antivirus programs run properly or whether any of your other efforts have any effect. Although security software manufacturers attempt to detect running rootkits, they are not always successful.

One good way to identify a rootkit is to use rescue removable media (such as a USB flash drive) to boot the computer. This way, the operating system is not running, which means the rootkit is not running, making the rootkit much easier for the external media to detect.

Unfortunately, because of the difficulty involved in removing rootkits, sometimes the best way to combat a rootkit is to wipe the drive and reinstall the operating system and all software. You might hear this referred to as "reimaging the machine." Generally, upon detecting a rootkit, a PC technician will do this because it usually is quicker than attempting to fix all the rootkit issues, and it can verify that the rootkit has been removed completely. However, this is really only an option if there is a backup for the data on the machine.

Software isn't the only method of defense and repair when it comes to rootkits. Newer motherboards equipped with UEFI take advantage of Secure Boot technology, which can help protect the preboot process against rootkit attacks. It means that a rootkit can potentially be stopped *before* it actually causes any damage.

Backup/Restore and Recovery Environments

A good security plan includes not only prevention methods but also solid backup procedures. Back up as often as you can. This could be done on a file-by-file basis, using built-in Windows programs such as File History as well as third-party programs; it can also include the imaging of storage drives and creation of a single file that incorporates the entire storage drive and all of its contents. Snapshots can be taken as well to mark a point in time (for example, by using System Restore). For any system that has important data on it, you should have a backup plan. Consider this whenever you build or deploy new systems. We'll be discussing backup plans further in Chapter 58, "Change Management and Backup Methods."

In the event that malware does infect a system, you have to quarantine it, remove it, and recover the system. A great way to do this is to "think outside the box" and boot the system to some type of recovery environment. This could

be a Linux-based repair disc/drive, or you could use the built-in Windows
Recovery Environment (RE). For more on this topic, see Chapter 53.

Cram Quiz

Answer these questions. The answers follow the last question. If you cannot answer
these questions correctly, consider reading this chapter again until you can.

1. Which of the following types of malware is designed to gain administrative-level
   control of a system?

   ○ **A.** Ransomware

   ○ **B.** Keylogger

   ○ **C.** Rootkit

   ○ **D.** Spyware

2. You have been tasked with implementing a virus prevention plan on a group of
   Windows client computers. Which of the following should you carry out? (Select
   all that apply.)

   ○ **A.** Update AV software.

   ○ **B.** Configure File History.

   ○ **C.** Update Microsoft Office.

   ○ **D.** Install a rootkit scanner.

   ○ **E.** Verify that a firewall is installed.

3. One of your customers complains of a problem: When browsing the Internet, multiple browser pages start opening automatically. You notice that the computer is
   performing poorly, even when not connected to the Internet. What should you do?

   ○ **A.** Enable a pop-up blocker.

   ○ **B.** Reboot the computer.

   ○ **C.** Install/scan with an anti-malware tool.

   ○ **D.** Update the antivirus definitions.

Cram Quiz Answers

1. **C.** A rootkit is designed to get administrative control of a computer system. The
   word *root* is synonymous with *administrator* in some systems (such as Linux and
   Unix). Ransomware is malware that encrypts a person's files so that they are not
   accessible. Keyloggers capture the keystrokes a person makes on a keyboard.
   They are used to steal passwords and other confidential information. Spyware is
   malware that is used to watch (and possibly record) what a person is doing on a
   system and on the Internet.

2. **A, C, and E.** First of all, update everything. Then verify that AV software and a firewall are installed and updated. Be sure to update the OS and apps as well. Microsoft Office is especially susceptible to malware, so if you run it, you have to keep a close eye on it. Configuring File History or any other backup methods won't prevent malware from occurring, but it is important to do this nonetheless. Remember, backup is not prevention. A rootkit scanner won't scan for viruses and won't prevent them; in fact, it won't prevent rootkits, but it might find them.

3. **C.** Chances are that the customer's computer does not have an antivirus or anti-malware program running. Install one (or enable one if it already exists). However, the problem is probably worse than that, and the system likely needs to be remediated (isolated, scanned, and so on). These are probably not just pop-ups; you normally see only one legitimate pop-up at a time. Plus, the computer is performing poorly, even when not connected to the Internet. Rebooting the computer can fix some issues, but it won't fix a malware-infected system. Updating the antivirus software is always a good idea, but the problem might not be caused by a virus. It is more likely that the system has no anti-malware program running. Note: If you ever determine that a system is infected with malware, it should be disconnected from the network right away and placed in isolation until it is repaired properly!

Well, another chapter is complete. Pat yourself on the back, review your notes, and then continue. Great job!

CHAPTER 46

Social Engineering

This chapter covers the following A+ 220-1102 exam objective:

▶ **2.4** – Explain common social-engineering attacks, threats, and vulnerabilities.

When it comes to information security, it's not just about technical attacks. We need to worry about people, too. One great way to improve your organization's security mindset is to employ the following epigram: "To know your Enemy, you must become your Enemy" (Sun Tzu). This means knowing your attacker's methods, techniques, and purpose.

This chapter embarks on a journey through some of the various social engineering methods as well as some technical attacks that you should know for the exam.

> **ExamAlert**
>
> **Objective 2.4** concentrates on the following: social engineering (such as phishing and shoulder surfing), threats (such as DDoS and zero-day attacks), and vulnerabilities (such as unpatched systems and EOL systems).

Social Engineering

Social engineering is the act of manipulating users into revealing confidential information or performing other actions that are detrimental to users. Almost everyone gets emails from unknown entities making false claims or asking for personal information (or money!); this is one example of social engineering. But there are a plethora of other ways to extract information from unwitting users. Let's discuss some of them now.

Phishing

Phishing is an attempt to fraudulently obtain private information. A phisher usually masquerades as someone else, perhaps another entity. Phishing is usually done via electronic communication. Little information about the target is necessary. A phisher may target thousands of individuals without much concern as to their backgrounds. An example of phishing would be an email that requests verification of private information. Clicking a link in the email will probably lead to a malicious website that is designed to give individuals a false sense of security and fraudulently obtain information from them. Such a website often looks like a legitimate website. A common phishing technique is to pose as a vendor (such as an online retailer or a domain registrar) and send individuals email confirmations of orders that they supposedly placed.

Specific groups of people might be targeted with more streamlined phishing campaigns; this is known as *spear phishing*. A campaign can even target specific individuals. A form of spear fishing, known as *whaling*, targets senior executives of corporations, though con artists use other techniques in addition to phishing when targeting a "whale."

Phishing is also sometimes attempted by telephone. Phone phishing, known as *vishing*, works in the same manner as phishing but is initiated via a phone call, often using an automated VoIP system or home-brewed private branch exchange (PBX). The phone call often sounds like a prerecorded message from a legitimate institution (bank, online retailer, donation collector, and so on). The message asks the unsuspecting person for confidential information such as name, bank account numbers, codes, and so on, under the guise of needing to verify information for the person's protection. It's really the opposite, of course, and many people are caught unawares by these types of scams every day. By using automated systems (such as the ones telemarketers use), vishing can be perpetrated on large groups of people with little effort.

As you can imagine, several different types of social engineering are often lumped into what is referred to as phishing, but actual phishing for private information is normally limited to email and websites. To defend against this, a phishing filter or add-on should be installed and enabled on a web browser. Also, individuals should be trained to realize that reputable institutions and businesses will not call or email, requesting private information. If individuals are not sure whether they're being targeted, they should hang up the phone or simply delete the email. A quick way to find out if an email is phishing for information is to hover over a link (but don't click it!). You will see a URL domain name that is far different from the institution that the phisher is claiming to be—probably a URL located in a distant country.

Evil Twin

An evil twin is a rogue, counterfeit, and unauthorized wireless access point that uses the same SSID name as a nearby wireless network, often a public hotspot.

Like an evil twin antagonist in a sci-fi book, the device is identical in almost all respects to the authorized WAP. While the antagonist in the sci-fi book usually has a beard or goatee, the WAP is controlled by a person with the same types of motives as the bearded evil twin. One of these motives is phishing.

For example, an attacker might attempt to fool wireless users at an Internet café to connect to a counterfeit WAP to gain valuable information and passwords from those users. If a user is unlucky enough to connect to the evil twin, all the information within the session can easily be recorded and digested later by the attacker. This type of attack can also be enacted on organizations. To protect against this, virtual private networks (VPNs) can be implemented and require external authentication outside the WAP. Administrators should scan the network often for rogue APs that might be evil twins. If it's feasible, users in general should be trained not to send passwords, credit card numbers, and other sensitive information over wireless networks.

Shoulder Surfing

With shoulder surfing, a person uses direct observation to find out a target's password, PIN, or other authentication information. The simple resolution for this is for the user to physically shield the screen, keypad, or other authentication-requesting devices. A technical method is to use a screen filter. A more aggressive approach is to courteously ask an assumed shoulder surfer to move along. Also, private information should never be left on a desk or out in the open. In fact, many organizations have a "clean desk policy" that states this explicitly. Computers should be locked or logged off when the user is not in the immediate area. Shoulder surfing and the methods described in the following several sections are examples of no-tech hacking.

> **ExamAlert**
>
> Use a screen filter to protect against shoulder surfing.

Piggybacking/Tailgating

With piggybacking, an unauthorized person tags along with an authorized person to gain entry to a restricted area—usually with the person's consent. Tailgating is essentially the same but with one difference: It usually occurs *without* the authorized person's consent. Both of these types of intrusions can be defeated through the use of access control vestibules (also known as mantraps). Remember that this is a small space that can usually fit only one person. It has two sets of interlocking doors; the first set must be closed before the other will open, creating somewhat of a waiting room where people are identified (and cannot escape).

Multi-factor authentication (MFA) is often used in conjunction with an access control vestibule. With MFA, two or more types of authentication are used for user access control (for example, using a proximity card and PIN at the first door and then using a biometric scan at the second). An access control vestibule is an example of a preventive security control. Turnstiles, double entry doors, and employing security guards are other less expensive solutions to the problem of piggybacking and tailgating and help address confidentiality in general.

Dumpster Diving

With Dumpster diving, a person scavenges for private information in garbage and recycling containers. Any sensitive documents should be stored in a safe place as long as possible. When they are no longer necessary, they should be shredded. (Some organizations incinerate their documents.) Information might be found not only on paper but also on storage drives or removable media. Proper recycling and/or destruction of storage drives is covered later in the book. Another way to deter a person from attempting Dumpster diving is to use security cameras and good lighting in the area where the dumpsters are located; some organizations keep their dumpsters indoors in a warehouse or similar area.

Impersonation

Impersonation involves presenting oneself as another person, imitating that other person's characteristics. By impersonating the appropriate personnel or third-party entities, a person hopes to obtain records about an organization, its data, and its personnel. IT people and employees should always be on the lookout for impersonators and should always ask for identification. If there is any doubt, the issue should be escalated to a supervisor and/or a call should be made to the authorities. Impersonation is often a key element in *pretexting*, in which someone invents a scenario and attempts to get a key person to reveal confidential information.

> **Note**
>
> This objective covers more than just social engineering, but the following techniques are sometimes used by attackers and malicious insiders in addition to social engineering, and they are therefore somewhat related.

Threats and Vulnerabilities

Because there are so many types of threats and vulnerabilities in today's computers and networks, there are many types of attacks as well. Let's briefly examine some more types of attacks and common vulnerabilities that a typical organization might have to face.

Network-Based Attacks

Network-based attacks include spoofing, on-path attacks, zero-day attacks and various denial of service attacks. Let's consider them now.

In a *spoofing attack*, an attacker masquerades as another person by falsifying information. This can be done as a social engineering attack, as in the previously mentioned phishing method, or it can be performed as a more technical attack, such as the on-path attack. In an on-path attack, an attacker intercepts data between a client and a server. It is a type of active interception. If the attack is successful, all communications are diverted to the attacking computer. The computer can at this point modify the data, insert code, and send it to the receiving computer. This type of eavesdropping is only successful when the attacker can properly impersonate each endpoint.

Some attacks exploit vulnerabilities that haven't even been discovered yet or that have been discovered but have not been disclosed through the proper channels so that security administrators can become aware of them. These are known as *zero-day attacks*. In this type of attack, an attacker exploits a vulnerability in an operating system or a network security device in such a way that makes it almost impossible to defend against. Because of this, zero-day attacks are a severe threat. Actually, most vulnerabilities are discovered through zero-day attacks, and the first group of systems that are attacked have very little defense. But once such an attack is detected, the development of a solution is not far behind (it could be days or even hours); the vulnerability (and attack) becomes known and is no longer a zero-day threat.

Most of the attacks and malware we have reviewed so far can be initiated by *zombies*—computers that distribute malware or participate in attacks without the knowledge of the owner. Zombies (also called robots or bots) can be grouped together by a central attacker to form a *botnet*. This is done to perpetuate large-scale attacks against particular servers. Distributed denial of service (DDoS) is an example of an attack committed by a botnet; it is designed to bring down a server or website. Let's talk about denial of service attacks a little more.

DoS

Denial of service (DoS) is a broad term applied to many different types of network attacks that attempt to make computer resources unavailable. Generally, it is done to servers but can also be perpetrated against routers and other hosts. Examples of DoS attacks include ping floods, Smurf attacks, SYN floods, Pings of Death, and fork bombs.

DDoS

An attacker (or group of attackers) may make use of a distributed denial of service (DDoS) attack. In this type of attack, a group of compromised systems attacks a single target, causing denial of service at that host.

A DDoS attack often utilizes a botnet—which is a large group of computers, known as *robots* or simply *bots*. Often, these are systems owned by unsuspecting users. The computers in a botnet that act as attackers are known as *zombies*. An attacker starts a DDoS attack by exploiting a single vulnerability in a computer system and making that computer the zombie controller, or DDoS controller.

This controlling system communicates with the other systems in the botnet. The attacker often loads malicious software on many computers (zombies). The attacker can launch a flood of attacks by all zombies in the botnet with a single command. DDoS attacks and botnets are often associated with exploit kits and ransomware.

DoS and DDoS attacks are difficult to defend against. These attacks can be prevented to some extent by keeping stateful firewalls, switches, and routers updated and implementing access control lists, intrusion prevention systems (IPSs), and proactive testing. Several companies offer products that simulate DoS and DDoS attacks. By creating a test server and assessing its vulnerabilities with simulated DoS tests, you can find holes in the security of a server before you take it live. An organization could also opt for a "clean pipe," which attempts to weed out DDoS and other attacks. This solution is offered as a service by some ISPs and other companies. Manual protection of servers can be a difficult task; to implement proper DDoS mitigation, your organization might want to consider anti-DDoS technology and emergency response from an outside source or from a cloud-based provider. Finally, if you realize that a DDoS attack is being carried out on your network, call your ISP and request that the traffic be redirected.

> **ExamAlert**
>
> In a DDoS attack, multiple systems are used to attack a server, website, or network.

Password Cracking

One way that attackers attempt to gain access to systems is through password cracking. This is usually done with the aid of password-cracking software. Two common methods of password cracking are the dictionary attack and the brute-force attack.

A dictionary attack uses a prearranged list of likely words, trying them all, one at a time. A dictionary attack can be used for cracking passwords, passphrases, and keys. It works best with weak passwords and when targeting multiple systems. The power of a dictionary attack depends on the strength of the dictionary used by the password-cracking program.

In a brute-force attack, a threat actor tries every possible password. This type of attack is often a last resort because of the amount of CPU resources it can require. It works best on shorter passwords but can theoretically break any password, given enough time and CPU power.

Using complex and long passwords is the best way to prevent these types of attacks from succeeding. But a system and its network should also be protected with the Internet security appliances mentioned previously.

Cryptanalysis Attacks

A *cryptanalysis attack* uses a considerable set of precalculated encrypted passwords located in a lookup table. Such a table is known as a *rainbow table*, and this type of password attack uses a *precomputation*, where all words in the dictionary (or a specific set of possible passwords) are hashed and stored. The goal of a cryptanalysis attack is to recover passwords more quickly. This type of attack can be defeated by implementing salting, which is the randomization of the hashing process. It usually incorporates key stretching, which means adding bits of information to a password to make it stronger.

For more information about key stretching and salting, see the video at https://dprocomputer.com/?p=1578.

ExamAlert

Know the differences between dictionary and brute-force attacks and understand how rainbow tables are used.

Additional Security Threats

There are some more security threats that you should know for the exam, including insider threats, SQL injection, and cross-site scripting (XSS). Let's start with insider threats.

Insider Threat

A malicious insider is one of the most insidious threats. Instead of impersonating personnel, as is done in pretexting, the person actually becomes personnel!

This attack is often used as part of a corporate espionage plan. Think that all IT techs are 100% honorable? In high tech, you will find an assortment of atrocities, including malicious insider threats. The insider might have been sent by a competing organization to obtain a job/consulting position with a certain company, or perhaps the person may be approached by the competing organization while already working for the company that is the target. Such an attack is often initiated by organizations from another country. Once an insider is situated, that person can easily get access to secure data, personally identifiable information (PII), financials, engineering plans, and so on and pass that information on to the infiltrating organization. Of course, the penalties for this are high, but the potential rewards can be quite enticing to properly "motivated" individuals. Companies therefore often run thorough background checks and credit checks and have human resources put a potential employee through a set of psychological questions. Then, when a person is hired, there is a sort of trial period during which the person is allowed very little access to secure data and secure environments.

Now, a malicious insider doesn't necessarily have to be a person. It could be a device or a bug that was inserted into the organization by a person using social engineering skills—for example, rogue PIN pad devices, audio and video sensors (bugs), keyloggers, and so on. Planting such devices requires physical access to the building in one way or another, so identification and authentication are of paramount importance.

Cross-Site Scripting (XSS)

One web application vulnerability to watch out for is cross-site scripting (XSS). XSS holes are vulnerabilities that can be exploited with a type of code injection. *Code injection* involves exploiting a computer programming bug or flaw by inserting and processing invalid information; it is used to change how a program executes data. In the case of an XSS attack, an attacker inserts malicious scripts into a web page in the hopes of gaining elevated privileges and access to session cookies and other information stored by a user's web browser. This code (often JavaScript) is usually injected from a separate "attack site." It can also manifest as an embedded JavaScript image tag, header manipulation (as in manipulated HTTP response headers), or other HTML embedded image objects within emails (that are web based).

Programmers can often defeat XSS attacks through the use of output encoding (JavaScript escaping, CSS escaping, and URL encoding), by preventing the use of HTML tags, and with input validation (for example, checking forms and confirming that input from users does not contain hypertext). On the user side, the possibility of an XSS attack's success can be reduced by increasing cookie security and by disabling scripts. If XSS attacks via email are a concern, a user could opt to set the email client to text only.

SQL Injection

Databases are just as vulnerable as other computer systems. The most common kind of database is a relational database, which is administered by a relational database management system (RDBMS). These systems are usually written in Structured Query Language (SQL). An example of a SQL database is Microsoft's SQL Server; it can act as the back end for a program written in Visual Basic or Visual C++. Another example is MySQL, a free, open source relational database program often used in conjunction with websites that employ PHP pages.

One concern with SQL is SQL injection attacks, which occur in databases, ASP.NET applications, and blogging software (such as WordPress) that use MySQL as a back end. In these attacks, user input in web forms is not filtered correctly and is executed improperly; as a result, an attacker is able to gain access to resources or change data.

For example, the login form for a web page that uses a SQL back end (such as a WordPress login page) may be insecure, especially if the front-end application is not updated. An attacker may attempt to access the database (from a form or in a variety of other ways), query the database, find a username, and then inject code into the password portion of the SQL code—perhaps something as simple as X = X . This will allow any password to be used for the user account. If the login script was written properly (and validated properly), it should deflect this injected code. But if it wasn't, or if the application being used is not updated, such an attack could work.

It is possible to defend against SQL injection threats by constraining user input, filtering user input, and using stored procedures such as input-validation forms.

> **Note**
>
> Injection attacks are on OWASP's "top 10 web application security risks" list. Learn more about these risks at https://owasp.org/www-project-top-ten/.

Vulnerabilities and Security Best Practices

Most organizations have policies regarding security best practices. The biggest vulnerability to an organization is the violation of those best practices (namely, non-compliant systems).

For example, an organization might have rules stating that all systems—operating systems, anti-malware applications, and so on—must be updated at particular intervals. If a single computer fails to be updated, it is no longer in compliance with policy. This one computer could be used by a hacker or malicious insider to cause all kinds of harm, even on systems that are updated, simply because the nonupdated system is behind the firewall (on the LAN) with the rest of the computers.

When updating systems, double-check that everything has indeed been updated. Use scanning software to find all systems on the network and review network documentation to make sure no systems have "fallen through the cracks." If you find some rogue systems, make sure they are legitimate systems. Verify that these systems have some kind of anti-malware program installed and that the program has been updated.

While scanning through a network of systems, it's also vital to check for outdated software. Remember that in Chapter 39, "Common Operating Systems," we talked about the end-of-life (EOL) date for operating systems such as Windows and macOS. If a computer on your network has passed the EOL date, then it most likely does not receive security updates anymore, and it is therefore a vulnerability to the entire network and infrastructure.

Finally, let's discuss some bring-your-own-device (BYOD) concerns. Around 2011, organizations began to allow employees to bring their own mobile devices into work and connect them to the organization's network (for work purposes only, of course). This BYOD concept has since grown into a popular method of computing for many organizations. It is enticing from a budgeting standpoint, but it can be very difficult on the security administrator—and possibly on the user as well.

For a BYOD implementation to be successful, the key is to implement storage segmentation—a clear separation of organizational and personal information, applications, and other content. The data ownership line must be unmistakable.

For networks with a lot of users, consider third-party offerings from companies that make use of mobile device management (MDM) platforms. These are centralized software solutions that can control, configure, update, and secure remote mobile devices that run Android, iOS, iPadOS, and Chrome OS, all from one administrative console. MDM software can be run from a server within the organization or administered within the cloud. It makes the job of a mobile IT security administrator at least manageable. From the central location, the security administrator can carry out tasks related to application management, content management, and patch management in a simplified manner and to multiple devices at once. This reduces the risks related to vulnerable systems on the network, increases the efficiency of devices, reduces the footprint of devices, and, ultimately, makes devices more secure.

Cram Quiz

Answer these questions. The answers follow the last question. If you cannot answer
these questions correctly, consider reading this chapter again until you can.

1. Which of the following is an attempt to guess a password by using a combination
   of letters and numbers?

   ○ **A.** Brute-force

   ○ **B.** Social engineering

   ○ **C.** Dictionary

   ○ **D.** Zero-day

2. A user clicked a link in an email that appeared to be from his bank. The link
   led him to a page that requested he change his password to access his bank
   account. It turns out that the web page was fraudulent. This an example of which
   of the following?

   ○ **A.** Impersonation

   ○ **B.** Dumpster diving

   ○ **C.** Phishing

   ○ **D.** Shoulder surfing

3. Several hundred infected computers simultaneously attacked your organization's
   server, rendering it useless to legitimate users. This is an example of what kind of
   attack?

   ○ **A.** Botnet

   ○ **B.** On-path attack

   ○ **C.** Tailgating

   ○ **D.** DDoS attack

   ○ **E.** Rainbow table

4. A hacker executed a coded attack against a vulnerability that has not yet been
   addressed by anyone. This is an example of what kind of attack?

   ○ **A.** DDoS attack

   ○ **B.** Spoofing attack

   ○ **C.** Zero-day attack

   ○ **D.** Brute-force attack

Cram Quiz Answers

1. **A.** A brute-force attack uses a combination of letters, numbers, and symbols to guess passwords, PINs, and passcodes. In contrast, a dictionary attack uses a list of words. Social engineering is an attempt to manipulate people into providing confidential information. A zero-day attack is an attack that has not yet been seen or documented, and it is very difficult to prepare for such attacks.

2. **C.** This is an example of phishing. Phishers use email to trick a person into divulging confidential information. While it could be said that the website that was accessed is impersonating the actual banking website, that would be more of a spoof; with true impersonation, a person mimics another person. Dumpster diving involves a person hunting through garbage or recycling to find confidential information. With shoulder surfing, a person attempts to get information by sight by, for example, looking over a person's shoulder as that person types in a password.

3. **D.** In a distributed denial of service (DDoS) attack, many computers (zombies) work together in an attempt to bring down a server or router. While it makes use of a botnet, not all botnets are necessarily bad, nor is a botnet an attack. An on-path attack is a type of spoof in which a person uses a computer to intercept and either use or change data that is captured. Tailgating is a type of social engineering attack in which a person attempts to enter a secure area by following another person without that person's knowledge. A rainbow table is set of precalculated encrypted passwords located in a lookup table.

4. **C.** A zero-day attack is an attack that exploits vulnerabilities that have not yet been discovered (besides by the attacker, that is). A DDoS attack is an attack that incorporates many systems in a collective attack against a server or network device. A spoofing attack involves technical impersonation; for example, a computer system sitting between a client and a server may impersonate the server in an attempt to retrieve user data. A brute-force attack is a password-based attack in which every conceivable password is attempted.

Now, some of things we talked about in this chapter may sound far-fetched, but they are real, and you need to proactively secure against them. Continue!

CHAPTER 47

Windows Security Settings

This chapter covers the following A+ 220-1102 exam objective:

▶ **2.5** – Given a scenario, manage and configure basic security settings in the Microsoft Windows OS.

More security? Yes, six more chapters to be sure, including this one, but it doesn't end there. You should always be thinking with your information security hat on.

This chapter gets into some fun Windows security settings such as Windows Defender Firewall, NTFS permissions, and BitLocker. It's important for you to be know how to navigate through Windows, find these various security tools, and use them appropriately. We could discuss Windows security for days, but we have limited space, so we'll stick to the basics! Let's go!

> **ExamAlert**
>
> **Objective 2.5** focuses on Defender Antivirus, Defender Firewall, users and groups, local OS options, NTFS vs. share permissions, Run as administrator vs. standard user, BitLocker, BitLocker To Go, and Encrypting File System (EFS).

The CIA of Computer Security

The main goals of information security are to keep data *confidential* and keep the *integrity* of data intact—all while preserving the *availability* of data. This is the *CIA triad* of computer security, and you should consider it whenever you are securing hardware, software, data, and the people who use that data. In this chapter, we'll contemplate security as it relates to OS tools, files, folders, users, permissions, and encryption. We'll start with two Windows Security tools: Defender Antivirus and the Defender Firewall.

Windows Defender Antivirus

Windows Defender Antivirus is Microsoft's built-in antivirus (and anti-malware) tool. It runs automatically when Windows is installed. This tool is part of the *Windows Security* suite of programs and settings. You can access Windows Security in several ways, including

- ▶ Go to **Start > Windows Security**.

- ▶ Search for **windows security**.

- ▶ Go to **Run** and type **windowsdefender:** .

- ▶ In Windows 10, Navigate to **Windows Settings > Update & Security > Windows Security**. Then click on the **Open Windows Security** button. (Note: In Windows 11, replace Update & Security with **Privacy & Security**.)

Once you have accessed Windows Security, click **Virus & threat protection**. From there, you can run a quick scan of the system for viruses and check for updates to the Defender Antivirus program. You can also click **Manage settings** to make configuration changes to the program. For example, perhaps your organization uses a separate third-party anti-malware suite. From Manage settings, you can turn off real-time protection so that the two programs do not conflict with each other. You can also enable cloud protection and modify how Windows alerts you about viruses.

Windows Defender Firewall

Windows Defender Firewall is meant to protect client computers from malicious attacks and intrusions, but sometimes it can be the culprit when certain applications fail. You can access Windows Defender Firewall in a couple of ways:

▶ The Windows Settings access method: Access **Windows Security** as described previously and then click **Firewall & network protection**.

▶ The Control Panel access methods:

▶ Select **Control Panel > All Control Panel Items > Windows Defender Firewall**.

▶ Select **Run > firewall.cpl**.

From here, you can enable or disable Windows Defender Firewall for the private network, public network, and domain network. (In the Control Panel, you will see **Guest or public networks** instead of *domain*.) By default, these are "on," or "connected." As with Defender Antivirus, you might decide to disable Windows Defender Firewall and instead use the third-party firewall that your organization uses. Always verify that at least *one* firewall is enabled!

When Windows Defender Firewall is on, the default setting is to shield all inbound ports (effectively closing them). This is a type of default *port security*, and it means that certain applications that need to communicate with a remote host might not work properly. Or if a client computer wanted to host some services (such as FTP or a web server), the firewall would block them. That's where exceptions come in. You can still use the firewall, but you can specify applications that are exceptions to the rule. Figure 47.1 shows an example of exceptions made on a Windows 10 Pro computer. To create exceptions in Windows Security, click **Allow an app through the firewall**. To create exceptions in the Control Panel version, click **Allow an app or feature through Windows Defender Firewall**. Either method takes you to the Allowed apps window.

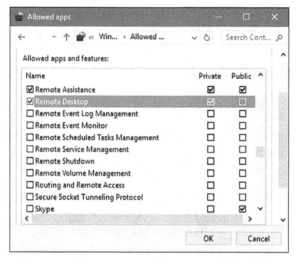

FIGURE 47.1   **Firewall exceptions**

Figure 47.1 shows that two applications are not blocked from incoming connections. Remote Assistance is not blocked at all—not on the Private profile and not on the Public profile. Remote Desktop is allowed only on the Private profile. So, as long as the firewall is enabled, this computer can make Remote Assistance calls to other users on the Internet. But if a person wants to connect to this system through Remote Desktop without an invitation, that person must be on the LAN to succeed. With these settings, you are not sacrificing the security of the entire system. All other incoming connections will be blocked.

Let's get more in depth with the firewall settings. By clicking the **Advanced Settings** link, you can make use of Windows Defender Firewall with Advanced Security (also available in Administrative Tools and as a snap-in in the MMC). You can also get to this by opening the **Run** prompt and typing **wf.msc**. From here, you can get more in-depth with application restrictions. For example, you can create inbound and outbound rules for individual applications based on the private network, the public network, or both. You can also configure the firewall with the **netsh** command or within PowerShell. (For more information, see https://tinyurl.com/WFDAS.)

If Windows Defender Firewall gives you errors when you attempt to update the firewall settings, add exceptions, or access the advanced settings, make sure the Windows Defender Firewall service is enabled and running in **services.msc**.

Essentially, a firewall is a packet filter that uses *access control lists (ACLs)* to specify what packets can pass through. ACLs are composed of source and destination IP addresses and ports, as well as the type of packets to be allowed or denied. ACLs are written differently depending on the device or program you are using. In Windows, they can be written using PowerShell or configured graphically using Windows Defender Firewall with Advanced Security.

Users and Groups

Users are what it's all about when it comes to Windows security. On a Windows client computer, you have two options: Microsoft accounts and local users. Microsoft accounts are accounts that are associated with email addresses. But you can also create local user accounts that do not need a email addresses or Microsoft accounts.

Both types of user accounts have a variety of logon options for authentication purposes. You can change your authentication method by going to **Windows Settings > Accounts > Sign-in options**. The following is a partial list of sign-in options in Windows:

▶ **Username and password:** This is often a default setting. When you log on to Windows, you select the user account from the screen (or type the username) and then type the password. The username/password authentication method has been the industry standard for decades, but it's important to use a complex password, as we will discuss in Chapter 48, "Windows Best Practices."

▶ **Personal identification number (PIN):** You can choose a numeric passcode to access Windows. This is not as secure as a password.

▶ **Fingerprint:** If your device has a biometric reader, you can incorporate fingerprint authentication. Some laptops have these readers built in, or you could use an external USB-based fingerprint reader.

▶ **Security key:** You can use a USB-based physical token that houses an encryption key for authentication purposes.

▶ **Picture password:** With this option, you select a picture to use and then "draw" on the touchscreen to have the system save your gesture. Every subsequent logon requires this gesture.

Objective 2.5 also makes mention of facial recognition and single sign-on (SSO). Facial recognition means that a camera-equipped system will attempt to scan your face as part of the authentication process. SSO means that you can use one logon to access all the systems and networks you need. To a certain extent, the Microsoft account is an example of SSO because it can allow a person access to the local computer as well as Microsoft OneDrive and other cloud-based resources.

> **Note**
>
> You can configure Windows users for enterprise-level single sign-on (SSO) authentication. This generally requires a domain, Microsoft Identity Manager, Azure, or OpenID Connect (and often a combination of these). For more information, see https://docs.microsoft.com/en-us/azure/active-directory/manage-apps/what-is-single-sign-on.

> **Note**
>
> The rest of this section shows how to work with local accounts.

You can accomplish basic user account creation from within Settings or the Control Panel, but in this section, we will be focusing on the more useful Local Users and Groups, which you can access from Computer Management or directly by going to **Run** and typing **lusrmgr.msc**.

There are four main types of user account levels you should know for the exam:

▶ **Administrators:** These users have full (or nearly full) control of an operating system. They are the most powerful accounts in Windows and have access to everything.

▶ **Standard users (also simply referred to as users):** These users are the normal accounts for people who can log on to the network. A standard user account has access to (owns) data but cannot access the data of any other user and, by default, cannot perform administrative tasks (such as installing software).

▶ **Guests:** These users have limited access to the system. A guest cannot install software or hardware, cannot change settings or access any data, and cannot change the password. A guest account is sometimes used for temporary workers or vendors who may need temporary access. The guest account is disabled by default.

▶ **Power users:** These users are included in Windows for backward compatibility with older versions of applications.

> **ExamAlert**
>
> Know the Windows user accounts and groups, including Administrator, Power User, Guest, and Standard User. Know what they can and cannot do!

All of these types of users are actually groups within Windows client operating systems (such as Windows 10). If you access the Local Users and Groups window and click the **Groups** folder, you will see these groups and many more (for example, Backup Operators, Remote Desktop Users, and so on). There are, however, individual administrator and guest accounts (located in the Users folder) that are built into the system.

You can create users by clicking the **Users** folder and then clicking **Action >** **New User** or by right-clicking in the user list work area and selecting **New User**. Either option brings up the window shown in Figure 47.2.

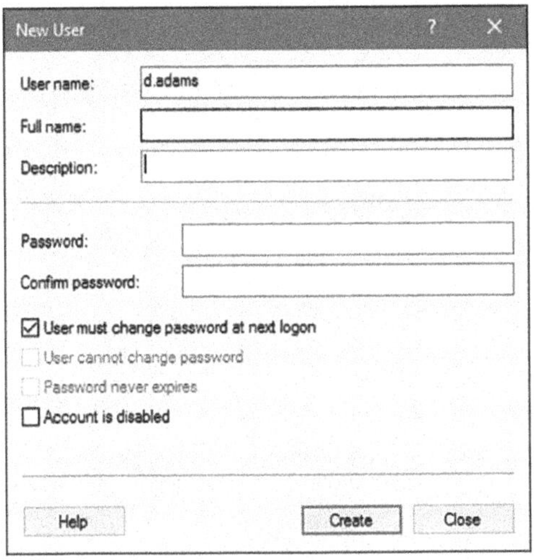

FIGURE 47.2 **New User window**

Try going through the process now. At a bare minimum, you'll be required to type a username. You can fill out other information as well, including the user's full name and a description of the user. By default, the option **User must change password at next logon** is selected, so you don't have to select a password. In some scenarios, the systems administrator supplies the password. With this option, you as the admin would have to type the password (and confirm it), deselect the first checkbox, and then select **User cannot change password**. The password will have to comply with any password policy that has been set (in terms of length, complexity, etc.). Keep in mind that this is not the most secure way to do things, but it might be necessary in some cases. Also note that there is a checkbox called Account is disabled. You can disable an account temporarily by using this option, but generally you would work with that setting after the account is created (from the account **Properties** dialog box > **Account** tab). For example, if a user fails to log on with the correct password after *x* number of attempts (as set in a Group Policy), the account will become disabled, and the administrator will have to deselect the checkbox to enable the user to log on. If a person leaves an organization or is terminated, you should immediately disable the account so that the user cannot log on anymore.

By default, when a user is first created, the user is automatically given group membership to the Users group and performs as a standard user. However, you can add members to other groups if you need to (for instance, if you need to have a second administrator). To do this, right-click the user account, select **Properties**, and then click the **Member Of** tab. The Select Groups dialog box pops up, as shown in Figure 47.3, and you can either type the name of the group you want to make the user a member of or browse for it.

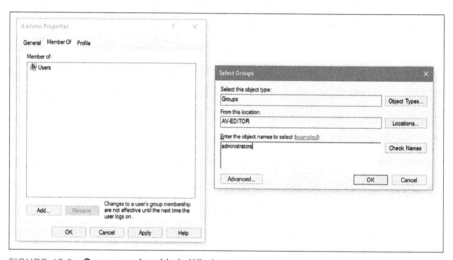

FIGURE 47.3 **Group membership in Windows**

In Figure 47.3, the user d.adams is currently a member of the Users group, but I am in the process of adding that user to the Administrators group. Be careful who you add as an admin as that person will now get full control!

Restrict Administrator Access!

Some end users like to play with systems—which can often result in disaster. Case in point: Have you ever heard of God Mode for Windows? It displays almost every configuration window an administrator could want in one big list. It's easy to access: Just create a new folder on the desktop (or anywhere else) and rename the folder to the following:

```
GodMode.{ED7BA470-8E54-465E-825C-99712043E01C}
```

That will create the custom control panel, and you will have access to *many* functions in one window. This is great for actual administrators, but a typical user can use it to wreak havoc.

So, I can't stress enough how important it is to restrict administrative access. Typical users should *not* be administrators—period. They shouldn't be added to the administrators group, nor should they be allowed to gain administrative privileges through UAC or by knowing an admin's password. Remember the principle of least privilege. Make sure that account privileges and permissions are set so that typical users get the least access necessary!

Permissions

Folders and files can be assigned permissions, which allow users a particular level of access to the data. There are two levels of permissions, which are configured in the Properties window of a folder or a file:

▶ **Share permissions:** These permissions can be accessed from the Sharing tab. By default, the Everyone group has Read (read-only) access. The other two permissions available are Change and Full Control.

▶ **NTFS permissions:** These permissions are accessed from the Security tab. There are six default levels of permissions, from Read to Write to Full control, as shown in Figure 47.4.

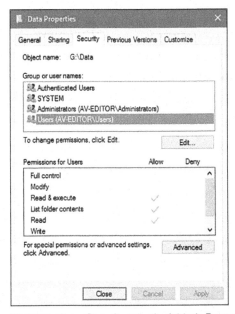

FIGURE 47.4 **Security tab of a folder's Properties window**

If you happen to be using both share and NTFS permissions, the most restrictive of the two will take precedence. So, for example, if a user was given Full Control access for Share permissions and only Read access for NTFS permissions, the user would ultimately have only the Read permission.

ExamAlert

NTFS permissions are modified in the Security tab of the folder's Properties window.

The weakest of the NTFS permissions is Read and the strongest, of course, is Full control. Administrators have Full control by default. Typical users have only Read, List folder contents, and Read & execute by default. Note the options Allow and Deny, which can be assigned for a particular user or for a user group (hence the term user-level security). Generally, when you want users to have access to a folder, you add them to the list and select Allow for the appropriate permission. When you don't want to allow them access, normally you simply don't add them. But in some cases, an explicit Deny is necessary. This could be because the user is part of a larger group that already has access to a parent folder, but you don't want the specific user to have access to this particular subfolder.

Permission Inheritance and Propagation

If you create a folder, the default action it takes is to inherit permissions from the parent folder. So any permissions that you set in the parent will be inherited by the subfolder. To view an example of this, locate any folder within an NTFS volume (besides the root folder), right-click it, select **Properties**, access the **Security** tab, and click the **Advanced** button. Figure 47.5 shows an example of this in Windows 10. (Names and navigation will be slightly different in other versions of Windows.)

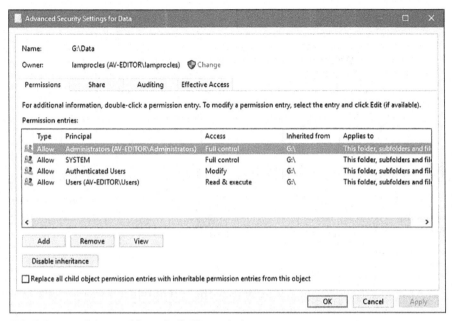

FIGURE 47.5   **Advanced Security Settings window**

What this all means is that any permissions added or removed in the parent folder will also be added or removed in the current folder. In addition, permissions that are inherited cannot be modified in the current folder. To make modifications in this case, click the **Disable inheritance** button (or deselect the corresponding checkbox in earlier versions of Windows). When you do this, you have the option to copy the permissions from the parent to the current folder or remove them entirely. So, by default, the parent is automatically propagating permissions to the subfolder, and the subfolder is inheriting its permissions from the parent. You can also propagate permission changes to subfolders that are not inheriting from the current folder. To do so, select the **Replace all child object permission entries with inheritable permission entries from this object** checkbox. (Again, names will vary according to the version of Windows.)

This might all seem a bit confusing. You will probably not be asked many exam questions on the subject. Just remember that folders automatically inherit from the parent unless you turn off inheriting—and you can propagate permission entries to subfolders at any time by selecting the **Replace** option.

> **Note**
>
> One other concept you should know that is not listed in the objectives is *ownership*. By default, Windows uses discretionary access control (DAC), which means the creator of a file or folder is the owner—and this means that only that person can assign permissions to that file or folder. However, an administrator can change who the owner is simply by clicking the **Change** link that is shown in Figure 47.5. So, the administrator can take ownership and subsequently change permissions if needed.

Moving and Copying Folders and Files

This subject (like the previous one) is actually an advanced Microsoft Windows concept, so we'll try to keep this section simple. *Moving* and *copying* folders and files have different results when it comes to permissions. Basically, it breaks down like this:

▶ When you copy a folder or file on the same volume or to a different volume, it *inherits* the permissions of the parent folder it was copied to (known as the target directory).

▶ When you move a folder or file to a different location on the same volume, it *retains* the original permissions.

▶ When you move a file to another volume, it *inherits* the permissions of the parent folder.

> **Note**
>
> Keep in mind that when you move data within a partition, the data isn't actually relocated; instead, the pointer to the file or folder is modified.

File Security

Files can be assigned four different attributes in Windows: read-only, hidden, compression, and encryption. To access these attributes, right-click any file and select **Properties**. On the General tab, you will see the Read-only checkbox; if this is checked, no one can save modifications to the file, but a new file can be saved with the changes. Checking the **Hidden** checkbox makes the file invisible to all users except the user who created the file. Admins can unhide files individually or for an entire system, as I will explain in a moment. When you click the **Advanced** button, you see two checkboxes: **Compress contents to save disk space**, which allows you to convert the file to a smaller size that takes up less space on the drive, and **Encrypt contents to secure data**, which scrambles the file content so only the user who created the file can read it. We'll discuss encryption later in this chapter.

> **Note**
>
> The **attrib** command at the Command Prompt can modify the read-only, archive, system, and hidden attributes for files and display the attributes for each file. This older command is still available in Windows but is not used often. For more information about this command, see https://dprocomputer.com/?p=811.

System files and folders are hidden from view by the OS to protect the system. In some cases, you can simply click the **Show the contents of this folder** link, but to permanently configure the system to show hidden files and folders, you need to navigate to the Folder Options dialog box. (An example of this is shown in Figure 35.2 in Chapter 35.) Then select the **View** tab and, under Hidden files and folders, select the **Show hidden files, folders, and drives** radio button. To configure the system to show protected system files, deselect the **Hide protected operating system files** checkbox, located below Show hidden files and folders. This enables you to view files such as bootmgr, pagefile.sys, and hiberfil.sys.

> **ExamAlert**
>
> To view files such as bootmgr, pagefile.sys, and hiberfil.sys, select the **Show hidden files** radio button and deselect the **Hide protected operating system files** checkbox.

Administrative Shares

Folders and files need to be shared so that other users on the local computer and on the network can gain access to them. Windows operating systems use an access control model for securable objects such as folders. This model takes care of rights and permissions, usually through discretionary access control lists (DACLs) that contain individual access control entries (ACEs). All the shared folders can be found by navigating to **Computer Management > System Tools > Shared Folders > Shares**, as shown in Figure 47.6. In this figure, you can see that I have shared a folder named Data, which is also known as a local share.

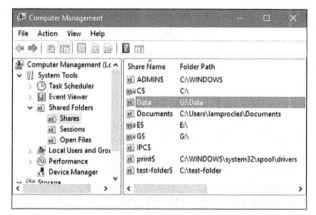

FIGURE 47.6 **Windows shares**

Here you can also see the hidden administrative shares, which can be identified by the $ on the end of the share name. These shares cannot be seen by standard users when browsing to the computer over the network; they are meant for administrative use. Note that every volume (C:, E:, and G:, for example) has an administrative share. Although it is possible to remove these by editing the registry, this is not recommended because it might cause other networking issues. You should be aware that only administrators should have access to these shares. Hidden shares can be created by simply adding $ to the end of the share name when enabling the share. Administrative/hidden shares can be accessed only if the user knows the exact network path to the folder and has permissions to access it.

ExamAlert

Hidden/administrative shares can be identified by the $ on the end of the share name.

Encrypting File System

Encryption is the process of converting information with the use of a cipher (algorithm), making it unreadable by other users unless they have the correct "key" to the information. Cryptography is the process of hiding information. In a cryptosystem, information is protected by being disguised.

A few different encryption technologies are used in Windows. For example, whenever you log on to a Windows network, that authentication is secured with the Kerberos protocol. As another example, when you want to encrypt one or more files or folders, Windows uses Encrypting File System (EFS), a component of NTFS. Follow these steps to encrypt a file in Windows:

1. Locate the file you want to encrypt, right-click it, and select **Properties**. This brings up the General tab within the file's Properties window.

2. At the bottom of the General tab, click the **Advanced** button. This brings up the Advanced Attributes window.

3. Check the box labeled **Encrypt contents to secure data**.

4. Click **OK** for both windows. (When you do so, the system should ask whether you want to encrypt the parent folder and the file or just the file. It's recommended that the file's parent folder be encrypted as well.)

To unencrypt the file and return it to normal, simply deselect the **Encrypt contents to secure data** checkbox.

> **Note**
>
> You can color code encrypted and compressed NTFS files. You do this in the Folder Options dialog box by clicking the **View** tab and selecting **Show encrypted or compressed NTFS files in color**. After you select that, a green filename indicates an encrypted file, and a blue filename indicates a compressed file.

If a file needs to be decrypted and the original user (the owner of the key or certificate) isn't available, an EFS recovery agent needs to be used. In many cases, the default recovery agent is the built-in administrator account. It is important to note a couple more items: EFS isn't designed to protect data while it is transferred from one computer to another; in addition, EFS is not designed to encrypt an entire drive.

BitLocker Encryption

To encrypt an entire disk, you need some kind of full disk encryption software. There are several options currently available on the market. One of them, developed by Microsoft, is called BitLocker, and it is available only on select editions of Windows (such as Pro, Pro for Workstations, and Enterprise). BitLocker uses a type of encryption known as *data-at-rest*. This means data that is stored on the local computer and not being transmitted through the network.

BitLocker software can encrypt an entire disk, which, after it's completed, is transparent to the user. However, there are some requirements for this. You need either of the following:

▶ A Trusted Platform Module (TPM) chip, which is a chip residing on the motherboard that actually stores the encrypted keys.

▶ An external USB key to store the encrypted keys and a storage drive with two volumes, preferably created during the installation of Windows. One volume (most likely C:) is for the operating system that will be encrypted; the other is the active volume that remains unencrypted so that the computer can boot. If a second volume needs to be created, that can be done in Disk Management, and the volume can then be accessed by BitLocker.

ExamAlert

Know the components necessary for BitLocker: a TPM or USB key.

To use BitLocker, you can search for it in Windows Settings or go to **All Control Panel Items > BitLocker Drive Encryption**. BitLocker software (like EFS) is based on Advanced Encryption Standard (AES) and uses a 128-bit key by default, though it can be increased to 256-bit in the Group Policy Editor. Keep in mind that a drive encrypted with BitLocker usually suffers in terms of performance compared to a non-encrypted drive and could have a shorter shelf life as well. By default, BitLocker is used to encrypt the internal drive of a system. However, you can also encrypt USB drives and other removable devices by using BitLocker To Go. This is also done in the same place that BitLocker is used. Once inserted, a USB drive or other removable media will be recognized by the program automatically.

Note

Need to increase BitLocker's AES cipher strength to 256-bit? Open the Local Group Policy Editor (**Run > gpedit.msc**) and go to **Computer Configuration > Administrative Templates > Windows Components > BitLocker Drive Encryption** and enable and configure the policy for your version of Windows.

Run As

Remember that standard users can't do very much in Windows. You need to run a lot of these configuration programs as an administrator—meaning in elevated mode. Generally, right-clicking an app and selecting **Run as administrator** is enough. For more options, see Chapter 31, "Microsoft Command-Line Tools, Part I." Also, Objective 2.5 makes mention of User Account Control (UAC), and we discuss UAC briefly in Chapter 44, "Logical Security."

Cram Quiz

Answer these questions. The answers follow the last question. If you cannot answer these questions correctly, consider reading this chapter again until you can.

1. You have been tasked with setting up encryption for a Windows computer. You are required to encrypt several shared folders within a partition so that they can't be read by other users. What tool should you use?

   ○ **A.** BitLocker

   ○ **B.** TPM

   ○ **C.** Administrative share

   ○ **D.** EFS

2. One of the users on your network is trying to access files shared on a remote computer. The file's share permissions allow the user Full Control, but the NTFS permissions allow the user Read access. Which of the following will be the resulting access for the user?

   ○ **A.** Full Control

   ○ **B.** Modify

   ○ **C.** Read

   ○ **D.** Write

3. You are the administrator for your network, and you set up an administrative share called Data$. Which of the following are necessary for another user to access this share? (Select the two best answers.)

   ○ **A.** The user must have permissions to access the share.

   ○ **B.** The user must know the decryption key.

   ○ **C.** The user must know the exact network path to the share.

   ○ **D.** The user must enable File Sharing in the Network and Sharing Center.

4. You are tasked with encrypting several laptops using BitLocker. However, some of the laptops do not have a built-in TPM chip. What should you implement to enable BitLocker on those laptops?

   ○ **A.** Firmware update

   ○ **B.** MFA

   ○ **C.** USB key

   ○ **D.** Encryption on the local drive

5. Which Windows account would you create for someone who needs to regularly install software, change settings, and take ownership?

- ○ **A.** Power user
- ○ **B.** Standard user
- ○ **C.** Guest
- ○ **D.** Root
- ○ **E.** Administrator

Cram Quiz Answers

1. **D.** Use Encrypting File System (EFS). This is easily done: Right-click the folder(s), select **Properties**, click the **Advanced** button, and check **Encrypt contents to secure data**. At this point, other users will not be able to read the files contained in those folders. BitLocker is used to encrypt an entire storage drive (or volume), but in the scenario, you only need to encrypt several folders. A Trusted Platform Module (TPM) chip is a chip that is required for using BitLocker, but it is not necessary for EFS. By creating an administrator share, you will effectively hide the contents from typical users, unless they know the admin password. If they do know the password, then they can read the files. Regardless, administrative shares do not encrypt data.

2. **C.** The user will get only Read access. If you are using both sets of permissions, the most restrictive set will take precedence. In this case, NTFS permissions are more restrictive than share permissions.

3. **A and C.** The user needs to have permissions to the share and must know the exact path to the network share because it is an administrative share. The question does not mention whether the file is encrypted. The user doesn't need to enable sharing; the person is trying to access a share.

4. **C.** If the laptops don't have a TPM chip, use a USB key to provide the encryption required by BitLocker. A firmware update won't help in this scenario; the TPM chip is an actual piece of hardware that is integrated to the motherboard. MFA stands for multi-factor authentication. While MFA is a good idea, this question deals with encryption, not authentication. Encrypting the local drive is the task at hand, but you need to get BitLocker to work first!

5. **E.** Administrators have full control of an operating system. Power users are included in Windows for backward compatibility with older versions, and are seldom used. Standard users are the normal default accounts for people who can log on to the network. Guests have limited access to the system. A guest cannot install software or hardware, cannot change settings, cannot access any data, and cannot change the password.

Remember, with great power comes great responsibility. In short, leave it to the admins. Continue!

CHAPTER 48

Windows Best Practices

This chapter covers the following A+ 220-1102 exam objective:

▶ **2.6** – Given a scenario, configure a workstation to meet best practices for security.

As a systems administrator, you have to make sure that users can only get access to what they need and that no one else can masquerade as a legitimate user. User accounts can be secured by using a combination of strong passwords, password policies, restrictions, account lockouts, and, in general, good account management, which requires not only solid configuration but also monitoring and auditing of user accounts. While many of the techniques in this chapter are designed for Windows, some of the concepts can be easily incorporated with any operating system.

> **ExamAlert**
>
> **Objective 2.6** concentrates on data-at-rest encryption, password best practices, end-user best practices, account management, changing the default administrator's user account/password, and disabling AutoRun/AutoPlay.

Usernames and Passwords

The username/password combination is the most common type of authentication for gaining access to computers. The username is known to all parties involved and can be seen as plaintext when typed. In some cases, the user has no control over their username; in other cases, the username might be a name or an email address or might be selected by the user. For example, you might use a sign-in to access the Microsoft Store for apps; in this case, it is typical to use your email address as your username. You can see this username, it shows up on the screen, and you can be identified by it. The password is either set by the user or created automatically for the user. This password, however, is not something anyone else should know or see.

It is common knowledge that a strong password is important for protecting a user account, whether the account is with a bank, at work, or elsewhere. But what is a strong password? Many organizations define a strong password as a password with at least 10 characters, including at least 1 uppercase letter, 1 number, and 1 special character. The best passwords have similar requirements but are 16 characters or more. Many password-checker programs on the Web can help you get an idea of what is considered "strong." Table 48.1 shows a strong password and a "best" password.

TABLE 48.1 **Strong and Stronger Passwords**

Password	Strength of Password
|Ocrian7	Strong
This1sV#ryS3cure	Very strong, or "best"

Notice that the first password in the table uses the | (pipe) symbol instead of the letter L. This is a special character that shares the \ (backslash) key on the keyboard. The second password uses 16 characters, including 3 capital letters, 2 numbers, and a partridge in a pear tree…um, I mean 1 special character. (Just checking whether you are still with me!) Although a partridge wouldn't help your password security, the other methods make for an extremely strong password that would take a supercomputer a long time to crack. (Of course, the passwords in the table are now weak because they have been mass printed and are *known*. They are just examples and should not be used on a system.)

Password length can go beyond 16 characters. In fact, the National Institute of Standards and Technology (NIST) says the longer the better, as long as your users are set up with a secure method of either remembering those passwords/ passphrases or pasting them from a password vault.

ExamAlert

Understand what is required for a strong complex password.

Note

As mentioned in Chapter 16, "Motherboards and Add-on Cards," BIOS/UEFI passwords are also very important, especially the administrative password. The same basic rules described here apply to BIOS passwords as well.

Password Policies

A password might need to meet certain requirements, or it might need to be changed at regular intervals, among other policies. Figure 48.1 shows an example of the default password policy in the Local Security Policy window on a Windows computer. To open the Local Security Policy window, go to **Administrative Tools** or go to **Run > secpol.msc**. Then navigate to **Security Settings > Account Policies > Password Policy**.

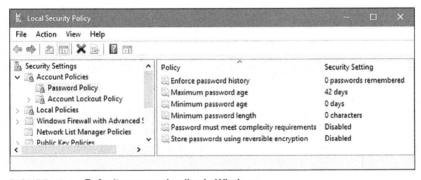

FIGURE 48.1 **Default password policy in Windows**

As shown in the figure, there are several items that you can configure (or that can be configured by the network administrator centrally if the computer is part of a domain). The important ones for the exam include the following:

▶ **Enforce password history:** When this is defined, users cannot use any of the passwords that are remembered in the history. If you set the history to 3, the last three passwords cannot be used again when it is time to change the password.

▶ **Maximum password age and Minimum password age:** These settings define exactly how long a password can be used. The maximum is initially set to 42 days but does not affect the default administrator account. To enforce an effective password history, the minimum must be higher than 0 days.

▶ **Minimum password length:** This requires that the password must be at least the specified number of characters. For a strong password policy, set this to between 10 and 16 (at least!).

▶ **Password must meet complexity requirements:** This means that passwords must meet three of these four criteria: uppercase characters, lowercase characters, digits between 0 and 9, and nonalphabetic characters (special characters).

> **Note**
>
> For more information on some password best practices, see
> https://www.microsoft.com/en-us/research/publication/password-guidance/
> and the NIST special publication SP 800-63B: Digital Identity Guidelines:
> https://pages.nist.gov/800-63-3/sp800-63b.html.

Account Management and End-User Best Practices

Now that you know more about secure passwords and password policies, let's talk about securing user accounts for Windows. There are a few things you can do to secure them, as described in the following list. Refer to Figure 48.2 while reading through the list:

▶ **Rename and password protect the Administrator account:** To config-ure this account, navigate to **Computer Management > System Tools >**

Local Users and Groups > Users and locate the Administrator account. Right-click the account, and you see a drop-down menu in which you can rename it and/or give it a password. (Just remember the new username and password!) It's great to have this additional Administrator account on the shelf just in case the primary account fails. Many organizations do just this and disable the original Administrator account. If the account is disabled, you can enable it if necessary. Right-click the account and select **Properties**. In the **General** tab, deselect the **Account is disabled** checkbox. Alternatively, open PowerShell or the Command Prompt (as an admin) and type **net user administrator /active:yes**. Of course, you have to have administrative privileges to perform these actions.

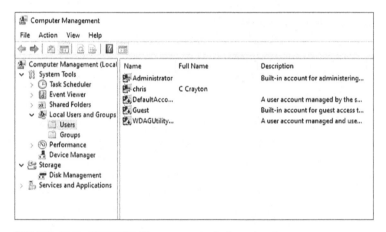

FIGURE 48.2 Computer Management window, showing users

▶ **Verify that the Guest account and other unnecessary accounts are disabled:** Navigate again to **Local Users and Groups > Users**, right-click the account in question, select **Properties**, and then select the checkbox **Account is disabled** (which is disabled by default in most versions of Windows). You can tell that it is disabled if it has a black down arrow over the account icon. You can also delete accounts (aside from built-in accounts, such as the Guest account); however, companies usually opt to have them disabled so that they can retain auditing information that is linked to those accounts.

▶ **Restrict user permissions:** Users are created as standard users by default, but it's always a good idea to audit the user accounts and make sure that they don't have any unnecessary group memberships that could give them more power than they require. This is part of the principle of least privilege: The less a user can do, the more secure the system will be.

▶ **Set logon time and computer restrictions:** In a Windows domain, you can allow and disallow certain hours of the day that a user can log on to the network. In the user's Properties dialog box, go to the **Account** tab and click the **Logon Hours** button. From there, you can configure when the user is allowed to log on. For example, in Figure 48.3, Bob can only log on to the domain Monday through Friday from 8 a.m. to 6 p.m. You can also specify individual computers that the user can log on to by clicking the **Log On To** button in the Properties dialog box. For temporary employees and contractors, it's a good idea to configure account expiration, which is at the bottom of the Account tab.

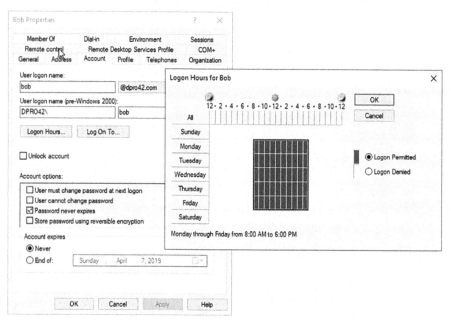

FIGURE 48.3 **Logon Hours setting**

▶ **Set the account lockout threshold:** If a user attempts to log on to a system and is unsuccessful (after a specified number of attempts), the user will be locked out of the system. The settings and thresholds for this can be configured in the Local Security Policy window. Navigate to **Security Settings > Account Policies > Account Lockout Policy**. From here, you can set the account lockout threshold to a certain number of invalid logons, set how long the user will be locked out, and set the amount of time until the lockout counter is reset. If an account is locked out and you need to unlock it immediately, follow one of the options at the end of the first bullet.

ExamAlert

Know how to enable/disable accounts, reset passwords, and modify password policy!

Note

Lockouts due to forgotten passwords are common in organizations. Sometimes a user will use several passwords to gain access to various systems, making the problem worse. Having several complex passwords can be confusing to a user and may lead to many tech support calls requiring accounts be unlocked. To combat this, use *single sign-on (SSO)*, or federated identity management. Remember that with SSO, a user needs only one password to gain access to two or more systems.

It's important to note that when logging on to a Microsoft network, the logon process is secured by the Kerberos protocol, which is run by the Active Directory domain controller. This adds a layer of protection for the username and password as they are being authenticated across the network.

Regardless of whether a user is part of a domain or not, when the user takes a break or leaves for lunch, the user should either log off or lock the computer. Locking the computer can be done by pressing Windows+L. The operating system then goes into a locked state, and the only way to unlock the computer is to enter the username and password of the person who is logged in to the computer. The difference between locking and logging out is that a locked computer leaves all the session's applications and files open; logging out closes all open applications and files.

Aside from locking a computer manually, a user can opt to put the computer to sleep after a certain period of time or enable a password-protected screensaver, both of which will force the user to log on when returning to the computer. Sleep settings can be accessed in Windows 10 by navigating to **Settings > Power & Sleep** or by navigating to **Control Panel > All Control Panel Items > Power Options > Edit Plan Settings**. Further configuration can be performed within the **Power Options** dialog box by clicking the **Change advanced power settings** link. To set the screen saver to require a password when the system resumes in Windows 10, for example, go to **Settings > Personalization** (or right-click the desktop and select **Personalize**). Then go to **Lock screen > Screen saver settings**. In the dialog box, check **On resume, display logon screen**.

Finally, end users should be educated about securing critical hardware and personally identifiable information (PII). For example, a laptop could be secured with a cable lock or, at the very least, put away in a laptop bag out of sight. And PII such as passwords, ID cards, and so on should not be left out on a desk or under a keyboard. These are the first places malicious insiders and other con artists will look. Anything that can trace back to the end user or the organization should be secured.

Disabling AutoPlay/AutoRun

If you disable AutoPlay, removable media won't automatically start its AutoRun application (if it has one), and any embedded malware won't have a chance to infect the system before you scan the media. To disable AutoPlay/AutoRun in Windows, you have a couple of options.

One way to do this in Windows 10 is to open **Settings** and then click **Devices**. Next, select **AutoPlay** from the left side. Finally, set the AutoPlay slider button to **Off**.

Or, to use the Group Policy Editor, complete the following steps:

1. Go to the **Run** prompt and type **gpedit.msc**. The Local Group Policy Editor appears. (This is not available in some editions of Windows.)

2. Navigate to **Computer Configuration > Administrative Templates > Windows Components > AutoPlay Policies**. From here you can modify how AutoPlay and AutoRun function.

3. Double-click the **Turn off AutoPlay** setting. This displays the Turn off AutoPlay configuration window.

4. Click the **Enabled** radio button and then click **OK**. When you do this, you are actually enabling the policy named Turn off AutoPlay.

ExamAlert

Know how to disable AutoPlay in Windows Settings and the Group Policy Editor.

Note

We discuss data encryption further in Chapter 47, "Windows Security Settings."

The Information Security Field Is Enormous

As you can see, you could configure security for Windows all day—and still have more to do. This is one of the reasons the computer security field is so massive—and this is just Windows. Remember, these last couple of chapters have given an overview of how to secure Windows and Windows networks. Keep reading and learning because there is a lot of work to do when it comes to computer and data security!

Cram Quiz

Answer these questions. The answers follow the last question. If you cannot answer these questions correctly, consider reading this chapter again until you can.

1. Which of the following is the strongest password?

   ○ **A.** |ocrian#

   ○ **B.** Marqu1sD3S0d

   ○ **C.** This1sV#ryS3cure

   ○ **D.** Thisisverysecure

2. Your boss is concerned that people who have been terminated will come back in the building and attempt to log on to the network using passwords that they used in the past. What should you do to help protect against this? (Select the two best answers.)

   ○ **A.** Set up a password length policy.

   ○ **B.** Configure an account lockout threshold.

   ○ **C.** Immediately disable the accounts of people who have been terminated.

   ○ **D.** Set logon time restrictions.

   ○ **E.** Disable the Guest account.

3. A customer complains that while he was away at lunch, someone used his computer to send emails to other co-workers without his knowledge. Which of the following should you recommend that the user do?

   ○ **A.** Enable a screensaver.

   ○ **B.** Unplug the network cable before leaving for lunch.

   ○ **C.** Use the Windows lock feature.

   ○ **D.** Enable the out-of-office message in email when leaving for lunch.

4. Which of the following best describes encryption?

  ○ **A.** Prevents unauthorized users from viewing or reading data

  ○ **B.** Prevents unauthorized users from deleting data

  ○ **C.** Prevents unauthorized users from posing as the original source sending data

  ○ **D.** Prevents unauthorized users from decompressing files

5. How can you prevent applications from automatically executing, and possibly infecting a computer with malware, when removable media is inserted?

  ○ **A.** Enable the account lockout threshold policy.

  ○ **B.** Turn on BitLocker.

  ○ **C.** Turn off BitLocker To Go.

  ○ **D.** Disable AutoPlay.

Cram Quiz Answers

1. **C.** This1sV#ryS3cure incorporates uppercase and lowercase letters, numbers, and special characters, and it is 16 characters long. That makes it the strongest password of the listed options. |ocrian# has special characters but is missing uppercase letters and numerals—and it is only 8 characters long. Marqu1sD3S0d does not have any special characters. Thisisverysecure is 16 characters long and has 1 capital letter but does not have any numerals or special characters.

2. **B and C.** The best answers are to configure an account lockout threshold and immediately disable the accounts of anyone who has been terminated. A common method is to use the "three strikes and you're out" rule for account lockout, meaning that a person can attempt to log on three times before the account is locked out. But, more importantly, you should disable (or lock) the accounts of people who have been offboarded or terminated. The other options are all good security options in general but won't help much with disgruntled former employees who are attempting to get into the system. Also, some type of authentication system should be in place so that these people cannot get access to the building.

3. **C.** Tell the customer to lock the computer (by pressing Windows+L or by using the Start menu) before leaving for lunch. As long as there is a strong password, other co-workers should not be able to access the system. Screensavers by themselves do not secure systems, but a user can enable the password-protected screensaver feature (but should be aware that there is a delay before the screensaver turns on). Unplugging the network cable is not a legitimate answer; plus, it can always be plugged back in. The out-of-office message will reply only to people emailing the user; it won't stop outgoing emails.

4. **A.** Encryption prevents unauthorized users from viewing or reading data. Properly configured permissions prevent unauthorized users from deleting data or attempting to decompress files. A strong logon password prevents unauthorized users from posing as the original source sending data.

5. **D.** If you disable AutoPlay, removable media won't automatically start its AutoRun application (if it has one), and any embedded malware won't have a chance to infect the system before you scan the media. The account lockout threshold specifies the amount of times a user can attempt to log on to Windows before being logged off. BitLocker and BitLocker To Go are used for encryption, not for blocking removable media from automatically executing files.

Fantastic! You're doing great. This important chapter wraps up Windows security. Be sure to review the chapter and your notes, take a break, and then continue!

CHAPTER 49

Mobile Device Security

This chapter covers the following A+ 220-1102 exam objective:

▶ **2.7** – Explain common methods for securing mobile and embedded devices.

Mobile devices need to be secured just like any other computing devices. But due to their transportable nature, some of the security techniques will be a bit different and can be more challenging for a systems administrator. I recommend that you prepare for the possibility of a stolen, lost, damaged, or compromised device. The methods in this chapter can help you recover from such problems and also aid you in preventing them from happening.

Screen Locks

Because mobile devices are expensive and could contain confidential data, they are often targeted by thieves. Plus, they are small and easy to conceal, making them easy to steal. However, there are some things you can do to prevent theft or loss, protect data, and attempt to get a mobile device back in the event that it is *misplaced*.

The first thing a user should do when receiving a mobile device is to configure a screen lock. Locking the device makes it inaccessible to everyone except experienced hackers (or someone who knows your unlock method). To unlock the device, the user has to be authenticated in one of several ways. There are several types of screen locks that a user can choose from to be authenticated. The screen lock can be something a user *knows*, such as a PIN or a password. It could also be based on something the person *is*; it might use fingerprint, voice, or facial recognition technology, which are collectively known as *biometrics*. Or, it could be something the person *does*, such as a basic swipe (which has no inherent security by itself), or a pattern that is drawn on the display, or a series of taps or knocks on the phone. Finally, in a secure environment, it could be a combination of these different methods, which is known as *multi-factor authentication (MFA)*. Figure 49.1 shows an example of an Android smartphone's screen lock options.

A complex password is often used as a secure form of screen lock. See Chapter 48, "Windows Best Practices," for more information about complex passwords. You can also select how long the device will wait after inactivity to lock (as part of the screen timeout). In a confidential environment, you might set this to the lowest setting—10 or 15 seconds.

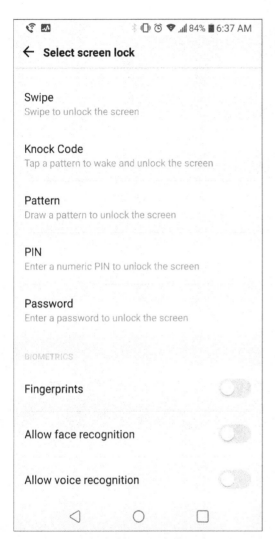

FIGURE 49.1 **Android screen lock options**

Speaking of passwords, some devices have the option to make the password visible (or to make the last character typed visible). This is almost never recommended because it makes the mobile device vulnerable to shoulder surfers (people looking over your shoulder to find out your password); it should be deselected so that only asterisks (*) are shown when the user types a password.

Aside from the default timeout, devices can also be locked by pressing the Power button quickly. If configured, the passcode must be supplied whenever a mobile device comes out of a sleep or lock state and whenever it is first booted.

Some devices may have an account lockout threshold. This means that if a user fails to be authenticated after a certain number of attempts (typically three or five), the device locks temporarily, and the user has to wait a certain amount of time before attempting to authenticate again. After that, if the user fails to be authenticated again, the timeout increases (on most devices). After a certain number of attempts, the device either needs to be connected to the computer it was last synced to or must be restored to factory condition with a hard reset (which can wipe the data). Many companies utilize a mobile device management (MDM) solution. In an MDM-controlled environment, the device and/or account might be locked in this scenario, and only an administrator will be able to unlock it.

Some devices have a setting to erase the device automatically after a certain number of incorrect authentication attempts. There are also third-party apps available for download for most mobile devices that can wipe the data after a specified number of attempts. Some apps configure a device to automatically take a picture of the user after three failed attempts and email the picture to the owner of the device.

Authenticator Applications

Authenticator apps can be installed to a mobile device to help in the process of authenticating an individual. They might be used as the only method of authentication or as part of a two-step authentication process. The latter is common.

For example, say that you are logging in to a service provider, such as Google. Further suppose that you have initiated two-step authentication, and you have to supply not only a username and password but also, in the second step, a code that is sent to you (often by way of text message or email). The authenticator app can be used to take the place of that second step by giving you a QR code, a numeric code, or something similar. The code is preinstalled to the mobile device, but it can allow a person to log on to a service or be otherwise authenticated to something even if Internet access is not currently available on the mobile device.

Two-Step Authentication

Two-step authentication is quite common, but it is not necessarily the most secure authentication. Don't mistake two-*step* authentication with two-*factor* authentication. Two-step authentication normally requires that the person logging in have two pieces of information that the person *knows*. True multi-factor authentication requires two or more different *factors* of information, such as something a person *knows* and something a person *is*.

Theft and Loss of Mobile Devices

There's an app for virtually everything. Imagine that a device is lost or stolen. If the user previously installed a locator application and the GPS/location service is enabled on the device, the user can track where the device is, and the organization can decide whether to get the police involved. One example is Google's *Find My Device*, but there are plenty of other locator and tracker apps available for Android and iOS.

Even if you track your mobile device and find it, it might be too late: A hacker might be able to get past passcodes and other screen locks. It's just a matter of time before the hacker has access to the data. So, an organization with confidential information should consider installing a remote wipe program on mobile devices. As long as a mobile device still has access to the Internet, the remote wipe program can be initiated from a desktop or laptop computer, deleting all the contents of the mobile device remotely. In some cases, the command that starts the remote wipe must be issued from an MDM server.

You should also have a backup plan in place so that data on a mobile device is backed up to a secure location at regular intervals. This way, if the data needs to be wiped, you are secure in the fact that most of the data can be recovered.

The type of remote wipe program, the backup program, and policies regarding how these are implemented will vary from one organization to the next. Be sure to read up on your organization's policies to see exactly what is allowed from a mobile security standpoint.

> **ExamAlert**
>
> Know what locator/tracker applications are and how remote wipes are used to erase confidential data in the event that a device is stolen.

Compromised and Damaged Devices

Theft and loss aren't the only risks a mobile device faces. You should protect against the chance that a mobile device will be damaged or that its security will be compromised. The device could be the victim of unauthorized account access, root access, leaked files, location tracking, camera/microphone activation, and so on. These problems could be due to a rogue application, malware installation, or other hijacking of the mobile device. You need to be prepared before such things happen.

Backups

Many organizations implement backup and remote backup policies. iOS devices can be backed up to a PC via USB connection and by using iTunes. Also, they can be backed up remotely to iCloud. In addition, you can use third-party apps for remote backup. Information can even be restored to newer, upgraded iOS devices. Various manufacturers of Android devices have their own proprietary cloud backup programs. Otherwise, almost all Android data and settings can be backed up in a collection of ways. First, Google Cloud can be used to back up email, contacts, and other information. If you use Gmail, then email, contacts, and calendars are backed up (and synchronized) to Google servers automatically. With a Google Cloud backup, if a mobile device is lost, the information can be quickly accessed from a desktop/laptop computer or another mobile device. Android applications can be backed up as long as they are not copy-protected. If you choose not to use Google Cloud to back up files or not to use the synchronization program that came with the device, there are plenty of third-party apps that can be used to back up via USB to a PC or to back up to the cloud.

Updates

One way to protect mobile devices from compromise is to patch or update the operating system. By default, you will be notified automatically about available updates on Android- and iOS-based devices. However, you should know where to go to manually update these devices as well. For Android, this is generally the About Device section, though actual navigation can change from version to version. You are usually notified of updates in the notification panel/status screen.

If you find that there are system updates or security updates available for download, you should probably install them right away. Security patches account for a large percentage of system updates because there are a lot of attackers around the world trying to compromise the Android operating system. But let's be real: Attackers will go for any OS if it catches their fancy, be it Android or iOS or any other operating system! Updates for iOS can be located at **Settings > General > Software Update** (or a similar path).

> **Note**
>
> Remember that the exact path to the update feature in a mobile OS can be different from one manufacturer to the next and from one device to the next. In addition, new versions of the software are constantly being released, resulting in changed paths and modified settings names. However, you can find out the path you need by consulting the software manufacturer's website (visit the following links), by going to the device manufacturer's website, or even by going to your cellular provider's website:
>
> ▶ **iOS:** https://support.apple.com/ios
> ▶ **Android:** https://support.google.com/android

> **ExamAlert**
>
> Know how to check for, and perform, Android and iOS updates.

Antivirus/Anti-malware/Firewalls

Updates are great, but they are not created to specifically battle viruses and other malware. So, just as there is antivirus/firewall software for PCs, there is antivirus/firewall software for mobile devices. There are a number of third-party applications that can be downloaded (and possibly paid for) and installed on a mobile device. Some examples for Android include Lookout (which is built into many devices), McAfee, Avast, Bitdefender, and Sophos. Different terms are used to describe the various protective software that is installed to a mobile device: antivirus, anti-malware, firewall, endpoint protection platform, and mobile intrusion prevention system (MIPS). Be ready to install and configure any of these on mobile devices.

iOS, on the other hand, is a tightly controlled operating system. One of the benefits of being a closed source OS is that it can be more difficult to write viruses for it; however, there is no OS that can't be compromised. For the longest time, there was no antivirus software for iOS—that is, until 2011, when a type of jailbreaking software called *jailbreakme* used a simple PDF to move insecure code to the root of a device, causing a jailbreak. Ever since, antivirus software has been a reality for iOS-based devices.

iOS *jailbreaking* is the process of removing the limitations that Apple imposes on its devices that run iOS. Jailbreaking enables users to gain root access to the system and allows the download of previously unavailable applications and software not authorized by Apple.

In the Android world, the act of gaining "superuser" privileges is known as *rooting*. Note that performing either rooting or jailbreaking could be a breach of the user license agreement. It can also be dangerous. These types of hacks might require a user to wipe out the device completely and/or install a special application that may or may not be trustworthy. Many phones are rendered useless or are compromised when attempting such a procedure. Applications that have anything to do with rooting or jailbreaking should generally be avoided.

> **ExamAlert**
>
> Understand the terms *jailbreaking* and *rooting*.

MDM and MAM

Any antivirus software for Android or iOS should be checked regularly for updates—if the device is not configured to automatically download updates, that is. Also, as previously mentioned, for large organizations that have many mobile devices, a mobile device management (MDM) suite can be implemented. An MDM server can take care of pushing updates and configuring hundreds of mobile devices from a central location. Decent-quality MDM software will secure, monitor, manage, and support different types of mobile devices across the enterprise.

MDM deals mostly with the device itself and the operating system. Contrast this with mobile *application* management (MAM), which concerns corporate-owned software and apps. Sometimes you will see MDM and MAM combined as *enterprise mobility management (EMM)*.

Full Device Encryption

If a device is stolen or lost, and the authentication method is defeated, then the attacker (or another person) will have access to the data unless some kind of remote wipe is initiated. However, sometimes remote wipe will not function; for example, if the device is out of range of a radio tower, or if the attacker takes it into a shielded area such as a Faraday cage. This is when encryption can help avoid data loss.

Some mobile device manufacturers allow for encryption of the entire storage area for select devices. In other cases, you will have the option to encrypt the SD card only. This is something to consider when deciding on the type of mobile devices to use in your organization. Careful planning is required when implementing encryption—not only planning the selection of the software to be used but also planning the process and knowing what to do in the event that decryption is necessary. For example, in many cases, if you encrypt an entire smartphone, the encryption process can be lengthy, taking up to an hour or two—depending on the speed of the device, the software used, and the amount of data to encrypt. One way around this is to encrypt only new data instead of all the data, as shown in Figure 49.2. That might be a viable time saver in a bring-your-own-device (BYOD) environment. Another consideration: It's important not to interrupt the encryption process as interruptions could cause files to be corrupted. You'll often simply encrypt new devices before they are given to a user, but that's not always the case; in any case, you should have a device fully charged before starting the process. Finally, if files need to be decrypted, you might need to initiate a factory reset or provide the key to the data, so be sure to have a decryption plan in place.

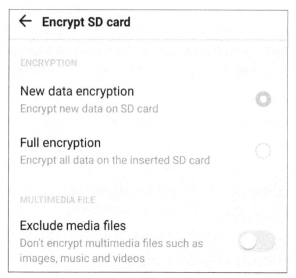

FIGURE 49.2 **SD card encryption screen on an Android-based smartphone**

The beauty of encryption is that it makes it very difficult to make sense of the files. If the proper encryption methods are used—for instance, AES-256—then a hacker would need a team of supercomputers working for a nearly infinite number of years to crack the cipher and decrypt the content (as of the writing of this book, of course). So, it is unlikely that a hacker will attempt to decrypt files unless the hacker guesses that a weak or compromised cipher has been employed. Instead, the hacker will use...*other* methods. (And don't ask me what "nearly infinite" means.)

Remember that encryption and any other techniques used to secure a device or data are not foolproof. A good security person will create a *threat model*—in essence, determine what the threats and vulnerabilities are within a particular system or data set and prioritize them from most threatening to least. After the threat model has been established, you can decide on the security techniques to implement.

Note

If you liked that last paragraph, then you might be interested in pursuing the CompTIA Security+ certification or other computer security–related certifications.

IoT Security

The Internet of Things (IoT) is a realm of technologies that is growing at an estimated rate of 1 million devices per day, and it has an economic impact measured in the trillions of dollars. In the home or at work, IoT devices need to be secured because they are potential targets for attackers. This is partially because many of them are easily accessible and partially because many IoT devices are not built with security in mind; this means that, out of the box, many of these devices are inherently insecure.

A lot of the techniques that we established in the previous several chapters can also be used for IoT devices: lengthy and complex passwords/passphrases, encryption, multi-factor authentication, and so on. But because of the lack of built-in security, IoT devices need a little more.

Speaking generally, we can do a few things to increase IoT security. First we need to be able to *see* the various IoT devices as some can easily go unnoticed. Next, we should attempt to segment the devices based on their risk levels. Finally, we need to protect through monitoring, policies, and periodic testing.

From a more technical standpoint, we can employ some specific security controls—for example, avoiding the built-in defaults, using the best password managers/vaults, keeping software (and firmware) up to date and considering automating that process, encrypting network connections (data in motion), and super-securing the Internet connection and connections to other network segments. That's right, *super-secure* it: the Internet connection, associated network cables, and any routers, cable modems, and other Internet-related devices. Remember this: The weakest link in your security chain is actually your strongest link. What I mean by this is that it only takes one weak link to allow an intruder access to your network. And don't forget to layer your security: Have a *defense-in-depth* mindset.

For larger environments, you have to think realistically. How in the world can one admin, or even a group of admins, spare the time to monitor and protect the cornucopia of IoT devices that potentially exist? In many enterprise environments, it's just not feasible. That's where third-party IoT infrastructure management tools and services come in. They use network access control (NAC) methods to see all devices, monitor the devices, and control access to and from the network. That last part goes well beyond the CompTIA A+, but it's something to consider as you progress in the IT world!

> **ExamAlert**
>
> Secure IoT devices! Know how many devices you actually have, use network segmentation to reduce the attack surface, always keep firmware up to date, and, in enterprise environments, monitor IoT devices at all times using real-time monitoring and alerting.

> **Note**
>
> For more information on IoT security, see
> https://www.nist.gov/itl/applied-cybersecurity/nist-cybersecurity-iot-program

Policies and Procedures

Well, at some point, we had to talk about rules and who sets them. Sometimes it's the systems administrator, and many times, it is an executive, upper management, or a committee. Whoever it is, you can bet that there will be policies and procedures to follow at your organization. Generally, these are designed to be helpful, but they can be somewhat challenging in a BYOD environment.

> **Note**
>
> Remember, BYOD = bring your own device.

In BYOD environments, a person can use his or her personal mobile device for work purposes. As you can imagine, this can create a lot of logistical problems. For example, an organization adopting BYOD has to carefully plan how data is to be separated; devices require different partitions, data access policies, data loss prevention (DLP) methods, and so on—not to mention data encryption. User agreements must be drawn up and signed by employees to acknowledge that they understand what they can and can't do with their devices while on company premises or during work hours. The organization should consider use of an MDM for the addition and removal of devices.

From a user perspective, the greatest concern is the loss of employee privacy. From a company perspective, the greatest concern is the leakage of data and any other security breaches related to mobile devices. As an entry point to a network, mobile devices have historically been less secure than typical workstation computers. That's a generalized statement, but what I am suggesting is being cautious when configuring mobile devices. There are a lot of other issues that can present whenever you mix business and personal. However, what is more important is what you can do about it.

First, I mentioned using an MDM solution, which can be used to remotely administer a host of devices. It gives the administrator the ability to lock down devices and create those separate partitions, perhaps virtual partitions, or use containerization. Such a solution should completely separate the work data *and* apps from the personal data and apps. An MDM solution can also be used to limit how and when a user works, defining the time and the place where work can be done. In addition, an organization needs to have a user agreement, in which it clearly explains that the work data on a mobile device can be accessed and monitored by the organization at any time. Organization is also important. Keep a log of all the BYOD devices on the network; it should be kept separate from any MDM software that is running to limit mobile device sprawl. Then, enact the best practices we have talked about in this book, such as complex passwords, automatic locks, DLP, encryption, MFA, and so on. Finally, carefully decide on who will be administering the devices and keep that list short!

> **Note**
>
> There are also corporate owned, personally enabled (COPE) devices. In a COPE environment, the order is reversed: Instead of a person bringing in a device that is already in use and having it adjusted for work, with COPE the organization owns the device, prepares it for work, and then offers it for personal use as well. It's similar to the idea of a company car.

Profile Security Requirements

For mobile device security, a good practice is to create *security profiles*, or templates that you can use on multiple devices, as long as they are on the same platform. Then you can create a template (or set of templates) for each type of mobile device. For the most part, this means using an MDM solution. MDMs often come with prebuilt profiles for administration, but they are usually not secured—especially for your organization's particular needs. So, it's best to start with a built-in profile and then build out the security from there, based on your overall security plan, threat model, and vulnerability assessment.

Once you have begun creating a profile, start configuring it securely. For example, choose the mode that it will use, such as authenticated (which might use Transport Layer Security [TLS]) or encrypted (which might use TLS and AES). Then select a certificate that will be used when the mobile device communicates with the MDM server; be sure that it is a valid certificate with the proper encryption bit level. Configure endpoint protection, which might include Windows Defender and BitLocker (for Microsoft devices) or other endpoint protection software. Your organization might also require that identity protection services be installed on the mobile devices. Think about kiosk settings (such as allow lists) to limit what a user can do on the mobile device and give the user access to the functionality that is required. Then, it's all about securely configuring services that we have talked about previously: email, VPN, Wi-Fi, DLP, and certificates. For example, Microsoft Intune supports Simple Certificate Enrollment Protocol (SCEP) and Public Key Cryptography Standards (PKCS) certificates to help with the authentication of users via Wi-Fi and VPN. Profiles can also be configured to govern how people utilize data through a cellular provider and whether or not hotspots can be created.

As mentioned, you can initiate allow lists and deny lists to either allow certain programs or disallow certain programs, respectively. Plus, consider configuring trusted and untrusted application sources for mobile devices. For example, an administrator might configure an Android-based profile that only allows users to download apps from Google Play or, better yet, doesn't allow users to install apps *at all*. Ultimately, the idea is to lock down the devices as much as possible but still allow users to perform their work. The more you can automate this process through the use of templates and scripts, the better.

> **Note**
>
> We'll be discussing policies and procedures further in the operational procedures section later in this book.

Cram Quiz

Answer these questions. The answers follow the last question. If you cannot answer these questions correctly, consider reading this chapter again until you can.

1. You want to prevent a user from accessing your phone while you step away from your desk. What should you do?

   - ○ **A.** Implement remote backup.
   - ○ **B.** Set up a remote wipe program.
   - ○ **C.** Configure a screen lock.
   - ○ **D.** Install a locator application.

2. Which of the following can be described as removing limitations in iOS?

○ **A.** Rooting

○ **B.** Jailbreaking

○ **C.** Geotracking

○ **D.** Antivirus software

3. Your organization is concerned about a potential scenario involving a mobile device containing confidential data being stolen. Which of the following should be recommended first? (Select the best answer.)

○ **A.** Remote backup application

○ **B.** Remote wipe program

○ **C.** Passcode locks

○ **D.** Locator application

4. You are concerned about the possibility of jailbreaks on your organization's iPhones and viruses on the Android-based devices. Which of the following should you implement? (Select the two best answers.)

○ **A.** Antivirus software

○ **B.** Firewall

○ **C.** Mobile device management

○ **D.** Device reset

5. There are Android-based smartphones in your organization that are part of the BYOD infrastructure. They need to be able to connect to the LAN remotely using a VPN. Which of the following should you incorporate into the MDM profile for the smartphones to connect to the VPN securely? (Select the best answer.)

○ **A.** Antivirus software

○ **B.** Certificate

○ **C.** Remote wipe

○ **D.** Authenticator app

○ **E.** Microsoft Intune

Cram Quiz Answers

1. **C.** You should configure a screen lock (either a pattern drawn on the screen, a PIN, a password, biometric recognition, or something else). Remote backup, remote wipe, and locator applications will not prevent someone from accessing the phone.

2. **B.** Jailbreaking is the process of removing the limitations of an iOS-based device so that the user gets superuser abilities. Rooting is a similar technique used on Android mobile devices. Geotracking is the practice of tracking a device over time. Antivirus software which is used to combat malware.

3. **B.** The remote wipe program is the most important option listed. This will prevent a thief from accessing the data on the device. Afterward, you might recommend a backup program (in case the data needs to be wiped), as well as passcode locks and a locator application.

4. **A and C.** You should implement antivirus software on the local mobile devices and consider MDM for deploying antivirus updates to multiple mobile devices remotely. This can protect against viruses and other malware as well as jailbreaks on Apple devices. As of the writing of this book, firewalls for mobile devices are not common, but that could change in the future. Device resets are used to restart mobile devices or to reset them to factory condition, depending on the type of reset and the manufacturer of a device. We'll discuss those more in Chapter 55, "Troubleshooting Mobile Operating Systems and Application Issues."

5. **B.** Use an encryption certificate to secure the VPN connection process from the mobile devices to the LAN. Consider powerful VPN technologies such as OpenVPN, IKEv2, RADIUS servers, and so on. Antivirus software is important for mobile devices, but it won't impact secure VPN connectivity. Remote wipe is an important theft/loss solution. Authenticator apps are used to verify a user to a system and are often used in place of the second step of two-factor authentication, but they are not as secure as using a certificate. Microsoft Intune can be used to administer mobile devices, but it is not inherently secure; the profiles therein need to be configured in a secure way.

Yes! You've made it to the end of another chapter. Know this: Learning never ends! Continue!

CHAPTER 50

Data Destruction and Disposal

This chapter covers the following A+ 220-1102 exam objective:

▶ **2.8** – Given a scenario, use common data destruction and disposal methods.

In this chapter, we'll cover how to properly repurpose, recycle, dispose of, and destroy storage devices. And, by the way, we'll be focusing on internal storage drives, but some of the methods herein can be applied to other devices that store data: USB flash drives, memory sticks, and so on. Be ready to protect all data, wherever it exists! There's lots to do, so *let's go already*!

Data Security 101

Storage drives that contain an organization's data can be a security threat. When a drive is removed from a computer, it needs to be either stored, repurposed within the company, recycled for use by another entity, or disposed of in a proper manner. Sanitizing the drive is a common way of removing data, but it's not the only way. The manner in which data is removed might vary depending on the proposed final destination of the device. Proper data removal goes far beyond file deletion or the formatting of digital media. The problem with high-level formats done within the operating system is the data remanence (or residue) that is left behind; with the help of third-party software, that residue can be used to re-create files. So, you have to plan how a drive will be repurposed and use some quality tools to make sure any existing data has been removed properly.

Warning

The tools and procedures described in the following sections will either remove all data on a drive or render a storage drive unusable. Proceed with extreme caution and at your own risk! Consider using virtual machines for testing.

Formatting Drives

Recall that we talked about formatting back in Chapter 34, "Microsoft Operating System Features and Tools, Part II." As mentioned in that chapter, Windows can perform quick formats and full formats; both of these are known as *high-level* formats, but they have different results. A quick format in Windows simply removes access to the files, but a full format writes zeros to the entire partition (zeroing out the drive). So, for repurposing a drive, the full format is the better option as it is a form of overwriting.

However, the CompTIA A+ objectives use the term *low-level format*. Also known as a physical format, a low-level format is something that is done to mechanical drives by the manufacturer. Modern hard disk drives are low-level formatted at the factory, and this technique should be done to a drive only once under normal circumstances; it physically creates the tracks and sectors on a hard disk drive. Older hard disk drives (from the 1980s and 1990s) could be low-level formatted from the BIOS in an effort to extend the life span of those drives, but low-level formatting can be damaging to a drive. Today, the term *low-level format (LLF)* has taken on a little more meaning for some people. Some consider commands such as **dd** (which can zero out the drive) and **hdparm**, programs such as GParted, and some other third-party tools to be LLF tools. However, the reality is that they either zero out a drive or simply remove and create partitions, so they are not really low-level formatting the drive. However, some of these tools *can* be more effective than a basic Windows format.

Regardless, all of these processes have to be performed from outside the partition and file system that is to be formatted or overwritten. So, for example, to rewrite a Windows system partition, you could boot a computer to a live Linux flash drive (running Ubuntu or another distro) and run the command or program required on the target Windows system partition.

Overwriting Drives

Let's talk about deleting vs. overwriting for a moment. If you delete a file on a drive, the OS will not be able to access it anymore. However, in most systems, the file remains until it is overwritten, either by another file or through another process. So, deleting data is not nearly enough to secure a drive that will be repurposed or recycled. Overwriting is a better option. This can be done with programs that write various data to the drive, but a common method is to *zero out* the drive. This means writing binary zeros over every sector and all the data on the drive.

You can zero out a drive in Windows in a few ways. First, you can use the full format option in the GUI that we mentioned previously. Second, you can use the **format** command in PowerShell or the Command Prompt. For example, the following command will format the E: drive as NTFS and zero out every sector of the drive in two passes, meaning that it will run the process twice. You have to be in elevated mode to perform this procedure:

```
format E: /fs:NTFS /p:2
```

You can increase the number of passes by changing the parameter **p:2** to whatever number you wish. A company may require a particular number of passes—perhaps three—depending on the organization and the policies that have been put in place. But remember that the more passes, the more time it will take, and the more stress that will be put on the drive.

> **Note**
>
> For more information about the **format** command and all of its parameters, type **format /?** at the command line and/or see https://docs.microsoft.com/en-us/windows-server/administration/windows-commands/format.

The third option is to use **diskpart**, but this utility wipes the entire drive, including any existing partitions, leaving you with unallocated space. To use this utility, enter **diskpart** (in elevated mode), list the disks (with the **list disk** command), select the disk you want to zero out (for example, **select disk 1**), and then type **clean all**. (You also have to type the name of the volume to proceed.) If you want to use the drive again, it will have to be initialized, partitioned, and formatted.

For all three of these options, the process can be very lengthy, depending on the size of the drive, the speed of the drive, and the amount of data on it. To test these commands quickly, use a virtual machine with a small secondary virtual drive that is around, say, 8 GB. Remember, you have to be outside the partition or drive that you want to zero out. So, for example, if you want to zero out the E: partition, you can do it from C:.

You can also zero out a drive in Linux and macOS. I mentioned that it can be done graphically with the GParted application (which has to be installed first), but you can also do it in Terminal with the **dd** command. For example:

```
sudo dd if=/dev/zero of=/dev/sdb1
```

where you replace *sdb1* with whatever drive and partition you want to zero out. This particular command will zero out the first partition of the drive *sdb* (a second drive in the system). The process can take a long time, and it gives you no warnings. To watch the progress of the procedure, use the **status=progress** parameter. Afterward, you will have to reformat the partition to the file system of your choice. Be very careful not to zero out the system partition. Use this method with extreme caution!

So, zeroing out the drive can be a potentially secure way of overwriting all the data so that the drive can be repurposed within an organization. But what if a drive is to be recycled for use by another organization, or what if you want to sell a personal computer? You might want to go further. And if your organization has highly sensitive data or stores personally identifiable information (PII), then a higher standard should be employed.

For example, the DoD 5220.22-M standard specifies *sanitizing* a drive. One implementation of this standard is to perform three passes: first, overwriting the entire drive with binary zeroes; second, overwriting the entire drive with binary ones; and third, overwriting the entire drive with a random bit pattern and verifying that final overwrite and logging that verification.

However, newer standards are more secure, such as NIST 800-88 Rev. 1, *Guidelines for Media Sanitization* (published in 2014). 800-88 is actually broken down into three categories: clear, purge, and destroy. Let's discuss those three categories now.

Clear

Clearing is the removal of data with a certain amount of assurance that it cannot be reconstructed. However, the data is actually recoverable with special techniques. With clearing, the media is repurposed and used within the company again. Zeroing out the drive and using bit-erasure software are examples of clearing. However, this method is not recommended for sensitive data.

Purge

Purging a drive, or wiping its data, is recommended for sensitive data and drives that will leave the organization. It can be done in two ways: with the Secure Erase option (or a similar technique) or by degaussing the drive.

Secure Erase is a command that can be run from the firmware of an ATA drive (accessed from the BIOS/UEFI or elsewhere). Or, you can use tools from Seagate (SeaTools), Western Digital (SSD Dashboard), or Samsung (Magician). Third-party tools such as Blancco Drive Eraser are also available. If you use any of these tools, the drive will still function. The question to consider is this: Will the tools meet the standards and policies set forth by your organization? Always follow your organization's guidelines, and if there are no guidelines, or if you are not sure, then purge the drive to the best of your ability, document the procedure, and store the drive in a secure location.

Note

Third-party tools such as DBAN can also wipe a drive, but they are designed for personal use and do not meet the requirements of NIST standards and so are not recommended for drives containing sensitive data.

It is also possible to degauss a magnetic drive (hard disk drive). This will render the data unreadable, and in most cases it will render the drive unusable, which is why some people refer to it as a method of "destruction." Machines such as electromagnetic degaussers and permanent magnet degaussers can be used to permanently purge information from a disk. The process rearranges the magnetic field of the disk so that the data is destroyed. This process is necessary for disks that cannot be accessed from a computer; if the drive can't be accessed, then zeroing-out methods cannot be performed. If a drive is designated to leave the organization, and the drive is damaged, this process might be used first before physical destruction. Some IT destruction companies always degauss first before physically destroying a drive. Keep in mind that degaussing is primarily used on magnetic-based drives.

Destroy

The destroy option means what it says: The storage media is physically destroyed. This could be done in a very basic way by using a hammer or similar tool or by drilling holes through the platters. But for drives containing sensitive data, a more robust destruction technique should be employed. Electromagnetic degaussing is one option, but, as previously mentioned, that is often used in conjunction with a complete physical destruction process, such as incineration or the more common *drive shredding* (also known as pulverization). At this point, the remnants of the drive can be disposed of in accordance with municipal guidelines.

Some organizations require a certificate of destruction to show that a drive has indeed been destroyed; in fact, the certificate is often required by data privacy laws. A destruction certificate is obtained from the third party that performs the drive destruction. A typical organization does not have the equipment necessary to perform proper destruction. That's why an outside vendor is usually contracted to do the work; those third-party vendors have mechanical degaussers and drive shredders designed specifically to meet NIST and DoD standards. Some of these vendors come onsite to perform the process of destruction in front of the appropriate company personnel. Then the personnel sign off on the procedure. It's not recommended that drives be mailed or otherwise transported to a vendor, but if they are, the organization should use properly insured and tracked postal options or secure couriers, and the entire process should be documented utilizing a chain of custody or similar process.

The type of data removal used will be dictated by the data stored on the drive. If there is no PII or other sensitive information, the drive might simply be cleared. But in many cases, organizations will specify purging of data if the drive is to leave the building and be reused. In cases where a drive previously contained confidential or top-secret data, the drive will usually be destroyed. Again, always follow the policies that have been developed by your organization. If they are unclear, ask for additional interpretation from the appropriate personnel.

Note

The NIST SP 800-88 document can be obtained from https://csrc.nist.gov/publications/detail/sp/800-88/rev-1/final.

Cram Quiz

Answer these questions. The answers follow the last question. If you cannot answer these questions correctly, consider reading this chapter again until you can.

1. A drive needs to be disposed of in such a way that no one can access the data Which method should be used?

   ○ **A.** **format E:**

   ○ **B.** Clearing

   ○ **C.** **diskpart**

   ○ **D.** Destruction

2. A drive is to be repurposed within your company. You have been tasked with zeroing out the drive three times from within Windows. Which of the following methods will accomplish this?

   ○ **A.** Degaussing

   ○ **B.** **format C: /fs:fat32 /p:3**

   ○ **C.** **diskpart > select disk 1 > clean all**

   ○ **D.** **dd if=/dev/zero of=/dev/sda1**

3. You have been tasked with purging a drive so that it can be recycled to a sister company. Which of the following should you perform before sending the drive out?

- ○ **A.** Clear the drive.
- ○ **B.** Degauss the drive.
- ○ **C.** Run Secure Erase on the drive.
- ○ **D.** Pulverize the drive.

Cram Quiz Answers

1. **D.** You should destroy the drive. You could do this with the use of a tool (such as a drive shredder), by incinerating it, or by degaussing it, although the first option is usually preferred. The **format E:** command will only format the drive to a new file system; that is not secure enough if the data has to be removed altogether. Clearing is the removal of data from a drive that is to be repurposed and used again within the organization. The **diskpart** utility can be used to clear the drive, but it is not appropriate for drive disposal.

2. **B.** The only option listed that will zero out the drive three times (from Windows) is **format C: /fs:fat32 /p:3**. This procedure formats the drive as FAT32 and runs the process three times (**p:3**). Degaussing a hard disk drive will render the data unreadable and, in most cases, will make the drive unusable. By default, the **diskpart** and **dd** processes listed will only zero out the drive once. They would have to be run with an additional parameter or run manually two more times to meet the criteria. Also, **dd** is run from Linux, not from Windows, so that is another reason that answer is incorrect. But be very careful: Note that the drive listed in the **dd** command is sda1. That will most likely be the system drive; if the command is run on that drive, the OS will be erased, which is what you want in this case. Just remember to use caution when erasing drives. Double-check what you are doing before you run any commands.

3. **C.** At a bare minimum, run the Secure Erase program (or a comparable program) to sanitize the drive; it needs to be completely wiped if it is to be reused. The rest of the answers are not examples of sanitizing or purging. Clearing the drive by formatting or zeroing out does not meet the requirements for sending the drive out to another company as standardized by NIST and the DoD. Degaussing the drive will render it useless. Pulverizing the drive (shredding it) will destroy it and will also render it unusable.

You need to know how to recycle, reuse, and if necessary, destroy storage drives. Go with standardized processes, and all will be well. Continue!

CHAPTER 51

SOHO Security

This chapter covers the following A+ 220-1102 exam objective:

▶ **2.9** – Given a scenario, configure appropriate security settings on small office/home office (SOHO) wireless and wired networks.

A small office/home office (SOHO) network is easy to set up. But if you don't secure it, you might as well just call up a hacker and ask that person to invade the network. The core of a SOHO network is the SOHO router. This device actually acts as a switch, router, firewall, and wireless access point (WAP). For the rest of this section, we'll talk about how to secure this device, and we'll refer to it simply as a *router*. Before you make any security configurations, it is highly recommended that you back up your settings and update the firmware. And don't forget to save the configuration when you are done!

ExamAlert

Objective 2.9 concentrates on home router settings, wireless-specific settings, and firewall settings.

Note

You can access online emulators for several different kinds of routers. It's good practice to run through these configurations on your own router or an emulator of some sort.

Changing Default Passwords

The first thing you should do to secure a router is to change the password. Some routers require that you change the password when you first log in. Other routers come with a blank password or have a basic password, such as *admin*. You need to connect to the router by opening up your favorite browser (your favorite should be the most secure one), typing the IP address of the router (for example, 192.168.0.1 or 192.168.1.1), and logging in. If the router has the option to create another admin account (or at least change the name), do it—and keep the original administrator account as the backup. No matter what router you're using, you will definitely be able to change the password— and you should change it! Make it something complex, based on the rules we discussed in Chapter 48, "Windows Best Practices." Save the settings (which will log you out) and then log in with the new password to make sure your new settings have taken effect.

ExamAlert

Remember to change the admin password first before you do anything else!

A router may also have a user password. Change this as well but change it to a different password than you used for the admin account.

Wireless-Specific Security Settings

Now we'll move on to some core radio and broadcasting security concepts, including the SSID, encryption, antennas, radio power levels, and WPS.

Changing and Disabling the SSID

The service set identifier (SSID) is used to name a wireless network. Default SSIDs are usually basic; it is wise to change the name of the wireless network before enabling wireless on the router. Names that include uppercase letters, lowercase letters, and numbers will be more challenging for casual wireless passersby to memorize.

After all wireless clients are connected to the network, consider disabling the SSID. Although this is not a perfect solution, it will mask part of the SSID broadcast, making it impossible to see with normal wireless locating software. Figure 51.1 shows a modified SSID named *Neptune8Network* and that it is not enabled.

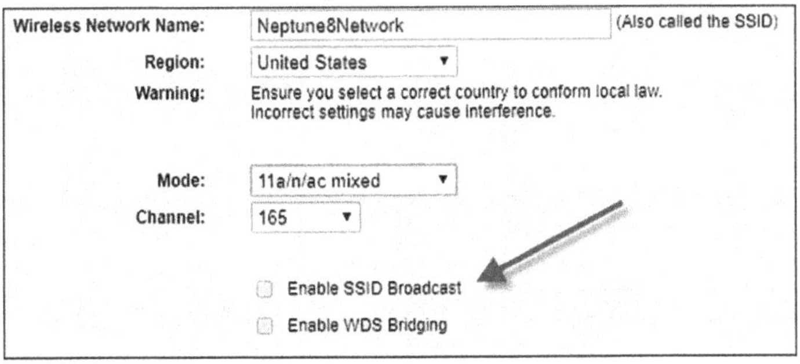

Wireless Network Name:	Neptune8Network	(Also called the SSID)
Region:	United States ▼	
Warning:	Ensure you select a correct country to conform local law. Incorrect settings may cause interference.	
Mode:	11a/n/ac mixed ▼	
Channel:	165 ▼	
	☐ Enable SSID Broadcast	
	☐ Enable WDS Bridging	

FIGURE 51.1 **Renamed and disabled SSID**

When the SSID is disabled, wireless clients won't see the SSID name when they scan for wireless networks. If you need to connect additional wireless clients, you will either have to enable the SSID broadcast or enter the wireless SSID manually when connecting. For example, to connect manually in Windows, open the Network and Sharing Center and select **Set up a new connection or network**. Then select **Manually connect to a wireless network**. (The wireless adapter must be installed with correct drivers for you to see this link.) You will have to type the SSID (also known as the *network name*), the security type, the encryption type, and the security key to get into the network.

> **Note**
> By the way, given the channel and mode listed in Figure 51.1, what frequency is this router transmitting on? The channel is 165, so its center frequency is 5.825 GHz. If a channel overlaps with a neighbor, consider changing the channel to one that is farther away.

Antennas and Radio Power Levels

It is important to strategically place your access point (AP). Usually, the best place for an AP is in the center of the building—if at all possible. This way, equal access can be given to everyone on the perimeter of the organization's property, and there is the least chance of the signal bleeding over outside the organization. If you need to reduce the broadcast range of the AP, you can attempt to reduce the transmission power levels of the antenna. For example, Figure 51.2 shows the transmission power of an AP set to Low, which for small offices is usually enough. The other options are Medium and High, or you might actually get a numeric option on some routers (measured in dBm). Test the signal strength by connecting with a laptop or another mobile device and moving to the perimeter of the building. If the lowest setting still allows access from the mobile device—with a decent data transfer rate—then there is no need to increase the power level.

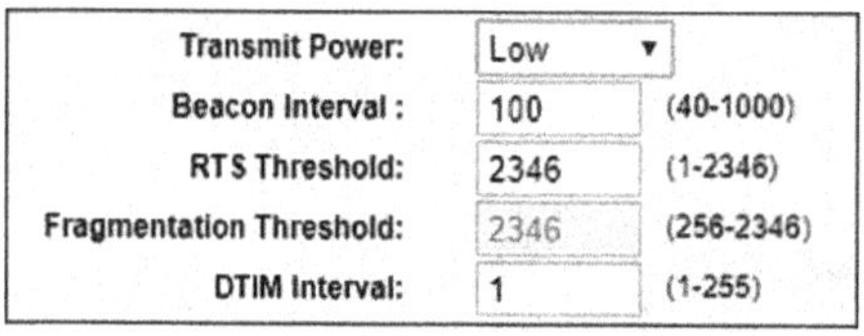

Transmit Power:	Low ▼	
Beacon Interval :	100	(40-1000)
RTS Threshold:	2346	(1-2346)
Fragmentation Threshold:	2346	(256-2346)
DTIM Interval:	1	(1-255)

FIGURE 51.2   **AP power level set to Low**

Also, to avoid interference in the form of electromagnetic interference (EMI) or radio frequency interference (RFI), keep WAPs away from any electrical panels, cables, devices, motors, or other pieces of equipment that might give off an electromagnetic (EM) field. If necessary, shield any device that is creating an EM field.

An AP's antennas can be rotated so that they are parallel to each other or at an angle to each other. For example, if you have two antennas, then 180 degrees is often a good orientation to sweep the area for wireless transmissions. The more antennas, the better (usually)—especially if they incorporate MIMO technology (described in Chapter 7, "Wireless Protocols") to combine multiple data streams.

By placing the AP and adjusting the antennas appropriately and lowering the radio power levels as far as possible, you can further secure your wireless network while still providing decent service to your users.

> **ExamAlert**
>
> Strategically place your access points and know how to adjust radio power levels and AP antennas.

Guest Networks

Wireless guest networks can be a great convenience for people who are visiting your home or place of work. A guest network allows those people access to the Internet but does not allow access to any internal resources or other wireless clients on the main wireless networks. Using a guest network is a good way to isolate your guests. It's also a good way to isolate IoT devices such as video cameras and music devices (which can be inherently insecure). However, the guest network can be a liability in and of itself, especially if it doesn't use strong passphrases or encryption. For many organizations, the policy is to disable the wireless guest network altogether unless it is absolutely necessary. Instead, if your organization has individuals who need guest access, install a completely different wireless access point used just for guests.

Disabling WPS

Wi-Fi Protected Setup (WPS) was originally intended to make connecting to a wireless access point easier for the average user. However, anything that is made simpler is often less secure as well. Case in point: WPS is vulnerable to brute-force attacks, which can lead to intrusions on the network. In a brute-force attack, threat actors try to guess passwords and codes by trying combinations of letters, numbers, and symbols. A WPS code is usually 8 to 10 digits long, which is not very difficult to crack. So, your best bet is to disable WPS altogether.

Enabling MAC Filtering and IP Filtering

A wireless access point might also have the capability to be configured for MAC filtering and IP filtering, which are basic forms of network access control. MAC/IP filtering can filter out which computers can (or cannot) access the wireless network (and wired network). An AP does this by consulting a list of MAC addresses or IP addresses that have been previously entered.

In some cases, a device might broadcast this MAC or IP table. If this is the case, look for an update for the firmware of the access point and attempt to fine-tune the broadcast range of the device so that it does not leak out to other organizations. Because MAC/IP filtering and a disabled SSID can be fairly easily circumvented using a network sniffer, it is important to also use strong encryption and possibly to consider other types of network access control (such as 802.1X) and external authentication methods (such as RADIUS).

> **ExamAlert**
>
> MAC filtering and IP filtering can be used to specify which computers are allowed or denied to the wireless network (and wired network).

Assigning Static IP Addresses

A SOHO router can be set to limit the number of DHCP addresses it hands out. If there are not enough addresses to go around, you might find that certain hosts (such as servers or printers) lose connectivity when there are more client computers on the network. First, consider increasing the scope of addresses that the router is configured to hand out to clients. Second, try assigning static IP addresses to the servers and printers—essentially, any hosts that share information or services. This way, if more clients obtaining dynamic addresses are added in the future, the servers and printers will not be affected.

By default, a SOHO router itself uses a static IP address on the LAN side; however, on the WAN side, it is usually set to obtain an IP address from an ISP dynamically, although you can change this to a static address if you wish. If you have servers that a SOHO router is port forwarding to, and if you have clients connecting to those servers from the Internet, you might consider requesting a bank of static IP addresses from your ISP and configuring the SOHO router's WAN port to use one of those static IP addresses. Or, at the very least, you might use a service such as DynDNS to forward your Internet domain name to your SOHO router's dynamically assigned IP address. This way, clients will be able to connect by domain name, even if the IP address changes over time. If you have clients connecting via a VPN through your SOHO router, using PPTP, L2TP, or OpenVPN, then the use of a static IP address is recommended, and it might even be required.

Firewall Settings and Additional Configurations

A SOHO router usually has a built-in firewall with some basic security functionality. Let's discuss a few of the common features you might find in such a router:

▶ **NAT:** Network address translation (NAT) is the process of transforming IP addresses as data crosses a router. NAT hides an entire IP address space on the LAN (for example, 192.168.1.1 through 192.168.1.255). If an IP address on the LAN needs to communicate with the Internet, the IP address is converted to the public IP address of the router.

▶ **Port forwarding:** This process maps an external network port to an internal IP address and port, enabling you to have a web server, FTP server, and other servers—but you need to have only one port for each of them open on the WAN side of the router. It can be any port you like; of course, you need to tell people which port they need to connect to if it is not a standard one. Some devices use what are called *virtual servers* to make the process a lot more user friendly. So, for example, you might have an FTP server running internally on your LAN; its IP address and port might be 192.168.0.100:21 (notice that the colon separates the IP address from the port), but you would have users on the Internet connect to your router's WAN address (for example, 65.43.18.1) and any port you want. The router takes care of the rest, and the forwarding won't be noticed by the typical user. Port forwarding is also referred to as destination NAT (DNAT).

▶ **Screened subnet:** A screened subnet, also known as a demilitarized zone (DMZ), is an area that is not quite on the Internet and not quite part of your LAN. It's a sort of middle ground that is for the most part protected by a firewall, but particular traffic will be let through. A screened subnet is a good place for web servers, email servers, and FTP servers because these are services required by users on the Internet. The beauty of a screened subnet is that users can access it without having access to your LAN—if it is configured correctly, of course. Quite often, a screened subnet is set up as the third leg of a firewall. The first leg connects to the LAN, the second leg connects to the Internet, and the third connects to the screened subnet. You need to know the ports that your servers will use, and you need to create rules within the firewall (or an all-in-one device, such as a SOHO router) to allow only the required traffic into the screened subnet.

▶ **UPnP:** Universal Plug and Play (UPnP) is a group of networking protocols that allows computers, printers, and other Internet-ready devices to discover each other on the network. It is a consumer-level technology designed to make networking easier for the user. For example, if you want easier accessibility and connectivity of a PC, a smartphone, and a printer that are all connected to the SOHO router, UPnP can provide that. However, it is often recommended to disable this function if you are concerned about security.

Content Filtering/Parental Controls

Most SOHO routers come with a parental control section where content can be filtered on a very basic level. The "parent" can select the MAC address of a particular computer and specify what domain names that computer is allowed to connect to—and when. Figure 51.3 shows an example of this.

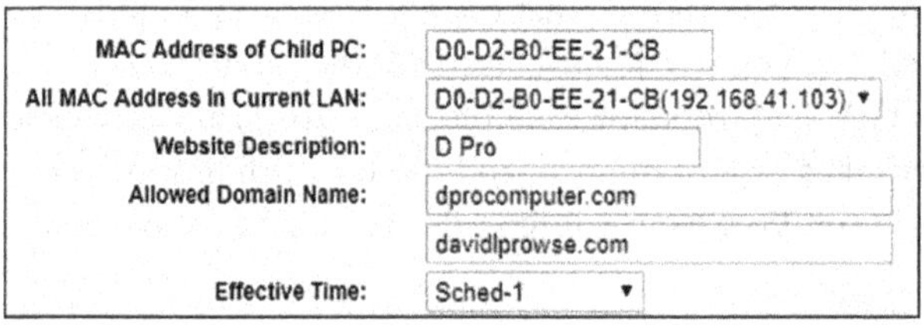

MAC Address of Child PC:	D0-D2-B0-EE-21-CB
All MAC Address In Current LAN:	D0-D2-B0-EE-21-CB(192.168.41.103) ▼
Website Description:	D Pro
Allowed Domain Name:	dprocomputer.com
	davidlprowse.com
Effective Time:	Sched-1 ▼

FIGURE 51.3 **Parental control entry**

In the figure, you can see that the MAC address D0-D2-B0-EE-21-CB has access to two domains (dprocomputer.com and davidlprowse.com, of course) and that Effective Time is set to Sched-1, a schedule I preconfigured that allows the "child" to connect from 8 a.m. to 4 p.m. on weekdays; scheduling is usually a component of parental control.

Because the MAC address of a computer can't be changed (by a typical user), this configuration follows the computer, even if it gets a new IP address later. This uses the same concept as MAC filtering, and in fact some parental control sections have MAC filtering built in.

Disabling Physical Ports and More Physical Security

A router might come with the capability to disable the physical ports on the switch portion of the device. Disabling physical ports is a wise precaution. If you disable unused physical ports, a rogue computer can be plugged into the router physically but won't have any hopes of accessing the network. This concept is a policy in most organizations. Unused router or switch ports are disabled so that a person can't connect a laptop to any old RJ45 jack on the premises.

> **ExamAlert**
>
> Disable any physical ports that are not in use!

Consider the physical security of a SOHO router as well. Can anyone in the building put their hands on it? That would be inappropriate, so you need to physically secure the device, which means keeping it in a locked area such as a wiring closet or, if that is not possible, above a drop ceiling (mounted properly) or against the ceiling if there is no drop ceiling. This way, the device will at least be more difficult to reach—as long as you don't have a ladder lying around. Anyone who uses a SOHO router is unlikely to have a server room, but a server room would be an optimal location.

A Final Word on SOHO Routers

Make sure that a router's firmware is kept up to date. Also, make sure the built-in firewall is always enabled. This firewall is going to be much more important than the Windows firewalls on the individual computers, though both are recommended. Most routers' firewalls are on by default, but you should check. If you do any kind of port forwarding, port triggering, screened subnet configuration, or remote connections, make sure the firewall is allowing traffic only through the specific port or ports you require and that all others are blocked. Check for updates every month or so, and while you are at it, change the administrator password for good measure.

Cram Quiz

Answer these questions. The answers follow the last question. If you cannot answer these questions correctly, consider reading this chapter again until you can.

1. Which of the following helps to secure a SOHO router? (Select the three best answers.)
   - ⭘ **A.** Change default passwords.
   - ⭘ **B.** Enable SSID.
   - ⭘ **C.** Enable MAC filtering.
   - ⭘ **D.** Enable WPS.
   - ⭘ **E.** Enable WPA3.

2. You want to prevent rogue employees from connecting a laptop to the SOHO router and accessing the network. How can you accomplish this? (Select the two best answers.)
   - ⭘ **A.** Enable MAC filtering.
   - ⭘ **B.** Create a screened subnet.
   - ⭘ **C.** Configure a complex SSID.
   - ⭘ **D.** Disable physical ports.

3. You want to prevent certain users from accessing particular websites. What should you configure on the SOHO router?
   - ⭘ **A.** MAC filtering
   - ⭘ **B.** Disable unused ports
   - ⭘ **C.** Port forwarding
   - ⭘ **D.** Content filtering
   - ⭘ **E.** Power levels

Cram Quiz Answers

1. **A, C, and E.** Changing default passwords, enabling MAC filtering, and enabling the latest version of WPA can all increase the security of a SOHO router. Enabling SSID broadcast makes a router visible. Enabling WPS makes it easier to connect to the router but has security implications.

2. **A and D.** By enabling MAC filtering, you can create a list of MAC addresses that a SOHO router will accept. Any other computers with different MAC addresses will not be allowed access to the network. This works for wired and wireless connections. You can also disable physical ports on the router; this blocks any physical signal from being sent to those unused ports. (You might also try reducing the transmitting power of the wireless channel being used.) A screened subnet (also

known as a DMZ) is used to host servers and acts as a separate area between the LAN and the Internet. A complex SSID is great but won't matter to a user connecting a laptop physically to the router because the SSID affects only wireless access.

3. **D.** By enabling content filtering (and parental controls), you can select computers—by MAC address—and select what websites (domains) those computers are allowed to connect to. MAC filtering by itself simply allows or denies computers access to the router based on the MAC address of the computer. Disabling unused ports is a good idea, but it will simply stop a computer from accessing the SOHO router if it is connected on that port. Port forwarding involves configuring a router to forward Internet-based IP addresses and ports to a computer or server that is on the LAN or the screened subnet. Power levels refer to the broadcasting power of an AP's radio. The lower, the better—as long as people on the perimeter of the building can still communicate with the router.

In this chapter, you read a lot about router security. If you employ these methods, you'll be on your way to a *super-secure* Internet experience! Continue!

CHAPTER 52
Browser Security

This chapter covers the following A+ 220-1102 exam objective:

▶ **2.10** – Given a scenario, install and configure browsers and relevant security settings.

Web browsers—everyone uses them. And they connect us to the Internet. Do I have to stress the need for web browser security? This chapter describes some basic techniques used to secure the most common browsers and shows how to safeguard users' browsing habits. In this chapter, we'll focus mostly on Microsoft Edge and Google Chrome.

And hey! This is the last chapter on security. Or is it? We should always be thinking in terms of security, as you will see as you progress through the rest of the book. But as far as Domain 2.0: Security is concerned, this is the last chapter.

ExamAlert

Objective 2.10 focuses on browser download/installation, extensions and plug-ins, password managers, secure connections/sites and valid certificates, and settings.

Browser Download/Installation

As you work with different operating systems, you will see that each of them favors a certain web browser that is installed as part of the system and works by default whenever you need to connect to the Internet.

For example, Windows has Microsoft Edge built in. Apple products have the Safari browser. Linux distributions often use Firefox. And Chromebooks use Chrome. You will find that Chrome is also heavily used by end users and many organizations as their main web browser. There are other web browsers, but these are the four you should know for the exam, with Microsoft Edge and Chrome at the top of the list.

If you use the default browser that comes with an operating system, then no download or installation is necessary; the browser just works. However, if you want to use a different browser, you need to download it, install it, and then set it as the default within the operating system. So, for example, if you are working in Windows 10 and want to use Chrome as the default web browser, you need to do the following:

1. **Search for the Chrome web browser:** A simple search in any Internet search engine for "Chrome web browser" will suffice. (Generally speaking, I recommend skipping through any ads displayed in the search results.) Click the download button or link.

2. **Download and install:** After clicking "Download," the installation usually begins automatically, regardless of the OS you are using. The installation of most web browsers is so user friendly that it happens almost like magic.

3. **Set Chrome as the default web browser:** A web browser often asks if you want to set it as the default web browser, and clicking yes makes it so. You can also perform this action in the browser settings. Or, you can change the default browser in Windows. For example, in Windows 10, you go to **Windows Settings > Apps > Default Apps**. Then, scroll down to and click the current web browser under the heading **Web browser** and select the browser you want to use—in this case Google Chrome.

For other web browsers, you might need to use slightly different download and installation methods. The important thing to know for the exam is how to change the default web browser in Windows.

ExamAlert

To change the default web browser (or other default programs) in Windows, go to **Windows Settings** > **Apps** > **Default Apps**.

Table 52.1 lists the download links for some popular web browsers.

TABLE 52.1 **Web Browser Download Links**

Browser	Link
Microsoft Edge	https://www.microsoft.com/en-us/edge
Chrome	https://www.google.com/chrome/
Firefox	https://www.mozilla.org/en-US/firefox/new/
Safari	https://support.apple.com/downloads/safari (macOS only)
Opera	https://www.opera.com/download
Chromium	https://www.chromium.org/getting-involved/download-chromium

All of the web browser links listed in Table 52.1 are considered to be trusted sources. It's important to download programs and files from trusted sources—that is, sources that you know are legitimate. However, keep in mind that the level of trust in a source may depend on the policy of your organization. Any website or app can be put on an untrusted list, and sometimes browsers are banned. For example, hackers tend to prefer browsers such as Firefox and Opera to do their dirty work. This might prompt an administrator to eliminate the ability to install those web browsers and place them on the untrusted list. We'll discuss trusted and untrusted sources more later in the chapter.

Note

Firefox has been the standard in privacy for a long time. But you might also be interested in the Tor Browser or Brave, as well as search engines such as DuckDuckGo or Startpage.

Hashing

In your travels, you will encounter file downloads that incorporate *signatures*. A signature allows you to check whether a file has been tampered with while in transit between the web server and your local computer. A signature could be considered a summary of a file to be downloaded. It is created using a cryptographic hashing technique.

Commonly used browsers such as Microsoft Edge and Google Chrome do not use signatures to verify the browser installation files. Instead, they rely on the mandatory usage of secure HTTPS connections before downloads can be initiated. However, other less commonly used web browsers might use signatures. A signature might also be referred to as a "hash" or as a "checksum." Essentially, you need to check the downloaded file's signature against the signature that is stored on the website. If the two match, then you can be relatively sure that your download has not been tampered with during transit. Of course, the process is more technical than that. Step-by-step processes are readily available on the Internet for hashing technologies such as SHA and PGP.

Settings

It's important to know how to access the settings for web browsers. Table 52.2 shows ways to get to the settings for Edge, Chrome, Firefox, and Safari.

TABLE 52.2 **Web Browser Settings Pages**

Browser	How to Get to Settings
Edge	▶ Click the menu button (three horizontal dots) in the upper-right corner of the screen and click **Settings**.
	▶ Type **edge://settings** in the address bar.
Chrome	▶ Click the menu button (three vertical dots) in the upper-right corner of the screen and click **Settings**.
	▶ Type **chrome://settings** in the address bar.
Firefox	▶ Click the menu button (three horizontal lines) in the upper-right corner of the screen and click **Preferences**.
	▶ Type **about:preferences** in the address bar.
Safari	▶ On the menu, click **Safari** > **Preferences**

Extensions and Plug-ins

To customize web browsers, you can use extensions and plug-ins. For the most part, Microsoft Edge and Google Chrome focus on extensions and have done away with the term *plug-ins*. But Firefox still uses both extensions and plug-ins (as of the writing of this book).

Extensions are software programs that add functionality to a browser. Extensions can be good or bad. The good ones make the browser better and don't use too much more of your computer's resources. The bad ones often use a lot of system resources, cause system failures, collect data, or perform malicious actions behind the scenes.

Some examples of extensions for Microsoft Edge and Google Chrome include Office Online, Adblock Plus, LastPass, Save to Pocket, and Dark Mode. These all add different types of functionality to the web browser. These extensions, once installed, are easily accessible from the main browser application.

To see what extensions are installed to Microsoft Edge, type **edge://extensions** in the Edge address bar. To see what extensions are installed to Chrome, type **chrome://extensions** in the Chrome address bar. From these locations, you can also search extensions and, most importantly, enable/disable them.

Once again, it's important to use a trusted source when obtaining extensions. In the Microsoft Edge extensions page, you can click the **Get extensions for Microsoft Edge** link. Doing so opens a new tab that brings you to the Edge Add-ons web page. For Google Chrome, use the Chrome Web Store.

To work with extensions in Firefox, click the menu button and select **Add-ons** (or press Ctrl+Shift+A). Then select **Extensions.** Or go to the following https://addons.mozilla.org/en-US/firefox/extensions/. The Firefox Add-ons page also shows plug-ins. While using an extension is the more common way to modify the Firefox browser, a plug-in might still be used, such as for a decryption module or a video codec for playback of certain types of video files.

Quite often, a web browser will warn you when you try to install an extension from an untrusted source. This is an example of a failsafe. Educate your users to read the messages that show up onscreen as these messages are often security related. An extension that comes from an untrusted source could cause system instability or could compromise the system altogether.

Password Managers

Beware! Passwords can be stored in a variety of places. The most common way is within some kind of password manager. A *password manager* is a program that stores all the passwords that you use for various websites and services. There are several types of password managers (or *password vaults*, as they are some-times called). They can exist as locally run programs or as third-party Internet-based services. A person could use Credential Manager (Windows) or Keychain (macOS) to store web credentials *and* OS credentials. Password managers also exist within most of today's web browsers. Because this chapter is about browser security, we'll focus in on web browser–based password managers.

By default, when you type a password to access a website, most web browsers ask you if you want the browser to save the password. If you click **Yes**, your machine saves it within the browser application in Settings, where you can later copy and paste them to the various websites you need to access. Some browsers may also offer to fill in passwords automatically when you next access websites. Depending on the browser and the settings, you might also have the option to have a password saved to your *account*. This means that the password is stored in the cloud with your user account (if you are logged in). The password can then move with you to other devices using the same browser and user account. All of the browsers will use encryption for the username and password.

A home user might like to let the browser manage passwords; I mean, who can remember all those pesky complex passwords today? However, most organiza-tions frown upon this practice because they deem it too great a security risk. So, you should know how to disable it. That means disabling two functions: the browser offering to save a password and the ability for the browser to autofill the password in the future. To disable these settings in Edge, go to **Settings > Profiles > Passwords** (or type **edge://settings/passwords**). To disable them in Chrome, go to **Settings > Autofill > Passwords** (or type **chrome://settings/passwords**).

Banning Web Browser Password Managers

If an organization bans web browser password managers, what are organizational users to do with their passwords? Well, there are a few options.

First, there are third-party password manager programs, such as LastPass, Keeper, Zoho, and KeePass2 (my personal favorite). An organization might consider using one of these programs as a more secure solution than storing passwords in a web browser. These programs typically encrypt passwords in a vault locally on the system. However, some of them can also integrate with the web browser. Some store passwords in the cloud to allow access from multiple devices. The key (pun intended) is to have a super-lengthy and complex passphrase that allows access to the entire vault. That's the *one* password that needs to be memorized. If that password is compromised, all the user's other passwords are compromised.

Second, an organization might choose to build its own password manager, using the programming language and cipher of its choice. An organization might build from scratch or—more likely—build on other work. For example, programs such as KeePass2 are open source, and the source code can be freely downloaded and modified at will.

Third, an organization might say *no* to passwords altogether, instead relying on other forms of authentication. Or the organization might simply disallow users from logging in to anything other than the organization's infrastructure. Technically, this would probably be accomplished using a single sign-on (SSO) system and various types of filtering. Fundamentally, this method would rely on the principle of least privilege, which, ultimately, reduces risk and simplifies the situation in one stroke.

Secure Connections

If an Internet session isn't secure, then clients, servers, and data in motion are all at risk. Let's discuss a couple of technologies and options for securing connections.

TLS

The first thing to consider is the type of connection made when connecting to a website. To secure a connection, you need to encrypt it. There are a variety of ways to do this. The most common way is to use Transport Layer Security (TLS).

TLS is a cryptographic protocol that provides secure Internet communications such as web browsing, instant messaging, email, and VoIP. This protocol relies on a public key infrastructure (PKI) for obtaining and validating certificates.

> **Note**
>
> A public key infrastructure (PKI) is an entire system of hardware and software, policies and procedures, and people. It is used to create, distribute, manage, store, and revoke digital certificates. If you have connected to a secure website in the past, you have been a part of a PKI! But a PKI can be used for other things as well, such as secure email transmissions and secure connections to remote computers and remote networks. A PKI is all encompassing: It includes users, client computers, servers, services, and, most of all, encryption.

Many people refer to the secure connections they make to websites as SSL, but actually most of them are TLS. TLS is a newer and more secure solution, and Secure Sockets Layer (SSL) has been deprecated. As of the writing of this book, the latest version of TLS is 1.3 (defined in 2018), though you will still see version 1.2 in use. However, what you should be most interested in is the strength of the cipher—which is something to keep in mind when inquiring as to TLS certificates. Let's talk about essentially how TLS works. Two types of keys are required when any two computers attempt to communicate with TLS: a public key and a session key. Asymmetric encryption is used to encrypt and share session keys, and symmetric encryption is used to encrypt the session data. A session key used by a protocol such as TLS is used only once; a separate session key is used for every connection.

> **ExamAlert**
>
> To learn more about cryptography, see https://www.nist.gov/cryptography.

Now, you may be called upon to verify that specific versions of TLS are enabled (or disabled) in the web browser settings. To do this for Edge/Internet

Explorer, open the Internet Properties dialog box (**Run > inetcpl.cpl**), go to the **Advanced** tab, scroll all the way down to the TLS settings, and select/ deselect the various versions of TLS. As of the writing of this book, TLS 1.3 is experimental in Windows, but it is sure to gain more acceptance as time moves on. Also, Google Chrome piggybacks the Windows settings for TLS, so you go to the same location for Chrome as for Edge.

> **ExamAlert**
>
> Know how to check the TLS version in Edge and in Chrome.

You might also work with specific security functions for TLS 1.3 and other security features. The Advanced tab is the place to be in this respect. In Chrome, there is another option: Open a new tab by clicking the plus symbol at the top of the browser or pressing Ctrl+T. Then type **chrome://flags** in the address bar. Search for "TLS 1.3" (or something similar), and you will see the option to enable/disable it. To do the same thing in Firefox, open a new tab and type **about:config** in the address bar. Search for TLS and look for the **security.tls.version.min** setting.

From a user education standpoint, you should instruct people not to enter any PII on a website that does not have a secure connection. The easiest way for a user to tell if the connection is secure is to look for the padlock in the address bar (and possibly the HTTPS protocol). If there is no padlock or if it's clear that HTTPS is not in use, the user should close the tab. To get even more information about a connection, a user could right-click on the padlock and view the details of the certificate used for the encrypted connection. The drop-down menu that appears when you right-click the padlock will state whether the certificate is secure. You can then view the details of the certificate. The details include the connection protocol (for instance, TLS), the certificate encryption type (for example, RSA), and the cryptographic hash (for example, SHA256), among other things. Viewing the details of the certificate goes a little beyond the A+, but it's something I recommend you take a look at when you get a chance.

Secure Sites and Tracking

You can modify the security level for a browser to affect which sites are accessed and the ways the browser allows those sites to track users.

For example, in Edge, go to **Settings** > **Privacy, search, and services** (or **edge://settings/privacy**) and locate the **Tracking prevention** section. For some organizations, the default Balanced option might not be secure enough, and you might be instructed to set this to Strict instead. Better yet, you can do this on multiple systems automatically with group policy (discussed in a little bit). You can also set exceptions for sites that you want to allow.

The Privacy section of Edge is the place to be if you are concerned about security. It has a *ton* of stuff for you to consider. Spend 5 or 10 minutes browsing that portion of Settings. For example, scroll down to the **Security** section and click on **Manage Certificates** to bring up the Certificates window, where you can import, export, and further manipulate certificates. You can view and *really* manage certificates by going to **Run** > **certmgr.msc** to bring up the Certificate Manager window. Try navigating to **Trusted Root Certification Authorities** > **Certificates** to see all of the certificate issuers for the system.

In addition, there are other settings scattered around Edge, such as the Cookies and site permissions section, where you can set the cookies you want to allow from web servers and view permissions for sites that have been visited.

Note

For a secure Internet browsing experience, you might also implement a proxy server or a virtual private network (VPN).

More Settings

You've already seen how to access some settings in Edge and Chrome. Remember **edge://settings** and **chrome://settings**? Table 52.3 shows some examples of browser settings, what they mean, and where to configure them in Edge and Chrome (using address bar paths).

TABLE 52.3 **Web Browser Configurations**

Setting	Meaning	Configuration
Pop-up blocker	Blocks unwanted windows that appear when a user clicks on a web page element.	**edge://settings/content** > **Pop-ups and redirects** **chrome://settings/content** > **Pop-ups and redirects**

Setting	Meaning	Configuration
Clear browsing data	Removes all website-based temporary files stored on the local system, such as browsing history, cookies, passwords, and cache.	**edge://settings/privacy** > **Clear browsing data** **chrome://settings/privacy** > **Clear browsing data**
Sign-in/data synchronization	If enabled, synchronizes logon and data across devices.	**edge://settings/profiles/sync** **chrome://settings/syncSetup**
Trusted/untrusted sites	Allows you to configure which websites the browser is allowed to connect to.	**Run** > **inetcpl.cpl** > **Security tab**

A user who doesn't want information about a browsing session to be stored locally can use private browsing, also known as incognito mode. In this mode, the browser disregards any cached information, logins, synchronized data, and so forth. And, by default, web caching, cookies, and so on are disabled (at least for that "private" session).

To enter private browsing mode, right-click the browser icon and select **New InPrivate window** (Edge) or **New Incognito window** (Chrome). Or, from within the browser, use the Ctrl+Shift+N shortcut (Edge/Chrome) or Ctrl+Shift+P (Firefox).

ExamAlert

Know how to initiate private browsing mode in Edge and in Chrome.

Note

Does private browsing mode mean the browsing history isn't stored anywhere? Not on your life! Know this: Just about everything today is tracked one way or another. Enough said.

Want to configure these settings in a policy-oriented system? Of course you do! Use the Local Group Policy Editor. Go to **Run** > **gpedit.msc** and navigate to **User Configuration** > **Administrative Templates** > **Windows Components** > **Microsoft Edge**. There you will find more policy settings than you could dream of. I recommend that you take a few minutes to explore these settings. You will discover that configuring browser settings (and Windows settings in general) can be performed more efficiently with the Local Group Policy Editor, especially if you need more advanced control and want to configure policies for multiple users/computers (for example, using Active Directory group policy).

General Browser Security Procedures

An organization should implement some general procedures, regardless of the browser it uses. These concepts can be applied to desktop browsers as well as mobile browsers:

▶ **Implement policies:** The policy could be handwritten, configured at the browser, implemented within the computer operating system, or, better yet, configured on a server centrally. Policies can be configured to manage add-ons and disallow access to websites that are known to be malicious. Or, a policy might state that all web browsers should be configured to delete all cookies and content daily. Another policy might state that if there is a browser misconfiguration, a technician should reset the browser to default settings and start fresh.

▶ **Train users:** User training is important when it comes to helping users know which websites to access, how to use search engines, and what to do if pop-ups appear onscreen. The more users you can reach with your wisdom, the better!

▶ **Use a proxy and content filter:** An HTTP proxy (also known as a proxy server) acts as a go-between for the clients on a network and the Internet. Basically, it caches website information for clients and thus reduces the number of requests that need to be forwarded to the corresponding web server on the Internet. An HTTP proxy is used to save time, make more efficient use of bandwidth, and help secure client connections. By using a content filter in combination with an HTTP proxy, specific websites can be filtered out, especially ones that may potentially be malicious that can waste users' time (you know what I'm talking about!).

▶ **Secure against malicious code:** Depending on your company's policies and procedures, you might need to configure an increased level of security concerning ActiveX controls, Java, JavaScript, audio/video media, phishing, and much more. Always be on the lookout!

Cram Quiz

Answer these questions. The answers follow the last question. If you cannot answer these questions correctly, consider reading this chapter again until you can.

1. You have been tasked with implementing ad blocking functionality within a web browser. Which of the following should you add to make ad blocking a reality?

   ○ **A.** Extension

   ○ **B.** Valid certificate

   ○ **C.** Pop-up blocker

   ○ **D.** Password manager

2. A user's computer is running very slow. You investigate and find out that there are many, many temporary files, caused by *excessive* browsing. Where would you go in Microsoft Edge to fix the problem?

- ○ **A.** edge://settings/profiles/sync
- ○ **B.** chrome://extensions
- ○ **C.** edge://settings/privacy
- ○ **D.** edge://settings/content

3. You want to verify that Google Chrome will connect to websites in a secure manner. Where should you go to confirm this? (Select the two best answers.)

- ○ **A.** PGP key
- ○ **B.** TLS setting (1.2 or higher)
- ○ **C.** Installation file signature from a trusted source
- ○ **D.** Incognito mode
- ○ **E.** Trusted zones in **Internet Properties** > **Security**

4. You are working for Geeks of the Future, a company that solves home user technology issues. One of your customers tells you that his computer is suffering from slow performance as well as browser crashes. These issues began after the customer clicked a "repair" pop-up while browsing the Web. Which of the following should you perform *first* to resolve the issue? (Select the two best answers.)

- ○ **A.** Enable the web browser's pop-up blocker.
- ○ **B.** Scan the storage drive's boot sector and RAM with an antivirus program.
- ○ **C.** Initiate a cold shutdown and then turn on the computer.
- ○ **D.** Uninstall any recently installed suspicious programs and browser extensions.
- ○ **E.** Run SFC and replace changed files with the original system files.

Cram Quiz Answers

1. A. Add an extension for the ad blocker of your choice. (Make sure it's relatively secure!) A valid certificate is required before a web browser establishes a session with a web server. Pop-up blockers are different from ad blockers in that they block pop-up windows in general; an ad blocker might happen to block some pop-up windows but only because they are ad based. A password manager stores passwords in an encrypted fashion within a vault on the local computer.

2. C. In the address bar, go to **edge://settings/privacy** and then click **Clear browsing data**. This will remove all of the temporary files that are potentially slowing down the system. **edge://settings/profiles/sync** is used for sign-in and data synchronization. **chrome://extensions** is where you would go to enable/disable extensions in Chrome, not Microsoft Edge. **edge://settings/content** is for blocking pop-ups.

3. **B and E.** Check the TLS setting in **Internet Properties** > **Advanced**. In most cases, you want to make sure that it is TLS 1.2 or higher. That is the secure protocol that launches the session. Also, check out the trusted zones section of **Internet Properties** > **Security**. This is where you can select the level of security and specify custom levels, if necessary. Both of these will work for Edge and for Chrome. Using a PGP key (or an installation file signature) is a good idea when you are installing a less-well-known browser; it lets you verify whether the installation file was tampered with during transit. Incognito mode, which is Chrome's private browsing mode, is great to use when you want to avoid having browser session information stored locally.

4. **A and D.** The *first* things you should do are to enable the web browser's pop-up blocker and uninstall any recently installed suspicious programs and browser extensions. The problem occurred when the customer clicked on a fake repair pop-up while browsing the Internet. Pop-ups should be disabled on today's web browsers by default, but users have a way of disabling that which protects them most! The act of clicking the pop-up probably initiated more problems—for example, the installation of unwanted browser extensions (which is common) or perhaps even undesirable programs. These extensions and/or programs are most likely causing the system to behave slowly because they are reaching out to the Internet to do malicious things. They should be removed. However, you should also scan the system for malware—not just the boot sector of the storage drive but the entire system and not just with anti*virus* software but with a full-fledged anti-*malware* program. And the *very* first thing you should do if malware is even a remote consideration is to quarantine/isolate the system. If you suspect malware, you might also need to run System File Checker (SFC) to repair OS files. (You might also opt to simply reimage the system, though that can be a tough sell with a home user.) Finally, a cold shutdown and boot is also known as a *graceful shutdown*, and it can help with various hardware and software issues; it is generally a good idea to perform a graceful shutdown as a final step when you are done troubleshooting a system.

You have finished this chapter and also the security section of this book. Well done! But remember, you should always have security on your mind! For a technician, security should be a primary consideration with any technology. Review your notes for this chapter and for the entire domain. Take a nice break, and I'll "see" you at the next chapter!

CORE 2 (220-1102)

Domain 3.0: Software Troubleshooting

CHAPTER 53

Troubleshooting Microsoft Windows

This chapter covers the following A+ 220-1102 exam objective:

▶ **3.1** – Given a scenario, troubleshoot common Windows OS problems.

Welcome to the first chapter of Domain 3.0: Software Troubleshooting.

Now for the toughest part of working with Windows: troubleshooting. Before beginning this chapter, I recommend that you review the six-step troubleshooting methodology presented in Chapter 23, "Computer Troubleshooting 101." As mentioned in that chapter, troubleshooting is probably the most important skill for a computer technician to possess.

Many different things can go wrong in a computer, and the majority of them are software related. This vital chapter endeavors to give you the tools, utilities, and skills necessary to troubleshoot the various boot errors, stop errors, and other Windows problems you might encounter.

This is one of the longer chapters in the book. Take breaks as you go and review your notes often.

> **ExamAlert**
>
> **Objective 3.1** concentrates on common symptoms and common troubleshooting steps in Windows.

Windows Recovery

There are many tools included with Windows designed to help you troubleshoot and repair just about any issue that might come up. Before getting into the exact issues you might face, let's discuss some of the repair and preinstallation environment repair tools, what they do, and where you can access them. We'll start with the Windows Recovery Environment.

Windows Recovery Environment (Windows RE)

Windows RE (or WinRE for short) is a set of tools included in Windows whose purpose is to recover Windows from errors that prevent it from booting. These tools can also be instrumental in fixing issues that cause a computer to "freeze up."

In Windows, you access WinRE through the Advanced Startup menu. You can get to Advanced Startup in a variety of ways, including the following:

► Hold the **Shift** key while selecting **Restart**. (This works with most power option locations in Windows.)

► In PowerShell or the Command Prompt, type **shutdown /r /o** and then press **Enter**.

► Go to **Start > Settings > Update & security > Recovery** and, under Advanced Startup, click **Restart now**.

► Boot to the appropriate recovery media.

► For suitably equipped devices, press the hardware recovery button or button combination designated by the maker of the device.

Once the system has rebooted, you should see the Choose an option screen. Select **Troubleshoot**, and you see several options, including

▶ **Reset your PC:** This option allows you to keep personal files *or* remove everything.

▶ **Advanced Options:** This option brings up the Advanced options screen, which shows the main tools that a technician can use to troubleshoot a system. Figure 53.1 shows the Advanced options screen that appears in Windows 10. The options might be listed differently, depending on your version of Windows. Table 53.1 describes these options, as well as other options that you can't see in the figure.

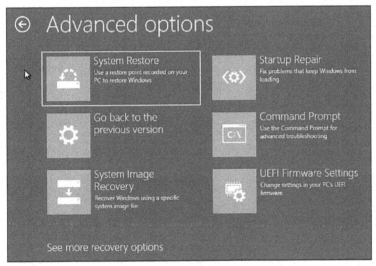

FIGURE 53.1   **The Windows 10 Advanced options screen**

TABLE 53.1   **Windows Recovery Options**

Recovery Option	Description
System Restore	This option restores the computer's system files to an earlier point in time. This option allows you to undo system changes to a computer without affecting the personal files on the computer, such as email, documents, or photos.
	Note: If you use System Restore when a computer is in Safe Mode, you cannot undo the restore operation. However, you can run System Restore again and choose a different restore point, if one exists. We discuss System Restore further later in this chapter.

Recovery Option	Description
Go back to the previous version	This option, which is available for only a limited time after an upgrade, allows you to go back to an earlier build of Windows. You can also do this from Settings in Windows. A similar tool is Uninstall Updates.
System Image Recovery	These programs are used to restore a storage drive from a backup in select editions of Windows.
Startup Repair	This option automatically fixes certain problems, such as missing or damaged system files that might prevent Windows from starting correctly. This can help with general system instability. Startup Repair scans your computer for the problem and then tries to fix it so your computer can start correctly. Most of the time, this is a great place to start when troubleshooting.
Command Prompt	Advanced users can use the Command Prompt to perform recovery-related operations and also run other command-line tools for diagnosing and troubleshooting problems. To use it, you must log on as an administrator.
UEFI Firmware Settings	This option allows a user to access the UEFI from the OS to make changes. (It requires UEFI-compatible BIOS.)
Startup Settings	This option enables you to boot to a variety of modes that are explained later in this chapter. To access this in Windows 10, you may have to click **See more recovery options**.

ExamAlert

Memorize the different Windows RE options.

Note

To learn more about WinRE, see https://docs.microsoft.com/en-us/windows-hardware/manufacture/desktop/windows-recovery-environment--windows-re--technical-reference.

Keep in mind that Windows attempts to do a self-repair if it senses a boot issue. This occurs first when you start, or restart, the system. If this automatic repair does not fix the problem, using WinRE is your next stop. However, in some cases, you need to boot the system in a different *way* to fix a problem. Let's discuss advanced booting now.

Startup Settings

If Windows is not functioning properly, the culprit might be a video driver, a new configuration, or another system issues. The Startup Settings portion of WinRE has several startup options—such as Safe Mode—that can aid you in fixing such problems.

F8

Historically, the Startup Settings options were accessed by pressing the F8 key immediately after the computer started up. For example, in Windows 7, pressing F8 would bring up the Windows Advanced Boot Options menu, which has essentially the same options as shown in Figure 53.1 but with slight differences in names and arrangement.

While the F8 keypress is still supported by Microsoft, it does not work in Windows 10/11 by default. To enable F8 functionality in Windows 10/11, type the following in the Command Prompt (as an admin):

```
bcdedit /set {default} bootmenupolicy legacy
```

That effectively replaces the Startup Settings version. To disable it and go back to the Startup Settings version in WinRE, use the same command but replace **legacy** with **standard**.

The Startup Settings window and the Advanced Boot Options menu have essentially the same options, with one difference: The Advanced Boot Options menu includes the **Repair Your Computer** option, which automatically attempts to fix Windows issues for you. This option is not included in the Startup Settings window because there are several automated repair options elsewhere in WinRE. You will most likely use Startup Settings more often, so I'll be focusing on that.

Figure 53.2 shows an example of the Startup Settings window in Windows 10. Table 53.2 describes the options listed in the Startup Settings window. Note that you can use the F1–F9 function keys to select the corresponding startup options.

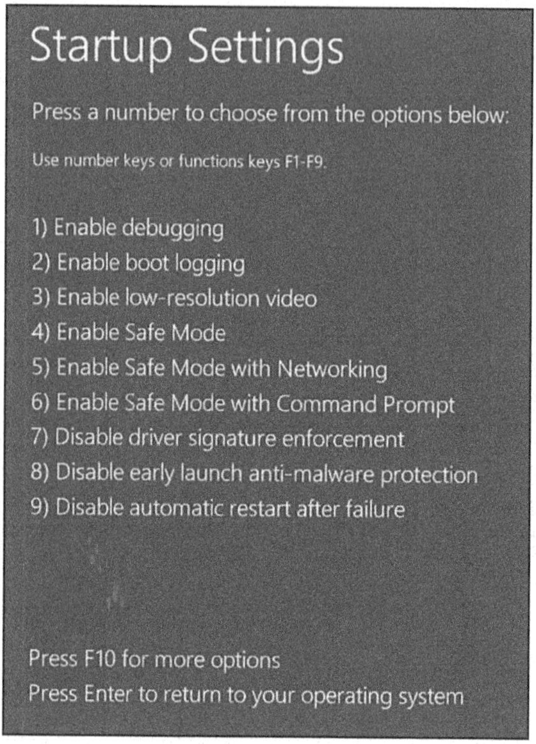

Startup Settings

Press a number to choose from the options below:

Use number keys or functions keys F1-F9.

1) Enable debugging
2) Enable boot logging
3) Enable low-resolution video
4) Enable Safe Mode
5) Enable Safe Mode with Networking
6) Enable Safe Mode with Command Prompt
7) Disable driver signature enforcement
8) Disable early launch anti-malware protection
9) Disable automatic restart after failure

Press F10 for more options
Press Enter to return to your operating system

FIGURE 53.2   **The Windows 10 Startup Settings screen**

TABLE 53.2   **Windows Startup Settings**

Startup Setting	Description
1) Enable debugging	Enables the use of a debug program to examine the system kernel for troubleshooting.
2) Enable boot logging	Logs the boot process and creates an ntbtlog.txt file that is stored in %systemroot%.
3) Enable low-resolution video	Uses a standard VGA driver in place of a GPU-specific display driver but uses all other drivers as normal, typically at 640×480 resolution.
4) Enable Safe Mode	Starts the system with a minimal set of drivers; used in the event that one of the drivers fails. Safe Mode is a good option when attempting to use System Restore and when scanning systems for viruses. It is also a good option if you encounter a blue screen of death (BSOD) error and need to roll back a driver.
	You can also initiate Safe Mode (and its derivatives) by opening the System Configuration utility (**Run** > **msconfig**), accessing the **Boot** tab, checking **Safe boot**, and restarting the computer.

Startup Setting	Description
5) Enable Safe Mode with Networking	Starts the system with a minimal set of drivers and enables network support.
6) Enable Safe Mode with Command Prompt	Starts the system with a minimal set of drivers but loads the Command Prompt instead of the Windows GUI.
7) Disable driver signature enforcement	Enables drivers containing improper signatures to be installed.
8) Disable early launch anti-malware protection	Disables anti-malware, when needed, to diagnose and fix the system. Rootkits can infect a system early on as it boots, and some anti-malware programs are designed to check for these programs early on in the boot process. This option disables anti-malware programs so that you can diagnose and fix the system, such as when using System Restore.
9) Disable automatic restart after failure	Prevents Windows from automatically restarting if an error causes Windows to fail. Choose this option only if Windows is stuck in a loop in which Windows fails, attempts to restart, and fails again repeatedly.

ExamAlert

Know the various settings under Windows Startup Settings (such as Safe Mode) and know what they do.

System Restore

The System Restore tool can be used to create a snapshot of the state of the operating system and store it for later retrieval. It can be very helpful when troubleshooting a system.

System Restore can fix issues caused by defective hardware or software by reverting to an earlier point in time. Registry changes made by hardware or software are reversed in an attempt to force the computer to work the way it did previously. Restore points can be created manually and are also created automatically by the operating system before new updates, applications, or hardware are installed.

To create a restore point in Windows, follow these steps:

1. Open the System Properties dialog box to the System Protection tab by selecting **Run** and typing either **systempropertiesprotection** or **sysdm.cpl ,4** (see Figure 53.3). For more information on the System Properties dialog box, refer to Chapter 36, "Windows Settings."

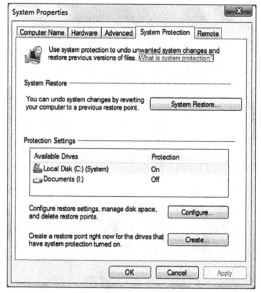

FIGURE 53.3   The System Protection tab of the System Properties dialog box

2. Click the **Create** button. The System Protection dialog box appears.

3. Type a name for the restore point and then click **Create**.

If System Restore is not available, it might be turned off. There are several reasons a person might turn it off (for example, if the system had been scanned for viruses recently).

To enable or disable System Restore in Windows, click the **Configure** button on the System Protection tab of the System Properties dialog box. Then click the radio button **Turn on system protection**.

Using System Restore is kind of like using a time machine (if one actually existed). It allows you to reset a computer to an earlier configuration—hopefully, one that functioned properly. To actually restore a computer to an earlier point in time, just click the **System Restore** button on the System

Properties/System Protection dialog box and then follow the instructions. But beware: Some applications might be removed, and drivers might be uninstalled.

> **Note**
>
> If a system won't boot normally, you can attempt to run System Restore from Safe Mode, or you can use WinRE or System Recovery Options.

> **ExamAlert**
>
> Understand how to enable and disable System Restore, how to create restore points, and how to restore a system to an earlier point in time.

Improper, Spontaneous, and Frequent Shutdowns

You've probably seen a Windows computer fail and reboot with a message such as "Windows was shut down improperly." Improper shutdowns and spontaneous shutdowns can happen for a variety of reasons, including brownouts or blackouts, power surges, hardware failures, a user inadvertently unplugging the computer, or perhaps a virus or other malware. This can be a disturbing phenomenon to users, and it may have been going on for a while before a user got you involved, so it is especially important to be patient with the user (and the computer) when troubleshooting this problem.

Some of the methods you can use to troubleshoot improper and spontaneous shutdowns include the following:

▶ **Check the Event Viewer:** Look in the System log to see if there are any alerts about hardware failures, service failures, and so on. If there is an alert, consider upgrading the driver for the affected hardware or upgrading the software that the service is dependent on. Ensure that the computer is running the latest updates.

▶ **Use MSConfig (the System Configuration utility):** On the General tab, select the **Selective startup** checkbox and the **Load startup items** checkbox. To weed out third-party program issues, click the **Services** tab, click the **Hide all Microsoft services** checkbox, and then click **Disable all**. Restart the system and see if the same issues return or if events are still written to the Event Viewer. Remember to restore Normal startup in MSConfig when finished troubleshooting.

▶ **Boot into Safe Mode:** Use Safe Mode to further investigate the problem. Safe Mode uses only the most basic drivers, so if a driver issue is causing the problems, Safe Mode could help you find out about it. Don't forget that you can also use Safe boot in MSConfig.

▶ **Run a virus scan:** Run a scan for malware and quarantine anything unusual. Update the antivirus software when you are finished.

▶ **Check power:** Make sure the AC outlet is wired properly and is supplying clean power. Verify that the power plug is firmly secured to the computer. If necessary, you might have to check the power supply. Intermittent and unexplained shutdowns can sometimes be linked to power supplies or other hardware failures.

▶ **Use Windows RE:** If necessary, use the Windows Recovery Environment to troubleshoot spontaneous shutdowns.

Stop Errors

A stop error (also known as a blue screen of death [BSOD]) is the worst type of error that can happen while Windows is operating. It completely halts the operating system and displays a blue screen with various text and code. You might also see a sad face with a QR code, among other things.

Anything you were working on when you get a BSOD is, for the most part, lost. In some cases, Windows reboots the computer after a memory dump has been initiated. (This is also known as auto-restart.) If not, you need to physically turn off the computer by pressing the Power button and then turn it back on. A BSOD may happen only once, and if that is the case, you need not worry too much. But if it happens two or three times or more, you should investigate. Quite often these errors are due to hardware issues, such as improperly seated memory or a corrupt driver file. If you see two columns of information on a BSOD with a list of drivers and other files, a driver issue could be the culprit. Look at the bottom of the second (or last) column and identify the driver that has failed (for example, ntfs.sys). Drivers can become corrupt for a variety of reasons, and those that are corrupt need to be replaced when you boot into Windows. Or, if you can't boot into Windows and Windows does not auto-repair the file, you can replace the driver from within Windows RE's Command Prompt. Less commonly, a BSOD might be caused by a memory error, and the screen will show additional code that you can research on Microsoft's websites: support.microsoft.com and docs.microsoft.com.

By default, three things happen when a stop error occurs:

1. An event is usually written to the System log within the Event Viewer, if that option has been selected in the Startup and Recovery window, as shown in Figure 53.4. When a stop error is written to the System log, it may be listed as an Information entry, not as an Error entry. The stop error will be listed as "The computer has rebooted from a bugcheck. The bugcheck was: *error number*." Use the error number to look up the problem—and hopefully find a solution—at one of Microsoft's support sites.

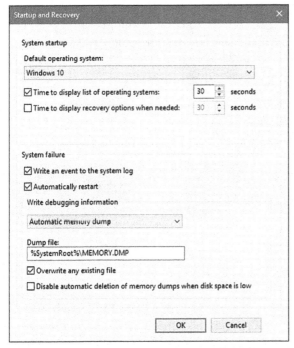

FIGURE 53.4   **The Startup and Recovery window**

The settings shown in Figure 53.4 can be accessed from the Advanced tab in the System Properties dialog box (which you can access directly via **Run > SystemPropertiesAdvanced.exe**). Click the **Settings** button in the Startup and Recovery area to access the Startup and Recovery window.

2. Windows writes debugging information to the storage drive for later analysis with memory dump debugging programs; this debugging information is essentially the contents of RAM. The default setting in Windows is to only write a portion of the contents of RAM; this is known as a kernel memory dump. The kernel memory dump is saved as the file %SystemRoot%\Memory.dmp. You can also select to create a small memory dump, which is written to %SystemRoot%\Minidump. Windows also enables you to do a complete memory dump, which dumps the entire contents of RAM to a file named Memory.dmp. To support a complete memory dump, the paging file must be large enough to hold all the physical RAM plus 1 MB.

> **Note**
>
> For more information about the various dump files, visit https://docs.microsoft.com/en-us/windows-hardware/drivers/debugger/varieties-of-kernel-mode-dump-files.

3. The computer automatically restarts (if the Automatically restart option is selected, which is the default in Windows).

> **ExamAlert**
>
> Know how stop errors occur and how memory dumps function.

Restoring Windows

There actually is something worse than a stop error. With a complete system failure, a system cannot be repaired. When this happens, the only options are to reinstall Windows or to restore Windows. There are several methods for restoring Windows, including

▶ **Repair option:** Boot to the Windows installation media (USB flash drive, DVD, etc.) and click the repair option. In the main Windows RE Advanced options (or System Recovery Options) window, select **System Image Recovery**. Provide backup media.

▶ **Reset the image:** Reset the system to a factory image stored on a separate partition of the storage drive. This commonly needs to occur on laptops, especially ones that do not have optical drives. Or you can use third-party tools such as Ghost or Acronis True Image. Remember that the image needs to be created *before* the disaster!

There are various other ways to access the utilities mentioned. Refer to earlier parts of this chapter for details or refer to the documentation that came with your third-party software.

Common Windows Symptoms and Solutions

We have already discussed a lot of issues and solutions, but there are a good number of other symptoms that you will encounter when working on Windows. What makes troubleshooting difficult is that there are often several potential solutions to a problem. Let's fill the gaps by listing some of those symptoms and potential solutions in Table 53.3.

> **ExamAlert**
>
> You will likely be tested on the common symptoms and solutions listed in Table 53.3. Given a scenario, know how to troubleshoot Windows OS problems well for the exam and in the field!

TABLE 53.3 **Windows Symptoms and Solutions**

Symptom	Potential Solutions
Slow or sluggish performance/slow bootup	▶ Use the built-in Windows Troubleshooter: Go to **Settings** > **Update & Security** > **Troubleshoot**. Note: In Windows 11, the troubleshooters can be found in **Settings** > **System** > **Troubleshoot**. Or Go to **Control Panel** > **System and Security** and click the **Troubleshoot common computer problems** link under Security and Maintenance. Then click **Additional Troubleshooters**. From there you can run a variety of troubleshooting tools.

Symptom	Potential Solutions
	Note: You can also see individual troubleshooting tools by navigating to **Control Panel** > **All Control Panel Items** > **Troubleshooting**.
	▶ Clean up and defragment the storage drive.
	▶ Reboot often.
	▶ Watch for numerous tabs opened in a web browser.
	▶ Uninstall unused programs.
	▶ Limit programs that run at startup. View the notification area to see what is running. Use **Task Manager** > **Startup** to disable programs.
	▶ Scan for malware.
	▶ End tasks in **Task Manager** > **Processes** (or with the **taskkill** command).
	Also, if you receive a "low memory" error:
	▶ Increase RAM (if possible).
	▶ If it is not possible to increase RAM, increase the virtual memory: **Run** > **systempropertiesadvanced.exe** > **Advanced** and click the **Settings** button under Performance to open the Performance Options dialog box, where you select the **Advanced** tab and click the **Change** button.
Limited or no connectivity	▶ Restart the system.
	▶ Reboot the router or modem.
	▶ Update the network settings, including the IP address and gateway address, and run **ipconfig /release** and **ipconfig /renew**.
	▶ Update the wireless network settings: SSID, encryption type, and so on.
	▶ Ensure that the system is not in airplane mode.
	▶ If necessary, boot into Safe Mode (or Safe boot) and roll back the network driver in the Device Manager.
	▶ Check the patch cable and look for a link light.
	▶ Go to **Settings** > **Update & Security** > **Troubleshoot** > **Additional troubleshooters** > **Internet Connections**.
No OS found/failure to boot	▶ Update the BIOS/UEFI boot order.
	▶ Repair the GPT or MBR or boot files in the system partition. (See the various repair options earlier in this chapter.)
	▶ Check hardware connections (drive cables, etc.). If necessary, roll back any changes or reimage/reload the OS.

Symptom	Potential Solutions
Bootmgr is missing	If the Windows Boot Manager file is missing or corrupt, try the following: ▶ Boot to WinRE and select **Startup Repair** to automatically repair the system. ▶ Rebuild the Boot Configuration Store (BDC) by entering **bootrec /rebuildbcd** in the Command Prompt in WinRE (and do a System Restore, if needed). ▶ Ensure that the C: partition is set to **active**. See this site for advanced troubleshooting of Windows boot problems: https://docs.microsoft.com/en-us/windows/client-management/advanced-troubleshooting-boot-problems.
Boot sector issues	Enter **bootrec /fixboot** at the WinRE Command Prompt.
Application/OS won't install or won't run	▶ Verify the requirements for the application or OS. ▶ Add resources (CPU cores, RAM, storage space, etc.). Note: If there is a RAM issue, run the Windows Memory Diagnostic program to troubleshoot it: **Run > mdsched**.
Application crashes	▶ Apply updates to the OS. ▶ Apply updates to the application. ▶ Repair the application: **Control Panel > All Control Panel Items > Programs and Features** and then right-click the application in question and select **Repair** (or reinstall if necessary). ▶ Run the application in program compatibility mode. Use the Program Compatibility Troubleshooter: Go to **Settings > Update & Security > Troubleshoot > Additional troubleshooters > Program Compatibility Troubleshooter**. Or right-click the program executable and change the compatibility settings. ▶ Temporarily disable the application from startup if it is interfering with other programs and the OS: **Task Manager > Startup**.
Missing or corrupt system files	▶ Use the System File Checker (**sfc**) tool. ▶ Use the **chkdsk** tool.
Blue screen/black screen	See the sections "Windows Recovery" and "Stop Errors," earlier in this chapter.
Printing issues	▶ Go to **Settings > Update & Security > Troubleshoot > Additional troubleshooters > Printer**. ▶ Configure settings in **Control Panel > All Control Panel Items > Devices and Printers**. ▶ Roll back device drivers for any devices that fail in Windows. (See Chapter 28, "Troubleshooting Printers," for more information.)

Symptom	Potential Solutions
Device issues	▶ Use the Troubleshooter.
	▶ Use the Device Manager to troubleshoot (**Run** > **devmgmt. msc**). Know the Device Manager icons:
	▶ Black arrow pointing down = Device is disabled. Simply reenable it to use the device. In rare cases, a hardware conflict can be caused by I/O settings or IRQs (for example, serial COM ports).
	▶ Exclamation point = Incorrect driver or hardware conflict. Try removing the device and let Windows reinstall it. If that does not work, download correct drivers from manufacturer's website.
	To troubleshoot further, open the Properties window for the device and locate the error code on the General tab or the Events tab. Cross-reference the code with the codes listed at https://support.microsoft.com/en-us/help/310123/ error-codes-in-device-manager-in-windows.
USB controller resource warnings	When you get warnings such as "Not Enough USB Controller Resources," try the following:
	▶ Manage and rearrange devices connected to USB ports.
	▶ Reserve USB 3.0 ports for USB 3.0 devices only, older devices should be connected to USB 2.0 ports.
	▶ Use a USB dock.
	▶ Add a USB adapter card.
	▶ Reinstall the USB Controller drivers in the Device Manager.
Services fail to start	▶ Start or restart services: **Run** > **services.msc**, right-click the service in question and choose **Properties**, and stop and start it within the Properties window. Or use the **net start** and **net stop** commands. Check for issues with other services that the affected service is dependent on. Also try modifying services in **MSConfig** > **Settings** or with the **Restart-Service** cmdlet in PowerShell. (See the following site for more on this cmdlet: https://docs.microsoft.com/ en-us/powershell/module/microsoft.powershell.management/ restart-service?view=powershell-7.2.)
	▶ Verify that the services have not been disabled in MSConfig or the Services console window.
Time drift	Time drift (or "clock drift") occurs when Windows is not synchronized to a time server properly, and the clock slowly drifts away from standard time. It might then synchronize to the motherboard's Real Time Clock (RTC). Try the following:
	▶ Use Network Time Protocol (NTP) to synchronize the Windows system to a time server.
	▶ Synchronize the Windows system to the domain controller (if the system is a member of that domain).

Symptom	Potential Solutions
Slow profile load	Slow profile loading is often due to a bloated user profile (especially roaming profiles). Check the following: ▶ Clean up temp files and cookies with cleanup programs and manually. For example: c:\Users\%username%\AppData\Local\Microsoft\Windows\ Temporary Internet Files c:\Users\%username%\AppData\Roaming\Microsoft\Windows\ Cookies ▶ Verify that the workstation's time is synchronized to the domain controller (if on a domain). Use the **net time** command. For example, log on locally and type **net time *domaincontroller*/set**. ▶ Check the User Profile service for issues. ▶ Watch for too many programs loading at startup. ▶ Configure policies via **gpedit.msc: Computer Configuration > Administrative Templates > System > Group Policy** (and similar policies). ▶ Run the Windows Troubleshooter. ▶ Roll back updates (if necessary).
Corrupted profile	▶ Copy the profile to a new account. Do this at **Run > systempropertiesadvanced.exe** and click the **Settings** button in the User Profiles section. Or copy the entire folder or just the ntuser.dat file, as required. ▶ Repair the user profile within the Registry Editor. ▶ Remove, rename, and/or rebuild the profile.

> **ExamAlert**
>
> Know how to get to the troubleshooters in Windows (**Settings** > **Update & Security** > **Troubleshoot** > **Additional troubleshooters**) and know the various troubleshooting tools, such as those for Internet connections, playing audio, printers, and so on.

> **Note**
>
> You can also use "God Mode" for troubleshooting. See Chapter 47, "Windows Security Settings," for a refresher. When you open that control panel, search "troubleshooting" or scroll way down to see all of the Windows troubleshooters.

A Final Word on Windows Troubleshooting

Here's the thing about troubleshooting: It goes on and on. Many problems may occur and there are usually multiple potential solutions to each problem. What works today on one version of Windows might not work tomorrow on another version of Windows. Be ready to think outside the box and use that six-step troubleshooting methodology as a guide while prioritizing the probable causes and potential solutions. Also, visit https://support.microsoft.com and https://docs.microsoft.com often.

Cram Quiz

Answer these questions. The answers follow the last question. If you cannot answer these questions correctly, consider reading this chapter again until you can.

1. Which option starts the operating system with a minimal set of drivers?

   - ○ **A.** Windows RE
   - ○ **B.** System Restore
   - ○ **C.** Safe Mode
   - ○ **D.** Debugging Mode

2. Which tool should be used if you want to use Startup Repair in Windows?

   - ○ **A.** File History
   - ○ **B.** Windows RE
   - ○ **C.** System Restore
   - ○ **D.** Safe Mode

3. Jack, an end user at your company, copied files from a USB thumb drive to his PC. When he was done, he updated his computer and restarted it. Then he received the error message "NO OS FOUND." Which of the following should you try *first* to fix the problem?

   - ○ **A.** Reboot the computer.
   - ○ **B.** Check the SATA cables.
   - ○ **C.** Check the BIOS/UEFI boot order.
   - ○ **D.** Uninstall, reinstall, and update applications.
   - ○ **E.** Perform a hardware diagnostics check.

4. One of your customers updated the software for a wireless adapter on a PC. After rebooting, the user logged in, and the computer displayed a blue screen. What should you do?

   ○ **A.** Install the device on a known good computer.

   ○ **B.** Reboot the computer and access debugging mode.

   ○ **C.** Purchase a new wireless adapter.

   ○ **D.** Roll back the device drivers in Safe Mode.

5. A technician suspects protected Windows system files may be corrupt. What should the tech do first to verify these suspicions and fix any potential problems?

   ○ **A.** Run a system file check.

   ○ **B.** Roll back updates.

   ○ **C.** Restart all services.

   ○ **D.** Rebuild Windows profiles.

6. A stop error could manifest as which of the following?

   ○ **A.** A BSOD

   ○ **B.** An Event Viewer error

   ○ **C.** An Action Center notification

   ○ **D.** An Edge error

7. Which tool can be used to restore a computer?

   ○ **A.** **bootrec /fixboot**

   ○ **B.** System Restore

   ○ **C.** Windows Troubleshooter

   ○ **D.** MSConfig

8. Which of the following might cause a blue screen?

   ○ **A.** A faulty USB port

   ○ **B.** A CPU without a fan

   ○ **C.** Bad drivers

   ○ **D.** A program compatibility issue

9. You are tasked with repairing an issue with a Windows client computer that is attempting to log on to a domain. The user informs you that it takes 5 minutes to log on to the domain, but logging in to the local machine takes only 15 seconds. What steps should you take to fix the problem? (Select the two best answers.)

- ○ **A.** Clean up temp files.
- ○ **B.** Disable unnecessary services in MSConfig.
- ○ **C.** Update the BIOS/UEFI boot order.
- ○ **D.** Synchronize the Windows client's time to the domain.
- ○ **E.** Run **ipconfig /release** and **ipconfig /renew**.

Cram Quiz Answers

1. C. Safe Mode starts the operating system with a minimal set of drivers. Windows RE (WinRE) is the recovery environment used to repair Windows; it exists outside the operating system. System Restore is used to revert the OS to an earlier point in time. Debugging mode is one of the Advanced boot options.

2. B. Windows RE includes Startup Repair. File History is the backup and restore feature of Windows. Safe Mode is part of the Startup Settings screen. System Restore is a different tool that is also available in Windows RE; it can be used to restore a computer's settings to a previous point in time.

3. C. Check the BIOS/UEFI boot order first. In the scenario, it is likely that the user left the USB flash drive in the USB port of the computer when he restarted the system. It follows that USB is set first in the BIOS boot order, and therefore the system could not boot to the main storage drive that houses the OS. While this could also be fixed by simply disconnecting the USB drive, the BIOS boot order should be changed immediately as having USB first is a security issue. Generally, end users should not be rebooting PCs (and you might even have a policy enforcing this); however, the user had already restarted the system. (By the way, end users usually should not update their systems, either.) Opening the computer and checking cables should be further down the troubleshooting list because these steps take time (and are most likely not the issue here). Uninstalling, reinstalling, and updating all applications could take an enormous amount of time and has very little to do with the problem. If removing the USB flash drive and modifying the BIOS boot order doesn't fix the problem, a hardware diagnostics check might be necessary.

4. D. You should boot into Safe Mode and roll back the drivers of the device in the Device Manager. The drivers that the customer installed were probably corrupt and caused the stop error. There's no need to remove the device and install it anywhere just yet. Debugging mode probably won't be necessary for this; it is more commonly used to analyze issues during boot. Never purchase new equipment until you have exhausted all other ideas!

5. A. The technician should first run System File Check (SFC) to verify whether or not operating system files are corrupt. The technician might also be tempted to check the physical integrity of the disk with the **chkdsk** command, but this is different from checking protected Windows system files. Rolling back updates might be necessary but could cause more issues than it solves. Plus, the idea here is to *check* the system files first without actually *doing* anything. Restarting all services would seem to be a bit extreme for this scenario, but it could be done in **MSConfig > Services** or with the PowerShell **Restart-Service** cmdlet. However, it would probably be wiser to focus on a few select services first instead of restarting all of them. Windows profiles are separate from the protected system files; the technician should rebuild these files if he suspects that there are problems with user accounts.

6. **A.** A BSOD (blue screen of death) results from a stop error in Windows. The proper name for it is a stop error.

7. **B.** System Restore is the tool used to restore a computer to an earlier point in time. While it doesn't completely restore from an image, it is still a form of restoration. The command **bootrec /fixboot** is used to repair the boot sector of the storage drive. The Windows Troubleshooter is a group of troubleshooting tools that can repair issues related to the Internet connection, printers, and so on. MSConfig is used to modify how Windows boots and which services are run.

8. **C.** Bad drivers could cause a blue screen error (stop error). Blue screens could also be caused by improperly seated RAM, among other hardware issues. A faulty USB port should not cause a blue screen. A CPU installed without a fan would overheat, causing the system to shut down. Incompatible programs simply don't run.

9. **A and D.** Apparently, the user's roaming profile is loading slowly, and the local profile is fine. This could be caused by a variety of things, including: a bloated roaming profile or the client not being synchronized to the domain properly. So, first try cleaning up temp files and cookies (either with a cleanup program or manually), cleaning up the login script, and otherwise reducing the size of the profile. Then make sure that the client computer's time is synchronized to the domain controller (which can also help with *time drift*). Do this with the **net time** (or **w32tm**) command. Disabling unnecessary services is always a good idea, but it is unlikely that doing so will improve the logon process to the domain very much, especially if the local logon is quick. Updating the BIOS/UEFI boot order isn't necessary because the system is booting to Windows just fine. Releasing and renewing the IP address shouldn't be necessary in this scenario, but it can be helpful when troubleshooting no (or limited) connectivity issues.

Remember that troubleshooting is what we technicians do. It's all about persistence: Keep searching for answers!

CHAPTER 54

Troubleshooting PC Security Issues

This chapter covers the following A+ 220-1102 exam objectives:

▶ **3.2** – Given a scenario, troubleshoot common personal computer (PC) security issues.

▶ **3.3** – Given a scenario, use best practice procedures for malware removal.

In Chapter 45, "Wireless Security and Malware," we discussed the types of malicious software you should know for the exam. Now that we've covered a lot more security information, as well as some Windows troubleshooting methods, let's get into how to resolve malware-based security issues and discuss proper malware removal.

In this chapter, we're covering two objectives because they are closely related. We'll be looking at Objective 3.3 first so that we can discuss the malware removal process. While going through this chapter, keep in mind that some organizations don't want to troubleshoot malware *at all*. They simply wipe a problematic system, re-image it, and restore the data afterward. That method has its place in the IT field, but in this chapter, for the most part, we will be concentrating on resolving malware issues via removal. You might hear the terms "antivirus software," "anti-malware program," "endpoint protection platform," and other similar terms. They are all essentially the same thing, and I will for the most part use the term *anti-malware*.

We'll also discuss some closely related security issues that may or may not be malware related. Sometimes, a security issue may appear to be malware related, but really it is something different or something that was designed to look like malware. So be ready to troubleshoot with an open mind (as always) and look for alternative causes for the problems you face.

ExamAlert

Objective 3.3 concentrates on the steps involved with identifying, researching, quarantining, and remediating malware, including end-user education.

ExamAlert

Objective 3.2 focuses on common PC security issues and symptoms of malware.

The CompTIA A+ Seven-Step Malware Removal Procedure

As much as you try to protect computers from malware, it will eventually affect—or *infect*—one or more systems on your network. At that point, it is important to think logically and methodically. CompTIA offers some best practices for malware removal.

Here is the CompTIA-recommended procedure for the removal of malware:

1. Investigate and verify malware symptoms.

2. Quarantine the infected systems.

3. Disable System Restore in Windows.

4. Remediate infected systems.

    a. Update anti-malware software.

    b. Scanning and removal techniques (e.g., safe mode, preinstallation environment).

5. Schedule scans and run updates.

6. Enable System Restore and create a restore point in Windows.

7. Educate the end user.

ExamAlert

Know the CompTIA A+ malware removal procedure.

Malware Removal Scenario

Let's take a look at an example of using the CompTIA-recommended seven-step process. In this scenario, a user in the marketing department contacts you and says he thinks his computer is infected. You initiate a trouble ticket and then walk over to the person's computer to investigate. To start, you need to gather information by analyzing the computer and talking to the user. Let's go through the steps now.

1. Investigate and Verify Malware Symptoms

Before you do anything else, you should investigate the problem and gather information about it. It's important that you verify that a problem is potentially malware based before you go any further with the malware removal process.

So back to the scenario: When you arrive at the user's computer, the user tells you that since this morning, the system has been booting and running much more slowly than usual. Also, you witness that he cannot open a couple of important applications that are stored locally. Based on this information, you decide that there is a chance that the computer is infected with a virus, as these are common symptoms of viruses.

> **Note**
>
> Before making any changes, make sure you back up any critical data!

2. Quarantine the Infected Systems

At this point, the computer should be quarantined—logically and possibly physically. The system should be taken off the network. If it is wired to the network, disconnect it. If it is wireless, put it in airplane mode or disable the wireless adapter in the Device Manager. In some cases, you will work on the computer where it is located, but if possible, shut it down and physically isolate it by taking it to the computer bench or some other lab environment where it can be worked on further.

> **Note**
>
> An organization might have a policy that states a system should be isolated immediately at the slightest mention of a virus or malware. So, depending on the situation, you might have to remotely shut down the system, take it off the network, or otherwise quarantine it before you even start this malware removal process.

3. Disable System Restore in Windows

System Restore can get in the way of proper analysis of a system, so it is recommended that you disable it before doing anything else. Do this by accessing the System Protection tab of the System Properties dialog box (**Run > systempropertiesprotection.exe**). Highlight any drives that have protection turned on (one at a time) and then click the **Configure** button. The System Protection dialog box for that particular volume appears, as shown in Figure 54.1. Click the **Disable system protection** radio button. Do this for each volume that has system protection enabled.

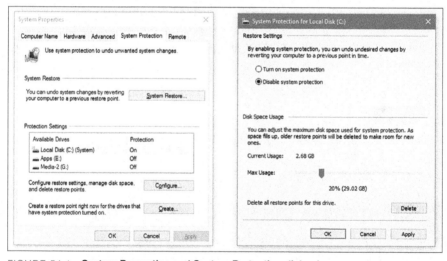

FIGURE 54.1   **System Properties and System Protection dialog boxes**

> **Note**
>
> Other systems, such as macOS and Linux, should have similar restoration programs disabled (if any). The idea is to disable any programs that might interfere with the scans you are going to run.

4. Remediate the Infected Systems

Check and update the anti-malware software on the machine. Is it running properly? Can it update? Verify that the update brings it to the latest version. Next, it's time to scan the system. This is best done from Safe Mode in Windows or from a preinstallation environment such as WinRE (see Chapter 53, "Troubleshooting Microsoft Windows," for details on how to access those) or from a bootable USB flash drive with its own OS or repair/recovery environment. These modes and environments reduce the chance that the virus (or other malware) will be able to interfere with your scans and remediation techniques.

> **Note**
>
> At this point, you might encounter problems performing the tasks required. Tougher malware is designed to stop a person from disabling System Restore or from updating (or even using) an anti-malware program. The toughest malware slows Safe Mode to a crawl or makes it difficult to otherwise use the system. If this happens, you should seriously consider re-imaging the system.

Once the anti-malware program has been updated, initiate a full scan of each volume systematically. These scans can be time-consuming, so be prepared to multitask. (Aren't you always ready to multitask anyway?) You might opt to scan the system from a separate OS running on a USB flash drive or on another system altogether. (You might have removed and isolated the target storage drive.) Working from an external system can be a powerful way to resolve problems and is a common practice. In any case, scan each volume individually and log the results.

Chances are that you will find one or more pieces of malware. If you do, quarantine, remove, and/or delete them as suggested in the anti-malware program (or programs) that you are using and according to organizational policy.

Scan the system again to verify that all malware has been taken care of. Then boot the system and make sure it does not have the same symptoms as before. The system should boot at the appropriate speed, and the programs that were problematic before should now run properly. If there are still problems, you will need to take additional measures, and, once again, you should consider re-imaging.

> **ExamAlert**
>
> Remember that the remediate step for removing malware includes using scanning and removal techniques in Safe Mode or from a preinstallation environment such as WinRE.

In less common scenarios, you might need to remove registry entries that were added by malware. In the case of a boot sector virus, you'll have to boot the system to external media or relocate the storage drive to your testing computer for full analysis.

5. Schedule Scans and Run Updates

If the system has been given the thumbs up and is now certified for use, you need to access the anti-malware program again and schedule periodic scans of the system. Also make sure that scheduled updates are turned on and are defined based on company policy. Many organizations use corporate-level, centrally managed antivirus solutions—known as *endpoint protection platforms*. These programs can push out updates to all the computers on the network at once. Create a profile for all the computers within a group that should be affected by these updates.

This step is all about preventive maintenance, and there are lots of other things you can do to make a PC stronger. For example, you can enable Secure Boot in the BIOS/UEFI (if it isn't already enabled); you can enable No-eXecute (NX) bit technology in the BIOS (for compliant CPUs), which can help stop viruses from infecting code; you can update the OS; and so on. Be ready to *harden* the computer system.

6. Enable System Restore and Create a Restore Point (in Windows)

Turn System Restore back on for all drives that require it. Then create a restore point. In the System Properties dialog box, you do this by clicking the **Create** button toward the bottom of the window (refer to Figure 54.1). This way, if a problem occurs in the future, you can go back in time, so to speak, to the point where the malware was removed and the system was functioning normally.

7. Educate the End User

At this point, the computer is ready for use. Reconnect the system to the network and explain to the end user what you did and why. Explain what happened to the system. In this particular scenario, there wasn't much that the user could have done to prevent the problem. However, sometimes end users click unknown links or attempt to install untrusted software. Explain in an amicable way that it is not good for a computer to take such risks. Educate the end user on how to safely operate the system.

> **Note**
>
> Educate users to watch out for rogue antivirus programs. These are malicious programs that appear to be antivirus programs, using similar names and logos as the real thing. Keep a sharp eye out for programs masquerading as other programs!

Symptoms of Viruses

The previous scenario mentioned a couple typical symptoms of viruses, but there are more. If a computer is infected by a virus, you want to know what to look for so that you can "cure" the computer. Here are some additional typical symptoms of viruses:

- ▶ Internet access, or network access is blocked or is redirected.

- ▶ You receive unusual error messages or security alerts, which are most likely false (for example, false alerts regarding antivirus protection).

- ▶ System files or personal files are altered. Perhaps they are missing or have been renamed. Maybe they have been corrupted, and perhaps folders are created automatically.

- ▶ Unwanted notifications occur within the operating system.

- ▶ Windows Update fails.

- ▶ The computer runs more slowly than usual.

- ▶ The computer/PC operating system locks up frequently or stops responding altogether.

- ▶ The computer restarts on its own or crashes frequently.

▶ Storage drives and applications are not accessible or don't work properly.

▶ Applications crash (which could also be a sign of a Trojan that has exhausted the resources needed to run the application).

▶ Permission to specific files and folders is denied, and "access denied" errors appear.

▶ Strange sounds occur.

▶ Display or print distortion occurs.

▶ New icons appear or old icons (and applications) disappear.

▶ There is a "double extension" on a file attached to an email that was opened (for example, .txt.vbs or .txt.exe). These are designed to trick a user into thinking the file attachment is a text file, when in reality it is a potentially dangerous script or executable.

▶ Antivirus programs do not run, can't be installed, or can't be updated.

Symptoms of Spyware

Spyware designed to spy on the user and attempt to gain confidential information. Be on the lookout for it. Here are some common symptoms of spyware:

▶ The web browser's default home page has been modified. This is a type of browser redirection, and it is a very common browser-related symptom.

▶ A particular website comes up every time you perform a search.

▶ Excessive pop-up windows appear. Rogue antivirus applications and security alerts seem to appear out of nowhere, supposedly scanning the system.

▶ The network adapter's activity LED blinks frequently when the computer shouldn't be transmitting data.

▶ The firewall and antivirus programs turn off automatically.

▶ New programs, icons, and favorites appear.

▶ Odd problems occur in Windows. For example, the system might be slow, applications might behave strangely, and so on.

▶ The Java console appears randomly.

More Symptoms of PC Security Issues and Potential Solutions

There are some more symptoms that we have not covered yet. Those symptoms and some potential solutions to them are listed in Table 54.1.

TABLE 54.1 **PC Security Symptoms and Solutions**

Symptom	Potential Solutions
Browser redirection	▶ Check for a redirect in the browser home page setting. For example, for Edge, go to **edge://settings/startHomeNTP**. For Chrome, go to **chrome://settings/onStartup**. ▶ Check for redirects in the hosts file (located in C:\Windows\system32\drivers\etc). ▶ Check whether websites have been added to the Trusted Sites section of the browser. ▶ Run anti-malware scans. Watch for spyware and viruses.
Invalid certificate issue/certificate warnings	▶ Analyze and verify installed certificates in the trusted root of the **Certificate Manager (Run > certmgr.msc) > Trusted Root Certification Authorities**. ▶ Analyze the Security log file in the Event Viewer for information on individual events concerning invalid certificates. ▶ Delete, export, revoke, and otherwise modify the certificates that are invalid and import new trusted certificates from a trusted certificate authority.
Invalid email certificate	If there is no malicious activity: ▶ Import new certificates for all parties concerned. For example, in Outlook, go to **File > Options > Trust Center > Trust Center Settings > Email Security**. Then import a new digital ID (certificate). (Be sure to select the **Add digital signature to outgoing messages** checkbox.) ▶ Publish the certificate appropriately if the certificate server being used is not properly integrated with other platforms on the network (for example, Microsoft Exchange Server). If there is potential malicious activity: ▶ Analyze the Event Viewer System, Application, and Security logs. ▶ If needed, revoke the current certificate, create a new one, and import it to all parties concerned. ▶ Scan the system and change account passwords.
Computer is being remotely controlled by an unknown entity	▶ Scan for malware, especially Trojans. ▶ Disable Remote Desktop and Remote Assistance, as well as any third-party remote-control software such as RealVNC.

Symptom	Potential Solutions
Ransomware hoax alerts	If it is real, then files are encrypted and locked. But there are many ransomware hoaxes as well that occur when a person stumbles onto an infected or malicious website. If this happens

  ▶ Block websites and domains from which the web pages are initiated.

  ▶ Check for browser redirection.

  ▶ Train users not to click the X button to close the browser. Instead, end the application or underlying background process within the Task Manager.

> **ExamAlert**
>
> Know the common symptoms of malware and how to troubleshoot and resolve them.

Cram Quiz

Answer these questions. The answers follow the last question. If you cannot answer these questions correctly, consider reading this chapter again until you can.

1. Which of the following are symptoms of viruses? (Select the three best answers.)
   - ○ **A.** A computer runs slowly.
   - ○ **B.** A computer is unable to access the network.
   - ○ **C.** Excessive pop-up windows appear.
   - ○ **D.** A strange website is displayed whenever a search is done.
   - ○ **E.** Unusual error messages are displayed.

2. Which of the following is the best mode to use when scanning for viruses?
   - ○ **A.** Safe Mode
   - ○ **B.** Reset this PC
   - ○ **C.** Command Prompt only
   - ○ **D.** Boot into Windows normally

3. You have been tasked with repairing a computer that is exhibiting the following symptoms:
   - ▶ Excessive pop-up windows appear.
   - ▶ A particular website comes up every time the user searches.

What is the most likely cause?

○ **A.** Spam

○ **B.** Virus

○ **C.** Social engineering

○ **D.** Trojan

○ **E.** Spyware

4. A co-worker technician is using certmgr.msc to analyze a problem with a computer. Which of the following issues is the technician most likely troubleshooting?

○ **A.** Trusted root CA

○ **B.** Hijacked email

○ **C.** Spyware

○ **D.** Browser redirection

5. You are tasked with removing malware from a Windows computer. You already performed research on the malware and have determined that it is a memory virus. Which step should you take next?

○ **A.** Educate the user.

○ **B.** Quarantine the affected system.

○ **C.** Remediate the affected system.

○ **D.** Disable System Restore points.

6. Several computers were infected with malware after end users clicked unknown links embedded in emails. You have successfully applied the first six steps of the best practice procedures for malware removal. What should you do next?

○ **A.** Schedule scans and run updates.

○ **B.** Enable System Restore and create a restore point.

○ **C.** Document findings, actions, and outcomes.

○ **D.** Educate the end users.

Cram Quiz Answers

1. **A, B, and E.** Symptoms of viruses include a computer running slowly, unexplained loss of network access, and unusual error messages. Excessive pop-ups and strange websites displaying after searches are symptoms of spyware.

2. **A.** Safe Mode should be used (if your anti-malware software supports it) when scanning for viruses. Safe Mode is found in the Startup Settings of WinRE. Other options found there include Command Prompt only, which offers command-line

access only; and the option to boot into Windows normally. Reset this PC is a WinRE option that reinstalls Windows; in Windows 10, it can delete data or keep it during the reinstall.

3. **E.** The computer is most likely infected with spyware. Spam is the abuse of email or other messaging system. A virus infects a system and has symptoms that might include slow performance, application crashes, and computer lockups. Social engineering is a group of attacks done on a social level, such as shoulder surfing, Dumpster diving, tailgating, and so on. A Trojan is malware that is often used to gain access to remotely control a system or that acts as a container for the actual malware payload.

4. **A.** The technician is most likely investigating a certificate issue—which is why the tech is using the Certificate Manager (certmgr.msc). The Trusted Root CA (Certificate Authority) section in the Certificate Manager contains all the certificates that were issued to the computer by third-party companies, as well as certificates that were created on the computer itself. When double-clicked, each certificate will display the issuer and the validation dates. Make sure certificates are still valid! Delete any that are not valid and notify the appropriate companies or personnel.

5. **B.** The next step you should take is to quarantine the system. You already completed the first step (investigate and verify malware) and ascertained that the problem is a memory virus, so step 2 (quarantine the infected systems) would be the next logical step. During this step, you might isolate the system in a lab that has no network connectivity.

   Disabling System Restore points happens during step 3—after quarantining but before remediation (which is step 4). Educating the user happens last, as step 7.

6. **D.** You should educate the end users next. This is step 7 (the final step) of the CompTIA best practice procedures for malware removal. In this scenario, the end users clicked unknown links. Explain to them why this is a bad idea and what the result was—downtime and loss of productivity. Then consider proposing written policies, security controls, and training programs to prevent the issue from happening again. "Schedule scans and run updates" is step 5. "Enable System Restore and create a restore point" is step 6. "Documenting findings, actions, and outcomes" is a great idea! However, that is step 6 (final step) of a separate process—the CompTIA troubleshooting methodology, not the malware removal process.

Now we're really cooking! Great work! Review, take a short break, and then continue.

CHAPTER 55

Troubleshooting Mobile Operating Systems and Applications

This chapter covers the following A+ 220-1102 exam objective:

▶ **3.4** – Given a scenario, troubleshoot common mobile OS and application issues.

The number of mobile devices in the workplace has been steadily growing for a long time now, and with more devices come more problems that will need your attention. There is a bit of overlap between this chapter and Chapter 3, "Mobile Device Accessories and Ports," and Chapter 4, "Mobile Device Network Connectivity and Application Support." That's because the hardware and the software of a mobile device are very closely linked; a problem that occurs could be due to software, hardware, or both! So, you might want to refer to those chapters to get a little refresher on mobile device hardware and communications. Let's get troubleshooting!

> **ExamAlert**
>
> **Objective 3.4** focuses on the following common symptoms of mobile OS and application issues: application fails to launch, application fails to close/crashes, application fails to update, slow to respond, OS fails to update, battery life issues, randomly reboots, connectivity issues, and screen does not autorotate.

> **Note**
>
> I discuss mobile device batteries elsewhere in the book, and mobile battery troubleshooting specifically in Chapter 27, "Troubleshooting Mobile Devices."

Wireless Troubleshooting

Wireless difficulties make a up a good percentage of the total problems you will face when it comes to mobile devices. This section goes into some detail about Wi-Fi, Bluetooth, NFC, and AirDrop.

Wi-Fi Troubleshooting

Failed Wi-Fi can cause all kinds of issues, from applications not working, to Internet access failures, to problems updating the OS on a device. When troubleshooting mobile device wireless connections, always perform the following basic wireless troubleshooting techniques:

- ▶ Check whether the device is within range.

- ▶ Ensure that the correct SSID is entered (if manually connecting).

- ▶ Ensure that the device supports the encryption protocol of the wireless network.

- ▶ Ensure that the device is not in airplane mode.

- ▶ Make sure the user didn't inadvertently connect to an unintended Wi-Fi network. It happens more often than you might think, given the number of open Wi-Fi networks available today. And let's not forget about rogue access points and evil twins.

▶ Watch for tethering and mobile hotspots. Make sure they are not conflicting with the wireless connection.

▶ Check whether the cellular connection is conflicting with the wireless connection.

If you still have trouble, here are a few more methods you can try to connect or reconnect to a wireless network:

▶ Power cycle the mobile device.

▶ Power cycle the Wi-Fi.

▶ Remove, or "forget," the particular wireless network and then attempt to connect to it again.

▶ Consider using a Wi-Fi analyzer app to locate the wireless network in question. Sometimes these analysis apps can give you more information that can help to solve the connectivity problem. They're also great security tools for checking your own WAP. Just be careful because some of them use up a good deal of system resources and could possibly cause the battery to run hot.

▶ Access the advanced settings and check whether there is a Wi-Fi sleep policy, whether Wi-Fi scanning has been turned off, whether there is a proxy configuration, or whether a static IP address is used. Also, Wi-Fi Direct and WPS might need to be configured properly or disabled. Any of these could possibly cause conflicts. You might also try renewing the lease of an IP address, if the device is obtaining addresses from a DHCP server (which it most likely is). Some devices also have the option Best Wi-Fi Performance, which uses more power but might help when connecting to distant WAPs. Another possibility is that the mobile device needs to have an encryption certificate installed, which is usually done from here as well. The advanced settings will vary from device to device, but an example is shown in Figure 55.1. Note that the IP address and MAC address are shown at the bottom of the figure; if you ever need to know either of those addresses, this is a good place to go.

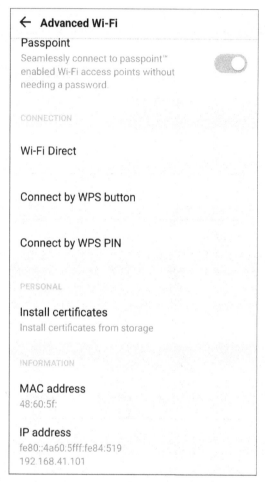

FIGURE 55.1 **Advanced wireless settings**

One of these methods usually works when troubleshooting a wireless connection, but if all else fails, a hard reset can bring the device back to factory settings. (Always back up all data and settings before performing a hard reset.) And if the mobile device still can't connect to any of several known good wireless networks, consider accessing the Developer options and the *super* advanced wireless settings (more on Developer options later) or take the device to an authorized service center.

You might also encounter issues where a device can connect to Wi-Fi but has a slow connection. In such a case, check the signal strength, the distance to the nearest AP, whether or not the device is connecting to the *correct* AP (if there is more than one option), and whether there are any obstructions.

ExamAlert

Know your Wi-Fi troubleshooting techniques!

Bluetooth Troubleshooting

If you have trouble pairing a Bluetooth device and connecting or reconnecting to Bluetooth devices or personal area networks (PANs), try some of the following methods:

▶ Make sure the phone or other mobile device is Bluetooth capable.

▶ Verify whether Bluetooth is enabled on the mobile device. Also, if applicable, verify whether it is enabled on the target device (for example, an automobile sound system).

▶ Verify whether your devices, especially Bluetooth headsets, are fully charged.

▶ Check whether you are within range. For example, Class 2 Bluetooth devices have a range of 10 meters.

▶ Restart the mobile device and attempt to reconnect.

▶ Check for conflicting Wi-Fi frequencies. Consider changing the channel used by the Wi-Fi network (if it is on 2.4 GHz).

▶ Use a known good Bluetooth device with the mobile device to make sure that the mobile device's Bluetooth is functional.

▶ Remove, or "forget," the particular Bluetooth device, turn off Bluetooth in general, restart the mobile device, and then attempt to reconnect.

▶ Check that the user didn't make an unintended Bluetooth connection. If a Bluetooth device doesn't have a passcode or other security methods implemented, it can easily be connected to another mobile device and vice versa.

ExamAlert

Know your Bluetooth troubleshooting techniques!

NFC and AirDrop Troubleshooting

A couple of other close-proximity wireless technologies that can cause headaches are NFC and AirDrop.

As mentioned in Chapter 3, near-field communication (NFC) allows mobile devices to communicate with each other by touching the devices together or by having them in close proximity to each other. If it fails to perform for a user, you can try a couple of things:

▶ Check whether the two NFC-compliant devices are in close proximity.

▶ Check whether the device is in airplane mode.

▶ Turn NFC off, wait five seconds, and turn it back on again.

▶ Try restarting the device.

▶ Attempt to clear any NFC cached data.

▶ Download updates for NFC or for the OS.

▶ Make sure the device is actually NFC compliant; it might not be, and if this is the case, the user will have to transfer data using other means.

AirDrop is a proprietary Apple protocol used to transfer files, images, and so on between two iOS devices and/or Mac computers that are in close range. It does this using a combination of Wi-Fi and Bluetooth technologies. AirDrop troubleshooting is similar to NFC troubleshooting in that you should make sure AirDrop is on, check for airplane mode, make sure that the devices are in close proximity to each other, and possibly restart the device. However, more specific to AirDrop, you should also take the following steps:

▶ Check Wi-Fi and Bluetooth individually because AirDrop relies on them both. Toggle them on and off if necessary.

▶ Check device compatibility. You will need a Mac computer using OS X (Yosemite) or later or a mobile device running iOS 7 or later.

▶ Check the different AirDrop levels of connectivity: off, contacts only, and everyone. For example, if a user has this set to "contacts only" and is trying send data to another person who is not in the contacts list, the transfer will fail.

▶ Try updating the device or resetting the network.

▶ If all else fails, do a hard reset.

Troubleshooting Email Connections

If you have trouble connecting an email account, try some of the following methods:

- ▶ Make sure the mobile device has Internet access. If connecting through the cellular network, make sure there is decent reception.

- ▶ Verify that the username, password, and server names are typed correctly. Remember that the username is often the email address.

- ▶ Check the port numbers. See Chapter 5, "TCP and UDP Ports and Protocols," for a list of ports. Be aware, however, that network administrators might decide to use non-default port numbers!

- ▶ Remember that secure email ports are preferred most of the time. Double-check whether security is required in the form of Transport Layer Security (TLS). For nonstandard port numbers and security configurations, check with your network administrator.

> **ExamAlert**
>
> When troubleshooting email connections on mobile devices, double-check all settings, such as username, password, server name, and port number.

You might also encounter issues where users cannot decrypt email communications. Encryption issues can happen on several levels, including at the server, during the email session, in individual emails themselves, and in attachments. Today, email sessions are based on TLS. The user's email account needs to log in to a secure server, making use of the correct protocol and port. We discuss that more in Chapter 5. If individual emails (or attachments) cannot be decrypted, then there is probably a certificate issue. If the problem affects only one user, the certificate should be checked at the mobile device; a new one will potentially have to be imported. In Figure 55.1, you saw an option in Android for installing certificates from storage. This can also be done from Encryption & credentials, as shown in Figure 55.2.

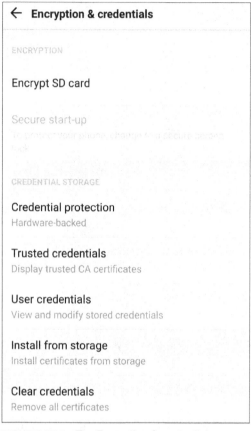

FIGURE 55.2 **The Encryption & credentials screen in Android**

From this screen, you can clear and install certificates and check trusted credentials. So, you could check whether a certificate has expired or has been revoked and import the new one if needed. Note that attachments might use a separate certificate from the main email certificate. With some mobile device management (MDM) solutions, certificates can be exported directly to mobile devices; just make sure to use an encrypted session between the MDM and a device to prevent the certificate from being compromised!

> **ExamAlert**
>
> If individual emails (or attachments) cannot be decrypted, then there is probably a certificate issue.

Troubleshooting and Stopping Applications

Sometimes applications fail to launch, close unexpectedly, or fail to update properly. Often, such issues call for a restart of the device, or possibly an update to the OS. In other cases, an application might need to be uninstalled and reinstalled; if this is the case, make sure that all data pertaining to the application is backed up accordingly.

You might encounter applications that continue to run in the background even after you close them. That behavior will continue unless you specifically turn off the apps within the OS or restart the device.

To turn off apps (or services) that are running on a typical Android-based system, go to App info or the Application Manager (or similar name). That screen displays all the currently running applications and services, though the services portion might be within a different tab of that screen. Like applications on PCs, mobile device apps use RAM. The more RAM that is used by a mobile device, the worse it will perform; high RAM usage makes a device slow to respond and eats up battery power. To close an app, you simply locate it on the list, tap it, and, on the next screen, tap **Force stop**. The left side of Figure 55.3 shows an example of an app info screen with the Force stop option. You can also stop services or processes in this manner. If you are not absolutely sure what a service is, do not initiate a Stop because it could possibly cause system instability. In the past, due to that instability, force stops were reserved for services; they are now an option on many devices for applications as well. Just remember that force stops can cause the OS to behave erratically. You can also clear the storage data and cache by tapping **Storage**, as shown on the right side of Figure 55.3. By clearing the data and cache, you can fix a lot of issues with applications.

To force quit an app on an iOS-based device, follow these steps:

1. From the Home screen, swipe up from the bottom of the screen and pause slightly in the middle of the screen.

2. Swipe right or left to find the app that you want to close.

3. Swipe up on the app's preview to close the app.

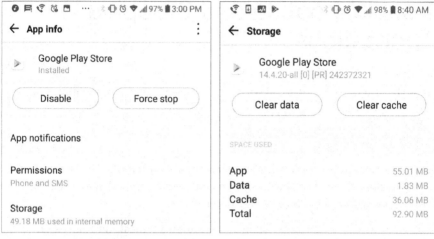

FIGURE 55.3 **The Force Stop option and Clear options in Android**

ExamAlert

Understand how to stop apps on Android and Apple devices.

There are third-party apps that can close down all the apps in one shot if you need to save time. However, these can cause erratic behavior. Finally, if an application is causing a device to lock up and you can't stop the app normally or through a force stop, then a soft reset or a hard reset will be necessary.

Initiating Resets

The screen on a mobile device may freeze so that tapping on the screen and pressing any buttons has no effect. To fix this problem, consider a soft reset. A *soft reset* is done by simply powering off the mobile device and powering it back on. (You might have to hold the Power button for longer than usual.) This resets the drivers and the OS. Soft resets are similar to shutting down a PC and powering it back up. Some technicians will also call this a *power cycle*. A soft reset can help when certain applications are not functioning properly or when network connectivity is failing. When a smartphone is still locked up when it is restarted, attempt a hard reset.

iOS-based devices can do a variety of more advanced software resets beyond a simple power cycle, such as Reset and Erase All Content and Settings. These are available by tapping **Settings** > **General** > **Transfer or Reset iPhone**.

A *hard reset* should be initiated only when things have gone terribly wrong—for example, when hardware or software has been compromised or has failed and a soft reset does not fix the problem. You need to make sure that all data is backed up before performing a hard reset because some hard resets will reset the mobile device back to the original factory condition.

> **Warning**
>
> All data will be wiped when a hard reset is initiated!

Hard resets (and forced restarts) vary from one device to the next. They can be initiated from within the OS, or they can be initiated by pressing a special combination of buttons, possibly while restarting the device.

> **Note**
>
> For more information on how to restart an iPhone X (or later) and an iPhone 8 (or earlier), visit https://support.apple.com/en-us/HT201559.
>
> For more information on how to restore an iPhone or iPad to factory settings, visit https://support.apple.com/en-us/HT201252.

More Mobile Application and OS Troubleshooting

The operating system and the loaded applications can give mobile device users some heartache—especially given how some people truly *love* their smartphones and tablets.

Updates: The Good and the Bad

We talked about keeping a device updated; in general, this is a good idea, especially for anti-malware applications. But sometimes, an update is not a good idea. For example, the latest version of a mobile OS might not work well on your device (even if the experts say it will). The older the device, the slower the CPU; and the newer the OS version, the more CPU resources it requires. Ultimately, the new version of an OS will not function as well on an older device. The same goes for the latest versions of apps, though not to such an extent. In the event that a device is updated and starts to work sluggishly, a downgrade may be necessary. This means going back to the original factory image for the device and usually requires a USB connection to a desktop computer, with USB debugging enabled. In order to enable USB debugging, some devices require you to enter developer mode, which can be done, for example, by tapping the build number (in About) seven times or using some other similar technique. Once you are in developer mode, you can enable USB debugging from Settings. Other devices allow you to select USB debugging when you first plug in the device via USB. You'll need to have a full battery before initiating a downgrade. Check your device documentation for more information or go to the manufacturer's website to find out how to enable USB debugging for a specific device.

Application Issues

Applications can also cause a mobile device OS to perform slowly or freeze the system altogether. If this happens, first restart the device. If that does not work, consider force stopping the application in question, uninstalling unnecessary apps, and possibly resetting the device. If you have previously enabled developer mode, you can access that and see a list of all running services and modify them from there.

Apps might also fail to load or might load very slowly. That could occur when there are too many apps open, or when the web browser has too many tabs open. It could also be a sign that there is no space left on the device. Close apps, close browser tabs, and remove and/or relocate apps to see if any of those actions fix the problem. On most Android devices, you can also clear the cache memory for the system and for individual apps. To clear the system cache, reboot the device into recovery mode (usually with a simultaneous button combination, such as Power, Volume Up, and Home) and then select **wipe cache partition** or an option with a similar name. Just be very careful not to select the factory reset option! It is often very close in proximity on the menu. Individual app cache (and app data) can be cleared on the same screen where force stops are performed.

Random Reboots

A device might randomly reboot. To troubleshoot this problem, try the following:

▶ Make sure the OS is up to date.

▶ Check storage and clear space, if needed.

▶ Close apps that are not being used.

▶ Remove the case and external batteries, if they are being used.

▶ Disable auto-restart.

▶ Check for bad apps, such as banned games or faulty untrusted apps, and uninstall them.

▶ Scan the device with an anti-malware program.

Poor Battery Life

We discussed battery life in depth in the 220-1101 section of the book, but it deserves a mention here, too. Poor battery life in smartphones may be attributed to the following:

▶ The battery is old (which often means the battery gets hot quite easily).

▶ The battery is damaged.

▶ Powerful applications are siphoning battery power (possibly running in the background).

▶ The battery is not charging properly. Check the charging cable and port.

▶ The phone is too hot. Powerful applications, GPS programs, and games could cause this and can make it more difficult for the battery to charge.

▶ The phone has wireless issues. For example, if it is in a signal dead spot, the phone will constantly attempt to search for signal, which causes the battery to drain. Additional wireless technologies such as GPS, Bluetooth, NFC, and so on, if running concurrently, can drain the battery.

See Chapter 27, "Troubleshooting Mobile Devices," for more information on how to conserve battery power.

Video Issues

If I had a dollar for every person who approached me with a video issue, I'd be a rich man. From dim displays to no display, damage to the screen, missing pixels, blinking screen, mobile devices can experience a number of video issues. Luckily, mobile device displays are more resilient today than they once were, but there are still some common issues that you should consider.

First is autorotate. It's amazing how easy it is to disable this function accidentally; users do it all the time. If a user is working on photos, videos, or apps that require autorotate, it can be a very frustrating to be without this function. The good news is that this particular fix is usually easy. For Android users, the solution is usually directly within the quick settings panel that can be swiped down from the top of the screen. In Android, this option is often called Rotation. In iOS, it is called Portrait Orientation Lock.

Earlier in the book, I said you can connect anything to anything else if you have the right adapter. That holds true for mobile devices. However, some adapters are made better than others. For example, it is wise to use an adapter made by Apple for connecting, say, an iPad's USB-C or Lightning port to an HDMI input. For Android devices, seek out quality adapters for connecting from USB-C-equipped Android devices to HDMI or to the USB port of an automobile. For both iOS and Android, make sure there is a solid connection and that you are using the correct adapter. Generally, this just works out of the box, even if screen sharing or screen mirroring is turned off because it relies on a cabled connection, not a wireless connection. The troubleshooting side of it is usually at the TV, monitor, or projector where the image is to be mirrored. Always remember to check the input option being used; it is usually part of the onscreen display (OSD).

> **Note**
>
> We discuss mobile video hardware and ports in the 220-1101 portion of this book.

On the software side of things, make sure that screen mirroring is enabled. Different Android devices have this setting in different places. One example is to go to **Network** > **Screen Sharing** (though Screen Sharing could also be in General, Display, or elsewhere, depending on the device). Verify that screen sharing is enabled. On the other end, make sure the device that is being shared to is accepting the connection. There could be a passcode required if you are connecting to some kind of casting device (Amazon Fire TV, Google Chromecast, Apple TV, and so on). Don't forget to check the volume on the mobile device as well. iOS devices use the Screen Mirroring option, which by default only connects to Apple TV devices, but there are third-party software offerings that can allow iOS devices to mirror to computer systems. Screen Mirroring can easily be found by double-tapping the **Home** button or swiping up from the bottom of the display.

> **Note**
>
> If a physical cable is connecting an iOS device to an external display, the Screen Mirroring name changes to Dock Connector. If you were to press **Stop mirroring**, you might need to restart the iOS device in order to enable mirroring again.

Cram Quiz

Answer these questions. The answers follow the last question. If you cannot answer these questions correctly, consider reading this chapter again until you can.

1. An application won't close on an Android smartphone. You've tried to force stop it—to no avail. What should you do?

   ○ **A.** Hard reset the device.

   ○ **B.** Stop the underlying service in Running Services.

   ○ **C.** Soft reset the device.

   ○ **D.** Take the device to an authorized service center.

2. Which of the following are valid Wi-Fi troubleshooting methods? (Select the two best answers.)

   ○ **A.** Power cycle the device.

   ○ **B.** Restart Bluetooth.

   ○ **C.** Use a static IP address.

   ○ **D.** Make sure the device is within range.

   ○ **E.** Rename the SSID of the AP.

3. A technician has turned the Portrait Orientation Lock off for an iPhone user. Which common mobile OS problem does this rectify?

   ○ **A.** The Camera app fails to launch.

   ○ **B.** The screen does not autorotate.

   ○ **C.** The OS fails to update.

   ○ **D.** The battery fails to hold a charge.

4. A user tells you that her iPad cannot send a large document to an iPhone that is in close proximity. The user can't use the Internet because the network connection is too slow. You start investigating and find that Wi-Fi and Bluetooth are disabled. After you reenable them, the document is sent with no problems. Which of the following technologies was the user most likely trying to work with?

- ○ **A.** NFC
- ○ **B.** AirDrop
- ○ **C.** Email
- ○ **D.** Bluetooth

Cram Quiz Answers

1. **C.** If you've already tried to stop the application within Running Services, attempt a soft reset. Hard resets on Android devices should be used only as a last resort because a hard reset will return a device to factory condition—wiping all the data. The question indicated that the application won't close, not that a service won't stop, though you could try finding an underlying service that might be the culprit. But you should try resetting the device before doing this or taking it to an authorized service center.

2. **A and D.** Valid Wi-Fi troubleshooting methods include power cycling the device and making sure the mobile device is within range of the wireless access point. Bluetooth could possibly cause a conflict with Wi-Fi. If you suspect that Bluetooth is interfering, simply turn off Bluetooth. Static IP addresses are one thing you can check for when troubleshooting. Normally, the mobile device should obtain an IP address dynamically from a DHCP server. Renaming the SSID of the access point could cause problems for all clients trying to connect. However, you should make sure that the correct SSID was typed if the connection was made manually.

3. **B.** If an iPhone's or iPad's screen won't autorotate, it is probably because the Portrait Orientation Lock setting is on and locking the display in place. Turning it off unlocks the option, allowing the screen to rotate. In Android, this is simply known as Rotation. If the Camera app fails to launch, you might need to restart and/or update the app or restart the phone. If the OS fails to update, you need to troubleshoot the Wi-Fi connection. If the battery fails to hold a charge, it will most likely need to be serviced.

4. **B.** The user is most likely trying to use the Apple AirDrop feature, which can send files between Apple devices in close proximity and relies on Wi-Fi and Bluetooth to function. NFC is similar and is commonly used on Android-based devices (though it can be used on Apple devices as well). If the user was trying to send a file between Apple devices that are in close proximity, then email is not necessary, though it would be a possible answer (if the Internet wasn't slow). While Bluetooth is instrumental in making connections between devices in order to use AirDrop (and is useful for connecting other devices, such as smart watches and earphones), it wouldn't be the first choice of an Apple device user.

Excellent. One more troubleshooting chapter to go! Review and then continue!

CHAPTER 56

Troubleshooting Mobile Operating Systems Security Issues

This chapter covers the following A+ 220-1102 exam objective:

▶ **3.5** – Given a scenario, troubleshoot common mobile OS and application security issues.

Okay, here's the last chapter on troubleshooting. This one continues on with mobile devices but concentrates more on security issues related to those devices. This is a short one, so take a seat. Ready? Learn!

> **ExamAlert**
>
> **Objective 3.5** concentrates on security concerns; Android package (APK) source, developer mode, root access/jailbreaking, bootleg/malicious application, and common symptoms; and high network traffic, sluggish response time, data-usage limit notifications, limited Internet connectivity, no Internet connectivity, high number of ads, fake security warnings, unexpected application behavior, and leaked personal files/data.

Mobile Device Security Concerns and Symptoms

Some of the most important security concerns are unauthorized access, loss of *authorized* access, and compromised or lost data. You need to protect against these things. In other words, you need to keep the bad guys out and the employees in—while preserving the data.

You can implement a variety of security measures, but you need to be careful not to *over-secure*. Too many hurdles for users can cause an unacceptable number of system lockouts. Lockouts translate to a loss of productivity for users and increased tech support calls to have accounts and/or devices unlocked. Over time, this costs the organization money and slows down projects.

That's why the "three strikes and you're out rule" is a good middle ground. It allows enough attempts for users to make some typos during the login process, but it provides a lockout for an attacker who tries to guess a user's password. This rule can be set up as a policy within an MDM and affect all mobile devices within the group. With a typical standalone mobile device, the lockout might last 15 minutes, and subsequent lockouts can be longer. However, when configuring this within an MDM, the lockout should be more severe, such as locking the account until an administrator confirms the user's identity and perhaps runs a quick interview. Even that might not be enough, however. Just because an account was locked out today doesn't necessarily mean it wasn't compromised previously. The simple fact that the lockout occurred should be a red flag. Many organizations will then launch an investigation at some level or at least do a basic analysis of the account. Logs should be checked for anomalous activity, resource usage should be looked into, and the admin should double-check for any unauthorized usage of the device, apps, or data.

Speaking of logs, be sure to view log files to ascertain whether any security issues have occurred within a mobile device's OS or applications. Some applications have their own logs that you can view. Many MDMs have log files that you *definitely* should review periodically. Finally, you can go deep into an individual mobile device programmatically. For example, with Android, you can use the Android SDK (software developer kit) and use the Android Debug Bridge (ADB) from a PC or another system—with USB debugging enabled on the mobile device. Look for errors and anomalous activity that might indicate a security breach.

> **ExamAlert**
>
> Periodically view log files to ascertain if any security issues have occurred within a mobile device's OS or applications.

Apps can be a real target. Remember I mentioned that every program installed on a computer increases the attack surface? One reason so many mobile devices get hacked is that there are a lot of apps out there, each of which poses a security risk to some extent. When you have the power to do so, limit the number of apps that users have access to. An attacker might attempt to gain information from an employee of a company by initiating unauthorized location tracking. This can be done with an app or through a backdoor of the OS or with malware, often a Trojan. If you suspect that this is happening, then disable location services until the problem is resolved.

Attackers may also attempt to take control of the camera/webcam and microphone of a mobile device to spy on a user. One way to tell if this is happening is by listening for shutter noises occurring when the user is not taking pictures. Temporary solutions include disabling (or unplugging) the camera/webcam, or covering the camera/webcam with masking tape, and force stopping any unknown applications. Another basic preventive action is to have the webcam indicate when it is in use, either with a light, tone, or message. Along those lines, you can also check application permissions. For instance, the Camera app will allow certain programs to make use of the camera. If there are any programs on that list that are not expected, are not desirable, or are potentially malicious, then disable them. For example, in Android, a typical navigation path would be **General > Apps & Notifications > App permissions**. From there, you will see the Camera app; tap it to find out which applications are using it and disable them as necessary.

As a security person, you need to look for high resource utilization or power drain on a mobile device. These can indicate that a Trojan has been installed that has taken control of the webcam or is working in a remote desktop manner. Another indicator is high data usage. When the data transmission for a device goes over the limit set by the cellular provider—or over a wireless transmission quota that your organization has set—it could be that the mobile device has been compromised and is working as a bot. It will cause the user to lose productivity.

If you suspect that there is unauthorized usage occurring on a mobile device, that device should be taken offline, isolated, scanned, and otherwise analyzed. In many cases, the device will have to be wiped (as per company policy) and re-imaged. If the device is used in a BYOD environment, re-imaging the company partition might be enough, but with some organizations, the device might be banned until the personal side is also re-imaged.

There are some additional concerns for Android and iOS specifically. The first is root access and jailbreaking. We discussed these issues in Chapter 49, "Mobile Device Security," but I have a few more thoughts on the subject. In a nutshell, Android rooting and iOS jailbreaking can be prevented through protection and detection. For example, an organization should use mobile devices that are "business-oriented"—that is, devices that use hardware protection that makes booting in a rooted fashion difficult. This hardware/firmware protection will analyze the OS as it boots and makes sure it hasn't been tampered with. This makes it nearly impossible to boot to any untrusted code. A sysadmin should use MDM software to scan for rooted devices. Many business-oriented mobile devices come with some type of attestation, which means they can reply to an MDM to reveal their true status and whether or not they are rooted. Also, there are third-party apps that can block rooting and/or jailbreaking. Users should also be careful about where they get software. When Android users obtain apps from Google Play and iOS users obtain apps from the Apple Store, these apps are usually scanned and are typically safe to use (though not always). However, Android users can also download application packages from other sources. The problem is that these other sources may or may not check the level of secure coding of an app. These Android packages (APKs) should be downloaded from trusted sources (such as APKMirror). Or an APK installer can be used instead.

> **ExamAlert**
>
> Know how to prevent rooting and jailbreaking.

You need to take the precautions described here when dealing with Android and iOS apps so that you can avoid rooting and jailbreaking and also to avoid malicious applications (and bootleg apps), as well as application spoofing. An app might look quite normal, but if it is downloaded from an untrusted source, it could actually be something else entirely.

Malicious apps can cause a variety of symptoms, some of which can have the same symptoms as malware—because, essentially, a malicious app *is* malware. Here are some symptoms that you might see:

▶ **Communications issues:** A device might have no or limited Internet connectivity, experience high network traffic volume, and get data-usage limit notifications.

▶ **Worrying messages:** A user might see a large number of advertisements and fake security warnings, which are often found when browsing to less-than-reputable websites.

▶ **Performance issues:** A user may experience sluggish response time of the OS in general or of specific apps, as well as unexpected application behavior.

▶ **Leaked personal files/data:** If this happens, the mobile device should be quarantined and isolated right away because this is a symptom of a larger and potentially devastating problem.

To summarize, you want to try to *prevent* the problems mentioned in this chapter from happening. Remember the old saying: "An ounce of prevention is worth a pound of cure." When it comes to mobile devices, prevention means updating anti-malware and firewalls, requiring strong passwords, disallowing public and open Wi-Fi hotspot connections, obtaining software from trusted sources, implementing anti-malware, using data loss prevention (DLP) to prevent leaked data, and, in general, locking down devices at the MDM workstation. These are some of the preventive measures you can take to protect the integrity of the data and keep it confidential while maintaining productivity of authorized users.

Cram Quiz

Answer these questions. The answers follow the last question. If you cannot answer these questions correctly, consider reading this chapter again until you can.

1. A user downloaded an APK from an untrusted source and installed it. Now the mobile device is suffering from slow performance. The user also shows proof that the device is leaking data. What happened to the device?

   - ○ **A.** Jailbreaking
   - ○ **B.** Application spoofing
   - ○ **C.** Developer mode
   - ○ **D.** Rooting

2. Which of the following could result from downloading something from an untrusted source? (Select all that apply.)

   - ○ **A.** Attestation
   - ○ **B.** Malicious apps
   - ○ **C.** Dead battery
   - ○ **D.** App spoofing

3. You suspect that a mobile device has been compromised and is now part of a botnet. What are some of the indicators that this has happened? (Select the two best answers.)

   - ○ **A.** High resource usage
   - ○ **B.** Notification of camera/webcam usage
   - ○ **C.** Apps force stopped
   - ○ **D.** Power drain
   - ○ **E.** Log files unavailable
   - ○ **F.** Locked user account

Cram Quiz Answers

1. **D.** Of the listed answers, the device has most likely been rooted, and someone else (or the application) has control of the system. The device should be taken offline, quarantined, and isolated immediately. The real issue is that the user downloaded a malicious application from an untrusted source. This application then took control of the system. A jailbreak occurs on iOS-based devices. We know that this is an Android-based device because the application downloaded was an Android package (APK). The user might have been fooled into thinking that the application was legitimate, but this isn't something that happened to the

device per se. Developer mode is used to take control of certain aspects of a mobile device, such as to enable USB debugging mode. While developer mode can be used maliciously, it is more likely that the primary issue here is that the phone was rooted.

2. **B and D.** Always download from trusted sources to avoid rooting and jailbreaking and also to avoid malicious/bootleg applications, as well as application spoofing. An app might look quite normal, but if it is downloaded from an untrusted source, it could actually be something devious. Many business-oriented mobile devices come with some type of attestation, which means they can reply to an MDM to reveal their true status and whether or not they are rooted.

3. **A and D.** If a mobile device has been compromised and added to a botnet, the user might know it but might experience high resource usage, power drain on the battery, and, less commonly, high data usage. You should check all of these things as well as any available logs. (If the logs are not available, then that could indicate other foul play.) Take the device off the network, isolate it, and run a scan of the device; you are on the hunt for Trojans especially. A notification of camera/webcam usage either means that the device is being used properly by the user or an attacker is attempting to spy on the user, but it doesn't mean that the mobile device has joined a botnet; it is possible but unrelated. If apps were force stopped, they might have been stopped by the user, or by a rogue app, or by an attacker who has taken control of the mobile device, but this is also a separate problem. If the user account was locked out, it could simply be that the user forgot the password and had too many failed attempts. Or, it could be that a hacker was attempting to guess the password, either directly or through covert means. Again, that's a separate problem. In all of these cases, the image should be preserved for later analysis, and the device should most likely be re-imaged to be sure that any bad apps, malware, and so on have been removed.

And that does it for the software troubleshooting section of this book. Well done. Review your notes for this chapter and for this entire section. Then break for a bit and recharge those little gray cells!

CORE 2 (220-1102)

Domain 4.0: Operational Procedures

CHAPTER 57

Documentation

This chapter covers the following A+ 220-1102 exam objective:

▶ **4.1** – Given a scenario, implement best practices associated with documentation and support systems information management.

Welcome to the first chapter of Domain 4.0: Operational Procedures. This domain is tied with Domain 3.0: Software Troubleshooting for the smallest percentage of the exam, but it's still packed with key information. So, as with all of the other domains, it is important that you understand the content.

We're shifting gears to the organizational, operational, and facilities side of things, so prepare for a bit of a different mindset. Because the goal is to prepare you for the A+ exam, we won't be going very deep into operational procedures, but you should know the basics.

Proper documentation is a key element of any organization. Without it, you have chaos. With it, you can at least bring some semblance of order to your networks, policies, and decisions. For you as a technician, the most important reason to have solid documentation is that it helps you troubleshoot problems. If a person on the team documents properly, that makes troubleshooting much easier for anyone else who encounters the same problem. If everyone documents well, it means increased productivity for the entire team. And one other thing: *Remember to leave documentation better than you found it.* If something is not accurate, make it so. Others will thank you, and you never know, you might thank yourself one day. (We all know that we technicians talk to ourselves sometimes!)

Types of Documents

There are all kinds of documents that you will work with in the IT field. In fact, with some organizations, the volume of documents is staggering. Here's one tip I need to give you right off the bat: Make use of your human resources department. Unless you are a compliance officer, chances are that you will not understand some of the documentation that your organization uses. Work with your HR department to navigate the sea of paper and e-paper that should be created, modified, and signed off on. Let them guide you to the personnel you will have to deal with on a day-to-day basis.

> **Note**
>
> Keep detailed notes. That's right: You need a document database to help you traverse the plethora of organizational documentation. It could be a simple paper notebook or an application such as OneNote, Evernote, or Joplin (my personal favorite).

Let's discuss some of the documents you will most commonly see and work with in the field, including network topology diagrams, incident report documentation, standard operating procedures, regulatory compliance requirements, acceptable use policies, and user checklists.

Network Topology Diagrams

To develop quality network documentation, an administrator should use network diagramming software, perhaps in conjunction with network mapping software. A good network diagram should show how computers and network devices are connected together—their *topology*. Figure 57.1 shows a basic example of a network diagram.

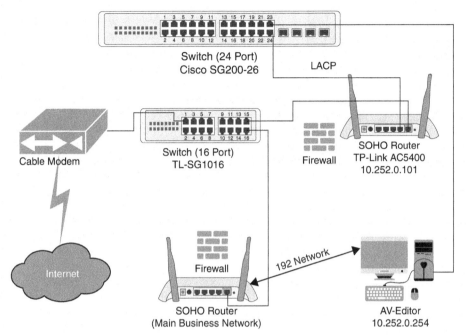

FIGURE 57.1 **Network diagram**

In the figure, you can see network switches, a couple of SOHO routers, a work-station, a cable modem, and the cloud/Internet. A topology is just one way of documenting a network; it doesn't show *where* the systems are, but it shows *how* they are connected. For example, in the diagram in Figure 57.1, there is a main switch that connects out to the Internet and has two other connections to separate firewalled LANs. My main workstation, *AV-Editor*, has access to both networks because it is a multi-homed computer, meaning it has two NICs. In general, a technician does not need to be overly concerned with the client computers, but it might be important to list particular workstations in the network diagram.

Figure 57.1 shows a high-level logical topology diagram; it shows IP addresses used by the LAN and certain systems, and it illustrates to which devices groups of computers are connected. However, sometimes diagrams get a little more detailed about the individual ports on switches and the actual physical connections; at that point, it might be referred to as a *physical network diagram*. A network diagram can focus on the physical, the logical, or both.

You can build a network diagram with a tool such as Microsoft Visio, or you can use network mapping software that will automatically search the network for hosts, including servers, routers, and switches. Combine the two, and you can come up with some pretty powerful network documentation.

> **ExamAlert**
>
> Network topology diagrams identify network components and how they are physically and/or logically connected.

You might also opt to use a spreadsheet to sort computers by name or IP address. Some companies use virtual notebooks or custom-made wikis for documentation that supplements network diagrams. And, of course, there are plenty of vendors that offer network documentation software solutions.

The whole point is to have solid documentation that you can refer to in the event of a problem or if you need to reconfigure network components or add or remove components to or from the network.

Incident Report Documentation

An *incident report* is a document that you maintain during the incident response process. It should be initiated at the onset of an event and continued through to the event's conclusion. If you know or even suspect that an incident is occurring, start recording all facts and information that you encounter. Use some type of logbook (hardcopy or digital, though I prefer hardcopy for this type of procedure), plus a mobile device with a webcam, another digital camera, an audio recorder, or a combination of these to record all the data you can.

Incident documentation is just a piece of incident response. We'll be discussing that process in more depth in Chapter 61, "Incident Response, Communication, and Professionalism."

Standard Operating Procedure

A *standard operating procedure (SOP)* is a document that shows, step-by-step, how to perform a routine operation, such as an installation of software, an upgrade, or an OS installation. Generally, in an effort to be software independent, an SOP should focus on the process at hand rather than on the tools to be used. The document should be written plainly so that just about anyone can understand it. Acronyms and technical jargon should be avoided.

For example, you as a technician may be called on to do custom software installations several times per week. The process can only be automated so much because the software installation process is customized for each system the software is installed on. Here's a basic SOP example for the installation of an application called *custom package #23*:

1. Log in to the target computer as a user with administrator privileges.

2. Verify that the target computer's operating system is up to date.

3. Download custom package #23 from the trusted intranet source.

4. Verify that the package has not been tampered with.

5. Begin the installation process.

   a. Answer the scripted questions based on the group that the particular computer is a member of. For example, computers with hostnames that start with *eng* are part of the engineering group. Note: Only users within that same group or organizational unit should be able to use this package.

   b. Once the files begin copying, start filling out Form #568 Rev B. Submit this to your manager when complete. Take note of any messages that appear on the screen and enter them into Form #568.

6. When the installation has completed, restart the computer.

7. Test package #23. Make sure it can connect to the main database.

8. Check for any errors or warning messages in the system's log.

9. Log off the target computer.

This is just off the top of my head, but you get the idea. An SOP is not technical, but it requires technical know-how, and some specific technology—such as using PGP or SHA to "verify that the package has not been tampered with." The procedure outlined in this SOP might seem simple, but when technicians are running many tasks at the same time, little things can be missed. That's one of the concepts of the SOP—to guide a tech step-by-step so that those "little things" are carried out properly. Remember that one little mistake can botch an installation, especially a custom installation of software.

Besides written SOPs, there are also software programs that can help you devise SOPs and store them in an organized fashion. This makes it easier when dealing with software installation policies that might include things such as the purpose, scope of work, records, privacy information, and specific policies for software to be installed. These policies might focus on more generic things that a tech needs to consider, such as installation options, upgrade considerations, data conversions, automated installations, terminal applications, and what to do if the software won't install properly.

Compliance and Regulatory Policy

Compliance is the process of making sure an organization and its employees follow the policies, procedures, regulations, standards, laws, and ethical practices that have been written by or that apply to an organization. The documentation related to compliance is called a *compliance policy*. Most corporations have one, and they are usually quite similar. This documentation is available to all employees, and it often includes principles of business conduct, such as no discrimination, integrity in business dealings, fair competition, proper record keeping, environmental sustainability, cooperation with authorities, and so on. Additional documentation will detail how to accomplish the compliance policy, such as with further policies and procedures. Generally, this type of documentation, or at least the overview, is publicly available via the Internet (as a PDF) and in print form.

Regulatory compliance might deal with the technical side of things as well. For example, to comply with an organization's marketing goals, you might be required to include a splash screen within a custom application. The splash screen is a window that contains a logo or other branding and that appears when an application is first started. In the background, the application gathers the resources necessary to function. To meet marketing objectives, the splash screen will have to be designed with the latest logo, trademark and registered symbols, and proper color scheme. Or, depending on the application (especially with in-house apps), an organization might deem splash screens an unnecessary waste of a developer's time.

There are organizations that create standardized policies and procedures. One example is the International Organization for Standardization (ISO). An organization that follows a particular ISO standard can be certified as ISO compliant for that standard, such as ISO 9001:2015, *Quality Management Systems—Requirements*, or ISO/IEC 27002:2013, *Information Technology—Security Techniques*. An organization has to be examined and accredited by an accrediting certification body to be deemed ISO certified. This is a rigorous process that an organization should not take lightly. Also, keeping up the standard can create *too much* documentation and could possibly bog down the organization in details and minutia if it doesn't have the appropriate compliance personnel.

These personnel must be well trained in the day-to-day operations of the organization and its procedures; have a strong understanding of information technology; and be well versed in how to read, update, and publish technical documentation.

For an organization that doesn't have the necessary personnel or wherewithal to certify to, or use, the ISO standards, it can still incorporate individual guidelines such as NIST SP 800-88 (*Guidelines for Media Sanitization*), which we spoke of in Chapter 50, "Data Destruction and Disposal." The National Institute of Standards and Technology (NIST) has plenty of guidelines such as this that an organization can use to model its IT infrastructure and overall security plan. These guidelines are freely available and can be integrated with an organization's documentation.

Regulatory policies of an organization attempt to achieve compliance with a government's objectives through laws and regulations. Now we're going beyond standards and moving into the realm of law. For example, in many organizations, compliance personnel must confirm that certain laws are being followed, especially as they pertain to personally identifiable information (PII)—for instance, the Privacy Act of 1974 (2015 edition), which establishes a code of fair information practice, and the Sarbanes-Oxley Act (SOX), which governs the disclosure of financial and accounting information. Most industries are regulated to some extent, and it falls to the compliance people to know about applicable laws.

> **Note**
>
> As a technician, you should take a look at regulatory laws to get a better idea of what is expected of an organization and what an organization might expect from you and any other employees and contractors. Also, consider looking at some of the compliance management software suites available on the Internet.

Acceptable Use Policy

Acceptable use policies (AUPs) define the rules that restrict how a computer, network, or other system may be used. They state what users are allowed to do when it comes to the technology infrastructure of an organization. Often, an AUP must be signed by employees before they begin working on any systems.

An AUP protects an organization, and it also defines to employees exactly what they should and should not be working on. If a director asks a particular employee to repair a particular system that is outside the parameters of the

AUP the employee signed, the employee should know to refuse. If employees are found working on a system that is outside the scope of their work, and they signed an AUP, that could be grounds for termination. As part of an AUP, employees enter into an agreement acknowledging they understand that the unauthorized sharing of data is prohibited. Also, employees should understand that they are not to take any information or equipment home without express permission from the various parties listed in the policy. The idea behind this is to protect the employee, the sensitive data (especially PII), the company systems (from viruses and network attacks), and the organization itself (from legal action).

User Checklists (Onboarding and Offboarding)

Most organizations have checklists for the setup of new users and for what to do when a user is terminated. For example, new users need a user account in the domain, need some type of system or device to work on, need access to certain areas of the building, and so on. Users who are terminated need to have their computer accounts disabled (not deleted) and their security clearances revoked. These checklists might be incorporated within onboarding and offboarding processes.

Onboarding is the process of adding an employee to an organization and to its identity and access management system. It includes training, formal meetings, lectures, and human resources employee handbooks and videos. It can also be implemented when a person changes roles in an organization. Onboarding is a socialization technique used to ultimately provide better job performance and higher job satisfaction.

Offboarding is the process of removing an employee from an organization's systems, restricting rights and permissions, and possibly debriefing the person or conducting an exit interview. This happens when a person changes roles within an organization or departs the organization altogether.

Knowledge Bases/Articles

Well, I've been referencing knowledge base articles throughout the book, especially Microsoft-related articles. But a knowledge base (KB) is more than articles written by a company; the information is also spread among community support, forums, and blogs. It's important to know *where* and *how* to find the information you seek.

The "where" I can answer with this: Go to the source! I say it often: Use the websites created by manufacturers of hardware and developers of software. For example, if you are supporting Windows 10 clients, use the Microsoft support sites. If you are using Western Digital storage drives, use the Western Digital support site. Remember this when using an Internet search engine. Often, you will get third-party results, which may or may not contain accurate data. So always start by going to the source. Doing so can help prevent information overload.

The "how" might differ depending on which vendor's site you visit, but for the most part, vendors' sites are internally searchable by phrase or by KB number. Once you get the knack for searching, you can learn how to do almost everything with a product by using the support website—from installation and configuration to security and troubleshooting. Let's take a look at a couple of examples, starting with Microsoft since it is so prevalent on the A+ exams.

The Microsoft Knowledge Base is spread among multiple websites and has hundreds of thousands of articles and posts from Microsoft employees and from the Microsoft "community." To search the Knowledge Base, simply go to one of the following sites and type in the search term or KB article number that you wish to learn more about:

▶ **Microsoft Support (https://support.microsoft.com):** This is the main support site that Microsoft offers for end users and for IT professionals. Over the years, a lot of content from other Microsoft sites has been redirected here. Also, Microsoft has moved away from the term "Knowledge Base" to a certain degree and often uses terms such as "help" or "support" instead. For example, the page at https://support.microsoft.com/en-us/help/322756 demonstrates how to back up and restore the registry in Windows. (It actually redirects to a more name-based web page.) In the past, this article would have been called KB #322756, and it is still searchable that way, but Microsoft has moved toward using more easily searchable URLs, as you will see if you follow the previous link. (Once you access the link, it will append it with the post name, which makes it more search engine friendly.) You'll find in your journeys that you sometimes end up at Microsoft Technical Documentation as well.

▶ **Microsoft Technical Documentation (https://docs.microsoft.com):** Historically, this was the support site designed with IT professionals in mind. It is based on what used to be called TechNet in the good old days. From this location, you can search for solutions within a mini-search engine or by using older KB article numbers. In addition, you can find community support, labs, a wiki, and blogs.

Here are a couple of other examples:

▶ **Apple (https://support.apple.com):** Here you can find support articles and community support for Apple products, including macOS-based systems and iOS-based mobile devices.

▶ **Android (https://support.google.com/android/):** Here you can learn about the Android OS and also get redirected to the major manufacturers that use it on their mobile devices.

▶ **Intel (https://www.intel.com/content/www/us/en/support.html):** This KB contains articles, posts, and discussions about all of Intel's products. Intel has a separate developer KB as well.

▶ **Western Digital (https://support-en.wd.com):** This site supplies written articles for the various storage drives and other products that WD manufactures, along with community support.

▶ **Ubuntu Community Support: (https://ubuntu.com/support/community-support):** This site offers support for Ubuntu Linux. One of the fabulous things about Linux is the quality of the support communities for distros such as Ubuntu and Arch—and these are just a couple of examples!

For security purposes, I suggest keeping an eye on knowledge bases that describe common vulnerabilities and exposures (CVEs). CVEs are lists of publicly available security flaws that you should be familiar with. For example:

▶ **Mitre:** https://cve.mitre.org

▶ **NIST National Vulnerability Database:** https://nvd.nist.gov/vuln

Try accessing some of these links and spend some time searching around the knowledge bases to get a feel for how they work. Think about some of the products and software you use at home or at work and locate support sites and knowledge bases for those products and software. You will find that some companies have better support and KBs than others. Some have superior technical documentation specialists and more efficiently structured community platforms. Over time, this kind of high-quality product documentation often leads to a higher level of customer satisfaction as well as trusted name recognition. This is the model to follow if your organization currently makes or decides to create its own knowledge base.

> **ExamAlert**
>
> Know how to research knowledge bases! If you can research within them, you can research pretty much anywhere.

Ticketing Systems

A *ticketing system* is software that manages issues from end users and customers. An organization might also refer to it as an *issue tracking system, trouble ticket system, incident ticket system*, or *support ticket system*. Examples of ticketing systems include Zendesk, Freshdesk, and ITSM. Or an organization might design its own or customize an existing open-source solution.

Ticketing systems are commonly used in an organization's call center for support purposes. Often, they are used to support hardware or software issues that arise. Issues are classified with different priority, or urgency, levels. A person working at a help desk is in charge of opening a ticket (unless it was opened by the system and customer already) and then works to fix the issue or escalates the issue to another person or department.

The Help Desk

Typically, ticketing systems are used by help desk support personnel and other types of IT technicians. We haven't talked much about the help desk in this book. A typical help desk station has a dual-monitor setup plus a separate laptop and a (possibly stressed out) person wearing a headset who is quickly working to solve problems for customers and end users. Multiply that by a couple dozen—or more or less, depending on the size of the organization. Employees use softphone applications so that they never have to take their hands off the keyboard. In many organizations, help desk personnel are expected to meet a quota and help out a specified number of customers per hour or resolve a certain number of tickets per hour. A help desk position can be an awesome experience (at the right organization), and—if you prove yourself—it can be a steppingstone to other IT positions.

While ticketing systems can be used in a variety of ways, we'll focus on the help desk as an example. An employee working at a help desk who opens a ticket might communicate with the customer by way of chat, email, or phone. The employee is responsible for collecting details about the user and information about the device or software that the end user or customer is using. All of this information is entered into the ticket. Most importantly, the employee must obtain a detailed description of the problem. (The solution is usually in the details!)

The help desk employee is also responsible for categorizing the issue and determining the severity of the issue. For example, a customer might state that a device won't charge. This would be a power-related issue, and the severity/urgency will probably be somewhat low. Or perhaps a co-worker's email client was affected by malware and is now spamming the entire company. That would be an in-house software/security issue, and the severity would be high.

While working to solve the problem, the employee should use clear, concise communication—written and verbal—so that other people will be able to quickly understand the status of the problem. That means making a detailed description of the problem, any progress so far, and the resolution.

In the event that the employee cannot resolve the problem, the problem needs to be escalated or perhaps moved laterally. It could be that the problem requires a help desk level 2 or level 3 technician, or perhaps it needs to be transferred to another department. The employee should track exactly who was brought in to work on the ticket before relinquishing control of the situation. In some cases, the original help desk employee may be required to follow up on the status of those opened tickets. One way or another, the goal is to close tickets (solve the problems) so that the end users or customers walk away happy!

> **ExamAlert**
>
> When working on a ticket, gather detailed information on the problem, use clear and concise verbal and written communications, and track the status of the problem from beginning to end.

A ticket system could be part of a larger set of software, such as help desk software, asset management (more on that in a bit), or IT service management. But for the exam, you should focus on the ticket portion of that software and how to properly create, manage, and resolve tickets. Consider checking out a trial version of a help desk ticketing system to get a feel for how one of these programs works.

Asset Management

Asset management—in particular, *IT asset inventory management*—is the process of supervising, tracking, and auditing IT equipment within an organization's infrastructure.

All companies are at risk of technology sprawl—meaning the disorganization of IT equipment and software that can occur over time. To reduce this risk, an organization should use written and software-based documentation to track all assets. This includes tracking the procurement and life cycle of client computers, servers, switches, routers, mobile devices, IoT devices, and other hardware, as well as tracking software that is installed, uninstalled, and updated. It also includes any items that are stored for later use. You might use asset tags for physically stored items. These could be written or printed tags, barcode stickers, or RFID tags. There are a variety of software packages available that can track all of this information. Most inventory tracking systems can read all of these types of tags and can communicate with handheld wireless and USB-based devices used to scan the tags. This software is part of your overall technical documentation.

> **ExamAlert**
>
> Asset tags and barcodes are used by inventory management systems and software to identify and keep records of company assets.

Asset-based documentation might also include things that you collect, such as device warranties and licenses for software. For example, Microsoft has used certificates of authenticity (COAs) and the client-access licenses (CALs) for ages. These commercial licenses come with software that is purchased and prove that the organization paid for the software or the additional client licenses to connect to that software (as is the case with Windows Server products). Many types of software use a standard end-user licensing agreement (EULA), a personal license that might be on paper or stored on the computer (or online) and might be a single personal license or multiple commercial licenses.

Let's not forget about the virtual side of things. VMs should be documented and tracked the same way that physical computers are. VM management helps you avoid virtualization sprawl. Virtualization sprawl occurs when the number of VMs expands beyond the manageable control of the administrator(s).

Often, an organization will use an asset management system. Such a system includes inventory lists and a database to organize assets more efficiently. A system such as this is key when assigning users devices in an enterprise setting.

Documentation Is Key

The bottom line is this: Document everything that you possibly can—within reason. Know how to access all the written and digital documentation. If the process for finding the information is not written, ask your manager or human resources department to help you and ask to put the process in writing. And remember: Leave the documentation better than you found it!

Cram Quiz

Answer these questions. The answers follow the last question. If you cannot answer these questions correctly, consider reading this chapter again until you can.

1. You have been tasked with fixing a problem on a Windows server. You need to find out which switch it connects to and how it connects. Which of the following types of documentation should you consult?

   - ○ **A.** Microsoft Knowledge Base
   - ○ **B.** Network topology diagram
   - ○ **C.** Incident documentation
   - ○ **D.** Compliance policy
   - ○ **E.** Inventory management

2. You work for an enterprise-level organization that is ISO 27002:2013 certified. You have been tasked with adding a group of Windows client computers with a new image configuration to the IT asset inventory database, and this task has a standard procedure. You must furnish a document to be signed off by two people. Who should you approach for signatures? (Select the two best answers.)

   - ○ **A.** Your manager
   - ○ **B.** Compliance officer
   - ○ **C.** IT director
   - ○ **D.** Owner of the company
   - ○ **E.** CISO

3. What do inventory management systems and software use to keep track of assets? (Select the two best answers.)

   - ○ **A.** Regulatory policies
   - ○ **B.** AUPs
   - ○ **C.** Asset tags
   - ○ **D.** Barcodes

4. You are working at a help desk and encounter an issue that has not been identified or worked on previously. You go through your troubleshooting methodology, research, and, finally, solve the problem. Which of the following should you do so that the issue can be addressed properly if it is encountered again?

- ○ **A.** Add your findings to the knowledge base.
- ○ **B.** Enter the resolution into the ticket and close it.
- ○ **C.** Escalate the issue to your immediate supervisor.
- ○ **D.** Email the rest of the technicians on the team, explaining the problem.

Cram Quiz Answers

1. **B.** Use a network topology diagram (if one is available). This documentation should graphically map out what switch the server connects to and how. An automated network map would work as well. While the Microsoft Knowledge Base is great for answering questions about Windows Server, Microsoft has no way of knowing exactly how *your* organization has set up the network—and you really don't want Microsoft to know unless perhaps you initiate a tech support call to Microsoft for another issue. Incident documentation is used during the incident response process. Compliance policy deals with adhering to guidelines, standards, and possibly law. Inventory management will help you find out things such as when the server was installed and possibly where it is physically located, but the best documentation to find out how network devices and servers are connected is the network topology diagram documentation.

2. **A and C.** Before you perform any work where ISO compliance requires signatures, always obtain the signature of your manager and any other parties that should be aware of what you are about to do. In this case, the IT director (or someone with another similar title) should be aware of anything substantial being added to the network as assets. You might also have a project manager, or someone in asset management or other departments, sign off as well. If you're using hardcopy documentation, make copies and store the documents in the appropriate location. If the documentation is digital, make sure the signatures are properly validated and store the e-docs in the proper secure locations. The compliance officer need not be involved unless there is a change concerning processes and procedures—and yes, that would be a procedure to change a procedure. The owner of the company shouldn't be bothered with these types of day-to-day operations (except in your weekly report). Also, an enterprise-level company will most likely have a group of executives instead of an owner. One of those might be the chief information security officer (CISO); however, this person will usually not be included because the IT director will either report to that person directly or be working closely with them.

3. **C and D.** Asset tags and barcodes are used in inventory management systems and software to identify and keep records of company assets. Regulatory policies of an organization attempt to achieve compliance with a government's objectives through laws and regulations. Acceptable use policies (AUPs) state what users are allowed to do with respect to the technology infrastructure of an organization.

4. **A.** You should add your findings to the knowledge base. Be sure to enter detailed information about the solution so that other techs can efficiently address the issue if they come across it in the future. You should also enter the resolution into the ticketing system and close that particular ticket, so that you have proof of how you solved the problem. However, the trouble ticket system might not be easily searchable. The knowledge base, on the other hand, is designed for anyone to easily search by issue or by solution. There is no need to escalate the problem as it's been solved! Emailing the rest of the technicians is not necessary; if everyone did this for every problem, the whole team would be swimming in email! Besides, that would defeat the purpose of the knowledge base—to store concise solutions to problems for easy reference later on.

You are doing *fantastic*! This chapter contains a lot of information. Be sure to review, take a break, sip your favorite beverage, and then continue on to the next chapter of this supertome.

CHAPTER 58

Change Management and Backup Methods

This chapter covers the following A+ 220-1102 exam objectives:

▶ **4.2** – Explain basic change management best practices.

▶ **4.3** – Given a scenario, implement workstation backup and recovery methods.

In this chapter, we will cover the fundamentals of change management and disaster recovery. As you progress to other certifications, and if you ascend into management, these concepts become more crucial.

Understanding Basic Change Management Best Practices

ExamAlert

Objective 4.2 focuses on documented business practices and change management concepts.

Change management is a structured way of changing the state of a computer system, network, policy, procedure, or process. The idea behind this is that change is necessary, but an organization should adapt with that change and be knowledgeable of it throughout its life cycle. Any change that a person wants to make should be introduced to each of the leaders of the various departments that it might affect. Those personnel must approve the change before it goes into effect. Before this happens, department managers will most likely make recommendations and/or give stipulations. There might even be a committee involved. When the necessary people have signed off on a change, it should be tested and then implemented. During implementation, it should be monitored and documented carefully.

In a larger organization that complies with various certifications such as ISO 9001:2015, this whole process can be a complex task. IT people should have charts of personnel, project managers, and department heads. There should also be current procedures in place that show who needs to be contacted about a proposed change.

The typical A+ technician doesn't need to know everything about change management but should understand the basics, including the basic plan for change, how to work within a change management system, and how to implement basic change management best practices. To that end, Table 58.1 gives definitions for change management terms that you should know for the exam. It also includes some examples that assume a scenario where you as an IT technician see a need to update the firewall software for a group of client computers.

TABLE 58.1 **Change Management Terms**

Term	Description
Documented business processes	Most likely, there will be forms involved that require the technician to state the reason for a proposed change. These are known as *change control forms* or *change request forms*. The technician should fill out the forms as accurately as possible, in plain English, with little or no jargon.

Term	Description
	These processes could possibly include the following:
	Rollback plan: To deal with the possibility that an installation, an upgrade, or a modification fails to perform as expected, a rollback plan is a set of procedures that will bring the application, system, or infrastructure back to the original state before the change was made.
	Sandbox testing: Detailed procedures explain how applications and systems will be tested in an isolated environment.
	Responsible staff member(s): It is important to list the person or people who will oversee the business process in question.
	Read on for more items that should be included in a change request.
Purpose of the change	The technician should give a basic description of the change and why the change should come about (although these might be separated on some forms). For example: "It is my contention that computers 251 through 299 are vulnerable to a certain type of attack that could be prevented by updating their firewalls."
Scope of the change	In describing the scope of a change, a technician goes into detail about what systems will be updated and the procedure that will take place, including who it will affect and when. For example, expanding or reducing the functionality of a networking technology might impact hundreds of systems; therefore, it is wise to perform these changes off-hours.
Risk analysis	Risk analysis (risk assessment) is an attempt to determine threats that could occur with computers and networks. It's a big topic, but a technician needs to simplify based only on the change that is proposed. The technician should state any vulnerabilities that can be mitigated as part of the change and any that could potentially occur due to that change. For example, the firewall update could possibly interfere with other installed applications, and it should therefore be tested in an isolated environment first before being deployed. By making a risk analysis, the technician (and the team) can define the risk level, or the amount of potential risk.
End-user acceptance	How will the end users be affected, and what are the chances that they will accept the change gracefully? This also applies to customers of the company if they are affected. The idea behind most of IT is that it should be transparent to the user—and in this scenario, that is what the technician is hoping for. Also, the firewall update should take place off-hours to prevent a loss of productivity. In cases where software is to be changed, the technician should work closely with end users/customers and gather their input on how the change should go forward.

Term	Description
Change board	Also known as a change control board or change advisory board, this group includes department heads, subject matter experts (SMEs), and project managers who will decide on whether a proposed change should be approved. In some cases, this group's approval is not necessary; for example, a technician might only need a manager signature to update a single computer's anti-malware platform. But in the scenario, multiple computers and users will be affected, so it will probably go to a committee that will review the change request form and all supporting documentation.
Backout plan	This is a set of procedures that will reverse any changes made quickly and efficiently. It should be enacted only if the change fails. It should include the contact information of all parties involved and a communications plan to make sure the backout goes smoothly. The failure should be well documented. You can reduce the chance of a backout plan/rollback plan ever being necessary by performing risk analysis and testing.
Document changes	Once approval is made, the technician should carefully document any changes that are made and when. Forms or a database are often used to facilitate this. The technician should note each step taken during the update of the firewalls and detail any anomalies or unexpected events that came up during the process.

ExamAlert

Know the change management terms and definitions in Table 58.1 for the exam.

Remember that some changes require more attention to change management than others. A basic change to a system might not even require a signature, or it might simply require a basic form with a manager's signature. But a more complex change that affects multiple systems and users will need a more developed change management approach. It might consist of stages, including planning, awareness, analysis, learning, and adoption. Keep an open mind. The point where advanced change management planning should occur and the particular procedures and naming conventions used will vary from one organization to the next.

Note

Here's a Microsoft-related example of a strategy for change management: https://docs.microsoft.com/en-us/microsoftteams/change-management-strategy.

> **Note**
>
> The Cram Quiz at the end of the chapter covers the material for both Objectives 4.2 and 4.3.

Implementing Workstation Backup and Recovery Methods

> **ExamAlert**
>
> **Objective 4.3** concentrates on backup and recovery, backup testing, and backup rotation schemes.

There's no need to go looking for disasters; they will come looking for you—that is, if you don't plan well and if you don't incorporate fault tolerance and redundancy whenever possible. The more you secure and provide redundancy, the more you reduce the risk of disaster. However, a disaster can happen. In the *unlikely* event that it does, you need to be ready. Be prepared with a disaster recovery plan (DRP).

The objective of a DRP is to ensure that an organization can respond quickly to an emergency and minimize the effects of the disaster on the organization, its employees, and its technology. A DRP could be a simple one-page document (for small offices) or an entire set of documentation including profiles, processes, and procedures (and more likely the latter).

> **Note**
>
> The following link leads to NIST SP 800-34 Rev. 1, *Contingency Planning Guide for Federal Information Systems*, which provides plenty of information about security in general, including DRPs: https://www.nist.gov/privacy-framework/nist-sp-800-34.

For the A+ exam, you need to be most concerned with one concept in the realm of disaster prevention and disaster recovery: backup and recovery.

Know this: Your data IS NOT SAFE! (Yes, I was screaming that.) So, backing up data is critical for organizations—as well as individuals! It is not enough to rely on a fault-tolerant array of storage drives or other redundancy methods. Individual files or the entire system can be backed up to another set of drives, to optical discs, or to tape. One way to do this in Windows is to use the File History application.

Using Windows File History and Recovery

File History is a file backup program that can be accessed from the Control Panel. After you turn it on, it automatically searches for accessible drives on the local computer or network that are potential candidates for backups. By default, it copies files from the Libraries location, Desktop, Contacts, and Favorites. You can select the copy destination that the File History program will use. You can also restore personal files from here. Access File History by navigating to one of the following:

▶ **In Windows 10: Settings > Update & Security > Backup**

▶ **In Windows 10 and 11: Control Panel > File History** (if in Category view of the Control Panel, **System and Security > File History**)

You'll need to enable file history, and you'll need a separate drive to back up to. If File History is no longer needed or desired, drag the slider to off (or click the **Turn off** button in the Control Panel).

> **ExamAlert**
>
> Know how to use File History to back up data in Windows.

> **Note**
>
> In Windows 11, you can also use Windows Backup, located at **Settings > Accounts > Windows Backup**.

In some cases, you might want to back up more than just personal files from specific locations; you might want to back up the entire system. One way to do this is to use the **System Image Backup** option (linked to in the bottom-left corner of the Control Panel File History window). This program can create an image of your system drive and user data files, and you can use this image to restore your system later on. You can also manually select additional information, such as the entire C: drive, as shown in Figure 58.1. There are third-party imaging products as well (for example, Ghost). Many organizations prefer to use them.

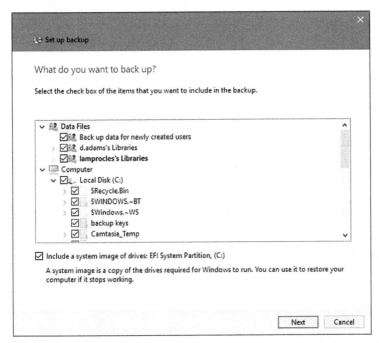

FIGURE 58.1 **File History > Backup screen in Windows with the C: drive selected**

Larger companies use more elaborate backup systems, which often back up to tape drives with large capacities, such as Linear Tape-Open (LTO). A typical LTO-9 tape can hold 45 TB of raw data. These drives come with their own programs that allow you to select various types of backups and verify those backups in several ways.

Backup Methods

There are several backup types you should be aware of for the exam, including full, incremental, differential, and synthetic. Most operating systems and third-party backup utilities support some or all of these types. Keep in mind that this list is not the end-all of backup types, but it gives a basic idea of the main types of data backups used in the field. When performing any of these types of backups, a technician must select what to back up. It could be a folder or an entire volume.

Full Backup

A full backup backs up the entire contents of a folder or volume, whichever is selected. A full backup can be stored on one or more tapes. If more than one is used, the restoration process would require starting with the oldest tape and moving through the tapes chronologically, one by one. Full backups can use a *lot* of space, causing a backup operator to use a lot of backup tapes, which can be expensive. Full backups can also be time-consuming if there is a lot of data. So, often, incremental (or differential) backups are used with full backups as part of a backup plan.

Incremental Backup

An incremental backup backs up only the contents of a folder that have changed since the last full backup or the last incremental backup. An incremental backup must be preceded by a full backup. Restoring the contents of a folder or volume requires starting with the full backup tape and then moving on to each of the incremental backup tapes chronologically, ending with the latest incremental backup tape.

> **Note**
>
> Some operating systems and backup systems associate an archive bit (or archive flag) with any file that has been modified; this indicates to the backup program that it should be backed up during the next backup phase. The incremental backup resets the bit after backup is complete.

Table 58.2 shows an example of a basic one-week backup schedule using the full and incremental backup types. A full backup is done on Sunday, and incremental backups are done Monday through Friday.

TABLE 58.2 Sample Incremental Backup Schedule

Day	Backup Type	Time
Sunday	Full backup	6 p.m.
Monday	Incremental backup	6 p.m.
Tuesday	Incremental backup	6 p.m.
Wednesday	Incremental backup	6 p.m.
Thursday	Incremental backup	6 p.m.
Friday	Incremental backup	6 p.m.

In this schedule, six backup tapes are required, one for each day, and the backups are done at 6 p.m. daily. Tapes might be reused when the cycle is complete, or the organization might opt to archive certain tapes each week—such as, the full backup tapes—and use new tapes every Sunday.

Let's say that this backup procedure is used to back up a server. Now, imagine that the server crashes on Wednesday at 9 p.m., and the storage drive data is lost. A backup operator arriving on the scene Thursday morning (or earlier) would need to review any logs available to find out when the server crashed. Then, the admin would need to fix the server, and the backup operator would need to restore the data. This would require starting with the Sunday full backup tape and continuing on to the Monday, Tuesday, and Wednesday incremental backup tapes. In this case, four tapes in total would be needed to complete the restoration.

Windows Server has a built-in program called Windows Server Backup (wbadmin.msc). After adding it as a feature in Windows Server, you can then back up data as you wish, optimize the backup performance, and select either full or incremental backups for individual volumes, as shown in Figure 58.2

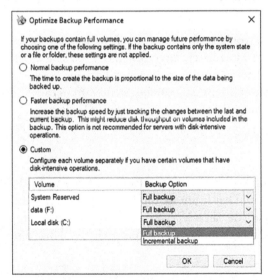

FIGURE 58.2 **Windows Server Backup screen set to full backup of the C: drive**

Differential Backup

A differential backup backs up only the contents of a folder that have changed since the last full backup. A differential backup must be preceded by a full backup. To restore data, a person would start with the full backup tape and then move on to the differential tape.

> **Note**
>
> Differential backups do not reset the archive bit when backing up. This means that incremental backups will not see or know that a differential backup has occurred.

Synthetic Backup

Synthetic backups are full backups that can simplify the restoration process. They can be incorporated into a full/incremental backup scheme like the one shown in Table 58.2. Let's say you run a full backup on Sunday and incremental backups on Monday through Friday. Now imagine that there is a problem on Friday evening. Without a synthetic backup, you would restore by using all the backup tapes as mentioned previously—first the full backup and then each of the five incremental backups, individually. But with a synthetic backup, you can simplify the process!

One way to use a synthetic backup would be to allow it to create another incremental backup on Friday and then, immediately after, generate a full synthetic backup, based on the original full backup and all incremental backups. Now, if there is a failure on Saturday, the entire backup can be restored from one tape—the synthetic full backup—instead of requiring six tapes of backup.

Backup Testing

After a backup is complete, it should be verified or validated in some way. Manufacturers of backup software and hardware solutions usually include some kind of verification mechanism that you can select during the backup process. This mechanism will verify that the backup was written properly to the backup media.

However, a verification mechanism isn't enough to satisfy a DRP. A backup operator needs to periodically test backups by actually restoring hand-picked backup jobs to test systems. This might seem like a shot in the dark, but you can logically select what to test by being included in the change management loop. Any substantial change proposals might need to notify the backup group so that those changes can be tested by way of a new backup/restoration.

When initially backing up a system, such as a Windows server, that backup should be *thoroughly* tested via a restoration and in-depth comparison of the original data to the restored data. But it goes further than that; restorations should be tested on simulated systems with simulated *failures*. So, for example, if you are concerned that the server's system drive (or array) could fail, then you could test that by setting up a test server with the same configuration and storage drive array and restore the system data or image to that test system. Or, if the IT budget doesn't allow for this, you could at least test it virtually. Quality virtualization software is a must in this case because it needs to emulate hardware appropriately.

Finally, consider the frequency of backup testing. For example, once a year is not enough. Some organizations require that backup testing be done monthly or even weekly.

ExamAlert

Perform backup testing to ensure that backups are actually being performed and that data can actually be restored!

Backup Rotation Schemes

There are a variety of schemes that you can implement when planning your backup schedule. Let's discuss a couple schemes and some best practices.

Grandfather-Father-Son (GFS)

The GFS backup rotation scheme is a very common backup method. When you use this scheme, three sets of backup tapes must be defined—usually they are daily, weekly, and monthly, corresponding to son, father, and grandfather. Backups are rotated on a daily basis; normally the last one of the week is graduated to father status. Weekly (father) backups are rotated on a weekly basis, with the last one of the month being graduated to grandfather status. Often, monthly (grandfather) backups, or a copy of them, are archived offsite.

10-Tape Rotation

The 10-tape rotation method is simple and provides easy access to data that has been backed up. It can be accomplished during a two-week backup period, and each tape is used once per day for two weeks. Then the entire set is recycled.

Generally, this is similar to the one-week schedule shown previously; however, the second Monday might be a differential backup instead of a full backup. And the second Friday might be a full backup, which is archived. There are several options; you would need to run some backups and see which is best for you, given the number of tapes required and time spent running the backups.

Onsite vs. Offsite Backups

Most of what we have discussed so far has been based on the backup of data to local storage. The beauty of local storage is that you own it (or your organization does). This means you can access it when you wish, it is physically available to you, and it can most likely be secured relatively easily. In addition, if there is a failure, the time to repair might be less than if you back up data to the cloud. Plus, simulations and testing can be run faster (in some cases). So being local has advantages. However, it can be costly: Servers, racks, drive arrays, tape drives, *electricity*, and so on can quickly break the bank. And don't forget about disasters such as theft, fire, flood, or natural disaster. If one occurs and it encompasses your building, then your data is done, and you just might be out of a job. It can make an IT person wonder if backing up to the cloud is a better solution—and sometimes it can be.

The big platforms such as Amazon Web Services (AWS), Microsoft Azure, Google Cloud, and so on have various cloud services plus storage, syncing, and backup solutions. These tend to be more secure than services such as Dropbox, Microsoft OneDrive, and Google Drive because they are designed for business use, especially enterprise-level business, where security is paramount. There are two keys to this: speed and resilience. You need to have a fast backup solution (and, more importantly, a rapid restoration process), regardless of the location of the backup. And whichever providers are used, the data needs to be redundant and accessible. How would you go about ensuring all this? Think about it for a moment.

Regardless of the solution you use, the backups should be well documented, and the backup accounts should have strong passwords/passphrases. This is all part of a data backup strategy where you are concerned with having onsite backups (for easy restoration), offsite backups (for disastrous situations), backup testing, and an organized storage system that is properly documented.

> **Note**
>
> Last thought on this: Smart companies "hedge. This means they will use onsite *and* offsite solutions together to reduce their risk as much as possible.

3-2-1 Backup Rule

The 3-2-1 backup rule is just about as old as the backup tape. Simply stated, it requires *three* copies of data. The first is the actual production data—the data in use. The second and third are backup copies. Those *two* should be stored on different media (such as disk and tape), and *one* of them should be stored offsite.

While this rule was used for years by many backup operators, it has limitations. For example, one backup stored offsite is not enough today, especially if you are storing it on the cloud.

> **Warning**
>
> The basic rule of cloud is this: DO NOT RELY SOLELY ON ONE CLOUD PROVIDER! There, I said it.

Another option is to scale the 3-2-1 rule. For example, make it the 3-2-2 rule, where you use two separate geographic regions to store your offsite backups. You might opt to store one backup with a cloud provider such as Microsoft, Google, or Amazon and store another backup at a colocation, or you might use two different cloud providers, as long as the data is stored in two different geographic areas. There are lots of possibilities when it comes to storage locations, and you could further scale the 3-2-1 rule as needed.

> **Note**
>
> For more information, see the following NIST link for guidelines on the backup (CP-9) and recovery (CP-10) of data, which are part of SP 800-53B: https://csrc.nist.gov/publications/detail/sp/800-53b/final.

Cram Quiz

Answer these questions. The answers follow the last question. If you cannot answer
these questions correctly, consider reading this chapter again until you can.

1. In a change management board meeting, you are discussing any vulnerabilities that can be mitigated as part of a recommended change and anything that
   could potentially occur due to that change. What best describes what you are
   discussing?

   ○ **A.** Purpose of change

   ○ **B.** Scope of the change

   ○ **C.** Backout plan

   ○ **D.** Document changes

   ○ **E.** Risk analysis

2. You have been tasked with backing up new user profiles in an enterprise environment. You propose to back up these user accounts to a new tape backup
   device. Which of the following procedures should you follow? (Select the two best
   answers.)

   ○ **A.** Change management

   ○ **B.** End-user acceptance

   ○ **C.** File History

   ○ **D.** Incremental backup

   ○ **E.** Backup testing

3. You work with servers and network infrastructure in an IT department. You are
   proposing a major operating system upgrade to a Linux server. You have completed the documentation for this, and it shows that the upgrade will impact your
   organization's web services. You finish the required risk analysis and document
   the processes that will be required. Which of the following should you complete
   next?

   ○ **A.** Rollback plan

   ○ **B.** Change request

   ○ **C.** Purpose of the change

   ○ **D.** Scope of the change

4. Which type of backup scheme uses two types of media, with one being stored offsite?

   ○ **A.** GFS

   ○ **B.** 10-tape rotation

   ○ **C.** 3-2-1

   ○ **D.** Cloud storage

5. You have implemented a backup solution that combines a full backup on Monday at 6 p.m. and incremental backups on Tuesday through Friday at 6 p.m.. If there was a storage drive failure on Saturday morning, how many backup tapes would be required to restore the entire backup?

   ○ **A.** 1

   ○ **B.** 2

   ○ **C.** 4

   ○ **D.** 5

6. Which of the following will bring a system back to its original state before a change was made? (Select the two best answers.)

   ○ **A.** A responsible staff member

   ○ **B.** Sandbox testing

   ○ **C.** Undocumented business process

   ○ **D.** Rollback plan

Cram Quiz Answers

1. E. You are discussing risk analysis, which is the attempt to determine what threats could occur with computers and networks. The purpose of a change is a basic description of the change and why the change should come about. The scope of a change is detail about what systems will be updated. The backout plan is a set of procedures that will reverse any failed changes made quickly and efficiently. Documenting changes happens once approval is made; the technician should carefully document any changes that are made and when.

2. A and E. Because this is a change (backing up to a new tape device), a change management document will probably be needed, listing procedures for usage of the new backup device and the backup of the new accounts. Backup testing should be done often, or at least periodically, and definitely when it comes to new data, as is the case in this scenario with new user profiles. You are not concerned with the end-user acceptance aspect of change management because the users should not be affected by this—it should be transparent to them—but if you were, that would be part of change management. File History is a Windows tool; in enterprise environments, you would use Windows Server Backup or a comparable third-party tool. Because these are new user profiles, you would want to do a full backup, not an incremental backup.

3. **B.** The technical assessments are finished, and you know how you would proceed with the process of upgrading the Linux server. Now it's time to actually fill out the paperwork required by your organization. This would most likely be a change request form. This and any supporting documentation and assessments will be presented to a change control board or committee. This document needs to be approached from a business standpoint and written in a way that your team, *and management*, can read easily. It will hopefully include many things, such as the purpose of the change, the scope of the change, a rollback plan (or backout plan), systems affected, and so on. As you see, by using the process of elimination, you reject the other potential answers in the question; remember this technique. It's awesome that you are using a Linux server to run web services—perhaps Apache web server or NGINX—and as a technician, you have the know-how to make the upgrade work. However, your proposal needs to "sell" the idea to the organization. The change request document needs to show that the process will not disrupt business operations (at least not too much) and that the organization's risk will be reduced as much as possible. It needs to show that everything is planned out step-by-step and that you have a contingency plan (backout plan) if something goes awry. Remember, even if you make no mistakes, issues can still occur.

4. **C.** The 3-2-1 rule is a backup scheme that specifies *three* copies of data: one in use and *two* others that are stored on different media types, with *one* of those being stored offsite. The grandfather-father-son (GFS) backup scheme uses three sets of backup tapes: daily, weekly, and monthly. 10-tape rotation uses two weeks' worth of daily tapes, which are reused after a two-week period. Cloud storage is a possible backup scheme for your data, and although it is offsite, it does not deal with different types of media.

5. **D.** You would need all five backup tapes to restore the entire backup. That would include the full backup from Monday, and the four incremental backup tapes from Tuesday through Friday. If you had also set up a synthetic backup on Saturday, then you would only need that one tape. If you had a different setup with a full backup on Monday and a differential backup on Friday (with incrementals between Tuesday and Thursday), only two tapes would suffice for the recovery: the full backup and the differential backup (and the incremental backups would not be necessary). If perhaps the failure occurred on Friday morning instead of Saturday, then you would only need four tapes: the full backup and the three incremental tapes from Tuesday through Thursday.

6. **A and D.** A responsible staff member is the person (likely you) who will oversee the business process in question. The business process in question here is a rollback plan that will bring the system back to the original state before the change was made. Sandbox testing is a detailed procedure that explains how applications and systems will be tested in an isolated environment, which is often a virtual machine (VM). An undocumented business process is just that: a business process that has yet to be documented.

Great work! You've completed yet another chapter. Before you know it, we'll be wrapping up this book. There was a lot of detail in this chapter, and it moved away from the computer tech side of things. So, review carefully, take a break, and then forge ahead!

CHAPTER 59
Safety Procedures

This chapter covers the following A+ 220-1102 exam objective:

▶ **4.4** – Given a scenario, use common safety procedures.

Safety first! Remember to put safety on the top of your priority list when dealing with computers, power, networking, and people. Protect yourself, protect others, and protect your computer. Proper grounding, electrical safety, physical safety, and fire prevention are the keys to a happy and healthy career.

ESD Prevention and Equipment Grounding

We'll start with electrostatic discharge (ESD) prevention. Guard those components! By using antistatic methods, you protect your computer's parts and keep *it* safe.

ESD occurs when two objects of different voltages come into contact with each other. The human body is always gathering static electricity—more than enough to damage a computer component (for example, that $500 video card you just purchased). ESD is a silent killer. When you touch a component without proper protection, the static electricity could discharge from you to the component, most likely damaging it without showing discernible signs of damage. Worse yet, it is possible to discharge a small amount of voltage to a device and damage it enough that it works intermittently, making it tough to troubleshoot. It takes only 30 volts or so to damage a component. On a dry winter day, you could gather as much as 20,000 volts when walking across a carpeted area! However, you can protect components from ESD by equalizing the electrical potentials in several ways:

▶ **Use an antistatic wrist strap:** This type of strap, which is inexpensive and takes only a moment to put on and connect, can protect a computer from accidental voltage spikes. In addition, almost all antistatic wrist straps come equipped with a resistor (often 1 megaohm) that protects the user from shock/electrocution hazards. Use one whenever working on PCs or laptops.

▶ **Use an antistatic mat:** Place the computer on top of the mat. Connect the mat via the antistatic cable the same way you do an antistatic wrist strap. You can also stand on a mat and connect it in the same manner.

▶ **Self-ground:** To further discharge yourself, touch the chassis of the computer before handling any components. Especially do this when an antistatic strap is not available.

▶ **Use antistatic bags:** Adapter cards, motherboards, and the like are normally shipped in antistatic bags. Hold on to them! When installing or removing components, keep them inside an antistatic bag until you are ready to work with them. Keep the bag on top of the antistatic mat.

▶ **Handle components properly:** If you are sitting at your desk without any ESD protection, there is no reason to be handling components, so don't. Handle components only when you are fully protected. When you do handle components, try to hold them at the edge. For example, when installing RAM, hold the module at the sides. This will inhibit any direct handling of the chips, contacts, and other circuitry. Hold adapter cards by the metal plate (bracket) or by the edge of the fiberglass board but never by the contacts. Never touch a CPU's lands/pins or the CPU cap if at all possible.

Some other ways to prevent ESD include using antistatic wipes, sprays, and gloves; keeping your feet stationary (to reduce friction); working in an uncarpeted area; and raising the humidity.

> **Note**
>
> Take a look at the various standards for static control at the following site: https://www.esda.org/standards/.

> **ExamAlert**
>
> Remember the main ways to avoid ESD: wearing an antistatic strap, using an antistatic mat, self-grounding (touching the computer case), and using antistatic bags.

Warning! Be Careful with Electricity!

Remember, the whole idea here is to equalize the electric potentials between the person and the equipment to reduce the risk of a discharge. But you have to be careful with electrical circuits. If you are not sure what you are doing, *hire a qualified and certified electrician* to help you. In my lab, I take off the alligator clips of the antistatic wrist strap and mats and connect them to a common point ground connector, which then plugs into a dedicated grounding outlet (although any properly wired AC outlet will do). In a bench or lab environment, it goes much further: There will be dedicated grounding outlet strips, the entire bench may be grounded, and all kinds of other techniques will be used, such as antistatic gloves, lab coats, special flooring, and so on. Be sure to follow whatever procedures your organization has set forth.

If you are still unsure or are concerned, simply take the electricity out of the mix. Connect the alligator clips of the antistatic strap and mat to the chassis of the computer and then touch an unpainted portion of the case before handling components. This is not as good as a properly grounded setup, but it does help to equalize the potentials.

It is also possible to equalize the potentials with the computer plugged in, but I do *not* recommend it—for a variety of reasons. For example, you might not know whether the AC outlet (or circuit) is wired properly. So, remember to keep the computer unplugged—by disconnecting the power or hitting the kill switch on the back of the computer (if there is one)—before working on the system. This way, you reduce the chance of an electrical shock.

It's also important to ground network racks in a server room or datacenter. This can be done by installing grounding bars to the racks/equipment and by using a thick, low-gauge grounding wire (for example, 6 AWG) and connecting it from the grounding bars to a grounded location, which might be the building's main ground wire, an I-beam, and so on. The key is to provide a path for electricity in the event of a power-related issue. Check your municipality's code to find out what is acceptable, and if you are not sure, get an electrician or the facilities department involved.

Electrical Safety

Electricity is a great energy that should be treated as such. *Always practice proper power handling.* Before working on any computer component, turn off the power and disconnect the device from the AC outlet. If a device such as a power supply or video monitor has a label that reads "No Serviceable Components Inside," take the manufacturer's word for it and send the component to the proper repair facility or simply replace the component. The message on the device is intended to keep a person out, usually because the internal components might hold electrical charge.

Be sure to use your power supply tester, receptacle tester, and other power testing equipment properly. If you do not know how to use these tools, escalate the issue to the facilities department or another person in your company. If you find issues with AC outlets or other types of AC equipment, refer the issue to your manager or building supervisor. Do not try to fix such issues. If you find an issue like this in a customer's home, tell the customer about the problem and recommend that the AC outlet be repaired by an electrician before going any further.

Do not open power supplies. As far as the A+ exam is concerned, if a power supply goes bad, you should replace it, even if you think it is just the fan and would be an easy repair. A power supply is known as a *field replaceable unit (FRU)* for a reason. Although it is possible to repair power supplies, it should be done only by trained technicians. Remember that a power supply holds a charge; this alone should be enough to keep you away from the internals of the power supply. In addition, the amount of time it would take a person to repair a power supply would cost more to a company than just buying a new one and installing it. However, be sure to recycle the old one according to municipal guidelines.

LCD monitors can also be dangerous. I can't actually tell you *not* to work on them, especially because laptops integrate them. Regardless, it is again recommended that a failed monitor (or laptop) be sent to the proper repair organization or to the manufacturer if the device is within warranty. However, if you do decide to work on an LCD, one thing to be careful of is capacitors, which are normally near the LCD power supply and hold a charge. Also, make sure that the device is turned off and unplugged; if it is a laptop, make sure the battery has been removed. One of the items that can fail on an LCD monitor is the backlight inverter. The inverter is usually mounted on a circuit board, and if it fails, either a fuse needs to be replaced or the entire inverter board needs to be replaced. The inverter is a high-voltage device; try not to touch it, and be especially sure not to touch it when the LCD device is on. (Keep in mind that LED-based LCD monitors don't have inverters, and these monitors are much more common as of the writing of this book in 2021.) A lot of this is common sense, but it is worthwhile to always be sure—like measuring twice before you cut.

> **Note**
>
> In the uncommon scenario that you come across a CRT monitor, don't open it as it carries a lethal charge. Instead, refer such a monitor to a company that specializes in monitor repair. If you need to dispose of CRTs, find a monitor repair company that will buy them or simply accept them without charge. Otherwise, they need to be recycled in compliance with local government regulations and/or municipal ordinances.

Another device that you need to make sure you turn off and unplug is a laser printer. A laser printer contains extremely dangerous high voltages. On a related note, if a printer was recently used, watch out for the fuser; the fuser runs hot!

Finally, it is important to match the power requirement of your computer equipment with the surge protector or uninterruptible power supply (UPS) that it connects to. Verify that the number of watts your computer's power supply requires is not greater than the amount of power your surge protector can provide; the same goes for the watts (or volt-amps) that the UPS can provide. In addition, be sure that you do not overload the circuit that you connect to. For additional information about electrical safety, see the electrical safety and health topics at the Occupational Safety and Health Administration (OSHA) website: https://www.osha.gov/electrical.

Electrical Fire Safety

Let's talk a little about electrical fire safety. The safest measures are preventive ones. Buildings should be outfitted with smoke detectors and fire extinguishers. The proper type of fire extinguisher for an electrical fire is a Class C extinguisher. For example, CO_2-based BC fire extinguishers are common and relatively safe to humans, but they can cause damage to computers. If equipment needs to be protected by more than a CO_2-based BC fire extinguisher, an ABC Halotron extinguisher should be used. Server rooms and datacenters are often protected by larger special hazard protection systems such as FM-200, which is based on the gaseous suppression agent heptafluoropropane. This clean agent won't cause damage to servers and other expensive equipment.

If you see an electrical fire, use the proper extinguisher to attempt to put it out. If the fire is too big for you to handle, then the number one thing to do is dial 911. Then evacuate the building. Afterward, you can notify building management, your supervisor, or other facilities people.

Hopefully, you will never come near a live electrical wire. But if you do, you want to attempt to shut off the source. Do not attempt to do this with your bare hands and make sure that your feet are dry and that you are not standing in any water. Use a wooden stick, board, or rope. If this is not possible, you need to contact your supervisor or building management so that they can shut down power at another junction. If you find an apparently unconscious person underneath a live wire, do not touch the person! Again, attempt to move the live wire with a wooden stick or similar object. Never use anything metal and do not touch anything metal while you are doing it. After moving the wire, call 911 and contact your superiors immediately. While waiting, attempt to administer first aid to the person.

> **Note**
>
> For more information about fire extinguisher types and their operation and fire protection and fire prevention in general, see https://www.osha.gov/sites/default/files/2019-03/fireprotection.pdf.

Physical Safety

Physical safety considerations include the following:

▶ Securing cables

▶ Using caution with heavy items

▶ Avoiding touching hot components

▶ Using safety equipment

▶ Considering workplace ergonomics

Cables can be a trip hazard. Employ proper cable management by routing cables away from high-traffic areas and keeping computer cables stowed away and tie-wrapped. Network cables should have been installed permanently within the walls and ceiling, but sometimes you might find a rogue cable. If you discover a cable on the floor or hanging from the ceiling, alert your network administrator or your manager. Do not attempt to reroute the network cable. You don't know what data is transferred on the cable. Because network cabling is monitored by municipalities the same way other electrical work is monitored, only qualified, trained technicians should take care of network wiring.

Lifting heavy items incorrectly can cause many types of injuries. As a general rule, if an item is heavier than one quarter of your body weight, you should ask someone else to help. When lifting something, stand close to the item, squat down to the item by bending your knees, grasp the item firmly, keep your back straight, and slowly lift with your legs, not your back. Be sure not to twist your body; keep the item close to your body. This helps to prevent back injuries. When moving items, it is best to have them stored at waist level so that minimal lifting is necessary. OSHA has plenty of guidelines and recommendations for physical safety at the workplace. Its website is https://www.osha.gov.

Be careful when handling components that might be hot. The best method when dealing with hot items (such as a laser printer's fuser, a burned-out power supply, or a CPU or storage drive that needs to be replaced) is to wait until they have cooled. To be safe, before replacing items, wait 15 minutes for them to cool. Servers and networking equipment can get quite hot as well, even when they are stored in a climate-controlled room. Take great care when working with these devices. Also, be careful with items that hold a charge. For the A+ certification, know that if a device has the possibility of holding a charge, you should not open it. This includes power supplies and CRT monitors. These types of electronics can be recycled in most municipalities. Programs might include curb-side pickup, drop-off centers, or recycling events. Usually these are free. There are also many donation programs for equipment that still functions.

Use safety equipment whenever necessary, including safety goggles, hard hats, air filtration masks, fluorescent clothing, and so on. Whenever you enter a work area, lab, construction site, or any other non-office environments in the field, be sure to follow safety instructions.

You probably won't get any questions on the exam about this, but ergonomics is important when operating a computer. Ergonomics can affect the long-term health of a computer operator. It is important to keep the wrists and hands in line with the forearms and to use proper typing technique. Keep the elbows close to the body and supported if possible. The lower back should be supported, the head and neck should be straight and in line with your back, and the shoulders should be relaxed. Keep the top of the monitor at or just below eye level. Take breaks at least every two hours to avoid muscle cramps and eyestrain. To further reduce eyestrain, increase the refresh rate of the monitor, if possible.

> **Note**
>
> For more information on ergonomics, see OSHA's information on computer workstations at https://www.osha.gov/etools/computer-workstations.

Cram Quiz

Answer these questions. The answers follow the last question. If you cannot answer these questions correctly, consider reading this chapter again until you can.

1. If a power supply fails, what should you do?

    ○ **A.** Replace it.

    ○ **B.** Repair it.

    ○ **C.** Use a different computer.

    ○ **D.** Switch it to a different voltage setting.

2. Which of the following are ways to avoid ESD? (Select three.)

    ○ **A.** Use an antistatic wrist strap.

    ○ **B.** Use a vacuum cleaner.

    ○ **C.** Use an antistatic mat.

    ○ **D.** Touch the chassis of the computer.

3. You walk into the server room and see a person lying on the floor with a live electrical wire draped over. What should you do first?

    ○ **A.** Run out and call 911.

    ○ **B.** Grab the wire and fling it off the person.

    ○ **C.** Grab the person and drag him out from under the wire.

    ○ **D.** Grab a piece of wood and use it to move the wire off the person.

Cram Quiz Answers

1. **A.** Replace the power supply. Trying to repair it can be dangerous and is not cost-effective to the company.

2. **A, C, and D.** Using antistatic wrist straps and mats and touching the chassis (self-grounding) of the computer are all ways to stop ESD. Vacuum cleaners can cause damage to components.

3. **D.** The first thing you should do is get a wooden stick, rope, or something similar (every server room should have one) and use it to CAREFULLY move the wire off of the person. In reality, the first thing you should do is breathe and not make any rash decisions in the heat of the moment. After the wire is removed, you should call 911 and then attempt to offer first aid to the victim. DO NOT ever touch a live wire or anything that the live wire is coming into contact with.

That was a shorter chapter, but it is very important for your livelihood and for the well-being of the computers you work on. Make it a point to always practice good safety procedures!

CHAPTER 60

Environmental Controls

This chapter covers the following A+ 220-1102 exam objective:

▶ **4.5** – Summarize environmental impacts and local environmental controls.

Environmental factors vary from one organization to the next. For the exam, you need to know how and why to control temperature and humidity, what an MSDS is and how to use it, and how to deal with dust and debris when it comes to computers. You should also have a basic understanding of some of the procedures that a typical organization puts into practice in order to meet government-based guidelines and regulations.

ExamAlert

Objective 4.5 focuses on material safety data sheets (MSDSs)/documentation for handling and disposal; temperature, humidity level awareness, and proper ventilation; and power surges, under-voltage events (brownouts), and power failures (blackouts).

Temperature, Humidity, and Air

You should be aware of the temperature and humidity measurements in your building. You should also think about airborne particles and proper ventilation. Collectively, OSHA refers to the removal of air contaminants and/or the control of room temperature and humidity as "air treatment." Although there is no specific government policy regarding air treatment, there are recommendations, including a temperature range of 68 to 76 degrees Fahrenheit (20 to 24 degrees Celsius) and a humidity range of between 20% and 60%. Remember, the higher the humidity, the less chance of ESD, but it might get a bit uncomfortable for your co-workers; they might not want to work in a rainforest, so a compromise will have to be sought. If your organization uses air handlers to heat, cool, and move the air, it will be somewhat difficult to keep the humidity any higher than 25% to 30%. That brings us to ventilation. An organization should implement local exhaust (to remove contaminants generated by the organization's processes) and introduce an adequate supply of fresh outdoor air through natural or mechanical ventilation.

For air treatment, organizations should make use of filtration devices, electronic cleaners, and possibly chemical treatments activated with charcoal or other sorbents (materials used to absorb unwanted gases). Most filtration systems make use of charcoal and HEPA filters. These filters should be replaced at regular intervals. Air ducts and dampers should be cleaned regularly. And ductwork insulation should be inspected now and again. For environments that still have a considerable number of airborne particles, portable air filtration enclosures can be purchased that also use charcoal and HEPA filters; you can also utilize ultraviolet light to eliminate particles. These are commonly found in PC repair facilities due to the amount of dust, debris, and dirt sitting in PCs that are waiting for repair. Some organizations even foot the bill for masks or respirators for their employees. Many PC workbenches are equipped with compressed air systems and vacuum systems (incorporating HEPA filters) that PC techs can use to blow out the dust and dirt from a computer and vacuum it up at the same time. Otherwise, it is usually best to take a computer outside to work on it (except in windy conditions).

> **ExamAlert**
>
> Protect yourself from airborne particles with air filtration enclosures and masks!

MSDS and Disposal

Products that use chemicals require material safety data sheets (MSDSs), which are documents that give information about particular substances (for example, the ink in inkjet cartridges). Information in an MSDS includes

▶ Proper treatment if the substance is ingested or comes into contact with the skin

▶ How to deal with spills and other hazards

▶ How to dispose of the substance

▶ How to store the substance

It's easy to find MSDSs; most companies have them online. You can search for them at a manufacturer's website or by using a search engine. An MSDS identifies a chemical substance and its possible hazards, fire-fighting measures, handling and storage, and so on. Make sure you have Adobe Acrobat Reader installed because most MSDSs are in PDF format.

It's important to know what to do if someone is adversely affected by a product that contains chemicals. A person might have skin irritation due to coming into contact with toner particles or with a cleaner that was used on a keyboard or mouse. As a technician, your job is to find out how to help the person. If you do not have direct access to the MSDS, you should contact your facilities department or building management. Perhaps the cleaning crew uses a particular cleaning agent that you are not familiar with, and only the facilities department has been given the MSDS for it. It's better to review all MSDS documents and be proactive, but in cases where you don't have access to the document, you need to collaborate with the facilities department to get the person who was affected the proper first aid and, if necessary, take the person to the emergency room. Finally, remove the affected device (such as a keyboard or mouse).

Replace it with a similar device until you can get the original device cleaned properly.

> **ExamAlert**
>
> Know that an MSDS contains warnings and safety information about chemical substances and hazards.

Generally, substances that contain chemicals should be stored in a cool, dry place, away from sunlight. "Cool" means the lower end of the OSHA guideline, approximately 68 degrees F (20 degrees C). Often, this will be in a storage closet away from the general work area and outside the air filtration system. This also allows the items to be stored in a less humid area.

Recycling and proper disposal are also important. Batteries should not be thrown away with normal trash because they contain chemicals. First, you should check your local municipal or EPA guidelines for proper disposal of batteries; in some cases, you will find that there are drop-off areas for them—either at the town municipal center or sometimes at office and computer supply stores. This applies to alkaline, lithium (for example, CR2032), lithium-ion, and other types of batteries.

> **ExamAlert**
>
> Check your local municipal and EPA guidelines for information on disposal of batteries and other equipment.

Ink and toner cartridges can usually be sent back to the manufacturer, or office supply stores and printer repair outfits often take them for recycling. Some municipalities have a method for recycling electrical devices in general.

Speaking of recycling and disposal, cell phones, smartphones, and tablets should be disposed of properly. However, unlike the devices we have spoken of so far, these devices contain data. Internal memory, SD cards, and SIMs should be wiped and, if necessary, destroyed (as described in Chapter 50, "Data Destruction and Disposal"). If a device is destroyed, the remains need to be recycled by the vendor that provided the destruction services or by the organization, in accordance with municipal guidelines. Phones and tablets that have been wiped properly—but not destroyed—might also be donated to various charities or given to electronics recycling companies or recycled at a county-wide recycling event.

Power Devices

Many of the issues that you see concerning power are due to lack of protection and improper planning, and you will see several questions (if not more) on the A+ exam regarding this subject.

Utilizing proper power devices is part of a good preventive maintenance plan and helps protect a computer. You need to protect against several things:

▶ Surges

▶ Spikes

▶ Sags

▶ Under-voltage events

▶ Power outages

A *surge* in electrical power means that there is an unexpected increase in the amount of voltage provided. This can be a small increase or a larger increase, known as a spike. A *spike* is a short transient in voltage that can be due to a short circuit, tripped circuit breaker, power outage, or lightning strike.

A *sag* is an unexpected decrease in the amount of voltage provided. Typically, sags are limited in time and in the decrease in voltage. However, when voltage reduces further, an under-voltage event could ensue. During an *under-voltage event*, the voltage drops to such an extent that it typically causes the lights to dim and causes computers to shut off. This reduction in power can be damaging to devices that aren't properly protected.

A *power failure* (blackout) is a total loss of power for a prolonged period. A problem associated with power failures is the spike that can occur when power is restored. In the New York area, it is common to have an increased number of tech support calls during July related to lightning storms! Quite often the issues are due to improper protection.

> **ExamAlert**
>
> A power surge is an unexpected increase in voltage. An under-voltage event is a drop in voltage that can cause computers to shut off. A power failure is a total loss of power for a prolonged time.

Some power devices have specific purposes, and others can protect against more than one of these electrical issues. Let's examine a few of these devices.

Surge Protectors

A *surge protector*, or *surge suppressor*, is a power strip that also incorporates a metal-oxide varistor (MOV) to protect against surges and spikes. Most power strips that you find in office supply stores or home improvement stores have surge protection capability. The word *varistor* is a blend of the terms *variable* and *resistor*.

> **ExamAlert**
>
> To protect against surges and spikes, use a surge protector!

Surge protectors are usually rated in joules, which measure energy; essentially, the more joules, the better. For computer systems, 1000 joules or more are recommended. This joule rating gives you a sense of how long the device can protect against surges and spikes. Surges happen more often than you might think, and every time a surge happens, part of the varistor is burned out. The higher the joule rating, the longer the varistor (and therefore the device) should last. Most of today's surge protectors have an indicator light that informs you if the varistor has failed.

Because surges can occur over telephone lines, RG-6 cable lines, and network lines, it is common to see input and output ports for any or all these on a decent surge protector. Higher-quality surge protectors have multiple MOVs not only for the different connections (such as AC and phones) but for the individual wires in an AC connection.

Uninterruptible Power Supplies

An *uninterruptible power supply (UPS)* combines the functionality of a surge suppressor with a *battery backup*. A UPS protects a computer not only from surges and spikes but also from sags, under-voltage events, and power failures.

> **ExamAlert**
>
> Use a UPS/battery backup to protect your computer from power outages! It can keep your computer running long enough to save your work and properly shut down the computer, if necessary.

But a battery backup can't last indefinitely! It is considered emergency power and typically keeps your computer system running for 5 to 30 minutes, depending on the model you purchase and the load being placed on the UPS. Workstation UPSs often have two types of outlets on the device: one group that is marked for battery backup and surge protection and one that is marked for surge protection only. Server room rack-mountable UPSs often only have battery backup outlets.

Most UPS devices also act as line conditioners, protecting from over- and under-voltage; they condition (or regulate) the voltage sent to the computer. If you happen to see a customer's lights flickering, this could indicate dirty power, and you should consider recommending a UPS for the customer's computers and networking equipment. If there is an alternating current (AC) failure, and the UPS stops receiving power from the AC outlet, the UPS monitoring program identifies the problem, either by beeping or with an LED visual indicator. Most UPS devices today have a USB-based connection so that your computer can communicate with the UPS. When there is a power outage, the UPS sends a signal to the computer, telling it to shut down, suspend, or stand by before the battery discharges completely. Most UPSs come with software that you can install that enables you to configure the computer with these options.

The output power capacity of UPS devices is rated in volt-amps (VA) and watts. Although you might have heard that volt-amps and watts are essentially the same, they are somewhat different. The volt-amp rating is slightly higher due to the difference between apparent power (when in battery backup mode) and real power (when pulling regular power from the AC outlet). For example, a typical UPS device might have a volt-amp rating of 350 VA but a wattage rating of 200 watts. Generally, this is enough for a computer, a monitor, and a few other devices, but a second computer might be pushing it with this wattage rating. The more devices that connect to a UPS, the shorter the battery lasts if a power outage occurs; if too many devices are connected, there might be inconsistencies when the battery needs to take over. Thus, many manufacturers limit the number of battery backup-protected receptacles on a UPS. Connecting a laser printer to a UPS is not recommended due to the high current draw of the laser printer; also, to protect a UPS from being overloaded, never connect a surge protector or power strip to one of the receptacles in a UPS.

ExamAlert

Do *not* connect laser printers to UPS devices.

A UPS has a battery (often lead-acid) that, when discharged, requires several hours to recharge. This battery is usually shipped in a disconnected state. Before charging the device for use, you must first either flip over the battery or otherwise make sure that the battery leads connect to the UPS; if the battery ever needs to be replaced, a red light usually appears and is accompanied by a beeping sound. Beeping can also occur if power is no longer supplied to the UPS by the AC outlet.

The "power" of a UPS can't be denied. It is a required component in server rooms and is very useful at users' computers as well, especially custom workstations. It's interesting to note that most power outages last for 15 minutes or less; often they are short blips. To continue using a desktop computer during a power outage of any length, the user needs to have not only the computer but also the monitor and some peripherals connected to the battery backup outlets of the UPS.

> **ExamAlert**
>
> For custom workstations, make sure that computers, monitors, and powered USB hubs are all plugged into the UPS.

Cram Quiz

Answer these questions. The answers follow the last question. If you cannot answer these questions correctly, consider reading this chapter again until you can.

1. What document can aid you if a chemical spill occurs?

   ○ **A.** HEPA

   ○ **B.** MSDS

   ○ **C.** OSHA

   ○ **D.** EPA

2. A co-worker complains that after the cleaning crew has come through, the keyboard irritates his hands and leaves some green residue. What should you do?

   ○ **A.** Call the fire department.

   ○ **B.** Contact the facilities department.

   ○ **C.** Contact the manufacturer of the keyboard.

   ○ **D.** Call OSHA and complain.

3. You are concerned with power outages that occur infrequently and for short periods of time. You don't want your users' computers to suffer from potentially harmful restarts. What device should you install for the users' computers?

- ○ **A.** Surge protector
- ○ **B.** Line conditioner
- ○ **C.** MSDS
- ○ **D.** UPS

4. What is the term for a total loss of power that lasts for a prolonged period?

- ○ **A.** Power failure
- ○ **B.** Surge
- ○ **C.** Spike
- ○ **D.** Under-voltage event

5. You want a *cost-effective* solution to the common surges that can affect your computer. Which device offers the best solution?

- ○ **A.** UPS
- ○ **B.** Surge suppressor
- ○ **C.** Power strip
- ○ **D.** Rack grounding

Cram Quiz Answers

1. **B.** A material safety data sheet (MSDS) defines exactly what a particular chemical substance is, what its potential hazards are, and how to deal with those hazards. HEPA stands for high-efficiency particulate air, as in a HEPA filter. OSHA stands for Occupational Safety and Health Administration. EPA stands for Environmental Protection Agency.

2. **B.** Contact the facilities department to see if it has the MSDS for the cleaner. You and/or the facilities department should then treat the irritation according to the MSDS. If this does not work and the problem gets worse, take the co-worker to the emergency room. Remove the keyboard from the work environment.

3. **D.** Use an uninterruptible power supply (UPS) to protect a computer from ungraceful shutdowns and restarts that can occur as a result of under-voltage events (brownouts), power failures (blackouts), and other AC failures—which the UPS will monitor for. A surge protector (suppressor) is a power strip that also incorporates a metal-oxide varistor (MOV) to protect against surges and spikes. A line conditioner can level out dirty power but won't protect against a power outage. An MSDS defines what a particular chemical substance is and how to deal with related hazards.

4. **A.** A power failure is a total loss of power for a prolonged period. The best protection against power failures is either a UPS (battery backup) or a generator. A surge in electrical power means that there is an unexpected increase in the amount of voltage provided. This can be a small increase or a larger increase, known as a spike—which is a *short* transient in voltage. A brownout is a drop in voltage (but not to zero) that can cause computers to shut off. It could be prolonged but is not a complete loss of power.

5. **B.** A surge suppressor (or surge protector) is the right solution at the right price. A UPS is a possible solution but costs more than a surge protector and is not necessary in this scenario. A power strip doesn't necessarily have surge protection functionality; it is simply a strip of outlets for additional connectivity. Rack grounding is done to protect networking equipment and servers that are installed into racks in a datacenter or server room.

This chapter and the last one were all about health, safety, recycling, and the environment—in essence, protection. You need to protect yourself, your co-workers, the organization's data and systems, and the environment. Do this, and you will have made the world a better place. Continue!

CHAPTER 61

Incident Response, Communication, and Professionalism

This chapter covers the following A+ 220-1102 exam objectives:

▶ **4.6** – Explain the importance of prohibited content/activity and privacy, licensing, and policy concepts.

▶ **4.7** – Given a scenario, use proper communication techniques and professionalism.

How will you respond to incidents? How will you communicate with customers? How will you deal with the best practices, regulations, and laws that your organization complies with? We'll answer these questions and more as we progress through this chapter.

A good technician not only knows how to work with technology but also how to deal with customers, tough problems, and imminent threats. It's the well-rounded technician that enjoys the most job security.

Understanding the Importance of Prohibited Content/Activity and Privacy, Licensing, and Policy Concepts

One of the goals of policies and procedures, best practices, and regulations is to prevent incidents from occurring. However, it is inevitable that incidents will happen. People are imperfect, and we create imperfect technologies. When the right criteria are met, small imperfections can pave the way for incidents to transpire. How we respond to these incidents and how we limit the damage are both important.

Incident Response

We need to differentiate between an event and an incident. An event is simply something that happens within a computer or on a network. It could be good or bad. For example, an event could be an administrator connecting a system to another system through a mapped network drive according to the organization's procedures. This is an occurrence that is positive. But there are adverse events as well, where negative consequences result—for example, unauthorized privilege escalation or execution of malware. Rev it up further to the computer security incident, which is an imminent threat or an outright violation of security policies and a security breach. An example of an incident is an attacker initiating a DDoS attack against a server, perhaps causing that server to crash. Another example is an attacker locking files on a computer with ransomware. A technician or a team of technicians is expected to respond to incidents quickly and efficiently.

How you follow up on an incident is a good measure of your ability to an organization. Incident response is a set of procedures that an investigator follows when examining a technology incident. How you first respond, how you document the situation, and your ability to establish a chain of custody are all important to your investigation skills.

First Response

When you first respond to an incident, your first task is to identify exactly what happened. You must recognize whether it is a simple problem that requires troubleshooting or whether it is an incident that needs to be escalated. For example, if you encounter a person who has prohibited content on a computer, this can be considered an incident, and you will be expected to escalate the issue to your supervisor (and law enforcement, if necessary) and report on exactly what you have found. Copyrighted information, malware, inappropriate content, and stolen information could all be considered prohibited. So, before you do anything else, you should report your findings to the proper channels and then make sure the data and affected devices are preserved. This may mean making a backup of the computer's image/storage drive and making sure the integrity of the data is preserved for future reference or as proof. Exactly what you do at this stage will depend on your organization's policies. Depending on the scenario, you might be told to leave everything as is and wait for a computer forensics expert or a security analyst. The idea here is that the scene will be preserved for that other person so that he or she can collect evidence.

> **ExamAlert**
>
> As a first responder, you identify an incident, report through the proper channels and escalate if necessary, ensure data/device preservation, and document everything!

Remember: Documentation Is Key

The bottom line is this: When an incident occurs, you need to document everything that you find and anything that happens after that. If your organization doesn't have any other methodology, write it down! When you leave the scene, you will be required to divulge all information to your supervisor. If you fixed the problem and no other specialists were required, the documentation process will continue through to the completion of the task and beyond when you monitor the system. You should also document any processes, procedures, and user training that might be necessary in the future.

Incident Response Life Cycle

Let's take it a bit further and discuss computer security incident response. Different organizations have different views on how incident response should be handled. One common method is to incorporate a four-phase life cycle:

1. **Preparation:** An organization with a well-planned incident response procedure, a strong security posture, and a knowledgeable chief information security officer (CISO) will be able to limit damage caused during an incident. Good communication is required, and the technician(s) should have access to secure storage facilities, digital forensic workstations, forensic software, and plenty of documentation.

2. **Detection and analysis:** This stage includes the identification of exactly what is happening during the incident. Because there are literally thousands of attack vectors (and perhaps many more), you can't create step-by-step procedures for every type of incident. However, you can categorize incidents to a certain extent and then take the appropriate steps based on the type of incident you have detected. For example, categories could include DDoS/brute-force attacks, web-based attacks, spoofing/on-path (aka MITM) attacks, and theft. Once you know what an attack is, you can analyze it using the right tools and methods. Of course, you will need to do a certain amount of thinking on your feet; as a technician, you should be ready to adjust your mindset and methodologies in real time. However, the process has to be quick so that you can contain the problem rapidly.

3. **Containment, eradication, and recovery:** First, isolate the problem: quarantine systems, isolate networks, place attackers' processes in padded cells or other holding areas (if at all possible), remove devices, and so on. Then you need to remove the threat by using other mitigation techniques. After that, you can retrieve data, reenable systems, and recover images and backups. Some organizations break this stage into multiple phases.

4. **Post-incident activity:** During this stage, you review what happened and why, finalize documentation, get signatures, and contemplate, with your team, the lessons learned.

> **Note**
>
> This life cycle is documented in great detail in NIST SP 800-61 Rev. 2, Computer Security Incident Handling Guide: https://csrc.nist.gov/publications/detail/sp/800-61/rev-2/final.
>
> The CompTIA A+ exam won't go far into the depths of this document, but if you are interested in a career that involves incident response, consider reading this document and have it on hand.

Remember that an organization might have use phases or break them up differently. In addition, an organization will describe its incident response process in much greater detail than what is shown here. Be ready to study your organization's documentation carefully!

Chain of Custody

If you are required to preserve evidence, one way to do it is to set up a chain of custody—a chronological documentation or paper trail of evidence. The chain of custody should be initiated at the start of any investigation. It documents who had custody of the evidence all the way up to litigation (if necessary) and logs the transfer of evidence from person to person. It also verifies that the evidence has not been modified or tampered with. The log should include identifying information for systems such as serial numbers, IP addresses, MAC addresses, and so on; the names, titles, and phone numbers of everyone who collects, analyzes, and handles evidence; the time and date (universal); and where and how evidence is stored.

> **ExamAlert**
>
> The chain of custody is a chronological, verifiable paper trail documenting who has possessed evidence.

As an A+ tech, you will probably not get too involved with incident investigations, but you should know the basic concepts first response, documentation, and chain of custody for the exam—and in case you find yourself in a real-life situation where you have found prohibited content or illegal activities. The bottom line is that many times your job will be to escalate the issue to the appropriate personnel.

Licensing/DRM/EULA

There are various types of licensing for software, hardware, support, and services. Let's focus on software licensing here. Licensing could be free or paid for. For example, we mentioned Microsoft Windows client licenses previously in the book. A license is considered to be valid (non-expired) as long as its expiration date has not passed. It's important to have licensing information well organized and accessible. Most proof of licensing today is digital, and it should be stored in a safe place (possibly encrypted), backed up, and digitally validated.

Licensing is important during incident response. Depending on the situation, you might need to locate valid licenses (or lack thereof) for software, client connections, and hardware. For example, you might need to be able to locate the client access licenses (CALs) being used to access a Windows server. License compliance violation can have legal ramifications, as well as availability and integrity repercussions.

There are two terms related to licensing that you should know for the exam:

▶ **EULA:** An end-user licensing agreement (EULA) is a contract or an agreement between a proprietary software vendor and an end user. In most cases, the end user is required to agree to the EULA before using the product. The EULA primarily defines the ways that the software can be used and asserts that the vendor has limited liability for issues and damages that occur through the use of the product. EULAs are usually lengthy documents, but if a company plans to use software products that require a EULA, the appropriate personnel should have a working legal understanding of these agreements.

▶ **DRM:** Digital rights management (DRM) is a group of security controls designed to restrict the usage or proliferation of copyrighted software and products. For example, various DRM controls can prevent illegal copying of software.

ExamAlert

EULA is a licensing agreement between a software vendor and an end user. DRM restricts usage or proliferation of copyrighted software and products.

Essentially, if a technician finds that a user or company is illegally copying, circumventing, or modifying software; is using software without the appropriate licensing; or is otherwise breaching the EULA or DRM agreement, the technician should report that finding to the appropriate personnel or authorities and log and document the situation in accordance with incident response procedures.

Software licenses can be commercial—for example, licenses for Microsoft or Apple software—or open source, as is the case with the GNU General Public License (GPL) for Linux software. In the case of commercial or closed source licensing, the user or organization using the software is usually not allowed to share or modify the software.

899
Understanding the Importance of Prohibited Content/Activity
and Privacy, Licensing, and Policy Concepts

There are also personal and enterprise-level licenses. For example, a home user might have a computer with a paid personal license to use Microsoft Windows 10 Home Edition, but a midsized to large organization will have corporate-use licenses (such as for Windows 10 Enterprise Edition) that are usually bought in bulk.

Software with open source licensing is usually free to use. With open source licensing, the user is allowed to study, modify, and share the software or even create new distributions of it and sell it for a profit.

> **ExamAlert**
>
> Know the difference between open source and commercial licenses. And know the difference between personal licenses and corporate-use licenses.

Be sure to organize and store licensing information properly, according to organizational policy, and know how to find licenses for your own organization or for a customer if you are contracted to perform work for a customer.

Regulated Data

Several types of data regulations are covered on the A+ exam. These regulations are designed to protect personal information and people. Here we'll briefly discuss PII, PHI, PCI-DSS, and GDPR.

PII

Personally identifiable information (PII) is something that every organization and technician should be concerned with because it affects us all. PII is information used to uniquely identify, contact, or locate a person. This type of information could be a name, birthday, Social Security number, biometric information, and so on. In Chapter 57, "Documentation," I mentioned the Privacy Act of 1974 and other laws, regulations, and guidelines that are designed to protect PII in a standardized way. However, organizations often have their own privacy policies (which may be based on these best practices) that go further to define how users' identities will be protected in a procedural manner.

An example of PII is personal government-issued information/identification. In the United States, this includes birth certificates, Social Security cards, driver's licenses, non-driver ID cards, passports, permanent resident cards, municipal

ID cards, and individual taxpayer ID numbers. There are a lot of ways that a person can be identified, and therefore, there is a lot of information that needs to be protected and secured.

PHI

Protected health information (PHI) is information that is protected under the HIPAA Privacy Rule. The Health Insurance Portability and Accountability Act (HIPAA) is a wide-ranging act, passed in 1996, that governs the protection of all kinds of health information. Any organization in the United States that requests, stores, or accesses health information must abide by the rules within HIPAA.

Best practices for PII and PHI are quite similar, so let's discuss a couple of them as they relate to digital records:

▶ Appoint a security admin (with compliance experience) to oversee the access and storage techniques used for PII and PHI records.

▶ Physically secure computers, servers, server rooms, datacenters, and network connections where records are being stored.

▶ Store records in an encrypted format and transmit records from one system to another or from a system to the cloud using end-to-end encrypted sessions. This way, data at rest, data in transit, and data in use can be protected.

In addition, make use of the many security best practices that we have documented within this book's security chapters and keep in mind that PII and PHI records are at the top of the list when it comes to logging, auditing, and monitoring.

PCI-DSS

The payment card industry (PCI) encompasses anything that concerns credit cards, debit cards, ATMs, point-of-sale (POS) machines, and so on, that organizations use or transact with when dealing with user cardholder data. The PCI Security Standards Council (PCI-SSC) developed a compliance program known as the Payment Card Industry Data Security Standards (PCI-DSS). These standards, and the varying levels of compliance, define how credit card data is to be transacted and stored. For example, system and audit logs that

901
Understanding the Importance of Prohibited Content/Activity
and Privacy, Licensing, and Policy Concepts

show access to stored data must be retained for at least one year. Afterward, all sensitive and credit card data must be destroyed if it is no longer required legally. (Keep in mind that these data retention requirements could change over time. See the links and references below to keep up to date on the latest PCI-DSS changes.)

The best practices for PCI-DSS include a lot of the security methods we have discussed previously in this book, but from a more high-level viewpoint, the PCI-SSC is looking for a sustainable security program; compliant policies and procedures; performance metrics (such as those defined in NIST SP 800-55 Rev. 1, Performance Measurement Guide for Information Security); specific assignments to qualified personnel (perhaps who certify to PCI-DSS); proper risk assessment and management techniques; monitoring of security controls (which is a big part of the compliance); maintaining evidence; incident response procedures; and generally maintaining security awareness.

PCI-DSS is important whether your organization is a five-employee office or an enterprise-level corporation.

> **Note**
>
> You can view the entire best practices document (updated to version 2.0 in 2019) as set forth by the PCI-SSC at https://www.pcisecuritystandards.org/documents/ PCI_DSS_V2.0_Best_Practices_for_Maintaining_PCI_DSS_Compliance.pdf.

GDPR

The General Data Protection Regulation (GDPR) is a European Union (EU) regulation that deals with data protection and privacy for people who live in the EU. However, it has wide-ranging implications for companies around the world (especially in the United States) that have transactions with EU citizens, requiring them to adopt policies and best practices that support the regulation. One common example of an industry that was "turned upside down" by GDPR is the email/mailing list industry. These lists contain personal data—meaning information related to an identified or identifiable natural person—and in many cases the way that data was handled was not compliant with the GDPR. The GDPR defines how transparency should function, the proper securing of data, the awareness of what data is being collected, and citizen rights such as the right to access and request erasure of personal data. This regulation was enforceable as of May 25, 2018, and at the time, it seemed that technical changes, written policies, and proper opt-in/opt-out lists became realities almost overnight for many companies. The GDPR affects my own business and every single company that I deal with.

> **ExamAlert**
>
> Know the types of regulated data and related concepts, including PII, PHI, PCI, and GDPR.

GDPR best practices are similar to what we have mentioned already in this chapter, and the security methods include much of what we have discussed in the security sections of this book. These best practices focus on the auditing data; securely managing data; assessing risk of data that is stored; assigning a data protection officer (for companies with 250 employees or more); training employees about GDPR best practices; and having in place a data breach and incident response plan.

> **Note**
>
> For more information on the GDPR, see https://ec.europa.eu/info/law/law-topic/data-protection_en.

Don't Be Too Alarmed by Data Regulations!

An A+ technician should know what data regulations and best practices are and should be ready to abide by them when employed by an organization. However, the simple truth is that most A+ technicians will have very little to do with the creation, modification, or enforcement of these regulations. The bottom line is that you should concentrate on identifying the threat model for your organization's data and implement strong security measures that hopefully will prevent data breaches, while monitoring the data carefully for any changes, anomalies, or attacks. If you are ever confused by a regulation, best practice, or written organizational policy, see the appropriate compliance or human resources personnel to get the record straight.

Cram Quiz

Answer these questions. The answers follow the last question. If you cannot answer
these questions correctly, consider reading this chapter again until you can.

1. You find illegal materials on a customer's computer. Your boss commands you to
   preserve computer evidence until he gets to the scene. What is your boss asking
   you to begin?

   ○ **A.** Documentation

   ○ **B.** Chain of custody

   ○ **C.** First response

   ○ **D.** GDPR compliance

2. Which of the following is not one of the steps of the incident response process?

   ○ **A.** Eradication

   ○ **B.** Recovery

   ○ **C.** Containment

   ○ **D.** Non-repudiation

3. Which of these is a group of security controls designed to restrict the usage or
   proliferation of copyrighted software and products?

   ○ **A.** EULA

   ○ **B.** Personal use license

   ○ **C.** DRM

   ○ **D.** Corporate use license

4. You are the security administrator for your organization. You have just identified a
   malware incident. Of the following, what should be your first response?

   ○ **A.** Containment

   ○ **B.** Removal

   ○ **C.** Recovery

   ○ **D.** Monitoring

5. Which type of regulated data is specifically protected under the HIPAA Privacy
   Rule?

   ○ **A.** PII

   ○ **B.** PCI

   ○ **C.** GDPR

   ○ **D.** PHI

Cram Quiz Answers

1. **B.** Your boss is asking you to begin the process of a chain of custody, which is a chronological paper trail of evidence. It is a specific form of documentation. You were the first responder. These cases will be rare, but you should understand the terminology and what to do if you find illegal materials.

2. **D.** Non-repudiation, although an important part of security, is not part of the incident response process. Non-repudiation means that you have irrefutable proof that a person did something; it might include logs, audit trails, and so on. Eradication, containment, and recovery are all parts of the incident response process

3. **C.** Digital rights management (DRM) is a group of security controls that restricts usage or proliferation of copyrighted software and products. An end-user licensing agreement (EULA) is a contract or an agreement between a proprietary software vendor and an end user. A personal use license is meant for one user. For example, a home user might have a computer with a paid personal use license to use Microsoft Windows 10 Home Edition. A midsized to large organization might have enterprise-level or corporate use licenses (such as for Windows 10 Enterprise Edition) that are usually bought in bulk.

4. **A.** Of the listed answers, most organizations' incident response procedures specify that containment of the malware incident should be first. Next would be the removal of the malware, then recovery of any damaged systems, and finally monitoring (which should actually be going on at all times). But before all of this is the preparation phase; in the scenario, identification was already performed.

5. **D.** Protected health information (PHI) is information that is protected under the HIPAA Privacy Rule. The Health Insurance Portability and Accountability Act (HIPAA) is a wide-ranging act that governs the protection of all kinds of health information. Personally identifiable information (PII) is information used to uniquely identify, contact, or locate a person. The payment card industry (PCI) encompasses anything that concerns credit cards, debit cards, ATMs, or point-of-sale (POS) machines. The General Data Protection Regulation (GDPR) is a European Union regulation that deals with data protection and privacy.

Using Proper Communication Techniques and Professionalism

> **ExamAlert**
>
> **Objective 4.7** focuses on the following: professional appearance and attire; using proper language and avoiding jargon, acronyms, and slang, when applicable; maintaining a positive attitude/project confidence; actively listening; taking notes; avoiding interrupting the customer; being culturally sensitive; being on time (and, if late, contact the customer); avoiding distractions; dealing with difficult customers or situations; setting and meeting expectations/time lines and communicating status with the customer; and dealing appropriately with customers' confidential and private materials.

Mind your customer service skills. You might be a super technician, but without people skills, your job market will be limited. By being professional and utilizing good communication skills, you increase the chances of receiving a good customer reaction. Also, these skills help you get to the heart of an issue and can help make you more efficient, saving time as you repair computer problems. Throughout the rest of the book, you have learned how to repair computers. If you put those abilities together with a professional demeanor and good communication skills, there should be no lack of new customers in your future.

Communication Techniques and Professionalism

For the CompTIA A+ 220-1102 exam, communication and professionalism consist of 10 categories:

▶ **Professional appearance and attire:** As they say, "dress for success!" The exact type of dress should be appropriate for the environment and situation. For example, formal dress might be required for a job interview. Formal dress in the workplace usually means a suit and tie for men and a business suit with pants or long skirt and jacket for women. The conventional colors for formal wear are black and navy blue. But this kind of ensemble isn't appropriate for other situations, such as day-to-day work at the office or fixing an end-user's cable Internet connection. In those scenarios (and many others), business casual is recommended. While there is no standard definition for business casual, we can site some examples: for women, skirt or dress slacks, blouse, sweater, twinset, jacket, and closed-toe shoes; for men, shirt and tie with dress slacks or sweater with chinos, and dark socks and shoes. Keep in mind that a company might have its own dress code, which might specify uniforms or other specific requirements. If you aren't sure, ask! Many HR departments will gladly share what is considered appropriate for the company and might even list this information on a website or in the company portal.

▶ **Use proper language and avoid jargon, acronyms, and slang, when applicable:** Speak slowly, clearly, and professionally so the customer can fully understand what you are saying. Refrain from slang and profanity. Avoid computer jargon and acronyms (for example, WPA3 or TCP/IP). If you use computer jargon, the customer might think that you are insecure and cannot clearly explain things. Stay away from techno-babble. The customer expects you to know these things technically but to explain them in a simple manner. That's the essence of a good teacher!

> **Note**
>
> Even if the customer hits you with something like this: "Hey, my VPN with static IP is using PPTP, but isn't that deprecated? And I really need DynDNS and a RADIUS right away!" you should still respond with as little technical jargon as possible. (This really occurred, but you'll note that the customer didn't actually need DynDNS, because they had a static IP address already.)

▶ **Maintain a positive attitude/project confidence:** Even if the customer thinks the situation is hopeless or the customer is frustrated, be positive. Sometimes problems that appear to be the worst have the easiest solutions! And there is always a solution. It's just a matter of finding it. Also, as part of being positive, try to project confidence. Be calm and assure your customer that the problem will be solved.

▶ **Actively listen (taking notes) and avoid interrupting the customer:** The more you listen, the better you will understand the problem. Write down key points related to the problem the customer is having. Don't interrupt the customer, even if you think you know what the problem is before the customer has fully explained the situation. Be respectful and allow the customer to completely explain the problem. The customer's tale just might give you clues as to what the real problem is. Listen carefully and be assertive when eliciting answers.

▶ **Be culturally sensitive:** Understand that customers come from all walks of life. Be aware that cultural differences and similarities exist. Be respectful and kind. Use appropriate professional titles when applicable and when possible. Make an effort to ensure that you and the customer understand each other and work toward a common goal. If you don't at first understand the customer or if there is a language barrier, kindly ask the customer to repeat themselves.

▶ **Be on time (and, if late, contact the customer):** Be punctual! Be on time! If a customer has to wait, the situation might become difficult before you even begin. If you are running late, contact the customer, say you will be late, and apologize.

▶ **Avoid distractions:** Phone calls should be screened and left to go to voicemail except in emergencies. The same goes for emails and text messages that arrive on your smartphone. If other customers call, explain to them that you are with a customer and will call them back shortly (or have your manager or co-worker take care of them, if they are available). Avoid talking to co-workers when dealing with customers. The customer wants to feel valued and wants to get the problem fixed in a timely manner. Try to avoid personal interruptions in general. And avoid using social media sites while working with customers or to communicate about customers.

▶ **Deal with difficult customers or situations:** By being patient, understanding, and respectful, you show customers that you are a professional and are serious about fixing their computer problems. Never argue with customers or take a defensive or offensive stance. This is one of those times in which I like to think of Mr. Spock. Approach customers' computer problems and complaints from a scientific point of view. Try not to make light of a customer's computer issues, no matter how simple they might seem, and avoid being judgmental about any possible user error. Try not to ask things such as "What did you do?" or "Who was working on this?" because these questions can come across as accusations. Ask computer-oriented, open-ended questions when eliciting answers from the customers (for example, ask "What is wrong with the computer?" or "What can you tell me about this computer?"). Stick with the senses; questions such as "What type of strange behavior did you see from the computer?" keep customers more relaxed and can help you narrow down the cause of the problem. Again, if a customer doesn't come across clearly, restate what you believe to be the issue or repeat your question so that you can verify your understanding and be on the same page as the customer. Clarify the customer's statements. Ask concise questions of the customer to further identify what the issue is and narrow the scope of the problem. When you think you understand what the problem is, you should clarify by repeating the problem back to the customer. Restate the issue to verify that everyone understands the problem. Again, do not disclose experiences via social media.

▶ **Set and meet expectations/timelines and communicate status with the customer:** When you have a clear idea of what the customer's trouble is, set a timeline; offer a reasonable assessment of how long it will take to fix the issue and what will be involved. Stay in contact with the customer, giving him or her updates at certain intervals—every half hour for smaller jobs and perhaps two or three times a day for larger jobs. If applicable, offer different repair or replacement options as the job progresses. At first, you might inform a customer that it appears a power supply needs to be changed. Later, you might find that an optical drive also needs to be replaced. Keep the customer up to date and offer options. Whatever the service, be clear as to the policies of your company and provide the proper documentation about the services you will be performing. After you finish the job, follow up with the customer to verify that the computer runs smoothly and that he or she is satisfied.

▶ **Deal appropriately with customers' confidential and private materials:** Do not look at or touch confidential information. Ask the customer to move confidential items to another area where you cannot see them. Do not look at or touch confidential materials located on a computer, desktop, printer, and so on. This could include bank statements, accounting information, legal documents, and other top-secret company information. Going beyond this, don't disclose any work experiences you had with an organization on social media.

Always remember to do the right thing. If a customer asks you to do something that you think is inappropriate, be sure to verify exactly what it is the customer wants you to do. Then take appropriate action. For example, if a customer asks you to install company software on his personal laptop, you should verify that the installation is allowed under the company's licensing agreements. If so, no harm is done. If not, you will have to politely refuse the customer. This type of customer behavior, while rare, should be reported to your manager.

ExamAlert

Be professional, punctual, and positive and practice all the other skills mentioned in this section. They are important for the exam—and crucial in the computer field.

Cram Quiz

Answer these questions. The answers follow the last question. If you cannot answer these questions correctly, consider reading this chapter again until you can.

1. How will speaking with a lot of jargon make a technician sound?
   - ○ **A.** Competent
   - ○ **B.** Insecure
   - ○ **C.** Smart
   - ○ **D.** Powerful

2. A customer experiences a server crash. When you arrive, the manager is upset about this problem. What do you need to remember in this scenario?
   - ○ **A.** Stay calm and do the job as efficiently as possible.
   - ○ **B.** Imagine the customer in his underwear.
   - ○ **C.** Avoid the customer and get the job done quickly.
   - ○ **D.** Refer the customer to your supervisor.

3. Which of the following are good ideas when dealing with customers? (Select two.)

○ **A.** Speak clearly.

○ **B.** Ignore them.

○ **C.** Avoid distractions.

○ **D.** Explain to them what they did wrong.

4. You are a field technician working at a customer's site. One of the workers asks you to load a copy of an organization's purchased software on a personal laptop. What should you do first?

○ **A.** Verify that the installation is allowed under the company's licensing agreement.

○ **B.** Act as though you are distracted and ignore the user.

○ **C.** Leave the premises and inform the police.

○ **D.** Tell the worker that installing unlicensed software is illegal.

○ **E.** Notify the worker's manager of a security breach.

5. You have been asked by a customer at a hospital to perform routine maintenance on a laser printer. Before you begin, you notice that PHI has printed out. What should you do first?

○ **A.** Ensure the paper tray is full so that everything can print.

○ **B.** Place the printed output in a secure recycle bin and begin maintenance.

○ **C.** Kindly warn the customer that printing PHI at work is a HIPAA violation.

○ **D.** Ask the customer to move the printed output to another area.

Cram Quiz Answers

1. **B.** Using too much computer jargon can make an end user think that you do not have the qualifications needed and are masking it with techno-babble.

2. **A.** There isn't much you can do when a customer is upset except stay calm and fix the problem! Remember, it's a job; it's not personal.

3. **A and C.** Speak clearly so that customers understand you and avoid distractions so that the customers know they have your complete attention.

4. **A.** You should check whether the company allows installation of paid software on personal computers or laptops. If it is allowed, go ahead and do the installation. If not, you should refuse and notify your manager of the occurrence. Refusal can be tough at times, so be strong and think about the consequences of your actions. They could directly affect you in a negative way.

5. **D.** Ask the customer to move the confidential information. Protected health information (PHI) is information that is protected under the HIPAA Privacy Rule. Before ensuring that the paper tray is full, you should first ask the customer to remove the private information. You should never throw away or recycle customer-printed output unless a customer asks you to. Printing PHI at a hospital is routine and not a HIPAA violation. Remember to always behave professionally and protect people's privacy. If you make this a regular practice, you will often receive a customer's gratitude, and as time goes on, you will increase your job security.

Nice work! That was a bit of a longer chapter, so review your notes and then take a break because we will be getting back into the more technical side of things in the next chapter. You are doing great!

CHAPTER 62

Basic Scripting, Part I

This chapter covers a portion of the following A+ 220-1102 exam objective:

▶ **4.8** – Identify the basics of scripting.

The goal of this chapter is to cover the basics of scripting construction. This chapter is not designed to make you a programmer; however, it should enable you to break down the components of some basic scripts. One of the goals of scripting is to make things faster and more efficient by automating processes, ultimately making your job as a technician easier. If you have any doubts about programming computers, let me just say: You can do this! Let's go!

> **ExamAlert**
>
> **Objective 4.8** concentrates on the following: script file types, use cases for scripting, and other considerations when using scripts.

Programming 101

Before we can get into specific scripting types, we need to cover some foundational programming concepts, including data types, script constructs, variables, and comments. This chapter provides a crash course on the basics of programming. We will cover specific scripting types (such as PowerShell and Bash) in the following chapter. Begin.

Basic Data Types

There are two basic data types that you should know: integers and strings. In computer programming and scripting, an integer is essentially the same as in mathematics. An *integer* is a whole number (no fractions or decimal places) that can be positive, negative, or zero.

Integer types can have different sizes, and you have no doubt heard of some of them—for example, the byte of information. Typically, a byte can be between 0 and 255. In binary, this would be 00000000 through 11111111. So, it can have 2^8 (that is, 256) values. But there are more integral data types, like the nibble (which is 4 bits) or a word (which is 16 bits), or the doubleword (which is 32 bits).

All programming languages from C++ and Java to Python and JavaScript use integers because all programming languages are based in mathematics.

> **Note**
>
> By the way, if you need fractions or decimal places (real numbers), then you need floating-point numbers rather than integers.

A *string* is a sequence of characters used as a constant (such as a "word" like *cat*) or as a variable (such as *x*). A *constant* is something that remains the same. A *variable*, on the other hand, is something that can change over time, but we reference it with something that does not change (for example, *x* or *y*).

As opposed to an integer, a string is designed to represent text instead of numbers. You'll also hear strings referred to as *alphanumeric strings*, which can include letters in the alphabet, digits, blank space, and special characters and punctuation.

Collectively, these data types are the building blocks for data within programming languages. Let's now focus on using these data types in scripting.

Basic Script Constructs

Scripting construct methods are essentially the same from one scripting language to the next. Let's use PowerShell as an example as we discuss some basic scripting constructs.

if Statement

One basic construct to use in scripting is the **if** statement. Here's an example of the general syntax:

```
if (conditional_expression) {
  statement_list
}
```

We use parentheses around the conditional expression, which can include things such as basic math—for example, (1 + 1)—or can point to code blocks, which would be contained in angle brackets (< >)—for example, **<test1>**. If the conditional expression is true, then the *statement_list* runs. For example, you might have a script write something to the screen or perform some kind of function within the OS, using a module from within PowerShell such as Write-Host or PSWindowsUpdate. Whatever it is, it should be confined within the curly braces{}.

This is a form of an **if-then** statement. While many programming languages use **if-then** statements, PowerShell doesn't actually incorporate the term **then**. Instead, if a condition is true, the code runs. If not, you use the **else** option to specify that other code runs.

Other constructs in PowerShell include **switch, for, break, continue, while,** and **do.**

Let's say that you want to repeat a task 10 times. To avoid typing the code 10 times, you can instead incorporate a loop. Two of the most common constructs used for looping in PowerShell are **for** and **while**. Let's discuss the **for** loop.

for Loops

A **for** loop is used to repeat a block of code as needed. These repetitions are also known as *iterations*. A **for** loop has two parts: a header specifying the iteration and a body that is executed once per iteration. Look at the following general syntax:

```
for (init; condition; repeat)
    {command_block}
```

In this syntax, ***init*** is the command that is run before the loop begins. Generally, it is used to initialize a variable. ***condition*** is whether the expression is true or false. If it is true, the command will continue to repeat until the loop is exhausted and the condition is changed to false. This is based on the number of iterations, which is also included. ***repeat*** reads the value of the variable and increments it…one at a time. ***command_block*** is the command or group of commands that will repeat. Here's an example of a **for** loop in PowerShell that will count to 10:

```
for ($i=1; $i -le 10; $i++)
    {Write-Host $i}
```

PowerShell always places a **$** before a variable—for example, **$i**. In this case, ***init*** is **$i=1**, so the variable **i** has been set to 1. This is where the counting starts. This loop will repeat 10 times, as set in the condition **-le 10**.

Try this last script and the following one in PowerShell:

```
for ($i=1; $i -le 10; $i++) {$i,"'n"}
```

Both of these scripts will count from 1 to 10, but there is a slight difference between them. Can you spot the difference?

For information on how to open and use PowerShell in Windows, see Chapter 31, "Microsoft Command-Line Tools, Part I."

Remember, we are using the **for** construct to create the loop and the **$i** variable for the integers to be displayed.

As you progress, you will combine **if-then** statements with **for** loops and other programming constructs.

Environment Variables

We have mentioned environment variables previously in the book; for example, %systemroot% (which is usually C:\Windows) and %username% (which is whatever user or users you are referring to). If you are working in the GUI or the Registry Editor, or if scripting in the Command Prompt, you use the *%variablename%* syntax. However, PowerShell has its own variables that start with **$** (which is similar to many other scripting languages)—for example, **$Env:*variablename***, where an actual value might be **$Env:Path**.

Path is a variable in Windows. It allows you to run programs from various locations in Windows without having to type the entire folder path to the executable. For example, a default path in Windows is C:\Windows\System32. You can run programs that reside within System32 in the Run prompt, the Command Prompt, or PowerShell just by typing the executable name. You can find out all of these path locations by executing the following in PowerShell:

```
Get-Item Env:Path
```

This displays any paths that have been added to the **Path** variable. However, this isn't functional only within the shell; **Path**, as well as other variables, can be added programmatically to scripts as well, which has a wide range of implications, from administration to development. Be ready to work with environment variables in Windows and in Linux.

Comment Syntax

Sometimes, you will want to add descriptions, warnings, links, or other information to your scripts that do not actually *do* anything other than give information to the person reading the script. These things can be accomplished by adding comment syntax to the code. You can also *comment out* certain lines of code if you want them to stop functioning temporarily for testing purposes.

Using comment syntax in PowerShell and Bash is as easy as adding a number sign (#) before each line. For example:

```
# this script will count to 100.
for ($i=1; $i -le 100; $i++) {$i,"'n"}
```

Other types of scripts, such as JavaScript, use the double slash (//) before each line, which I'll demonstrate in the JavaScript section in the next chapter.

ExamAlert

For the exam, know how to comment out code with # (in PowerShell and Bash) or // (in other commonly used scripting languages).

Cram Quiz

Answer these questions. The answers follow the last question. If you cannot answer these questions correctly, consider reading this chapter again until you can.

1. Which of the following is an integer? (Select the two best answers.)
   - ○ **A.** 16
   - ○ **B.** cat
   - ○ **C.** string
   - ○ **D.** 00000001

2. You want to list a variable number 16 times but don't want to type 16 lines of code. Which of the following techniques should you use?
   - ○ **A.** if-then
   - ○ **B.** Looping
   - ○ **C.** Environment variables
   - ○ **D.** Comment syntax

3. What should you type to comment out syntax in PowerShell?
   - ○ **A.** $
   - ○ **B.** #
   - ○ **C.** //
   - ○ **D.** ()

Cram Quiz Answers

1. **A and D.** The number 16 is an integer (any whole number is), and the binary number 00000001 is an integer that is equal to one 8-bit byte of information. Cat is an example of a string, which is a sequence of characters.

2. **B.** Make use of looping, which allows you to write one line of code based on math that will output the 16 lines of code required. In this example, it would be a *conditional loop*, where the operation is repeated until a specific requirement is met. **if-then** statements are used as conditional expressions. Environment variables are variables that define items within the system such as the environment path. Comment syntax is used to temporarily disable lines of code.

3. **B.** Use the number sign (#) to add comments or comment out lines of code in PowerShell and Bash. (The # symbol on the keyboard is also known as the pound sign or hash.) The **$** is used to denote a variable in many languages and scripting tools, including PowerShell and Bash. The double-slash (**//**) is used to add comments or to comment out individual lines of code in JavaScript (and several other types of languages). Parentheses ( ) contain pieces of code, such as a conditional expression within an **if-then** statement.

Embrace the Power of Programming

All right! Our Programming 101 crash course is now complete. Take a deep breath! If these topics are new to you, then I recommend that you review what you have learned so far before continuing on. And for those of you feeling a strange sensation right now, it could be that you are starting to realize the power of programming and scripting. With tools such as PowerShell, Bash, and others, you get complete control over a system and can automate processes, which will save you time and make you a more efficient tech. I mentioned it previously in the book: The command line is where real technicians live. And scripting takes the command line to the next level. Embrace the power.

CHAPTER 63

Basic Scripting, Part II

This chapter covers a portion of the following A+ 220-1102 exam objective:

▶ **4.8** – Identify the basics of scripting.

Now let's move into scripting types that you will undoubtedly see in the IT field. There are six scripting types listed in the A+ objectives. Probably the most important of them for the exam are Windows-based Power-Shell scripts (.ps1) and Linux-based Bash scripts (.sh). Let's start with those.

PowerShell and .ps1

PowerShell is Microsoft's main command-line and scripting environment for Windows. It is a much more powerful shell than the Command Prompt and is the preferred method for administration, scripting, and developing. Go ahead and open PowerShell in elevated mode now in your version of Windows.

Note

If you plan to use PowerShell often, I recommend creating a shortcut on the desktop (with an associated keyboard shortcut) or have it start automatically when you log on by adding it to the Windows Startup folder or the Task Scheduler.

To begin, you need to make sure that you are running a current version of PowerShell. To find out the version, type the following in the shell:

```
$PSVersionTable
```

For my version of Windows 10 (21H1), the PowerShell version (PSVersion) is 7.0.2. As this book ages, that version will become dated. You will want to upgrade to the current version of PowerShell. To find out more about the current version and to upgrade, see https://docs.microsoft.com/en-us/powershell/.

You will note additional information when running the **$psversiontable** command, such as the OS version (from a programmatic standpoint); at the writing of this book, mine is Microsoft Windows 10.0.19043.

One of the main reasons to use PowerShell is to automate processes or at least make them faster. For example, if you wanted to create a user in Windows, you would have to go through a lengthy process in Settings or in Local Users and Groups, using both the keyboard and the mouse. However, you can also create users in PowerShell. Take a look at the following command:

```
New-LocalUser "user1" -FullName "Test User" -Description "Test user
account."
```

New-LocalUser is a *cmdlet*—that is, a lightweight command that is used in the PowerShell environment. This cmdlet (and ensuing parameters) would result in a new user being created, called *user1*, with the name *Test User*. PowerShell would then ask you to type a password for the account, and then the account would be created and placed in the Users folder; you can easily test it by typing **net user**, which will display the users on the computer (though you also get verification from PowerShell after the command is run).

Boom, done, and you didn't have to go through the GUI—so already you can see that PowerShell is a boon for sysadmins.

Now, running commands in PowerShell is super fun, but what if you want to create a script? A *script* is used to run multiple commands in rapid succession and to initiate **for** loops and other programmatical constructs. You could write and run a PowerShell script directly in PowerShell, but it is usually wiser to build a script by using a tool. You could use a basic text editor, such as Notepad (**Run > notepad**), or you could use an integrated development environment (IDE) such as Visual Studio Code (VSC), which you can download for free from https://code.visualstudio.com.

When you are done writing a script, you save it as a .ps1 file. The .ps1 extension identifies a file as a PowerShell script. .ps1 is not the only extension you can use, but it's the one we will focus on for the A+ exam.

> **ExamAlert**
>
> Know that PowerShell scripts are identified by the .ps1 extension!

Which Tool to Use?

That's up to you. Notepad is built into Windows, and it's super easy to use. Feel free to work with that tool or another text editor if you like. However, you need to run Notepad and PowerShell separately, and every time you want to test your code, you have to switch between the two applications. Windows Snap can help somewhat, but you still have to use Alt+Tab or the mouse to switch between apps. That's where an IDE comes in. If you really want to get busy, use VSC. It *integrates* PowerShell (or other shells) right into the program that you code in. Pure genius, right? Downloading and installing it is a breeze. Also, it's cross-platform, so there are downloads for Linux and macOS as well—if you prefer those platforms over Windows. Or, you might find that you like a different IDE better; I use a couple different IDEs. There are a lot of options, and which one you choose depends on what kind of work you will be doing. But I *strongly* urge you to check out using VSC as a method for working effectively with PowerShell (and other scripting types).

Let's take it to the next level. Figure 63.1 shows an example of a .ps1 script that adds multiple users at once.

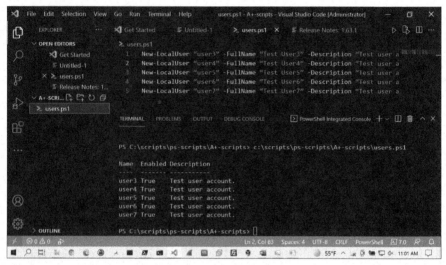

FIGURE 63.1   **users.ps1 script example.**

I wrote this script in VSC (as an administrator). I created a new .ps1 file called users.ps1, which you can see in the left-hand pane (known as the Explorer). The actual script is the five lines of code you see in the coding area at the top. In VSC, the code can be executed (or run) by clicking the play button or pressing Ctrl+F5. The results are displayed in the integrated PowerShell console at the bottom. You can see that user3 through user7 were all added at once.

In this example, I added the password during user creation. To create the password first and store it securely, you could use the following code in PowerShell:

```
$Password = Read-Host -AsSecureString
```

…and type the password that you want. Then reference it later during the user creation process in the script with the following:

```
-Password $Password
```

-Password is the parameter, and **$Password** is, wait for it…a *variable*. It will grab the password that you previously stored. In PowerShell, a variable name always begins with a dollar sign (**$**).

However, the script in Figure 63.1 is *very* basic. It's really just for educational purposes. You could take it further by using more variables, **for** loops, **if-then** statements, and tables (arrays) of information and then adding more and more lines to the script. Then you could save the whole adventure for later use, again as a .ps1 file. This is scripting in a nutshell.

Here's another example of PowerShell usage. Say that you want to test whether a computer is alive on the network. You could run the **ping** command, but PowerShell also offers the **test-connection** cmdlet, which enables you to ping multiple systems and in many ways. Try the following command in PowerShell:

```
test-connection example.com, dprocomputer.com
```

If you have a working Internet connection, the results will show the IP address of each website and that each was pinged four times successfully. Because it is a PowerShell-specific command, you could use the **test-connection** command in a .ps1 script as needed. It could be a basic script that simply runs the command with the options you desire—and even that would be a time saver if it is a test you run often. Or, you could combine it with the programming constructs we described in the previous chapter to make your tech world even more efficient.

Take it to the next level, and you could run your pings in an *actual* script by using a **for** loop and Microsoft class structures. Instead of using the **ping** or **test-connection** command, you could go straight to the source and make use of the Win32_PingStatus class in PowerShell. This might go beyond the A+ exams, but I show exactly how to do this in the video at https://dprocomputer.com/?p=3110.

> **Note**
>
> For more information about PowerShell, start here: https://docs.microsoft.com/en-us/powershell/scripting/overview.

Challenge 6: Use PowerShell and VSC!

As mentioned, these challenges are optional, but they are designed to help you grasp the concepts in the A+ objectives as they apply to the real world. So, if you have the time, try the following on a test machine:

1. Update to the latest version of PowerShell.
2. Create a shortcut to PowerShell on the Desktop (as an administrator).
3. Add a user with the **New-LocalUser** command.
4. Ping a domain on the Internet with the **test-connection** command.
5. Download and install VSC and play around with it for a little bit. If you are feeling brave, write a basic script and save it as a .ps1 file.

.bat and Batch Files

For a long time, we DOS/Windows users (aka dinosaurs) would write batch scripts (sometimes complicated and temperamental) to map network drives, add users, perform a series of pings, and so on and then save them as .bat files. Often these files would be written in the Notepad program or something similar and run in the Command Prompt. Here's a basic example:

```
net use Z: \\mach1\superdata
```

This command, when run as a batch process (by executing the .bat file), would map the Z: drive of the local system to the *superdata* share on the *mach1* server. You could then add the batch file to the startup process of the operating system. This would be handy if the drive needed to be mapped every time the system booted. But it's not necessary on today's Windows systems. By the way, to make this command persistent, meaning that the drive would remain after a reboot, you add this option: **/Persistent:Yes**. However, **net use** is the old method. Later on in the chapter, we'll look at the newer PowerShell method.

You can still create batch files today within Notepad, and some Windows users still do, but PowerShell makes the process much easier and more configurable. Personally, I left .bat files in the dust many years ago, but they are listed in the A+ objectives, so there you have it!

Bash and .sh

In the Linux, world, you can create scripts with a text editor (such as nano, Vim, or gedit) or an IDE. IDEs in Linux work in the same manner as in Windows, which we showed previously in the PowerShell section. So, for this section, let's focus on using text editors in the Linux Terminal.

In Linux, you can type commands and run text editors directly within Terminal. (Remember: Terminal is the command line for Linux.) This program utilizes one of a variety of shells. (Essentially, the shell is the command line interpreter.) The default shell in many Linux distributions is called Bash. To find out what shell is being used, type the following command:

```
echo "$SHELL"
```

Bash is also where you can save scripts by default. The path is /bin/bash, though you can save them elsewhere if you wish. Normally, bash scripts are saved with the .sh extension (short for shell).

ExamAlert

Know that the .sh file extension represents a Linux/Unix shell scripting file.

Let's look at how to build a basic and traditional "Hello, World" script. First, you need to access Terminal. If you are on a Linux desktop, press the super-user key (the Windows key), start typing **terminal**, and Terminal appears. Alternatively, some distros (such as Ubuntu) let you use the keyboard shortcut Ctrl+Alt+T to go straight to Terminal. A Linux server does not usually have a desktop environment, and therefore you are already working in the command line—essentially Terminal.

Once you have opened Terminal, you can open the text editor where you will build your scripts. There are two main options in Linux: nano and Vim.

nano is built in to most Linux distros and is the easier tool to use. It is quite similar to Notepad in Windows (but is keyboard only by default). For example, to create and edit a file with nano, you could type **nano testscript.sh**. This command opens the nano program, and you are ready to start typing into your file. You will note several keyboard shortcuts at the bottom of the screen. To save a file and exit out of nano, you press Ctrl+X on the keyboard and then press **y** to save the changes to the file. If you wanted to modify the file later, you could simply repeat the entire process. As you can see, nano is easy to use.

However, many technicians prefer Vim because it is heavily customizable and can provide for excellent workflow. However, it is more cryptic in its usage if you are not used to it.

Vim is based on the original (and ancient) Unix text editor vi but is a bit easier to use. Vim is vi *improved*. vi is included in almost all distributions of Linux, and Vim is included in many as well. However, if Vim is not available in yours, you can install it by using a command like **apt install vim** (in Debian/Ubuntu) or **dnf install vim** (in Fedora/Red Hat). I recommend that you use Vim rather than vi because of its comparative ease of use and because it is very adaptable.

> **Note**
>
> For a basic video tutorial on Vim, see https://www.prowse.tech/vim/.

To create or modify a file in Vim, type **vim** and then the filename—for example, **vim helloworld.sh**. This opens the Vim editor, and you can get to work. However, to use Vim, you need to know special keystrokes to perform certain actions. For example, to actually enter information, you have to first press a key on the keyboard—most commonly the i key. (Think *i* for insert.) Table 63.1 lists some basic key commands. Most of these will work in Vim or in vi.

926

CHAPTER 63: Basic Scripting, Part II

TABLE 63.1 **Common Vim Tasks and Keystrokes/Commands**

Task	Keystroke
To enter insert mode for editing (before you can write a script)	Press Esc and type **i**
To go to command mode (for saving, exiting, and so on)	Press Esc
To save a file	Press Esc and type **:w** *filename*
To quit	Press Esc and type **:q**
To save and quit at the same time	Press Esc and type **:wq**

Keep in mind that you need **sudo** (superuser or equivalent) access to perform some of these actions (unless you are working as root). For more information on **sudo** and the root account, see Chapter 42, "Linux."

To try building the "Hello, World" script, follow these steps:

1. In Terminal, type **vim helloworld.sh**.

2. Press Esc and type **i** to enter insert mode (remember that this is the editing mode).

3. Type the following:

```
#!/bin/bash
echo "Hello, World!"
```

4. Press Esc to exit insert mode.

5. To save the file, type **:w** and press Enter.

6. Quit Vim by typing **:q** and pressing Enter. This will bring you back to the standard Bash terminal. Note that you could instead combine steps 5 and 6 by typing **:wq**.

7. Set permissions so that the script will run. For example:

```
chmod +x helloworld.sh
```

8. Run the script by typing **./helloworld.sh**.

You should now see the text that you placed in quotes within the script "Hello, World." Great job! That is an example of the most basic of Linux-based scripts.

Now let's take it up a notch. Here's a script that uses looping and displays the quoted text five times:

```
#!/bin/bash
for i in 1 2 3 4 5
do
  echo "Looping $i"
done
```

If you type this exactly, and use **chmod** with it, you should see the looped results. This script also makes use of the variable **$i**, which changes from 1 to 2 to 3 to 4 to 5 on each line.

Now, here's an example of an **if-then** statement as it would work in Bash:

```
if <condition>;
then <commands>
fi
```

This is a little different from the PowerShell-based *if* statement shown in the previous chapter. It uses an **if-then-fi** statement—also known as **if...fi**—to make decisions and execute statements conditionally. The condition is based on what you type in *<condition>*, and the *<commands>* are what will occur if the condition is met. Here's an example:

```
#!/bin/bash
age=21
if [ $age -gt 18 ]
then
  echo "You can now vote in the United States."
fi
```

In this example, the condition is that the **age** number must be greater than 18 for the command to work. The command is a simple **echo** command that displays the text "You can now vote in the United States." I created a variable where **age=21**, so the condition will be met. It's a bit of a silly script, but it's a quick way of showing how an **if-then** statement works in Bash.

Scripts often run automatically as cron jobs in Linux. Cron jobs can be created by using the **cron** utility, which is a time-based job scheduler. (See Chapter 42 for other scheduling and automation tools.)

To comment out in Bash, you add the number sign (#) before each line that you want commented out, just as you do in PowerShell. For example, I might type something like this:

```
# test script for voting age - exceptions apply!
```

This would describe what the script is meant to do, but it won't have any impact on how the script functions.

> **Note**
>
> You might have noticed that the Bash scripts started with **#!/bin/bash**. This is known as the shebang, or "bang," line. This is not a comment; rather, it tells Linux to interpret the script using the Bash shell and specifies the absolute directory path to that shell, which is /bin/bash. So, **#!** is different from just **#**.

> **ExamAlert**
>
> Know how to use Bash, including Terminal, nano, and Vim, for the exam!

Challenge 7: Linux, Nano, Vim, and Bash

Linux is a super-important tool for all kinds of techs: sysadmins, developers, and engineers. Practice with it by doing the following on a test system or virtual machine:

1. Create a basic Bash script with nano or Vim that will display text on the screen using the **echo** command.

2. Use **chmod** to apply executable permissions to the script and run it!

> **Note**
>
> If you enjoy working with Linux, check out my website https://prowse.tech. It's all about Linux and Linux servers.

Use Cases and Other Considerations for PowerShell and Bash

There are a lot of use cases for scripting within PowerShell or Bash. To start, you can create scripts to do basic automation of tasks such as file backups. This way, you don't have to manually run them each time. You can also build scripts to gather data about files, software, users, and so on. If these are the kinds of things that you do on a daily or weekly basis, then automating is the way to go.

There are some other use cases as well. Take a look at Table 63.2 for some examples. Any of these commands can be placed in a script to run when and how you want.

TABLE 63.2 **Typical Scripting Use Cases**

Use Case	Shell	Sample Commands (or cmdlets)
Restart a machine	PowerShell	**Restart-Computer**
	Bash	**reboot**
Restart multiple machines	PowerShell	**Restart-Computer -*ComputerName server01, server02, server03***
	Bash	**for *host* in $(< *inputfile*.txt);** **do** **ssh $*host* reboot now** **done**
Map network drive	PowerShell	**New-PSDrive**
	Command Prompt/Batch file (.bat)	**net use X:*server\share***
Install new applications	PowerShell	**Invoke-CimMethod**
	Bash	**apt install <*programname*>** or **dpkg -i <*packagename*>** or **dnf install <*programname*>**
Initiate updates	PowerShell	**Install-module PSWindowsUpdate** (if it isn't installed already) Then, **Install-WUUpdates**
	Bash	**apt update && apt upgrade -y**

These are just examples. You can modify and augment these examples in a million ways. Note also that most of the time, you don't need all the capital letters in the PowerShell commands, but that is how they are normally presented in documentation.

Mapping a Drive in PowerShell

Here's an actual example of mapping a drive in PowerShell using the **New-PSDrive** cmdlet. Type everything below as one line:

```
New-PSDrive -Name "K" -PSProvider FileSystem -Root
"\\mach2\megadata" -Persist
```

This would map a K: drive to the *megadata* share on the *mach2* server and make the connection persistent. For more on the **New-PSDrive** cmdlet, see https://docs.microsoft.com/en-us/powershell/module/microsoft.powershell.management/new-psdrive?view=powershell-7.2.

Keep in mind that scripts can be used for productive or malicious purposes, so they should be tightly controlled. For example, when you used the **chmod +x** command on a Bash script, you made it executable. You have to be careful what scripts you allow to execute, and you need to be very aware of the user and group permissions that you set for those scripts.

Here's the thing: A poorly designed script, or a script with weak permissions, can introduce chaos to your systems and networks. You might unintentionally introduce malware because it might be seeking out weak scripts. Another consideration is that you could inadvertently change system settings. Or, if a script is not designed well, it could mishandle the resources of the system (CPU, RAM, and so on), potentially causing web browsers and other applications—or even the entire system—to fail.

One way to avoid these pitfalls when developing scripts and entire applications is to implement *secure coding concepts*—that is, best practices used during software development to increase the security of the script or application being built; secure coding hardens code. An example of secure coding is working within a software development life cycle (SDLC) such as the agile model. SDLC models have a few core principles, including maintaining confidentiality, preserving integrity, and protecting availability (the CIA triad). There are several things that scripters/programmers can do to incorporate those core principles. The following are some of them, and they apply to all the scripting types in this chapter and programming in general:

▶ **Follow the principle of least privilege:** Users should have access only to what they need. Processes and scripts should run with only the bare minimum access needed to complete their functions.

▶ **Follow the principle of defense in depth:** The more security controls, the better. Also known as layered defense.

▶ **Ensure that applications never trust user input:** Input should be validated carefully.

▶ **Minimize the attack surface area:** Every additional feature that a person adds to a script or an application increases the attack surface and increases risk. Unnecessary functions should be removed, and necessary functions should require authorization.

▶ **Establish secure defaults:** Out-of-the-box offerings should be as secure as possible. Permissions should default to "no access" and should be granted only as they are needed.

▶ **Provide for authenticity and integrity:** For example, when deploying applications and scripts, use code signing in the form of a cryptographic hash with a verifiable checksum for validation.

▶ **Fail securely:** At times, applications fail. How they fail determines their security.

▶ **Fix security issues correctly:** Once found, security vulnerabilities should be thoroughly tested, documented, and understood. Patches should be developed to fix the problem but not cause other issues or application regression.

You get the idea. Always be thinking with that CIA triad in the back of your mind when it comes to scripts—or anything else technology related.

Python and .py

While PowerShell and Bash are heavily used, they aren't the only scripting tools in town. Case in point: Python.

Python is a high-level object-oriented programming language. While it can be used for scripting, it is a general-purpose programming language that can be used to build in-depth programs, making it more powerful than PowerShell,

Bash, JavaScript, and VBScript but slightly less powerful than languages such as C, C++, and Java. That's because Python requires an interpreter. In general, Python is very flexible and is used in a variety of ways.

To use Python in Windows or Linux, you first have to install it; you can grab it from https://www.python.org. After you install Python, you can access the Python console by simply typing **python** at the command line. You can test your Python commands there or build a Python script in a text editor or an IDE. When scripting in Python, you save the script as a .py file.

> **ExamAlert**
>
> Python scripting files use the .py file extension.

Python uses statements similar to those in other languages, such as **if**, **for**, and **while**, and it makes use of variables in a similar fashion.

Here's an example of a Python script that displays random six-sided die rolls.

```
import random
number = random.randint(1,6)
print("Your die roll is: " + str(number))
```

Let's say you saved this script as a file called rpg6sider.py. You could then run the script directly from the command line. To do so, you would type **python rpg6sider.py**. The script then runs, and it should randomly select a number between 1 and 6 and display it on the screen. (Gaming night just got geekier!)

Instead of programming everything from scratch, this script imports a module called **random**. This module includes all the math code needed for a pseudo-random generator and saves you a *ton* of time as you don't have to code that yourself. There are many modules and libraries like this. Take advantage of them.

As of the writing of this book, the current version of Python is version 3. (Version 2 is considered deprecated for the most part.) For Python documentation, see https://docs.python.org/3/. If you wish to program more in Python and want to use an IDE, consider using PyCharm or VSC.

> **Note**
>
> Interested in learning more? Check out *Intro to Python for Computer Science and Data Science* by Paul Deitel and Harvey M. Deitel. It's good.

Remember that Python is designed for small and large projects, and therefore it can be a great scripting tool in Windows and Linux, regardless of its differences from PowerShell and JavaScript.

JavaScript and .js

If you are going to have a powerful and interactive front end to your website, you will most likely be using JavaScript. Though it can be used in other environments, JavaScript is best known for being used to develop web pages. A good web developer knows to use HTML to define the content of web pages, CSS to work with the layout of web pages, and JavaScript to program how the web pages will behave and to add functionality. For example, if you wanted to have a quiz or a calculator on your website, you could use JavaScript.

You can work with JavaScript in any text editor but will probably have better luck with an IDE such as Eclipse, VSC, or one of the many others that are available. Regardless, when you are finished creating a script with JavaScript, save it as a .js file.

> **ExamAlert**
>
> Remember, JavaScript files use the .js file extension.

To comment out code in JavaScript, use the double-slash method (//), by adding the double-slash before each line to be commented out. // is designed for single lines of code. For multiple lines, use /* at the beginning of the comment and */ at the end. JavaScript will ignore any text between them. This is also common in other programming languages, such as C++, as well as markup languages.

> **Note**
>
> Speaking of markup languages, as a technician, you will want to learn a little bit about JavaScript Object Notation (JSON), which was derived from JavaScript. This markup language is used by many programs and systems for configuration files and analysis. Other good markup languages to know include YAML, HCL, and especially Markdown. Trust me on this.

By the way, if you are scripting in JavaScript, you will probably also be working in HTML. If you are working on an HTML web page and you want to leave a comment or comment something out, you use **<!--   -->** with the comment in the middle. A similar, newer programming language that you might encounter is TypeScript (which uses .ts files). It is a superset of JavaScript, which means that all .js files can run within it.

Regardless of what you use, you'll find that all scripting is based on math and common sense—once you get past the syntax and naming conventions, that is!

Visual Basic Script and .vbs

A file with the extension .vbs is a Visual Basic script, or VBScript file. VBScript is an object-based scripting language, and it was historically used in Windows environments (.NET and Office) and in web pages. You can build VBScript scripts within the Windows Notepad program or using any other text editor or IDE. Then simply save the script as a .vbs file. Visual Basic is also heavily used in Microsoft Office (namely Excel) with the included Visual Basic Editor.

> **ExamAlert**
>
> A file with the .vbs extension is a Visual Basic script, or VBScript file.

> **Note**
>
> In Windows, a lot of what was once done in VBScript is now done with PowerShell. On the Internet, it is more likely that you will use JavaScript or some other tool. However, VBScript still has a place in .NET (though many developers prefer C#) and especially within Microsoft Office. See this site for a tutorial about using the Visual Basic Editor within Microsoft Office, known as Visual Basic for Applications (VBA): https://docs.microsoft.com/en-us/office/vba/library-reference/concepts/getting-started-with-vba-in-office.

A Final Word on Scripting

You should be able to identify the various types of scripts and file extensions listed in this chapter, but I suggest that you focus primarily on PowerShell and Bash as those are specifically designed for systems administration with Windows and Linux, respectively.

Cram Quiz

Answer these questions. The answers follow the last question. If you cannot answer these questions correctly, consider reading this chapter again until you can.

1. A technician just finished scripting a sequence of code and saved the script as a .sh file. What system is the technician working in?

   - ○ **A.** PowerShell
   - ○ **B.** Linux
   - ○ **C.** JavaScript
   - ○ **D.** Python
   - ○ **E.** Batch file

2. You are scripting in PowerShell and need to incorporate a construct that will repeat an operation until a specific requirement is met. What construct should you use, and which extension should you use to save the script?

   - ○ **A.** **if-then** logic and .sh
   - ○ **B.** String variables and .py
   - ○ **C.** Conditional loop and .ps1
   - ○ **D.** Integers and .vbs

3. Which of the following can you use to map a network drive in PowerShell?

   - ○ **A.** **apt install**
   - ○ **B.** **for** loop
   - ○ **C.** **restart-computer**
   - ○ **D.** **Install-WUUpdates**
   - ○ **E.** **New-PSDrive**

4. Which of the following extensions identify files that can be run as scripts? (Select all that apply.)

   - ○ **A.** .ps1
   - ○ **B.** .exe
   - ○ **C.** .bat
   - ○ **D.** .docx
   - ○ **E.** .vbs
   - ○ **F.** .py
   - ○ **G.** .txt
   - ○ **H.** .sh

Cram Quiz Answers

1. **B.** The technician is working on a Linux system and making use of Bash (perhaps vi). When you work in Bash, it is accepted as a best practice to save the scripts as .sh files. PowerShell uses .ps1 by default. JavaScript is .js. Python is .py. Batch files are used for scripting in Windows and are saved with the .bat extension—but remember that using PowerShell is recommended over using batch files.

2. **C.** The construct required to repeat an operation until a specific requirement is met is a conditional loop (such as a **for** loop). If you are working in PowerShell, then you will most likely save the script as a .ps1 file. **if-then** statements use conditions such as true, false, else, and so on. .sh is used by Bash. Strings are sets of alphanumeric characters, and variables take the place of particular pieces of data. .py is used by Python. Integers are whole numbers, and .vbs is used by Visual Basic Script.

3. **E.** Use the **New-PSDrive** cmdlet to map a network drive in PowerShell. While the **net use** command still works in PowerShell, using **New-PSDrive** is the newer way. **apt install** is used in Linux (Debian/Ubuntu) to install or upgrade packages. A **for** loop is used to repeat a process in programming. The **Restart-Computer** cmdlet in PowerShell will, well, restart the computer. The **Install-WUUpdates** cmdlet in PowerShell will initiate Windows Update.

4. **A, C, E, F, and H.** .ps1 files are PowerShell scripts. .bat files are batch file scripts. .vbs files are Visual Basic scripts. .py files are Python scripts. .sh files are Bash scripts. The incorrect answers are .exe (executable files), .docx (word processor files), and .txt (text files).

This is a monster chapter to be sure, but you did it. There was a lot of content in here that at times might have thrown you for *a loop*! So, review carefully. You might not get a lot of questions on the exam about these concepts (though I can almost guarantee some), but they are super important skills for the IT field. Exceptional work!

CHAPTER 64

Remote Access Technologies

This chapter covers the following A+ 220-1102 exam objective:

▶ **4.9** – Given a scenario, use remote access technologies.

Here we have the last of the 220-1102 chapters. It's awesome that you've made it this far. Just a little farther to go.

Why walk or drive to another computer when you can control it remotely? Unless there is a networking or hardware issue, always try to remote into a system to repair it. It will be faster and more efficient than physically going to the device. Tools such as RDP, SSH, and RealVNC are some of a sysadmin's best friends.

Remote Desktop

Remote Desktop software, included with Windows, enables a user to see and control the GUI of a remote computer. It enables users to control other computers on the network or over the Internet without leaving their seats. It aids technicians in their attempts to repair computers because they don't have to go to a system that needs repair.

To have a Remote Desktop session, you need to configure the software. You can configure Remote Desktop within Settings or in the System Properties dialog box:

▶ **Settings:** Open **Settings > System > Remote Desktop**. From here, you can enable Remote Desktop simply by dragging the slider and selecting users who are allowed to connect to the local system. There are also advanced options, including options for configuring network-level authentication.

▶ **System Properties dialog box: Run > systempropertiesremote**. This option gives you a little more fine-grained control of Remote Desktop. There are two sections in this window: Remote Assistance and Remote Desktop. Let's examine those two parts now.

Remote Assistance

In the Remote Assistance section, the **Allow Remote Assistance connections to this computer** checkbox is selected by default. This means that connections can be made via Remote Assistance invitations, by email, or via instant messaging. These invitations can ask for help or offer help. This option is often implemented in help-desk scenarios in which a user invites a technician to take control of his or her computer so that it can be repaired. Invitations are made by accessing the Windows Remote Assistance program (simply type it into the Search field). For this to function, in addition to having the checkbox checked,

Remote Control must be enabled by clicking the **Advanced** button and selecting the **Allow this computer to be controlled remotely** checkbox. When the proper settings are enabled, Remote Assistance calls flow right through Windows Defender Firewall. Collectively, this functionality is known as Microsoft Remote Assistance.

Remote Desktop Connection

In the Remote Desktop Connection section, you can select whether other users can connect to, and control, your computer at any time *without* an invitation from you. There are options to disable remote connections, enable connections with any version of Remote Desktop, and enable connections running Remote Desktop with network-level authentication for security. The option to connect is disabled by default, but if it is enabled, remote users can make connections to your system by computer name or by IP address. Finally, you can select the users who are allowed to connect to your computer. If your network is a workgroup, then any local user account you select is just that: local. For a remote user to connect, the remote computer must have an identical account (the same username and password) as the one you selected on your computer, and the remote user must know the username/password. If the network is a domain, this is not an issue due to centralized administration of accounts.

> **ExamAlert**
>
> Be able to explain the difference between Remote Assistance and Remote Desktop and use them both.

Connecting with Remote Desktop

To make a Remote Desktop connection to a remote computer, you need to make sure the remote computer has Remote Desktop enabled. Next, open the Remote Desktop Connection program. In any version of Windows, simply type **remote** in the Search field and select Remote Desktop Connection. (In Windows 10, you can also go to **Start > Windows Accessories**.) Remember, Home editions of Windows only allow the client side of Remote Desktop, so consider using Windows Pro or higher to have full Remote Desktop capabilities.

Click **Show Options** to get the logon settings shown in Figure 64.1. To make a connection, you need to supply the computer name or the IP address of the remote computer and the username and password for an account on the remote computer.

FIGURE 64.1 **The Remote Desktop Connection window**

Click **Connect**, and the screen of the other computer should show up on your local display. At this point, you can control the remote computer as if you were sitting at it locally. By default, when you connect, the remote computer's physical screen locks; it can be unlocked only with a username/password.

> **Note**
>
> Remote Desktop is based on Remote Desktop Protocol (RDP, which it is often referred to by techs). When Remote Desktop is enabled, this protocol is allowed through Windows Defender Firewall using TCP port 3389 (by default), which is a well-known port. Give *strong consideration* to using network-level authentication when allowing Remote Desktop connections. It is enabled by default for good reason. And, for further security, consider implementing FIPS 140 compliance with TLS and making use of port 443 (configured in Group Policy).

> **ExamAlert**
>
> Know how to use Remote Desktop to make connections to remote computers. I can guarantee you will get exam questions on RDP!

You can also use the **mstsc** command. If you use this command by itself, it will simply display the Remote Desktop Connection program, just as before. However, you can use it solely at the command line and add options. For example, you can perform custom Remote Desktop connections, edit existing Remote Desktop configuration files, and migrate old connection files to newer systems. If you wanted to remotely control another system with the **mstsc** command in full-screen mode, you type the following:

```
mstsc.exe /v:computername /f
```

> **Note**
>
> For more information on the **mstsc** command, visit https://docs.microsoft.com/en-us/windows-server/administration/windows-commands/mstsc.

Need to control more than one computer remotely at the same time? Consider using the Remote Desktop Connection Manager. I use it all the time. It's an extra download for Windows that is available from https://docs.microsoft.com/en-us/sysinternals/downloads/rdcman.

Remote Monitoring and Management (RMM) and Desktop Management Software

Take it to the next level with remote monitoring and management (RMM) solutions. These are software tools (often third-party tools) that are designed to remotely monitor and manage client endpoints, networks, and computers. These remote IT management solutions go beyond single RDP connections and allow a technician to have a more wholistic view of systems and networks, all displayed in one window. Examples include LogMeIn Central and NinjaOne.

RMM solutions are similar to desktop management software (and the two terms are sometimes used interchangeably). Desktop management software focuses more on the client OS management and *security*. In contrast, an RMM might also be used to track customer information, assets, inventory, and so on. Be ready to use RMM tools if you plan to work in an enterprise setting.

SSH

I can't tell you how many times I've typed **ssh**, and I can't stress enough how important this tool is for your resume or CV. We briefly discussed the Secure Shell (SSH) protocol way back in Chapter 5, "TCP and UDP Ports and Protocols." Consider reviewing that information before continuing.

Using SSH is typically considered a secure way to connect to remote systems, network devices, and more (as long as it is configured properly). Once you connect via SSH, you can control the remote system from the command line.

For example, from time to time, I securely connect to a pfSense firewall (which is FreeBSD based) from my Windows client using PuTTY, a common SSH client program. Take a look at Figure 64.2.

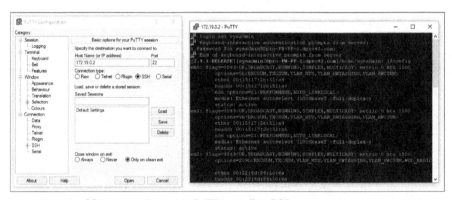

FIGURE 64.2 **SSH connection using PuTTY to a FreeBSD system**

On the left, you see the PuTTY client program configured to connect to the host 172.19.0.2 on port 22 (the default port for SSH). When you click the Open button, you get a text window like the one on the right in the figure. From the top down, it shows that I logged in as sysadmin, and then I typed the command **ifconfig** just show some information in the command line. That's it: Full remote control from the command-line. When you are done, type **exit** to end the session.

However, most of the time, I use SSH directly at the command line, usually by making use of OpenSSH. OpenSSH is a free, open source tool that is available on Windows, macOS, and Linux. Here's an example of an SSH connection from a Windows system to a remote system:

```
PS C:\Windows\System32> ssh user@10.42.0.15
```

```
user@10.42.0.15's password:
Welcome to Ubuntu 20.04.3 LTS (GNU/Linux 5.4.0-91-generic x86_64)
Last login: Tue Nov 30 18:18:14 2021 from 10.42.0.253
user@telemetry:~$ hostnamectl
   Static hostname: telemetry
  Operating System: Ubuntu 20.04.3 LTS
            Kernel: Linux 5.4.0-91-generic
      Architecture: x86-64
user@telemetry:~$
```

Now, I removed *a lot* of content from these results to save space and concentrate on only what you need to know here. I started in the Windows PowerShell and typed the command **ssh user@10.42.0.15**. That means that I am using the SSH protocol to connect, and I am connecting to a computer with the IP address 10.42.0.15. (You could also connect by computer name, of course.) I connected as the user account called, simply, *user*. That is one of the accounts that exists on the remote computer. SSH then requested the password for the *user* account. I typed that and was granted access to the remote system. (Keep in mind that I will only have access based on the *user* account permissions.) What kind of system did I connect to? If you said Linux, you'd be correct. To be precise, it is an Ubuntu Linux server, version 20.04. You can see that because I typed the Linux command **hostnamectl**, which provides the hostname of the computer, *telemetry*, and a set of additional information, including the OS and Linux kernel used by that OS.

The *user* account is a standard, restricted account, so at this point I can only accomplish basic things on this Linux server. If I wanted full control of the remote Linux system, I would have to log in as root or go the more recommended and secure route of logging in as a user account with **sudo** privileges. For more on **sudo** and the root account, see Chapter 42, "Linux." Also, there are more secure ways of connecting via SSH, such as by using SSH keys. This gets a bit beyond the A+ certification, but it gives you an idea of the power and depth of SSH. It should be used carefully and secured appropriately.

> **Note**
>
> For an OpenSSH how-to video, see https://www.prowse.tech/ssh/.

There are plenty of other SSH clients available, but note these two important things:

▶ You must have SSH *installed* on the target device (consider OpenSSH if nothing is already installed).

▶ The SSH service must be turned on at the computer (or network device) that you want to remote into.

You should also be aware that other protocols and their tools can make use of SSH and port 22—for example, Secure Copy Protocol (SCP), Secure File Transfer Protocol (SFTP), and rsync. For the IT field, I strongly urge you to learn more about these tools and SSH in general.

> **ExamAlert**
>
> You will *definitely* see exam questions on SSH! Understand why you would use SSH and know how to use SSH client software to make connections to remote computers.

More Third-Party Tools

Plenty of other tools are available for the remote control of systems. I routinely make use of a Virtual Network Computing (VNC) product such as RealVNC to remotely control Linux computers, macOS systems, and Android-based smartphones and tablets. Other remote control tools include LogMeIn, TeamViewer, NoMachine, AnyDesk, and Chrome Remote Desktop. (I do not endorse any of these tools, and as always, you should use third-party tools with caution.)

You can also share your screen with other systems, which works well for collaboration and education. For example, use Miracast on Windows Surface systems or utilize a web-based webinar system such as Cisco Webex or ON24; these live-stream platforms are great for training and presentations. Or, you might share your screen using video conference software such as Microsoft Teams, Zoom, FaceTime, or Skype. Just make sure that the remote users cannot take control of *your* system (unless you want them to and give them permission to do so).

The key with any of these tools is to make sure that they are secure. If you are connecting over the Internet, you need a secured session. Whether that is done by way of VPN for direct connections or by using an encrypted certificate when connecting via a browser (with TLS, RSA, and AES, for example), you need to make sure that the session is secure and that passwords are lengthy and hard to guess. Also consider using MFA if it is a viable option for the software you are using.

VPN

We discussed virtual private networks (VPNs) briefly in Chapters 8, "Networked Hosts," and 37, "Windows Networking." In essence, a VPN provides a way of tunneling through the Internet securely instead of relying on the security (or lack thereof) of your ISP. Microsoft Windows VPN connections can be made with the following protocols: Point-to-Point Tunneling Protocol (PPTP), Layer 2 Tunneling Protocol (L2TP), Secure Socket Tunneling Protocol (SSTP), or Internet Key Exchange version 2 (IKEv2). At this writing (early 2022), the preferred methods for Windows clients are SSTP and IKEv2. Certain Windows VPN security features only work with IKEv2; for example, LockDown VPN secures a computer in such a way that traffic can flow only over the VPN connection, and no other network connections or adapters, while the VPN session is active. You can also configure traffic filtering rules based on protocols and using port and IP address ranges.

When signing into a VPN from a Windows client, you need to know the server name or IP address (which is often a public IP address), and you need to configure the VPN type (such as IKEv2). Then you have to specify the sign-in information, which could be the typical username and password or might use a smart card, an OTP, or a certificate.

ExamAlert

Know that VPNs use secure tunneling protocols to connect secure private networks (or devices) together through public (unsecured) networks such as the Internet.

Note

Some organizations use VPN servers or appliances that are not quite compatible with the Windows VPN client. In such cases, always-on VPN services such as OpenVPN can be used, but a separate client has to be downloaded and installed to the Windows computer.

> **Note**
>
> You might opt to run RDP or SSH through a VPN for added security, especially if you are remoting to a computer on the Internet. Some people use OpenSSH with OpenVPN tunneling.

Cram Quiz

Answer these questions. The answers follow the last question. If you cannot answer these questions correctly, consider reading this chapter again until you can.

1. Which program enables a user to invite a technician to help repair their computer remotely?

   ○ **A.** Remote Desktop Connection

   ○ **B.** Remote Assistance

   ○ **C.** RDP

   ○ **D.** Remote connectivity

2. You have been tasked with making a command-line-based remote connection to an Ubuntu Linux computer located on your LAN so that you can run two scripts on it as an administrator. What protocol should you use? (Select the best answer.)

   ○ **A.** RDP

   ○ **B.** mstsc

   ○ **C.** SSH

   ○ **D.** VPN

3. You are in charge of setting up the administrators' connections to remote Windows computers located at satellite offices using RDP. What are some of the ways to make these connections more secure? (Select the three best answers.)

   ○ **A.** Use strong passwords

   ○ **B.** Use OpenSSH

   ○ **C.** Use network-level authentication

   ○ **D.** Use PuTTY

   ○ **E.** Use L2TP and IKEv2

4. You are tasked with updating a network switch at a customer location. You need to make sure that data is not sent in plaintext over untrusted networks. Which of the following protocols should you implement? (Select the two best answers.)

   ○ **A.** RDP

   ○ **B.** SSH

⚪ **C.** FTP

⚪ **D.** SCP

⚪ **E.** Telnet

⚪ **F.** VNC

5. You are a technician working on a help desk. One of your customers installed a program to Windows that requires a license key. After the user contacted you, you accessed the customer's system and entered the license key manually. Which tool did you use to accomplish this?

⚪ **A.** SSH

⚪ **B.** FTP

⚪ **C.** RDP

⚪ **D.** rsync

Cram Quiz Answers

1. **B.** Remote Assistance calls can be made from users to invite other users to help fix problems for them. Remote Desktop connections are the connections that a computer makes to a remote computer to control it.

2. **C.** Use Secure Shell (SSH) to connect to the Ubuntu Linux computer, take control, and run the scripts as required (within Vim or your favorite text editor). You could also incorporate a VPN, but if both systems are on the LAN, a VPN might not be necessary. RDP is the protocol (and commonly used name) behind the Windows Remote Desktop Connection software. **mstsc** is the command-line executable for Remote Desktop Connection.

3. **A, C, and E.** Always use strong passwords (based on length, complexity, or a mixture of the two), as well as network-level authentication, which requires the user's credentials from the client computer. Also, because the connections in this case are to remote offices, consider using a virtual private network (VPN). Layer 2 Tunneling Protocol (L2TP) is a decent solution for a VPN (if configured properly), but OpenVPN or another always-on VPN service is usually better. Internet Key Exchange version 2 (IKEv2) is the preferred VPN protocol on Windows computers. OpenSSH and PuTTY are used for SSH connections, but they wouldn't be used in this Windows-based scenario because the task requires RDP—meaning the Remote Desktop Connection program.

4. **B and D.** One secure method for moving data over a network is to use Secure Copy Protocol (SCP). This rides on SSH and so, in essence, it means you are using both SCP and SSH. RDP is used to remotely control a Windows system. File Transfer Protocol (FTP) is another method for moving data but is not inherently secure. Using Telnet is an older and deprecated way of connecting to remote systems; SSH should be used instead. VNC is another remote control tool.

5. C. You most likely used the Remote Desktop Connection program, which is based on RDP. This program would allow you to remotely control the customer's system and add the license key (which perhaps only your team has access to). SSH is used for controlling remote systems from the command line. It is unlikely that you would use SSH to enter a license key. But it is quite likely that you would use it to connect to a Linux-based system in a datacenter or in the cloud. FTP and rsync are used to transfer entire files (or groups of files) but not to perform tasks such as entering license keys into an application.

Great Job!

If you have come this far, I congratulate you! This is the last chapter of actual CompTIA A+ objective-based content. 64 chapters is quite a lot, even for super-heroes. Well done!

Directly following this chapter, you will find the 220-1102 practice exam, and then the final chapter, where I give some tips for passing the exam and close out the book. Take a break (you deserve it), and then continue on to the practice exam!

If you are planning on taking the actual CompTIA A+ Core 2 (220-1102) exam, be sure to go through the 220-1102 checklist, located in "Introduction to Core 2 (220-1102)," just before Chapter 30.

A+ Core 2 (220-1102) Practice Exam

The 90 multiple-choice questions provided here help you to determine how prepared you are for the actual exam and which topics you need to review further. Write down your answers on a separate sheet of paper so that you can take this exam again if necessary. Compare your answers against the answer key that follows this exam. Read through the explanations and also the incorrect answers very carefully. If there are any concepts that you don't understand, go back and study them more.

Exam Questions

1. Which of the following commands will display the MAC address of a computer?
   - ○ **A. ping**
   - ○ **B. netstat**
   - ○ **C. ipconfig /all**
   - ○ **D. ipconfig /renew**

2. You plug a 32 GB flash drive into a Windows laptop. The flash drive has multiple smaller partitions that are not writable. Which of the following **diskpart** commands can be used to remove the partitions so that you can later format the drive to full capacity?
   - ○ **A. repair**
   - ○ **B. clean**
   - ○ **C. merge**
   - ○ **D. extend**

3. Which command is used to list the contents of a directory in the Command Prompt?
   - ○ **A. cd**
   - ○ **B. dir**
   - ○ **C. ping**
   - ○ **D. ver**

4. You are a technician working at a help desk in tier 1 support, and you receive a call from a user whose computer is suffering from BSODs. Just as you receive the call, you realize that you are scheduled to take your break. What should you do next?
   - ○ **A.** Ask another technician to take the call for you.
   - ○ **B.** Ask the user to call back.

   ○ **C.** Send the user to help desk tier 2.

   ○ **D.** Troubleshoot the problem for the user.

5. Your company has multiple users who work with the same commercial software. What is the best type of license to purchase so that your company is in compliance with the EULA?

   ○ **A.** Seat license

   ○ **B.** Commercial license

   ○ **C.** Enterprise license

   ○ **D.** Open source license

6. Which of the following is a risk of implementing BYOD?

   ○ **A.** Encryption mismatches

   ○ **B.** Increased risk of phishing attacks

   ○ **C.** Introduction of malware onto the network

   ○ **D.** DHCP failures

7. One of your co-workers tells you that whenever she returns to her desk, she has to type her username and password to unlock the computer. She says she cannot modify the screensaver. After analyzing the system, you notice that the screensaver and the screen lock options are indeed grayed out. Which of the following is the most likely reason for this?

   ○ **A.** Incorrect local-level user policies

   ○ **B.** Domain-level group policies

   ○ **C.** Antivirus domain-level policies

   ○ **D.** Corrupted registry

8. Which of the following features in Windows allows the following command to run?

`$PSVersionTable`

   ○ **A.** Compatibility mode

   ○ **B.** OneDrive

   ○ **C.** Windows Defender Firewall

   ○ **D.** PowerShell

9. You have been tasked with printing a Group Policy configuration report to an HTML file for offline review. Which of the following commands will enable you to do this?

   ○ **A. gpresult**

   ○ **B. gpupdate**

   ○ **C. gpedit.msc**

   ○ **D. secpol.msc**

10. Which of the following commands should you use to find out what edition of Windows is running?

   ○ **A. pathping**

   ○ **B. winver**

   ○ **C. ls**

   ○ **D. hostname**

11. You have identified malware on a customer's laptop. Based on malware removal best practices, which of the following should you do next?

   ○ **A.** Educate the user.

   ○ **B.** Update antivirus software.

   ○ **C.** Enable System Restore.

   ○ **D.** Isolate the infected system.

12. One of the users in your company frequently leaves her workstation and wants to make sure that her confidential data is not accessed by anyone else. However, the user does not want to turn off the computer when she leaves work in the evening. Which of the following is the best solution for securing the workstation?

   ○ **A.** Implement a password and fingerprint lock for after-hours login.

   ○ **B.** Set a strong password that requires a renewal every 30 days.

   ○ **C.** Apply a screen lock after 5 minutes of nonuse and set login time restrictions for after-hours.

   ○ **D.** Run a screensaver after 1 minute of nonuse and a fingerprint lock for after-hours.

13. A manager suspects that a user has obtained movies and other copyright-protected materials through the use of a BitTorrent client. The incident response tech confirms the suspicion; the user is in violation of company policy. What should the incident response technician do next?

   ○ **A.** Immediately delete all unauthorized materials.

   ○ **B.** Secure the workstation in a limited-access storage facility.

   ○ **C.** Reprimand the user and apply a content filter to the user's profile

   ○ **D.** Document the incident and purge all policy-violating materials.

14. You are required to update a Linux server in a remote datacenter. Company policy states that you must connect in a secure fashion, using the command line only. Which of the following tools should you use?

   ○ **A.** RDP

   ○ **B.** SFTP

   ○ **C.** VNC

   ○ **D.** SSH

15. You work for an organization that uses various permissions for individual user accounts. One of the managers with a restricted user account receives the following message:

Windows Update cannot currently check for updates because the service is not running.

The manager contacts your organization's help desk to report the error. You connect to the manager's computer and identify the problem. What action should you take next to quickly resolve the problem?

- ○ **A.** Reboot the computer.
- ○ **B.** Roll back the device drivers.
- ○ **C.** Restart the appropriate service(s).
- ○ **D.** Rebuild the Windows profile.

16. Your security team needs to satisfy the following requirements of a disaster recovery plan:

- ▶ The last month of backups should be easily accessible and preferably on-premises.
- ▶ Long-term backups should be stored offsite.
- ▶ There should be minimal use of hardware.

Which of the following answers will best meet the requirements?

- ○ **A.** Store backups with a cloud provider and onsite.
- ○ **B.** Store 30 days' worth of backups onsite and store anything older than that with an offsite cloud provider.
- ○ **C.** Store all backups with a cloud provider.
- ○ **D.** Store backups onsite and use cloud bursting if the backup hardware demands more resources.

17. You have been asked to set up a new networking closet, and you notice that the humidity level in the room is very low. Which of the following tasks should be done before rack-mounting any networking equipment?

- ○ **A.** Install grounding bars.
- ○ **B.** Set up a dehumidifier.
- ○ **C.** Use an ESD strap.
- ○ **D.** Implement a fire suppression system.

18. Which of the following security techniques is most closely related to a user entering a username and password once for multiple applications?

- ○ **A.** Propagation
- ○ **B.** MFA
- ○ **C.** SSO
- ○ **D.** Inheritance

19. Jason from accounting reports that when pressing Ctrl+Alt+Del to log on to a Windows workstation, he is asked for a PIN. Which of the following should you tell Jason?

- ○ **A.** "Enter all the passwords that you have used previously."
- ○ **B.** "Reboot the computer."

- C. "Check the network cable."
- D. "Please verify that you are using your smart card."

20. A surge suppressor safeguards connected equipment by directing surges to the
    - A. path of least resistance
    - B. path of shortest conductance
    - C. path of lowest inductance
    - D. path of highest voltage

21. By default, a file or folder receives its NTFS permissions from the parent folder. Which of the following terms is used for this process?
    - A. Permission propagation
    - B. Single sign-on (SSO)
    - C. Client-side virtualization
    - D. Proxy settings
    - E. Recovery image
    - F. Inheritance

22. Which of the following are examples of physical security? (Select the two best answers.)
    - A. Directory permissions
    - B. OTP hardware tokens
    - C. Principle of least privilege
    - D. Privacy filters

23. You have been given technical documentation from the network administrator that details the switch ports that you need to use for an upcoming network upgrade. Which of the following documents did you receive?
    - A. Change control form
    - B. Process diagram
    - C. Network topology diagram
    - D. Fiber backbone diagram

24. Which of the following will help protect an organization from further data exposure *after* a list of passwords has already been leaked due to a policy breach? (Select the two best answers.)
    - A. Require strong passwords.
    - B. Use multi-factor authentication.
    - C. Educate end users.
    - D. Enable file encryption.
    - E. Restrict user permissions.

25. A user is reporting that his web browser is not going to the site he is trying to access. Which of the following statements describes the best way to resolve this?

   ○ **A.** Ensure that the user is not using a proxy server.

   ○ **B.** Remove all Internet shortcuts.

   ○ **C.** Delete all Internet cookies.

   ○ **D.** Clear all Internet cache.

26. A customer wants to use FTP to push configurations to a couple of switches that the customer is updating. The customer can use the FTP program on a laptop and can place the configurations in the proper directories of the switches. But the switches cannot communicate to the PC with FTP. How can you resolve the problem?

   ○ **A.** Change the laptop's IP address to dynamic.

   ○ **B.** Make sure that the laptop's IP address is in the correct VLAN.

   ○ **C.** Generate a static DNS entry on the server for the laptop.

   ○ **D.** Create an exception in the local firewall of the laptop.

27. A customer's mobile device seems to be losing battery life rapidly, and the device is very warm. It is a relatively new mobile device, so the customer believes it must be defective. You inspect the device and find the following:

   ▶ Storage: 48 GB used

   ▶ Display: Brightness: Auto

   ▶ Mail: Pull every 15 minutes

   ▶ Privacy: Maps: always enabled

Which of the following should you modify to fix the problem?

   ○ **A.** Storage

   ○ **B.** Display

   ○ **C.** Mail

   ○ **D.** Privacy

28. Which of the following are ways to remove data from a storage drive through destruction? (Select the two best answers.)

   ☐ **A.** Disabling ports

   ☐ **B.** Shredding

   ☐ **C.** Drilling

   ☐ **D.** Using low-level formatting

   ☐ **E.** Purging

29. Which of the following Internet Options tabs should you access to enable TLS in Internet Explorer?

   ○ **A.** Security

   ○ **B.** Privacy

    ○ **C.** Advanced

    ○ **D.** Connections

30. You are attempting to install a Windows 64-bit OS within a VM, but you keep receiving errors. The specifications for the VM include

    ▶ Four 1 GHz CPUs

    ▶ 4 GB of RAM

    ▶ 15 GB storage drive space

    ▶ 720p screen resolution

Which of the following should you do to resolve this issue?

    ○ **A.** Increase the number of CPUs.

    ○ **B.** Increase the amount of memory.

    ○ **C.** Increase the amount of drive space.

    ○ **D.** Increase the screen resolution.

31. Your organization's network consists of 25 computers that are wired to a switch. Your boss is interested in employing a file server with network shares and a print server. Which of the following Windows network setups should you recommend?

    ○ **A.** Workgroup

    ○ **B.** Ad hoc

    ○ **C.** Spoke-hub

    ○ **D.** Domain

32. Which of the following is the best example of the use of chain of custody?

    ○ **A.** The technician notes the date, time, and who was given the computer.

    ○ **B.** The technician remembers when and who he or she gave the computer to.

    ○ **C.** The technician uses a third party to hand over the computer to the proper authorities.

    ○ **D.** The technician calls the supervisor after the computer has been transferred.

33. You just installed a new updated driver for a network interface card (NIC). Now you want to test its data transfer rate. What tool should you use to run your test?

    ○ **A.** Device Manager

    ○ **B.** Local Security Policy

    ○ **C.** Performance Monitor

    ○ **D.** System Information

34. You just got your first IT job working at a help desk. You get a call from a user about an issue you have never seen before, and you are not sure where to begin troubleshooting. What is the first course of action you should take?

    ○ **A.** Tell the customer that this is the first time you have encountered this problem and to please be patient.

    ○ **B.** Tell the customer that the problem needs to be escalated to a higher-tier technician.

    ○ **C.** Tell the customer to please hold while a senior technician is consulted regarding the problem.

    ○ **D.** Ask the customer if he or she would mind holding for no more than two minutes to check resources.

35. One of your company's users just purchased an Android smartphone and is attempting to access a public hotspot. The user receives a message that a page cannot be displayed. The user notices a question mark (?) in the radio icon in the toolbar. The user has activated Bluetooth and verified that airplane mode is turned off. Tethering is turned on. The user is using the smartphone to call in to the help desk for assistance. Which of the following is the most likely issue?

    ○ **A.** The user has exceeded the data allowance.

    ○ **B.** There is unauthenticated wireless connectivity.

    ○ **C.** It is an un-rooted smartphone.

    ○ **D.** The SIM card is not activated.

    ○ **E.** The smartphone is only 3G capable.

    ○ **F.** A data plan was not purchased.

36. Which Windows utility can be used to see which user is currently logged on?

    ○ **A.** MSConfig

    ○ **B.** Disk Management

    ○ **C.** Task Manager

    ○ **D.** Administrative Tools

37. Which of the following tools are commonly used to remove dust from the inside of a computer? (Select the two best answers.)

    ☐ **A.** Compressed air

    ☐ **B.** Cotton and alcohol

    ☐ **C.** Feather duster

    ☐ **D.** Antibacterial surface cleaner

    ☐ **E.** Vacuum

38. You have been tasked with downloading an operating system image to be installed to a virtual machine. Which of the following file types will you most likely download?

    ○ **A.** EXE

    ○ **B.** appimage

○ **C.** ISO

○ **D.** VDI

39. Which of the following is a common symptom of a problem that can occur while starting up the Windows operating system?

○ **A.** Spontaneous shutdown/restart.

○ **B.** invalid boot disk.

○ **C.** WinRE won't start.

○ **D.** The BIOS/UEFI's time is not synchronized to a time server.

○ **E.** The emergency repair disk doesn't boot.

○ **F.** Regsvr32 has failed.

40. Which of the following are possible symptoms of malware? (Select all that apply.)

○ **A.** Security alerts

○ **B.** Windows Update failures

○ **C.** Preinstallation environment

○ **D.** Renamed system files

○ **E.** Rogue antivirus

○ **F.** User error

41. One of your company's users complains that his smartphone is making shutter noises even when he is not taking pictures. What should you do first to determine the cause of the problem?

○ **A.** Update all applications on the smartphone.

○ **B.** Run OS updates.

○ **C.** Uninstall the camera installation.

○ **D.** Check the application permissions.

○ **E.** Reset the phone to factory settings.

42. You are troubleshooting a Windows system that is suffering from poor performance. The Event Viewer states that the file system is corrupt. What should you do next?

○ **A.** Reload the OS using FAT32 instead of NTFS.

○ **B.** Run **chkdsk** with the **/R** option and reboot the system.

○ **C.** Open the **defrag** utility and run the drive analysis.

○ **D.** Change the drive from basic to dynamic.

43. Which type of fire extinguishing technology should be used during an electrical fire?

○ **A.** Overhead sprinkler systems

○ **B.** Water-based fire extinguishers

○ **C.** Class B fire extinguishers

○ **D.** Non-water-based fire extinguishers

44. You attempt to install a legacy application on a computer running Windows. You receive an error that says the application cannot be installed because the OS is not supported. Which of the following describes the first step you should take to continue installing the application?

   ○ **A.** Purchase the latest version of the application.

   ○ **B.** Install the application in Safe Mode.

   ○ **C.** Install the application in compatibility mode.

   ○ **D.** Install the latest security updates.

45. A user tells you that his new smartphone is suffering from poor battery life. The user has been using the phone for a short time and has installed several apps lately. Which of the following is the most likely cause of the problem?

   ○ **A.** Unauthorized root access

   ○ **B.** Battery needs to be replaced

   ○ **C.** Defective SD card

   ○ **D.** Signal drop or weak signal

   ○ **E.** Slow data speeds

46. You have been tasked with setting up a SOHO wireless network in a small health-care office that cannot afford a server. The wireless users require the highest level of security available, and various other levels of desktop authentication for access to cloud-based resources. Which of the following protocols and authentication methods should you implement? (Select the two best answers.)

   ☐ **A.** WPA

   ☐ **B.** WPA2

   ☐ **C.** WPA3

   ☐ **D.** TKIP

   ☐ **E.** RADIUS

   ☐ **F.** TACACS+

   ☐ **G.** SSO

   ☐ **H.** Multi-factor

47. A customer calls to report that when she walks away from her laptop for an extended period of time, she has to reconnect to wireless upon returning. Which of the following will most likely correct this issue?

   ○ **A.** Replace the wireless card.

   ○ **B.** Install a higher-capacity battery.

   ○ **C.** Adjust the power settings.

   ○ **D.** Disable the screensaver.

959
Exam Questions

48. You work as an end-user technician working for a computer support company. A typical customer says that he is concerned about the privacy of his home laptop and the security of the network in general when browsing the Internet. Which of the following should you discuss with the customer to educate him while addressing his security concerns? (Select the two best answers.)

   ○ **A.** Antivirus
   ○ **B.** Proxy servers
   ○ **C.** Firewalls
   ○ **D.** VPNs
   ○ **E.** Advanced TCP/IP settings

49. Which of the following commands should be used to search for a specific string in a filename?

   ○ **A. sudo**
   ○ **B. grep**
   ○ **C. chmod**
   ○ **D. wget**

50. You are working on a computer that is displaying a black screen. You restart the computer, but the operating system will not load. After talking with the user, you find out that the operating system was patched the previous evening. Which of the following should you attempt next?

   ○ **A.** Repair the Windows registry.
   ○ **B.** Configure boot options in the BIOS.
   ○ **C.** Reboot into Safe Mode and roll back the updates.
   ○ **D.** Disable Windows services.

51. You are required to replace a desktop power supply. Which of the following tasks should be performed first?

   ○ **A.** Remove your watch and jewelry.
   ○ **B.** Review local regulations for disposal procedures.
   ○ **C.** Read the MSDS.
   ○ **D.** Check for environmental concerns.

52. Your customer has a computer (named comp112) that has been infected by a virus. The virus has propagated to at least 30 other computers on the network. Which of the following tasks should be performed before attempting to remove the virus from the comp112 computer?

   ○ **A.** Log the user off the system.
   ○ **B.** Boot the system in Safe Mode.
   ○ **C.** Run a full virus scan.
   ○ **D.** Disconnect the network cable from the computer.

53. You are working at a computer and see the following at the beginning of a script:

`#!/bin/bash`

What type of system are you working at?

○ **A.** Windows

○ **B.** Linux

○ **C.** iOS

○ **D.** JavaScript

54. Which of the following tools allows you to change the number of CPU cores that Windows uses?

○ **A. perfmon**

○ **B. dxdiag**

○ **C. msconfig**

○ **D. taskmgr**

55. A user is unable to view office network files while working from home. Which of the following is the most likely cause of the problem?

○ **A.** Outdated anti-malware protection

○ **B.** Inactive VPN

○ **C.** MDM policies

○ **D.** Untrusted software

56. One of your co-workers is attempting to access a file on a share located on a remote computer. The file's share permissions are set to allow the user full control; however, the NTFS permissions allow the user to have read access. Which of the following will be the user's resulting access level for the file?

○ **A.** Read

○ **B.** Write

○ **C.** Modify

○ **D.** Full Control

57. You are installing an older 32-bit program on a 64-bit version of Windows. Where does the program get installed to?

○ **A.** C:\

○ **B.** C:\Program Files

○ **C.** C:\Windows

○ **D.** C:\Program Files (x86)

58. A home user needs to reinstall Windows on a home computer but cannot find the operating system media that came with the computer. Which of the following would allow the home user to install the operating system?

○ **A.** System Restore

○ **B.** Recovery partition

○ **C.** Linux rescue media

○ **D.** Primary partition

59. You have been tasked with running updates on a Windows computer. Some of the updates go through fine, but one of them fails. While troubleshooting, you restart the computer and attempt to install the failed update, but it continues to fail. Which of the following should you do first?

○ **A.** Analyze the Event Viewer for more information about the failures.

○ **B.** Download the failed updates to install it manually.

○ **C.** Visit the Microsoft Update website to see if there is an issue with a specific update.

○ **D.** Look up the error number associated with the failed update.

60. You are working on a client computer and receive a message that says the trust relationship to the domain has been broken. Which of the following steps should be taken to resolve this problem from the client computer?

○ **A.** Update the BIOS using the latest version.

○ **B.** Run **chkdsk**.

○ **C.** Rejoin the computer to the domain.

○ **D.** Reboot the PC as the domain will automatically rebuild the relationship.

61. You are configuring a friend's iPad. He needs to access his work email. In order to do this, you require information from the IT department. Which information should you ask for?

○ **A.** Server and gateway

○ **B.** IP address and domain

○ **C.** IP address and DNS

○ **D.** Server and domain

62. You need to write a script that checks data one line at a time until the end of the file being searched. Which of the following constructs should you use?

○ **A.** Integer

○ **B.** Loop

○ **C.** String

○ **D.** Variable

○ **E.** **if-then**

63. A co-worker has asked for a solution that will prevent file corruption by ensuring a graceful shutdown in the event of a power outage. The user would like at least one hour of uptime if the power goes out. Which of the following should you recommend?

○ **A.** Surge protector

○ **B.** Power strip

    ○ **C.** Uninterruptible power supply

    ○ **D.** Power distribution unit

64. As you are investigating a customer's Windows laptop, you find the following:

    ▶ Windows Update was disabled.

    ▶ Malware replaced a few Windows operating system files.

You complete a malware scan to remediate the problem. Which of the following commands should you run next before enabling Windows Update?

    ○ **A. sfc**

    ○ **B. chkdsk**

    ○ **C. gpupdate**

    ○ **D. robocopy**

    ○ **E. grep**

65. A customer reports to you that a file shared on her computer for another user is not accessible to that third party. The customer says that the third party was given Allow rights for Read and Write access to the file. Which of the following could be a reason the third party cannot access the file?

    ○ **A.** The parent folder has explicit Allow rights set for the third-party user.

    ○ **B.** The parent folder has explicit Deny rights set for the third-party user.

    ○ **C.** The user forgot to share the parent folder and shared only the specific file.

    ○ **D.** The parent folder likely has the archive attribute enabled.

66. Which of the following tools is used to type recovery commands into a Linux box?

    ○ **A.** Backup/Time Machine

    ○ **B.** Shell/Terminal

    ○ **C.** Restore/Snapshot

    ○ **D.** Command/CMD

67. You are part of a security team that is auditing an organization's server room. You find that a USB drive was previously inserted into three of the servers. There were many login attempts that were successfully performed using common login information. What should you do to prevent the vulnerability from being exploited again? (Select the two best answers.)

    ☐ **A.** Remove admin permissions.

    ☐ **B.** Modify the AutoRun settings.

    ☐ **C.** Install a software-based firewall.

    ☐ **D.** Disable the Guest account.

    ☐ **E.** Change default credentials.

    ☐ **F.** Run operating system security updates.

68. You are tasked with creating a new script in PowerShell. You need to add notes to the script to explain to the engineering group what each portion of the script is meant to do. Which of the following should you make use of?

  ○ **A.** End-user documentation

  ○ **B.** Inline comments

  ○ **C.** Variables and **if-then** statements

  ○ **D.** Change management documentation

69. In a SOHO wireless network, which of the following prevents unauthorized users from accessing confidential data?

  ○ **A.** Enabling MAC filtering

  ○ **B.** Changing the SSID name

  ○ **C.** Setting encryption

  ○ **D.** Reducing broadcast power

70. Which Control Panel utility is best used to remove a Windows application?

  ○ **A.** Disk Cleanup

  ○ **B.** Administrative Tools

  ○ **C.** Folder Options

  ○ **D.** Programs and Features

71. You receive a tech support call from a user on your corporate network about an Internet connection that is not working. You analyze the system and find out that the user's system has a valid IP address, can connect to network shares, and can view local intranet pages in the web browser. However, when you attempt to access a public website, the connection times out. Which of the following should you investigate next?

  ○ **A.** Proxy settings

  ○ **B.** IPv6 settings

  ○ **C.** Hosts file

  ○ **D.** DNS server

72. You have been tasked with setting up an AP in a small office that is in the middle of a crowded building. What should you do to increase the security of the wireless network? (Select the two best answers.)

  ☐ **A.** Configure WPA encryption.

  ☐ **B.** Disable the DHCP server.

  ☐ **C.** Reduce the transmit power.

  ☐ **D.** Reduce channel availability.

  ☐ **E.** Enable QoS management.

  ☐ **F.** Disable the SSID broadcast.

73. A computer has been infected with multiple viruses and spyware. Which of the following tasks should be performed before removing this malware?

- ○ **A.** Disable System Restore.
- ○ **B.** Disable network cards.
- ○ **C.** Run Windows Update.
- ○ **D.** Run the **chkdsk /R** command.

74. One of your customers has set up a perimeter firewall and has implemented up-to-date AV software. She asks you what else she can do to improve security. Which of the following will have the greatest impact on her network security? (Select the two best answers.)

- ☐ **A.** Conduct a daily security audit.
- ☐ **B.** Use strong passwords.
- ☐ **C.** Install additional antivirus software.
- ☐ **D.** Assign security rights based on job roles.
- ☐ **E.** Disable screensavers.

75. Which of the following statements describe how to demonstrate professionalism when dealing with a customer? (Select the three best answers.)

- ☐ **A.** Avoid distractions.
- ☐ **B.** Retain a chain of custody.
- ☐ **C.** Avoid being judgmental.
- ☐ **D.** Leave documentation to the customer.
- ☐ **E.** Meet expectations that the customer sets for you.

76. You previously installed a new application for a customer and added three new services. Today, the customer informs you that the application will not start. You find out that one of the three new services has failed to start, and manual attempts to start it fail. Where should you look next for information? (Select the two best answers.)

- ☐ **A.** Registry
- ☐ **B.** Event Viewer
- ☐ **C.** %systemroot%\System32\Drivers
- ☐ **D.** Log files for the new application
- ☐ **E.** Task Manager

77. Your organization has hired a new IT firm to manage its switches and routers. The IT firm is located in another state and will need to be able to remotely access the devices. Which of the following should be implemented to provide secure access from the IT firm to the switches and routers?

- ○ **A.** RDP
- ○ **B.** Telnet
- ○ **C.** SSH
- ○ **D.** VNC

78. Which of the following is the best way to maintain data security for a mobile device that has been lost or stolen?

- ○ **A.** Passcode lock
- ○ **B.** GPS
- ○ **C.** Remote wipe
- ○ **D.** Login attempt restrictions

79. Look at the following syntax:

```
net use Z: \\servername\sharename
```

Which of the following file types would you expect this syntax to be located in?

- ○ **A.** .vbs
- ○ **B.** .bat
- ○ **C.** .js
- ○ **D.** .py

80. One of your customers connected a tablet computer to her personal mobile hotspot device for Internet access to be used in a public location. The device running the hotspot shows that there are two connections instead of just one. Which of the following actions can they perform to prevent this unauthorized access to the device *immediately*? (Select the two best answers.)

- ☐ **A.** Access the intruder's device and shut it down.
- ☐ **B.** Add the intruding device to a blocked access list.
- ☐ **C.** Set up a Wi-Fi analyzer to identify the intruding device.
- ☐ **D.** Change the SSID to a different broadcast name.
- ☐ **E.** Shut down the device until the intruder is no longer in the area.

81. Which of the following would most likely cause apps to load slowly or fail to load at all on a mobile device? (Select the best three answers.)

- ☐ **A.** Too many apps open
- ☐ **B.** GPS is disabled
- ☐ **C.** An unintended Bluetooth connection
- ☐ **D.** No space left on device

82. Your company is growing to the point where you need a better solution to remotely manage a vast array of client systems, servers, and networks. What monitoring solution would best meet your needs?

- ○ **A.** RMM
- ○ **B.** RDC
- ○ **C.** **mstsc**
- ○ **D.** Remote Assistance

83. You receive an error message stating "remote desktop can't connect to remote computer" when trying to assist a remote customer. Which of the following can help you correct this problem? (Select the two best answers.)

   ☐ **A.** Have the customer reboot the computer.

   ☐ **B.** Run Windows Update to ensure that the system is updated.

   ☐ **C.** Change the firewall settings.

   ☐ **D.** Change settings to allow remote connections to this computer.

84. Your upgrade attempt from Windows 10 Pro to Windows 11 Pro fails. Your system has the following specs:

   ▶ 64-bit Intel Core i9 3.70GHz CPU

   ▶ 16 GB RAM

   ▶ 100 GB Storage

   ▶ UEFI Secure Boot enabled

   ▶ TPM sub-version 1.38

   ▶ Graphics card DirectX 12 with WDDM 2.0 driver

   ▶ Display high definition (720p)

   Which of the following is preventing you from performing the upgrade to Windows 11 Pro?

   ○ **A.** The processor does not meet the minimum requirements.

   ○ **B.** There is not enough RAM.

   ○ **C.** The graphics card does not meet the minimum requirements.

   ○ **D.** The TPM is incompatible.

85. You go to the store and put your bank card into an ATM and enter your PIN. What examples of multi-factor authentication have you exhibited? (Select two.)

   ☐ **A.** Something you are

   ☐ **B.** Something you have

   ☐ **C.** Something you know

   ☐ **D.** Somewhere you are

86. You are responsible for setting up a web server and an email server on a secure part of your network, using private IP addresses. Which of the following should you implement?

   ○ **A.** A screened subnet

   ○ **B.** DHCP reservations

   ○ **C.** IP filtering

   ○ **D.** A static WAN IP address

87. One of the users on your network logs on to the Windows domain from a laptop. The user tells you that the computer is taking a long time to log on and that a technician made changes recently. You look at the latest tickets for the user/computer and find out that the user's account was recently switched to a

roaming profile. The user says that, previous to that, the laptop started up quickly. What should you check to troubleshoot the issue?

- ○ **A.** The amount of RAM in the laptop
- ○ **B.** The size of the paging file
- ○ **C.** The amount of data in the user's desktop
- ○ **D.** The free space on the network share

88. When handling internal computer components, which are best practices to avoid ESD? (Select the two best answers.)

- ☐ **A.** Keep the environment dry.
- ☐ **B.** Ground yourself before touching the components.
- ☐ **C.** Verify that the device is plugged into a grounded outlet.
- ☐ **D.** Handle adapter cards by the edge.
- ☐ **E.** Wear eye protection.

89. One of your customers works on a Windows laptop. She downloaded an application from a website that you have never heard of. The customer saved the download, but she can't find the executable file to install the application. What is the most likely reason for this?

- ○ **A.** The .exe file is not compatible with the operating system.
- ○ **B.** File permissions were set so that the user could not access the executable.
- ○ **C.** The executable was quarantined by the anti-malware program.
- ○ **D.** A host-based firewall blocked the download.

90. A user wants to protect all of the data at rest on a Windows laptop. You analyze the laptop and find that it has a TPM chip. Which of the following should use to secure the data while taking advantage of the TPM?

- ○ **A.** BitLocker
- ○ **B.** SFTP
- ○ **C.** ACLs
- ○ **D.** EFS
- ○ **E.** Hardware security module

Answers at a Glance

1. C
2. B
3. B
4. A
5. C

6. C

7. B

8. D

9. A

10. B

11. D

12. C

13. B

14. D

15. C

16. B

17. A

18. C

19. D

20. A

21. F

22. B and D

23. C

24. B and C

25. A

26. D

27. D

28. B and C

29. C

30. C

31. D

32. A

33. C

34. D

35. B

36. C

37. A and E

38. C

39. B

40. A, B, and D

41. D

42. B

43. D

44. C

45. A

46. C and H

47. C

48. C and D

49. B

50. C

51. A

52. D

53. B

54. C

55. B

56. A

57. D

58. B

59. D

60. C

61. D

62. B

63. C

64. A

65. B

66. B

67. B and D

68. B

69. C

70. D

71. A

72. C and F

73. A

74. B and D

75. A, C, and E

76. B and D

77. C

78. C

79. B

80. B and D

81. A and D

82. A

83. C and D

84. D

85. B and C

86. A

87. C

88. B and D

89. C

90. A

Answer Explanations

1. Answer: **C. ipconfig /all** displays the MAC address of a computer. Whereas **ipconfig** shows the IP address, subnet mask, and gateway address, **ipconfig /all** gives you more information: the MAC address (called the physical address), the DNS server IP address, whether or not DHCP is enabled, and additional information. See Chapter 32, "Microsoft Command-Line Tools, Part II," for more information.

   Incorrect answers: **ping** is used to test whether other computers are available on the network. **netstat** displays all the network sessions to remote computers. **ipconfig /renew** is used with **/release** to reissue DHCP-obtained IP addresses.

2. Answer: **B.** The **clean** option in **diskpart** removes all partitions. This way, you can later format the drive to full capacity. As per the docs.microsoft.com **diskpart** page: "clean removes any and all partition or volume formatting from the disk with focus." See Chapter 31, "Microsoft Command-Line Tools, Part I," for more information.

   Incorrect answers: The **repair** option can repair software-based RAID 5 arrays. The **merge** option can be used with virtual drives. The **extend** option extends a volume or partition (along with the file system) into free space on the drive.

3. Answer: **B. dir** is used to list the contents of a directory in the Command Prompt or PowerShell. You might also use the **tree** command to show the tree of directories. See Chapter 31, "Microsoft Command-Line Tools, Part I," for more information.

   Incorrect answers: **cd** is short for change directory and is used to navigate. **ping** is used to verify whether another computer is available on the network. **ver** shows the version number of the Windows operating system—in the Command Prompt, but not PowerShell. (**winver** gives more information in a graphical format.)

4. Answer: **A**. The best answer listed is to ask another technician to take the call for you. In a typical help desk environment, breaks are scheduled, and you don't want to miss your break because you probably won't be able to take it later! See Chapter 61, "Incident Response, Communication, and Professionalism," for more information.

Incorrect answers: Asking the user to call back, even if done politely, is not good customer service; if the user does call back, it could be to complain to your manager. Sending the user to tier 2 support is not necessary yet because you haven't even attempted to troubleshoot the problem. You never know, multiple BSODs could be a tier 2 problem, but it needs to be analyzed first before you escalate it. Whatever you do, don't put the user on hold or attempt to help the user while taking your break!

5. Answer: **C**. You would want to get an enterprise license (sometimes referred to as a "corporate use" license). This allows multiple users to install the software on their systems, and each can accept the end-user licensing agreement (EULA) individually. See Chapter 61, "Incident Response, Communication, and Professionalism," for more information.

Incorrect answers: The terms "seat" and "commercial" licensing might be used for other types of licenses, but generally, the term "enterprise" is widely used when there are many end user licenses required (for example, when you are dealing with Microsoft operating system and Office software). An open source license (or open license) doesn't require a purchase. It can be downloaded and freely modified, based on the rules of the open source licensing agreement.

6. Answer: **C**. The most common issue when implementing bring-your-own-device (BYOD) as a policy to your organization is the possibility that malware from someone's smartphone, tablet, or laptop could be introduced to the network and spread to other systems. So, every BYOD device needs to be equipped with anti-malware software and kept up to date. Also, it would be wise to remotely administer these devices with a mobile device management (MDM) solution so that anti-malware updates can be streamed from a central source. See Chapter 49, "Mobile Device Security," for more information.

Incorrect answers: If you implement the system correctly, encryption of company-owned data can be the same across the board—and it should be. Devices in general will probably become more secure because they are initiated into a corporate BYOD network, so the level of phishing attacks should be the same or possibly reduced. DHCP failures should not increase unless your IP scope (range of IP addresses) can't handle the additional devices on the network. As always, you should consult your network documentation and see if your DHCP server's IP scope can handle all the clients that you plan to introduce to the network.

7. Answer: **B**. The most likely reason for this is that domain-level group policies have been implemented by the administrator. This is by design so that end users cannot enable screensavers. This cannot be changed by the end user. See Chapter 44, "Logical Security," for more information.

Incorrect answers: As mentioned, these domain-level group policies are by design; they are not incorrect policies, although it is possible to implement a similar security feature with the local computer policy of a system. Antivirus policies that are instituted at the domain level would affect the antivirus software of a group of systems on the network but should not affect Windows settings. A corrupted registry could cause problems with the logon, but what is happening in the scenario is a specific setting designed to secure the workstations on the domain.

8. Answer: **D**. PowerShell is an advanced command line in Windows that goes beyond the Command Prompt. It is designed for administrators so that they can run scripts, batch commands, and snippets, and save the work as .ps1 files (by default). The command **$PSVersionTable** will tell you the version of PowerShell, the Windows version, and more. The "PS" in the command stands for "PowerShell"! See Chapter 63, "Basic Scripting, Part II," for more information.

    Incorrect answers: Compatibility mode is a mode in Windows that allows you to run older programs within newer versions of Windows. OneDrive is Microsoft's cloud service. The Windows Defender Firewall is the built-in software-based firewall that blocks unwanted intrusion.

9. Answer: **A**. Use the **gpresult** command, which allows you to view the results of the Microsoft Group Policy configuration and print it to various file formats if you wish. See Chapter 31, "Microsoft Command-Line Tools, Part I," for more information.

    Incorrect answers: **gpupdate** takes care of updating settings on a computer regarding the computer policy configuration. **gpedit.msc** opens the Local Group Policy Editor window. **secpol.msc** opens the Local Security Policy window.

10. Answer: **B**. Use the **winver** command to find out the version and edition of Windows that is running. This opens a window that displays the information graphically. You could also use the **ver** command in the Command Prompt or **$psversiontable** in PowerShell. See Chapter 31, "Microsoft Command-Line Tools, Part I," for more information.

    Incorrect answers: The **pathping** command displays the route from the local system to the remote system on another network; it is similar to the **tracert** command. **ls** is a Linux command that displays the contents of the current directory. **hostname** shows the name of the computer.

11. Answer: **D**. You should isolate the infected system in a lab or another secure area that has no network connectivity. This is the first thing you should do after you have identified that there is malware. Know your malware removal steps! See Chapter 54, "Troubleshooting PC Security Issues," for more information.

    Incorrect answers: After quarantining the system, you would disable System Restore, remediate the infected system (if at all possible), schedule scans and run updates to the anti-malware program, enable System Restore, and finally, educate the user.

12. Answer: **C**. The screen lock and login time restrictions are your best bet. This way, the computer will lock after five minutes, even if the user forgets to lock it manually (with a quick Windows+L on the keyboard). Set the login restriction hours within the system or on the domain so that no one can log in after a certain time (such as 5 p.m.). See Chapter 48, "Windows Best Practices," for more information.

Incorrect answers: Every system should have a password, and it is required when the computer is first turned on, if the person logs off and logs back on, or if the system is unlocked. To avoid logging off and losing work, use the screen lock option. That will require the password when the user comes back to the computer. A strong password is important but does not meet the requirements when it comes to the person leaving the workstation frequently and the issue of not turning off the computer. A screensaver is not enough because this does not necessarily require a password. The screen lock is a much more secure method in general.

13. Answer: **B.** The incident response technician should secure the workstation in a limited-access storage facility until the matter is sorted out. A company can be liable for what its employees download, so the workstation should be securely stored and not disturbed until the matter has been investigated thoroughly. The incident response technician should also contact the network administrator (or network security administrator) and inform them that the user was able to download a BitTorrent client and figure out a way to block the usage of those. See Chapter 61, "Incident Response, Communication and Professionalism," for more information.

Incorrect answers: Because there are legal ramifications (for the user and for the company), the incident response tech should not delete anything and should store the computer securely for the time being. At some point, the tech will probably be called upon to image the drive, and the investigation can then be carried out. Reprimanding the user is up to the manager, but applying a content filter would probably be done for the entire network, not just that individual user's profile. The tech should definitely document the incident—that is of utmost importance—but the tech should not purge the downloaded materials. Instead, quarantine the computer in a safe location until the investigation is complete. If the user was working with a BitTorrent client, there is the chance that the user was performing other illegal acts, so the computer should be thoroughly analyzed, and the drive should be stored indefinitely in a secure place for future reference.

14. Answer: **D.** Use the Secure Shell (SSH) utility. Linux admins use it *all* the time. It allows you to log in to remote systems in a secure way (as long as those systems have an SSH server running). By the way, once you are logged in to the Linux server, use **apt update** or **dnf update** to update the server (depending on the distribution of Linux).

Incorrect answers: Remote Desktop Protocol (RDP) is the commonly used name for the Remote Desktop Connection program in Windows. It is used to connect to remote Windows systems. Secure File Transfer Protocol (SFTP) is a secure tool (that works on SSH), but it is designed to transfer files, not update a Linux server. Virtual Network Computing (VNC) is another way of remotely controlling systems, but it is a *graphical* desktop-sharing system, not a command-line system.

15. Answer: **C.** It is likely that the Windows Update service stopped. It can be restarted (along with RPC, which it is dependent on) within the Services console window in Computer Management (or **Run > services.msc**) or within the PowerShell/Command Prompt by typing **net start wuauserv**. However, it might be that Windows Update was disabled on purpose as part of company policy. Always check your organization's policies and procedures first before starting

services. See Chapter 49, "Mobile Device Security," for more information. See Chapter 34, "Microsoft Operating System Features and Tools, Part II," for more information.

Incorrect answers: Rebooting the computer will most likely result in the same issue later on, when Windows Update needs to update the OS. There are no device drivers that will affect the Windows Update service. Rebuilding the user profile is also not necessary here; plus, it is a lengthy process and definitely not a quick solution.

16. Answer: **B**. Store 30 days (1 month) of backups onsite (on-premises, or "on-prem") and store older backups with a cloud provider that is offsite (and preferably in a different geographic location). This meets all the requirements in the question: The last month of backups is easily accessible because it is onsite, long-term backups are stored offsite (cloud provider), and there is minimal use of hardware because you don't have to use as many tapes, disk arrays, and NAS boxes because the cloud is storing all backups older than 30 days. Of course, the cloud provider will use a lot of hardware, and that's part of the point of using the cloud. All that said, it's a good idea to have your 30 days of on-premises backups duplicated and stored offsite as well. Remember the 3-2-1 rule? See Chapter 58, "Change Management and Backup Methods," for more information.

Incorrect answers: Storing backups with a cloud provider and onsite is not specific enough. Storing all backups with the cloud provider is not a good answer because requirements say that only the long-term backups should be stored offsite. Storing backups onsite and using cloud bursting will probably entail using too much hardware.

17. Answer: **A**. All networking racks should be grounded, either to grounding bars or an I-beam in the ceiling or using some other grounding method. This should be done before installing any equipment to the racks to prevent any damage from electrostatic discharge (ESD). See Chapter 59, "Safety Procedures," for more information.

Incorrect answers: A dehumidifier would make the problem worse by removing additional humidity from the air. An ESD strap will provide some protection to the devices while you work on them, but it won't help once you disconnect. Fire suppression systems are important but won't protect against ESD.

18. Answer: **C**. With single sign-on (SSO), a user account's username and password can be used to gain access to multiple applications, systems, or networks (instead of the user having to memorize multiple passwords). SSO is often used in a federated identity management system. See Chapter 47, "Windows Security Settings," and Chapter 48, "Windows Best Practices," for more information.

Incorrect answers: Propagation and inheritance deal with NTFS permissions. By default, child objects (such as subfolders) inherit their NTFS permissions from the parent folder; conversely, the parent folder propagates those permissions to the child folder. MFA stands for multi-factor authentication; MFA is in place, for example, when a user is required to log on with two types of identification such as a password and a fingerprint.

19. Answer: **D**. You should tell Jason to make sure he is using his smart card. In a multi-factor authentication system, you might have a combination of a physical

smart card requiring that a personal identification number (PIN) be typed and then the password. So, you want to make sure that users are swiping (or inserting) their smart card before entering the PIN code. Of course, it depends on the type of authentication (or MFA) system that is in place. In this scenario, and with the answers listed, verification of the user's smart card is the best answer. See Chapter 44, "Logical Security," for more information.

Incorrect answers: The user probably hasn't gotten to the authentication stage where the password needs to be entered, but in any case, it is not a good idea to suggest entering all past passwords. Rebooting the computer can fix many problems, but in situations such as this one, it will simply result in the same issue. The network connection shouldn't play into the PIN requirement.

20. Answer: **A**. Surge suppressors (otherwise known as surge protectors) safeguard the equipment that is connected to them by directing surges to the path of least resistance. Electrical resistance is the measure of difficulty to pass an electric current through a conductor and is measured in Ohms (Ω). It usually means redirecting the current to ground. So, the metal-oxide varistor (MOV) within the surge suppressor will normally redirect to the ground wire of the AC circuit because there is no resistance on that wire. See Chapter 59, "Safety Procedures," for more information.

Incorrect answers: Electrical conductance deals with current and how easily it flows; it is the inverse quantity of resistance. Inductance deals with changes in current flowing through a circuit. The path of highest voltage is just that—for example, the hot wire of an AC circuit (120 V). You would not want a surge to be redirected to high-voltage areas, and you should always redirect surges and spikes to the ground.

21. Answer: **F**. Inheritance means that a file or folder receives its NTFS permissions from the parent folder. It is the default setting of the Advanced configuration dialog box within the Security tab of a file or folder. In Windows, it is shown as a button that can enable or disable inheritance (also described as "Include inheritable permissions from this object's parent" in older versions of Windows). See Chapter 47, "Windows Security Settings," for more information.

Incorrect answers: This is different from permission propagation in that with propagation, a parent folder forces the permissions to the subfolder. It can be initiated by the user, it is a separate configuration, and it is not necessarily configured to work by default. SSO is a type of authentication method in which a single username/password combination (or another single authentication scheme) is used to gain access to multiple different resources. With client-side virtualization, a client operating system (such as Windows) is run in a virtual machine. The virtual software applications that house VMs have their own set of requirements, as do the VMs themselves. For example, Windows running within a VM will not require as many resources as Windows running on a physical computer in a standard installation. Proxy settings are Internet connectivity settings that are set up on a computer running an OS such as Windows. The proxy setting is usually an IP address of a special computer on the network that acts as a go-between for the client computer and the Internet. It stores web information so that the client computer can gain access to the information faster while conserving Internet bandwidth. A recovery image is an image file that can recover an operating system. It is created by a manufacturer or by a user as a form of preventive maintenance in the event of a system crash and can be saved to an optical disc, a USB flash drive, or a special partition on the storage drive.

22. Answers: **B and D**. One-time password (OTP) tokens are usually implemented as hardware-based tokens that a person carries with them. The passcode changes periodically (for instance, every 60 seconds). A privacy filter is a filter placed in front of a monitor to reduce the viewing angle and make it more difficult for shoulder surfers (social engineers) to discern information from the screen. Another example is an RSA token. An RSA token can be a physical device, either located within a smart card or a key fob. This is intelligent technology that communicates with the security system, transferring information such as identification, dynamic passcodes, and more, allowing for a more secure authentication method. See Chapter 44, "Logical Security," for more information.

Incorrect answers: Directory permissions are the rights granted to users within Windows, allowing or denying them access to files, folders, printers, and other resources. The principle of least privilege states that a person should only have access to what is absolutely necessary; the concept "need to know" is part of this principle.

23. Answer: **C**. A network topology diagram shows network devices, such as switches and their individual ports (among other things.) This documentation is designed to help describe where computers and other networking equipment should connect, on a port-to-port basis. Often, a network topology diagram deals with physical connections, but it can also detail logical connectivity—for example, the IP addresses used by a LAN and what device that group of computers connects to. This might also be referred to as a logical topology diagram. See Chapter 57, "Documentation," for more information.

Incorrect answers: A change control form is used to document business processes during change management. A process diagram is a diagram that shows a step-by-step procedure or troubleshooting process. A fiber backbone diagram shows high-speed connections, often from one network to another. It wouldn't be required for an upgrade that concerns switch ports, which most likely implies standard 1 or 10 Gbps switches.

24. Answers: **B and C**. You should implement a multi-factor authentication system (such as one that uses usernames/passwords and also a smart card). You should also educate end users about company policies regarding the usage and storage of files and databases that can include passwords and personally identifiable information (PII). See Chapter 44, "Logical Security," for more information.

Incorrect answers: The strength of the password was not the problem here. The organization might have already instituted a policy that requires complex passwords; it's the password file or database that was leaked (most likely by an employee, possibly a malicious insider). But strong passwords are nonetheless important. File encryption is also a good idea, but it won't help with authentication strength. Restricting user permissions is important, too, but if the password list that was leaked includes administrator passwords, game over. You would need to implement an organizationwide password reset (right away).

25. Answer: **A**. Make sure the user is not using a proxy server within the browser before attempting anything else. A proxy address (whether added by malware or by the user) can redirect the browser to unwanted websites (often malicious in nature). See Chapter 37, "Windows Networking," for more information.

Incorrect answers: Internet shortcuts that were added without the user's knowledge could also be a culprit, so they should be checked, and the browser should also be cleared of cookies and cache, if necessary. But check that proxy setting first!

26. Answer: **D**. You most likely need to create an exception in the local firewall of the laptop. Outbound connections from the laptop are working fine, but that doesn't necessarily mean that inbound connections will work; in fact, most host-based firewalls have an implicit deny on all incoming traffic, while outgoing traffic is allowed. See Chapter 47, "Windows Security Settings," for more information.

Incorrect answers: You shouldn't need to change the IP address of the laptop. If it can push the configurations to the switches via FTP, then you know you have a valid network connection. That means a specific VLAN is not necessary either because connectivity has already been established. (However, a specific management VLAN is a good idea!) No static DNS entry is needed in this scenario, which made no mention of servers or DNS in general. DNS is extremely important in today's networks, but there is no evidence that DNS has failed here. In addition, sometimes technicians and administrators who need to perform technical tasks, such as pushing configurations via FTP, do so via IP address directly—skipping DNS altogether.

27. Answer: **D**. Disable Maps in the privacy settings. If Maps is always on, then it will drain the battery quickly, which subsequently makes the device considerably hotter. It's not just GPS; any powerful application (games, virtual reality programs, mobile OS update programs, and so on) can cause the battery to drain quickly and cause the device to heat up rapidly. See Chapter 55, "Troubleshooting Mobile Operating Systems and Application Issues," for more information.

Incorrect answers: Many mobile devices will come with 32 or 64 GB of storage. Using up 48 GB should not cause the battery to drain quickly, nor should the device heat up in the manner described in the question. Stored data is data at rest; it isn't doing anything with the other resources of the system—*unless* it is opened or used by an application. Having the display brightness set to auto is a good thing; it allows the device to monitor the ambient lighting and reduce or increase the brightness of the screen as necessary; this is actually a power-*saving* feature. Likewise, 15 minutes between mail pulls would not cause a power drain. If, however, it were set to automatic or real time, that could cause a drain on the battery, but it would still not cause as much drain as the GPS program that is always on in the scenario.

28. Answers: **B and C**. A drive shredder or drill can be used to physically tear the drive into multiple pieces or to make holes in the platters of the hard drive, thus making it inoperable. It can then be disposed of according to municipal guidelines. This is one of several ways to physically destroy a drive and is only performed when the drive has met the end of its life cycle, is not going to be recycled within the organization, and is to be disposed of. However, shredding (or pulverizing) is the best way to destroy a drive; vendors offer services to perform this work and provide a certificate of destruction when complete. See Chapter 50, "Data Destruction and Disposal," for more information.

Incorrect answers: Disabling ports is done on a firewall or SOHO router to block access into (or out of) a network. A low-level format is a type of formatting procedure done in the BIOS/UEFI of a system (on older drives), through the use of special removable media, or is done at the manufacturer. It removes more data than a standard operating system format but does not destroy the drive (though it can cause damage to particular sectors if performed too often). Many technicians also refer to data wiping as a method of low-level formatting.

29. Answer: **C**. Use the Advanced tab to enable TLS 1.2/1.3 (and other security protocols) within Internet Explorer. See Chapter 35, "Windows Control Panel Utilities," for more information.

Incorrect answers: This is a bit of a trick question. At first glance, you would think that TLS is a security feature; and while it is, the Security tab deals with zone *security*, not specific protocol-based security options. The Privacy tab deals with blocking cookies. The Connections tab concerns setting up Internet connections, VPNs, and proxy server connections.

30. Answer: **C**. The storage drive space is not large enough for Windows 10 or 11. 64-bit installations of Windows 10 require 32 GB of storage drive space. Windows 11 installations require 64 GB of storage drive space. This holds true for physical installations and virtual installations. The virtual machine (VM) installation will fail until the VM's drive space is increased. In fact, 15 GB is not enough for Windows 8 either, though chances are you won't be seeing much of that since its EOL is January 2023. See Chapter 30, "Comparing Windows Editions," for more information.

Incorrect answers: The rest of the listed specifications for the VM are enough for Windows 10 or Windows 11, so the rest of those do not need to be modified.

31. Answer: **D**. You should recommend the Microsoft domain setup. This means installing a server that acts as a domain controller, where all logon authentication is centralized. This way, all access to network shares and print servers is also centralized. A domain controller is a server that is running a version of the Windows Server operating system and has Active Directory Domain Services (AD DS) running. See Chapter 37, "Windows Networking," for more information.

Incorrect answers: A workgroup is a good choice for networks with 20 or fewer computers. Once you exceed 20 computers, it is wise to configure a domain. The main reason for this is that a single Windows client computer can handle only 20 connections simultaneously. Storing all your data on one computer for every user to access is fine for networks with 10 to 15 computers. But as you increase your network to 20 computers or more, you are forced to store resources on multiple computers, which can create confusion. Ad hoc means that no one computer is in control; this especially applies to wireless networks and is sufficient for a few systems but definitely not for 25 computers. Spoke-hub (also known as hub-and-spoke, or the older star topology) refers to the network topology or how computers are connected. This isn't covered in the A+ objectives, but it essentially means that the computers are wired in such a way that all of them physically connect to a central connecting device (such as a switch) or wirelessly connect to a wireless access point. This is easily the most common way that computers connect to a wired network. You wouldn't recommend this because it already exists! This will be the wired network configuration in the vast majority of scenarios. However, in this 220-1102 practice exam, the question is assessing your understanding of the Windows solution for how the data will be shared.

32. Answer: **A**. Chain of custody is the chronological documentation (written) of evidence pertaining to a computer or other technical device that has prohibited content or has been confiscated. The technician should write (or type) the date, time, and who took custody of the computer next. It's important for the technician to adhere to the chain-of-custody rules when storing the computer or data. It's also important to verify that the chain of custody remains intact, so as to ensure evidence is admissible in legal proceedings. See Chapter 61, "Incident Response, Communication, and Professionalism," for more information.

    Incorrect answers: Committing such important facts to memory is not enough; this will not stand up in court as evidence. A "third party" will break the chain of custody. Calling the supervisor is part of first response; it's not part of chain of custody.

33. Answer: **C**. Use Performance Monitor (**Run > perfmon.exe**) to analyze a device. In this example, you can find out how many bits per second the NIC can transfer (that is, the data transfer rate). You can also use this tool to monitor all of the other devices (objects) on the system and save and report on those findings in a variety of ways. Another useful tool is Resource Monitor. See Chapter 33, "Microsoft Operating System Features and Tools, Part I," for more information.

    Incorrect answers: Device Manager is where you would go to install or uninstall a device or roll back the driver for that device. Local Security Policy (**Run > secpol. msc**) is where you would go to enable or disable rules (policies) on a Windows client computer. System Information (**msinfo32**) gives you the Windows system summary for hardware resources, components, and the software environment, but it cannot perform tests.

34. Answer: **D**. Most help desks' standard policy is to have their techs research new problems for a couple minutes before escalating them to higher-level techs. Often this proves to be the right course because the technician is often able to find the answer within two or three minutes. Of course, if you do place the customer on hold, watch the time (I suggest a timer app) and be sure to get back to that person when that time is up. See Chapter 61, "Incident Response, Communication, and Professionalism," for more information.

    Incorrect answers: It's better to tell the customer that you are checking resources than to tell the customer that you have never encountered the problem before because it instills more confidence. If you can't find the answer in two minutes, then inform the customer that you will have to escalate the problem.

35. Answer: **B**. The question mark (?) on the icon or elsewhere in the wireless connection properties normally indicates an unauthenticated connection, meaning that the user is connecting to an "open" public hotspot; this, in turn, means that the user did not have to log on and might not be using any encryption to connect

via Wi-Fi. When this is the case, certain web pages and sites may not open. For example, if the user was trying to connect to the company VPN or something similar, the company's infrastructure might see that the smartphone does not have an authenticated connection and deny access. The same can happen with some websites. See Chapter 45, "Wireless Security and Malware," for more information.

Incorrect answers: Data allowance has to do with a cellular connection, not a Wi-Fi connection. In addition, many providers offer "unlimited" data transfer, which really means that you can send and receive a specified amount of data (for instance, 20 GB) before the connection is throttled down—but again, that is based on cellular connectivity, not Wi-Fi connectivity. Un-rooted is what you want! That is a normally functioning phone. A rooted phone, on the other hand, is one that has been configured to gain root-level access in order to run certain programs and make changes to the phone. However, that shouldn't affect data usage or connectivity (unless the rooting led to a hack). If the SIM card was not activated, then the user would not have been able to call in to the help desk. 3G is a cellular data technology, not Wi-Fi. A user normally can't purchase a smartphone without a data plan, but even if the user could, that plan deals with cellular data, not Wi-Fi connections. As you can see, most of the incorrect answers concern cellular data, but the scenario refers to a Wi-Fi connection.

36. Answer: **C**. In Windows, the Task Manager Users tab shows any currently logged-on users and their status. The Task Manager shows the percentage of resources that are being used by each user. See Chapter 33, "Microsoft Operating System Features and Tools, Part I," for more information.

Incorrect answers: MSConfig (System Configuration) is used to change boot settings and disable services. Disk Management is used to monitor the status of drives and to work with partitioning/formatting. Administrative Tools is a collection of tools used to configure the OS, but it does not offer a quick way to see which users are logged in to the system.

37. Answers: **A and E**. Compressed air and a vacuum are tools commonly used to remove dust and debris from inside a computer. Of course, when you use compressed air, consider doing this outside because the dust and dirt will fly all over the place. Use a vacuum to clean up after you are done. If you do use a vacuum inside a computer, make sure it is an antistatic, computer-ready vacuum, and, importantly, don't touch any of the components inside the system! See Chapter 60, "Environmental Controls," for more information.

Incorrect answers: Cotton and alcohol (or a 50/50 mix of alcohol and water) might be used to clean a printer's rubber rollers, the bottom of an ink cartridge (if it is very dirty), or a display. A feather duster would cause electrostatic discharge (ESD) and should be avoided; it is not a good tool for the job. Antibacterial surface cleaner should only be used on the outside of a computer case.

38. Answer: **C**. Using an ISO image (.iso) is a common way to allow for the download of operating systems such as Windows, Linux, and so on. It can be easily read by virtualization programs to install operating systems into virtual machines. An ISO image is designed to take the place of an entire optical disc. See Chapter 40, "Operating System Installations and Upgrades," for more information.

Incorrect answers: .exe files are executable programs. An appimage is an image of an application that can run without needing to be installed; it is common in Linux. .vdi is the default extension used in VirtualBox for virtual storage drives.

39. Answer: **B**. An invalid boot disk error is a common symptom of a problem loading the Windows operating system. It could be caused by removable media inserted into the computer (an optical disc or USB flash drive) that is not bootable. This could be avoided by setting the storage drive to first in the BIOS/UEFI boot order. Another possible symptom of problems loading the operating system would be if a RAID array was not detected during bootup or during installation of the OS. Either way, the storage drive, or RAID array of drives, should be inspected for faulty connections. See Chapter 53, "Troubleshooting Microsoft Windows," for more information.

Incorrect answers: A spontaneous shutdown and restart indicates either a problem with the power supply or the possibility of malware on the system. Note that the question refers to "starting up" Windows; a shutdown or restart can only happen when the system has already booted. WinRE is the Windows Recovery Environment, which includes System Recovery Options such as Startup Repair and System Restore. WinRE is not accessible during a routine bootup of Windows but can be initiated by booting from a special partition on the storage drive or by booting from a USB flash drive (or, in older versions of Windows, from an optical disc). Whether or not the BIOS/UEFI is synchronized to a time server shouldn't matter. However, it is important to sync Windows time to a time server. An emergency repair disk (or disc) should only be booted to in the event that there is a problem with Windows. A failure to boot to an emergency repair disk is not a common symptom of a problem starting Windows, but you might use a recovery disc to fix the problem. REGSVR32 is a tool used in the Command Prompt to activate or deactivate ActiveX controls, none of which should stop Windows from booting.

40. Answers: **A, B, and D**. Malware can have many symptoms. Viruses are especially prevalent in today's society; there are millions of different kinds. Fake security alerts, failure to update Windows, and renamed system files are all possible symptoms of malware—specifically, viruses. See Chapter 54, "Troubleshooting PC Security Issues," for more information.

Incorrect answers: Windows has a preinstallation environment known as Windows PE or simply WinPE; this is a lightweight version of Windows that is often used to deploy the operating system. It can be booted from optical disc, USB flash drive, over the network via PXE, or by the storage drive. It is an add-on to Windows available with the Windows Assessment and Deployment Kit (ADK). It can be used to run recovery tools such as Windows RE and for running drive-cloning utilities. Rogue antivirus programs are not symptoms of malware; they *are* malware! A rogue antivirus program can often be something that appears to be legitimate when it is not. Or it could be a part of a rogue security software suite, which deceives the user into paying for fake malware protection. User error is not a symptom of malware, but it could very well be the cause. If a user surfs to a malicious website or opens an unknown email attachment without verifying the source of the email first, malware could be—and often is—the result. Educate the end user when it comes to screening emails and surfing the Web. Show the user how to be responsible when accessing online information.

41. Answer: **D**. It could be that another program (quite possibly malicious) is using the camera on its own, without user intervention. So, the best first thing to do is to check the application permissions. For example, in Android, a typical navigational path would be **General > Apps & Notifications > App permissions**. From there, you will see the Camera app; tap it to find out which applications are using it. Then, you can deselect whichever apps you need to. You might also find that a malicious or unwanted program is on the list and enabled for camera usage; if so, it should be removed. See Chapter 55, "Troubleshooting Mobile Operating Systems and Application Issues," for more information.

Incorrect answers: Updating all applications is a bit premature. You may want to do that at some point, though, as long as company policy allows it. OS updates should be checked as well at some point but not first because that does not get to the root of the problem. Uninstalling the camera application won't change how other apps can use the camera. You will simply be preventing the user from using the camera. Resetting the phone is one of the last options to try, but it could be a reality if the smartphone has been compromised, which is a distinct possibility in this scenario. If resetting is necessary, your company might also require a few overwrites of data first.

42. Answer: **B**. The only option that would help the situation would be to run the **chkdsk** command with the **/R** option. **/R** locates bad sectors and recovers readable information, which is the only option listed that might fix the file system corruption (keyword *might*). **/R** implies **/F** as well, which fixes basic errors on the drive. Though not listed in the A+ objectives, you might also use the dism tool to repair a slowly running Windows system. See Chapter 31, "Microsoft Command-Line Tools, Part I," for more information.

Incorrect answers: Reloading the OS would wipe all data (on the system partition at least), so it is not recommended. In addition, you wouldn't normally go from NTFS to FAT32; it's recommended to use NTFS. Plus, if the file system were corrupt, a reinstall of the OS (using NTFS again) would fix those issues. Opening the **defrag** utility and running a drive analysis doesn't really change the drive; it simply tells you if the drive is fragmented. Changing the drive from basic to dynamic is done so that you can resize partitions.

43. Answer: **D**. Non-water-based fire extinguishers should be used during an electrical fire. This could be a CO2-based fire extinguisher such as a Class C extinguisher, a Halotron fire extinguisher, or an FM-200 overhead system. See Chapter 59, "Safety Procedures," for more information.

Incorrect answers: Standard overhead sprinkler systems use water. They should not be present where expensive computer equipment is located (for example, in server rooms). Regular water-based fire extinguishers should not be used. Class B extinguishers are meant for burning gases and liquids, whereas Class C are meant for electrical fire (think "C" for "copper," like the copper inside electrical wiring).

44. Answer: **C**. Attempt to install legacy (older) applications in compatibility mode. Select the older OS that the application was originally written for. See Chapter 35, "Windows Control Panel Utilities," for more information.

Incorrect answers: Your first step should never include the word *purchase*; besides it is not necessary in a system such as Windows, where compatibility mode exits. Normally you wouldn't install an application in Safe Mode; you might run the application or troubleshoot the system in that mode. Security updates probably won't have an effect on this scenario either.

45. Answer: **A**. Of the listed answers, the most likely cause in this scenario is that there has been unauthorized root access. Whether this was done by the user on purpose or without his knowledge by one of the newly installed apps is still something you need to discover. Unauthorized root access by an app or by a user could cause the phone to perform unwanted actions, which would most likely drain the battery quickly. See Chapter 55, "Troubleshooting Mobile Operating Systems and Application Issues," for more information.

Incorrect answers: It is unlikely that the battery needs to be replaced since it is a new phone, but it is something you can investigate after determining whether the phone has been rooted. A defective SD card probably won't affect the battery. Weak signal could cause battery drain (especially if the user is in a basement or other unfavorable wireless location), but short battery life is more likely caused by root access, by powerful apps pulling too much power, or by a bright display that has been configured to not shut off. Slow data speeds are an annoyance, but they're not something that should cause the battery to drain quickly.

46. Answers: **C and H**. For the highest level of wireless security, use WPA3 (and AES). For authentication, select multi-factor authentication (MFA). Many health-care providers are required to log on with a username/password and a smart card (or biometric). See Chapter 45, "Wireless Security and Malware," for more information.

Incorrect answers: Out of WPA, WPA2, and WPA3, WPA3 is the most secure. Protocols such as WEP, WPA, and TKIP are especially vulnerable; they are out-dated examples of encryption protocols. RADIUS and TACACS+ are example of authentication servers—and the scenario mentioned that the company can-not afford a server. It is unknown what the cloud contains; there is probably an authentication server there (connected to via secure VPN), but it is not something that *you* would implement at the SOHO office. SSO stands for single sign-on, and it quite possibly is already set up in the cloud as it is very common in the healthcare industry.

47. Answer: **C**. Try adjusting the power settings so that wireless connections will not time out as quickly. This can be done in Windows in Power Plans and the Power Options dialog box. See Chapter 35, "Windows Control Panel Utilities," for more information.

Incorrect answers: If the wireless card was faulty, the customer would never be able to get onto a wireless network, so there is no reason to replace the wireless card. The capacity of the battery will not affect wireless connections. Disabling the screensaver will also not affect the wireless connection; however, you can get to some of the power options necessary to solve the wireless problem indirectly from the screensaver window.

48. Answers: **C and D**. You should discuss firewalls (for the general security of the network) and a VPN (for security while browsing the Internet). These two

concepts can help make the home user's network and laptop more secure and will protect the user's privacy. See Chapters 47, "Windows Security Settings," and 64, "Remote Access Technologies," for more information.

Incorrect answers: Antivirus and anti-malware programs help with malicious programs, but not with privacy. A proxy server can be used in multiple ways: by an organization to act as a go-between and a caching device for multiple clients and by an end user who *really* wants to protect his or her privacy. This is not something you would bring up with a typical customer. Remember your professionalism best practices: It's not a good idea to bring up heavily technical concepts (such as advanced TCP/IP settings) with a customer.

49. Answer: **B**. **grep** is the Linux command used to search for matching information in a file, files, or filename. See Chapter 42, "Linux," for more information.

    Incorrect answers: Other Linux commands include **sudo**, which is used to allow a user to execute a command as another user (for example, an administrator); **chmod**, which is used to change the permissions of a file or folder; and **wget**, which retrieves content from web servers (as opposed to the **get** command, which is often used to obtain files from an FTP server).

50. Answer: **C**. Chances are that the update caused an issue with the computer; perhaps the video driver or another driver was updated, resulting in the black screen. Booting into Safe Mode can help figure out the problem. If Safe Mode displays properly, you can be fairly certain that there is a video driver issue or some other driver issue; the driver can be rolled back. If you aren't sure what was affected, you can roll back the entire update. See Chapter 53, "Troubleshooting Microsoft Windows," for more information.

    Incorrect answers: The registry is rarely the first place to go when troubleshooting problems, and it definitely would not be first in this case. The registry is where you go to make advanced configuration changes to the OS. Many times, when you take exams, two answers will look plausible; that's the case here with "Configure boot options in the BIOS." Often, if there is a black screen, it might be accompanied by a message such as "invalid boot device" or "No OS found." If that is the case, then it could very well be that the BIOS boot priority needs to be changed. However, in the scenario, there is no mention of a message of any sort, but you did get information that there was an update the night before. (It could be that the video card is simply displaying a black screen.) Disabling Windows services is a possibility, but you would want to boot into Safe Mode first and diagnose the system further before disabling any services.

51. Answer: **A**. Remove watches, jewelry, and any other metals when working on a computer so they are out of the way and do not pose any threats while working on the computer. See Chapter 59, "Safety Procedures," for more information.

    Incorrect answers: You should review local regulations and check for environmental concerns when disposing of storage drives, batteries, and toner cartridges. Read the MSDS (material safety data sheet) when you encounter a fluid spill or other unknown chemical.

52. Answer: **D**. Before you do anything else, disconnect the network cable from comp112. This can help isolate the problem. You might also decide to disconnect the network cables from any other systems that were infected by this

virus. Sometimes, it is easier to do this at the server room. See Chapter 54, "Troubleshooting PC Security Issues," for more information.

Incorrect answers: After the network cable is disconnected, the computer should be shut down (which will log off the user anyway) and rebooted into Safe Mode. Then the virus should be isolated and quarantined. Finally, a full virus scan should be run. This, of course, is just a quick example; you probably need to do more to resolve this problem on all computers concerned.

53. Answer: **B**. This is a Linux, Unix, or macOS system. When it comes to Linux, Unix, and similar systems, a lot of technicians simply refer to them as *nix, meaning anything ending in "*nix*." Many Linux distributions use the Bash shell by default. This is where scripts are run. This default line tells the system the path and how to interpret the upcoming script. See Chapter 63, "Basic Scripting, Part II," for more information.

Incorrect answers: Windows uses PowerShell. Saved scripts (such as .ps1 files) don't use this type of line to identify the shell interpreter. iOS doesn't use Bash or Terminal the way that macOS and Linux do. JavaScript is not a system at all; instead, it is a type of scripting language that is often used with websites.

54. Answer: **C**. The System Configuration utility (**msconfig**) can be used to change the total number of CPU cores used by Windows. This can be found by going to the **Boot** tab and clicking the **Advanced options** button. From there, check the **Number of processors** checkbox and select the number of CPU cores (or the actual number of CPUs if you have more than one). This is usually done to troubleshoot the CPU or Windows; in most cases, Windows will use all CPU cores available to it by default. See Chapter 33, "Microsoft Operating System Features and Tools, Part I," for more information.

Incorrect answers: The Performance Monitor (perfmon.exe) is used to analyze system performance and can view each core in real time, as can the Task Manager (taskmgr.exe). The DirectX Diagnostics tool (dxdiag.exe) is used to analyze audio and video DirectX components in the system.

55. Answer: **B**. Of the listed answers, the most likely cause is an inactive virtual private network (VPN) connection. If the user did not log in through the VPN, or if the VPN session timed out, then the user will not be able to get access to the files stored at the office LAN. See Chapter 44, "Logical Security," for more information.

Incorrect answers: Outdated anti-malware protection could possibly allow a virus to get into the system, and a symptom of this might be missing or renamed files on the local computer. Mobile device management (MDM) policies are designed to configure or restrict mobile devices. However, you don't know what type of computer the person is using from home, but you can guess that it is a laptop, and not a smartphone or tablet. Untrusted software is any application that an organization does not trust and does not want installed to systems. It's possible that untrusted software could cause the VPN connection to fail, but it is less likely as an indirect cause of the problem.

56. Answer: **A**. The user will have only read access to the file. Remember that the more restrictive permissions take precedence, so in this case, the NTFS "Read"

permission level takes effect. See Chapter 47, "Windows Security Settings," for more information.

Incorrect answers: It is possible for the user to get write, modify, or full control access—but only if the NTFS permissions are configured to allow the user to do so. As it stands, the user has only read access.

57. Answer: **D**. The program would be installed to C:\Program Files (x86). This is the default folder for 32-bit programs when installed to a 64-bit version of Windows. See Chapter 38, "Application Installation and Configuration Concepts," for more information.

Incorrect answers: 64-bit programs are installed to the C:\Program Files folder. The operating system is installed to C:\Windows. Finally, C:\ is the root of the drive. A few system files are placed in the root, but otherwise the OS and applications are installed to folders within the root. x86 is the general term applied to 32-bit computers, whereas x86-64 (or simply x64) is the term applied to 64-bit computers.

58. Answer: **B**. If the computer has a recovery partition, then the reinstallation of Windows can be accomplished from there. This is often a partition that was placed on the storage drive by the computer manufacturer for just this type of scenario. See Chapter 40, "Operating Systems Installation and Upgrades," and Chapter 53, "Troubleshooting Microsoft Windows," for more information.

Incorrect answers: System Restore is an example of Windows functionality that can bring the system back to an earlier point in time but does not reinstall the entire OS. Linux rescue media (flash drive or boot disc) might work, but only if a Windows image is available somewhere, so the answer is not specific enough. (You might also use a flash drive with a Windows image.) The primary partition is where Windows is installed *to*. It does not normally contain recovery data or a recovery Windows image.

59. Answer: **D**. The first thing you should do is look up the error number. If an item fails during Windows Update, an error log called WindowsUpdate.log can be written to C:\Windows\Logs\WindowsUpdate, but only if you have run the **Get-WindowsUpdateLog** cmdlet in PowerShell first. (In previous versions of Windows, it was in the %systemroot%, usually C:\Windows.) An example of an error code is 0x80243FFF, which is a user interface error. (It might show up in the log without the 0x.) You might also need to access the CBS.log file, which is located in %systemroot%\Logs. See Chapter 36, "Windows Settings," for more information.

Incorrect answers: While the Event Viewer can be very handy for analyzing system file, application, and security issues, it is not the first and best place to go when troubleshooting Windows Update errors. The Event Viewer is more generic (problem-wise), whereas the WindowsUpdate log files and CBS.log files are very specific. Downloading the failed update and installing it manually will probably result in the same error. You need to dig deep and find out what the real cause of the problem is. You do want to visit the Microsoft website, but you will most likely be going to https://support.microsoft.com or https://docs.microsoft.com (or both); there is no Microsoft Update website per se (as of the writing of this book).

60. Answer: **C**. You must rejoin the computer to the domain. This can be done by navigating to the **Computer Name** tab of the System Properties dialog box,

which is accessed from the **Advanced settings** link from the System window or by executing **systempropertiescomputername.exe** at the Run prompt. You might also use the **netdom** command in the Command Prompt if you have Remote Server Administration Tools (RSAT) enabled on the Windows client or are working directly on a Windows server. See Chapter 37, "Windows Networking," for more information.

Incorrect answers: Updating the BIOS/UEFI to the latest version will help with any firmware issues but won't have any effect on trust relationships within Windows. Running **chkdsk** will check for errors on the storage drive. Rebooting the PC will not automatically rebuild the relationship; you must manually rejoin the computer to the domain.

61. Answer: **D**. Your friend might have an address such as thomas_r@abc-company. com. To enable the iPad access to this email account, you'll need the type of server that handles email (be it SMTP, POP3, IMAP, or an Exchange server) and the domain name that the server resides on. Often, this will be the same domain name as the email address, but not always. An example of an SMTP mail server might be mail.abc-company.com. A POP3 server might be pop.abc-company.com. See Chapter 55, "Troubleshooting Mobile Operating Systems and Application Issues," for more information.

Incorrect answers: IP addresses aren't necessary when configuring an email account on an iPad, an Android device, a PC, or any computer, really. This is because the email account software will automatically attempt to resolve the mail server name to the IP address, in the same manner a web browser does when you type in a web address. The gateway address and DNS server are only necessary when attempting to connect a device to the Internet. This most likely won't be an issue with an iPad, but it can be configured in the networking settings, if necessary.

62. Answer: **B**. You want to use a loop construct, such as a **for** or **while** loop, that will loop through a command block until the condition changes from true to false (the end of the file). See Chapter 62, "Basic Scripting, Part I," for more information.

Incorrect answers: An integer is any whole number. A string is one or more characters. A variable is something that refers to something else and can change over time (for example, $x = 42$). Integers, strings, and variables can be used *within* conditional loops. And a loop might be used within an if-then statement, which can be described as a statement that contains a hypothesis followed by a conclusion. In programming, it provides a secondary path of execution when the if portion is evaluated as false.

63. Answer: **C**. You should recommend an uninterruptible power supply (UPS). This meets both requirements: It enables the system to gracefully shut down in the event of a power outage, which protects files from corruption, and it can provide an hour of uptime (though that will require a fairly powerful UPS of at least 1500 VA). See Chapter 60, "Environmental Controls," for more information.

Incorrect answers: A surge protector and power strip don't meet either of the two requirements. A power strip simply allows for more outlets, while a surge protector can help protect a computer against surges or spikes. A power distribution unit (PDU) is a device with multiple outlets that can come in many forms, including as a strip; however, it is much more than a power strip in that it can be monitored and controlled. PDUs are often used in datacenters and server rooms and are also known as main distribution units (MDUs).

64. Answer: **A**. You should run the system file checker (SFC) utility. This will check and possibly replace damaged or missing Windows operating system files. See Chapter 31, "Microsoft Command-Line Tools, Part I," for more information.

Incorrect answers: **chkdsk** checks the drive for errors and may try to fix those errors, depending on the options you supply with the command. **gpupdate** makes changes to group policy take effect immediately (instead of waiting for user logoff and logon). **robocopy** is used to copy groups of files or folders. **grep** is a filtering tool in Linux.

65. Answer: **B**. The best answer listed is that the parent folder has explicit Deny rights set for the third-party user. If this is the case, then by default, that permission will *propagate* to any subfolders and files within the parent. This can also be expressed as the default action for a subfolder (also known as a child folder) to *inherit* its permissions from the parent. Basically, you should remember two things: A folder inherits its permissions from the parent, and Deny rights will always override Allow rights. See Chapter 47, "Windows Security Settings," for more information.

Incorrect answers: If the folder were set with Allow rights, the third party should be able to access the data. If the user forgot to share the folder, the third party would not be able access the data. However, it's the second part of that answer that is impossible because you can't share a specific file; you can only share folders. The archive attribute would simply create a backup copy of a file or folder. Permissions questions can be some of the toughest on the A+ exam, but if you remember a few basic rules (such as the ones mentioned here), you should survive them!

66. Answer: **B**. The most common Linux shell program is the Terminal utility, which uses the Bash shell by default on most Linux distros. (This is also available in macOS.) This utility allows the user to enter commands of all types—including recovery commands—to be executed by Linux. See Chapter 42, "Linux," for more information.

Incorrect answers: The equivalent of the Terminal utility in Windows is the PowerShell or Command Prompt. By the way, the Command Prompt is often referred to as CMD because it can be opened with the **cmd.exe** executable. Backup and restoration programs, such as macOS's Time Machine, Windows System Restore, and so on, cannot have recovery commands typed into them. You require some kind of text interface to do so.

67. Answers: **B and D**. Modify the AutoRun settings and disable the Guest account. Modify AutoPlay/AutoRun by disabling it in the Group Policy Editor. (Also, the use of USB drives and other removable media should be disabled in the BIOS/UEFI.) Disable the Guest account within Local Users and Groups (or within Active Directory Users and Computers if on a domain). The problem with the Guest account is that it has no password by default, and it could be used to attempt privilege escalation. See Chapter 48, "Windows Best Practices," for more information.

Incorrect answers: Removing admin permissions is somewhat vague. An administrative account has administrative permissions for a reason: so that the admin can access the server. Removing a user from the Administrators group would result in a standard user account, which is great from a principle of least privilege perspective, but that person could no longer log in to the server, making it pointless. A software-based firewall would not have prevented this exploit because the user was local (behind the firewall) using a USB stick. You could change the default credentials of the Guest account, but it is better to either give it a strong password (if you have to use it) or, better yet, disable the account altogether. OS security updates should be run on a regular basis, but this is an issue that goes beyond updates.

68. Answer: **B**. Use comments to describe what the script is doing. In PowerShell, Bash, and many other scripting systems, use the number sign (**#**) to start a comment. Remember, comments don't actually *do* anything other than provide explanation. See Chapter 62, "Basic Scripting, Part I," for more information.

Incorrect answers: End-user documentation is an important element to include in any software. However, that is better developed as a PDF file or online documentation (readthedocs, mkdocs, and so on). In addition, end users usually won't see your scripts; in the scenario, the comments are designed for the engineers who might actually look at the script. Variables and **if-then** statements are components of a script that actually do something (unlike comments). Change management documentation would be required if you were to make changes to the script.

69. Answer: **C**. Encryption (for example, WPA3 with AES) prevents unauthorized users from accessing confidential data that is transmitted over the wireless network. One of the best ways to protect confidentiality of data in general is through encryption. Use the highest level of encryption possible on a SOHO wireless network to eliminate this threat. See Chapter 51, "SOHO Security," for more information.

Incorrect answers: Enabling MAC filtering looks like a good answer. However, it is used to stop unauthorized computers from accessing the wireless network. While a good idea, it does nothing to protect the actual data. Plus, a good hacker can get past MAC filtering. If that happens, encryption is going to be the savior anyway. While anything is hackable, breaking the AES cipher will require a powerful computer and a lot of time. Changing the SSID name only modifies the name of the wireless network. However, by default, the SSID is broadcast from most SOHO routers, which is easily found by various wireless scanning software packages. Reducing the broadcast power is a smart idea as well, but this simply reduces the distance the SOHO router sends its wireless signal. If the hacker is within this range, they will have access to the network. The key here is confidential. To protect confidentiality, use encryption.

70. Answer: **D**. Programs and Features is the place to go in the Control Panel (CP) to remove an application in Windows. You can also open this by entering **appwiz. cpl** in the Command Prompt. Or you could access **Settings > Apps > Apps & features**. See Chapter 35, "Windows Control Panel Utilities," and Chapter 36, "Windows Settings," for more information.

Incorrect answers: Disk Cleanup is used to remove temporary files; it's not used to remove applications. Administrative Tools is a group of tools, such as Event Viewer, Task Scheduler, and Computer Management. Folder Options (or File Explorer Options) is where you can go to change how folders are displayed.

71. Answer: **A**. Check the proxy server settings in the browser. A large network may use a proxy server to facilitate the caching of web pages—often for external, or *public*, websites only. It could be that the proxy server was not configured properly or wasn't configured at all. See Chapter 37, "Windows Networking," for more information.

Incorrect answers: You shouldn't have to modify the IPv6 settings because the question says the system has a valid IP address. The hosts file is an older text file used to statically resolve hostnames to IP addresses. Although this file still exists in some versions of Windows, it is rarely used, except for malicious purposes. If it was used for malicious purposes, the browser probably wouldn't be able to connect to any websites—external or internal. A DNS server performs domain name-to-IP address resolution; if other pages are working on the intranet, then chances are that the DNS server is not the issue.

72. Answers: **C and F**. Of the listed answers, you should reduce the transmitting power of the AP and disable the SSID broadcast. Reducing the power prevents signal bleed to other offices; usually this can be set to "low" or something similar. Disabling the SSID or network name of the AP makes it so a typical user cannot scan for and locate the wireless network. Other smart ideas are to put a strong password on the admin account, use WPA2/AES, implement MAC filtering, and disable WPS. See Chapter 51, "SOHO Security," for more information.

Incorrect answers: WPA is generally avoided because WPA3 (or at least WPA2) is better. Disabling the DHCP server won't do much for security, but it will hamper availability because most end users' computers will obtain IP addresses automatically. Most SOHO routers can modify the channel width but can't reduce the channel *availability*. Users can either connect or not. When enabled, quality of service (QoS) can help to prioritize traffic from specific computers or applications.

73. Answer: **A**. For proper quarantining and removal of malware, you usually have to disable System Restore first because it can get in the way of the anti-malware scanning and removal processes. See Chapter 54, "Troubleshooting PC Security Issues," for more information.

Incorrect answers: You might ask, "Well, what about disabling the network cards so that the malware doesn't spread?" While this might work, the best way is to physically disconnect the computer from the wired network and turn off any wireless on/off switches if at all possible. Or remove the wireless antenna from the computer. It's just impossible to tell if a virus or other type of malware is playing tricks on the Windows option to disable a networking card. Windows Update should be run after quarantining and removal processes are complete. You can run **chkdsk /R** to locate bad sectors and recover readable information, if necessary, after the malware removal is complete.

74. Answers: **B and D**. Among other things, you should recommend using strong passwords and assigning security rights based on job roles. Strong passwords are important on routers, wireless devices, switches, computers, and anything

else that can be logged into. Role-based access control means rights and permissions are assigned based on the person's job in a company—accounting, marketing, and so on. See Chapter 48, "Windows Best Practices," for more information.

Incorrect answers: Daily security audits might be a good idea, but they do not increase security; they only determine whether there is a threat or vulnerability that needs to be attended to. The customer already said that their antivirus software is up to date, so additional antivirus software should not be necessary. In fact, you shouldn't run any more than one type of antivirus software because they can have conflicting results that can slow down the system. Disabling screensavers doesn't really increase the security of the network, but setting up a password lock within the screensaver can make the individual systems more secure.

75. Answers: **A, C, and E**. Professionalism comes in many forms. When dealing with a customer, you should avoid distractions, avoid being judgmental, and meet expectations that are set. Also, avoid arguing, talking to co-workers, and personal interruptions. Be positive and listen to the customer. See Chapter 61, "Incident Response, Communication and Professionalism," for more information.

Incorrect answers: It is important to retain a chain of custody, but this has more to do with tracking evidence and less to do with professionalism. Documentation is important as well and should be developed by you as the technician; it should not be left to the customer.

76. Answers: **B and D**. You should look in the Event Viewer (Application log) and look for any other log files that are created by that new application. These might contain clues about why the service won't start. Perhaps the service is dependent on another service or perhaps a particular file needs to be replaced. See Chapter 33, "Microsoft Operating System Features and Tools, Part I," for more information.

Incorrect answers: The registry contains all of the parameters of the operating system, but it won't give you error information. %systemroot%\System32\Drivers contains drivers for hardware. The log file might lead you to believe that a driver needs to be replaced, but it isn't the first place you should look. Task Manager shows the performance of the CPU and RAM and shows what services are running. You might have attempted to start the service from there (or the Services Console) as part of the scenario.

77. Answer: **C**. Secure Shell (SSH) is the best of the listed answers. It allows for secure sessions from a client to a server or to a network device. SSH needs to be installed/enabled on the switches and routers, and then the IT firm employees need to connect with a secure SSH client (such as OpenSSH, PuTTY, or something similar). See Chapter 64, "Remote Access Technologies," for more information.

Incorrect answers: RDP stands for Remote Desktop Protocol; it is a commonly used term to refer to Microsoft's Remote Desktop Connection program, which can only be used to connect to Windows clients and servers. Telnet is an insecure protocol that was the predecessor to SSH. It is disabled on most client systems, and some switches and routers don't incorporate its functionality at all. Virtual Network Computing (VNC) is used most often to connect to remote client computers such as Windows, macOS, Linux, and Android, but SSH is the pre-ferred method for connecting to network devices such as switches and routers.

78. Answer: **C**. The best answer to maintain data security is to initiate a remote wipe on a device that has been lost or stolen. That will delete the data and make it very difficult to reconstruct. See Chapter 49, "Mobile Device Security," for more information.

Incorrect answers: Passcode locks and login attempt restrictions will only hamper a hacker who has appropriated the device. GPS (or location services) can help to find the device; however, if a device has been stolen or lost, time is of the essence, and the data should be remotely wiped right away.

79. Answer: **B**. The syntax shown is one way of mapping a network drive in Windows. **net use** is the command, the drive letter to be used is Z:, and the path to the share is *servername\sharename*. This type of command would histori-cally be found in a batch file in Windows; it uses the .bat extension. However, PowerShell is the newer, and better, tool to work with; it uses the .ps1 file exten-sion by default. And while you can still use the **net use** command, PowerShell uses the newer **Get-PSDrive** cmdlet. See Chapter 63, "Basic Scripting, Part II," for more information.

Incorrect answers: .vbs indicates Visual Basic script, which can be used in Windows but is not necessary for basic networking procedures such as mapping network drives. .js indicates JavaScript, which is often used in websites. .py indi-cates Python, which is used for a variety of things, but again, is not necessary for mapping network drives.

80. Answers: **B and D**. To immediately prevent unauthorized access from the intruder, you could add the intruding device to a blocked access list. This might be done using the IP or MAC address and can be accomplished within some mobile devices directly within the hotspot configuration settings or with a third-party app. The other correct answer is to change the SSID. By changing the SSID, the other user will be disconnected in a short period of time. However, that other user could scan for networks and try to connect again. So, the best thing to do is to require encryption (WPA2/WPA3 and AES) and use a strong password (although this will take more time). You could also disable the SSID broadcast altogether on some devices. This would stop the average user from connecting, but if the person has a Wi-Fi analyzer, they might still be able to connect. In addi-tion, disabling the SSID can have unforeseen consequences. For example, your own mobile device that is connecting to the hotspot might be kicked off, and then you would have to reconnect it manually. See Chapter 51, "SOHO Security," for more information.

Incorrect answers: Accessing the intruder's device and shutting it down is not a good idea for a variety of reasons, especially if the intruder is malicious or expe-rienced with technology. Also, it is not an *immediate* solution. Neither is setting up a Wi-Fi analyzer to identify the intruding device; in fact, that might not be a solution at all. Shutting down the device is not a solution because now you, the user, have lost access as well. However, if you find you are in a situation in which you can't block the intruder, even with strong encryption, then shutting down the device might be your only option.

81. Answers: **A and D**. Apps might also fail to load or might load very slowly. That could be because there are too many apps open, or perhaps the web browser has too many tabs open. It could also be a sign that there is no space left on the device. Remove and/or relocate apps to see if that fixes the problem.

    Incorrect answers: Disabled GPS or an unintended Bluetooth connection would not likely cause apps to load slowly (or not at all). However, a disabled Wi-Fi connection could be another reason for failing apps.

82. Answer: **A**. Remote monitoring and management (RMM) solutions are software tools that are designed to remotely monitor and manage client endpoints, networks, and computers. These remote IT management solutions go beyond single RDP connections and allow a technician to have a more wholistic view of systems and networks, all displayed in one window. See Chapter 64, "Remote Access Technologies," for more information.

    Incorrect answers: Use Remote Desktop Connection (RDC) in Windows to make a single Remote Desktop connection to a remote computer. Use the **mstsc** command to simply display the Remote Desktop Connection program or to make full connections to remote systems from the command line. Remote Assistance calls can be made from Windows users to invite other users to help fix a problem for them.

83. Answers: **C and D**. Windows Defender Firewall may be blocking the connection to the remote system. (By the way, RDC uses port 3389.) Have the customer ensure that Remote Desktop is allowed through the firewall. Also check that remote connections are allowed by going to the Search field and typing **allow remote connections to this computer**. Look for option **Change settings to allow remote connections to this computer**.

    Incorrect answers: Rebooting the computer or running Windows Update simply won't address the problem at hand. Either the firewall is blocking the connection or the system isn't configured to accept remote connections. Also, it wasn't specified who would be running Windows Update, but it certainly couldn't be you because you have been blocked by the remote computer.

84. Answer: **D**. Your system does not meet Trusted Platform Module requirements. According to Microsoft's Windows 11 Pro minimum requirements (as of January 2022), TPM version 2.0 is required to upgrade your system to Windows 11 Pro. To fix the problem, you would have to upgrade the TPM firmware and possibly flash the BIOS/UEFI. See Chapter 40, "Operating System Installations and Upgrades," for more information.

    Incorrect answers: As of January 2022, the Windows 11 installation requirements in general are 1 GHz or faster processor with 2 or more cores on a compatible 64-bit processor or System on a Chip (SoC), 4 GB RAM, 64 GB or larger storage device, UEFI Secure Boot capable, Trusted Platform Module version 2.0, Graphics card compatible with DirectX 12 or later with WDDM 2.0 driver, and high def (720p) display. Your system meets all requirements with the exception of the TPM requirement.

85. Answer: **B and C**. An automated teller machine (ATM) is a common example of a multi-factor authentication system. Usually, an ATM requires "something you

have" (your ATM card) and "something you know" (personal identification number [PIN]). See Chapter 44, "Logical Security," for more information.

Incorrect answers: "Something you are" is incorrect because that includes a biometric factor—for example, a fingerprint, retinal pattern, or hand geometry. "*Somewhere* you are" is incorrect because that would include authenticating to a specific network in a specific geographic area or boundary, using geofencing or GPS, for example.

86. Answer: **A**. Use a screened subnet (also known as a DMZ) to house the servers. This will secure them by isolating them from the LAN. See Chapter 51, "SOHO Security," for more information.

Incorrect answers: In a DHCP scope, DHCP reservations are IP addresses that are reserved for specific devices or computers. While it is possible that you might assign the servers reserved addresses in the scope, it is more likely that the servers will use static IP addresses (as most servers do). IP filtering is a mechanism in which particular types of IP datagrams and packets are discarded. A static WAN IP is a public address (one that faces the Internet), and it does not change. This is something that you would apply to the Internet side of your router or a server that faces the Internet. But the question asked for private IP addresses, so these servers will not face the Internet directly.

87. Answer: **C**. Check the amount and type of the data stored on the user's desktop. When a user is set up with a roaming profile, some of the local profile information (and desktop data) is *merged* with the roaming profile to the network. This can cause logging on and logging off to take a long time. That time can be reduced by checking for (and possibly moving) data on the user's desktop and elsewhere. Speed can also be increased if you properly configure how roaming profiles work. The idea is to ultimately have small, compact roaming profiles because they follow the user around the network. See Chapter 44, "Logical Security," for more information.

Incorrect answers: While there are other things that can slow down the computer—including limited RAM, limited paging (swap) file, improper time synchronization, DNS issues, and so on—the rest of the answers are less likely to be the problem, especially because the laptop was working quickly until the user's account was changed to roaming. A network share is used to store user data centrally at a server, on a NAS, on a SAN, in the cloud, and so on. That is where you would probably want to move some of the data from the user's laptop.

88. Answers: **B and D**. First, ground yourself. The best way is to use an antistatic strap and other antistatic measures, including touching the chassis of the computer. Second, handle adapter cards and other electronics by the edge to avoid making contact with any of the circuitry—but don't touch the slot connectors! See Chapter 59, "Safety Procedures," for more information.

Incorrect answers: A dry environment actually increases the chance of ESD; keep the humidity higher and use a hygrometer to measure it. It is not recommended to plug the device into an outlet when working on it. Wearing eye protection is a good idea when working with hazardous materials and particulate matter, but it is not always necessary when working on electrical components.

89. Answer: **C**. Chances are that the anti-malware program quarantined the executable file. If the anti-malware program deems the file malicious, it will place it in a different location than the normal Downloads folder. See Chapter 45, "Wireless Security and Malware," for more information.

Incorrect answers: .exe files are most definitely compatible with Windows; .exe is the most common extension for executable files. It could be that file permissions denied the user access to the file, but the file should still *exist* where the user expects it to be. However, this is unlikely because the user will most likely download the file to the Downloads location, which the user has full control over by default. Host-based firewalls do not usually block a download such as this. But if the host-based firewall or web browser blocked the download, that would be logged, and the user would see a message about it.

90. Answer: **A**. Use BitLocker to encrypt the data on the laptop. As long as the laptop has a Trusted Platform Module (TPM) chip (or uses USB keys), BitLocker can be implemented to encrypt entire volumes/drives (data at rest) using AES. See Chapter 47, "Windows Security Settings," for more information.

Incorrect answers: Secure File Transfer Protocol (SFTP) is used to transfer data from a client to an FTP server—that's data in motion—and one way to protect that is by using SFTP, which makes use of SSH for security. Access control lists (ACLs) are rules that allow or disallow access on a firewall. Encrypting File System (EFS) is also found in Windows; it is used to encrypt individual files or folders and does not need a TPM. A hardware security module (HSM) can create secure boot keys; it must be enabled properly within the BIOS/UEFI; it is a different technology than TPM in that it is not (usually) included *within* the computer out of the box; instead, it is a standalone device or an add-on adapter card.

A Final Word About the 220-1102 Exam

After taking this practice exam, if you are unsure or unconfident in any way, then I urge you to step back and continue studying the 220-1102 objectives before attempting the real exam. And don't forget, if you purchased the print version of this book, you have a bonus practice exam waiting for you on the companion website (as well as other bonus materials). See the Introduction of this book for details. For even more practice questions, check out the A+ Exam Cram *Practice Questions* book.

Be ready for anything! I can't tell you *exactly* what will be on the exam because that would violate the CompTIA NDA, and the questions can change at any time! But the bottom line is this: If you know the concepts, you can pass any test. Use the official CompTIA A+ objectives as your guide. Review this book thoroughly. Finally, I challenge you to study in a hands-on manner on real computers and investigate all the concepts to the best of your ability. This will help you not only for the exam but also in the real world!

CHAPTER 65

Getting Ready for the Exams, and Farewell

This chapter provides some additional tools and information to help you be successful when preparing for and taking the CompTIA A+ Core 1 (220-1101) and Core 2 (220-1102) exams:

▶ Getting ready for the exams

▶ Tips for taking the real exams

▶ Beyond the CompTIA A+ certification

> **ExamAlert**
>
> **Warning!** Don't skip this chapter! I impart some of the most vital things you need to know about taking the real exams here.

Getting Ready for the Exams

The CompTIA A+ certification exams can be taken by anyone; there are no prerequisites, but CompTIA recommends one year of experience as an IT support specialist. For more information on CompTIA and the A+ certification, visit https://www.comptia.org.

Also visit my A+ page, at https://dprocomputer.com, for information, additions, and updated errata.

To acquire your A+ certification, you need to pass two exams: the Core 1 (220-1101) and the Core 2 (220-1102). These exams are administered by Pearson VUE (https://home.pearsonvue.com). You need to register with Pearson VUE to take the exams.

> **ExamAlert**
>
> I strongly suggest that you do not take both exams on the same day. Instead, take them a week or so apart (at least). Trust me on this.

> **Note**
>
> If you haven't already, make use of the step-by-step checklists for each exam, located in the 220-1101 and 220-1102 introductions in this book.

Each exam consists of two types of questions:

- ▶ **Multiple choice:** This type of question poses a question and asks you to select the correct answer (or answers) from a group of four or more choices. These questions are similar to the questions you've seen throughout this book.

▶ **Performance based:** This type of question asks you to answer a question, complete a configuration, or solve a problem in a hands-on fashion. The questions might ask you to drag and drop information to the correct location or complete a simulation in an emulated or virtual system.

To become proficient at both types of questions, you will need to have a deep understanding of the theory, and you will also need hands-on skills. So, use the companion website materials (described in the Introduction) and practice on actual computers as much as possible. This is, of course, imperative for the exams, but it is even more important for the real world. The more you install, configure, and troubleshoot real systems, the better you will be prepared for job interviews as well as whatever comes your way once you have acquired a position within an organization.

ExamAlert

You've been warned! Practice as much as possible on the following:

▶ Real desktop/laptop computer hardware and software

▶ A SOHO router

▶ Smartphones and tablets

▶ Printers, displays, and other peripherals

An Important Note Regarding Exam Questions

This book does not offer the exact questions that are on the exam. There are two reasons for this:

▶ CompTIA reserves the right to change the questions at any time. Any changes, however, will still reflect the content within the current A+ objectives.

▶ The contents of the CompTIA A+ exams are protected by a nondisclosure agreement (NDA). The NDA states that the questions within the exams are not to be discussed with anyone, and anyone who sits for an exam has to agree to this NDA before beginning a test.

So I cannot tell you exactly what is on the exams, but I do cover all of the exam objectives within this book in order to give you the best chance of passing the exams.

In addition to using the tear-out cram sheet in the beginning of this book (print version), one great way to study is to compile and use a "cheat sheet." I am not saying to cheat (nor do I condone it); I'm saying you should create a *key facts* document, containing things that you want to memorize or have a hard time memorizing, such as numbers, acronyms, procedures, minimum requirements, and so on. Include whatever you feel would help you most.

Table 65.1 provides a partial example of a cheat sheet that you can create to aid in your studies. Fill in the appropriate information in the right column. For example, the first step of the six-step troubleshooting methodology is "Identify the problem."

TABLE 65.1 **Example Cheat Sheet**

Concept	Fill in the Appropriate Information Here
The six-step troubleshooting methodology	1.
	2.
	3.
	4.
	5.
	6.
List of commonly used ports	
The laser imaging process	
The malware removal process	
Windows editions and their differences	
Commands and descriptions (For example, **ping** tests to see whether other systems on the network are live.)	
Etc. *	

* Continue Table 65.1 in this fashion on paper. The key is to write down various technologies, processes, step-by-step procedures, and so on to commit them to memory.

Tips for Taking the Real Exams

You might be new to certification exams. This section is for you. If you have taken certification exams before, feel free to skip this section or use it as a review.

Certification exams are conducted on a computer and are composed of multiple-choice and performance-based questions. You have the option to skip questions. If you do so, be sure to mark, or "flag," them for review before moving on. Feel free to mark any other questions that you have answered but are not completely sure about. This is especially recommended for the performance-based questions. In fact, you might choose to leave all of the performance-based questions until the end. That, of course, is up to you.

When you get to the end, you will see an item review section, which shows you any questions that you did not answer and any that you flagged for review. Be sure to answer any questions that were not completed.

The following lists share tips and tricks that I have developed over the years. I've taken at least 20 certification exams over the past two decades, and the following points have served me well.

General Practices for Taking Exams

▶ **Pick a good time for the exam:** It appears that the fewest number of people are at test centers on Monday and Friday mornings. Consider scheduling during these times. Otherwise, schedule a time that works well for you, when you don't have to worry about anything else. Keep in mind that Saturdays can be busy. You might also choose to take the test online. See the following links for more information about taking a test from home:

https://home.pearsonvue.com/Test-takers/OnVUE-online-proctoring.aspx

https://home.pearsonvue.com/comptia/onvue

https://www.comptia.org/testing/testing-options/take-online-exam

Very important: *Don't schedule the exam until you are ready to take it.* I understand that sometimes deadlines have to be set, but in general, don't register for the exam until you feel confident you can pass. Things come up in life that can sometimes get in the way of your study time. Keep in mind that most exams can be canceled as long as you give at least 24 hours' notice. (To be sure, though, check that time frame when registering.)

▶ **Don't overstudy the day before the exam:** Some people like to study hard the day before; some don't. My recommendations are to study using the Cram Sheet and your own cheat sheet, but in general, don't overdo it. It's not a good idea to go into overload mode the day before the exam.

▶ **Get a good night's rest:** A good night's sleep (seven to nine hours) before the day of the exam is probably the best way to get your mind ready for an exam.

▶ **Eat a decent breakfast:** Eating is good! Breakfast is number two when it comes to getting your mind ready for an exam, especially if it is a morning exam. Just watch out for the coffee and tea. Too much caffeine for a person who is not used to it can be detrimental to the thinking process.

▶ **Show up early:** The testing agency recommends that you show up 30 minutes prior to your scheduled exam time. This is important; give yourself plenty of time and make sure you know where you are going. Know exactly how long it takes to get to a testing center and account for potential traffic and construction. You don't want to have to worry about getting lost or being late.

Stress and fear are the mind killers. Work on reducing any types of stress the day of and the day before the exam. By the way, you do need extra time because when you get to the testing center, you need to show ID, sign forms, get your personal belongings situated, and be escorted to your seat. Have two forms of ID (signed) ready for the administrator of the test center. Turn off your cell phone or smartphone when you get to the test center; they'll check that, too. Showing up early applies to online testing as well. You will have to go through a similar information check and other things that will require time before the scheduled start time for the exam.

▶ **Bring ear plugs:** You never know when you will get a loud testing center or, worse yet, a loud test taker next to you. Ear plugs help to block out any unwanted noise in the location where you take the exam. Just be ready to show your ear plugs to the test administrator.

▶ **Brainstorm before starting the exam:** Write down as much as you can remember from the Cram Sheet and your cheat sheet before starting the exam. The testing center is obligated to give you something to write on; make use of it! Getting all the memorization out of your head clears the brain somewhat so that it can tackle the questions.

▶ **Take small breaks while taking the exam:** Exams can be brutal. You have to answer a lot of questions (typically anywhere from 65 to 90) while staring at a screen for an hour or more. Sometimes these screens are old and have seen better days; and any monitor can cause strain on your eyes if you stare at it too long. I recommend taking small breaks and using helpful breathing techniques. For example, after going through every 25 questions or so, close your eyes and slowly take a few deep breaths, holding each one for five seconds and then releasing each one slowly. Think about nothing while doing so. Remove the test from your mind during these breaks. This type of break takes only about half a minute but can help to get your brain refocused. It's almost a Zen type of thing. When I have applied this technique properly, I have gotten a few perfect scores. It's amazing how the mindset can make or break you. This leads to my last and most important point:

▶ **Be confident:** You have studied hard, gone through the practice exams, created a cheat sheet. You've done everything you can to prep. These things alone should build confidence. But actually, you just have to be confident for no reason whatsoever. Think of it this way: You are great.... I am great... (to quote Dr. Daystrom). But truly, there is no disputing this! That's the mentality you must have. You are not being pretentious about this if you think it to yourself. (Acting that way around others, well, that's another matter.) Build that inner confidence, and your mindset should be complete.

Smart Methods for Difficult Questions

▶ **Use the process of elimination:** If you are not sure about an answer, first eliminate any answers that are definitely incorrect. You might be surprised how often this works. This is one of the reasons it is recommended that you not only know the correct answers to the practice exam questions but also know why the wrong answers are wrong. The testing center should give you something to write on; use it to write down the letters of the answers that are incorrect to keep track. Even if you aren't sure about the correct answer, if you can logically eliminate anything that is incorrect, the answer will become apparent. The character Sherlock Holmes summed this up well: "When you have eliminated the impossible, whatever remains, however improbable, must be the truth." There's more to it, of course, but from a scientific standpoint, this method can be invaluable.

▶ **Be logical in the face of adversity:** The most difficult questions are those where two answers appear to be correct, even though the test question requires you to select only one answer. Real exams should not rely on "trick" questions. Sometimes you need to slow down, think logically, and compare the two possible correct answers. Also, you must imagine the scenario that the question is a part of. Think through step by step what is happening in the scenario. Write out as much as you can. The more you can visualize the scenario, the better able you will be to figure out which of the two answers is the better one.

▶ **Use your gut instinct:** Sometimes a person taking a test just doesn't know the answer; it happens to everyone. If you have read through a question and all the answers and used the process of elimination, sometimes gut instinct is all you have left. In some scenarios, you might read a question and instinctively know the answer, even if you can't explain why. Tap into this ability. Some test takers write down their gut instinct answers before delving into the question and then compare their thoughtful answers with their gut instinct answers.

▶ **Don't let one question beat you!** Don't let yourself get stuck on one question, especially a performance-based question. Skip it and return to it later. When you spend too much time on one question, your brain gets sluggish. The thing with these exams is that you either know it, or you don't. But don't worry too much about it; chances are you are not going to get a perfect score. Remember that the goal is only to pass the exams; how many answers you get right beyond that is irrelevant. If you have gone through this book thoroughly, you should be well prepared. You should have plenty of time to go through all the exam questions with time to spare to return to the ones you skipped and marked.

▶ **If all else fails, guess:** Remember that the exams might not be perfect. A question might seem confusing or appear not to make sense. Leave questions like this until the end. When you have gone through all the other techniques mentioned, make an educated, logical guess. Try to imagine why the test would bring up this topic, as vague or as strange as it might appear. However, remember this: The more you study, the less you will have to guess.

Wrapping Up the Exam

Review all your answers. If you finish early, use the time allotted to you to review the answers. Chances are you will have time left over at the end, so use it wisely! Make sure that everything you have marked has a proper answer that makes sense to you. But try not to overthink! Give it your best shot and be confident in your answers. You don't want to second-guess yourself!

Beyond the CompTIA A+ Certification

CompTIA started a policy on January 1, 2011, which says that a person who passes the A+ exams will be certified for three years. To maintain the certification beyond that time, you must either pass the new version of the exams (before the three years are up), pass a higher-level CompTIA exam (such as the Network+ or Security+), or enroll in the CompTIA Continuing Education (CE) Program. This program has an annual fee and requires that you obtain Continuing Education Units (CEUs) that count toward the recertification. There are a variety of ways to accumulate CEUs. See CompTIA's website for more information: https://www.comptia.org/continuing-education.

After you pass the exams, consider thinking about your technical future. Not only is it important to keep up your current technical skills sharp but technical growth is important as well; consider expanding your technical horizons by learning different technologies.

Usually, companies wait at least six months before implementing a newly released version of an OS or application on any large scale, but you will have to deal with it sooner or later. Windows, Linux, macOS, Android, and iOS are always coming out with new versions. Consider keeping up with the newest versions and obtaining access to the latest software and operating systems. Practice installing, configuring, testing, securing, maintaining, and troubleshooting them.

To keep on top of the various computer technologies, think about subscribing to technology websites, blogs, RSS feeds, and periodicals—and read them on a regular basis. Check out streaming video tech channels on the Internet. Join computer Internet forums and attend technology conventions. A technician's skills need to be constantly honed and kept up to date.

But the *best* advice I can give is for you to do what you love. From an IT perspective, I usually break it down by technology, as opposed to by the vendor or certification. For example, you might want to learn more about email systems, or securing internetworks, or you might prefer to work on databases, build websites, develop apps—who knows! You are limited only by your desire.

Final note: I wish you the best of luck on your exams and in your IT career endeavors. Please let me know when you pass your exams. I would love to hear from you! Also, remember that I am available to answer any of your questions about this book via my websites:

https://dprocomputer.com

https://prowse.tech

Sincerely,

David L. Prowse

Index

Symbols

Numbers

A

I

To receive your 10% off
Exam Voucher, register
your product at:

www.pearsonitcertification.com/register

and follow the instructions.